How the West Was Won

Brill's Studies in Intellectual History

VOLUME 188

How the West Was Won

Essays on Literary Imagination, the Canon, and the Christian Middle Ages for Burcht Pranger

Edited by

Willemien Otten
Arjo Vanderjagt
Hent de Vries

BRILL

LEIDEN • BOSTON
2010

On the cover: "Citing Gothic", photograph by Arjo Vanderjagt of the Rothman Winter Garden, Chicago Booth School of Business, University of Chicago, Chicago, USA.

This book is printed on acid-free paper.

Library of Congress Cataloging-in-Publication data

How the west was won : essays on the literary imagination, the canon, and the Christian middle ages for Burcht Pranger / edited by Willemien Otten, Arjo Vanderjagt, Hent de Vries.
   p. cm. -- (Brill's studies in intellectual history ; v. 188)
  Includes bibliographical references and index.
  ISBN 978-90-04-18496-1 (hardback : alk. paper) 1. Christian literature. 2. Christianity and literature. 3. Literature, Medieval. 4. Canon (Literature) 5. Europe--Intellectual life. I. Otten, Willemien. II. Vanderjagt, Arie Johan. III. Vries, Hent de. IV. Title. V. Series.

BR53.H59 2010
270.5--dc22

2010004393

ISSN: 0920-8607
ISBN: 978 90 04 18496 1

Typeset by CHS:P [Leiden, Netherlands]

Mixed Sources
Productgroep uit goed beheerde bossen
en andere gecontroleerde bronnen.
www.fsc.org Cert no. CU-COC-803902
© 1996 Forest Stewardship Council

PRINTED BY DRUKKERIJ WILCO B.V. - AMERSFOORT, THE NETHERLANDS

CONTENTS

THE CANON

THE CHRISTIAN MIDDLE AGES

PREFACE

If the concept of winning the West in this volume entitled *How the West was Won. Essays on Literary Imagination, the Canon, and the Christian Middle Ages for Burcht Pranger* appears daunting, the idea of his reaching retirement is only slightly less difficult to fathom for those who know Burcht well. Burcht has been an active member of the University of Amsterdam since his student days in the mid-1960s, receiving his Ph.D. a day before he turned thirty in 1975. Since 1994 he has been Professor of Theology and the History of Christianity at this same institution. I well remember his inaugural lecture on that occasion. Entitled *The Artificiality of Christianity* ('De kunstmatigheid van het christendom'), it was later expanded into a book, which dealt with the embeddedness of medieval theology and Christian thought within the encyclopedic tradition of the liberal arts as one of its often neglected and underrated aspects. Most other modern scholars of religion have characterized the tradition of medieval theology and religion as one of rote and ritual, of the heart rather than the mind, of devotion and spirituality. A case in point is the way in which Anselm of Canterbury's hyper-rational approach in such works as *Proslogion* ('Address to God') and *Cur Deus Homo* ('Why God Became Man')–the subject of Burcht's dissertation–is usually cordoned off into a separate corner of scholarship meant to be reflected on only by the logically-trained happy few. But this is precisely what Anselm with his outspoken preference for arguing on the basis of the so-called *usus loquendi*, the common usage of speech, did *not* want when in these works he tackled such difficult issues as the existence of God or Christ's incarnation. Anselm wanted Christianity and Christian faith not only to be open, rather than resistant, to logical thinking, but even more to common sense. In his view there was nothing of value to believe in the Christian religion that could not be rationally anchored and defended, and, hence, was not also simply worth *knowing*.

Anselm unfolded his preference for the *usus loquendi* in a way that allowed him to continue the tradition of *sermo humilis*, a term defined just after the second World War by the German literary scholar Erich Auerbach. Using the newly coined phrase of *sermo humilis* Auerbach–who never mentions Anselm to my knowledge–tracks the radical course of rhetorical reduction with which Jewish and Christian authors, ranging from the biblical authors of the Old and New Testaments, to Augustine, Gregory of Tours, Bernard of Clairvaux, and Francis of Assisi, broke through the sound barriers of ancient civilization with its precisely defined and supremely timed division and alternation of rhetorical styles. In this classical division the elevated style was reserved for the treatment of lofty matters of imperial, divine, or philosophical importance. The common style could be used for the burlesque and for rowdy farce, while the intermediate style required the speakers to navigate circumspectly between the two. Beginning with Augustine, who was well-trained in the rhetorical curriculum himself but felt increasingly drawn to the stubborn expressiveness of biblical language, Christian authors would come to favor a mixture of styles instead, preferring omission to parataxis, silence or hyperbole to circumscription, violence to order. This mixing of styles and all this entailed stood in the service of what Auerbach called *mimesis*, the 'thick' representation of reality rather than any 'thin' mirroring of it, with faithfulness of representation as the goal of *sermo humilis*. In this sense it is no accident that Auerbach as he was tracing the use of *sermo humilis* and the tradition of *mimesis* from the Middle Ages to such modern authors as Virginia Woolf wrote his work just after the Second World War from a position situated on the margins of classical European civilization, employed in Turkey rather than at a German research university.

The Netherlands does not have German-style research universities. Whatever ivory towers the country may have, the University of Amsterdam has always breathed a more cosmopolitan and more mundane air–not least in its now defunct theological faculty between 1877 and 1997–, which suited Burcht Pranger fine. More sadly, it seems that since the late 1940s the study of Christian thought has not had an easy time in the Netherlands. In the end there is nothing tragic about this, as fields flourish and go out of existence, and the rapid secularization of Dutch society could not fail to cause a decline of theological enrollments. But like Anselm, Burcht Pranger never felt any need either to change direction or to compromise. On the contrary, he came from an Auerbachian background and was inspired in this course by two University of Amsterdam luminaries representing two majestic sides of the study of classic European civilization, the theologian and historian of Christianity Conrad W. Mönnich, who was Burcht's Doktorvater and remained his lifelong conversation partner, and the classical scholar Christine Mohrmann, who was his first and female supervisor. In this atmosphere, Burcht found himself intellectually well-prepared to continue his analysis of and quest for *sermo humilis,* even if this entailed a gradual moving away from theological or religious studies as a segregated field.

Hence it is no surprise that he increasingly sought out the company of scholars in the humanities: historians, philosophers, classicists, as well as linguists. From the start Burcht had been a staunch supporter of the formation of a Humanities faculty at the University of Amsterdam, which soon became a forerunner of what is now a widely shared national development. For many years Burcht paid more than his fair share of administrative dues by serving as Director of its Research Institute for Culture and History. For him it went without saying that the work that needs to be done still needs to be done, intellectually and administratively, under whatever rubric one chooses to organize it. More importantly, tackling the identity of western civilization and its religious past is today more than ever a matter of pressing social and intellectual debate in the Netherlands.

Lodging the study of these issues of western identity within a larger Humanities faculty–entailing literary studies, history, theology and philosophy–does not in itself provide a panacea. The Humanities are no longer seen as a respected but harmless treasure trove of *Bildung,* and they are not 'solid' enough perhaps to form an unbroken front of critical enquiry which is able to handle the intense and in large part financial competition with the other sciences (Medical, Physical, Social) without sacrificing the commitment to its own venerable tradition of self-reflection and introspection. The problem then of how to bring the past into the future looms large. This background explains Burcht Pranger's recent shift of interest to the issue of temporality in his grant-funded research project *The Pastness of the Religious Past.* In this project he is attempting a razor-like approach to the past by regarding it from the position of a present which is not only seen as post-Christian or post-secular–words which seem to be used as material synonyms even if they are to some extent oppositional–, let alone as a present that can lay claim to any kind of neutrality, but which will allow us to monitor the unfolding of history by keeping the pulse of time itself. 'Time' is taken by Burcht no longer as the punctual contraction of divine presence–as in the Anselmian *punctum* or Bernard of Clairvaux's *verbum abbreviatum*–but increasingly he analyzes it in, if you will, its soteriological quality: that is, its ability to overcome the distance between nothingness and matter in creation, and to connect the voices of the human and the divine through incarnation, miracle, or mystical union. The exercise of making the religious past available to a wider audience without insisting on religious claims is one that is intellectually highly ascetic, precisely because the stakes are high and the abyss is deep. For how can one take religion seriously without being forced to adopt the perspective of either insider or outsider? When Burcht embarked on his project, he surely had no mind to proselytizing, which would by all accounts be a very un-Prangerian move and one whose teleological nature would defy the contingency of time and would sound out the fragility of voice. If anything, he wants to convey a deep understanding of how the age-old religious ideas and institutions of western Europe have tended to process change by resisting it through a strategy of subversion that is as subtle as it is effective: the massive and monumental quality of tradition tends to trick adherents and opponents alike into conflating time with sempiternity.

Accepting time not just as a religious positive but as a valuable category of analysis through which to analyze and provide access to the religious past has led Burcht Pranger back also to his early interest in ordinary language. Now it is no longer only Anselm's *usus loquendi* but especially the ordinary language philosophy of Stanley Cavell which attracts him. Cavell's masterful refutation of skepticism as a kind of life-long tango with it for Burcht closely approximates the intellectual quest undertaken by Augustine himself, who is the subject of his latest book. Cavell, moreover, does something else as well, for he has brought Burcht back to the fragility of the human voice and the difficult task of cultivating it not only in religion–with Augustine's *Confessions* as the finding of voice contrasted with Calvin's predestination as its suppression–but also in entertainment, what the French like to call 'divertissement.' This is another aspect of medieval theology which is often overlooked but brought out by Burcht especially in his teaching; in seminars with theology students in the early '80s he would shed light on Bernard's sermons on the Song of Songs as both technical and improvised by comparing them to the vaudeville approach that the Marx Brothers applied to Hollywood scripts in such films as *Night at the Opera* or *Duck Soup*. Thus putting the embeddedness of religion in the liberal arts in a new guise, Burcht has proven himself one of the world's few historians of Christianity who is able through this kind of 'desegregation' of religion to seriously engage–and, when needed, challenge–contemporary thinkers such as Cavell, Hent de Vries, or Jean-Luc Marion from the perspective of the past itself. It is a pity in a way that the Humanities faculties in the Netherlands have so far not adopted a liberal arts program, where such an approach to Bernard and the Marx Brothers together would thrive, preferring instead in unmedieval fashion to keep the liberal arts separated in expensive University Colleges as something for the wealthy few. This does show, however, that in culture and religion progress is a relative category.

Temporality, ordinary language philosophy, 'divertissement,' the arts, and the culture of the Middle Ages: these are some of the themes with which this volume deals as a kind of anthology of the interests which Burcht Pranger has pursued over the course of his career. In a postmodern fashion which he may or may not appreciate, the volume catches 'traces' of these interests rather than treating them exhaustively–traces, however, which like the Augustinian-Bonaventuran tradition of *vestigia* allow the reader to come ever closer to what makes the scholarship of their creator tick. For, what the volume's three main parts, on Literary Imagination, the Canon, and the Christian Middle Ages respectively, ultimately strive to do is to pay tribute to the enormous creativity of Burcht Pranger's mind, as one that ranges as easily from Augustine to the Marx Brothers as it does from Gregory of Nyssa to Pierre Boulez. It is tempting to call his mind a humanist one, but for someone having consistently breathed Amsterdam air, that city's own branch of cosmopolitanism provides explanation enough.

The editors of the volume thank all the contributors for their prompt and collegial collaboration as well as for their rich essays. A special word of thanks goes to Mr. Jeremy Thompson of the University of Chicago for his careful correction of the English of this volume and his copy-editing. All these labors together have made this volume into the concrete gift of a Festschrift dedicated to Professor M. Burcht Pranger.

Willemien Otten
(on behalf of the editors)

PUBLICATIONS OF BURCHT PRANGER

Monographs

Consequente Theologie; een studie over het denken van Anselmus van Canterbury (Assen: Van Gorcum, 1975), 145 pp.

Bernard of Clairvaux and the Shape of Monastic Thought. Broken Dreams, Brill's Studies in Intellectual History 56 (Leiden: Brill, 1994), 376 pp.

The Artificiality of Christianity. Essays on the Poetics of Monasticism, Figurae: Reading Medieval Culture (Stanford: Stanford University Press, 2003), 352 pp.

Eternity's Ennui. Temporality, Perseverance and Voice in Augustine and Western Literature (forthcoming).

God (1000-1300) en andere essays over literaire aspecten van het Christendom (forthcoming).

Edited books

S. de Boer and M.B. Pranger, eds., *Saecula saeculorum; Opstellen aangeboden aan C.W. Mönnich* (Amsterdam: Polak en van Gennep, 1982).

B.S. Hellemans, W. Otten, and M.B. Pranger, eds., *On Religion and Pastness* (forthcoming).

Articles

"Petrus Damiani de kluizenaar; het leven als kunstwerk," *Tijdschrift voor Theologie* 17, no. 3 (1977): 250-263.

"Quelques remarques historiographiques concernant le principe d'individuation," *Nederlands Theologisch Tijdschrift* 35 (1981): 7-31.

"Masters of Suspense: Argumentation and Imagination in Calvin, Anselm and Bernard," *Assays: Critical Approaches to Medieval and Renaissance Texts* 1 (1981): 15-33.

"Terret me vita mea; een analyse van Anselmus' Ie meditatie," *Bijdragen; tijdschrift voor filosofie en theologie* 43 (1982): 63-83.

"Barokke Vroomheid; dynamiek en beweging bij Pierre de Bérulle," *Bijdragen; tijdschrift voor filosofie en theologie* 43 (1982): 306-318.

"Literaire Schroom; Bernardus' 23e preek over het Hooglied," in S. de Boer and M.B. Pranger, eds., *Saecula saeculorum* (Amsterdam: Polak & Van Gennep, 1982), 151-181.

"*Studium Sacrae Scripturae*: Comparaison entre les méthodes dialectiques et méditatives dans la première méditation d'Anselme," in *Les mutations socio-culturelles au tournant des XIe-XIIe siècles*, Etudes Anselmiennes, Colloques Internationaux du Centre de la Recherche Scientifique (Paris: CNRS, 1984), 469-490.

"Augustinus *De civitate dei*," *Werkschrift voor leerhuis en liturgie* 5 (1984): 24-28.

"La langue: corps de la théologie médiévale," in H. Hillenaar, ed., *Le roman, le récit et le savoir* (Groningen: University of Groningen, 1986), 149-158.

"Figuurstudies; een beschrijving van Bernardus' tractaat *De gradibus humilitatis et superbiae*," *Nederlands Theologisch Tijdschrift* 41 (1987): 99-117.

"Anselm's Brevitas," in *St-Anselm and St-Augustine Episcopi ad Saecula*, Anselm Studies 2 (White Plains, NY: Kraus International Publications, 1988), 447-458.

"Bernardus van Clairvaux, de laatste der Vaders?," *Millennium; Tijdschrift voor middeleeuwse studies* 2 (1988): 447-458.

"The Virgin Mary and the Complexities of Love-Language in the Works of Bernard of Clairvaux," *Citeaux: Commentarii Cistercienses* 40 (1989): 112-138.

"Reve, God en Bernardus van Clairvaux," *BZZLLETIN* 170/171 (1989): 91-99.

"Verborgen vormen van liefde in Bernardus' Hooglied preken," in E.K. Grootes and J. de Haan, eds., *Geschiedenis, godsdienst, letterkunde; Opstellen aangeboden aan dr. S.B.J. Zilverberg* (Roden: Nehalennia, 1989), 17-21.

"De kracht van het lot; een essay over lot en voorbeschikking bij Calvijn en Hartmann von Aue," *Kerk en Theologie* 42 (1991): 145-154.

with Willemien Otten, "Over middeleeuwen en patristiek in de theologiegeschiedenis," *Millennium, Tijdschrift voor Middeleeuwse Studies* 4 (1991): 143-152.

"Mystical Tropology in Bernard of Clairvaux," *Bijdragen; Tijdschrift voor filosofie en theologie* 52 (1991): 428-435.

"*Perdite vixi*: Bernard de Clairvaux et Luther devant l'échec existentiel," *Bijdragen; tijdschrift voor filosofie en theologie* 53 (1992): 46-61.

"Mystiek en lyriek bij Juan de la Cruz en Bernard van Clairvaux," in F. Tilmans, ed., *Taal van verlangen; Kanttekeningen bij Juan de la Cruz* (Haarlem: Gottmer, 1992), 34-72.

"The Concept of Death in Bernard's Sermons on the Song of Songs," in J.R. Sommerfeldt, ed., *Bernardus Magister*, Papers Presented at the Nonacentenary Celebration of the Birth of Saint Bernard of Clairvaux (Kalamazoo, Michigan: Cistercian Institute Publications, 1992), 85-93.

"The Rhetoric of Mystical Unity in the Middle Ages. A Study in Retroactive Reading," *Theology and Literature, An Interdisciplinary Journal of Theory and Criticism* 7 (1993): 33-49.

"De kloostermystiek van Bernard van Clairvaux," in J.L.M. van Schaik, ed., *Mystiek in onze tijd* (Zeist: Vrij Geestesleven, 1993), 44-53.

"Anselm Misunderstood: Utopian Approaches towards Learning in the Eleventh Century," in J. Zumr and V. Herold, eds., *The European Dimension of Anselm's Thought*, Proceedings of the Conference Organized by the Anselm-Society and the Institute of Philosophy of the Academy of Sciences of the Czech Republic (Prague: Institute of Philosophy, 1993), 163-87.

"Augustinianism and Drama: Jansenius' Refutation of the Concept of *natura pura*," in M. Lamberigts, ed., *L'Augustinisme à l'ancienne Faculté de théologie de Louvain*, Biblioteca Ephemeridum Theologicarum Lovaniensium 111 (Leuven: Leuven University Press, 1994), 299-309.

"Monastieke toekomstverwachting," *Millennium; Tijdschrift voor Middeleeuwse Studies* 8, no. 1 (1994): 18-35.

"God," in M. Stoffers, ed., *De middeleeuwse ideeënwereld van 1000 tot 1300* (Heerlen-Hilversum: Verloren, 1994), 93-117.

"De school als utopie: van klooster- naar stadsschool," in R.E.V. Stuip and C. Vellekoop, eds., *Scholing in de Middeleeuwen* (Hilversum: Verloren, 1995), 205-221.

De kunstmatigheid van het Christendom, inaugural address, Amsterdam 1995, 24 pp.

"De ongenaakbaarheid van de Bijbel: over de verhouding tussen christendom en literatuur," *Tijdschrift voor theoretische geschiedenis* 22, no. 4 (1995): 394-404.

"The Mirror of Dialectics: Naked Images in Anselm of Canterbury and Bernard of Clairvaux," in D.E. Luscombe and G.R. Evans, eds., *Anselm: Aosta, Bec and Canterbury*, Papers in Commemoration of the Nine-Hundredth Anniversary of Anselm's Enthronement as Archbishop, 25 September 1093 (Sheffield: Sheffield University Press, 1996), 136-148.

"André Malraux, Charles de Gaulle and Bernard of Clairvaux on Action and Contemplation," in J.E. Caraway, ed., *Mediterranean Perspectives,* vol. 1 (Oakdale: Dowling College Press, 1996), 131-143.

"*Sic et non:* Patristic Authority Between Refusal and Acceptance: Anselm of Canterbury, Peter Abelard and Bernard of Clairvaux," in I. Backus, ed., *The Reception of the Church Fathers in the West* (Leiden: Brill, 1997), 165-193.

"Narrative Dimensions in Gregory of Nyssa's *Life of Macrina,*" *Studia Patristica* 32 (1997): 201-7.

"Monastic Violence," in H. de Vries and S. Weber, eds., *Violence, Identity, and Self-determination* (Palo Alto: Stanford University Press, 1997).

"Killing Time: An Essay on the Monastic Notion of Speed," in Carolyn Muessig, ed., *Medieval Monastic Preaching* (Leiden: Brill, 1998), 319-335.

"De *Confessiones* herlezen," *Nederlands Theologisch Tijdschrift* 52 (1998): 206-24.

"De onpartijdigheid van de rechter vanuit religieus perspectief," *Rechtsgeleerd Magazijn Themis* 159 (1998): 35-41.

"Tranen in het antieke christendom," in R.E.V. Stuip and C. Vellekoop, eds., *Emoties in de Middeleeuwen* (Hilversum: Verloren, 1998), 29-48.

"Narratieve superioriteit; Petrus Venerabilis' *De miraculis* I,1," *Millennium. Tijdschrift voor middeleeuwse studies* 12, no. 2 (1998): 136-48.

"L'eucharistie et la prolifération de l'imaginaire aux XIe et XIIe siècles," in A. Haquin, ed., *Fête-Dieu (1246-1996)* (Louvain-la-Neuve: Publications de l'Institut d'Etudes Médiévales, 1999), 97-117.

"Reading Anselm," in R. Majeran and E.I. Zieliński, eds., *Saint Anselm, Bishop and Thinker,* Papers Read at a Conference Held in the Catholic University of Lublin on 24-26 September 1996 (Lublin: The University Press of the Catholic University of Lublin, 1999), 157-73.

"Apocalyptiek als stijlkwestie," in Theo Clemens, Willemien Otten and Gerard Rouwhorst, eds., *Het einde nabij? Toekomstverwachting en angst voor het oordeel in de geschiedenis van het christendom* (Nijmegen: Valkhof Pers, 1999), 109-23.

"Nachttaal. Het realisme van Gregorius van Tours," in M. de Jong, E. Rose, and H. Teunis, eds., *Rondom Gregorius van Tours* (Utrecht: University of Utrecht, 2000), 17-25.

"Reden über die Religion," *Krisis, tijdschrift voor Empirische Filosofie* 1, no. 4 (2000): 18-25.

"Unity and Diversity in Anselm of Canterbury," in *Anselm Studies,* vol. 4: *Proceedings of the Anselm Conference, Paris 1990: Saint Anselme: Pen-*

seur d'hier et d'aujourd'hui (Millwood, NY: Kraus International Publications, 2000), 317-341.

"Christine Morhmann, classica," *Lampas* 33, no. 4/5 (2000): 412-419.

"Saint Bernard et la mort," *Revue des sciences religieuses* 75, no. 2 (2001): 175-189.

"Time and Narrative in Augustine's *Confessiones*," *The Journal of Religion* 81, no. 3 (2001): 377-394.

"Images of Iron: Ignatius of Loyola and Joyce," in Hent de Vries and Samuel Weber, eds., *Religion and Media* (Palo Alto: Stanford University Press, 2001), 182-198.

"The Unfathomability of Sincerity: On the Seriousness of Augustine's *Confessions*," in *Actas do Congresso International As* Confissões *de santo Agostinho 1600 Anos Depois: Presença e Actualidade* (Lisboa: Universidade Católica Editora, 2002), 193-242.

"Normative Centering and Decentering as a Textual Process: Calvin, Ignatius, Eckhart," in Rudolph Suntrup and Jan R. Veenstra, eds., *Normative Zentrierung* (Frankfurt am Main: Peter Lang, 2002), 65-85.

"Religieuze onverschilligheid of het probleem van de christelijke middeleeuwen," *Millennium, tijdschrift voor middeleeuwse studies* 16 (2002): 3-16.

"Predestination and the Loss of Drama from Augustine to Calvin," in Z. von Martels, ed., *Antiquity renewed: Late Classical and Early Modern Themes* (Leiden: Brill, 2003), 79-103.

"Elective Affinities: Love, Hatred, Playfulness, and the Self in Bernard and Abelard," in Stephen Gersh and Bert Roest, eds., *Medieval and Renaissance Humanism* (Leiden: Brill, 2003), 55-72.

"Augustine and Henry James on Still Life," *Modern Language Notes* 119 (2004): 1-15.

"On Devotional Historiography," *Dutch Review of Church History/Nederlands archief voor kerkgeschiedenis* 84 (2004): 523-536.

"De schriftuitleg van Gregorius de Grote en Beda Venerabilis," *Schrift* 220 (2005): 133-140.

"Medieval Ethics and the Illusion of Interiority: Augustine, Anselm, Abelard," in I.P. Bejczy and R.G. Newhauser, eds., *Virtue and Ethics in the Twelfth Century* (Leiden: Brill, 2005), 13-33.

"Augustine and the Return of the Senses," in G. de Nie, K.F. Morrison and M. Mostert, eds., *Seeing the Invisible in Late Antiquity and The Early Middle Ages* (Turnhout: Brepols, 2005), 53-69.

"Anselm and the Refusal of Gift," in G.M.E. Gasper and H. Kohlenberger, eds., *Anselm and Abelard: Investigations and Juxtapositions* (Toronto: PIMS, 2006), 122-35.

"Politics and Finitude: The Temporal Status of Augustine's *civitas permixta*," in Hent de Vries and Lawrence Sullivan, eds., *Political Theologies* (New York: Fordham University Press, 2006), 113-121.

"The *Persona* of the Preacher in Bernard of Clairvaux," *Medieval Sermons Studies* 51 (2007): 33-40.

"Religious Indifference: On the Nature of Medieval Christianity," in H. de Vries, ed., *Religion Beyond a Concept* (New York: Fordham University Press, 2007), 513-523.

"Time and the Integrity of Poetry," in W. Otten and K. Pollmann, eds., *Poetry and Exegesis in Premodern Latin Christianity* (Leiden: Brill, 2007), 49-64.

"Devotion and the Present: Memory and Oblivion," in Mette B. Bruun and Stephanie A. Glaser, eds., *Negotiating Heritage: Memory of the Middle Ages* (Turnhout: Brepols, 2008), 239-248.

"Anselm, Calvin and the Absent Bible," in Alasdair A. MacDonald, Zweder R.W.M. von Martels and Jan R. Veenstra, eds., *Christian Humanism. Essays in Honour of Arjo Vanderjagt* (Leiden: Brill, 2009), 457-69.

"The Authenticity of the Devil in Gregory the Great, Anselm of Canterbury and Heinrich von Kleist," in Carry Nederman, ed., *Mind Matters* (Turnhout: Brepols, 2010).

NOTES ON CONTRIBUTORS

MARCIA L. COLISH, Ph.D. (1965), Yale University, retired as Frederick B. Artz Professor of History at Oberlin College in 2001, having taught there since 1963. Since 2001 she has been Visiting Fellow and sometime Visiting Professor and Lecturer in History at Yale University. She has published extensively on medieval intellectual history, on topics such as epistemology, the Stoic tradition, patristics, Peter Lombard, and early scholasticism.

PETER CRAMER published a study on the shifting perception and effect of baptism in the early Middle Ages (*Baptism and Change*, Cambridge 1993), and is at present interested in aspects of the history of religion and society in Europe from the twelfth to the fifteenth centuries. He teaches History, History of Art and Literature at Winchester College in the UK.

ROKUS DE GROOT, Ph.D. (1991), University of Utrecht, held a personal chair for "Music in the Netherlands since 1600" at the University of Utrecht (1994-2000). Since 2000 he has been Professor of Musicology at the University of Amsterdam. He has published extensively on the aesthetics and techniques of contemporary music composition, on the re-use in contemporary music of past religious concepts, and on Edward Said's concept of polyphony and counterpoint. He is also a composer, working with musicians from different cultural backgrounds on projects of mutual learning (*Song of Songs: The Life of Mirabai*, Delhi 2005; *Layla and Majnun*, Amsterdam 2006; *ShivaShakti*, Chennai 2009).

ALASTAIR HAMILTON, Professor Emeritus of the History of the Radical Reformation at the University of Amsterdam and former Louise Thijssen-Schoute Professor of the History of Ideas at Leiden University, is currently Arcadian Visiting Research Professor at the School of Advanced Study, London University, attached to the Warburg Institute. He has written extensively on European ecclesiastical history in the sixteenth and seventeenth centuries and on relations between Europe and the Arab world.

ANSELM HAVERKAMP is Professor of Philosophy and Literature at New York University, the European University Viadrina in Frankfurt/O and Ludwig-Maximilians-Universität München. Among his recent publications are *Fig-*

ura cryptica (Suhrkamp 2002), *Latenzzeit* (Kadmos 2004), *Metapher* (Fink 2007), *Metaphorologie* (Suhrkamp 2009), *Begreifen im Bild* (August 2009), *Genealogies of Power: Law and Latency in Shakespeare* (Routledge 2010).

BABETTE HELLEMANS, Ph.D. (2006), École des Hautes Études en Sciences Sociales (Paris) and Utrecht University, is a postdoctoral and assistant professor at Utrecht University. She has published on historiographical themes, such as the anthropology of eschatology in western medieval culture, including modern theories of temporality, semantics and images. Her current project involves the historical status of temporality within religious speech. In her forthcoming book on the 'language of *intentio*' in the work of Peter Abelard she examines the multifaceted nature of his oeuvre from an interdisciplinary viewpoint.

ERNST VAN DEN HEMEL completed a research MA in Cultural Analysis in 2006, and he has been a Ph.D. student at the University of Amsterdam since that time. In his doctoral work he combines an emphasis on literature and philosophy to analyze the poetic structure of John Calvin's *Institutes of the Christian Religion*. He is the author of *Calvinisme en Politiek: Tussen Verzet en Berusting* (Boom 2009).

MADELEINE KASTEN, Ph.D. (2001), University of Amsterdam, is affiliated with Leiden University, where she has lectured in the Literary Studies Department since 2004. She has published on medieval allegory, on Shakespeare, and on literary translation.

BRAM KEMPERS, Ph.D. (1987), University of Amsterdam, has been Professor of Sociology of Art at the University of Amsterdam since 1989. Prior to that he worked for the Ministry of Culture and taught at the University of Groningen. His dissertation was translated into German, French and English (*Painting, Power and Patronage*, 1992 and 1994). His main field of interest is the social context of art, in particular patronage, the art market, cultural policy and sponsoring. He has published many articles on medieval and Renaissance art in Italy and on modern art in the Netherlands. Some of his publications are devoted to Dutch art in the sixteenth and seventeenth centuries. Currently, he works on Pope Julius II and his great artistic projects.

HELMUT KOHLENBERGER (Dr.phil., Universität Tübingen, 1969), has been University Lecturer in Tübingen, Vienna and Salzburg, and served as an editor and translator. His publications focus on the history of ideas of the Middle Ages (especially Anselm of Canterbury) and the twentieth century, and include questions of religion, history, law, and literature in the Central European tradition of authors such as Jan Patočka and Leszek Kolakowski.

FRANS-WILLEM KORSTEN, Ph.D. (1998), University of Amsterdam, has held the chair in Literature and Society at the Erasmus University in Rotterdam since 2007. He also works at the department of Literary Studies in Leiden. He has written a new introduction to literary studies that is historical, theoretical and analytical (*Lessons in Literature*, Vantilt: Nijmegen, 2002, 2005, 2009). From his seventeenth-century study on *Sovereignty as Inviolability* (Hilversum: Verloren, 2009) his research now moves to the interstices between literature, law and politics in relation to the concept of dignity.

PAOLA MARRATI, Ph.D. (1995), Marc Bloch University of Strasbourg, has been Professor of Humanities and Philosophy at the Johns Hopkins University since 2003. She has published extensively on modern and contemporary philosophy, particularly on Derrida, Deleuze, and Cavell. Her current project includes an analysis of the relation between skepticism and immanence in the philosophy of Deleuze and Cavell.

BERNARD McGINN is the Naomi Shenstone Donnelley Professor emeritus at the University of Chicago Divinity School where he taught for thirty-four years. He has written extensively on medieval theology, especially on the history of apocalypticism and Christian spirituality and mysticism. He is currently at work on the fifth volume of his history of mysticism under the general title, *The Presence of God*.

GISELLE DE NIE, Ph.D. (1987), University of Utrecht, held the position of Senior Lecturer in Medieval History at the University of Utrecht. Her research has focused upon early medieval and late antique religious mentality, especially as regards the perception of miracles. Her current project examines the reactions to, and imaginative descriptions of, the 'return'–after a perceived absence of a few hundred years–of contemporary Christian miracles in the period 386-460 CE.

WILLEMIEN OTTEN, Ph.D. (1989), University of Amsterdam, was Professor of the History of Christianity at Utrecht University from 1997. Since 2007 she has been Professor of Theology and the History of Christianity at the University of Chicago. She has published on western medieval and early

Christian theology, including the continuity of (Neo) Platonic themes. Her current project involves a comparison between Johannes Scottus Eriugena and Ralph Waldo Emerson on the role of nature and the self.

PETER RAEDTS, D.Phil. (1984), University of Oxford, has been Professor of Medieval History at the Radboud University, Nijmegen, since 1994. He has just finished a book on the reception and representation of the Middle Ages in modern Europe. He is starting a new research project on the memory of Rome in medieval society.

PIET DE ROOY, Ph.D. (1979), University of Amsterdam, was Professor in Contemporary History (1985-1997) and in Dutch History (1997-2009) at the University of Amsterdam. He has published on the political and cultural history of the Netherlands and the city of Amsterdam during the nineteenth and twentieth centuries. He is currently writing an overview of Dutch political culture in an international perspective.

JOKE SPAANS, Ph.D. (1989), University of Leiden, is Senior Lecturer in Church History at Utrecht University. She has published extensively on the embeddedness of institutional and individual religion in the society and culture of the Dutch Republic. She is currently finishing a book on graphic satire and religious change, and embarking on a new project on the emergence of enlightened Protestantism around 1700.

INEKE VAN 'T SPIJKER, Ph.D. (1990), Utrecht University, is an independent scholar in Cambridge, United Kingdom. She has published on medieval hagiography, biblical exegesis, and medieval ideas about self-fashioning and interiority, including *Fictions of the Inner Life. Religious Literature and Formation of the Self in the Eleventh and Twelfth Centuries* (Turnhout: Brepols, 2004). She currently works on medieval perceptions of inner and outer as they relate to knowledge of self and other.

LEEN SPRUIT, Ph.D. (1987), University of Amsterdam was research fellow at the Universities of Amsterdam and Utrecht (1985-92) and is currently Lecturer of Dutch Language and Literature at the *Sapienza* University in Rome. His research interests concern the history of cognitive psychology, and the censorship of science and natural philosophy in the early modern period. Publications include *Il problema della conoscenza in Giordano Bruno* (Naples 1988); *Species intelligibilis. From Perception to Knowledge* (Leiden 1994-95); and, with Ugo Baldini, *Catholic Church and Modern Science.*

Documents from the Roman Archives of the Holy Office and the Index, vol. 1 of 4: *The Sixteenth Century*. (Rome 2009). He is also editor of works by Jarig Jelles and Raimondo di Sangro.

ASJA SZAFRANIEC, Ph.D. (2004), University of Amsterdam, is a postdoctoral fellow in the Department of Philosophy at the University of Amsterdam. She is the author of *Beckett, Derrida and the Event of Literature* (2007) and of articles on the relation between continental and ordinary language philosophy, on the question of the specificity of the nature of philosophical discourse, and on the relation between philosophy and various forms of literary experiment. Her current research on the work of Stanley Cavell focuses on contemporary philosophy's response to the questions of skepticism, faith and religion.

ARJO VANDERJAGT, Ph.D. (1981), University of Groningen, is Professor Emeritus of the History of Ideas of the University of Groningen. He has published on Anselm of Canterbury, the literary culture and political thought of the fifteenth-century Burgundian court, and on the Christian humanism of the northern Low Countries.

HENT DE VRIES holds the Russ Family Chair in the Humanities and is Professor of Philosophy at The Johns Hopkins University and the Director of The Humanities Center. He is also Professor Ordinarius of Systematic Philosophy and the Philosophy of Religion at the University of Amsterdam and Program Director at the Collège International de Philosophie, Paris. He is the author of *Minimal Theologies: Critiques of Secular Reason in Adorno and Levinas* (2005), *Religion and Violence: Philosophical Perspectives from Kant to Derrida* (2002), and *Philosophy and the Turn to Religion* (1999). Among the volumes he has co-edited are, with Lawrence E. Sullivan, *Political Theologies: Public Religions in a Post-Secular World* (2006), with Samuel Weber, *Religion and Media* (2001) and *Violence, Identity, and Self-Determination* (1998). Most recently, he edited *Religion Beyond a Concept* (2008).

IRENE E. ZWIEP, Ph.D. (1995), University of Amsterdam, was a postdoctoral Frances Yates fellow at the Warburg Institute, London. Since 1997 she has been Professor of Hebrew, Aramaic and Syriac languages and cultures at the University of Amsterdam. Her research interests include medieval and early modern Jewish linguistic thought and the history of Jewish scholarship in the eighteenth and nineteenth centuries. She is currently preparing a study of Ashkenazi linguistic thinking between 1600 and 1900.

LITERARY IMAGINATION

"MOVESI UN VECCHIEREL CANUTO ET BIANCO…": NOTES ON A SONNET OF PETRARCH

PETER CRAMER

I

Towards the end of book 2 of the *Secretum*, written (it is thought) between 1347 and 1354, Petrarch, agonising over why it is he is so sorely afflicted with *accidia*, or what Cicero called *aegritudo*, passes, in response to the probing questions of his interlocutor 'Augustinus', from one possible cause to another.[1] The problem is not easily fathomed. Perhaps this condition of spiritual sickness, of which one distant root is evidently the Greek adjective ἀκηδής, 'uncared for', used for example for the unburied body of Hector and, in this context, suggesting the lack of closure afflicting Priam as a result of ritual neglect,[2] was in Petrarch (or his fictional double who appears in the *Secretum* as 'Franciscus') the tearful memory of the expropriation by greedy executors of Ser Petracco's, his father's, house–and with it Petrarch's own books, including his copies of Virgil and Isidore of Seville. Or at least this is what the dialogue seems to be referring to.[3] Yes, this sadness might play its part. But it is nothing that cannot be kept at bay by reading Seneca's *De tranquillitate animi*, or other such consoling books, provided they are read, as Franciscus and Augustinus agree, with the right kind of practical attentiveness.[4]

Might *accidia* be the effect of ambition for high office, which will after all always bring disappointment, whether at success or failure? Surely not, protests Franciscus: I have always sought mediocrity, he insists, and have never deluded myself with the delusions of office. And yet, he confesses, it is true that the contrary seems to be the case: it is as if I were still deluded.

---

1 Francesco Petrarca, *Secretum*, ed. and trans. Enrico Fenzi (Milan: Mursia, 1992), 2.106 (p. 176): "Habet te funesta quedam pestis animi, quam accidiam moderni, veteres egritudinem dixerunt." The dating remains a problem. In his introduction Fenzi argues for a text begun in 1347, finished with revisions in 1354.

2 *Iliad* 24.554. I am grateful to John Falconer for this reference.

3 *Secretum*, ed. Fenzi, p. 190; see Fenzi's n. 229 on p. 350.

4 Ibid., p. 192.

Already, a certain elusiveness in the spiritual condition of *accidia* has begun to make itself felt. Augustinus calls it *perversa opinio*, this seeming ambition.[5] It becomes apparent though, that *accidia*, rather than a sickness over any specific misfortune or error of judgement, is an anxiety with no identifiable material origin. It is a sluggishness in the will which comes in large part from not knowing the cause behind it. It is an *anxietas*, a dispersal of powers which undermines every project, and which unlike the other vices brings no fruit, no prize or pleasure. It is a memory of cruelties inflicted in the past by the 'avarice' of fortune, and it is the fear of possible future intrusions by this same faceless oppressor. Yet it has in it a certain *atra voluptas*, as if it were a kind of vertigo at the edge of the abyss.[6] No doubt Petrarch was unaware of the Homeric sense, but the complex history of *accidia* which would have made diverse senses available to him gives his own usage a possible but problematic richness. It is the *taedium vitae* of Cassian, the torpor of the desert monk for whom at noon the sun, and so time itself, seems to stand still, the dullness which is the shadow-side of a sustained rhythm of life. Again, it is the widening of this monastic malady to the bigger world, where *accidia*, in an evolution running from Gregory the Great's *tristitia* to the thirteenth century, becomes *indevotio*, the sin of 'despair pertaining to spiritual good' (Aquinas), the sloth that follows on failure to recognize God's love.[7]

The sense of *accidia*, both in its longer history and in Petrarch, is something of a crux. The great researches of Klibansky, Panofsky and Saxl concerning melancholy touch on the problem, but reserve a fuller scrutiny for another day, taking note, for the time being, of a promising relation of melancholy and *accidia*.[8] Siegfried Wenzel, who did make a systematic enquiry into the history of *accidia* (*accidie*, *acedia* etc.), concluded that Petrarch casts it (chiefly in the *Secretum*) as a secular-humanist complexion:

> Franciscus' *accidia* takes on the features of Petrarch's personal experience. It is not the layman's shrinking from the performance of religious duties, nor the monk's boredom with the cell, but refers to the humanist's grief caused by the miseries of the "human condition" (which are not attributed to orig-

---

5 Ibid., pp. 185-6.

6 Ibid., pp. 188-90.

7 On these senses, S. Wenzel, "Petrarch's *Accidia*," *Studies in the Renaissance* 8 (1961): 36-48.

8 R. Klibansky, E. Panofsky, and F. Saxl, *Saturne et la mélancolie. Études historiques et philosophiques: Nature, Religion, Médecine et Art*, trans. [with some editorial changes] by F. Durand-Bogaert and L. Évrard (Paris: Gallimard, 1989), 395-9.

inal sin, but to the instability of fortune) and to his oversensitivity, which chafes against conditions that are incompatible with the life of a scholar and man of letters. In sum, I believe we are justified in considering the *accidia* of Petrarch's *Secretum* as a secularized form of the medieval capital sin.[9]

This humanist interpretation makes apparent sense of the story as a whole, and falls in with a reading of the Renaissance–indeed with some secularising readings of the Middle Ages–which have their root in Jacob Burckhardt.

Yet something doesn't fit. The context of Petrarch's introduction of *accidia* is the relation of the spiritual and the temporal–of spirit and body, of spiritual love and erotic love, of the desire for fame and the self-sufficiency of the solitary life. (It never really becomes clear, in the course of the *Secretum*, whether the analogy of physiological illness for the condition of *accidia* is merely an analogy. The tradition associating it with *aegritudo*, passing back through Cicero to the Stoics, would make the condition a material passion in the soul.) It does not take long with the text before one begins to suspect a monastic content in Petrarch's *accidia*, as well as a turning of the scholastic notion of spiritual negligence. The equilibrium of soul, the evenness of mind sought in the *Secretum*–and which, it might also be, gives dramatic coherence to the sensual turbulence of the *Rime sparse*, the 366 vernacular poems which he long continued both to lament and carefully to edit–is the stillness of the cell. Perhaps the *accidia* of Petrarch is a part of the contribution of monasticism to what we now (though more tentatively than we used to) call humanism.

This is sketching (with a view to one day painting in); but I hope one more speculative gesture is permissible. The explicit handling of *accidia* by Petrarch is in the latter part of book 2 of the *Secretum*. In the third and last book, however, Franciscus comes to the question of his love for the now dead Laura. (She died in the plague in 1348.) He defends this love against Augustinus' scepticism, calling on the Virgin as his witness, and maintaining that the only mistake he had made in his love for this face–for there was nothing crass in the love, as there was nothing crass in the face of the beloved–was in the failure to put a limit on it. "Put some measure on it, and nothing more beautiful can be thought."[10] Augustinus' retort to this, two or three pages later, creates something like a lurch in the progression of the conversation. Rather as one had come to see, with a

---

9 Wenzel, "Petrarch's Accidia," 47.
10 *Secretum*, ed. Fenzi, 3.143 (p. 212): "Adice modum; nichil pulcrius excogitari nequit."

queasy realisation of the depth opened up, the futility of seeking a name-able cause of *accidia*, here the possibility one had relied on that human and sensual love might be *transfigured* into the experience of divine love, is briskly withdrawn.[11] For Franciscus has loved the Creator insofar as He has created this creature which is Laura. "You have turned the order up-side down," says Augustinus. The stress is wrong. The right way up would be to love God first, then his creatures because they are his, to love them thus derivatively (though perhaps as strongly).[12] Is there not in this de-cisive intervention of Augustinus a reminiscence of that Old Testament lurch–or breach–in a long assumed wisdom, the Book of Job? "Doth the hawk fly by thy wisdom and stretch her wings towards the south?" (Job 39:26) Justification is no settled procedure of fair judgements on the ba-sis of mutual covenant, of the kind Job had appealed to with his: "Let me be weighed in an even balance, that God may know mine integrity" (Job 31:6). One would have had to be there at Creation itself really to know how things are ordered. In the absence of this possibility, the best recourse is to hold all Creation in suspension. A cheerful version of this is related by Chaucer in the epilogue of *Troilus and Criseyde*. Troilus, slain, finds himself aloft and looks down:

> And down from thennes faste he gan avyse
> This litel spot of erthe, that with the se
> Embraced is, and fully gan despise
> This wrecched world, and held all vanite
> To respect of the pleyn felicite
> That is in hevene above... [13]

Tragedy, as Chaucer hints, looks from this height like comedy. And here there is not so much breach as re-alignment, made possible perhaps by the cosmological optimism of Boethius.

---

11   *Triumphus eternitatis*, ll. 143-5; see *Rime, Trionfi e poesie latine*, ed. F. Neri, G. Mar-tellotti, E. Bianchi and N. Sapegno (Milan: Riccardo Ricciardi Editore, 1951), 559: "che, poi ch' avrà ripreso il suo bel velo,/se fu beato chi la vide in terra,/or che fia dunque a rivederla in cielo (Whom, when she will have drawn aside her beautiful veil, if he was blessed who saw her in earthly life, what will he become on seeing her again in heaven!)."

12   *Secretum*, ed. Fenzi, 3.148 (p. 216): "Augustinus: At pervertit ordinem. Franciscus: Quonam modo? Augustinus: Quia cum creatum omne Creatoris amore diligendum sit, tu contra, creature captus illecebris, Creatorem non qua decuit amasti, sed miratus artificem fuisti quasi nichil ex omnibus formosius creasset, cum tamen ultima pulchritudinum sit forma corporea."

13   *Troilus and Criseyde*, bk. 5, ll. 1814-19; see *The Riverside Chaucer*, ed. Larry D. Ben-son, et al. (Boston: Houghton Mifflin, 1987), 584. Dr Paul Dean pointed out this passage to me, and made a number of telling remarks about its relation to the rest of *Troilus and Criseyde*.

Augustinus' remark to Franciscus in the *Secretum* is more undermining, closer, for all the difference in style and temperament, to the fierce observation made by (Petrarch's older contemporary) Eckhart in *Vom abgescheidenheit*. If *abgescheidenheit* or detachment is a being-receptive-to-nothing-other-than-God, the risk it entails is that the world becomes waste–or nothing. Only God, says Eckhart, is fine enough to find a way between the state of detachment and nothing.[14] *Accidia*, in this light, would be the spiritual dryness that sets in when the risk of detachment fails to pay off. The world is in suspension, and the effect is not comedy, but an anxiety (Petrarch's *anxietas*) with no cause behind it. "I may drift, hanging on the hope of the doubtful hour" (quoting Horace, *Letters* i.18.110: *fluitem dubie spe pendulus hore*).[15]

II

In no. xvi of the *Rime sparse* or *Scattered Rhymes*, Petrarch writes of an old man's disappointment:

Movesi il vecchierel canuto et bianco
del dolce loco ov' à sua età fornita
et da la famigliuola sbigottita
che vede il caro padre venir manco;

indi traendo poi l'antico fianco
per l'estreme giornate di sua vita,
quanto più po col buon voler s'aita,
rotto dagli anni, et dal camino stanco;

et viene a Roma, seguendo 'l desio,
per mirar la sembianza di colui
ch' ancor lassù nel ciel vedere spera.

Così, lasso, talor vo cercand' io,
Donna, quanto è possibile in altrui
la disiata vostra forma vera.[16]

---

14   Meister Eckhart, *Vom abgescheidenheit*, in Eckhart, Werke, vol. 2, ed. N. Largier, Bibliothek des Mittelalters 21 (Frankfurt am Main: Deutscher Klassiker Verlag, 1993), 436.
15   *Secretum*, ed. Fenzi, 2.116 (p. 186). Of this 'suspension', he then uses the word *anxietas*: "Si haec anxietas tollatur..."
16   I have used the edition of Robert M. Durling, *Petrarch's Lyric Poems. The Rime sparse and Other Lyrics* (Cambridge, MA, and London: Harvard University Press, 1976), adapting his translations.

("Pale, white-headed, small, the old man sets out from the sweet place he
has tended for his late years, and from the stricken little family which stands
gazing after the dwindling back of a dear father; and dragging thence the
aged side through the end-days of his life, presses on with all the good will
he can gather, broken by the years and tired from the road; and he comes to
Rome, following the desire he has to look upon the likeness of the One who,
up there in heaven, he yet hopes to see. This, Lady–alas–is how I sometimes
go seeking, as far as can be done in another, your longed-for true form.")

The form of the sonnet, a kind of *verbum abbreviatum*, allows an infinite
desire to be affirmed within limits. One might say that Eckhart uses the
sermon to achieve a like effect–and in his German sermon no. 86, with a
marvellous *désinvolture* which turns the tradition upside down, he places
the older sister Martha (the active life) above the younger Mary (the contemplative) because Martha's duties in the kitchen, her pots and pans, sta-
bilise the infinite longing which she still feels, but which her sister has not
learnt to steady. Mary abandons herself to tears at Christ's feet, while Martha gets on with the cooking–and 'gets on with it' is about right, for she
is "among things, not in them (bî den dingen, und niht in den dingen)."[17]
In some ways the brevity of the sonnet, the fact that it can only refer, with
metaphorical intensity, and not develop likenesses at epic length, gives it
the greater reach. Here, Petrarch presses the whole epic of pilgrimage-fa-
tigue into his few lines, and into the single sentence which runs the first
eleven lines, treading over the pattern of division into octet and sextet,
a pattern nonetheless kept by the rhyme-scheme. The orthodox sonnet
form of 4, 4, 3, 3 is used to set off and stop, set off and stop, like a walker
who is old and tired of the road, till the final, but only apparently satisfactory arrival of "la disiata vostra forma vera," with its resolutely equal syl-
labic plod. In the first four lines, the white-haired old pilgrim sets off, and
it is as if we are witnessing it from the point-of-view of the sad family left
behind. The slow stepping rhythm of "che vede il caro padre venir manco"
gives the sad picture of the old man's back dwindling for good. (It looks as
if this is his last journey.) The picture might be an inversion of the Prodi-
gal Son. Instead of a homecoming which ends wandering, a departure on
a wandering with no definite end. For this is the pilgrim as *pendulus*, in
suspension. The second quatrain puts it to us not only that the road is ex-

---

17 *Predigt* 86, in *Meister Eckharts Predigten (60-86)*, vol. 3 of *Die deutschen Werke*, ed.
and transl. Josef Quint (Stuttgart: Kohlhammer, 1976), 487-92, at 485, ll. 5-6. And: "Aber
Marthâ stuont in hêrlîcher, wol gevestenter tugent und in einem vrîen gemüete, unge-
hindert von allen dingen (But Martha stood in nobler, firmer-footed virtue and in a free
spirit, unencumbered by all things)" (at p. 489, ll. 30-31).

hausting, but that the exhaustion might simply be the dragged feet of old age: "rotto dagli anni." And the stumbling effort of the tired will ("quanto più po col buon voler s'aita"–in contrast with the sprightly *bona voluntas* of the shepherds' journey to the Nativity in Luke's story) is in an all-too-true-to-life apposition with the aching limbs of the (almost Apocalyptic?) "estreme giornate di sua vita." Then the coming in to Rome, "et viene a Roma," at the opening of the sextet, begins the slowed movement again, with the *allegrezza* of arrival at the shrine. And the 'doubting hope' of Horace quickens, for just as this shrine, the *vera icona* or Veronica, the cloth held up by the woman Veronica to Christ's face on his way to Calvary, is–it now becomes obvious –no more than an image of the real thing, however painfully proximate to the reality ("la sembianza di colui/ch' ancor lassù nel ciel vedere spera"), so the glimpsed memory of the Donna, the beloved face of Laura, is only at second hand, by way of the glimpses of other faces. (Compare Dante's *donna gentile*, appearing at the end of the *Convivio* as consolation for the death of Beatrice.)

The sonnet's double-take–the getting there which is not quite getting there–establishes a gap, an interval, which because of the layering of quick-slow rhythm, the rapid succession of tired limbs and bright hopes, has an effect of density. There is, through this effect–the building up of hope and loss on one another in *lassù/lasso*, or in the slow gait of the "estreme giornate" which equally recalls the vigilance in the days before the end ("Quick, quick, the day of the Lord is round the corner," Wisdom 1:14)–what might be called the density of absence. Sometimes behind the poem is the very different canon of a hankering after the corporal presence of the holy which forms the core of Hans Belting's study of *Bild und Kult*.[18] If in the eastern churches the icon manages to represent the holy as aloofness, the western, from roughly the turn of the millennium, is inclined to a dialectic of absence and presence within the same image (whether sculpted in wood or in stone or painted). Something of this kind is evident in the prayer attributed (by Matthew Paris) to Pope Innocent III written for the Veronica cloth in 1208.[19] The relic was then housed in the Hospital of Santo Spirito, a part of the complex of S. Maria in Saxo in Rome, and in Innocent's time this location became the *statio* of a procession. When the cloth, bearing its *vera forma* and no doubt protected by a frame of some kind, "turned on its head by its own power, so that the forehead was beneath

---

18　Hans Belting, *Bild und Kult: eine Geschichte des Bildes vor dem Zeitalter der Kunst*, 2nd ed. (Munich: Beck, 1991).

19　For what follows, see Belting, *Bild und Kult*, 246-52, and Appendix 37 (pp. 602-5).

and the beard above," Innocent thought it advisable to stop the prayers for
a period of ten days and make a special prayer to honour this relic of relics. "Lord–went Innocent's prayer–you have left for us, we who are signed
(*signatis*) with the light of your face, the image impressed on this sweat-
cloth of Veronica (*sudario impressam imaginem*) as a memorial (*memori-
ale*). Protect us by your passion and cross, that as we now pray before and
honour this image as through a glass darkly (*in speculo et aenigmate*), so,
steadfast, we might see you as judge face-to-face (*facie ad faciem*)."[20]

The anxiety over presence of which this prayer is born echoes the stren-
uousness, the anxious spiritual yearning, which is both responsible for and
follows from the teaching of real presence in the eucharist. In Petrarch's
pilgrimage sonnet, a disappointed finality constitutes a critique of image–both erotic and religious–which throws the yearning soul back onto
the twists and turns of the path. The tiredness of old age binds the suggestions of detachment and desire which settle in the acquiescence of "quanto
è possible" in line 13. In no. xviii, again a sonnet, "Quando io son volto
in quella parte," the turning away from the "bel viso di Madonna" leaves
the light from the face a memory in the thought (*pensiero*) of the beholder,
which, being loss of original light, destroys thought from within and causes a blindness to set in. The blindness is a self-imprisonment, a narcissism
one could say, itself a form of desire (its primordial form?). Again, the image asserts itself by absence–in the devastating slightness of a turn of the
head or a leave-taking–throwing the *pensiero* back on to the dismay of desire. Here a comparison offers itself with *Paradiso* xxi where the refusal to
smile–for the smile of Beatrice, at this height of the heaven of Saturn,

> se non si temperasse, tanto splende,
> ch 'l tuo mortal podere, al suo fulgore,
> sarebbe fronda che trono scoscende[21] –

has the effect not of the blindness of a turning inward, but of an enlightened, exact vision, as if the mind is looking into the perfectly lucid mirror
of the eyes, which reflect what is there to be seen. A lover's repudiation in
Dante brings on clarity of outward seeing; in Petrarch it imprisons light
and is a cause of blindness.

---

20 Quoted in Belting, *Bild und Kult*, 604.
21 Ll. 10-12: "the smile...were it not tempered, would shine so bright that your mortal
powers, caught in the bolt, would be like a branch destroyed by thunder."

III

It seems, meanwhile, that the doctrine of real corporal presence in the species of bread and wine undergoes a shift, at least among the theologians of St Victor in Paris and among the Franciscans, which displaces the stress of presence from the physical process of transubstantiation, with its concentration on the material objects of bread/wine and body/blood, to what might be called an ethical presence. The theological line which insisted, from the late 1050s, on the *verum corpus*, tended, as de Lubac showed in his *Corpus mysticum*, towards an estrangement of the liturgical assembly from what had become objective eucharistic event: the *sui generis* metamorphosis of bread and wine into body and blood.[22] A ritual of participation becomes a ritual of observance, a turn which belongs with a marked tendency to clericalisation with its roots in the Reform movement of the eleventh century. But the response to this estrangement was stalwart. What seems to have happened in the end was that the social rigidification into priest and layman, sacred and profane, reflected in the ritual order of things and especially in the setting apart of real presence, became the source of a renewed accent on intention, both collective and individual. Gary Macy, in his illuminating essays on this, thinks of the process as one of 'negotiation' between laity and clergy over access–ultimately over the right continually to create and re-create the social body by ritual means–to the sacred grounds of the social. On the theology of the eucharist itself, the centre of his attention, he has this to say of the Victorine strain (which had far greater purchase, he believes, than the line taken by Aquinas, often perceived, in the slip-stream of modern Thomism, as the last word in the theology of material presence in the Mass):

> For most medieval theologians, however, a mere recognition of the Real Presence in the ritual of the Eucharist did not itself offer any aid in salvation. The Real Presence alone, in fact, had no spiritual effect. In the language of the School of St. Victor, the Real Presence was the *res et sacramentum*, but not the *res* of the ritual. That is to say that the whole point of the ritual, which the Latin word *res* implies, resided not in the Real Presence. That presence itself was a symbol pointing beyond itself to another far more important reality, the *res*, the thing itself, the point of the entire exercise. Theologians from the twelfth century on were nearly unanimous in their agreement that the *res*, the end result of the Eucharist, was spiritual communion and that this form of communion could and did take place apart

---

22 Henri de Lubac, *Corpus mysticum. L'eucharistie et l'église au Moyen Âge. Étude historique* (Paris: Aubier, 1944).

from the sacramental reception. Most commonly, this *res* was described as living a life of faith and charity. In effect, the predominant theology of the Eucharist in the late Middle Ages understood the liturgy as intimately and intrinsically tied to the moral life.[23]

The *res* of the eucharist, rediscovered under strain from an overly objectified body, stands in apposition to Petrarch's reversion to the interval which is pilgrimage.

IV

Against the objection of the *libertins* that the Bible lacks order, Pascal brings the order of love, 'l'ordre de la charité.' Saint Augustine did the same, says Pascal: "Cet ordre consiste principalement à la digression sur chaque point qui a rapport à la fin, pour la montrer toujours."[24] As a way of reading Augustine, this is suggestive. The end is present as digression in each stage. The disorderly, digressive, nature of story in the *City of God* book xix comes to mind. Story is, in this thinking of Augustine, the place where redemption takes place; only we cannot see how or quite where. In Petrarch's poetry–and in the digressions involved in dialogue in the *Secretum*–there is something similar going on. The end is 'always demonstrated' in the fragments, in each point on the way. But just as we cannot quite see how the City of God is at work in the earthly city in Augustine, so in Petrarch, who goes further in this sense, there is throughout a danger of imprisonment in the desire for the end: for some fullness. An imprisonment in the desire itself. The pilgrim falls back from "likeness/*sembianza*," mere image or face, to the density and no doubt weariness of the 'last days' and the intermittence of will-power on the path. His feet are clarty. He moves heavily. Or rather, it is more than this. He has got to Rome: "et viene a Roma." He has seen the likeness, the Veronica. The Veronica confirms that his vision is in a glass darkly, that in this way he is still a traveller. Lightness and weight, light and obscurity, accompany one another, as in Dürer's engraving of peasants dancing. The likeness of the true face places the desiring soul of the pilgrim in the indefinite interval separating likeness from truth, "the others" from the Donna herself. Even the irony

---

23   Gary Macy, "The Eucharist and Popular Religiosity," in *Treasures from the Storeroom. Medieval Religion and the Eucharist* (Collegeville, MN: The Liturgical Press, 1999), 172-95, at 179.

24   Fragment 280, *Pensées*, ed. Michel Le Guern (Paris: Gallimard 2000), 647.

which makes itself felt in the bitterness of a later sonnet, *Rime sparse* lxxv, is an intrigue which ensnares:

> I begli occhi ond' i' fui percosso in guisa
> Ch' e' medesmi porian saldar la piaga...[25]

There is a lightness which touches everything lightly; or another which exists in the lee of the sublime, as the whispering breeze heard by Elijah on Mount Horeb. Here in this sonnet, there is something else again. Lightness binds. The lightness with which the conceit is accomplished is no release from, but a tightening of the predicament. Fenzi, in a salient footnote to his edition of the *Secretum*, observes how Petrarch shies, on the whole, away from the *donna angelicata* of the Stilnovisti, the remote 'bel viso leggiadro' which stoops, like a Platonic form, from some heaven (see *Rime sparse* clix, lines 1ff.), and prefers to see her as an illusion to be put aside for a sturdier, more mythic presence:

> Quante volte diss' io
> allor, pien di spavento:
> 'Costei per fermo nacque in paradiso.'
> Così carco d'oblio
> il divin portamento
> e 'l volto e le parole e 'l dolce riso
> m'aveano, et sì diviso
> da l'imagine vera,
> ch' i' dicea sospirando:
> 'Qui come venn' io o quando?'
> credendo esser in ciel, non là dov' era.[26]

The putting away of heavenly illusion, though, still has in it the danger of entrapment. The density which comes from the desire for what is glimpsed in the metamorphoses of the forest is simply a more immediate and sensual imprisoning. In the last lines of no. cxxvi, Petrarch speaks to his poem:

> Se tu avessi ornamenti quant' ài voglia,
> poresti arditamente
> uscir del bosco et gir infra la gente.[27]

---

25 Ll. 1-2: "The beautiful eyes with which I was struck in such a way that they themselves were able to heal the wound."

26 *Rime sparse* cxxvi, ll. 53-63 : "How often did I say then, full of fear, She was born in paradise, for sure. And so, heavy [as I was] with forgetting, the god-like movements, the face, the speech, the sweet smile, cut me off so from the true image that I went sighing, How did I get here, when?, thinking I was in heaven, not where I was."

27 Ll. 66-68: "If you had the finery to go with your will, you'd walk boldly out of the wood and go among the crowd."

And the solitude of the poet will be no less than that of his poem.

V

The relation of eros and the spirit is a vexed question, in its reverberations more *mystère* than *problème* (in Gabriel Marcel's distinction, i.e., it is beyond the kind of thing that can be solved, for example by invoking 'allegory' or 'metaphor'). Burcht Pranger gave an exact and brilliant account of it in his commentary on St. Bernard's *Sermon on the Nativity of the Virgin*, of which the argument turns on a double-image, obvious but astonishing, of the *beata possessio* of the lovers in the Song of Songs and the fight till dawn of Jacob and the angel:

> 'Fight with the angel lest you succumb' (Genesis 32:24), for the kingdom of Heaven suffers violence and the violent take it by force (Matthew 11:12). Or, is this not a fight: 'My beloved is mine, and I am his' (Song of Songs 2:16)?[28]

In what follows, Bernard brings home this twofold image, even makes a step towards explaining it through the struggle with God, who tries the soul by withdrawing favour from it, while the soul, whose sins have after all not overwhelmed Him, on its side holds Him fast nonetheless. Seen in this way, the unlike of love which is a wrestling-match becomes like. Its difficulty returns more forcibly than ever, however, if we think of this wrestling till dawn in its probable setting of the breaking of night-silence in the monastery by the song of lauds at dawn. The shadowiness of a fight which is a lovers' embrace is all the more for its being recited at night's intersection with day. It is no mere conceit of the imagination, but an experience of the senses. ("Animum cum corpore amavi," confesses Petrarch with Ovid, letting slip the whole agon of his poetry in four words quoted at the pained Augustinus.[29]) The abiding matrix which holds in place 'the different and seemingly incoherent images' is that of the Virgin; and Bernard thinks of her as shadow: *umbra*. The Father is in Heaven. He is securely brightness.

> The mother, however, gave birth to the same splendour, but in the shadow with which the Most High overshadowed. And so the church, not the church of the saints in heaven and in splendour, but the church on earth, still under-

---

28   *In nativitate b. Mariae*, in *Sancti Bernardi opera*, ed. J. Leclercq and H. Rochais, vol. 5 (Rome: Editiones cistercienses, 1968), §16 (p. 286), quoted in M.B. Pranger, *Bernard of Clairvaux and the Shape of Monastic Thought. Broken Dreams*, Brill's Studies in Intellectual History 56 (Leiden: Brill, 1994), 150-62, at 150.

29   *Secretum*, ed. Fenzi, 3. 149 (p. 218).

way with pilgrimage, is right to sing: Thus in the shadow of Him for whom I have been longing I sat down, and his fruit is sweet to my palate.[30]

In the glass darkly of the Veronica-cloth, eros is fused with an austere version of enlightenment. The risk of incoherence in placing together the Veronica-face and the face of the Donna is shadow.

St Bernard has the advantage, living within the austere lines of Cistercian architecture, of being able effortlessly to associate shadow with a lucid contour capable of re-shaping what light there is as 'an endless stream of images.' Such is the grey light of lauds, its chiaroscuro. Language, in Bernard's usage, exists in the shadow of silence, but like the bleak light of dawn, is already in some way at once fulfilment of desire and its continuation. Lyric sensuality and ascetic restraint are bound in one.[31]

The predicament of Dante is not the same. "Ever since Augustine," says John Freccero,

> the Middle Ages insisted on the link between eros and language, between the reaching out in desire for what mortals can never possess and the reaching out of language toward the significance of silence. To refuse to see in human desire an incompleteness that urges the soul on to transcendence is to remain within the realm of creatures, worshipping them as only the Creator was to be worshipped. Similarly, to refuse to see language and poetry as continual *askesis*, pointing beyond themselves, is to remain within the letter, treating it as an absolute devoid of the spirit which gives meaning to human discourse.[32]

This *askesis*, Freccero observes, is borne out in the *Divine Comedy* by the Virgilian element and its historicity. For Dante learns from Virgil the renunciation of self required in order to get from the *folle amore* of Dido to the submission made by Aeneas to historical destiny. Submission to history means a tempering of desire; it is the prelude to the transfiguration of desire into the higher love of which, in Dante, Beatrice is the occasion. And the deepest expression, and the fullest, of the consonance of history or biography and "the spirit which gives meaning," is the harmony exist-

---

30 *In nativitate b. Mariae*, ed. Leclercq and Rochais, §2 (pp. 275-6): "At Mater sane eumdem ipsum splendorem genuit, sed in umbra, non nisi ea tamen qua obumbravit Altissimus. Merito proinde canit Ecclesia, non illa quidem Ecclesia Sanctorum, quae in excelsis et in splendore, sed quae interim peregrinatur in terris: Sub umbra eius quem desideraveram sedi, et fructus eius dulcis gutturi meo (Cant. 2:3)."

31 M.B. Pranger, *Bernard of Clairvaux*, 162.

32 J. Freccero, "Medusa: The Letter and the Spirit," in idem, *Dante. The Poetics of Conversion*, ed. Rachel Jacoff (Cambridge, MA, and London, England: Harvard University Press, 1986), 119-135, at 131.

ing in Dante's poem between the experiences of the exile who has lost his way on the path and the knowledge of the author who knows the whole shape of the poem as he sets it out line by line, episode by episode. The ascetic task of the reader, led on by this glimpsed concinnity of exile and author, pilgrim and knower, is to see through the veil of material history to the sense beyond it, through sensuality to sense, through shadow to light. At one marvellous juncture of Botticelli's drawings of the *Divine Comedy*, at *Paradiso* xxi, he has gone ahead of the story and shown Dante and Beatrice twice, once at the base of Jacob's ladder and again in the process of climbing it higher into heaven, but he has then gone back and scored this part of the drawing out with a sharp point, leaving only the two figures at the bottom of the ladder, in Dante's case (as we know from the text) still a pilgrim, unable to see to the top of the ladder. Here is the impulse of the reader to see beyond, and the asceticism which corrects it, telling him he must wait for the story to unfold. The unfolding, though, is not in doubt.

Petrarch is different again. The shadow of peregrination, of the interim between image and true form or between eros and spirit, is where the substance of the thing lies. But this interim space is neither shaped by the equal light of dawn nor by the clarity of a vision whose source is elsewhere, and strong enough to gather what still seems dispersed. Petrarch's method, so nearly the narcissism of self-pity–"Virgin, how many tears I have already spent, how many pleadings and how many prayers said in vain"[33]–is perhaps in the end that of drawing from the claustrophobia of an obsession the possibility of repentance.

---

33 *Rime sparse* 366, ll. 79-80 (to the Virgin): "Vergine, quante lagrime ò già sparte,/ quante lusinghe et quanti preghi indarno..."

MOMENTS OF INDECISION, SOVEREIGN POSSIBILITIES: NOTES ON THE *TABLEAU VIVANT*

Frans-Willem Korsten

1. Introducing "or"

Probably the best known and still most widely read medieval knight's tale of the Low Countries is *Karel ende Elegast*.[1] As is common in the Middle Ages, the written version of the tale (the best known dates from around 1350) builds from an older oral story. There is no question that the older oral variant was one out of many. We have testimony of different kinds of versions, ranging from epic tales to fairy tales and from prose to poetry, that have been found all over Europe.[2] In the particular Dutch version I am focusing on, Charlemagne is at the height of his power and is summoned, by an angel, to go out stealing. The angel has to repeat his request three times before Charles obeys. The latter gets dressed, takes his weapons, sneaks out of the castle and mounts his horse, plunging into the woods where he will meet a black knight. First thinking that he encounters the devil, Charles will soon learn that his adversary is one of his vassals, whom he had expelled for a trivial reason. Since he was banned, Elegast, as the vassal is called, lives the life of a robber, although it is ex-

---

1 I will be using the edition made by A.M. Van Duinhoven, *Karel ende Elegast. Diplomatische uitgave van de Middelnederlandse teksten en de tekst uit de Karlmeinet-compilatie*. Dl. 1 (Assen: Van Gorcum, 1969). That edition also formed the basis for an online edition that can be found at http://www.dbnl.org/tekst/_kar001kare01_01/colofon.htm. In 1998 the same edition was used in a book that also offers a translation in modern Dutch by Karel Eykman, *Karel ende Elegast–Het mooiste Nederlandse ridderverhaal uit de Middeleeuwen* (Amsterdam: Prometheus/Bert Bakker, 1998).

2 For the German reception, see Duijvestijn, "Middelnederlandse litteratuur in Duitse overlevering. Een arbeidsveld voor neerlandici," in F.P. van Oostrom and Frank Willaert, eds., *De studie van de Middelnederlandse letterkunde: stand en toekomst* (Hilversum: Verloren 1989), 153-168. For versions in other countries and regions, see, for instance, M.C.A. Brongers, "*Karel ende Elegast* en de Oudnoorse *Karlmagnûs saga*," *Nieuwe taalgids* 65 (1972): 161-180; or Van den Berg, 'De omzwervingen van *Karel ende Elegast*'. *Rapiarijs* (Utrecht: Instituut de Vooys, 1987), 9-11. A.M. van Duinhoven offers the most concise overview in the 1998 edition, pp. 13-15.

plicitly stated that, to his honour, he only robs the wealthy. This night, now, Charles and Elegast will go out stealing together.

In the story several moments of interruption play a decisive role, the status of which in relation to history is what concerns me. One such interruption can be found at the very beginning, when the angel summons Charles for the first time. Charles has just fallen asleep and is abruptly woken. This interruption on the level of action, or the *fabula*, takes place when the angel speaks as follows:

> … "Rise noble man.
> Dress yourself as quick as you can.
> Take your weapons and go out stealing,
> God ordered me to summon you,
> Who is lord in the empire of heaven,
> Or you lose your life and honour."
> (*Karel ende Elegast*, ll. 19-24) [3]

As one can see it is not just a matter of Charles being interrupted in the act of sleeping. The interrupting act is itself interrupted, for the angel speaks and then temporarily breaks off with: "God ordered me to summon you/Who is lord in the empire of heaven". The "who" obviously refers to God, here, but grammatically it can also refer to "you": Charles. The latter would then be lord of heaven. The resulting ambiguity is related to another one, concerning line 21 and 24. Taken together, these lines form the sentence: "Take your weapons and go out stealing//or you lose your life and honour". That sentence may be puzzling for Charles or for the uninformed listener, since both will wonder why on earth a king should go out stealing. Still, the sentence itself is perfectly grammatical. Due to the interruption, however, the sentence becomes awkward rhythmically and semantically. The effect is that the "or" in line 24 turns into an icon for what is at stake. The flow of action is caught in a freeze that puts emphasis on the "or" as an alternative line of action and, consequently, a different history.

It would not be very difficult to argue that these interruptions are a sure sign of an oral text, in which a skilful story-teller might use all kinds of interjections. Indeed, throughout the text, moments of interruption occur that can be traced by means of a change in an ongoing rhythm and pace manifesting itself on the level of the action, on the level of telling, or

---

3 All translations are mine, FWK. In the original the text is: "Ende seyde staet op edel man. / Doet haestelic v cleeder an / Wapent v ende vaert stelen. / God die hiet mi v beuelen / Die in hemelrike is here / Of ghi verliest lijf ende eere."

on the level of speaking. In some particular cases, however, the action appears to be distinctly *frozen* for a certain moment. A good case in point is this passage, where the consequent "or" after "Take your weapons and go out stealing" has to wait to materialize due to the frozen moment coming before it. It is as if Charles and the listeners have to hold their breath for a certain moment before being able to continue. In a sense this is simply a matter of suspense. Yet, I think such frozen moments, not just in this text but also in general, have another potential, that would even acquire a generic shape in the course of the coming centuries, namely as the *tableau vivant*. That is to say: I consider such frozen moments, as they appear in *Karel ende Elegast*, to be the embryonic form of the *tableau vivant*.

When, in this passage, the angel states that Charles must go out stealing, he does so without giving any explanation or reason. The angel simply calls upon the highest authority, God, who, apparently has something in store for the future. But what? The interruption results in an affectively heightened moment of awareness, or an intensified connection between audience and subject in relation to time. The major question, here, is how the freeze or *tableau vivant* functions to intensify a particular, decisive, moment. This intensity, so I will argue, cannot be explained entirely by considering the frozen moment only in relation to a well-known, or pre-ordained history. Partly the intensity is dependent upon a well known history. Partly, also, it is related to an as yet unknown future. Even when this future is known, the *tableau vivant* destabilizes it, and points to the possibility that it is not known. The frozen moment or tableau vivant is an in-between, a medium that, as such, forms an excellent carrier of affect. Aesthetically, in terms of affect, the *tableau vivant* helps to connect us with a distinctive historical moment in a particularly intense way.[4]

The intensity may also be the result of the way in which the frozen moment or *tableau vivant* embodies a moment of constitution. In its singularity and as a form of frozen action in the developing action, the moment captured is constitutive. It is, for instance, an expression of an as yet not established or not realized sovereignty: a sovereignty-in-the-making. In the case of this passage the moment of constitution is made explicit by a description of God as the supreme power. One might argue that such an appeal to God's sovereignty surely is a sign of an already established power. God's supreme power needs no moment of constitution. But that

---

4 I am thinking of Deleuze's conceptualization of affect here, as it is developed in the two studies on cinema: *Cinéma*, vol. 1: *L'image-mouvement* (Paris: Minuit, 1983) and vol. 2: *L'image-temps* (Paris: Minuit, 1985).

would be an argument that is specifically post nineteenth-century. Many medieval texts testify of the struggle to establish God's sovereignty. Often his sovereignty is emphatically proclaimed. The emphasis is needed because God's sovereignty is still in the making, or can never become a natural given. It needs to be artificially realized time and again. This specifically medieval artificiality was one of the main topics of interest in the work of Burcht Pranger.[5]

In relation to constitution, the frozen moment, as later the *tableau vivant*, may also serve to rigidify a distinct order or to radically open it up. History, in this case, is not what has happened with hindsight but what can be made by actors that act as the sovereign force in the production of history. In the case of *Karel ende Elegast*, it may be hard to consider Charles as a sovereign actor since he clearly appears to be the object of God's commands. But there is a split, here, between what happens in the story and the way in which the story is used or received politically. Whereas God may be commanding history in the story, he himself may well be used rhetorically to justify the sovereign actions of distinctly earthly actors. Let me consider this first.

2. Making (One's) History

When Charles has plunged into the dark wood at the beginning of the story, he meets, as has already been said, Elegast. The two challenge one another and start a fight that ends inconclusively. They then start to talk and decide to go out stealing together. This relieves Charles, who is rather worried about his capacities as a thief. In order to help himself, Charles first suggests going to Ingelheim, to the castle that he is familiar with. Elegast is shocked. He could not steal from his own king! No, they had better go to the castle of Eggeric, Charles' brother-in-law and a treacherous man, according to Elegast. The latter, having noticed that his companion is not a particularly skilful thief, enters Eggeric's castle alone, even for a second time. This is when he overhears a quarrel in the bedroom between Eggeric and his wife–Charles' sister. From that quarrel he learns that Eggeric plans to assassinate the king the next day. When Charles hears this, he immediately understands why he had to go out stealing. He was summoned by God, of course, in order to discover this act of treason. Likewise the

---

5 Notably in M.B. Pranger, *The Artificiality of Christianity: Essays on the Poetics of Monasticism* (Stanford, CA: Stanford University Press, 2003).

audience is supposed to understand that Charles' rule must be divine in nature, then.

All commentators accept the logic of this. Firstly, it is logical that Charles has to wonder why he has to go out stealing, since he, as he himself expresses, has no need to do so. He has everything he wants already. Secondly, it becomes logical that Charles has to go out stealing, because he has to learn about the plot against him. In relation to this, the common presupposition is that God's sovereignty is supreme, and that Charles is just his instrument. If we were to simply accept this logic, however, we would have a hard time explaining why the entire text is structured by trickery and thievery. Charles acts as a thief and tricks Elegast as to his true identity, Elegast has to trick and steal in order to make a living, Eggeric acts as the loyal brother-in-law, to then take the king's life in order to steal the kingdom. More generally even, stealing is a dominant theme in the text, or becomes so through the text.

One peculiar passage is telling. From ll. 204 to 273 Charles has just entered the dark wood. He is thinking by himself how he used to hunt thieves relentlessly. Now, rather suddenly, he grows to understand them. Then, before he has even met Elegast, the latter is already on Charles' mind. The reason is that Elegast had to become a thief because Charles had robbed him of his lands and possession for a trivial reason. Here Charles appears not only as a man who feels guilty about what he has done to a former vassal, but also as someone who has taken another's possessions without real justification. In a sense he has stolen from Elegast what was rightly his. With respect to the issue of the king taking the possessions of others, notably vassals, there is more historical material that is relevant and that works back on the story.

In the Dutch version of the story it is emphasized twice at the beginning that Charles is at Ingelheim, near the Rhine. Historically Charlemagne indeed had a castle there. The place serves as a realistic detail, then. Yet, there's more in the plot that resonates with Ingelheim–and with history. As A.M. Duinhoven explains the story may have two insurgencies against Charles for its working material.[6] The first insurgency is the one by count Hardrad, in 785, who had his powerbase at "the other side" of the Rhine. In Sigebertus' *Chronographia* from the late 11th century this Hardrad is called Hardericus, which in German becomes Harderic or

---

6 *Karel ende Elegast*, 19-25. On Tassilo, see also Rosamond McKitterick, *Charlemagne: The Formation of a European Identity* (Cambridge: Cambridge University Press, 2008), 118-127.

Herderic. That's already closer to Eggeric. Even more important is the in-surgence of Tassilo, duke of Bavaria, who was a cousin of Charles and one of his vassals. When Charles held court at Ingelheim in 788 he decided to remove Tassilo. The latter and his men were invited and captured when arriving in the castle. This is precisely what happens with Eggeric and his men at the end of *Karel ende Elegast*. In the story, and in relation to the historical event, the element of family-relations is shifted from Tassilo's being the sun of Charles' father's sister, to Eggeric's being the husband of the sister of Charles himself.

Historically, the interesting thing is that there is no real evidence that Tassilo plotted against the king. As the duke of Bavaria, he was extreme-ly successful, though, in extending his power. As a result he became the competitor that Charles did not want. This is why Charles made him ex-press his loyalty as a vassal two times, which Tassilo did. Apparently that was not enough. Of course Frankish sources want him to be a renegade that needed to be punished. But the Frankish sources are remarkably con-tradictory and there are other reports that clearly refer to a show trial. In this context the capture of Tassilo at the court of Ingelheim can be seen as a treacherous act by Charles, who had invited Tassilo to a feast only in order to be able to remove him from power and reassert Charles' claim to the lands that were, in a sense, Tassilo's.

In the light of this, one is tempted to shift the family relations one step further, from nephew (Tassilo), to brother-in-law (Eggeric), to brother. In all stories about Charlemagne his younger brother, Carloman, plays almost no role. This is not surprising since the man left the field before Charles had become Charlemagne. Or perhaps it is better to say that only because Carloman left the field Charles could become "the Great"–the one and only. In fact usurpation is what made the entire house of Charles into the house that it was. Charles' grandfather, Charles Martel, was not a king, but a king's mayor (from *maior domus*), as his fathers had been. It was this grandfather who may have decided to make an end to the farcical situa-tion of mayors acting like kings without being one, since in some docu-ments he is already described as "king." "Better be a king myself," is what his son Pippin III may have thought in 751, when he had himself anointed as king. The latter left his realm in 768 to both his sons: Charles and Car-loman.[7] As could be expected the two of them were not of one mind. Pa-

---

7   For the history of the Merovingian kings and mayors, see I. Wood, *The Meroving-ian Kingdoms* (London: Pearson, 1994), or P. Fouracre, *The Age of Charles Martel* (Harlow: Longman, 2000).

pal sources mention disharmony amongst the Frankish kings. In a papal letter from Pope Stephen III it is mentioned how relieved he was to learn from the brothers themselves how they had put aside their quarrels in order to preserve order and to guarantee the protection of the church. To accept this as a sign of the fact that the two brothers had no serious quarrel, as Rosamond McKitterick does, is not convincing to anyone familiar with the subtle language of diplomacy.[8]

We happen to know that Carloman suddenly dies in 771 and is immediately buried. We are informed that his wife and her two small sons immediately flee to Italy. This flight surely does not testify of much trust in the protection of Charles, or perhaps it expresses worse: the fear that Charles would come after them. Finally there is the fact that Carloman is very shortly dealt with in all the chronicles about Charles' life. This all suggests something different. Carloman had to make way so that Charles could be one and only king. It is possible that Carloman died a natural death. It is equally possible that he did not, in which case Charles stole half of the kingdom. Historically, therefore, Charles may have been an enormously skilled and well-trained thief.

As funny as the text of *Karel ende Elegast* may be, especially in the passages in which Charles shows himself a clumsy fool, as when he takes a farmer's plough as a burglar's instrument, the burlesque or carnivalesque elements point in the opposite direction. The political question is how Charles constituted his reign, how he came to occupy the seat of king and emperor, or how he constituted himself as Charles "the Great".

The chronicles show enough cases of people trying to get rid of Charles, including his eldest son Pippin the Hunchback in 792. Charles himself is depicted as solely noble–a marvellous case of successful "spin." As for this son Pippin, it is telling that in *Karel ende Elegast* Charles has an easy hand in distributing female family members. At the end of the story his sister is given to Elegast without much ado. In contrast Pippin the Hunchback was never allowed to marry, as was the case with most of Charles sons and daughters–nineteen in all. This, no doubt, would have led to too much competition, which is why most of them ended up in a monastery or in some other ecclesiastical position.

The cover up of histories, the spin given to histories, hence the making of history is always a precarious thing. This becomes clear at the very end of the play, when Eggeric and Elegast fight one another in a God's verdict.

---

8 McKitterick, *Charlemagne*, 78-79.

The battle has started "shortly before vespers" but is still going on "long after vesper time." Charles then asks God to put an end to this fight "in accordance with reason and justice" (l. 1439). So we get to the final, decisive moment, when Elegast has raised his sword:

> Elegast has raised it
> And struck a blow so mighty
> With the help of God almighty
> And so it is all in His honour
> And the prayer of the king
> which he did for Elegast
> So that he robbed him
> Of the biggest half of his head
> He dropped dead from his saddle.
> (*Karel ende Elegast*, ll. 1445-1453)[9]

As one sees, the theme of thievery has returned, explicitly, though perhaps hardly noticed. Elegast "robs" Eggeric of half his head. One could see this as a metaphorical way of speaking quite common in European languages. One can rob some other of his life. Still, the metaphor points to a sovereignty that is in place, even when the robbing is done with the sanction of God. With regard to the momentousness of life the "so that" in l. 1451 gets an intensely precarious quality, like the "or" in the previous passage. The tenses of the verb indicate the freeze in this passage. First present perfect (has raised), then a past (struck) which is frozen for a moment in the present of the interruption (so it is), after which we have the past of history (did) of Charles' prayer, after which there is the past of the provisional result (robbed, dropped). In the passage from line 47 to 50, and most intensely in the present tense of line 48, the sword remains hanging in the air for a moment. In this sense the passage gets the quality of a *tableau vivant*, or in this sense the passage embodies the precarious status of history being made. "And struck a blow so powerful…" has to wait for four lines before we see what the effect will be, or better: will have been.

In its rigidity or frozenness lines 47-50, the lines-in-between, function as a counterbalance to the precariousness of the moment. When the weight comes down it's done. It has come down. Life retakes its course. Eggeric is hanged, Elegast is re-installed as Charles' noble vassal and he gets Eggeric's wife. May God reward us all like this, the narrator wishes, "and now say ye all 'amen.'"

---

9 "Elegast, die hever verheven / Ende sloech enen slach so sere, / Bi Gods hulpe onsen Here / Dus ist al bi sere / Ende des conincs gebede / Die hi over Elegast dede, / so dat hi hem rovede / Die meeste helft van den hovede. / Hi viel doot uten gereide."

3. Freedom and the Opening Up of History

The popularity of *Karel ende Elegast*, and the many variants that circulated throughout Europe, has many reasons. One reason may be the issue of the nature and constitution of Charles' political sovereignty. With respect to this political sovereignty, a determining and troubling force was that Christianity could not accept politics–if politics was to be based on the idea of a somehow free moment, or a choice to act in a certain way, opening up a historical potential, or the potential of history. Within Christianity human beings are the object of God's actions. Sinful human beings are charged with a guilt that makes their actions principally not-free. They have failed their God, are in debt, and the only option offered is to keep paying him back. Even if one considers moral freedom, as Catholics would be inclined to do, God remains the determining subject of history, as a result of which history is closed, or geared towards the ultimate goal of a Last Judgement. Consequently, on a conceptual level, Christianity was and had to be opposed to the idea of the political, as the possibility that a guiltless life might exist in relation to a history that is radically open.

Let me turn, a little later, to a telling moment in 1324 when Marsilius of Padua's *Defensor Pacis*, or *The Defender of the Peace*, is brought out in the open. Before getting to him more needs to be said first about the nature of this political and historical openness.

In the course of the Middle Ages the moment of interruption in an oral story would contribute to the development of an independent genre: the *tableau vivant*, performed both inside and outside of the theatre. On average, *tableaux vivants* captured a charged moment in a well-known history. With respect to this, the *tableau vivant*, although being clearly a form of representation, was distinctly non-representative. It came to be a time-image that differs from, for instance, a photograph. It radiates with the warmth of living bodies that remain motionless in front of an audience that can almost touch them. As for the warmth, it is realized in a different way as well. Although the frozen moment of the *tableau vivant* represents some kind of temporary end in a historical development, it is alive in that it upholds what follows. It is truly momentous in this respect, literally breathtaking. It is also momentous, however, and perhaps figuratively breathtaking, with regard to the future, to which the *tableau vivant* remains effectively, radically open. Carrying the weight of a history, embodying the charged relations between live actors, whilst not showing but containing the potency of what is to happen, the *tableau vivant* is particularly intense in terms of affect. As such, and with regard to its momentous-ness and openness toward the future, the *tableau vivant* may capture the nature of the political *moment*, which is the topic that directs my argument.

Looking for a powerful image that may illustrate how the political ultimately is an act of a particular kind of freedom, Fabio Vighi and Heiko Feldner, authors of *Žižek beyond Foucault*, give the example of what, according to some, must be the best goal in the history of soccer. It concerns the second goal of Diego Maradona at the world championship of 1986: Argentina against England. Let's have a look at it again, keeping in mind Žižek's particular conceptualization of freedom:

> Freedom is not the freedom to do as you like (that is to follow your inclinations without any externally imposed constraints), but to do what you do not want to do, to thwart the 'spontaneous' realization of an impetus.[10]

In the first line of this quote Isaiah Berlin's two classical conceptualizations of freedom are condensed: positive freedom, indicating that you are enabled to act freely according to your will, and negative freedom, indicating that there are no forces outside of you that hinder or restrict your actions.[11] Žižek's ignores the antithesis between the two because both ideas of freedom concern a (political) subject who is, as an autonomous, conscious actor, able to *make* politics, or history. For Žižek, in the context of the totalitarian power of capitalism, political freedom cannot be considered in terms of such conscious and willful actions, but only in relation to a drive. Such a drive is not free in itself, on the contrary, but without it the opening up of a new possibility is impossible. That opening up cannot be a matter of strategy either, for then we are talking about politics in terms of achievable goals, and the very idea of achievability implies a form of historical closed-ness.

With respect to all this, Maradona's action is an example of what it might mean to grab the political moment, driven by something, and opening up history. Attacked by one English player in his back and by one in a slight angle to the right before him, whereas a third player blocks an escape to the left, Maradona's rational option is to pass the ball to one of his players in front of him. But instead the inconceivable happens, through what Vighi and Feldner call "an impromptu pirouette," an act of

---

10   Slavoj Žižek, *The Parallax View* (Cambridge, MA: MIT Press, 2006), 202.

11   Berlin's inaugural lecture from 1958, "Two Concepts of Liberty," has been republished in Henry Hardy, ed., *Liberty: Incorporating Four Essays on Liberty* (Oxford: Oxford University Press, 2002), 166-217.

virtuosity.[12] Having frozen the moment just before this act we have an image that partly resembles a *tableau vivant*. We know what it represents, recognize the temporary end, and we are aware of what will happen. So, how can the scene still work? Like this: it is as if we can sense the radical openness of history, and perhaps more fully now than at the historical moment itself, in 1986.

Five related issues can be derived from this scene. One: freedom consists in an entanglement of acting and being acted upon. This entanglement remains open, or can be opened up, through a drive. Maradona *produces* freedom through his pirouette. He does not *have* it in the sense of a free will that determines his actions beforehand, nor is he free from opposing forces. Acting, and simultaneously being the object of others' actions, he operates freely, suddenly. Two: the nature of the political moment is such that we do not know beforehand what an actor is going to do. Only with hindsight, the course of history will appear to have been changed. Yet, and that's three: the political moment is momentous, even on the slightest time-scale and whether we speak about micro-politics or macro-politics. Whereas with the *tableau vivant* we take the time, freezing the movement as if we hold our breaths, there is something in the political moment as well, perhaps in a split second, that has this breathtaking quality. Four: in relation to both the type of freedom-in-acting and the political moment, affects play a pivotal role. Driven by affects, affecting others and affected by others, caught in an intensified moment, subjects act. However, five: the moment at which an act becomes decisively political, it gets charged aesthetically, as a result of which it can be judged both politically and aesthetically.

In the last decades, the idea that affects have an important, positive role to play in relation to aesthetics and politics did not appear out of the blue. On the contrary, affects have been, perhaps still are, at the core of a vehement struggle that goes a long way back. One of the dominant players in that struggle was Christianity, in its different institutional shapes. In relation to both earthly politics or the realization of history, the Christian *doxa* was that affects or passions inevitably will become excessive. Consequently they are considered as vices that form a moral threat, and a threat to social harmony. Funny thing is, of course, that Christianity itself starts with, and is fueled by a passion: the passion of Christ. Whilst being driven by passion itself, then, Christianity passionately fought and fights against the powers of affects.

---

12 Fabio Vighi and Heiko Feldner, *Žižek Beyond Foucault* (Houndmills/New York: Palgrave MacMillan 2007), 225-229.

A prominent target of Christian attacks was the Greek philosopher Epicurus. In his philosophy not just the senses, and aesthetics, played a positive role, but also the *pathe*, feelings, which were part and parcel of man's ability to *know*. In the Roman and early Christian era the aspect of knowledge in relation to *pathe* would be downplayed and *pathos* would get three translations: *passio*, *perturbatio*, and the twin set *affectio* and *affectus*. The fact that these were recurrently used indiscriminately in later times can be attributed to Augustine, who elaborated on the translations in his *City of God*.[13]

Of the three *affectio* and *affectus* would prove to be least prone to negative connotations. As a result they could be reconsidered positively in later times, especially in the seventeenth century. *Passio* and *perturbatio* acquired more negative connotations. *Perturbatio* would imply disturbance, unrest, imbalance, and disharmony. With *passio* the way in which one was being affected could easily become a form of infliction or suffering, like in Christ's passion. And whereas his passion was valued immensely, other manifestations of passions weren't. Susan James describes, in her pivotal study *Passion and Action*, how they were considered as forces "that are at once extremely powerful and actually or potentially beyond our control. They perturb the economy of body and soul in ways that we are sometimes unable to prevent... [they] are rebels who rise up against reason and understanding, make secessions, raise mutinies."[14] The imagery is distinctly political. A question might therefore be why that would disturb Christianity, as a religion.

For Christianity affects were first of all vicious and unacceptable because they could corrupt the morality of man or could disrupt social order. But equally important was the fact that they embodied a radical freedom: a political potency or openness towards the future. Accordingly, those who looked for ways of opening up a domain of politics proper or who wanted to consider the principal openness of human history, had to re-conceptualize the notion of affects.

Enter Marsilius of Padua, who lived from around 1275 to 1342. Just a year after Marsilius' death Pope Clement VI expressed his extreme satisfaction that this "heresiarch" was dead. He had never read "a worse her-

---

13 Augustine, *City of God* 9.4; see the translation of Henry Bettenson (London: Penguin, 2003), 345-58.

14 Susan James, *Passion and Action: The Emotions in Seventeenth Century Philosophy* (Oxford: Oxford University Press, 1997), 11.

etic than that Marsilius."[15] The latter's heresy was specified partly as Aver-
roism, one of the usual suspects at the time. No mistake: neither Marsilius, nor the twelfth century Andalusian-Arabian scholar Averroes, or Abu
al-Walid Muhammad Ibn Ahmad Ibn Rushd, would have accepted the
truth of revelation and the truth of science to be equal or competitive. The
position of both scholars can better be described as what we now would
call a "difference within." Still, they themselves, and their enemies as well,
sensed rightly, that this difference-within would lead to a radically different routing, or to an opening up of history.[16]

4. Grabbing the Moment

Defensor pacis is typically scholastic in that it consists of an exhaustively
elaborated argument. Its theme, however, is distinctly atypical. Three discourses, entire books on their own, address the discrepancy that whilst
Christianity is not able to accept politics it is *doing* politics, either by divine intervention, as when God sends his son to intervene in history, or
by papal intervention in earthly matters of all sorts. Against the first, Marsilius does not, probably could not, have an argument. He is more outspoken when turning to the church. For Marsilius the development of the
papacy is "one long and exploitative process of illicit encroachment upon
the civic sphere, both in the form of owning property and in the form of
exercising coercive jurisdiction."[17] Why illicit? Because the encroachment
on the civic sphere by the church was not a matter of politics. Filling in
the political domain, the church veiled itself as a political player as a result
of which it could not be questioned on political terms. It hollowed out the
political domain, whilst having political aims: the control of property and
the claim to sovereign juridical coercion.

The hollowing out of the political domain by the church had to lead,
according to Marsilius, to disharmony. His major question then is how
to restore the possibility of a harmonious society through politics. In the
context of that question affects play a crucial role. Marsilius' *affectio* partly

---

15   Annabel Brett, Introduction of Marsilius of Padua, in Marsilius of Padua, *The Defender of the Peace*, ed. and trans. A. Brett (Cambridge: Cambridge University Press, 2005),
ix.

16   Even in a watered down version, as when Marsilius would defend the possibility of
a secular or temporal truth of reasoning against the divine or spiritual truth of belief, his
enemies could claim that thus he subverted the existence of one truth, and one truth only.

17   Brett, Introduction, xxviii.

went back to Cicero's, who contrasted *affectio* with *habitus–affectio* meaning a temporary change in the state of the body due to some cause. However, William of Moerbeke's translation of Aristotle's *Politics* plays a role as well, in which *affectio* was the equivalent of Greek *kédeia*, which meant some form of social tie, or alliance–hence faction. In relation to this relational or social aspect, it is of interest that affects are systematically considered in relation to actions.

Going back to Aristotle, Marsilius considers actions and affects within the dynamics of activity and passivity, hence of cause and effect. For Marsilius already holds what would become dominant in the seventeenth century, which is that: "To classify a state as passion or affect is to say something about its metaphysical and causal status, and something about its epistemological credentials; at the same time, it is to place it in a hierarchical structure of human thoughts and feelings and a broader topography of the mind and the body, each replete with moral significance."[18] And let me use this quote, in passing, to emphasize that for almost all of the thinkers concerned, Descartes included, there is never a simple split between soul and body, of which the latter would be the domain of emotions. Nor do they equate affects with emotions. Let me also note that passivity in this context does not mean the absence of action, but the fact that a body needs something else first that acts upon it in order to be affected.

In Marsilius' text affects are predominantly internal, but "they can issue in external or 'transitive' actions."[19] Indeed, after having stated that action and affects can be not-commanded or commanded (*Discourse* I, ch. 5), Marsilius subdivides the latter between those that are immanent and those that are transitive. Those are called immanent that take place within a body. Those that are transitive happen between bodies. So, affects may be doing something inwardly, but they can also concern the action towards or relation with other things and bodies.[20] This is all, according to Marsilius, entirely natural. Being natural, however, both actions and passions can be excessive, just like the weather can be. When the transitive ones become excessive, they threaten the web of social relations and the harmony within social order. Therefore a political solution is needed:

---

18 James, *Passion and Action*, 29.

19 Brett, Introduction, xxi.

20 See Marsilius of Padua, *The Defender of the Peace*, trans. A. Brett (Cambridge: Cambridge University Press, 2005), 214: "...insofar as they do not cross over into a subject other than the one producing them. All pursuits of things we desire, on the other hand, and all omissions of these (as their privations), and all movements produced by some exterior organ of the body (especially if it is moved in respect of place) ... are called 'transitive.'"

forms of coercion are necessary, handed over to a judge. For the temporal world, this judge must be the prince.

Yet, the prince is not simply a coercive power. It is also an animating one, and perhaps more than that. Using Aristotle's definition of man as a political animal, Marsilius reverses that definition by exploring the political element *as* an animal one (*Discourse* I, ch. 15). The constitutive parts of human society, imitating nature, are formed analogous to an animal. The question then is: what is "the efficient and determining cause of the parts of the city"? It is the "heart, or something analogous to the heart."[21] This organ has *virtus*: it is the source of a body's power or vigour. Later *virtus* is equated with law, and that which animates the law is the judging prince. Bringing the metaphor to its end, Marsilius will say that this heart is supposed to harmonize all actions that take place in the city. If it would cease its actions, this would disturb order: "And because of this the action of the prince in the city must never cease, just as the action of the heart in the animal must not."[22]

So, yes, in accordance with the medieval view affects or passions easily become excessive and therefore should be controlled, coerced, or balanced by a ruling power. However, in connecting affects principally to transitive action, Marsilius considers affects as the driving force within the body of human society. Affects are needed for the ongoing activity, for social *life*, in the city. In that context Marsilius does not define excessive affects as vices, as would be obligatory in Christianity, but as something natural. The third remarkable element, expressed metaphorically, is that at the very centre of the social body there is a force operative of which it remains unclear how it is commanded–if it is commanded. Qualifying the prince as the embodiment of *virtus*, or vigorous force, Marsilius has defined the prince as both the immanent and transitive power behind harmonious life in the *polis*. And with power and harmony both politics and aesthetics are in play.

Moreover, in relation to both, something else is at stake as well. Considering the prince as the heart that constantly and through ceaseless action invigorates and harmonizes the animal, Marsilius suggests that there is something in politics that escapes commandment, and therefore the moral rule of Christianity. The implication of the metaphor of the animal's heart with its vigorous, natural action is that there is another kind of freedom than the one related to empire or commandment. It is a type of free-

---

21   Ibid., 91.
22   Ibid., 96.

dom that Marsilius could not, or dared not, specify explicitly.[23] This would change, however. Let me turn to the conceptualisation of political drive, and the constituting *moment* of that drive in looking at Machiavelli's definition of *virtus*, or *virtù*.

Since the twelfth century scholastic thinkers had defined *virtus* as a crucial prerequisite for any ruler. Rulers had to shun violence (*vis*), and had to avoid vices such as avarice and exuberance. Instead they had to practice the four cardinal virtues that were the embodiment of *virtus*: justice, prudence, courage (*fortitudo*) and temperance. An issue on which the medieval scholastics and the later humanists would start to differ was the personal gain of this all. Whereas the scholastics tended to emphasize that the ruler needed to remain a humble servant of the community, the Italian humanists would emphasize that a ruler had to strive for fame and glory. It may be clear that Marsilius' definition of *virtus* is distinct from both. With Marsilius *virtus* indicated vigour, a force of animation, or an animating force. This element will be developed further by Nicollo Machiavelli, in *Il Principe*, from 1513. For him the virtuous shifts into the *virtuoso*. And in chapter 18 of *Il Principe*, an animal-metaphor plays an important role in the argumentation also.

Cicero had claimed that a just ruler must avoid brute force. He must not act beastly, neither with the raw force of the lion nor with the cunning guile of the fox. Machiavelli answers that one can indeed distinguish between human and beastly actions. But we do not live solely in a humane world. Men can act beastly. The classics had a good point in depicting the prince as a *kentauros*: half man, half beast; and appropriating Cicero's metaphors, Machiavelli then states that an effective ruler might best use both the force of the lion and the cleverness or skilfulness of the fox. For there is such a gap between how people ought to live and how they *do* live that a virtuous prince in the scholastic sense would not be able to preserve himself or the community. Faithfulness, in the temporal or spiritual sense of the word, fine; but vices may be necessary in order to rule, for it is not morals, but necessity that determines a ruler's actions. This is where Machiavelli's *Principe* becomes revolutionary:

---

23 When Marsilius explains the difference between commanded and not-commanded he says that "we do not have full liberty or empire over non-commanded acts as to whether they happen or not, whereas according to Christian religion, power over commanded acts lies in us" (*The Defender of the Peace*, 214). Here full liberty is equated with conscious ruling power (empire) and it is localized in the domain of commanded actions (*imperatus*) that is, within the Christian frame.

... it offers, in effect, a new analysis of what should count as *virtuoso* behaviour in a prince... A prince of true *virtù* will rather be someone who, in the proverbial phrase, makes a virtue of necessity. He will be ready at all times 'to turn and turn about as the winds and variations of fortune dictate'.[24]

In Machiavelli we meet a thinker, then, who considers the political *moment* as an intense entanglement of activity and passivity, or a simultaneous occurrence of action and being acted upon. Consequently the political is not a matter of wilful actions and strategies, but a ceaseless readiness and drive to act without beforehand knowing what action that will have been suited to what happens. That does not mean that Machiavelli is advocating brutish survival. *Virtù* counts, with its implications of skilfulness: art–aesthetics. Here politics' dominant task is not to keep in check affects; its very power becomes a matter of aesthetics and affects itself.

In this context a remark on affects by Gilles Deleuze is of importance: "Every mode of thought insofar as it is non-representational will be termed affect. A volition, a will implies, in all rigor, that I will something, and what I will is an object of representation, what I will is given in an idea, but the fact of willing is not an idea, it is an affect because it is a non-representational mode of thought."[25] If I translate this to my argument, the force of the political moment does not depend on individual will, volition, and on forms of representation, but on the affective drive of the subjects involved; all of them affected by others and affecting others. Let me consider, finally, what that will bring me when I turn to what can be called the century of affect, the seventeenth–with its *tableaux vivants*.

5. *The Moment of Politics*

In 1659 playwright Joost van den Vondel, published *Jeptha ofte offerbelofte–Jephthah or the vow to sacrifice*. The play reworks, expands on, and alters a short passage in the Bible, *Judges* 11-12:7. There, Jeptha is a bastard son of Gilead.[26] After the death of his father, Jeptha is disowned by

---

24 "Dictate", indeed, for in the original it says: "E però bisogna che elli abbi uno animo disposto a volgersi secondo ch' e' venti e le variazioni della fortuna li comandono." See Skinner, *Visions of Politics: Regarding Method* (Cambridge: Cambridge University Press, 2002), 147.

25 "Deleuze on Spinoza, Cours Vincennes–24/01/1978," http://www.webdeleuze.com/php/texte.php?cle=14&groupe=Spinoza&langue=2

26 The Dutch Authorized Version of the Bible calls Jeptha 'son of a whore' – although a few lines later he is the son of 'another woman'. So, probably father Gilead had at least one partner whom he had not married officially. The text in the Bible is, as it so often is, ambiguous when it comes to the qualification 'whore'; compare Mieke Bal, *Death and Dissymmetry: The Politics of Coherence in the Book of Judges* (Chicago: University of Chicago Press, 1988).

his half-brothers. He leads the life of a robber, until he is called upon by
the eldest of his tribe to take up leadership as the judge who gives direction to his lost people. Before a battle with the Ammonites, he promises
God that he shall celebrate victory with a sacrifice, namely the first being he meets coming out the door of his house. This turns out to be his
daughter. Even though it is his daughter and despite the ban on human
sacrifice, Jeptha keeps his word. His daughter is given two months to bid
her life farewell. In the meantime, Jeptha goes to war with a 'brother tribe',
the Ephraimites. He defeats them too. On his return, he kills his daughter,
who is called Ifis in the play.[27]

Act I of the play is concerned mainly with getting the mother out of
the house. When that has happened, Ifis and Jeptha can enter the stage.
With them acts II, III, and IV concentrate on discussions about the justifications for, or principal injustice of Jeptha's deed. In between act IV and
V Jeptha slaughters Ifis. In act V he feels remorse, and flees, also because
the mother returns. All the while Jeptha has had his doubts, for sure. But
throughout the play he talks of himself as an active, intentional individual.
Even when filled with self-disgust at times, he is preparing the murder
that, finally, he will carry out with his own hands. So, where is the political
moment?

Thanks to a chorus in the text and a performance of the play in the
seventeenth century it acquires a shape: in a *tableau vivant*, designed by
theatre director Jan Vos, who followed the description of the place of the
crime and the clothing and adornments of Ifis that are given in the text
(ll.1236 and following). So we see the sacrificial altar covered with small

---

27 In *Judges*, the daughter has no name and does not act. With Vondel, she appears as
a powerful character in four acts of the play, and she has a name: Ifis. The name is probably
taken from George Buchanan's *Jephte sive votum*, from 1554, who in turn took the name
from Ovid's *Metamorphoses* in which there is a story about a girl Iphis who grows up, disguised as a young man, in order to then change into a real young man (*Metamorphoses* ix, ll.
666-797, ed. Madeleine Forey and trans. Arthur Godling [Baltimore: Johns Hopkins University Press, 2002]). She had to disguise herself as a man because her father had declared to his
wife that the child she was bearing had better be a boy – for he would kill it if it were a girl.
Most plausible, then, is that Buchanan's Iphis and Vondel's Ifis are given this name because,
as a girl, she is not permitted to live by their father. As to the namelessness of the daughter,
put at a disadvantage by her namelessness because she can give less reason for identification, see also Bal, *Death and Dissymmetry*, 43. Bal calls the daughter Bath – daughter. That
Vondel's Ifis is more than a secondary character is argued by Van Dael, "Een toonbeeld van
gehoorzaamheid: Ripo en Vondels *Jeptha of offerbelofte*," *De zeventiende eeuw* 11:1 (1995),
89. Van Dael sees Ifis as a prefiguration of Christ – and has strong arguments for this. Ifis is
the 'sacrificial lamb' (l. 404) and is called 'rose of Jericho.' The 'rose of Jericho' exists in reality:
Anastatica Hierochuntica, or 'resurrection plant' – a plant whose dry bud is brought to life
by water. Because of this, the plant symbolizes Jesus' resurrection after death.

branches of wood to catch the blood. Common periwinkle is strewn every-where, the plant that stays green forever (symbol of virginity). Festoons of flowers are hanging on all the walls. Ifis is lying on the altar. Jeptha stands with sacrificial sword at the ready. And then there's a third figure, added by Vos: a lady representing Religion, who, perhaps horrified, turns her face away from the intended act.

With all the actors thus in place, they freeze for a moment: a temporary end in a development. One can argue that they are just on display, fasci-nating, perhaps thrilling an audience that knows what will happen: that sword will come down. However, the inevitability of this, or the closed-ness of this history, is countered by the chorus at the end of act IV. It de-scribes a history that on the level of action freezes into a *tableau vivant*:

> See them there, together.
> The altar stands, it's built,
> Isaac, the blessing of his father,
> is kneeling on the sacrificial wood.
> Abraham draws the sword
> to hit, when he
> by the Angel with his voice
> from heaven, is stopped.
> (*Jeptha*, ll. 1658-1666)[28]

The crucial sentence, here, is line 1664: "to hit, when he." Stop. He was about to hit when he–what? Did he, or didn't he? This is the moment in time where history may be altered from what seemed to be destined. Sud-denly a warmth of possibilities can be felt. Someone may act differently than we had expected, not out of his own free will, but in a situation of simultaneous acting and being acted upon.

It is such a moment also that is caught in Vos' *tableau vivant*. Whereas earlier I stated that both the *tableau vivant* and the political moment are not about representation, one could argue that here we have a distinct-ly representative, allegorical figure: Religion. Indeed so, but the nature of her representing something is one thing. The other is her frozen ac-tion. She has turned away, or better: she is being turned away. The being turned away of Religion is intrinsically political in relation to the future. It tells that what is about to happen will not be sanctified. Besides, as for what is about to happen, the impossible question is: Will it? We seem to

---

28   "Zietze bey te gader. / 't Outer staet gebout. / Isack, 's vaders zegen, / Knielt op 't of-ferhout. / Abram treckt den degen / Om te slaen, als hem / d'Engel met zijn stem / Uit den hemel tegenhiel."

know. The moment that is being captured is the one "just before." Intensifying that moment, however, the scene is breathtaking, momentous, in that there still is the possibility that it will not happen. Jeptha can decide, driven by whatever affect, not to kill his daughter. All that can be felt by a live audience, sensing the vigour of the bodies capturing the moment. Both actors and audience are in this breathtaking moment. Once the actors disentangle, get out of their pose, the moment is gone. Something momentous will have taken place. The daughter is dead, or she lives. The son is dead, or he lives. The father killed his child, or not.

I read Vondel's play with its *tableau vivant* of Abraham and Isaac, or the *tableau vivant* by Vos as embodiments of a positive re-conceptualisation of affects in the seventeenth century. This is not to say that Vondel or Vos endorsed the flourishing materialist philosophy that was allowed to develop in the Dutch Republic. Yet, their art had taken in what was discussed publicly and privately. And one of the most radical contributors to that discussion was Spinoza, who defined *affectus* as the continuous variation of the power of acting.[29] With "power" politics is implied, with "variation," or intensity, aesthetics. Indeed, affect is intrinsically related to both, or is on the crossroads between politics and aesthetics. This ties in with the way in which Spinoza defines *affectio*, in the analysis of Deleuze, as "a mixture of two bodies, one body which is said to act on another, and the other receives the trace of the first."[30] That is: affects are about the intensity and power of relations.

Now, Spinoza was only one of several thinkers who would change European thinking on affects and the way in which human beings act in the world. Before Spinoza, for instance, Franco Burgersdijk (1590-1635), who was teaching philosophy at Leiden University from the 1620s onwards, considered affects "not as the dark side of man, as flesh opposed to spirit, but as the material upon which man can develop his potentialities" as Hans Blom states.[31] Considered within the frame of potency the nature of the political subject would start to change. Hannah Arendt grasped adequately what was behind Machiavelli's ideas on this subject, when she said that "Nobody knows whom he reveals when he discloses himself in deed

---

29 Benedict de Spinoza, *Ethics*, trans. E.M. Curley (London: Penguin, 2004), 113-159.

30 "Deleuze on Spinoza," http://www.webdeleuze.com/php/texte.php?cle=14&groupe=Spinoza&langue=2

31 Hans W. Blom, *Morality and Causality in Politics: The Rise of Materialism in Dutch Seventeenth Century Political Thought* (Utrecht: University of Utrecht, 1995), 77.

and word."[32] Coincidentally, the conceptualisation of freedom would be subject to change as well. It no longer needed to be defined by individual will and volition, but could be determined by affect, drive, relation and choice.

Why would all that be so relevant politically? Or why *is* it? Let me end with quoting Deleuze here when he talks about Spinoza's idea of affects as intensifying the potency of a body, joyously, or lessening it, saddening it:

> ...how does it happen that people who have power, in whatever domain, need to affect us in a sad way? The sad passions are necessary. Inspiring sad passions is necessary for the exercise of power. And Spinoza says, in the *Theological-Political Treatise*, that this is a profound point of connection between the despot and the priest–they both need the sadness of their subjects. Here you understand well that he does not take sadness in a vague sense, he takes sadness in the rigorous sense he knew to give it: sadness is the affect insofar as it involves the diminution of my power of acting.[33]

Perhaps our current interest in affects might help us to better sense certain diminutions of our powers to act. Surely, as may have become clear, our interest in affects will not show us a clear-cut political way out. But our study of affects could give us a better, a fuller, a sharper, a more intense sense of what politics might mean again. Or it could help us to be prepared better, on any political level, and with respect to issues ranging from big to small, in order to be able to act, virtuously, at the given political moment.

---

32   Arendt, *The Human Condition* (London/Chicago: University of Chicago Press, 1989 [1958]),180.
33   "Deleuze on Spinoza," http://www.webdeleuze.com/php/texte.php?cle=14&groupe =Spinoza&langue=2

HISTORY AND THE VERTICAL CANON: CALVIN'S *INSTITUTES* AND BECKETT

Ernst van den Hemel

In his *The Western Canon: The Books and School of the Ages* (1994) Harold Bloom discusses the absence of Gore Vidal's literary work in the literary canon. Bloom suggests that it is because Vidal's oeuvre consists mostly of 'historical novels' that the spirit of the times denies one of Bloom's favourite authors a place in the canon. Our age no longer values historical novels greatly: "History writing and narrative fiction have come apart, and our sensibilities seem no longer able to accommodate them one to another."[1] Vidal's failure to achieve truly canonical status problematizes Bloom's project of providing a canon of Western culture because it points to the shifting form of the canon. In admitting that for our age the 'subgenre' of the historical novel is "no longer available for canonization,"[2] Bloom has to answer once again the question of the dangerously temporal nature of forming a canon: What is the value of the canon if it is merely a discursive snapshot of a *zeitgeist*? Is the canon not merely a reiteration of dominant values? Bloom's problem is that he writes a canon in the period that Bloom calls the Chaotic Age (the other two ages that Bloom forms his canon with are the Aristocratic and the Democratic). The Chaotic Age contains such writers as Freud, Proust, Joyce, Woolf and Kafka. The section in which Bloom describes this age starts with a diatribe against Marxism, Freudian and Foucauldian theories of interpretation, and it ends with a warning that a great writer such as Beckett should be saved from these "New Theocrats"[3] that see in literature nothing more than class-struggle, sublimation or power-structures. The message is clear: The Chaotic Age tries to do away with canon-formation. Bloom explicitly wants to depart from Foucauldian, Derridean, post-modern criticisms of canonicity. These exponents of the 'School of Resentment' are, according to Bloom, for a

---

1 Harold Bloom, *The Western Canon: The Books and School of the Ages* (New York: Riverhead Books, 1995), 21.

2 Ibid., 21.

3 Ibid., 514.

large part responsible for the deplorable state of literary criticism in our Chaotic Age. Bloom is, he writes with self-pity, "a literary-critic in what I now regard as the worst of all times for literary criticism."[4] Bloom presents himself as the savior of canonicity in a time of cultural relativism. In order to do this, however, he needs to separate literature from the claims of history. Over against the 'anti-canonizers' Bloom asserts the eternal supremacy of that which makes a literary work a literary work: its "irreducible" aesthetic quality. The prime example is, of course, Shakespeare:

> You cannot illuminate him with a new doctrine, be it Marxism or Freudianism or Demanian linguistic skepticism. Instead, he will illuminate the doctrine, not by prefiguration but by postfiguration as it were: all of Freud that matters most is there in Shakespeare already, with a persuasive critique of Freud besides (…) Shakespeare's eminence is, I am certain, the rock upon which the School of Resentment must at last founder.[5]

Shakespeare needs to be saved from the resentment of those who see in canonization nothing but an affirmation of power-structures: "Shakespeare, whose aesthetic supremacy has been confirmed by the universal judgment of four centuries, is now 'historicized' into pragmatic diminishment."[6]

In short, what Bloom's introduction brings to light is the inherent tension in the idea of literary canon-building in the Chaotic Age: in order to write a proper canon of literature, one has to incorporate eternity into linear time, and our time has rigidly separated the two. In order to save literature from these historical arrogations, Bloom presents the truly literary work as absorbing history, as resisting history's attempts to totalize it: "something irreducible does abide in the aesthetic."[7] But here important questions are left unanswered: if the literary work is indeed irreducible to linear time, is then not the linear nature of the canon obsolete? What are the implications of this for the practice of the historian who works with literary texts? Is the 'irreducible' element in literary texts completely out of reach for the historian, or is it possible to incorporate non-linearity in the practice of history? If Shakespeare can contain fin-de-siècle Freud, 20th-century Marxism as well as deconstruction, shouldn't history be able to make the same leaps and bounds? If Bloom is concerned with the status of literature in the Age of Chaos, what of the practice of history? Bloom

---

4 Ibid., 22.
5 Ibid., 25.
6 Ibid., 23.
7 Ibid., 24.

is too preoccupied with claiming the autonomy of literature to formulate answers to these questions.

In his *The Artificiality of Christianity* (2003) Burcht Pranger tackles precisely this problem:

> I rather want to raise the following question. Granted the fact that any form of history writing, or, for that matter, any form of writing about past sources whether historical or fictional, historicizes, that is, flattens the original source material in the process of squeezing a "literal" account out of it, is there a way back to the microlevel of the literary artifacts (that is, the sources) from which it springs?[8]

In his book, Pranger argues for a process of doing history with a sensitivity for the way in which a historical source relates itself linguistically speaking not merely to horizontal notions, such as context or influence, or direct linear meaning, but also to the more vertical dimension of literary appraisal:

> is it possible for the historian by applying "vertical" notions such as tragedy, comedy (…) to have time move backwards rather than forwards, to have it shrink rather than extend, to have it curve and follow a serpentine rather than a straight path?[9]

For Pranger, this could mean that when one evaluates historical texts such as, say, the *Confessions* by Saint Augustine, writers like Eliot and Beckett can become "part of the historical source material."[10] Using these literary texts as historical sources can foreground the idiosyncratic literary dimension in a historical text. By using such 'vertical notions' the linear nature of the canon becomes problematic. The challenge is then to formulate a non-linear canon that nonetheless has historical validity.

In Bloom's separation of the literary canon into linearly arranged periods he risks closing off the possibility of these vertical connections. Important stagings of such vertical notions such as tragedy, time and speed, as they occur for instance in medieval texts, run the risk of being excluded from the literary canon, and an important element of these texts risks being undervalued. If indeed, a canon is to remain open-ended, the separation between literature and history should continually be re-evaluated, not just horizontally, in the sense of shifting aesthetic preferences, but also

---

8   Burcht Pranger, *The Artificiality of Christianity* (Stanford, CA: Stanford University Press, 2003), 20-21.

9   Ibid., 21.

10   Ibid., 22.

vertically. Drawing vertical lines between texts can be an important aid in assessing the linguistic movements that together constitute a historical source. In this sense "the worst age to be a literary critic" might just be an age of possibilities for historians.

In this article this possibility, of doing history without excluding the literary, is explored by means of a discussion of the style of John Calvin. Calvin is indeed well-suited for such an endeavour. Calvin's 'literariness' has been a stumbling block for modern commentators. Calvin's style has often been described as "iron,"[11] and as austere. Yet at the same time his seamless blend of scriptural evidence and authorial authority has an elegance and eloquence that has ensured Calvin's place in many canons of French literature.[12] Furthermore, the failure to see in Calvin a pure systematic theologian has resulted in scholars looking for unifying principles of his theology in his style.[13] Drawing out 'vertical notions' in Calvin's text might therefore shed new light on this discussion. Before drawing a vertical line between the prose of Calvin and that of Samuel Beckett, I will discuss some key moments in the history of Calvin scholarship. I will conclude with some reflections on the impact that an emphasis on the serpentine elements of textuality could have for the canon.

Calvin's Style

In his early 1922-lectures on the theology of John Calvin, Karl Barth remarks that in the work of Calvin we can see an unusual tension between the demand of engagement in the world on the one hand, and an emphasis on the renunciation of human capacity on the other. Barth states that this tension is part of a typical conflation of 'time and eternity': the theol-

---

11   Barth and Weber both have used the metaphor of iron to describe not only Calvin's theology but also his style. Max Weber speaks of 'the iron consistency' of Calvin's doctrines; see Max Weber, *The Protestant ethic and the "spirit" of capitalism and other writings*, ed. and trans. Peter R. Baehr and Gordon C. Wells (New York: Penguin Classics, 2002), 93.

12   To name but one: Jean-Joseph Julaud, *La Littérature française pour les nuls* (Paris: Éditions Générales First, 2005), includes a chapter "La Belle Prose de Jean Calvin."

13   Commentators such as Richard A. Muller in *The Unaccommodated Calvin* (New York: Oxford University Press, 2002), 3-4, Heiko A. Oberman in his article on Calvin's stance on the eucharist, "The 'extra' dimension in the theology of John Calvin," in *Dawn of the Reformation* (Edinburgh: T&T Clark, 1992), 234-58, esp. 254-55, François Wendel in *Calvin* (London: Collins, 1965), 174, William J. Bouwsma in *John Calvin* (New York: Oxford University Press, 1989), 2, and Alister E. McGrath in *A life of John Calvin* (Oxford: Blackwell Publishers, 1990), 18-19, have suggested that the quest for logical and systematic coherence in Calvin's theology is problematic. This realization has led to a search for different unifying principles of which 'style' is but one.

ogy of Calvin fuses the earthly sphere and the divine to such an extreme degree that the believer needs to be made of iron in order not to buckle under its pressure. "There is nothing wooing, inviting, or winning here. It is almost all proclamation, promise, threat, either-or."[14] The text, according to Barth, because of its radical and earnest claim of taking sin seriously cuts away the access to its own workings,[15] and thus is unable to open up to subjective structures such as wooing, inviting or the guarantee of winning. For Barth, Calvin's theology is characterized by the unbearable weight it breathes: "The seriousness that was alive in this man and that emanated from him was a bitter and almost unbearable seriousness."[16] The seriousness of the demand placed on the believer resulted in the apparent inaccessibility of the notions of love and peace: "If what he represents is love and peace, then these things must be very different from what we think. What we find is a hard and prickly skin. The blossom has gone, the fruit has not yet come. An iron cage has come that calls for iron believers."[17]

Barth placed the 'iron' style of Calvin in a historical and dialectical framework. The Calvinist conflation of time and eternity is presented by Barth as a necessary and progressive departure from the exclusive religious space of the medieval monastery. In the work of later scholars, Barth's classification of Calvin as a necessary stroke of genius in the dialectical development of modern religiosity has been fiercely criticized for anachronistically forcing a Barthian framework onto a historical situation. This is not far-fetched. For instance, the break between a medieval religiosity and the theology presented by Calvin is rightly perceived to be highly exaggerated. Barth emphasized the genius of Calvin and thus neglected his embeddedness in a late medieval world.

The work that paved the way for modern Calvin scholarship by breaking with hagiographic tendencies[18] was Wendel's *Calvin: The Origins and*

---

14 Karl Barth, *The Theology of John Calvin* (Grand Rapids, MI: Eerdmans Publishing, 1995), 117.

15 It would be interesting here to execute a comparison between the modes of access that is granted to the reader in the work of, for instance, Melanchthon, Luther or Zwingli. Because of the limited space available here, I refer to my forthcoming dissertation *Calvin's Institutes: the Fundaments of Reading*.

16 Ibid.,117.

17 Ibid., 117.

18 Nineteenth- and early twentieth-century Calvin scholarship consisted mostly of partisan historical hagiographies of John Calvin. In the work, for instance, of Emile Doumergue, a strong defensive tone is present: "The diversity, the clashes, the contrasts, the dualism, the defects of logic, the contradictions if you like, the elements which entered into the composition of Calvinism, constitute precisely its originality, its richness, its force, in a word, its own peculiar life." See Emile Doumergue, *Jean Calvin. Les Hommes et les choses de son temps*, vol. 4 (Lausanne: Bridel, 1910), 278.

Developments of His Religious Thought, published in 1950. This work still remains one of the strongest and clearly-written introductions to Calvin's thought, and it signaled a turning point in Calvin scholarship. In contrast with Barth and most nineteenth-century scholars, Wendel tends not to emphasize Calvin's work as a stroke of genius, as a bolt from the sky that changed history, or as a specific personal invention, but as a continuation of previously existing currents of thought and a reworking of influences dominant in the sixteenth century. Notwithstanding Wendel's remarks in the beginning of his work that "whatever relations can be established between Calvin and his predecessors, they are not those of a disciple eager to reproduce the thought of his masters and alarmed at the very thought of changing the smallest feature of it,"[19] Wendel's book is primarily a historical study concerning the intellectual origins of Calvin than a search for the unicity of Calvin. As a result, the emphasis on Calvin's style (or, in the case of Barth on the use of linguistic affirmation in his theology) tended to fade into the background in favor of a search for the roots of Calvin's writings.

Wendel's approach was highly influential. Scholars like Ganoczy tend to avoid large sweeping statements about the person, the genius, the impact of Calvin and/or Calvinism and instead to focus on detailed historical data to prove for instance that a certain train of thought as it occurs in Calvin is in fact a rewriting of Stoic influences.[20] Whereas Barth spoke of the "iron age that has come for iron believers," Ganoczy and Wendel focused on the possibility of Stoic influence in Calvin's formulation of his theology. Thus, the 'iron style' becomes a rewriting of stoic philosophy.[21]

Partly as a counter-reaction to the 'historicizing' of Calvin, that was inspired by Wendel's *Origins and development,* William Bouwsma published probably the second most-cited interpretation of Calvin of the twentieth century, *John Calvin: A Sixteenth Century Portrait* (1988). In this work the historicizing tendency to interpret Calvin in the light of a large theological and philosophical tradition was resisted, in order to bring to the fore exactly what the title suggests: a portrait, a sixteenth-century portrait, but

---

19 François Wendel, *Calvin,* 11 (as in n. 13).

20 As an example one can read Alexandre Ganoczy's *Le jeune Calvin. Genèse et évolution de sa vocation réformatrice* (Wiesbaden: Steiner, 1966) as well as the volume that Ganoczy edited together with K. Müller, *Calvins Handschriftliche Annotationen zu Chrysostomus* (Wiesbaden: Steiner, 1981). In these works Ganoczy goes to great lengths to prove that Calvin's notion of 'Weltverachtung' hails from his knowledge of Stoic philosophy.

21 As an example of the tracing of the sources of Calvin's style to rhetorical influences, see O. Millet, *Calvin et la Dynamique de la Parole* (Geneva: Slatkine, 1992).

an individual portrait of Calvin as a singular figure nonetheless: "I believe that one of the basic tasks of humanistic scholarship is to discover the personal, and therefore historical, flavor that constitutes the humanity of all cultural artifacts."[22] In this work, Bouwsma emphasizes the personal subjective drive that lies behind Calvin's theology. Although admitting Calvin's historical embeddedness, Bouwsma believes that in order to understand the historical Calvin, one has to focus on the singularity of his personality as it is present in the text. The relentless affirmation that so confronts the reader is interpreted as a symptom of what is basically an anxiety disorder. Calvin's personality was dominated by a fear of the labyrinth and the abyss. These two dangers were to be avoided at all costs by clarity and directness. Bouwsma perceived two Calvins at work in the text: one scholarly, philosophical, rational, that tended "toward static orthodoxy" and craved for "order, certainty,"[23] and the other rhetorical, humanistic, skeptical, that tended to give primacy to experience over theory. The affirmative hardness and confidence deployed in Calvin's texts then becomes for Bouwsma the result of the idiosyncratic combination of these two Calvins: the deeply skeptical Calvin cannot allow any labyrinthine argumentation while the deeply rational Calvin suffers from fear of the abyss of the loss of meaning. The result is an obsessively rational voice that covers up its own anxiety.

The psychologizing tendency in Bouwsma's work is a little over the top, and Bouwsma's fancy for excavating Calvin's personality frequently leads him to make historically disputable claims. The work must be seen in light of the theological-historical situation of the late eighties, in which, as Bouwsma states, it was still a rare occasion to see a work that tries to approach Calvin from a point of view that is not biased to a certain vision of history or religion. In Bouwsma's eyes, one cannot approach the text of Calvin without keeping in mind the personality of the author. Both the theory and the practice of history have caught up with Bouwsma on this point, and many of his reflections on the style of Calvin have been so tainted by his vivid image of the author's personality that the link to scientifically valid theological or historical interpretations often seems beyond reach.

In what can be seen as one long well-crafted argument against all too eager accommodations of Calvin into anachronistic frameworks, Richard A. Muller's *The Unaccommodated Calvin* (2000) set a new landmark in Calvin scholarship. Muller opens the attack on scholars that seek a unify-

---

22 William J. Bouwsma, *John Calvin*, 3 (as in n. 13).
23 Ibid., 231.

ing factor in Calvin's theology. Muller argues that quests for the systematical coherence of Calvin's theology all too often end up with "the meaning or significance of the historical issue being examined in the doctrinal consciousness of the historian's or dogmatician's present rather than in the intellectual, exegetical, polemical, or political context of the historical issue itself."[24] The nineteenth century theologians that tried to make Calvin into a theologian whose theology was intended as a completely rational system simply ended up with a nineteenth century portrait of the reformer. Unfortunately, such 'accommodations' of Calvin's thought to theoretical structures alien to the specific sixteenth-century context have, according to Muller, not been abolished since the nineteenth century. On the contrary, Muller states, "'Barthian' 'Schleiermachian' or even 'Derridean' readings" have replaced the dogmatic interpretations of the nineteenth century. Over and against these 'accommodations' Muller argues for a reading that places Calvin back into his "medieval humanistic background."[25] It is only after careful study of the terms employed in sixteenth-century writings and how they were actually defined and used in their time that can one come close to making a historical evalution of Calvin's work. The historian that undertakes such an endeavour could end up with conclusions that might not be exciting, or even relevant,[26] but "in any case, the genuine usefulness of Calvin's thought to the present can be assessed only when his thought is rightly understood."[27]

Although Muller rightly criticizes Bouwsma for violating historical data in order to support his psychological portrait, the embeddedness of Calvin in sixteenth-century history does not preclude Calvin from having a singular idiosyncratic style and voice. Furthermore, the problems Bloom faces with the canonization of the literary are here effaced in the name of 'right understanding.'

In a second thread of recent scholarship, more and more emphasis is placed on the role of Calvin's way of presenting his theology in assessing the theology itself. In a larger framework this emphasis fits into a reappraisal of the Reformation as an era in which not only literal but also literary truth is at stake. For instance, in the work of Brian Cummings,

---

24 Richard A. Muller, *The Unaccommodated Calvin*, 5 (as in n. 13).

25 Ibid., 11.

26 Muller, ibid., 10-11, warns overexcited historians: "contemporary theologians who desire historical and textual accuracy in their representations of Christian doctrine need to be prepared to acknowledge that, on any given point, Calvin may have no direct influence and, indeed, no clear relevance to contemporary discussion."

27 Ibid., 11.

Grammar and Grace: The Literary Culture of the Reformation, a call is made to read the writings of the Reformers as making a literary as well as a theological claim. Similarly, in Ehrensperger's *Reformation Readings of Romans* (2008), the claim is made that what distinguishes the Reformers' interpretation of Paul's letter to the Romans from their precursors is not so much theological content but a new linguistic dimension that was added to theological activity:

> Inasmuch as they were looking for ways of understanding Romans in a meaningful way, in and for their particular contexts, they did not perceive themselves as creating something new. (…) The sixteenth century interpreters are aware of the fact they are in conversation with traditions and acknowledge this (…) Thus, their respective contributions to the interpretive conversations were shaped by choices concerning their diachronic conversation partners from tradition as well as by choices concerning key theological factors which supposedly guided their interpretation. It is significant to note how explicitly aware many of the interpreters were concerning this aspect of interpretation.[28]

Ehrensperger cites Calvin's preface to his interpretation of Romans, where Calvin admits a degree of fallacy in his own interpretations:

> This, however, I trust, will be allowed–that nothing has been done by men so absolutely perfect, that there is no room left for the industry of those who succeed them, either to polish, or to adorn, or to illustrate.[29]

According to both Cummings and Ehrensperger, the historian should take into account in what way the context is put into effect in each text, and both historians come up with an approach to texts that focuses not so much on literal content, but on what we can anachronistically call the literary structure of the text.

After having seen a sensitivity to Calvin's style been accommodated to a Barthian framework, after the work of pedigree-oriented historians, and after the psychologically oriented historians such as Bouwsma, one can see now that a possibility is beginning to form that preserves the historical embededness of Calvin and yet is able to bring to the fore 'vertical' notions such as movement, rhythm, and performativity as well. This article is too short for a full discussion of this argument. In a short concluding

---

28 Kathy Ehrensperger and R. Ward Holder, *Reformation Readings of Romans* (London: Continuum International Publishing Group, 2008), 194-195.

29 John Calvin, *Calvin's Commentaries*, 22 vols. (Grand Rapids, MI: Baker Books, 2005), 19: xxv. The quote is taken from "The Epistle Dedicatory to Simon Grynaeus" of the commentary on Romans.

example I will therefore attempt to bring the work of Samuel Beckett in *rapport* with the work of John Calvin through a short discussion of his presentation of the innate human capacity for knowledge of God.

Sensus Divinitatis

> But though experience testifies that a seed of religion is divinely sown in all, scarcely one in a hundred is found who cherishes it in his heart, and not one in whom it grows to maturity, so far is it from yielding fruit in its season. (…) Mingled vanity and pride appear in this, that when miserable men do seek after God, instead of ascending higher than themselves, as they ought to do, they measure him by their own carnal stupidity, and neglecting solid inquiry, fly off to indulge their curiosity in vain speculation. Hence, they do not conceive of him in the character in which he is manifested, but imagine him to be whatever their own rashness has devised.[30]

In this paragraph Calvin presents his doctrine of the innate knowledge of God, the *sensus divinitatis*. The exact status of the *sensus divinitatis* has been disputed in academic scholarship. On one end of the spectrum it is claimed that Calvin was a natural theologian.[31] His references to the presence of God in the natural order have been interpreted as natural theology by Emil Brunner and B.B. Warfield amongst others. On the other end of the spectrum the point of view is defended that Calvin rejected the formulation of knowledge on the basis of the created order in its entirety. Karl Barth famously denied that Calvin held any natural theological position. This variety of positions on the *sensus divinitatis* is made possible by the unclear status of the knowledge of God: is the knowledge of God the Creator rationally deducible from nature, or is the knowledge of God the Redeemer necessary for this knowledge to be brought to completion? By emphasizing again the definition of knowledge as a moral activity rather than a correct logical definition of God, the parameters for the correct knowledge of God are hard to define. First of all Calvin states that even pagan tribes and the ancient Greeks experienced the effect of the *sensus divinitatis*. Their polytheistic religion was of course far from true doctrine, but in acknowledging that there is indeed a divine presence, they none-

---

30   John Calvin, *Institutes of the Christian Religion*, trans. Henry Beveridge (Grand Rapids, MI: Eerdmans Publishing, 1989), I.4.1 (p. 46).

31   For an excellent unbiased study into the role of nature and the natural order in Calvin, see Susan Schreiner, *The Theater of His Glory: Nature and the Natural Order in the Thought of John Calvin* (Grand Rapids, MI: Baker Academic, 1991).

theless gave expression to the universal innate knowledge of a creator. In the Commentary on the Acts of the Apostels Calvin comments as follows: "When Virgil says that all things are full of Joy," he expressed, according to Calvin, the existence of God, "but through error he put in the wrong name."[32] Calvin hints at the *sensus divinitatis* as a universal cognitive presence. If experience is reflected on correctly, according to Calvin, an awareness of religion is undoubtedly encountered. This seems to be the interpretation of Alvin Plantinga:

> The basic idea, I think, is that there is a kind of faculty or a cognitive mechanism, what Calvin calls a *sensus divinitatis* or sense of divinity, which in a wide variety of circumstances produces in us beliefs about God. These circumstances, we might say, trigger the disposition to form the beliefs in question; they form the occasion on which those beliefs arise. Under these circumstances, we develop or form theistic beliefs–or, rather, these beliefs are formed in us; in the typical case, we don't consciously choose to have those beliefs. Instead, we find ourselves with them, just as we find ourselves with perceptual and memory beliefs.[33]

Things get even more complicated when Calvin emphasizes that knowledge is only true knowledge if it moves the believer into the correct speculation: "we see many, after having hardened in a daring course of sin, madly banishing all remembrance of God, though spontaneously suggested to them from within, by natural sense."[34] The *sensus divinitatis* then functions as a constant reminder that God exists, and as a constant reminder of human fallibility: "it follows, that every man who indulges in security, after extinguishing all fear of divine judgment, virtually denies that there is a God."[35] The believer, when correctly 'listening' to the *sensus divinitatis*, is to realize that God exists, and that "he is no spectre or phantom, to be metamorphosed at each individual's caprice."[36] The *sensus* is further defined as a knowledge that leaves no man without excuse: "His essence indeed, is incomprehensible, utterly transcending all human thought; but on each of his works his glory is engraven in characters so bright, so distinct, and illustrious, that none, however dull and illiterate, can plead ignorance as their excuse."[37]

---

32 John Calvin, *Calvin's Commentaries*, 19: 170 (commentary on Acts 17:28).
33 Alvin Plantinga, *God and Other Minds* (Ithaca, NY: Cornell University Press, 1990), 172-173.
34 John Calvin, *Institutes of the Christian Religion* I.4.2 (p. 47).
35 *Institutes* I.4.2 (p. 47).
36 *Institutes* I,4.3 (p. 47).
37 *Institutes* I.5.1 (p. 51).

The *sensus divinitatis* then, is both the security of God's existence, as well as the insecurity of man's tendency to capricious idolatry. Of course, there is more to say on the knowledge of God in the theology of Calvin,[38] but for the time being, let us limit ourselves to locating a peculiar conflation of security and insecurity, felicity and failing in the presentation of the *sensus divinitatis*. The description of the *sensus divinitatis* is an example of the use of rhetorical structure that is not just a trope or figure of speech, but that almost becomes a performance of what it means to convey:

> But though experience testifies that a seed of religion is divinely sown in all, scarcely one in a hundred is found who cherishes it in his heart, and not one in whom it grows to maturity, so far is it from yielding fruit in its season.[39]

The rhetorical figure used here is called the *katabasis*, the descent into the deep. Again, this figure is usually used either to describe a grim situation, from bad to worse so to speak, or to describe the situation as bleak as possible only to offer the only suitable solution. In the chapter on the *sensus divinitatis*, Calvin clearly seems to present an example of the second. Only lines after the *katabasis*, Calvin states that the only object should be the "true knowledge of him." Yet in the description of the innate knowledge of man, so much has been cut out of the equation that the "true knowledge of him" is of an unclear status.

Negativity and Performativity: Beckett and Calvin

It is tempting, for a literary critic of the Chaotic Age such as myself, after having traveled all this way, to read the phrase in which Calvin presents the *sensus divinitatis* as a performative, as indeed some commentators have tried to do,[40] in which the problematic ground for logical proof and knowledge is enacted before the reader. In the *katabasis*, the descent to the deep, the reader is offered a sense of security that is immediately deconstructed until there is no security left; "not one in whom it grows to maturity," the reader experiences so to speak that which otherwise could

---

38 For a discussion of the role of the knowledge of God in Calvin's theology, see Edward A. Dowey, *The Knowledge of God in Calvin's Theology* (New York: Columbia University Press, 1952).

39 *Institutes* I.4.1 (p. 46).

40 Cf. Serene Jones, *Calvin and the Rhetoric of Piety* (Louisville, KY: Westminster/John Knox Press, 1995), 29: "He typically identifies the disposition associated with a particular doctrine only after he has already taken the reader through a process of reading which itself *produces* that disposition."

only be offered with descriptive language. Since any true failing of human knowledge cannot be expressed in definition alone, it seems plausible that by deconstructing senses of security, Calvin took recourse to more literary forms of expression. This could mean that the grim prose of Samuel Beckett would offer a more suitable pair of glasses with which to read Calvin's texts. Beckett's textual experiments in human failing and the literary form in which he presented them could offer valuable inspiration into the failure of linguistic expression and its effects on the practice of writing. All anachronisms aside, the universes of Calvin and Beckett have a seriously limited capacity of man in common. Could Calvin be read along the lines of Beckett's phrase "I can't go on I must go on"? Can Calvin, to the extent that he employs literary mechanisms such as the *katabasis*, be characterized by a performativity of failing? If one could establish a rapport between the structure of the language and the logically inexplicable knots in Calvin's description of the *sensus divinitatis*, considerable progress would be made. However, such an interpretation fails on multiple levels. Although there is sufficient ground for tracing the textual movements in order to explore Calvin's unwavering sense of security in spite of logical inconsistencies, recourse to a performative dimension of failing is not quite enough. Or, one could say, such a comparison is not quite complete. A comparison between the possible performative dimensions of Calvin and Beckett might not solve the problem, but it might bring us a little closer to the strange combination of failure and 'iron' consistency in Calvin's rhetoric.

Failing Performativity?

Literary scholars have seen in Beckett's endless continuation of human failing not so much a description of the human incapacity to bring the endless demand for meaning to a close, but a performance of it. According to Gilles Deleuze, the universe of Samuel Beckett is a universe of endless possibilities: "there is no existence other than the possible."[41] Possibility, being the only state of existence, can never be brought to a close.

The result of this is that language is unable to express this infinite potentiality. All language can do is momentarily seize the endless possibilities and present a false transparency and apparent fixity to what is in fact an endless play of potentiality. Beckett's oeuvre can be seen not merely as an attempt

---

41 Gilles Deleuze, "The Exhausted," in *Essays Critical and Clinical* (Minneapolis: University of Minneapolis Press, 1997), 152-174.

to show the endless possibilities in which existence unrolls itself, but also as an attempt to perform the failing of presenting this endlessness. The strategy that Deleuze perceives in the oeuvre of Beckett is *exhaustion*. By presenting the endless possibilities in the world, Beckett presents the constant failing of bringing any of them to a close, which has as a result an experience of exhaustion which, according to Deleuze, might not succeed in putting an end to the problem, but at least succeeds in performing its failing. For indeed, exhaustive situations abound in the work of Beckett. Beckett's characters continually play with exhaustive situations. In the novel *Murphy* the hero ponders over the possible combinations in which he can eat the five flavors of biscuits that he is used to having for lunch. Murphy, in brooding over the 120 possible orders in which he can consume his lunch, is overtaken by exhaustion:

> Overcome by these perspectives Murphy fell forward on his face on the grass, beside those biscuits of which it could be said as truly as of the stars, that one differed from another, but of which he could not partake in their fullnes until he had learnt not to prefer any one to any other.[42]

The countless apparition of orders can then be seen as one entire apparatus aimed at exhausting. The idea of this is that one can indefinitely go on. Indeed, in expressing human fallibility to exhaust, one needs to continue exhausting. In being exhausted, there is no rest. Also, on a more rhetorical level, many apparent securities are undermined or stripped away in Beckett's texts:

> It is midnight. The rain is beating on the windows. It was not midnight it was not raining.[43]

Similarly, in the *Texts for Nothing*:

> But I am silent, it sometimes happens, no, never, not one second.[44]

> But it will end, a desinence will come, or the breath fail better still better still, I'll be silence, I'll know I'm silence, no, in the silence you can't know, I'll never know anything. But at least get out of here, at least that, no? I don't know.[45]

---

42   Samuel Beckett, *Murphy* (New York: Grove Press, 1957), 97.
43   Samuel Beckett, *Three Novels, Molloy Malone Dies, the Unnamable* (New York: Grove Press, 1958), 176.
44   Samuel Beckett, *The Complete Short Prose* (New York: Grove Press, 1995), 131.
45   Ibid., 132.

These examples share a similar structure to the description we have seen of Calvin's *sensus divinitatis*: the *katabasis*. In the light of human fallibility, and the tendency to consolidate matters in a false safe framework, the text undermines security by first presenting a security, and then undermining it. However, for Beckett, the process of exhaustion is never finished. In this sense, Beckett's texts go on forever, never arriving at closure. In Deleuze's interpretation of Beckett, Beckett's oeuvre works progressively toward an exhaustion first of language, then of words, then of voice, and finally of the image[46] in order to arrive at a limit-experience:

> The image is that which extinguishes itself, consumes itself: a fall. It is a pure intensity, which is defined as such by its height, that is, by its level above zero, which it describes only by falling.[47]

In its negativity, such a movement would find its equivalent in Calvin's "not one in whom it yields fruit." Thus, in the paragraph following his presentation of the *sensus divinitatis*, Calvin writes:

> It follows, that every man who indulges in security, after extinguishing all fear of divine judgment, virtually denies that there is a God.[48]

In presenting his view of mankind as failing, Calvin presents his language as failing as well. The phrases cited above could therefore be seen as a performative of man's falling nature, continuining endlessly. In the Beckettian universe, the text continues endlessly. The reader can tap into the endless flow of words in order to experience if not the end, at least its impossibility. In this sense the performative of failing in Beckett is felicitous.

In Calvin, however, the emotional entrance that the performative utterance could yield is blocked off. The performative utterance in Calvin is not felicitous. In its way stands the demand placed on the reader to stop questioning, to stop falling and to experience a consistency in the failing. In this sense, Calvin's language stands squarely in the way of the reader experiencing failing as continuous. In its stead stands the knowledge, infused with faith, of God as Redeemer that can only be presented as a block. Whereas Beckett's project can be characterized as deconstructing any fixity behind human failing (which does not preclude a religious sentiment), Calvin's style does not allow for such a movement in the text. The

---

46 Deleuze sees the entirety of Beckett's oeuvre, from the plays to the works for television, as a progressively developing project of exhausting. Deleuze identifies three languages in which language, words and space are exhausted. See "The Exhausted," 173.

47 Deleuze, "The Exhausted," 170.

48 *Institutes* I.4.2 (p. 47).

movement in Calvin is hinted at, but not brought to its continuation. Instead, the road of despair, which, paradoxically, creates an entrance for the reader in the case of Beckett, is blocked off with the appeal to the "character in which He is manifested." The performative is non-felicitous in Calvin's language. The result is a language whose seamless style generates a desparate reader, yet the text does not allow for despair. After cutting away the value of description and order, Calvin denies the reader entrance into the text in a way that Beckett was able to.

Concluding: Vertical Canonicity

Bloom's emphasis on the gap between historical relativism and aesthetic value results in a series of important questions: if the value of the canon lies not solely in historically determined power-relations, but also in the singular manner in which a certain work is able to absorb the roads into its aesthetic value, if the canon is to defended, is the literary-oriented historian merely to stand in awe of eternal aesthetic value? This would result in what we started out with: the uneasy tension between the practice of history and literary appraisal. Or is there a way of doing history that resists the flattening out of historical material into a literal account?

Although the emphasis on Calvin's idiosyncratic style has been claimed by scholars such as Barth and Bouwsma for projects that were more of their own design than Calvin's writings could allow for, the climate is ripening for an inclusion of 'vertical' notions such as movement, tension, access to the reader, and the staging of failing performatives. In the case of Calvin the scholar can retain the arguments of scholars such as Muller who argue that Calvin should be seen from the perspective of the sixteenth century while at the same time attempting to craft a poetical tool that can render Calvin's particular mode of sixteenth-century textuality visible.

If the canon is indeed based on a fusion of linear time and aesthetic eternity, perhaps this should be seen not as a limitation of history, but as a challenge, a challenge to find a mode of doing history that combines both aspects of the textual object: the challenge would be to think the time-bound existence of a historical source together with the vertical components that make up its canonical existence in the presence.

CHRIST'S CASE AND JOHN DONNE, "SEEING THROUGH HIS WOUNDS": THE STIGMA OF MARTYRDOM TRANSFIGURED

Anselm Haverkamp

Christ's Case

Martyrdom and stigmatization[1*] are two motives interwoven in religious representation, related but opposed in a shared logic of manifestation, the one quite literally soaked in the *experimentum crucis*, the other mystically withdrawn but nevertheless involved in an "expressism" of what seems to amount to the same literal blood. The former, martyrdom, enjoys an on-going political actuality; the latter, stigmatization, surfaces from secretive hiding and challenges the political service of the former through a virtuosity of its own.

One of the crucial questions raised by the proliferation of martyrdom is its religious and, more problematic, Christian character. Is it a religiously motivated strategy, most efficiently exploited by the first Christians and gathering a new momentum in the early modern period of religious wars, that finds itself secularized, generalized, globalized? The possible purposes of martyrdom in general are as unclear as the question from where it comes and how much it carries, in the very crypt of its saints, the secret of its motif, the motif that is–but is it?–self-sacrifice. Like most rhetorical devices, martyrdom works without begging the question, by sheer evidence. The martyr performs by suffering, by submitting him or herself actively to that passion called martyrdom, or blood-witnessing. The paradox, and the secret, in fact, of a performance of passion, modelled upon Christ's performance, on the cross, of salvation is–in a second paradox that turns out to be proliferating like a racing metonymy–followed, or imitated, in an *imitatio Christi*, by witnessing the performance of deliverance; in adding, that is, to the evidence of what is to be witnessed.

---

1 * The following train of thought was developed in contributions to a series of conferences organized by the *Amsterdam School of Cultural Analysis* and the Postgraduate Program on *Representation, Rhetoric, Knowledge* of the European University Viadrina on "Martyrdom" (1999), "Stigma" (2000) and "Political Theology" (2001). Burcht Pranger's expertise was important on all occasions.

In adding to the evidence, the secret of the performance is sheltered rather than explained: it is encrypted, and the crypt is painted with the evidence of witnesses, their blood; it is reiterated, re-instituted as a crypt and re-inscribed with a renewed narrative in blood. Christ's cross has been called a triumph of representation, and the martyr's cross is a dramatic reenactment of his passion's paradoxical performance. Witnessing the witnesses, we come to witness in the martyrs' performance a strange splitting of the witness, a doubling pretty close to heresy. The martyrs' testimony splits, even rivals, the authorized mode of representation as it finds itself instituted by Christ's own word in the instituting moment of the mass; it strips the secret of the institution of its sublime veil. The martyr jumps to a conclusion that comes, in Christ's case, only after the word has been spoken and the New Testament established, on the cross.

The *martyrium* of the martyrs following Christ reads the sequence of word and act backwards, upside down. The martyrs' blood turns the transubstantiated *corpus* back into the matter that had been left behind in bread and wine, before the cross was literally erected and Christ's literal blood literally spilled. The martyrs literalize what had never been intended as a literal end in itself; but they do so on purpose, in order to make use of the performative force hidden in the literal event of the *martyrium*. It is the imitation of Christ that invests the event with its originary force in bringing this force out into the open. The singularity of the unbelievable event that is salvation, its salvific potential, becomes palpable only through the representation of a non-palpable presence. In short, the representational logic of this dialectic is a result of Greco-Roman rhetoric and no Judeo-Christian feature; it replaces, or invests, the New Testament *kerygma* with Greco-Roman rhetoric. What we have to add to the success of Christian martyrs–of what not-yet-Christians may have found attractive and persuasive in martyrdom–is the rhetorical supplement, or supplementary logic, operative in the Christian triumph of representation and its narratology.

The late, decidedly post-religious, name of this supplementary structure is sadomasochism, a signifier as universal and global as martyrdom. Taken at its most basic, structural level, both sadomasochism and martyrdom are the result of superimpositions of an analogous pattern-formation. The martyr rests on the Christian, more precisely the Greco-Roman interpretation of the fulfillment of Jewish history, an interpretation which leaves behind its founding moment by superimposing the universalizing rhetoric of the Greco-Roman empire on the singular event of some non-rhetorical–not in the same Greco-Roman sense rhetorical, though not necessarily pre-rhetorical–primal scene of Christian interpretation. Christianity left its roots, the Judaic prophecy of the Messiah, right from the start; in the longer run, it did not allow for much more than the fleeting memory of something like an early Jewish church.[2] The early Roman Christians may have looked like a Jewish sect at the beginning, but they decidedly were not. Accordingly, the discovery of Christian sadomasochism is not free to allow for a phase of genuine Christian masochism without the founding projection of some primal pagan sadism. Christian masochism, new as it was, needed mythical violence in order to internalize the story of this salvation masochistically, in terms of the cross that is, rhetorically speaking, the chiasmus of imitation, the sadomasochistic double bind of following Christ's cross without ever being able to imitate the crucial act that came to allow for the *imitatio* in the first, not the second place.

Freud's conception of sadomasochism is historically close, even faithful–that is to say, it is more than historical irony–to the unreadability of the Christian primal scene, insofar as he revises his earlier notion of "primary sadism"–notoriously the sadism of the Greek gods–and replaces it with the vicissitude of an even "more original" masochism which found itself in the historical position, under the sign of the cross, to put the blame on pagan sadism which, in turn, was created in that same chiastic reversal.[3] Thus the rhetorical supplement, the supplementary logic of the chiasmus, took over the cross and produced the double bind of Christian martyrdom, Christian *religio* as enacted in martyrdom. But how Christian, if at all, is the Greco-Roman triumph of representation that makes martyrdom Christian vis-à-vis the Roman susceptibility to Greek *trauma*? Mythical violence *avant la lettre*, before the epic cultivation of narratives, lays the sadomasochistic foundation of all interiorization and produces–at the very time when early Christian martyrs were asking for domestic trouble–a new type or prototype of what early modern philosophy came to develop as the 'subject'–the individual subjected to traumatization, and established on the premises of traumatizing losses.[4]

---

2   For the new economy, or rule of representation, initiating and governing the Christian church see Giorgio Agamben, *Le règne et la gloire – Homo sacer* II,2 (Paris: Seuil, 2008), where the politico-theological trajectory is fully unfolded.

3   See the outline in Jean Laplanche and Jean-Baptiste Pontalis, *Vocabulaire de la psychanalyse*, 2nd ed. (Paris: PUF, 1967; repr. 1998), 231-32, 428ff.; translated into English as *Language of Psychoanalysis*, trans. Donald Nicholason-Smith (New York: Norton, 1973), 244, 400ff.

4   See here in particular Guy Rosalato, *Le sacrifice: Repères psychanalytique*, 2nd ed. (Paris: PUF, 1987; repr. Quadriga, 2002), 28ff.

The history of subjectivity in this sense leads to a phase that should not be omitted in this account, the role of the martyr for *Renaissance Self-Fashioning*. Stephen Greenblatt's case study of that title adds to the individual rather than collective aspect of the Christian martyr's evidence. The individualized martyr, however, is already a product of a dislocated medieval meditation rather than of early modern politics. Bernard of Clairvaux's sermons had been exemplary; he placed the martyr's soul as always ecstatically involved outside of his body, within the heart of Jesus whose literal wounds provided mystical access to the *corpus mysticum* of the church (*Sermo* LXI).[5] The early modern martyr is an individual subjected to the new collective challenge of the church. The "seizure of symbolic initiative," as Greenblatt describes the performance of Protestant martyrdom in Foxe's *Book of Martyrs* of 1563, draws heavily on the allegorical modes of such mystical identification. The notorious "Oldcastle," Lord Cobham, who was finally martyred, "consumed alive in the fire" in 1419, had been an heretical nuisance for some years; he had famously performed more than once before his inquisitors the "symbolic victory" of the powerless in the face of institutional coercion.[6] When he was confronted with the sign of the cross, he refused to recognize it just as the early Christians had refused to recognize the cult of the Caesars, but he did so by literally incorporating the cross, performing the cross with his own body. He "spread his arms abroad," and said "This is the very cross, yea, and so much better than your cross of wood, in that it was created of God, yet will not I seek to have it worshipped."[7]

In other words, the confrontation of power cannot very well have been as trivial as it seems to be. It entails a state of cultivation which accounts not so much for the power of the martyr's enormous endurance–the endurance is, on the contrary, the motif of allegorical narration for Bernard of Clairvaux–but for the representational logic of public sadism which is checked by the masochistic standard post-Roman, modern institutions. The totalizing, globalizing power of the most recent, postmodern surge of martyrdom seems to draw its power of provocation qua endurance or

---

5 See Caroline Walker Bynum, *Jesus as Mother* (Berkeley, CA: University of California Press, 1982), 117, elaborating the complementary aspects of "maternal imagery" in Bernard of Clairvaux.

6 Quotes from Stephen Greenblatt, *Renaissance Self-Fashioning from More to Shakespeare* (Berkeley, CA: University of California Press, 1980), 78-81.

7 The Oldcastle Controversy is most conveniently documented in Barbara Hodgdon's edition of William Shakespeare, *The First Part of King Henry the Fourth: Texts and Contexts* (Boston, MA: Bedford, 1997), 349-391, quote at 369.

strain from the fundamentalist recourse to the supplementary logic of denied violent foundations whose religious transmission is, precisely, this
denial: the systemic, alias Roman, *méconnaissance* of early Christian *religio*, namely, this religion's exemplary, double-binding force.[8]

Thus, the "seed of blood," *semen est sanguis* in Tertullian's famously infa-
mous words, seems nothing but–but could it be more?–the rhetorical supplement exposed. In this, it is not just bloody but verbal: committed to the
Verbum. The very same logic of representation which causes, as Benjamin
has put it so pointedly in his *Critique of Violence*, "something rotten" (as in
the state of Denmark), needs the blood of the scaffold in order to present
itself; and at the same time the mere reiteration of this mastery of power,
which is this order itself, the "ethical order" of Hegel, shies away from such
fundamentalist decomposition, the bloody travesty, that is, of this blood's
orderly shedding.[9] In the sadomasochistic logic of representation which
underlies the martyr's rhetorical *actualitas* and *enargeia*, the martyr is a
winner *par force*, no loser or victim at all. And as such, as the winning type,
the winning Christ's *typos*, the martyr becomes a protomodern figure, and
his most effective age of representation the Baroque. Benjamin's book on
the Baroque *Trauerspiel* shows him as the tyrant's true twin.[10]

The opposite strategy of representation and congenial logic, stigmatization, stems in its performative "rigor" from the same source.[11] Saint
Francis was the first to receive *stigmata* in order to overcome, compensate
and outdo the missing martyrdom. He takes back and seems to internalize with the wounds received the over-ostentatious, latently heretic structure of an all too literal reenactment of Christ's passion in martyrdom.
Structurally, this taking back is not so much a deepening–and certainly
no subjectivizing–of the sadomasochistic pattern but seems its allegorical
virtualization or even "Aufhebung." Giotto's first and ever after paradigmatic visualization of the scene exposes the net of sublation, sublation in
a network of correspondences. The stigmatized Francis–*ad imaginem et*

---

8 Unlike Emile Benveniste, *Le Vocabulaire des institutions indo-européennes* (Paris: Minuit, 1969), 2: 267-273, who prefers *reading* as the underlying force in *religio* – "le rapport
entre *religio* et *legere*" (271) – I give priority to the double-binding force of *re-ligio* in a reading re-bound in and by the binding – "l'explication de *religio* par *religare*" (272).

9 See Anselm Haverkamp, "How to Take it (and Do the Right Thing): Violence and
the Mournful Mind in Benjamin's Critique of Violence," *Cardozo Law Review* 13 (1991):
1159-1171.

10 Walter Benjamin, *Ursprung des deutschen Trauerspiels*, in *Gesammelte Schriften*, vol.
1 (1928; Frankfurt: Suhrkamp, 1974), 250ff.

11 See Jean-Luc Marion, "Le dernière rigueur," in *Dieu sans l'être*, 2nd ed. (Paris:
Fayard,1982; repr., Paris: PUF Quadriga, 2002), 259-277; see esp. 274ff.

similitudinem nostram–is no inverted, self-centered martyr who would, as it were, relocate the scene of triumph from public scandal to private auto-eroticism.[12] (As a matter of fact, this may have become much of its later attraction in the eighteenth, nineteenth and twentieth centuries, in the growing success of the deepest self-misunderstanding of stigmatization.)

Originally, in the primal scene of its Franciscan conception–shaped in the exemplary design of Bonaventura's *Legenda maior* which amounts to no lesser ambition than the complete revision of Christ's case and its testament through the Life of Francis–the stigmata are a breathtaking tour de force of re-metaphorization: the bold attempt at taking back, in the manner of mystical reflection, what was preposterously given away in the literal-minded fallacy of martyrdom proper: *non per martyrium carnis, sed per incendium mentis* is Francis fully transformed, *totum in Christi crucifixi similitudinem transformandum.*[13] In adding individual evidence, I said, the modern martyrs remained within the influence of a dislocated medieval meditation; they became the victims of modern politics in the vault of this dislocation: "The heretic is enrolled in a virtual *theater* of torments," Greenblatt says, a theatre whose heretical involvement had been renounced by the mystical wounds of Francis. The history of stigmatization seems to oscillate between a theatrical competition with martyrdom and its definitive refutation.

John Donne, "Seeing through his wounds"

Interestingly, and not unlike the reflection of martyrdom in Shakespeare's Henriad, the laying bare of the logic of representation in the Franciscan spiritualization of the *imitatio Christi* is echoed in the performance of poets, sometimes poetical sideshows of the stigmatized virtuosos themselves, whose writing, in the case of Teresa or John of the Cross, seems the flip side of their mystic experience. The post-allegorical *experimentum crucis* of the dying Donne in his *Devotions Upon Emergent Occasions* of 1624 is, although he does not speak of stigmata, a case in point, an at-

---

12 Chiara Frugoni, *Francesco e l'invenzione delle stimmate: Una storia per parole e immagini a Bonaventura e Giotto* (Torino: Einaudi, 1993).

13 S. Bonaventura, *Legenda maior S. Francisci Assisiensis et eiusdem Legenda minor*, XIII.3 (Firenze: Quaracchi, Collegium S. Bonaventurae, 1941), 108. The medieval German reception of the *Legenda* shows already signs of the modern reduction to empathic imitation; see *Franziskanisches Schrifttum im deutschen Mittelalter*, ed. Kurt Ruh (München: Beck, 1965), 1: 21.

tempt at a fundamentally new poetics along fundamentally old, classical lines, to which I would now like to turn because of its continued fundamental thrust.[14] What comes through along those lines, as outlined in Bernard's mystical experience, is not the more or less triumphant rhetoric of self-fashioning–a distorted self-perception, in any event–but a freedom of no lesser modernity than the reformed spirit of literal-mindedness will allow and is used to give into.

Donne's *Devotions* do not deal with stigmata, only with the medical symptoms of a deadly illness. But the emergency of these physically manifest signs to be deciphered by physicians does not provoke any "Überspannung der Transzendenz" in Benjamin's sense of incurable *melancholia*, the hallmark of tyrants and martyrs alike. Rather Donne, once the author of a *Pseudo-Martyr*, is ready to perceive mystically in the emergence of death in his body the signs of the cross. The last words of his last sermon, given "at Whitehall, before the King's Majesty, in the beginning of Lent, 1630," highlights this meta-physical sense of quasi stigmatization in a manner quite striking for those interested in the history of stigmata. His last word is "blood," to be followed only by the final "Amen," and the blood is "his (Christ's) incorruptible," which is the "price" of his compassion and "so manifested as that you may *see* them (the embodied vessels of compassion) *through his wounds*."[15] The meditative transfer whose medium is the blood shed on the cross follows and deepens a metaphorological logic of mystical transport and is not to be confused with the symptoms of physico-medical literalness. Not just bloody but committed to the Word, Tertullian's "seed of blood" belongs to a "Rücksicht auf Darstellbarkeit" in which *semen* and *sanguis* transcend *silva*, the printed matter of books. Their reading may be the only imitation possible, but the rigor, as in *rigor mortis*, of this mode of reading leads beyond the matter witnessed. The notorious sensuality of Donne's Metaphysical Poetry, therefore, does not simply emancipate the pleasures of this world but transforms a mystical discourse, whose interiorizing force had found in stigmatization its privileged experience. A more and more dubious model of expression, this experience would suffer from the same distortions of literalization as the future realm of aesthetics.

---

14 Kate Gartner Frost, *Holy Delight: Typology, Numerology, and Autobiography in Donne's 'Devotions Upon Emergent Occasions'* (Princeton, NJ: Princeton University Press, 1990), 76.

15 John Donne, "Death's Duel" (1630), *The Sermons of John Donne*, ed. Evelyn M. Simpson and George A. Potter (Berkeley, CA: University of California Press, 1953-62), 10: 237-248, quote at 247-48, last sentences (the text's emphasis).

But there was more to be said after Donne's death, which turned–as if articulating his very own intentions–into a watershed between old and new, ancient and modern. At the end of the day, "his lifelong preoccupation with the resurrection of the flesh"–the resurrection of his very own flesh, to be sure–seems to resemble "neither an early modern Protestant nor an early modern Catholic so much as a medieval church father."[16] A Bernard of Clairvaux's mystical elaboration of what might appear in Donne's language as the ecstasy of lived experience may very well mark both his distance from the medieval church father and the poetic difference achieved in that distance.[17] What was more to be said after Donne and the mise-en-scène of his death as the monumental proof of his preaching is a kind of writing, namely, the Word preached. In preaching, Donne's foremost duty, the Word enjoys a self-performative exhibition, which is, in this case, not so far from the blasphemously literal performance of the old Oldcastle's martyrdom. When at the end of "Death's Duel" a punning resonance of the Word–far from being Donne's wit only–rejoices "in that blessed *dependance*, to *hang* upon him that *hangs* upon the Crosse" (my emphasis), this resonance does not just co-produce some self-reflective, linguistic effect; the act of exhortation repeats, mimes and sublates at the same time, within the flow of resonating words, the mimesis, which the stigmatized Saint Francis once had performed: "there bathe in *his* teares, there suck at *his* woundes, and lye downe in peace in *his* grave ..." (again, my emphasis).

Thus, Stanley Fish's thesis of Donne's self-erasure in his preaching performance of the Word is not the whole story.[18] What is always on Donne's mind is the self-transcendence of self-resurrection, a self-transcendence as and in self-resurrection. Radical kenosis putting itself on paradoxical display is only the one, rhetorical side of Donne's last performance. It hides his poetical point and insight, a stunning curiosity in Christ's case that surmounts his triumph in "seeing through his wounds." The poetics of the compassionate flesh–"those bowels of compassion" *seen* "through

---

16 Ramie Targoff, *John Donne, Body and Soul* (Chicago, IL: Chicago University Press, 2008), 154, 172 (last chapter on "Death's Duel"); for the following see 173, 183.

17 See in detail Burcht Pranger, "Mystical Tropology in Bernard of Claivaux," *Bijdragen: Tijdschrift voor Filosofie en Theologie* 52 (1991): 428-435.

18 Stanley Fish's theory of *Self-Consuming Artifacts: The Experience of Seventeenth-Century Literature* (Berkeley, CA: University of California Press, 1972), can contain "Death's Duel" in this conclusion only superficially (68ff.), but Fish exposes in great precision the forced double bind of response in Donne's case.

his wounds"–drawn from Bonaventura and Bernard's interiorized *imitatio Christi* come to the rescue of the poet's desire for more than an unspecified, bodiless life after death. The life to be resolved and restituted is indistinguishable from this life's speculative instruments and their corporeal seat in life. Not only is "the prospect of dying and rising" for Donne everything but abstract, in its urgency it is "personal and imminent," as Ramie Targoff insists: personal in its imminence. In the end, Donne's poetics of valediction turn into a poetics of imminence, which is able to perceive through Christ's wounds the life within death. In that sense Donne confronts Benjamin's melancholy-bound "over-extension of transcendence" with its saving opposite, an over-extension of immanence, and the melancholy show of valedictions he had put on and played with for a while is shed off. The melancholy of leaving is left behind, and the aesthetic point of what Targoff lucidly recognizes in "Death's Duel" becomes "the moment preceding." It goes back to "his Mistris going to Bed," but it leads us also forward to another late Christ figure, the Romantic Keats facing his death in what Kenneth Burke has aptly called "pre-ecstasy"–"an eternal prolongation of the state just prior to fulfilment."[19] This, in short, is what modern poetics has in stock beyond melancholia.

P.S.

There is more than one afterthought to be followed in modern poetry. T.S. Eliot's complaint, in his partisan appreciation of the "metaphysical poets," about a lamentable "dissociation of sensibility ... from which we have never recovered" stated in fact a conflict originating in the specific Christian crux of double mimesis.[20] Literal imitation in martyrdom was spiritualized in stigmatization, whereby the rush to stigmatization during the centuries of Eliot's complaint literalized what had come to the highest metaphorological bloom in Donne. Milton, on the other hand, who was more congenial to Eliot's mind, manifests the split in most remarkable sobriety, whereas Keats, a far cry from Eliot's charge–"they thought and felt by fits, unbalanced; they reflected"–seems more in Donne's

---

19 Kenneth Burke, "Symbolic Action in a Poem by Keats" (1939), in *A Grammar of Motives* (Berkeley, CA: University of California Press, 1969), 447-463, quote at 449-50.

20 T.S. Eliot, "The Metaphysical Poets" (1921), *Selected Prose of T.S. Eliot*, ed. Frank Kermode (London: Faber & Faber 1975), 59-67, esp. 64-65. See also "Milton I (1936)" and "Milton II (1947)", ibid., 258-74.

than in his beloved Shakespeare's vein and thus would be able and ready to escape together with Donne the unmarked visual fallacy, for which the subtle Eliot fell for "a long, a last" time in Christ's wake.[21]

---

21 See the trajectory to *Finnegans Wake,* last lines, in Burcht Pranger, *The Artificiality of Christianity: Essays on the Poetics of Monasticism* (Stanford, CA: Stanford University Press, 2003), 281-82.

PLAYING WITH HISTORY: THE SATIRICAL PORTRAYAL OF THE MEDIEVAL PAPACY ON AN EIGHTEENTH-CENTURY DECK OF PLAYING CARDS

Joke Spaans

Somewhere at the beginning of the eighteenth century, an educational cardgame was published in the Dutch Republic. French Huguenot exiles had introduced the genre into the Amsterdam printing business. Besides the colours and values that made them playable games, their individual cards presented finely engraved pictures, useful in professional or moral instruction, often accompanied by an explanatory rhymed stanza. The subjects ranged from geography and fortification techniques to famous personages and moralistic satire. The idea behind this concept was, of course, that the element of play would make the instruction enjoyable, the ideal combination of *utile et dulce*.[1]

This particular card game, however, had chosen a curious subject matter for its 'pleasurable lesson.' Its jokers promised a satire on the bull *Unigenitus*, promulgated by Pope Clement XI in 1713 to end the Jansenist controversies in France. The history leading up to *Unigenitus* and its protracted sequel, as we know it, is hardly a laughing matter: *Unigenitus* marked a decisive stage in a theological battle over key matters of Catholic doctrine and ecclesiology. It inaugurated the persecution of dissenting clergy as well as political upheaval in the French state, and led to a schism in the Dutch Catholic community. Much of the literature on the conflicts surrounding *Unigenitus*, and especially on Dutch Jansenism, is quite technical–anything but playful.

A closer look at the pictures on the cards shows that *Unigenitus* itself is only an auxiliary issue in in this *Constitution game*. More than half of the cards are devoted to episodes from the history of the medieval papacy. The game as a whole presents a, necessarily selective, and moreover high-

---

1 H.A. Kenter and A.A.M. Rijnen, *In de kaart gekeken. Europese speelkaarten van de 15e eeuw tot heden* (Amsterdam: Museum Willet-Holthuysen, 1976), 16-17, 65-74; Detlef Hoffmann *Kultur- und Kunstgeschichte der Spielkarte* (Marburg: Jonas-Verlag, 1995), 70-71, 170; P.J. Buijnsters and Leontine Buijnsters-Smet, *Papertoys. Speelprenten en papieren speelgoed in Nederland (1640-1920)* (Zwolle: Waanders, 2005), 15-19.

The Constitution game *contrasts the good death of Pasquier Quesnel, represented by
a serene memorial with those of his opponents Louis XIV and Clement XI.
The latter obviously go to Hell.*

ly partisan and satirical, history of priestcraft from Pope Gregory I until
somewhere in the 1720s: the eight, seven and six of spades refer to the
deaths of Louis XIV (†1715), Pasquier Quesnel (†1719) and Clemens XI
(†1721) respectively. Who would make a game like this, and for whom?
How do the game and its content fit our understanding of Dutch Jansenism? And what exactly was the lesson it set out to impart?

Some background

The first two decades of the eighteenth century were an important period
for Dutch Jansenism. In 1724, after a long drawn-out stalemate between
the States of Holland and the Roman Curia over who was fit to govern the
Dutch Catholic community, Cornelis Steenoven was consecrated bishop
of the Jansenist Church of Utrecht, an autocephalous church independent
of Rome. This effectively caused a local schism in the Catholic church, a
schism which had its roots in the specific situation of Catholics living as a
tolerated community in the officially Reformed Dutch Republic.

From the late sixteenth century, a closely-knit group of Catholic priests
had worked to rebuild ecclesiastical institutions and a ritual and devotional life in accordance with the reforms formulated at the Council of
Trent. They had been highly successful in this endeavour. Formally, however, the institutions they rebuilt lacked full canonical status. Formally

the Northern Netherlands had reverted to the status of a mission field after the Reformation. Instead of bishops, Rome appointed apostolic vicars as overseers of this *Missio Hollandica*. The most prominent of these apostolic vicars, Johannes van Neercassel (1663-1686) and his close confidants–a circle of wealthy and well-connected native-born priests, who had assumed the positions of canons in the formally lapsed but effectively revived chapters of Utrecht and Haarlem–had ignored these canonical limitations to their authority. They imposed a rule of discipline on priests and laypeople that was stricter than what was usual in a mission situation. They consciously applied the full rigour of canon law, as they considered themselves and their flocks the legitimate heirs and guardians of the medieval Dutch church-province. This inevitably led to jurisdictional squabbles with regular priests, operating under the direction of the superiors of their orders residing outside the Republic, and who applied the somewhat laxer procedures proper for missions.[2]

The penitential regime favoured by the apostolic vicars was in line with the rigourism taught in Leuven, the university where Cornelius Jansenius had written his *Augustinus*. Most of the leading priests of the Holland Mission had studied in Leuven.[3] They carefully kept aloof from discussions about whether Jansenius had overstepped the bounds of orthodoxy in his formulation of Augustine's doctrine of grace. This very reticence made them suspect in the eyes of anti-Jansenist hard-liners. In 1699 Petrus Codde, apostolic vicar since 1688, was summoned to Rome to account for his doctrinal position and for his administration of the Holland Mission. The examination did not go well, and although not formally accused of heresy, Codde was suspended in 1702 and finally deposed in 1704. Rome appointed the anti-Jansenist Theodorus de Cock as his substitute until a new apostolic vicar could be installed. Codde's supporters in the Republic had succeeded, however, to convince the States of Holland that the Jansenist faction within the Catholic church was truly patriotic, whereas their opponents' loyalty to the Protestant government was more questionable. Henceforth, the States of Holland banished De Cock from the Republic, and would not condone the appointment of a new apostolic vicar unless he were duly elected by the (self-proclaimed) chapters of Utrecht and Haarlem. Rome, however, could never agree to a Jansenist as head of the Holland Mission.

---

2 Charles H. Parker, *Faith on the Margins, Catholics and Catholicism in the Dutch Golden Age* (Cambridge, MA, and London: Harvard University Press, 2008).

3 Gian Ackermans, *Herders en huurlingen: bisschoppen en priesters in de Republiek (1663-1705)* (Amsterdam: Prometheus/Bert Bakker, 2003).

Thus, a stalemate was reached. Three successive Roman appointments were vetoed by the States of Holland. Grievances from both sides were aired in dozens of pamphlets. In 1706 and 1707 a satirical print series, aptly titled *Roma Perturbata* as it was devoted to these troubles, was also brought on the market. *Roma Perturbata* eulogized Petrus Codde as a true shepherd and a living saint, while poking wicked fun at all his opponents–notably the Pope, the Jesuits and Theodorus de Cock. Mixed in with mostly *ad hominem* invective against the agents of Rome were statements about the pastoral strategies of the Jansenists that stressed their similarities with Protestant piety, such as their abhorrence of elaborate ritual, their rigourist morality and their advocacy of lay use of the vernacular Bible for private reading. Throughout, the prints emphasised how for Codde and his friends loyalty to the Republic came before their obedience to the Pope. In this way, the satire played upon Protestant as well as on Jansenist sentiments–a strategy undoubtedly devised to maximise profits for the publisher.[4]

Fruitless negotiations over the appointment of a new apostolic vicar continued for years, and the Mission devised ways to carry on without one. Joan Christaan van Erckel, priest in Delft and a staunch Jansenist, devised ecclesiological models for the Dutch Catholic community that closely resembled the Gallican position in France: emphasising the local, national character of the Catholic church under the aegis of its sovereign prince or government, against the more centralist policies of the papacy. Van Erckel's work met with considerable sympathy within Dutch regent circles. The commotion that broke out in France after the promulgation of the bull *Unigenitus* in 1713, in which no less than 101 theses based on the widely used devotional manual *Moral Reflections on the New Testament* by the Jansenist Pasquier Quesnel were condemned, gave an enormous boost to French Gallicanism. In turn, this stimulated Dutch Jansenists to implement Van Erckel's ideas on their own turf. The election of Steenoven was the result.[5]

---

4 Trudelien van 't Hof and Joke Spaans, *'Het Beroerde Rome'. Spotprenten op de paus in een pleidooi voor een Nederlandse katholieke kerk* (Hilversum: Verloren, 2010).

5 For French Jansenism: W. Doyle, *Jansenism: Catholic resistance to authority from the Reformation to the French Revolution* (Basingstoke: Macmillan, 2000); Joseph Bergin, *Church, Society and Religious Change in France, 1580-1730* (New Haven and London: Yale University Press, 2009), 394-423; for the Dutch counterpart: P. Polman, *Katholiek Nederland in de achttiende eeuw*, vol. 1 of 3 (Hilversum: Brand, 1968); M.G. Spiertz, "Jansenisme in en rond de Nederlanden 1640-1690," *Trajecta* 1 (1992): 144-167; id., "Anti-jansenisme en jansenisme in de Nederlanden in de zeventiende en achttiende eeuw," *Trajecta* 1 (1992): 233-251; Ackermans, *Herders en huurlingen*; D.J. Schoon, *Van bisschoppelijke cleresie tot Oud-Katholieke Kerk* (Nijmegen: Valkhof Pers, 2004); on Van Erckel: J.Y.H.A. Jacobs, *Joan Christiaan van Erckel (1654-1734): pleitbezorger voor een locale kerk* (Amsterdam: APA-Holland Universiteits Pers, 1982).

This time, the pamphlet discussions were more muted than in the Codde affair. In fact, anti-Jansenists and Jansenists had lived in a virtual schism ever since the turn of the century. The election of Steenoven simply formalized the actual situation. Despite the support of the Protestant political elite, the Jansenists–or Episcopal Clergy, as they called themselves, to mark their continuity with the pre-Reformation church–remained a small minority. The Catholic faithful favoured the clergy that remained loyal to Rome. The election of Steenoven did, however, provoke a new wave of satirical prints. Unlike the satire produced twenty years earlier, these new prints did not focus on indigenous clergy, but elaborated upon verse satires concerning the bull *Unigenitus*, produced at the time in France.[6] Besides allegorical prints, satirical goose boards apparently sold very well, as several versions were produced. The *Constitution game*, with its satirical version of church history, fits this situation very well. It also saw two editions.[7]

A ludic history of the popes

The playing cards of the *Constitution game* each contain a finely engraved allegorical picture, combined with two lines of rhymed text. The cards were printed on six sheets, nine pictures to a sheet: fifty-two playing cards and two jokers. The buyer was expected to clip out the pictures and paste them each onto a piece of sturdy paper or thin cardboard in order to create a useable deck. At the time all card–and boardgames were produced in this manner. On the other hand, educational games, because they had a story to tell, could also be left intact, to be 'read' like a text. Buyers could either use these games as 'paper toys', or include the uncut sheets in print albums or hang them on a wall as decoration.[8] In the *Constitution game*, the pic-

---

6 *Réceuil de poësies de differens auteurs, faites au sujet de la Constitution de N.S.P. le Pape, portant condamnation des Réflexions du Père Quesnel sur le Nouveau Testament* (no place, [1714]); *Poésies sur la Constitution Unigenitus. Recueillies par le Chevalier de G****, 2 dln. (Villefranche [= Amsterdam]: 'chez Philalete Belhumeur,' 1724).

7 See A.H.M. van Schaik, R. Auwerda and P.P.W.M. Dirkse, *Katholiek Nederland en de paus, 1580-1985* (Utrecht: Rijksmuseum het Catharijneconvent, 1985), 82; Van 't Hof and Spaans, "Het beroerde Rome," ch. 4.

8 Hoffmann, *Kultur- und Kunstgeschichte der Spielkarte*, 70-71; Buijnsters and Buijnsters-Smet, *Papertoys*, 15-19; Jan van der Waals, *Prenten in de Gouden Eeuw, van kunst tot kastpapier* (Rotterdam: Museum Boijmans-van Beuningen, 2006), 40-42. For a recent example see Claudia Kammer, "Gebruik geen graffiti, waarschuwt klaver drie. Defensie en UNESCO lichten soldaten voor over omgang met cultureel erfgoed in oorlogsgebied," *NRC Handelsblad*, 26 maart 2009, 11.

tures on consecutive cards are often set against a backdrop that forms a
continuous panorama–a pictorial suggestion of their continuous story line.
The full name of the *Constitution game* reveals the lesson it was meant to
impart to its players: *New Constitution Cardgame devoted to the so-called
infallibility of the Popes, founded on fury and blindness*.[9] If left uncut, the
print sheets present a graphic history of papal fallibility, from Gregory the
Great on the king of hearts to an allegory of successfully accomplished
reform on the ace of spades –the ace was the lowest value in early modern
card games, the Dutch word 'aes' means 1. It is, unsurprisingly, a very biased history. A chronological portrait gallery of suitably unedifying popes
is interspersed with more general allegorical figures supporting the general drift of the argument contained in the series as a whole. The composition is cleverly done: the images are well-conceived, and the makers have
taken care that the four queen cards all sport female figures. The queen
of hearts shows three women riding a griffin, allegories of Domination,
Superstition and Ignorance. The queens of diamonds and of clubs portray
the notorious Marozia and Lucretia Borgia, and the queen of spades is
again an allegory of Arrogance.

For the game to be funny, the player or viewer had to be familiar with
(learned) iconology, and with the biographies or the legends woven
around the personages represented on the cards. The format of the playing card leaves very little room for explanation: the rhymed captions have
just a few words with which to identify the historical or allegorical figures
and their contribution to the 'fury and blindness' that underlay the reign
of the popes. Yet, the depicted histories or legends should be easy enough
to recognize. The publisher had to make a profit, and must have seen a
market for this game. Both the modest price of paper toys and the captions in the vernacular made the game accessible to the general reader. Its
style and general format closely parallel those of a card game published in
or shortly after 1720 on the theme of the South Sea Bubble, an item that
figured prominently in the media at the time.[10] This suggests that with the
Constitution game the publisher aimed at the repetition of a successful
formula and corresponding sales success.

---

9   Dutch title: *Nieuwe Constitutie Kaart van 's Paussen gewaande onfeilbaarheid, gestigt
op dolheid en blindheid*. See Frederik Muller, *De Nederlandsche geschiedenis in platen*, 4
vols. (Amsterdam: F. Muller, 1863-1882), 2: 138 (cat. nr. 3709); G. van Rijn, *Atlas van Stolk*,
10 vols. (Amsterdam: F. Muller, 1895-1931), 5: 7-9 (cat. no. 3549).

10   Kenter and Rijnen, *In de kaart gekeken*, 74; Van Rijn, *Atlas van Stolk*, 4: 364-376
(cat. no. 3520) and 425-430 (cat. no. 3525).

The unknown maker of the deck has taken care that the four queen-cards all show female figures.

This begs the question what the intended audience could know about the history of the popes. The Republic boasted a well-informed general public. Books were readily available as the country, especially heavily urbanized Holland, was a main centre of printing, publishing and book trade in Europe. Civil administration, international trade and specialized manufactures each demanded a well-educated work force. Societies and correspondence networks, chambers of rhetoric, bookstores, coffee shops and, of course, homes and gardens offered people from different walks of life occasions to discuss common interests ranging from the news of the day to radical philosophies.[11] If we look at the available works on the lives of the popes in Dutch only, and analyse what each of them could have contributed to the narrative contained in the card game, this should produce an image of the previous reading experience that could reasonably be expected among lay readers, the probable buyers of the game, and thus of the perspectives of the intended public itself.

The standard compendium of Lives of the Popes at the time was the work of the Vatican librarian Bartholomew Platina (1421-1481). Based on medieval collections of Lives, Platina's *De vitis pontificorum Romanorum*, later expanded by other hands to conclude with the life of Clement VIII (1592-1605), was a truly humanist work of history, critically evaluating

11   Paul Hoftijzer, "Metropolis of print: the Amsterdam book trade in the seventeenth century," in Patrick O'Brien, ed., *Urban achievement in Early Modern Europe. Golden Ages in Antwerp, Amsterdam and London* (Cambridge: Cambridge University Press, 2001), 249-263; Willem Frijhoff and Marijke Spies, *1650: bevochten eendracht* (Den Haag: Sdu Uitgevers, 1999), 237-238, 258-264.

the achievements of individual popes, with due attention to their relations with secular rulers and their contributions to high culture. The popes were portrayed as initially dependents of the Roman and Byzantine Emperors, but in the course of the Middle Ages as their successors in all but name. The authors, although loyal to the chair of Peter, were often critical about the worldly aspirations of the popes. This ensured *De vitis* a certain popularity in humanist circles, both Catholic and Protestant.[12] It was translated into Dutch in 1650 as *'T Leven der Roomsche pauzen*.[13] Apparently the subject met with a lively interest, as four years later a conveniently pocket-sized and much abridged version was published. It offered an anthology of no more than one hundred biographical sketches, and omitted most of the 'good' popes, like Gregory I the Great and Gregory VII. It seems aimed at a popular, anti-papal, Reformed readership.[14]

Although *'T Leven der Roomsche pauzen*, or the abridged version, must have been a prime source of information on papal biography for Dutch lay readers, it did not provide the background knowledge that went into the *Constitution game*. This is apparent from the very first card in the series, devoted to Pope Gregory I, the Great (590-604). This pope had a very good press in each and every history of the papacy. Yet the king of hearts card shows him surrounded by the flames of Hell, while a sinister masked figure with a bellows, the usual depiction of evil counsel, approaches him from behind. The rhymed caption of this card states that Gregory received the papal crown, and with it the preeminence of Rome, from Hell and through hypocrisy.

The only likely reference is to the *Institutes* of John Calvin. The reformer of Geneva found an avid readership in the Reformed Dutch Republic. With more than ten Dutch editions from 1578 to 1720, his *Institutes* must have been continually in print. Book IV, on the Church, contains a chapter on the rise of the papacy. According to Calvin, the concept of one universal bishop ruling over the entire Church was invented in the time of Gregory the Great, by patriarch John of Constantinople. Gregory had called such a title profane, blasphemous and a sure sign of the advent of the Antichrist. Yet in fact, the see of Rome functioned as a court of appeal

---

12   Bartholomeo Platina, *Lives of the Popes*, ed. Anthony F. D'Elia, 4 vols. (Cambridge, MA: Harvard University Press, 2008-), 1: ix-xxxi.

13   B. Platina van Cremona, *'T Leven der Roomsche pauzen, van Jezus Christus onze Zaligmaker af, tot aan Sixtus de Vierde* (Amsterdam: Lodowijk Spillebout, 1650).

14   Abraham Wilsenius P.F., *Het kleyn tooneel van hondert pausen* (Middelburg: Isaac de Vreught, 1654).

The characterization of Pope Gregory I is derived from Calvin's Institutes: *despite his own misgivings he has become the founder of the 'papal monarchy'.*

for Western Christendom–not because of any formal preeminence, but for purely practical reasons: the Roman emperors delegated ecclesiastical questions put before them to the bishop of their capital. All this nicely fits the king of hearts: the flames of Hell, from which a tiara rises up towards Pope Gregory, and the sinister figure behind him convey the diabolical nature of the papal monarchy–a monarchy unwanted by Gregory himself, but cast upon him nonetheless and welcomed by his less scrupulous successors.[15]

The rest of the deck is equally revisionist in its depiction of the popes. The jack of hearts shows Phocas, the murderer of emperor Maurice, being crowned emperor by Gregory I. As he kneels before the pope to receive his crown, Phocas in turn holds up to him a papal tiara. The caption to this image states that Gregory crowned this impostor in order to gain the triple crown for the popes. This representation again does not derive from Platina, but is a fairly close rendering of a passage in Gottfried Arnold's *Unpartheiische Kirchen–und Ketzergeschichte*, translated into Dutch in 1701.[16] Arnold upbraids Gregory for the use of an elaborate doxology in the crowning ceremony, thereby making God Himself responsible for Phocas' evil deeds before and after his coronation.[17]

---

15 Jean Calvin, *Institution de la religion chrestienne*, ed. Jean-Daniel Benoit, 5 vols. (Paris: Vrin, 1957-1963), IV.7.4-16 (pp. 124-137).

16 Godfried Arnold, *Historie der kerken en ketteren, van den beginne des Nieuwen Testaments tot aan het jaar onses Heeren 1688*, 2 vols. (Amsterdam: Sebastiaan Petzold, 1701).

17 Arnold, *Historie* 6.1.19 (1: 434-435).

The designer(s) of the *Constitution game* did use Platina for the seven of hearts, showing Emperor Leo III on a tottering throne, but gave his biography a new twist. In the picture, priests removing the statues of the saints undermine Leo's seat. Pope Gregory–either II (715-731) or III (731-741)– is portrayed standing behind the imperial throne, receiving the removed statues, and holding up his hand to catch Leo's falling crown. The caption declares that the pope assumed imperial aspirations himself. The card refers to the westward turn of the papacy. Making common cause with the emerging kingdoms of the west compromised their loyalty to the Byzantine emperors after their falling out over Leo's iconoclasm.[18] Unlike Platina and most church histories, however, the sympathy of the *Constitution game* is with the emperor, and the opposition of both Gregories is seen as treason against his legitimate sovereignty.

The six of hearts is again incomprehensible without Calvin. In the *Institutes*, he compares the alliance of popes and Carolingian kings with a pact among highwaymen. Rome had collaborated with Pepin in overthrowing the Merovingian dynasty, and the two had shared the spoils of their crime. Over time, the unholy alliance of kings and popes degenerated into an insupportable and unchristian papal imperialism, culminating in the, equally unfounded, claim of infallibility.[19] The card shows a pope juggling a (French) crown, while in the background priests grab clerical habits from a–supposedly stolen–chest. The caption presents the claim of papal infallibility, combined with the leeching of French wealth by the clergy, as a wry joke.

So the makers of the card game were highly eclectic in their use of sources, from the late medieval papal librarian Platina, to the founder of Calvinism and the Enlightenend church historian Arnold. For many of the later histories references can be traced to the staunchly Reformed Petrus Cabeljau (†1668), minister of Leeuwarden and Leiden. He also served as Regent of the States College, founded by the States of Holland for students of theology beneficed with a scholarship. Cabeljau, a life-long anti-Catholic controversialist, wrote a compendium to provide the Reformed faithful with ammunition against Catholic claims of embodying the true church. In this hefty tome Cabeljau also provided a biographical lexicon of popes, based on a wide range of sources, including Platina.[20]

---

18 Platina, *'T Leven der Roomsche pauzen*, 259; cf. Eamon Duffy, *Saints and Sinners. A history of the popes* (London and New Haven: Yale University Press, 1997), 62-64.

19 Calvin, *Institution* IV.7.17-20 (4: 137-141); cf. Duffy, *Saints and sinners*, 68-69, 98.

20 Petrus Cabeljau, *Catholiick Memory-Boeck der Gereformeerde, gestelt tegen het Roomsch-Memory-Boeck der Paus-gesinde* 2 vols. (Leiden: Pieter Leffen, 1661). The lexicon of popes from Adam to Alexander VII (1655-1667) is at 1: 470-658.

Reliance on these non-Catholic sources may mean that the anti-papal satire of the *Constitution game* was conceived by Protestants. The question of probable authorship is best left for later, but at this point we have seen enough to notice that satire in the *Constitution game* specifically focuses on key elements of Jansenist piety: the rejection of papal monarchy and papal infallibility and the tacit approval of Emperor Leo's iconoclasm chime harmoniously with the Jansenist outcry against *Unigenitus*, their preference for a national church loyal to the worldly sovereign, and their disgust with baroque devotions.

The series continues in this way, presenting a canon of papal depravity. We see Sergius II (844-847), who introduced the custom whereby popes drop their own name and assume the name of one of their predecessors in office;[21] the notorious legendary popess Joan, giving birth during a procession;[22] Nicholas I (858-867) with Emperor Lotharius humbly walking besides his horse and leading it by the reins.[23] The 'dark age of the papacy,' from the turn of the ninth century to the beginning of the eleventh, when the empire was weak and the papacy had fallen into the rapacious hands of powerful Roman families, provided material for a number of cards. A central figure in this period was the redoubtable Marozia, who, according to legend, poisoned Stephen VIII[24] in order to bring her son John XII by Pope Sergius III (911-913) to the papal throne. Sergius III was notorious for his violence: he is shown on the king of diamonds while he tramples the naked body of pope Formosus (891-896), whom he had exhumed, defiled, and thrown into the Tiber.[25] Marozia herself is the queen of diamonds.[26]

The eleventh century, when the papacy again enjoyed imperial patronage, started hopeful, with the learned Gerbert d'Aurillac on the papal throne as Sylvester II (999-1003). According to legend, however, he practiced the dark arts. The *Constitution game* depicts him as a sorcerer, surrounded by magic symbols and flying demons.[27] As the power of the Ot-

---

21   4♥. See Cabeljau, *Catholiick Memory-Boeck*, 1: 542-543; cf. Duffy, *Saints and Sinners*, 296: this pope was confused with Sergius IV (1009-1012).

22   3♥. For the legend see Cabeljau, *Catholiick Memory-Boeck*, 1: 433-456, 543-544.

23   2♥. See Cabeljau, *Catholiick Memory-Boeck*, 1: 544-545.

24   1♥. See Cabeljau, *Catholiick Memory-Boeck*, 1: 552-553. The chronology and numbering of the popes are confused here.

25   Cabeljau, *Catholiick Memory-Boeck*, 1: 551; Duffy, *Saints and Sinners*, 84.

26   Platina does not mention Marozia, but Cabeljau does, *Catholiick Memory-Boeck*, 1: 551-553.

27   The legend appears both in Platina, *'T Leven der Roomsche pauzen*, 375-377, and in Cabeljau, *Catholiick Memory-Boeck*, 1: 375-376. Cabeljau endorses the legend against the more critical approach of later authors.

tonian emperors declined, however, Roman factions again took the upper hand. The rivalry between Benedict IX, Sylvester III and Gregory VI again produced a scandalous episode (1024-1044). The card devoted to this 'evil troika' shows the three popes sitting on three thrones, arranged in a triangle. The arrangement of the three thrones must have been inspired by the work of Cabeljau, where it is claimed that the three popes reigned at the same time, each from one of the Roman churches: Benedict from the Lateran church, Sylvester from St. Peter's and Gregory from Our Lady's. Platina's *De vitis* sternly condemns these popes, but describes their reigns as an elaborate round of musical chairs–highly unedifying, but with at least only one pope reigning at a time.[28]

The representation of the great reform pope Hildebrand, who took the name Gregory VII (1073-1085), on the nine of diamonds is remarkable. Usually highly praised, here Gregory is an outright tyrant. He is shown sitting on a throne, next to the Countess Mathilda of Tuscany, similarly enthroned. She holds the keys of Peter, while the pope himself holds a naked sword and his mouth spews a thunderbolt. A fox, the symbol of deceitful cunning, peeps from behind his throne. This image is again based on Cabeljau, who brushes Gregory with the blackest of tars. Cabeljau's entry on this pope starts with a pun on his name: Hildebrand = Hellebrandt (Dutch for hellfire). Cabeljau dwells at length on the alleged scheming that gained Hildebrand the papal crown, symbolized by the wily fox. He characterizes his reign as a period of conflict with the higher clergy and, of course, with Emperor Henry IV, abusing the papal office by wielding his power of excommunication (the thunderbolts coming from his mouth) and naked power (the sword in his hand) against personal rivals. Lavishly quoting German pro-imperial and anti-papal sources, Cabeljau accuses Gregory of fornication with Mathilda. This was the more scandalous because Gregory outlawed concubinage for the clergy–symbolized on the nine of diamonds by a group of women, spatially separated from a group of secular priests. Mercifully, or perhaps from sheer lack of space, the *Constitution game* omits Cabeljau's assertions that Gregory was also an accomplished sorcerer, a true pupil of his evil predecessor Sylvester II.[29]

Popes who strengthenend the throne of Peter at the expense of emperors–Alexander III (1159-1181), Celestinus III (1181-1198) and, of course,

---

28   10♦. See Platina, '*T Leven der Roomsche pauzen*, 384-387; Cabeljau, *Catholiick Memory-Boeck*, 1: 560-561.
29   9♦. See Cabeljau, *Catholiick Memory-Boeck*, 1: 566-574; cf. Duffy, *Saints and Sinners*, 90-99.

Pope Gregory VII bans clerical concubinage, while consorting with Countess Mathilda himself.

Boniface VIII (1294-1303)–are censured.[30] Alexander IV (1254-1261) is accused of rapacity. The cards devoted to these popes are all based on Cabeljau, who, in the case of Alexander VI, quotes extensively from English sources on the burden of ecclesiastical taxation under this pope, even accusing him of 'selling' absolution for the most heinous crimes in order to fill his coffers.[31] This period, however, also contained a first spark of reform: the six of diamonds shows Petrus Waldus, who translated the Bible into the vernacular for the edification of the laity. This ensured Waldus a place in the genealogy of Protestants and Dutch Jansenists alike, because both recommended Bible-reading for the common faithful. The history of Waldus and of the persecution of the Waldensians was available to a Dutch vernacular readership in Arnold's *Historie der kerken en ketteren*.[32]

From Boniface VIII the *Constitution game* jumps to the Renaissance popes Pius II Aeneas Sylvius (1458-1464) and Alexander VI Borgia (1492-1505). The first is shown on the king of clubs as half-cardinal, half-pope. The caption explains that Aeneas made a good cardinal, but once elevated to the papal throne he turned out proud and violent.[33] The queen of clubs

---

30 8♦, 7♦ and 3-1♦ respectively. Cf. Cabeljau, *Catholiick Memory-Boeck*, 1: 582-584, 586, 599-601.

31 4♦. Cf. Cabeljau, *Catholiick Memory-Boeck*, 1: 592-593.

32 Arnold, *Historie der kerken en ketteren* 12.5.6 (1: 640-41).

33 On this genre of image see Frans Grijzenhout, "Janus' betrouwbaarheid. Over een beeldmotief in de politieke grafiek," in Bram Kempers, ed., *Openbaring en bedrog. De afbeelding als historische bron in de Lage Landen*, (Amsterdam: Amsterdam University Press, 1995), 125-146.

is Lucretia, the daughter of Alexander VI, and the jack of clubs is Alexander himself. He is depicted at an outdoor banquet, accidentally drinking the poisoned wine destined for his guests. Again, the source of the images can be traced back to the work of Cabeljau who, like the proverbial spider, collected the most venomous material from the history of the popes and the legends woven into their biographies.

In praise of reform

The depravity of the medieval papacy is, however, only part of the lesson contained in the *Constitution game*. In stark contrast with the 'dark Middle Ages', it presents a swelling tide of reform from the sixteenth century, a tide heralded earlier by the Waldensians. The ten of clubs presents Emperor Charles V, who urged the convocation of the Council of Trent. The following cards, nine through five of clubs, refer to the reforms introduced by Luther and Calvin. They are not presented as the heroes of Protestantism, but as forerunners of Jansenism.[34] They opposed indulgences, gained free access to the Bible for the laity, removed idolatrous images, and defended the authority of secular princes to withstand the pope–all items applauded by the Jansenists. The four of clubs introduces the real hero of the game: Pasquier Quesnel, the leader of the Jansenist party after the death of Antoine Arnauld. Quesnel spent long years in exile in the Netherlands and exerted a strong influence on the Episcopal Clergy in the Holland Mission.

The three lowest clubs cards and the entire spades series are a sustained eulogy of Quesnel. He defended the rights of the French Crown against papal ambitions. He was the champion of truth against the superstitions of Rome. He was a martyr for true piety. Quesnel's opponents are not so much the popes as the Jesuits, also depicted as proud and lusting after power, vain and avaricious, patrons of superstition and oppressors of pious souls. The Constitution *Unigenitus* figures less than the name of the game leads us to expect, and it appears in curious places. On the jack of clubs it is held by a demon who contemplates the death of Pope Alexander VI. On the ace of clubs it is casually dangled from the hands of a Jesuit, busily raking money from an open chest, surrounded by flying demons.

---

34 Cf. *The Pope's Bull, condemning the New Testament with moral reflections done by Father Quesnel, the present Luther of France. With the several texts expounded by his propositions* (London, 1714), in Eighteenth Century Collections Online: http://www.gale.cengage.com/DigitalCollections/products/ecco/index.htm

Quesnel is shown writing in defence of truth, keeping popish tyranny at bay.

On the ten of spades a fool, his cap and bells topped by a cardinal's hat, carries it to Paris, whipped on by a Jesuit. *Unigenitus* is simply one of the instruments of oppression brought to bear against Quesnel and the Jansenist reforms.

Quesnel's martyrdom has won him eternal glory: the seven of spades shows a memorial in his honour. Its elegance and serenity contrast sharply with the sinister deathbed scene of Louis XIV and the outright lugubrious tomb of Clement XI on the cards immediately preceding and following it. Like the followers of Petrus Waldus, the Jansenists suffer persecution: the lower spades cards show both the war of books and the actual violence against the followers of Quesnel.[35] The last card of the game, the ace of spades, however, predicts that eventually antichristian priestcraft will be banished from Christendom. All in all, the Bull *Unigenitus* is mocked as a mere annoyance, unable to impede Jansenist reform.

Whose laughs?

The *Constitution game* emphatically presents Quesnel and the Jansenists as a reform party, dedicated to the eradication of a medieval heritage of priestcraft and superstition. An anthology of black legends, culled from medieval chronicles, Protestant controversialists and Enlightenment cri-

---

35 Various forms of persecution are depicted on 5♦, the card following the picture of Waldus, and on 5-2♠, following the sequence on Quesnel.

*The constitution Unigenitus, after which the deck was named, actually plays a minor role.
Of course it is vilified and ridiculed.*

tique provides ammunition against Rome and the Jesuits. Anti-papal satire
supported the Jansenist cause in the Republic; it justified the decision to
elect a bishop independently of Rome, and celebrated the achievement of a
national Catholic Church of Utrecht, supported by the Dutch government.

With its fulsome praise for Quesnel, it seems likely that Jansenists inspired, or at the very least had a hand in, its composition. The game must
have aimed first and foremost at a Jansenist audience. This was, however,
only a small niche market. The choice of sources also suggests a Reformed
connection. Calvinists who knew their classics and anti-Catholic polemic
would find much that was familiar. The tiny Church of Utrecht was no
threat to them, and they had common enemies. A flood of pamphlets had
brought the internal troubles of the Catholic community to nationwide
attention in the early years of the century, and the cause of Jansenism enjoyed considerable sympathy among Dutch Reformed regents.[36] A more
popular Protestant audience was conditioned to see the pope and the Jesuits as historical enemies of Dutch liberty.

Such a crossing of confessional divides was not unusual. Mixed mar-
riages connected Jansenists and Reformed, especially within the urban
elite. There was a lively interest in the tenets of other faiths. Cabeljau's
Catholiick Memory-Boeck der Gereformeerde, that informed many of the

---

36 Cf. Polman, *Katholiek Nederland*, 1: 266, 307.

cards of the *Constitution game*, testifies to that: it reproduces in full the Catholic primer it was meant to refute, assuming that his Reformed readers would like to know more about Catholic 'superstitions' before being convinced that they were wrong. It is highly likely that Catholics in turn read Cabeljau's book. This form of 'comparative religion' even engendered a certain convergence in religious practice, a shared notion of what constituted decent religion.[37] Jansenism, unlike the Catholicism of Rome and the Jesuits, would be perceived by many mainline Protestants as decent religion, as it meshed with the still predominantly humanist intellectual culture, civic morals and patriotic sensitivities common in the Dutch Republic.[38] For this very reason, Jansenists were accused by anti-Jansenists of Calvinist heresy.

The emphasis on the priestcraft of Rome, however, indulged in over the lengthy presentation of the meddling of medieval popes in the secular realm, culminating in the bull *Unigenitus*, must have struck less confessionally defined chords as well. Early Enlightenment authors invested much ingenuity and energy in reconfiguring the nature of churches and of religion in general. Often they asserted the need for a public church, upheld by political authority. They considered religion the cement of society and the foundation of morality. True religion, however, was first and foremost *civil* religion. They rejected clerical power as fanaticism, and confessional doctrines and precise rituals as superstition. Historiography served to support their claims: the history of Christianity was rewritten as a history of decline, or as a succession of false turns, in which true religion had fallen victim to fanaticism and superstition.[39]

The *Constitution game*, culminating in a vision of future reform, that would banish all antichristian accretions from religion, appealed to a wide variety of early eighteenth-century sentiments. Its judgement on the me-

---

37 Frijhoff en Spies, *1650. Bevochten eendracht*, 351-359; Spaans, "Stad van vele geloven," 464.

38 Peter van Rooden, *Religieuze regimes. Over godsdienst en maatschappij in Nederland 1570-1990* (Amsterdam: Bert Bakker, 1996), 78-120; Pasi Ihalainen, *Protestant Nations Redefined. Challenging Perceptions of National Identity in the Rhetoric of the English, Dutch and Swedish Public Churches, 1685-1772* (Leiden and Boston: Brill, 2005).

39 J.A.I. Champion, *The Pillars of Priestcraft Shaken. The Church of England and Its Enemies, 1660-1730* (Cambridge: Cambridge University Press, 1993); S.J. Barnett, *Idol Temples and Crafty Priests. The Origins of Enlightenment Anticlericalism* (London & New York: St. Martin's Press, 1999); Peter van Rooden, "Vroomheid, macht, Verlichting," *De Achttiende Eeuw* 32 (2000): 57-75; cf. Joke Spaans, "Hieroglyfen. De verbeelding van de godsdienst," in Henk van Nierop, ed., *Romeyn de Hooghe. De verbeelding van de Gouden Eeuw* (Amsterdam: Waanders, 2008), 48-57.

dieval papacy and on the revival of its worst sins in the bull *Unigenitus*
could serve Jansenists, Protestants, and the early Enlightenment in justify-
ing their various reform projects. Ironically, it chose to do so in the form
of a card game: a pastime condemned by all churches as dishonest and
even sinful, a danger to public order and a waste of valuable time.[40]

---

40   Buijnsters and Buijnsters-Smet, *Papertoys*, 25; Herman Roodenburg, *Onder cen-
suur. De kerkelijke tucht in de gereformeerde gemeente van Amsterdam, 1578-1700* (Hilversum: Verloren, 1990), 334.

FROM EAST TO WEST: JANSENISTS, ORIENTALISTS, AND THE EUCHARISTIC CONTROVERSY

ALASTAIR HAMILTON

Few movements were further removed from oriental studies than Jansenism when it started in the 1630s with the Abbé de Saint-Cyran's efforts to reform the convent of Port-Royal in Paris. Its teaching was based on that of a Church Father who met with particular favour in the West, St Augustine.[1] Even as its ideals expanded, they were essentially confined to the western Church and western problems–to combating the Jesuits, to arguing against Molinism and probabilism, and, ultimately, to bringing about a fundamental reform of the Church itself. And this is equally true of the origins of the eucharistic controversy. To start with it was an exclusively western concern, prompted by the publications, in the late 1620s and early 1630s, by Huguenot ministers such as Edme Aubertin, in defence of the Calvinist teaching on the eucharist, which denied that the bread and wine underwent any transformation at the consecration.[2] In 1659 the two Jansenist leaders, Antoine Arnauld and Pierre Nicole, replied by restating the Catholic belief in transubstantiation in a brief preface to the eucharistic liturgy for use by the nuns of Port-Royal. Although they were still mainly concerned with the Church of the West, they added a long section with passages from the Fathers, many of whom were Greek, and wrote that the teaching of transubstantiation "was so universally established, not only in the entire Church of Rome but also in all the communities which were separated from it, such as those of the Greeks and the Armenians, that no trace or memory suggests that there had ever been a different view."[3]

---

1 As nobody knows better than Burcht Pranger. See, for example, his "Augustinianism and drama: Jansenius' refutation of the concept of *natura pura*," in M. Lamberigts, ed., *L'augustinisme à l'ancienne faculté de théologie de Louvain* (Leuven: Leuven University Press, 1994), 299-308.

2 Jean-Louis Quantin, *Le Catholicisme classique et les Pères de l'Eglise: Un retour aux sources (1669-1713)* (Paris: Institut d'Etudes Augustiniennes, 1991), 291-39.

3 *L'Office du S. Sacrement pour le jour de la feste, et toute l'octave...* (Paris: Pierre le Petit, 1659) sig.a4r.

Jean Claude, the Huguenot minister of Charenton, responded. He claimed that the current Catholic teaching could not be traced back any earlier than the tenth or eleventh centuries, "the darkest and most polluted centuries, the most lacking in men of piety and learning, which Christianity has ever known."[4] Claude, moreover, denied that the Greeks had had a consistent belief in transubstantiation and expressed grave doubts about whether the other Christians of the East had either.

To Claude's somewhat questionable sources for this claim we shall return. Arnauld and Nicole took up the challenge with enthusiasm. For this there were many reasons. First of all it allowed them to indulge in their favourite pursuit–polemic. This, their refusal to let any argument drop, to continue discussions way beyond their point of exhaustion, was to be one of the causes of their undoing.[5] But in this case the polemic was different from the ones to which they were accustomed. They normally devoted their energy to contesting the teaching of the Jesuits or to replying to the strictures of the papacy. Now, however, they could attack Protestantism. This had immense advantages. It meant that they could prove their own orthodoxy and spring to the defence of a teaching shared by the Roman Catholic Church as a whole. Rather than defending themselves against charges of heresy, they could appear as champions of the Church to which they never ceased to profess their devotion. And besides, defence of the eucharist could also serve as an answer to those of their enemies incensed by the publication in 1643 of *De la fréquente communion*, the work in which Arnauld rejected the widespread view, greatly encouraged among the Jesuits, that communion should be taken as frequently as possible. Arnauld justified his opposition by his deep veneration for the eucharist and his insistence on the need of a particular preparation before the faithful could partake of it. His enemies had noted with horror that the number of communicants had dropped appreciably as a result of his publication, and that he was encouraging not respect, but contempt, for the sacrament.

In their first edition of *La perpetuité de la foy de l'Eglise catholique touchant l'eucharistie* of 1664 the Jansenist leaders still concentrated all but entirely on the western tradition. Only at the very end did they turn briefly to the eastern Churches, criticising Claude's sources and maintaining again that there was no doubt that "all the schismatic communions

---

4 Jean Claude, *Réponse aux deux traitez intitulez la Perpétuité de la foy de l'Eglise Catholique touchant l'Eucharistie*, 7th ed. (Paris: Antoine Cellier, 1668), 9.

5 This is justly emphasised in Antoine Adam, *Du mysticisme à la révolte: les Jansénistes du XVIIe siècle* (Paris: Fayard, 1968), 157.

of the East are in agreement with the Church of Rome on the matter of transubstantiation."[6] In order to bear out this last point, however, they would require assistance. Fine scholars, they were sufficiently acquainted with the Greek Fathers to fend for themselves,[7] but they also wished to prove that the Christians of the East in their entirety had always believed in transubstantiation and still did so. Jean Claude had already suggested that "every Greek on the face of the earth" be interrogated about whether he recognise any general law in his Church establishing the teaching of transubstantiation.[8] Arnauld and Nicole followed his advice. They set about collecting attestations. Among the first men to be approached was Arnauld's nephew, Simon Arnauld, marquis de Pomponne, who had been dispatched on an embassy to Stockholm, where he arrived in 1666. It was there, in 1667, that he assembled information about the Russians and their unswerving belief in transubstantiation.[9] In the following year a declaration was also submitted by the Greek archbishop of Cyprus,[10] and, in 1669, by the Nestorian community in Diarbekir.[11] But Arnauld and Nicole spread their net considerably further. Through the French ambassadors, consuls and missionaries posted throughout the Levant they requested attestations, signed by the various priests and prelates of all the eastern Churches, and they consequently needed a scholar who could translate the material collected.[12]

The Embassy in Istanbul

Their choice fell on a young man who was going to become one of the greatest Arabists of his generation, Antoine Galland. Born in Rollo in Picardy in 1646, Galland had received his early education, which included the rudiments of Hebrew, in Noyon, and, in 1661, was sent to Paris to continue his studies. After attending the Collège Duplessis he decided

---

6 Antoine Arnauld and Pierre Nicole, *La perpetuité de la foy de l'Eglise catholique touchant l'eucharistie* (Paris: C. Savreux, 1664), 495.

7 See the analysis of the controversy in Quantin, *Le Catholicisme classique et les Pères de l'Eglise*, 321-56.

8 Claude, *Réponse*, 442.

9 His declaration would be included in Antoine Arnauld and Pierre Nicole, *La perpétuité de la foy catholique*, 3 vols. (Paris: C. Savreux, 1669-74), 1:423-51.

10 BNF MS Arménien 145, fols.21-2.

11 Ibid., fos.26-7.

12 Alastair Hamilton, *The Copts and the West 1439-1822. The European Discovery of the Egyptian Church* (Oxford: Oxford University Press, 2006), 152-9.

to satisfy his interest in antiquity at the Collège Royal where he seems to have been taught some Arabic by Pierre Vattier, the translator of Avicenna and al-Makin, and to have improved his Hebrew under Valérien de Flavigny. Thanks to the vice principal of the Collège Duplessis, Nicolas Bouthillier, he was introduced to Nicolas Petitpied, a specialist in canon law who occupied various ecclesiastical and juridical posts and who became Galland's first advisor and patron. Through him Galland obtained access to the library of the Sorbonne and took part in compiling the inventory of the oriental manuscripts in Richelieu's collection. He also made the acquaintance of numerous scholars and found his way into the circle of Port-Royal in which members of the Petitpied family would play an increasingly prominent part. What recommended Galland particularly to Nicole and Arnauld was his competence as a Latinist and his knowledge of Greek and Arabic, for an embassy was preparing to leave for Istanbul led by another fervent Jansenist, Charles Olier, marquis de Nointel, who had agreed to collect the professions of faith of the eastern Churches. Nointel, whose mother had sought spiritual guidance from the *solitaires* of Port-Royal and whose three sisters were nuns at the Abbaye du Bois, was a learned man, but he required a secretary who knew some of the eastern languages.[13] This was to be Galland.

Nointel's embassy set out in August 1670.[14] For Arnauld and Nicole it was something of a triumph since their plan of sounding out the eastern Churches had the full support of the king and the French Church. For Galland it was a decisive experience. He spent three years in Istanbul on the first of what were to be a number of visits to the Near East. Besides learning Turkish, Persian and modern Greek, he improved his Arabic by frequenting the teacher of the *jeunes de langues*, the young interpreters for whom Colbert was endeavouring to set up a school. He also acquired the taste for eastern tales which paved the way to the achievement on which his reputation largely rests–the introduction into Europe, and the translation, of the so-called *Arabian Nights* nearly thirty years later.

Galland and Nointel were tireless in their service to the Jansenists. Just as Arnauld had approached his nephew in Sweden, so the ambassador and his secretary asked the opinion as to the Greek view of the eucharist of numerous European diplomats and residents in Istanbul. The at-

---

13   Mohamed Abdel-Halim, *Antoine Galland, sa vie et son oeuvre* (Paris: A.G. Nizet, 1964), 11-28.

14   The best study of the embassy as a whole remains Henri Omont, *Missions archéologiques françaises en Orient aux XVIIe et XVIIIe siècles*, 2 vols. (Paris: Imprimerie nationale, 1902), 1:175-221.

testations they assembled included those of the Polish ambassador; [15] the apostolic vicar; [16] the members of a Ragusan embassy who arrived in the Ottoman capital in October 1671; [17] the Genoese resident; [18] the Venetian bailo; [19] and the community of western merchants and interpreters living in Pera.[20] They also obtained support from less expected quarters. A German Calvinist merchant assured the ambassador repeatedly that the Greeks did indeed believe in transubstantiation and that Jean Claude had no business to doubt it.[21] He would, he said, have attested it himself in writing were it not for his fear of being excommunicated if he ever went to Charenton. The Austrian diplomatic representative, on the other hand, was far less cooperative. Described by Galland as being "de basse naissance et originaire de Milan,"[22] he flatly refused to provide a signed document, thereby confirming the traditional hostility between the Habsburg and the Valois embassies.

But Nointel and Galland relied above all on the missionaries and the French consuls. The ambassador would appear to have sent out a letter which informed the heads of the various Christian communities what the Protestants thought they believed about the eucharist, which specified the Catholic teaching, and which asked them to state their true belief. In Egypt the learned Capuchin Elzéar de Sanxay (who compiled a catalogue of the eastern manuscripts collected by the French chancellor Pierre Séguier) persuaded the Greek patriarch of Alexandria to submit a confession of faith contradicting Claude's assertions.[23] Also in Egypt the French consul in Cairo, Ambroise de Tiger, obtained statements from the Coptic patriarch of Alexandria, Matthew IV,[24] and from the Armenian bishop.[25] They were witnessed by what would seem to have been the entire Roman Catholic community in the city–the merchants of the French Levant Company, the missionaries, and the consular staff. In Persia the distinguished representative of France and French interests, the Capuchin mis-

---

15   BNF MS Arménien 145, fol.24
16   Ibid., fol.41.
17   Ibid., fol.47.
18   Ibid., fol.43.
19   Ibid., fol.57.
20   Ibid., fol.50.
21   Antoine Galland, *Voyage à Constantinople (1672-1673)*, 2 vols. (Paris: Maisonneuve et Larose, 2002), 1:34, 44.
22   Ibid., 2:2.
23   Ibid., 1:19.
24   BNF, MS Arabe 226.
25   BNF, MS Arabe 227; Galland, *Voyage*, 1:111, 235.

sionary Raphael du Mans, invited the Armenian community at New Julfa, just outside Isfahan, to provide a confession of faith which he witnessed.[26] In Mingrelia it was the Theatine missionary Giuseppe Maria Zampio who wrested an attestation from the Georgians which he himself translated into Latin.[27] Other French consuls obtained confessions of faith from the Greek communities in the islands.[28] Declarations were also submitted by the Greek archbishop of Milos;[29] the Greek bishop of Chios;[30] the Greek and the Jacobite patriarchs of Antioch;[31] the Armenian bishop of Sis;[32] the Greek archbishop of Mount Sinai;[33] the Greek metropolitan of Izmir;[34] and many others.

Nointel and Galland themselves scoured the area around Istanbul and exploited their trips to nearby cities such as Adrianople (Edirne).[35] Nointel proudly reported his visit to the monastery of St George in Büyükada, the largest of the Princes' Isles in the Sea of Marmara, where he interrogated systematically "the abbots and the monks" about their belief in "the mystery of the eucharist."[36] In a letter to Louis XIV he insisted still further on the thoroughness of his researches. He had followed Claude's advice to the letter, and had not only attended every possible religious service but had questioned "patriarchs, archbishops, bishops, priests, gentlemen and private individuals, even the popes and people in the country." They all expressed their abhorrence of the Calvinist accusations and affirmed their faith in transubstantiation.[37]

Galland too was personally engaged in canvassing Greek ecclesiastics. In a village close to Istanbul, for example, he went up to the local Greek

26   Ibid., 167. See also Francis Richard, *Raphaël Du Mans, missionnaire en Perse au XVIIème siècle*, 2 vols. (Paris: Société d'histoire de l'Orient, 1995), 1:81-91; BNF MS Or. Arménien 141.

27   BNF, MS Arménien 145, fols.71-5. Cf. Galland, *Voyage*, 2:126.

28   BNF, MS Arménien, fols.38, 34, 36, 45, 78.

29   Ibid., fol.55.

30   Galland, *Voyage*, 1:60.

31   Ibid., 146, 177.

32   Ibid., 214.

33   Ibid., 235.

34   Ibid., 2:105.

35   Ibid., 1:29-50.

36   BNF, MS Arménien 145, fol.29.

37   Ibid., fol.85v: "J'ay assisté a leur ceremonies, et a leurs liturgies, ou cette Verité paroist dans un éclat Invincible; Et les Patriarches, Archevesques, evesques, prestres, les gentilhommes, et les particuliers, mesme les Papas, et le peuple a la campagne, me l'ont certifié avec execration contre ceux qui Leurs Imputaient Une autre croyance, les traittans de calomniateurs et d'heretiques." Cf. Omont, *Missions archéologiques françaises*, 1:180.

priest and asked him about his views on the eucharist.[38] His main task, however, was to translate into French the attestations in Greek[39] and to write in the ambassador's name to the Greek patriarchs and metropolitans. The attestations produced by the Greeks in Istanbul were the most important of all. Galland and Nointel could count on the assistance of Panaiotis Nicousios from Chios, from 1669 to his death in 1673 the Grand Dragoman, or interpreter to the sultan. A man of letters of the greatest distinction, Nicousios, educated by the Jesuits, had assembled an important library and had formerly acted as personal physician to the Grand Vizir and interpreter to the imperial and other foreign embassies.[40] It was Panaiotis who procured for the French ambassador a letter from Nektarios, former Orthodox patriarch of Jerusalem, to Paisios, the patriarch of Alexandria, confirming his belief in transubstantiation.[41] More significant still was the declaration the ambassador and his secretary received from Parthenius IV, the patriarch of Constantinople and head of the Greek Church.[42]

Nointel and his secretary had every reason to be pleased with their achievements in the Ottoman Empire. Not only had they obtained an astonishing number of declarations, but some of them were documents of extraordinary beauty. The attestation of the Coptic patriarch of Alexandria, for example, is a magnificent illuminated scroll of paper on green silk.[43] The illuminated confession of faith of the Armenian catholicos, Hagop IV, is an even more splendid document.[44] Galland wrote at length about the beauty of the attestation provided by the Greek metropolitans

---

38 Galland, *Journal*, 1:104: "Je vis le papas du village auquel je demanday, de la part de S.E., ce qu'il croyoit de l'Eucharistie. Il me dit que c'estoit le corps et le sang de Jésus Christ, et luy ayant demandé s'il resoit encore du pain, il me respondit qu'il n'en restoit pas et que la substance du pain estoit changée en la substance du corps de Jésus Christ, et la substance du vin en celle de son sang."

39 Ibid., 58.

40 Damien Janos, "Panaiotis Nicousios and Alexander Mavrocordatos: the rise of the Phanariots and the office of Grand Dragoman in the Ottoman administration in the second half of the seventeenth century," *Archivum Ottomanicum* 23 (2005/6): 177-96. See also Galland, *Voyage*, 1:18, and Steven Runciman, *The Great Church in Captivity: A Study of the Patriarchate of Constantinople from the Eve of the Turkish Conquest to the Greek War of Independence* (Cambridge: Cambridge University Press, 1968), 363-4.

41 BNF, MS Arménien 145, fols.67-8.

42 Ibid., fols.13-16; Galland, *Voyage*, 1:19.

43 BNF, MS. Arabe 226; Gérard Troupeau, *Catalogue des manuscrits arabes. Première partie. Manuscrits chrétiens. Tome I. Nos.1-323* (Paris: Bibliothèque nationale, 1972), 193-4.

44 BNF, MS Arménien 145, fol.7. Cf. Annie Vernay-Nouri, *Livres d'Arménie. Collections de la Bibliothèque nationale de France* (Paris: Bibliothèque nationale de France, 2007), 16-17.

of Athens and Adrianople,[45] and of the profession from the Armenians of New Julfa, both richly illuminated.[46] They were later to become some of the most prized possessions of the French national library.

Galland returned to Paris in 1673 and would make two other extensive journeys to the Near East before settling in France for good, ending his career as professor of Arabic at the Collège Royal, venerated in the French drawing rooms for his translation of the *Arabian Nights* and admired in the world of scholarship for his many translations from Turkish, Persian and Arabic and his discoveries as an antiquarian and numismatist. He was, above all, a scholar, an exemplary citizen of the Republic of Letters for whom confessional allegiance was only of secondary importance when compared to the standard of a man's learning. He was not a theologian and he never indulged in confessional polemic. His friends had different religions. The scholar to whom he was closest, Jacob Spon, was a Huguenot. He had cordial relations with Anglican residents in the Ottoman Empire who, as we shall see, argued against the Greek belief in transubstantiation. He corresponded affectionately with Dutch members of the Reformed Church, and he included among his friends a number of Danish Lutherans.[47] He took employment wherever he could find it. Some of his patrons, such as the members of the Bignon family, were committed Jansenists, but others were not.[48] He himself said that he was sceptical by nature in every field except for religion,[49] but his own piety, deep though it ran, remained an essentially private matter.

---

45   BNF, MS Grec 431; Galland, *Voyage*, 1:54-5: "Elle estoit écrit sur un grand papier de soye collé sur de taffetas orné de peintures et principalement d'une lettre initiale qui représentoit d'un costé St Chrysostôme et St Basile de l'autre, en acte d'adoration envers un petit Jésus couché sur une patène couvert d'un voile à demy corps et un calice avec trois Chérubins qui estoient representés au dessus. Signée du Patriarche lui-même, de trois autres ses prédécesseurs et de celuy d'Alexandrie et d'un grand nombre de Mètropolites et bullée d'un grand sceau d'argent doré… Ce bulle pesoit quarante cinq dragmes."

46   BNF, MS Arménien 141; Vernay-Nouri, *Livres d'Arménie*, 18-19; Galland, *Voyage*, 167: "Elle estoit addressée à Sa Majesté en forme de lettre et on y avoit peint un Prestre à l'autel, levant le pain consacré devant le peuple à genoux avec beaucoup de dévotion, et les premières lettres représentoient en miniature assez délicate plusieurs figures d'animaux. La marge estoit ornée d'une belle vignette diversifiée fort industrieusement d'or et de couleurs fort proprement appliqués."

47   For his friends see Abdel-Halim, *Antoine Galland*, 34-5, 54-7, 106, 131-3, and for his tolerance, 424-5.

48   Ibid., 81-97.

49   Ibid., 113. He described himself as being "sans fard, cherchant la droiture, aimant la vérité, et la soustenant lorsque je puis la connoistre, scepticien (je mets la religion à part) dans les choses où elle ne m'est pas apparente, et cela pour me conserver dans une tranquillité d'esprit don't j'ai grand besoin, estant né Picard, je veux dire avec la teste chaude."

The attestations which Nointel had gathered in Istanbul were sent back to France,[50] and Antoine Arnauld made instant use of them. In 1669 he had started to issue a new edition of the *Perpétuité de la foy*. The small single volume of 1664 turned into three volumes. In the first volume he had already made use of the work of the Maronite Abraham Ecchellensis to confirm the belief in transubstantiation of the Nestorians,[51] and in the third, which came out in 1674, he included all the attestations assembled in Istanbul (and elsewhere). A more thorough exploitation of the new material, however, was due to Eusèbe Renaudot. The grandson of the Protestant physician Théophraste Renaudot, Eusèbe was a man of letters, a friend of Boileau, Racine, La Bruyère and Bossuet, but he was also a theologian, once a member of the Paris Oratory, an institution that had proved strongly sympathetic to Jansenism. His own commitment to the movement cost him the appointment as custodian of the royal library.[52] In Renaudot the Jansenist leaders had at last found someone who was both an orientalist and a theologian, and who was ready to document their theory about the ubiquity and antiquity of the teaching of the Catholic teaching on the eucharist. Opinionated and argumentative, he was, like Nicole and Arnauld, always prepared to polemicise, and in his hands the three volumes of the *Perpétuité de la foy* turned, many years later, into six.

Renaudot's additional volumes started to appear in 1711, well after the deaths of Nicole and Arnauld, and even if his first objective was to prove that all the eastern Churches shared the belief in transubstantiation, he in fact produced a study of eastern Christianity in its entirety–of the Melkites, the Nestorians, the Jacobites, the Copts and the Ethiopians. This was a fundamental contribution to the subject, and its importance was heightened by Renaudot's critical approach to other earlier and contemporary studies. In 1709 Renaudot had already published the homilies on

---

50 The most important collection is now at the BNF, MS Arménien 145 and others. These manuscripts, used by Arnauld and Nicole, were then passed on to Eusèbe Renaudot. At his death they entered the library of Saint-Germain-des-Prés, and, after the French Revolution, the Bibliothèque Nationale. Nointel, however, also had a copy made of most of the papers in Arménien 145 which is now in the library of Rouen. BNF Arménien 145 is described by Henri Omont, "Confessions de foi des églises orientales," *Bibliothèque de l'Ecole des Chartes* 55 (1894): 567-70, and the Rouen manuscript, also by Henri Omont, "Confessions de foi des églises orientales," *Bibliothèque de l'Ecole des Chartes* 45 (1884): 235-6.

51 Loubna Khayati, "Usages de l'oeuvre d'Abraham Ecchellensis dans la seconde moitié du XVIIe siècle: controverses religieuses et histoire critique," in Bernard Heyberger, ed., *Orientalisme, science et controverse: Abraham Ecchellensis (1605-1664)* (Tournai: Brepols, 2010), 192-203.

52 Antoine Villien, *L'Abbé Eusèbe Renaudot: Essai sur sa vie et son oeuvre liturgique* (Paris: V. Lecoffre, 1904), 29-33.

the eucharist by Gennadius I, patriarch of Constantinople when the city fell to the Turks. In 1713 he made a further contribution to oriental studies with his *Historia Patriarcharum Alexandrinorum Jacobitarum a D.Marco usque ad finem saeculi XIII*, the first extensive history of the Coptic patriarchs of Alexandria based entirely on Arabic sources, and in 1716 he published the first volume of his *Liturgiarum orientalium collectio* containing the liturgies of the Coptic and Ethiopian Churches. The second volume would follow ten years later with the liturgies of the Jacobites and the Nestorians.

Protestant Reactions

By the time Renaudot was writing the eucharistic controversy had spread far outside the French borders. But to follow it we must go back in time—to Jean Claude's original attack on the Jansenists and his assertions about the eastern Churches. When he maintained that the eastern Christians did not believe in transubstantiation his position was decidedly weak. For his description of the observances of the Abyssinians Claude drew on Damião de Goes (who claimed that they never exposed the eucharist)[53], but for information on most of the other eastern Churches he seems to have relied on Edward Brerewood's *Enquiries touching the Diversity of Languages, and Religions, through the Chiefe Parts of the World*, published posthumously in 1622. In fact Brerewood had little to say about beliefs in the eucharist, but when he came to the Armenians he stated that "they denie the true body of Christ to be really in the sacrament of the Eucharist under the Species of bread and wine."[54] As his source he gave the fourteenth-century Carmelite Guido Terrena, also known as Guy de Perpignan, whose inquisitorial activities as bishop first of Elna and then of Majorca bore fruit in his *Summa de haeresibus*. His long section on the Armenians is extremely interesting,[55] but, as Arnauld and Nicole pointed out, he was altogether alone in denying their belief in transubstantiation.[56]

For the Greek Church, on the other hand, Jean Claude advanced evidence which, at first sight, was considerably more convincing. This was

53 Claude, *Réponse*, 297-8.

54 Edward Brerewood, *Enquiries touching the Diversity of Languages, and Religions, through the Chiefe Parts of the World* (London: Iohn Bill, 1622), 173.

55 Guy de Perpignan, *Summa de haeresibus, et earum confutationibus* (Paris, 1518), fols.29v.-42r. For the eucharist, fols.38v.-39r.

56 Arnauld and Nicole, *Perpétuité de la foy* (1664), 494.

the confession of faith by Cyril Lucaris, five times patriarch of Constantinople. As the head of the Orthodox Church, Lucaris seemed a reliable spokesman of Greek views. Born in Crete, educated, like a number of promising young Cretans, in Venice and later in Padua, well acquainted with northern Europe, he had been sent as the deputy of the patriarch of Constantinople to the Council of Brest-Litovsk in 1595 to defend the interests of the Greek Orthodox community in Poland menaced by the advance of the Church of Rome. In the course of his travels he had had much to do with Protestants, and, as patriarch of Alexandria but resident in Istanbul, he had been befriended by Protestant diplomats and scholars.[57]

One of Lucaris's main concerns was to block the many attempts of the Catholic Church to win the Greeks over to union with Rome, and it was this that made his friendship with the European Protestants ever firmer. The outcome was a confession of faith published in 1629. Both here,[58] and in his letters to his Protestant friends,[59] Lucaris stated that the Greek Church did not accept the doctrine of transubstantiation.

Lucaris was strangled on the sultan's orders in 1638. He had a small number of disciples who continued to defend his views, and the Greeks who travelled to Northern Europe were usually prepared to please their Protestant hosts by saying that they did not share the Roman Catholic view of the eucharist.[60] Otherwise, Lucaris's confession of faith was all but unanimously rejected by the Greeks in the East. Nointel, we saw, had little difficulty in eliciting statements which clearly contradicted those of Lucaris, but the document which suited his purpose best was earlier. This was the so-called confession of Moghila, the *Orthodoxa Confessio Fidei* named after Petrus Moghila, the Paris-educated Moldavian metropolitan

---

57 Steven Runciman, *The Great Church in Captivity*, 259-88; Gerhard Podskalsky, *Griechische Theologie in der Zeit der Türkenherrschaft 1453-1821* (Munich: C.H. Beck, 1988), 162-80.

58 *La Confession de foy de Cyrille patriarche de Constantinople* (Sedan: Iean Iaques de Turene, 1629), 12. Of the eucharist he wrote, "nous confessons et faisons profession de recognoistre una vraye et reelle presence de Iesus Christ nostre Seigneur. Mais telle que la foy nous la presente, et non pas celle que nous enseigne la controuvée Transsubstantiation. Car nous croyons que les fidele mangent le corps de Iesus Christ en la Cene du Seigneur, non point en la brisant de la dent materielle, mais en le percevant par le sens de l'ame, veu que le corps de Iesus Christ n'est pas ce qui se presente à nos yeux au Sacrement, mais ce que nostre foy apprehende spirituellement, et qu'elle nous baille: D'où s'ensuit qu'il est veritable que si nous croyons, nous mangeons et participons, et si nous ne croyons pas, nous sommes destituez de tout fruict."

59 Jean Aymon, *Monumens authentiques de la religion des Grecs...* (The Hague: C. Delo, 1708), 118.

60 Runciman, *The Great Church in Captivity*, 289-309.

of Kiev who contributed, in 1640, to a slight revision of an existing confession which would be endorsed at the Orthodox Councils of Kiev in 1640 and Jassy in 1642. Published in Amsterdam in 1666, again thanks to Panaiotis Nicousios [61] it was transmitted to Nointel in a bilingual, Latin and Greek, manuscript by Nicousios himself, in 1671.[62] The statement about the eucharist could hardly have been less equivocal. "The holy Eucharist," it runs in the eighteenth-century English translation attributed to Philip Lodvel, "or the Body and Blood of our Lord Jesus Christ, under the visible Species of Bread and Wine: Wherein, really and properly, and according to the Thing itself, Jesus Christ is present."[63]

Despite such apparently obvious evidence about the eastern belief in transubstantiation the Protestants refused to give in. The material contained in the third volume of the new edition of the *Perpétuité de la foy* in 1674 prompted Claude to undertake the very same research, and he drew up a questionnaire, which was dispatched to Protestant chaplains in the Ottoman Empire, intended to determine the views on the eucharist of the Greeks and other eastern Christians. The questionnaire is reproduced in full in *Some Account of the Present Greek Church* published by John Covel in 1722. Covel spent many years in Istanbul, acting as chaplain to the English ambassador from 1670 to 1677 and, like most of his colleagues, he had a low opinion of the education of the Greek clergy. In the case of Claude's questionnaire he was particularly sceptical. Claude, he wrote, "supposed by his Queries, that the Greeks and Easterlings were learned and well versed in this Controversy; whereas I never met with one amongst them who ever pretended fully to understand, much less ever offer'd clearly to answer any of them."[64] And indeed, Claude's text, steeped in scholasticism, would have been totally incomprehensible to anyone without a western theological training. The Protestants with more experience of eastern Christianity, in other words the Englishmen who had been posted, or who had travelled, in the Ottoman Empire, chose a different approach.[65]

Thomas Smith, Covel's predecessor as chaplain at the English embassy in Istanbul where he stayed from 1668 to 1671 and who played an

---

61   Podskalsky, *Griechische Theologie*, 229-36.

62   Galland, *Journal*, 1:19. The manuscript is now BNF, MS Grec 1265.

63   *The Orthodox Confession of the Catholic and Apostolic Eastern Church from the version of Peter Mogila*, ed. J.J.Overbeck (London: Thomas Baker, 1898), 79-80.

64   John Covel, *Some Account of the Greek Church* (Cambridge: Cambridge University, 1722), vi.

65   Runciman, *The Great Church in Captivity*, 306-10.

important role in the idealisation of Cyril Lucaris that occurred in the Protestant world, denied the antiquity of the Greek belief in transubstantiation on philological and terminological grounds. He claimed that the term μετουσίωσις was a recent novelty, whereas the words to be found in the ancient liturgies of Basil and Chrysostom, such as μεταποίησις and μεταστοιχείωσις "do not infer such a substantial Change, that is, that the Elements notwithstanding their Conservation retain their essence and nature, though they are, as they are justly said to be, the Body and Bloud of Christ, is clear."[66] He also insisted that, in Greek services, the eucharist was not consecrated by the words of the priest, but by the descent of the Holy Ghost on the elements on the altar.[67]

Paul Rycaut spent over fifteen years in the Ottoman Empire, first attached to the English embassy in Istanbul and then, from 1667 to 1678, as consul in Izmir. Few Europeans knew the Ottoman world better than he did, and his *Present State of the Greek and Armenian Churches, Anno Christi 1678* was published shortly after his return to England.[68] On many points he agreed with Smith and Covel. Like Smith he emphasized the novelty of the term μετουσίωσις, but he also made it quite clear that "the Greeks detest that Confession of Faith, supposed to be wrote by Cyrillus, their Patriarch of Constantinople."[69] Like Covel he had some contempt for the piety of the Greeks.[70] And he had even more contempt for the Armenians, "being in most things of a dull and stupid apprehension, unless in Merchandise and matters of gain."[71] Where the belief in transubstantiation was concerned Rycaut was hesitant to reach a definite conclusion. The Armenians, he wrote, "hold Transubstantiation as do the Papists from whom the Priests readily accepted of such a Doctrine as tends to their Honour and Profit... Howsoever this Tenet of Transubstantiation is held as discussed but of late years amongst them and is not altogether Universally accepted; some of them will pretend to maintain, and others to deny it."[72] Nor had it been much discussed by the Greeks. "The question about Transubstantiation hath not been long controverted in the Greek Church, but

---

66 Thomas Smith, *An Account of the Greek Church, as to Its Doctrine and Rites of Worship* (London: Miles Flesher, 1680), 147.

67 Ibid., 144.

68 Sonia P. Anderson, *An English Consul in Turkey. Paul Rycaut at Smyrna, 1667-1678* (Oxford: Clarendon Press, 1989), 216-29.

69 Paul Rycaut, *Present State of the Greek and Armenian Churches, Anno Christi 1678* (London: For John Starkey, 1679), sig.a5r.

70 Ibid., sig.a1r.-v.

71 Ibid., 387.

72 Ibid., 433-4.

like other abstruse notions, not necessary to be determined, hath lain quiet
and dissentangled, wound upon the bottom of its own Thread, until Faction, and Malice, and the Schools, have so twisted and ravelled the twine,
that the end will never be found."[73] Even if the Greeks did at least seem to
accept transubstantiation, Rycaut, like Claude before him, pointed out that
their devotion to the eucharist was very different from that of the Church
of Rome: there were no eucharistic processions, no feast days devoted to it,
no prostrations at its appearance, and no exposition in public.[74]

Where the English participants in the eucharistic controversy agreed
was on the widespread theological ignorance of the eastern Christians,
and particularly of the Greeks. This was a point stressed by John Covel, who reported his urbane discussions with Nointel in the halls of the
English embassy. Having studied the attestations gathered by the French
ambassador Covel concluded that, in many cases, the signatories were
making no more than a gesture of obeisance to the powerful emissary of
a powerful monarch, and had certainly not understood the theological
niceties of the questions put to them. The members of the higher clergy
who signed, on the other hand, had, according to Covel, all been educated in Italy. Some–like Lucaris–had benefited from the ancient links with
Venice, and had studied there and in Padua. Others had been trained at
the Greek College in Rome founded by Gregory XIII in 1577, where, in
marked contrast to the Maronites, they benefited from the best teachers
the Society of Jesus had to offer.[75] There they had been imbued with Roman Catholic teaching.

Eastern Beliefs

But was Covel right? And what did the eastern Christians really believe? On one point the Anglicans were indisputably correct. The eastern
Churches had always been reluctant to discuss the consecration of the
eucharist. It was a mystery, a part of the liturgy, and, as such, was never
an object of theological speculation as it was in the West. The Greeks, admittedly, had devoted more attention to it since the Reformation, largely
because of their links with Europe.[76] Where those Churches situated in ar-

---

73   Ibid., 181.
74   Ibid., 182-3. Cf. Claude, *Réponse*, 444-5.
75   Covel, *Some Account*, xi-xxii.
76   For Greek discussions see Podskalsky, *Griechische Theologie*, 82-3, 121-2, 132-3,
155, 158, 187-8, 191, 197-8, 212-13, 226-7, 235, 240-1, 272-3, 281, 289-92, 329.

eas which had fallen to the Arabs in the seventh century were concerned, namely Syria and Egypt, theological discussion had been largely limited to subjects about which the Christians were in particular disagreement with the Muslims. These did not include the eucharist, and the few works in which the eucharist was discussed before the eighteenth century tend to be mainly concerned with the manufacture of the bread involved.[77] Yet, we see from the rubrics of the early fifteenth century that, in contrast to what certain Protestants might claim, the Coptic congregations not only believed in transubstantiation, but worshipped the elevated eucharist with just as much veneration as the Roman Catholics, prostrating themselves and begging for the remission of their sins by striking their breasts and "with tears and supplications."[78]

The shortage of disquisitions on the eucharist in the East meant that there was always room for a case against belief in transubstantiation. The answers given by the members of the eastern Churches to the question of whether they shared the Catholic belief depended to a large extent on the way in which the question was put. The antiquarian George Wheeler encountered a young monk in a monastery in Levadhia in Boeotia. Although he was from Zante, the monk had left his birthplace when he was too young to have had any traffic with Roman Catholicism. "When I asked him, Whether they believed that the Bread and Wine was changed into the Body and Blood of Christ? He answered me, Whether I thought them so much Beasts, as to believe such an Absurdity?"[79] Although he "could not find, that transubstantiation hath been heard of, except among those that have conversed with the Roman Church,"[80] Wheeler, who regarded the entire debate as disruptive of Christian unity, preferred to suspend judgement.[81] The German Lutheran Hiob Ludolf had a similar experience some years earlier. Ludolf, who had devoted himself to the study of Ethiopic under the protection of the duke of Saxe-Gotha, Ernest 'the

---

77   The Coptic belief in transubstantiation is clearly stated in a tract dating from the late fourteenth century, Alfonso 'Abdalla, O.F.M., *Un trattato inedito sulla SS. Eucaristia (MS. Vat. Ar. 123, 1396 A.D.). Testo originale e traduzione, Studia Orientalia Christiana Aegyptiaca: Collectanea* 12 (Cairo: Edizioni del Centro Francescano di Studi Orientali Cristiani, 1967), 345-464. For the use of unleavened bread see the extensive section 389-97, 448-59. For the best general discussion see Gabriele Giamberardini, O.F.M., *La conscrazione eucaristica nella Chiesa Copta* (Cairo: Edizioni del Centro Francescano di Studi Orientali Cristiani, 1957), 11-123.

78   Alfonso 'Abdallah, *L'ordinamento liturgico di Gabriele V – 88° patriarca copto, 1409-1427* (Cairo: Edizioni del Centro Francescano di Studi Orientali Cristiani, 1962), 194, 379.

79   George Wheeler, *A Journey into Greece* (London: printed for William Cademan, Robert Kettlewell and Awnsham Churchill, 1682), 198-9.

80   Ibid., 197.

81   Runciman, *The Great Church in Captivity*, 309-10.

Pious,' had managed to invite to Gotha an Ethiopian monk, Abba Gregorius, whose help he enlisted in compiling an Ethiopic dictionary. When he asked Gregorius about the real presence in the eucharist, Gregorius said he knew about the teaching, but that it concerned an abstruse mystery. Questioned more closely about the Catholic doctrine of transubstantiation, Gregorius added that it was unknown to the Abyssinians, but that his compatriots would never dream of unravelling the intricate problems involved in so mysterious a process. He himself believed that the elements were purely representative of the body and blood of Christ.[82]

But however vague eastern ideas on the eucharist may have been, was there any substance to Covel's persuasion that confessions were submitted solely to please the Catholic powers? There is no doubt that in certain cases this was so. The splendour of some of the manuscripts brought back to France is striking. The Armenians in Persia had clearly taken infinite pains to produce a document which not only affirmed their belief in transubstantiation but which was also an object of beauty. There had long been conflicting currents in the Armenian Church, some strictly orthodox, and some tending towards Roman Catholicism. The signatories of the attestations were, by and large, sympathetic to the Church of Rome, and the community of New Julfa drew up the confession of faith in a manifest effort to please Louis XIV at a time when they needed his protection. The Armenians in Persia, who had once benefited from the tolerance of Shah Abbas, had been in danger, ever since 1654, of being expelled from Persian territory, and it was their ejection from Isfahan which had led them to settle in a distant suburb. Taxes had increased under Shah Suleyman, Armenians had been imprisoned, and in 1672 the entire city of Isfahan was closed to them.[83] The French king, whose recent military victories had led to his being respected by the Turks, had always presented himself as the protector of the Christians in the Ottoman Empire, and even if his help never materialised, he could still raise the hopes of persecuted communities. Another fine document, as we saw, is the illuminated scroll containing the attestation of the Copts of Egypt and signed by the patriarch of Alexandria, Matthew IV. The head of the Coptic Church had little to expect from the king of France and the Copts owed Rome no favours, but Matthew had strong intellectual sympathies for the Roman Catholic Church–it was, after all, partly at his instigation that the German Lutheran scholar Johann

---

82 Hiob Ludolf, *Historia Aethiopica* (Frankfurt: J.D. Zunner, 1681), sigs. Aa4r.-v.
83 Richard, *Raphael du Mans*, 1:40-1, 55-7, 81-91.

Michael Wansleben, dispatched by Ernest the Pious to explore Ethiopia, converted to Catholicism in 1665.[84]

But to suggest that all the attestations were signed to curry favour with the Catholics of the West is wrong. One of the best pieces of evidence is the confession of faith submitted by Parthenius IV, the patriarch of Constantinople himself.[85] Far from being an attempt to prove the proximity between Orthodox and Catholic beliefs, the patriarch started his attestation by listing those tenets which his Church did not share with Rome. When he came to the question of transubstantiation, however, he fully accepted the Catholic position.

Conclusion

The eucharistic controversy sustained by the Jansenists continued for some thirty years after the deaths of Arnauld and Nicole and petered out, on the Protestant side, in a spirit of uncertainty, in the third decade of the eighteenth century.[86] Yet it made a deep impression on oriental studies in the West. Not only did it give Antoine Galland his first taste of the East, but it drew scholars of every confession all over Europe. Anglicans, Calvinists and Lutherans joined the debate in the North, while Catholics who could hardly be considered Jansenists, such as Richard Simon,[87] did so in France. Renaudot was immensely influential. One of the foremost students of Coptic at the time, the Augustinian Guillaume Bonjour, was close to him and, in Rome, encountered patrons and scholars who also had Jansenist leanings. Bonjour himself established a tradition of Coptic studies in the Augustinian Order which can be traced down to the twentieth century.[88] But the Jansenists did not limit themselves to interest in the eastern Churches. The section of the immense academy planned by Colbert which was to include orientalists such as Barthélemi d'Herbelot (whose *Bibliothèque orientale* was edited by Galland) and the elder François Pétis de la Croix, collapsed, partly because it was rumoured to have Jansenist sympathies,[89]

84 Hamilton, *The Copts and the West*, 143-4.

85 BNF, MS Arménien 145, fols.13-16.

86 For a general survey of the controversy see Podskalsky, *Griechische Theologie*, 392-6.

87 Richard Simon, *Fides ecclesiae orientalis seu Gabrielis Metropolitae Philadelphiensis opuscula* (Paris: G. Meturas, 1671; repr. Amsterdam: Rodopi, 1970), 84-143.

88 Hamilton, *The Copts and the West*, 229-32.

89 Nicholas Dew, *Orientalism in Louis XIV's France* (Oxford: Oxford University Press, 2009), 57-8.

and, however difficult such sympathies may be to document, there is little doubt that Jansenism left its mark, for many years to come, on a number of scholars studying different aspects of the East.

LABOURING IN REASON'S VINEYARD: VOLTAIRE AND THE ALLEGORY OF ENLIGHTENMENT

Madeleine Kasten

1. Introduction: Allegory Old and New

According to a long-standing critical tradition, Western European literature in the later eighteenth century witnessed a shift to a new aesthetic
devoted to the cult of the symbol.[1] The defining characteristic of this–secularized–symbol as described by one of its earliest advocates, Goethe, is
that it joins an image to an idea in such a way that the idea remains active
in the image without ever being exhausted or wholly expressed by it. The
symbol as envisaged by Goethe *is* and *means* at one and the same time, yet
defies attempts to say exactly *what* it means, and precisely this ineffable
quality determines its suitability to the poetics of Romanticism.

Like other Romanticists, Goethe develops his definition of the symbol
in contradistinction to allegory, thereby suggesting that the contemporary
aesthetic can establish itself only at the expense of the old. Allegory, he
claims, links an image to a *concept* which, unlike the idea, is limited and
may therefore be fully expressed by its metaphorical vehicle. While Goethe
thus associates the symbol with the active and inexhaustible realm of the
imagination, allegory is relegated to the province of intellectual abstraction
where the metaphorical transaction depends not on the spontaneous play
of the idea, but on culturally and historically determined convention.[2]

---

1 An earlier, shorter version of this argument appeared in a special issue of the magazine *Primerjalna književnost* (2006): 81-91, 253-63.

2 See Johann Wolfgang von Goethe, *Maximen und Reflexionen*, in *Goethes Werke:
Hamburger Ausgabe*, vol. 12: *Kunst und Literatur*, ed. Erich Trunz (München: Beck, 1981),
365-547, and esp. 470-71 for the following quotation: "Die Symbolik verwandelt die Erscheinung in Idee, die Idee in ein Bild, und so, dass die Idee im Bild immer unendlich wirksam
und unerreichbar bleibt und, selbst in allen Sprachen ausgesprochen, doch unaussprechlich
bliebe."[…] "Die Allegorie verwandelt die Erscheinung in einen Begriff, den Begriff in ein
Bild, doch so, dass der Begriff im Bilde immer noch begrenzt und vollständig zu halten und
zu haben und an demselben auszusprechen sei." For a lucid account of the genesis of the
allegory-symbol antinomy see Hans-Georg Gadamer, *Truth and Method*, trans. and ed. Joel
Weinsheimer and Donald G. Marshall (London and New York: Continuum, 1975), 61-70.

The Romantic allegory-symbol antinomy as it was construed by Goethe and others was to have a lasting impact on western culture. Nevertheless Paul de Man, in the first part of his famous essay "The Rhetoric of Temporality," claims that the victory of the symbol over its allegorical counterpart was by no means a foregone conclusion at the time. Discussing the relationship between the subject and nature in literature of the pre-romantic period, he notes that the symbolic specificity of the natural image often gives way to plainly conventional, allegorical descriptions. These shifts, in which he detects the "true voice" of early Romanticism, do not fail to affect the poetic subject-object relationship, since "the prevalence of allegory always corresponds to the unveiling of an *authentically* temporal destiny."[3]

Unlike the language of later Romanticists who will fall prey to the symbolic "cult of the moment,"[4] the diction of 'naturalists' such as Rousseau or Wordsworth testifies to their awareness that the lyrical subject can never coincide with the natural surroundings from which it draws inspiration. After all, where nature is subject only to the change of seasons–Goethe's *Dauer im Wechsel*–we mortals must inevitably resign ourselves to the temporality which is our authentic destiny, that is, to our mortality. And the figure most proper to this realization is allegory, a form of indirect speech ruled by convention where, through a conscious decision of the mind, anything may be made to represent anything else.[5]

The allegorist may take his reader by the hand and lead him up an enticing garden path, as Rousseau does in Part Four of his *Julie*, but the treasures he has in store typically belong to the moral rather than the physical world. The very language of the nature descriptions he brings into play alerts his reader to their distinctly *textual* origin. For the allegorical sign, dependent as it is on convention for its interpretation, necessarily owes its meaning to a sign which precedes it.

However, as de Man recognizes, allegory's very reliance on pre-established, historically determined meaning also entails its liability to historical change. The essential difference between the secularized allegory of the eighteenth century and its literary forebears, he claims, resides in

3 Paul de Man, "The Rhetoric of Temporality," in *Blindness and Insight* (1969; London: Methuen, 1983), 187-228, and 206 for the quotation (my italics).

4 Ibid., 204.

5 Walter Benjamin, *The Origin of German Tragic Drama*, trans. John Osborne (London: NLB, 1977), 175.

"the suppression [...] of the analogical and anagogical levels,"[6] that is, in the loss of the eschatological perspective which had once enabled a poetic language that was *both* symbolical and allegorical. Hence,

> [t]he meaning constituted by the allegorical sign can [...] consist only in the *repetition* (in the Kierkegaardian sense of the term) of a previous sign with which it can never coincide, since it is of the essence of this previous sign to be pure anteriority.[7]

Elsewhere, I have argued that this representation of cultural history, for which de Man draws implicitly on Walter Benjamin's *Origin of German Tragic Drama*, amounts to a gross simplification. Thus it fails to account for the ambivalent attitude towards allegory displayed in a fourteenth-century work such as William Langland's *Piers Plowman*, which closes the door on any unproblematic vision of the ways of God to man.[8] In this article I will take issue with de Man's corresponding theory of eighteenth-century allegory as a masochistic or at best therapeutic pastime conducted in the spirit of Kierkegaardian repetition. For in presenting allegory as an exercise in mortality not unlike the Freudian *Fort-Da*-game, a way of immunizing oneself against the pain of loss, de Man seems to ignore its importance as a cognitive instrument to explore the world. Despite the undeniable change in cultural outlook dividing eighteenth-century allegory from its pre-modern predecessor I would contend that this cognitive function, often dismissed as allegory's didactic penchant, was as vital in the age of Rousseau and Voltaire as it had been in Langland's.

The allegorical quest typically unfolds as a reading process in which the protagonist learns to cope with life's perplexities by interrogating his position as the subject–in a double sense–of his own text. Indeed, many narrative allegories incorporate this reading process as their main theme, grafting themselves as they do onto a prior text whose authority they either seek to uphold or to debunk through relentless satire. This is true of Voltaire's *Candide* no less than of Langland's *Piers Plowman*, even if the name of Voltaire's titular hero appears to mark him out as an allegorical representative not of a text but of its opposite, the blank slate. But then of course the *tabula rasa* is itself an ancient philosophical concept, and Voltaire's Enlightenment reading of it owes much to his admiration for a

---

6 De Man, "The Rhetoric of Temporality," 207.
7 Ibid., 207.
8 Madeleine Kasten, *In Search of 'Kynde Knowynge': Piers Plowman and the Origin of Allegory* (Amsterdam and New York: Rodopi, 2007), 207.

specific text that was considered highly controversial in his day, Locke's *Essay Concerning Human Understanding.*[9]

In this article I examine Voltaire's use of allegory as a means both to explore the world and to establish an identity in and through narrative. I will begin by highlighting those aspects of his philosophy which made narrative the vehicle *par excellence* for his thought. To this end, I propose to analyse one of his best-known fables, "L'Homme aux quarante écus." In my conclusion I will broaden my historical perspective by drawing a brief comparison between two emblematic gardens: the half-acre where Langland's medieval ploughman sets the world to work, and the garden whose cultivation is the final task undertaken by the indefatigable Candide.

2. The Philosopher and the Storyteller

What is the relationship between philosophy and the art of storytelling? Can one be a philosopher and a storyteller at one and the same time, or even in one and the same text? If so, then how does the medium affect the message? Walter Benjamin, in a well-known essay, characterizes the storyteller as a craftsman with the ability, growing increasingly rare, to share experiences.[10] A born communicator, the storyteller is someone who offers counsel to his listeners. This counsel tends to be either of a practical or moral nature, and it typically takes the form of a proposal as to how the story that is being told might continue. What is thus imparted to the audience is neither information nor some abstract truth but *wisdom*, "the epic side of truth," in which counsel is inextricably interwoven with the matter of real-life experience.[11]

Benjamin's eulogy of the storyteller as a mediator between life and truth might well make one forget that the art of performing truth in narrative has not always found similar favour among western philosophers. Yet it is important to remember that already Plato, in Book Two of his *Republic*, banishes fiction from his ideal state because of its potential for cor-

---

9   See letter 13 of the *Lettres philosophiques*; the following quote is from Roger Pearson, *Voltaire Almighty: A Life in Pursuit of Freedom* (London: Bloomsbury, 2005), 98: "I am no more disposed than [Locke] to imagine that a few weeks after my conception I was a very clever soul who knew a thousand things that I then forgot when I was born."

10   Walter Benjamin, "The Storyteller: Observations on the Works of Nikolai Leskov," trans. Harry Zohn, in *Selected Writings*, ed. Howard Eiland and Michael W. Jennings, vol. 3 (Cambridge, MA, and London: Belknap Press of Harvard University Press, 2002), 143-66, esp. 142.

11   Ibid., 145-46.

rupting public morals.[12] Along with the poet, the sophist, too, is dismissed as a tale-monger who abandons the cause of truth for the vulgar objective of persuasion.

Michel Foucault assigns Plato's attempt to distinguish between true and false discourse to a fundamental turning-point in human history, where the opposition true/false itself comes to function as the single most important mechanism for the control of human speech.[13] Indeed we find this observation well supported by the tradition of western philosophy, where the notion of 'falsehood' is frequently equated with that of 'fiction.' Ever since Plato, the relationship between philosophy and narrative has been an uneasy one, even if some celebrated philosophers–including, ironically, Plato himself–earned themselves a reputation as powerful storytellers.[14]

The case of François-Marie Arouet, *alias* Voltaire (1694-1778), appears to compound this difficulty. A tireless champion of the Enlightenment, he was likewise a man of many and diverse talents, who combined his literary output with his historical and philosophical work as well as his scientific interests. As is testified by Voltaire himself, he did not conceive of his various kinds of writing as radically different from one another. "J'écris pour agir,"[15] he declared, an adage which fits the purpose of his *Dictionnaire philosophique* (1764) as well as that of the twenty-six *contes philosophiques* which he left the world, and which today constitute the cornerstone of his literary reputation.

The common application of the term 'conte philosophique' to Voltaire's stories might suggest that he, for one, did not subscribe to the opposition

---

12   See the excerpts of Plato's *Republic* printed in D.A. Russell and M. Winterbottom, eds., *Ancient Literary Criticism: The Principal Texts in New Translations* (Oxford: Clarendon Press, 1972), 50-74, esp. 74.

13   See Michel Foucault, *The Order of Discourse*, trans. Ian McLeod, in *Untying the Text: A Post-Structuralist Reader*, ed. Robert Young (Boston: Routledge and Kegan Paul, 1981), 51-78, esp. 54. However, Foucault makes it clear that this opposition will reveal its aspect of arbitrary violence only when it is viewed from a position *outside* the discourse which it aims to regulate. *Within* a given discursive community, the need to distinguish between truth and falsehood can only appear self-evident (ibid., 54).

14   See the excerpts from Plato's *Republic* in Russell and Winterbottom, *Ancient Literary Criticism*, 74: "[...] there is an old quarrel between poetry and philosophy. I could quote a lot of passages for that: 'the yapping bitch that barks at her master,' 'a great man amid the vanities of fools,' 'the rabble of know-all heads,' 'thin thinkers starve,' and so on. However, let us make it clear that if poetry for pleasure and imitation have any arguments to advance in favour of their presence in a well-governed city, we should be glad to welcome them back. We are conscious of their charms for us. But it would be wrong to betray what we believe to be the truth."

15   The quotation is from a letter by Voltaire to Jacob Vernes dated 15 April 1767. See Roger Pearson, *Fables of Reason* (Oxford: Clarendon Press, 1993), 7.

between truth and fiction outlined above. However, Roger Pearson points out that the author himself rarely made use of it, even though the Quarto edition of his works published in 1771 contains two volumes whose contents are classified under the title *Romans, contes philosophiques*, etc. Moreover, he employed terms such as 'conte,' 'fable,' and 'roman' indiscriminately to denote miraculous chapters in biblical history, the metaphysics of fellow philosophers as far back as Plato, and the fabulous historiography of the ancients.[16] It seems safe to conclude, then, that Voltaire did not automatically endorse Aristotle's view of the poet as one concerned with the expression of a higher, more philosophical kind of truth than the historian, the chronicler of mere facts.[17]

This conclusion is confirmed by the article on history which Voltaire wrote for the *Encyclopédie*. He begins his contribution by drawing a conventional distinction between historiography, "le récit des faits donnés pour vrais," and the fable, "qui est le récit des faits donnés pour faux." Whoever might be inclined to interpret the word 'faux' in the neutral sense of 'fictitious' here is quickly disabused. In the fourth paragraph, the author observes that historiography has its roots in stories ("récits") passed on from one generation to another; a process in which the story gradually loses all probability. What remains is a "fable" in which the truth has been lost ("la vérité se perd"); hence, "toutes les origines des peuples sont absurdes."[18] Herodotus' *Histories*, he notes, represent a curious hybrid of the true things he has heard and the "contes" he has from hearsay; at times the work reads like a novel ("roman"). Those historians who, like Voltaire's older contemporary Charles Rollin, are inclined to admire the wisdom ("science") and truthfulness ("véracité") of these stories had better consider that time is too precious, and history too immense, to saddle their readers with such fictions.[19]

Not only do stories lack factual truth. Voltaire's last remark suggests that even where a story does contain a 'higher' truth, this might have been more efficiently conveyed through other means. The very term 'conte philosophique' thus presents itself as a potential problem in the context of his oeuvre, a circumstance which alone warrants a closer investigation

---

16 Pearson, *Fables of Reason*, 5-6.

17 See Aristotle's *Poetics* in Robert Con Davis and Laurie Finke, eds., *Literary Criticism and Theory: The Greeks to the Present* (New York and London: Longman, 1989), 66-67.

18 Voltaire, *Les Oeuvres alphabétiques*, vol. 1: *Articles pour l'Encyclopédie*, ed. Jeroom Vercruysse, Oeuvres complètes de Voltaire 33 (Geneva: The Voltaire Foundation and Taylor Institution, 1968- ; this volume, 1987), 164-65.

19 Ibid., 170.

into his actual practice of the genre. There may well be truth in Pearson's claim that Voltaire's general dislike of stories was grounded in his conviction that many of these stories prevent people from seeing things as they really are.[20] What Voltaire does, according to Pearson, is to penetrate the realm of fiction so as to destroy it from within by replacing the fable with a more authentic story. Far from pandering to his audience's craving for illusions, his stories present themselves as allegories which each reader must apply to his or her personal situation. This didactic design, it may be noted, conforms entirely to Voltaire's belief that the most useful books are those which are written jointly by the author and the reader.[21] At the same time it confirms the author's conception of the *conte philosophique* as a hybrid structure whose philosophical meaning emerges only indirectly, at the precise point where it turns the fables concocted by others–philosophers, scientists, legislators, the Church– against themselves.

In the following sections I will examine the role of narrative for Voltaire's thought through an analysis of one of his more successful *contes*, "L'Homme aux quarante écus" (1768). My enabling assumption is that what compelled Voltaire to a narrative approach was his view of the Enlightenment as a radically *historical* development. Ever suspicious of philosophical systems, he saw the Enlightenment project in terms of an open-ended process that could only unfold itself in the workings of the individual mind. "Lisez, éclairez-vous," one of the narrators in "L'Homme" exhorts both the protagonist and the external reader[22]–without, characteristically, providing any titles for the curriculum. Reading, an *occupation* and as such marked by temporality, is an important theme in this *conte*, where the hero's steadily increasing appetite for books presents itself as

---

20 Pearson, *Fables of Reason*, 4.

21 See Voltaire, *Dictionnaire philosophique*, 2 vols., ed. Christiane Mervaud, Oeuvres complètes 35 and 36 (Geneva: The Voltaire Foundation and Taylor Institution, 1968- ; these volumes, 1994-95), 164-65. In the preface to the *Dictionnaire philosophique* I Voltaire claims that "[l]es livres les plus utiles sont ceux dont les lecteurs font eux-mêmes la moitié; ils étendent les pensées dont on leur présente la germe; ils corrigent ce qui leur semble défectueux, et fortifient par leurs réflexions ce qui leur paraît faible" (1: 284). The author's view of the connection between fable and allegory is borne out by the first sentence of his article on fables in the same work: "*Les plus anciennes fables ne sont-elles pas visiblement allégoriques?*" (2: 99). Elsewhere in the same article he wonders whether "l'ancienne fable de Vénus, telle qu'elle est rapportée dans Hésiode, n'est [...] pas une allégorie de la nature entière" (2: 101).

22 Voltaire, "L'Homme aux quarante écus," in *Romans et contes*, ed. Henri Bénac (Paris: Garnier, 1960), 284-342, and 327 for this quotation. Unless stated otherwise all quotations are from the edition by Henri Bénac.

an allegory for his attempts to read life.[23] To read in this broader sense is to enlighten oneself, a way of performing reason through a constant dialogue with the baffling text that is the world.

My analysis focuses on the question how, that is, by what formal means, Voltaire's *conte* seeks to perform reason in and through narrative, as well as on the consequences of this narrative approach for the philosophical truth thus conveyed.

3. Mr Average[24] Learns to Read

"L'Homme aux quarante écus" is the story of a man's quest for knowledge. As such, it coincides with his individual growth towards a narrative identity.[25] Before proceeding to the question of form I will give an outline of this typically Voltairean plot.

"L'Homme" opens with a lament in the *ubi sunt* tradition, as an old man compares the present state of France's economy to its more glorious past. The main reason he gives for this decline is the current scarcity of agricultural labour owing, among other things, to the fact that so many French citizens have turned to different occupations nowadays.

In the chapter following this prologue we are acquainted with the disaster that has befallen the protagonist, a smallholder whose land would afford him an annual income of forty écus were it not for a tax reform recently introduced by "quelques personnes qui, se trouvant de loisir, gouvernent l'État au coin de leur feu."[26] The newly-appointed ministers, it turns out, have imposed a single tax on land while exempting all those who gain their income from different sources, and as a "seigneur terrien" our hero is bound to renounce half of his annual income to the state.[27]

---

23 Compare the following quotation from "L'Homme," 336, which appears near the end: "Comme le bon sens de monsieur André s'est fortifiée depuis qu'il a une bibliothèque! Il vit avec les livres comme avec les hommes [...]."

24 I borrow this translation of l'Homme's 'name' from Pearson, *Fables of Reason*, 22.

25 Compare Paul Ricoeur, *Oneself as Another*, trans. Kathleen Blamey (Chicago: University of Chicago Press, 1992), 147-48: "The narrative constructs the identity of the character, what can be called his or her narrative identity, in constructing that of the story told. It is the identity of the story that makes the identity of the character."

26 Voltaire, "L'Homme," 286.

27 The tax system as described here did indeed exist in Voltaire's day, but only as a theory advanced by a group of economists who styled themselves the 'Physiocrats.' Their idea, based on the belief that cultivation of the soil is the best way to ensure economic wealth, was that France needed to develop its agriculture. The proposal for a single tax to be levied on land came from Le Mercier de la Rivière, but was never actually put in practice in France; see Pearson, *Fables of Reason*, 21). Voltaire may thus be seen to ground his own story in an economic fable concocted by others.

Having served a term in prison for being unable to pay his due, he meets a puffed-up capitalist who tries to convince him of the justice of the new system: "Payez mon ami, vous qui jouissez en paix d'un revenu clair et net de quarante écus; servez bien la patrie, et venez quelquefois diner avec ma livrée."[28]

The capitalist's apologia sets *l'homme* thinking–a rare activity in his part of the country.[29] Yet he finds that thought alone does not provide him with the answers necessary to refute an argument he cannot believe in, so he calls in the help of two successive "géomètres."[30] His first consultant, who practises a metaphysical variant of geometry, merely confuses him by trying to make him disbelieve the evidence of his own eyes. Fortunately, his second mentor, a "citoyen philosophe," assures him that "la véritable géometrie est l'art de mesurer les choses existantes."[31] Through a number of statistic calculations, this 'true' measurer of things figures out that if the total amount of France's arable land were to be divided by the estimated number of its population, everyone would have an income of forty *écus* a year. At this point, then, *l'homme* discovers himself to be France's exact Mr Average. He soon comes to regret this position when learning that the average Parisian has a life expectancy of twenty-three years, including only three years of a tolerable existence: "Quarante écus, et trois ans à vivre! Quelle ressource imagineriez-vous contre ces deux malédictions?"[32]

Straightaway his counsellor, an eminently practical man, launches into a remarkably modern-sounding programme for the improvement of public health and hygiene: provide cleaner air, make the people eat less and do more exercise, encourage breastfeeding and inoculation against smallpox. As to the matter of fortune, he can only advise Mr Average to get married and have four children, since "five or six miseries put together make a very tolerable household."[33] After some more jests the *géomètre* delivers a lecture on good government. What is required, he asserts, is a system where the entire population, including the new industrials, is made to do its stint to relieve the national treasury. Having reached the end of his discourse, he ironically commends Mr Average to the grace of God.

---

28 Voltaire, "L'Homme," 287.

29 Ibid., 285.

30 In French, the word means both 'geometrician' and 'surveyor,' a professional who examines the conditions of land and establishes property lines. The narrative, which I identified earlier as the account of a reading process, may be seen to effect a shift from the first to the second sense.

31 Voltaire, "L'Homme," 292.

32 Ibid., 291.

33 Ibid., 292.

Average's answer shows that he is already beginning to reap the benefits of education: "On passe sa vie à espérer, et on meurt en espérant."[34]

Rendered destitute by the new tax legislation, our hero finds himself snubbed by a Carmelite whom he begs for food. A visit to a public session of the inspector general, before whom he hopes to present his case, provides him with further proof of how the country is ruled by iniquity. When he finally seizes his chance to demand justice he is told that he has been the victim of a hoax. In recompense, he receives a substantial sum and is exempted from tax for the rest of his life.

An anonymous correspondent, having read an account of Mr Average's vicissitudes and knowing him for an avid reader, sends him an issue of an economic journal. Since the writer himself has been ruined by the advice contained in such journals, however, he warns Mr Average to put no trust in the new economic theories and agricultural systems he will find expounded there: "Gardez-vous des charlatans."[35]

This embedded story of a man who learned to read too late is followed by another, allegedly drawn from the manuscripts of an old recluse in whom it is hard not to recognize an *alter ego* of Voltaire. This narrator shifts the topic from the creators of new governmental systems to those who aim to displace God by re-creating His universe after the fact. Thus he recounts a dialogue with a descendant of Thales who tried to convince him that the world was originally covered over with water and that the globe itself is made of glass. However, "plus il m'indoctrinait, plus je devenais incrédule."[36] Metaphysical system-builders–Leibniz, Descartes–and the explorer Maupertuis, who proposed to build a city at the centre of the earth, fare no better with this confirmed sceptic.

Meanwhile Mr Average has come a long way on the road to education. Possessed of a small fortune, he marries a pretty girl who soon gets pregnant. His approaching fatherhood triggers new questions, so he returns to his *géomètre* to find out how children are engendered. The latter denies any direct knowledge of the matter, but offers to give him the thoughts of some philosophers on the subject: "that is, how children are *not* made."[37] Various theories are reviewed, ranging from Hippocrates' ideas concerning the blending of male and female semen to Harvey's hypothesis that women, like all mammals, breed from eggs that ripen in the ovaries. Just

---

34 Ibid., 301.
35 Ibid., 307.
36 Ibid., 308.
37 Ibid., 311.

when the prospective father has avowed that his wife's eggs are very dear
to him, his instructor dampens the atmosphere by announcing that science has grown weary of this system, and that children are made differently nowadays.[38] There follows a round of new speculations which meet
with growing criticism on part of the student. When the *géomètre* declares
that in the end scientists may have to "return to the eggs," Mr Average
asks what the use of all these debates has been. The answer is: doubt. Scientists, says the *géomètre*, have an important advantage over theologians
in that they can hold different views without knocking each other's brains
out. Although he does not make the advantages of doubt for science itself explicit he counsels Mr Average to doubt everything in life–except, of
course, the basic principles of geometry.[39]

As he proceeds to put this advice into practice, Mr Average encounters
ever new evils and idiosyncrasies in the world. By keeping an open mind
and taking nothing for granted, however, he gradually succeeds in per-
fecting his own education. As his progress is attended by financial gain he
even manages to start a library of his own. But perhaps his most important feat is that he at last acquires a name for himself: henceforth, "notre
nouveau philosophe" will be known as Monsieur André.[40]

In his new capacity as a man of wisdom, Monsieur André quickly gains
a reputation as a mediator in conflicts. When a seemingly insoluble dis-
pute arises among theologians about the question whether the soul of the
virtuous pagan emperor Marcus Aurelius resides in heaven or in hell, he
invites both parties to supper and tactfully persuades them to leave the
emperor's soul *in statu quo*, "pending a definitive judgement."[41] Interestingly, he manages to break the ice by telling his guests a *conte*.[42] The last
episode finds him and his wife presiding over a banquet where the guests,
all of whom represent different religious denominations and walks in life,
nevertheless manage to spend a most enjoyable evening together. For his
part, the narrator of this final scene is convinced that the occasion yields
in nothing even to Plato's feast.[43]

---

38 Ibid., 313.
39 Ibid., 315.
40 Ibid., 332.
41 Ibid., 334.
42 Ibid., 334.
43 Ibid., 342.

4. Voltaire's Allegory of Enlightenment

Paul Ricoeur, in his monumental study *Time and Narrative*, defines human identity as being constituted essentially through narrative. As human agents, we live in a continuous present of historical time where we determine our actions on the basis of past experience and expectation of the future. In order to give expression to this complex historical present we need stories. Only by refiguring historical time through narrative can we situate our individual experience in the interpersonal context of the world we inhabit. For unlike the historical present, a story is not a sequence of unconnected events. In telling a story, we impose a unifying plot structure onto a succession of discrete events and incidents, thereby creating an illusion of logical and causal coherence. "Time becomes human," says Ricoeur, "to the extent that it is articulated through a narrative mode, and narrative attains its full meaning when it becomes a condition of temporal existence."[44] Stories enable us to synthesize the heterogeneity of experience into an intelligible whole. At the same time they help us come to terms with the finitude of our lives, in that they permit us to construct a prehistory and imagine a possible sequel to our existence. In short, we need stories to make *sense* of our lives.[45]

Judging from the outline of "L'Homme" given above, one might get the impression that the story provides a perfect illustration of Ricoeur's theory. Like *Candide*, Voltaire's most famous *conte*, "L'Homme" too unfolds as a *Bildungsroman* in which a man, struck by initial disaster, outgrows his role as a passive figure–in the case of the future Monsieur André, a *literal* figure–and gradually develops an identity which allows him to take his fate into his own hands.[46] Yet how could this triumph of education be demonstrated but in a narrative, Benjamin's "epic side of truth"? As in any *Bildungsroman*, the very illusion that the protagonist has fulfilled his quest for self rests on the fact that his story *ends* at a certain point, thereby imposing a unifying seal on his biography.

---

44 Paul Ricoeur, *Time and Narrative*, vol. 1, trans. Kathleen McLaughlin and David Pellauer (Chicago and London: University of Chicago Press, 1983), 52.

45 See ibid., 67: "First, the configurational arrangement transforms the succession of events into one meaningful whole which is the correlate of the act of assembling the events together and which makes the story followable. Thanks to this reflective act, the entire plot can be translated into one 'thought,' which is nothing other than its 'point' or 'theme.'"

46 From the point of view of identity, the story of Mr Average's transformation to Monsieur André seems the more spectacular of the two, as his change of name indicates that he exchanges his allegorical status for the identity of a man of flesh and blood.

A comparison between "L'Homme" and *Candide* yields further interesting correspondences. Both *contes* are anti-fables in that they employ the narrative mode to ridicule existing systems of thought. In this respect they differ from more conventional philosophical tales where the story merely serves to *illustrate* a truth, a genre for which Aesop's fables provided the western prototype. We have seen how "L'Homme" offers Mr Average and the external reader a course in exposing the unfounded certainties of others. Just as in *Candide*, 'true reading' here is never a matter of simply exchanging one system for another. Rather, the quest structure of the narrative serves to displace truth from one textual chain onto the next, finally to disappear beyond the horizon of the story. What lends the banquet *chez André* its convivial atmosphere is precisely his guests' ability to engage in spirited conversation while refraining from trying to convert each other, so that the evening yields no weightier conclusion than a jolly song which one of the company has composed for the ladies.

Yet there are also important differences to be observed between both *contes*. In my opinion the most conspicuous of these concerns the levels of narration and focalization.[47] In *Candide* as in "L'Homme," an initial stroke of fate lands the protagonist in a maelstrom of disjointed experiences where nothing seems to make sense anymore, and which leaves him for the time being out of control. Yet where narrative unity in *Candide* is throughout ensured by the presence of an external narrator who integrates the embedded stories into a single perspective, such unity is totally absent in "L'Homme."

In the prologue we meet a personal narrator who questions the old man. Only in the next episode does this narrator identify himself as the protagonist, who proceeds to tell his own story up to and including the scene where the inspector general relieves him of his pecuniary trouble. So far, Mr Average seems to be running the show of his own story, if not of his destiny. At this point, however, his account is interrupted, first by his anonymous correspondent–who claims to have *read* the story of Mr

---

47   See Mieke Bal, *Narratology: Introduction to the Theory of Narrative* (Toronto: University of Toronto Press, 1997), 5-7, who draws a narratological distinction between three different types of agency in a text: telling, seeing, and acting. She relates these different functions to three corresponding narrative levels, i.e., the text, the story, and the *fabula* respectively. By *fabula*, she understands the material or deep structure of a narrative, "a series of logically and chronologically related events that are caused by *actors*." The presentation of this *fabula* takes places on the level of the *story* and involves the agency of *focalization*, that is, of presenting the story from someone's perspective. Finally, the story reaches the external reader in the form of a *text* which is related by a *narratorial* agent.

Average's disaster and subsequent good fortune!–and then by the excerpt from the manuscript of the "vieux solitaire," Voltaire's fictional counterpart, who does not lose the opportunity to refer his readers to some of Voltaire's other writings.

The following episode, where Mr Average receives his crash course in biology, marks another shift, since the beginning is related by an external narrator. Here, Mr Average appears for the first time as the focalized object of another narrator. Before long, the text switches to the dramatic mode, until another personal narrator ('Voltaire'? The *géomètre*?) takes over. While the dialogic element is retained in the next scenes the protagonist is increasingly focalized by others. Once more the story is broken off, this time to accommodate a series of excerpts from a–historical–document on criminal justice written by an actual contemporary of Voltaire. In the final sections, the unidentified narrator is once more in firm command. By that time, the tense begins to shift from past to present, thereby suggesting the convergence of narrated time with the time of narration.

Summing up these observations, we might say that Mr Average's transformation to Monsieur André is counterbalanced by his gradual change from a narrative subject and focalizer into a narrated character and object of focalization, and this latter change accounts for our impression that the protagonist has reached his enlightened destiny at the story's conclusion. However, this would be putting things rather too neatly, considering the text's lack of narrative unity caused by the alternation between different, often unidentified narrators. The resulting sense of incoherence is yet reinforced by the medley of different texts, discourses, and genres which present themselves to the reader in quick succession. On the level of fabula, finally, the discrepancy between the practical nature of our hero's interests and the overtly fabulous nature of his change of fortune threatens to destroy any suggestion of *vraisemblance*.

Should we ascribe these *faux pas* to the ramblings of the author's old age? After all, Voltaire was seventy-four when he wrote "L'Homme." In my opinion there is a more interesting possibility. The very lack of formal coherence as well as the truly Bakhtinian cacophony of voices in the story may also be read as part of its allegorical meaning. Thus interpreted, "L'Homme" conveys the truth that reality itself is irreparably fragmented, and that any suggestion of internal unity can only be the result of emplotment.

On the other hand, Voltaire's *conte* also demonstrates that internal difference may be productive. After all, Monsieur André himself owes his genesis to this divided text. Nor need difference always be synonymous

with discord, as is shown in the closing scene. The mutual differences between the guests do not prevent them from enjoying each other's company; on the contrary, they help to fuel the conversation. Here, we might
remember the *géomètre*'s lesson that scientists, too, can learn to live with
their disagreements.

Difference is an indispensable condition for Voltaire's own view of the
Enlightenment as an open-ended process resisting any attempt to fix its
meaning. By the same logic, however, it will be clear that he needs stories
to press this philosophical point. The result, in "L'Homme," is an allegory
which continues to fascinate for its daring performance of reason.

5. Epilogue

The chief butt of Voltaire's satire in *Candide* is the monadology of Leibniz,
particularly the latter's optimistic belief that since God created the universe, we can only assume to be living in the best of possible worlds.[48] The
character who is made Leibniz' mouthpiece is Candide's tutor, the learned
Doctor Pangloss, who has been appointed to instruct his pupil in "méta-
physico-théologo-cosmolo-nigologie."[49] In the course of the story the
venerable doctor finds himself afflicted by all conceivable evils, yet he remains steadfast in his conviction that Leibniz cannot possibly be wrong.[50]
Not so Candide, whose own peregrinations lead him to the famous but
cryptic conclusion that "il faut cultiver notre jardin."[51] Bitter experience
has taught him to abandon his philosophical as well as his physical quest,
renouncing both for a life of labour in his postlapsarian garden. Reasoning is thus supplanted by the *performance* of reason, a task which holds
no guarantees for a happy future and whose allegorical meaning must be
supplied anew by each reader.[52]

In my thesis on *Piers Plowman*, for which Burcht Pranger acted as a
supervisor years ago, I venture a reading of an obscure passage where the

---

48   For an excellent yet accessible account of Leibniz' metaphysical thought see G.
MacDonald Ross, *Leibniz* (Oxford: Oxford University Press, 1984), esp. ch. 5-6.

49   Voltaire, *Candide ou l'Optimisme*, ed. Frédéric Deloffre (Paris: Gallimard, 2003), 28.

50   Ibid., 146.

51   Ibid., 153.

52   Deloffre, in the preface to his edition of *Candide*, in *Romans et contes*, vol. 2 (Paris: Gallimard, 1992), 22, suggests a possible link between Candide's garden and Voltaire's
own private 'vineyard of the Lord' (Matt. 21:28), i.e. his project to join forces with Diderot,
D'Alembert, and others at his rural estate of Ferney to ensure the completion of the *Encyclopédie*. Cf. Pearson, *Voltaire Almighty*, 269-72, who notes that Voltaire had reserved a field
on the estate which he used to work himself until well into his eighties.

mysterious Piers takes charge of a host of penitents in search of St. Truth. As the pilgrims do not know where to look for the saint's shrine Piers offers to show them the way, on condition that they first help him plough and sow his half-acre. In the course of this scene it gradually transpires that the ploughing is to replace the intended journey, which never takes place. The notion of pilgrimage itself is thus critically revised; a revision which is etymologically supported by the roots of the Latin word *peregrinus*.[53] Piers' actions demonstrate that like Candide, he too rejects the idea of travel, choosing instead to serve Truth as a simple worker or *travailer* on his acre. His only reward, satirically presented in the form of a pardon, is Truth's command to do well. Again, we are reminded of Candide, who stubbornly keeps reciting his injunction to work without providing any reasons.

Towards the end of *Piers Plowman*, the farmer's labour acquires apostolic dimensions as he establishes the Church before vanishing from his own text. In *Candide*, this figurative potential remains significantly unrealized. But this is not my point. What I would emphasize is that both texts employ narrative to achieve their didactic design rather than resorting to philosophical argument. In performing their message allegorically, they subject their protagonists and their external readers to a reading exercise whose educational purpose, in Voltaire's eighteenth century as in Langland's fourteenth, is to help them shape, test, and reshape their narrative identities.

---

53   The root of the Latin word *peregrinus* is the adverb *peregri* or *peregre*. This adverb is itself a compound made up of the preposition *per* ('through,' also in the instrumental sense) and the noun *ager* ('land,' especially 'cultivated land' or 'acre'). It takes the case of the locative and correspondingly carries the meanings 'abroad' and 'on the land.' However, *peregri* may also denote movement; it then means 'to/from foreign lands.' The word 'pilgrim' thus admits of two radically different interpretations – one predicated on movement, the other on stability; see Kasten, *In Search of 'Kynde Knowynge,'* 138.

The Canon

THE SEARCH FOR THE CANON AND THE PROBLEM OF BODY AND SOUL

Piet de Rooy

In 2000 the United States decided "to preserve sound recordings and collections of sound recordings that are culturally, historically, or aesthetically significant, and for other purposes." As part of the Library of Congress a National Recording Registry was established. Anyone can nominate a recording of any kind, as long as it is at least ten years old and informs or reflects 'life in the United States.' Every year a board decides on the entry of up to 25 items at the most. In 2004, for example, a 1939 recording of tenor saxophonist Coleman Hawkins playing "Body and Soul" was entered, a song originally written in 1930 by Edward Heyman, Robert Sour, Frank Eyton and Johnny Green. The record was considered "one of the best–known recorded jazz performances in history."[1] It was the sound of love, and has become a standard since then. All in all this was an agreeable and justifiable result from a transparent and satisfying procedure. This example makes one wonder: why should the recent canon of Dutch history and culture have to be a body without a soul?

Troubled history

Until a few decades ago Dutch historical writing reflected the segmentation of society. Caesar once began a book with the famous sentence "Gallia est omnis divisa in partes tres." Likewise, one of the most striking characteristics of Dutch society today is that it was divided. At the end of the nineteenth century four 'pillars' each organised a part of the population. That process was initiated by Catholics and orthodox Protestants, emulated by social-democrats and demurely followed by the liberal bourgeoisie. During World War I this 'unity in discord' became generally accepted. The state as such was weak; authority resided at the tops of those pillars, which guaranteed each cultural group a modicum of recognition as part

---

1   www.loc.gov/rr/record/nrb-home.html

and parcel of the nation. Here the nation-building process, as analysed in Eugen Weber's *Peasants into Frenchmen* (1976), was hampered by the fact that the conscripted army was small and primary education was divided between state-owned and 'free' schools, the latter mostly of a specific denominational affiliation. From 1878 onwards Dutch history was a required subject in the school curriculum, but generally speaking, this resulted in three different stories of the past: a liberal, a Protestant and a Catholic one. People lived together between animosity and politeness, and they prided themselves on the unworldly level of 'tolerance' toward one another that they had achieved. So far so good.

In the so-called *sixties* however, as part of the societal and cultural revolution, these pillars crumbled, burying the different varieties of history. History lost its inspirational meaning and significance; popular opinion even gave the impression that history was only a tale of exploitation of the populace, the proletariat, the women, the colonies and so on. The past had become a foreign country. In this sudden void the state did not step in with a new curriculum, as in 1878, although all schools were obliged to teach at least World War II. The lessons to be drawn from the War were thought to furnish the moral basis of society. In general, the consequence of this situation was that the teaching of history shifted from facts to skills, from knowledge to tricks. The author Rudy Kousbroek had lived long enough in Paris to have experienced a very different kind of relationship with the past, and he wrote after his return to Amsterdam that Dutch culture seemed 'to lack a dimension.'[2] Rather than to be alarming, however, this was considered a happy situation, whereas 'nationalism' was perceived as the root of all evil in the twentieth century. From this perspective, not knowing one's own history could be seen as a contribution to everlasting peace. Of course, this description is exaggerated, but only mildly unfair. Let us now turn to some recent efforts to strike a new course.

Un-Dutchables

In June 1988 Prime Minister Ruud Lubbers returned home from a European summit at which he had discussed the next steps in the political and cultural integration of the Union. Thus, he wondered about the future of Dutch culture in an integrated Europe. This led to a large research programme of the Netherlands Organisation for Scientific Research (NWO):

---

2   Rudy Kousbroek, *Is het zoo geschied?* (Groningen: Wolters-Noordhoff, 1995) 25.

'Dutch Culture in a European Context.' This project ran from 1991 until 2001; ten universities participated and five major publications and a host of monographs and research papers were produced.[3] A striking aspect of the series, however, was that, while attention was almost exclusively directed to the Netherlands, the European context remained well-nigh invisible. The Netherlands was presented in terms reminiscent of the Shire, that famous area, settled exclusively by Hobbits–also originally divided into four Farthings–as described by Tolkien. It was a small but beautiful land, its population allowed itself some quarrels and arguments but, compared to the dangerous and belligerent world around it, it was peaceful on the whole. As one commentator remarked: "the smoke of a pipe came from these pages, the smoke of gunpowder was hardly to be smelt."[4] The historical community of the Netherlands was not very amused with these results: the political community appeared to have taken no notice of them. Moreover, it played no role whatsoever in the public debate around the referendum on the European 'constitution' in 2005. This programme was, however, the first sign of the idea that it might perhaps be worthwhile to search for a Dutch 'identity,' that some essence lay hidden in the past and had to be preserved in the turmoil of capitalist transformation, societal renewal, loss of sovereignty to 'Brussels' and, perhaps most important of all, mass immigration.

For a long time, the effects of mass immigration from Turkey and Morocco had not been openly discussed in the Netherlands. Until the end of the twentieth century, even discussing this subject was almost considered a form of 'racism,' a direct violation of the moral lessons drawn from World War II. While frustration with the 'new' immigrants had risen for almost two decades in working-class quarters, the silence among respectable people was broken at last in 2000 by an article in a respected newspaper: "The multicultural tragedy" by the left-wing intellectual Paul Scheffer.[5] This piece made an important contribution to a change of attitude:

---

3 Translations of the major publications were completed in 2004. They were published by Van Gorcum (Assen) and Palgrave-Macmillan (Basingstoke and New York): Willem Frijhoff and Marijke Spies, *1650: Hard-won Unity*; Joost Kloek and Wijnand Mijnhardt, *1800: Blueprints for a National Community*; Jan Bank en Maarten van Buuren, *1900: The Age of Bourgeois Culture*; Kees Schuyt and Ed Taverne, *1950: Prosperity and Welfare*; Douwe Fokkema and Frans Grijzenhout, eds., *Accounting for the Past: 1650-2000*.

4 Karel Davids, "In opdracht van de tijd?," *Bijdragen en Mededelingen Betreffende de Geschiedenis der Nederlanden* 117 (2002): 544-556.

5 Paul Scheffer, "Het multiculturele drama," *NRC Handelsblad*, January 29, 2000. Paradoxically, this article made the populist politician Pim Fortuyn more or less respectable in the way that it was conceded that 'he has a point.'

emphasis shifted from association to assimilation. No longer were immigrants allowed to live their own lives on their own islands within Dutch society; now they had to respect Dutch 'identity' and conform to the values of that society. This change of policy, however, required a clear view with respect to the essential characteristics of Dutch culture. That clarity, however, was nowhere in sight, because Dutchmen had refused to regard themselves as a special branch of mankind but considered themselves cosmopolitans.[6] Now in some quarters, the need for an explicit 'Dutch identity' was urgently felt.

In May 2005 a Committee for the Development of a Dutch Canon was created by the minister of Education. The first sentence of the instruction runs as follows: "Societal transformations during the last years give reason to reflect again upon the identity of the Netherlands. [...] In wide circles the need for a new Tale of the Netherlands is felt."[7] A little while later, parliament decided that this Tale was also to function as the backbone of a new National Historical Museum. For the first time in decades politicians took a keen interest in the way Dutch history was presented, combining current political concerns with nostalgia for a homogeneous and peaceful Hobbit Shire. In a way it is understandable that when the loyalty of different groups within society is in doubt (after 9/11), the chasm seems to widen and the politics of difference and/or diversity–'multiculturalism'–no longer produce peace and harmony. In the past, history has served lesser goals and gods. But is a 'new' tale of Dutch identity not doomed to fall on barren grounds?

Historical ignorance

An opinion commonly held in respectable circles was that 'no one' any longer knew anything about history in general and Dutch history in particular. Paradoxically this situation was in some ways satisfying, since it allowed an elite to use knowledge of the past as a symbol of belonging to better circles of society. Useless knowledge served as a mark of distinction. But the resulting peace of mind was broken by an inquiry into his-

---

6 For example, Abram de Swaan, *Perron Nederland* (Amsterdam: Meulenhoff, 1991).

7 *De canon van Nederland. Rapport van de commissie ontwikkeling Nederlandse canon* (Amsterdam: Amsterdam University Press, 2006), 95. The direct impulse to create this committee was at the advice of the Council on Education to construct a canon, in order to attract attention for "the valuable parts of our history." This suggests it is worthwhile or even possible to resolve 'our history' into valuable and non-valuable factors.

torical knowledge among the members of Dutch parliament. The *Historisch Nieuwsblad* (Historical Tidings) ran an article in the summer of 1996 that made it obvious that the political elite as such was not very familiar with basic historical facts. Of course, this examination was slightly unfair, as extreme results could only boost the visibility of the journal, but it ended everyone's complacency. It was true! No one knew anything about 'our' history; all those history lessons in primary and secondary education had been wasted, pearls before swine. This situation demanded some heavy artillery. In 1997 a Committee was created to advise the government on a better way of teaching history. Their 2001 report argued for a shift from teaching skills to teaching some structured basic knowledge.[8]

Although the report was warmly received in general and was even gradually implemented by the Ministry of Education, this was somehow not enough. It would take several years before results would become noticeable, and sometimes politicians cannot resist the urge to pull seedlings out of the soil in order to examine the growth of the roots. Perhaps it was best, so it was thought, to combine the creation of that New Tale of the Netherlands with the construction of a minimal knowledge of history, geography, culture and tradition: a 'canon' to be taught in primary education and the first grades of secondary school, as a combination of enforced assimilation and the struggle against historical ignorance. Thus the canon became a cure for all ailments. In several quarters people now started to produce canons–about music, provinces, cities, Christian religion, etc.[9]– and a pandemic of 'canonitis' swept over the country. What was it that made a canon so attractive?

Silent background

The Committee for the Development of a Dutch Canon made official reports in 2006 and 2007. Fifty well-chosen 'icons,' ranging from the Stone Age to the present, were presented as the basic structure of the New Tale and served as a minimum of knowledge at the same time. The chairman of the Committee, Professor Frits van Oostrom, who was at that time president of the prestigious Royal Netherlands Academy of Arts and Sci-

---

8 *Verleden, heden en toekomst. Advies van de Commissie Historische en Maatschappelijke Vorming* (Enschedé: SLO, 2001). It is fair to confess that the present author chaired that committee.

9 Another confession: the present author was responsible for the construction of a canon for the city of Amsterdam and contributed to the canon for the city of Haarlem.

ences, kept a careful distance from tricky concepts such as 'identity', preferring the more neutral term 'collective memory'. His use of the icon as a window was a seminal strategy for explaining the larger context of each chosen person or object. This method perhaps contributed most to the success of this canon; it offered a model of presenting parts of the past in an attractive way. This might explain the explosion of canons that followed. But did the fifty icons, taken together, tell a New Tale or, put another way, did they add up to a history?

The answer has to be negative, and this largely explains the gradual disenchantment of this venture in 2008 after its initial success. First of all, the Minister of Education had to withdraw his proposal to make the canon obligatory in secondary education by making it part of the final examinations. Such a requirement would have put the state in the position of deciding on the content of historical instruction, which in the tradition of the pillarisation in the Netherlands was anathema and also ran against the professional pride of the teachers. The minister was forced to declare that the canon was to be seen as "an inspiration." Second, the two directors of the new National Historical Museum let it be known that they considered a canon unsuitable to the purpose of building a museum. The significance of the canon would be reduced to 'a silent background'–a fine example of euphemism. And so neither of the two goals of that canon, enhancing knowledge and presenting a New Tale, was achieved. In the troubled political climate–with a sharp rise in support for right-wing populist politicians–the canon was perhaps authoritative; no one offered a fundamental critique or proposed a radically different set of icons. But neither was the canon able to surmount the main problem: the absence of a certain level of historical consciousness in public debate. It is very hard to compose a new tale, when there is not an old one to build on and when even a certain tradition of storytelling is lost. In essence, the weakness of the canon was its inability to connect the fifty icons into a historical pattern, into a real story: it was a body without a soul. And that leaves the original problem unsolved.

Social amnesia

Currently there is a substantial popular interest in history, but at the same time a lack of historical consciousness–and knowledge–is unmistakable. The process of depillarisation in the sixties stripped the past of its relevance; academic history did not prove to be an alternative.[10] Academic

10   J.H. Plumb, *The Death of the Past* (Harmondsworth: Penguin Books, 1969).

history has taken advantage of the depillarisation, which implied a lifting of responsibilities, viz. legitimating the respective pillars by becoming more 'scientific'.[11] In that process a mass readership was lost. Current interest in history and the past is more like a new form of tourism, of crossing a border into a foreign country. It may offer interesting experiences, but it remains a digression, with reality waiting back home. Historical arguments play no role in political debate and a marginal one in public debate in general. Society suffers from social amnesia, after the happy phrase of Russell Jacoby.[12]

To this deplorable situation canons might have brought some relief. Their popularity suggests that we are dealing with an innovative genre of historical writing: short, well-illustrated, referring to places to visit–in virtual and real space–and written in crystal-clear prose. So this method, like a body attached to a soul, can be used to reach a wider audience, to connect books with historical sites, to give an analysis with nostalgic feelings of 'things remembered'. By recognising a canon as a new genre and by systematically exploring and exploiting this type of connection, history might regain some of its former importance. As far as content is concerned, I would suggest that not the icons themselves but the criteria for their selection are the most important aspects of constructing a canon. For example, it is important to explain *why* the Reformation is an inevitable part of the canon. This can be done by making Luther an icon, as well as Calvin, Hus or Melanchthon, and even Erasmus will do. A canon is most fruitful if it succeeds in explaining the reasons behind its selection. In this way a canon can teach discernment and add insight to knowledge. There the body might meet the soul. And all this, of course, hopefully will lead to a more general feeling that the past still lingers on, that the present world is a continuation of a former one and not a stage where everyday curtains are raised for a new play.

---

11   Paradoxically however, 'grand interpretations' of Dutch history had to come from foreign historians: for example, Simon Schama, *The Embarrassment of Riches: an Interpretation of Dutch culture in the Golden Age* (London: Collins, 1987); Jonathan Israel, *Radical Enlightenment: Philosophy and Making of Modernity 1650-1750* (Oxford: Oxford University Press, 2001). The only Dutch historian who came close to such an interpretation was Ernst Kossmann, *The Low Countries 1780-1940* (Oxford: Clarendon Press, 1978), but a mocking irony is the dominating style of this work.

12   Russell Jacoby, *Social Amnesia: a Critique of Conformist Psychology from Adler to Laing* (Boston: Beacon Press, 1975).

MUSIC AT THE LIMITS:
EDWARD SAID'S MUSICAL ELABORATIONS*

ROKUS DE GROOT

Music at the Limits

More than anywhere else, it was in his involvement with music that Edward Said showed himself to be a man of rationality and passion. Music occupied a privileged place in his life and work, not comparable even to literature. Music was a highly ambiguous art to him. He observed that music was the most inward, most private of the arts, and at the same time, as performance, a highly public event. While seemingly "autonomous from the social world," he emphasized music also as an elaboration of civic society.[1] To him music was also an ambiguous art in the sense that it requires a highly specialist training,–in Said's own words "a discipline rather like that of a Jesuit"–, which turns it into a hardly accessible, even mysterious and esoteric endeavor, while on the other hand, it makes a very powerful immediate effect.[2]

For Said, music was an experience at the limits of thought, social practice and life. First of all it was European classical music which greatly attracted him, a tradition of composing, performing and listening which has a rather small number of dedicated listeners worldwide. It is moreover a tradition which, much to Said's regret, has lost its former authority among intellectuals and a more general public alike.[3]

Even within that rarified tradition, Said was enchanted by exceptional compositions of resistance and intransigence, like 'late works', and compositions almost at the edge of social context. He viewed these kinds of music as constituting an emancipatory act. In *Musical Elaborations* he speaks of a "relatively rare number of works [...] making their claims entirely *as music*, free of many of the harassing, intrusive, and socially ty-

---

* This text is partly based on the Edward Said Memorial Lecture 2009, delivered at the American University of Cairo, October 31, 2009.

1 E.W. Said, *Musical Elaborations* (New York: Columbia University Press, 1991), xiv.

2 D. Barenboim and E.W. Said, *Parallels and Paradoxes* (New York: Vintage Books, 2002), 121.

3 Said, *Musical Elaborations*, 15-6.

rannical pressures that have limited musicians to their customary role as
upholders of things *as they are*." These works express

> a very eccentric kind of transgression, that is, music being reclaimed by un-
> common, and perhaps even excessive, displays of technique whose net effect
> is not only to render the music socially superfluous and useless–to *discharge*
> it completely–but to recuperate the craft entirely for the musician as an act
> of freedom.[4]

Apart from Mozart's *Così fan tutte*, he mentions as a phenomenal example
Bach's *Canonic Variations on 'Von Himmel hoch.'*

Furthermore, Edward Said was fascinated by music performance as an
extreme occasion, concentrated, rarified, often conspicuously discontinu-
ous with ordinary life, in which the highest standards, utter specialization
and complex production processes lead to a single event. Again, here too
he was attracted by exceptional figures, like Glenn Gould, in whom he
noted an elusive inaccessibility to the routine demands of human life as
lived by other human beings.[5]

Said placed himself firmly within the secular tradition of rational humanism of the eighteenth-century European Enlightenment, with its
aspirations to universality. This made him greatly appreciative of the rationality of Johann Sebastian Bach's music. Yet music also brought him to
the edge of rationality. Once Said observed about Bach that, while there
must be some rational law that explains his music, it was always drawing
away at the moment when he actually felt getting closer to it.[6] Similarly he
was fascinated by the music of Beethoven, who, though an Enlightenment
man, was inspired by rapturous states of mystical experience.[7] And again,
Said was enchanted by Glenn Gould, who with all his fervor for control
was given to ecstasy which Gould himself characterized as "the state of
standing outside time and within an integral artistic structure."[8] Said even
positively confessed to be highly intrigued by works of art and religion,
such as by Bach and Messiaen, by Ibn Arabi and Juan de la Cruz, which
seem to testify to the powerful conviction to *embody* the divine.[9]

All this is quite striking for a man who claimed to be totally not religious. His secular stance prevented him from really accepting the no-

---

4   Ibid., 71.
5   Ibid., 21-34.
6   Barenboim and Said, *Parallels and Paradoxes*, 123.
7   Ibid., 164.
8   Said, *Musical Elaborations*, 31.
9   Barenboim and Said, *Parallels and Paradoxes*, 123.

tion of the divine on earth, since reference to such an extra-human force would bring the experience down a notch.[10] Nevertheless, these musical experiences at the limits led Said at least to acknowledge meta-rationality. And it seduced him into entertaining utopian ideas.

To him, music played a role at the limits also in the political sense. Together with Daniel Barenboim, he took the initiative to organize in 1999 the West-Eastern Divan Workshop, bringing together Arab and Jewish musicians, inspired by Goethe for whom art "was all about a voyage to the 'other', and not concentrating on oneself."[11] The music which Said and Barenboim chose as the center of attention of this workshop has already been characterized above as being situated at the limits: European classical music.[12]

Music was also at the limits of life to Said. His wife Mariam relates that, when faced with death in the life of others as well as in his own life, language stopped being a significant mode of communication. It was music which he needed here most, music about the 'muteness' of which he had expressed his wonder time and again, music, which itself is a constant resistance as well as surrender to silence.[13] So when we speak of Edward Said and music, it is music in a heightened sense, musical composition, performance and listening of exceptional intensity, music *at the limits*.

Among the musical phenomena that fascinated Said most were polyphony and counterpoint. He used these terms more or less interchangeably. In his writings they rank among the most frequently used musico-technical terms. Viewed in the context of music practices worldwide, the musical possibility of polyphony as elaborated in the compositions favored by Said may in itself be viewed as at the limits. Finally, it is significant to point in this context to a statement by Said that music gave him the courage to develop new ideas in criticism.[14]

Polyphony: A Definition

Defining now the concept of polyphony in music, we take it as referring to the simultaneity of two or more 'voices' which, in the perspective of simultaneity, differ in their melodic and rhythmic shapes. By voice I mean

---

10   Ibid., 158.
11   Ibid., 11.
12   To place this initiative in the 'at the limits' perspective is a suggestion of Kiene Brillenburg Wurth, personal communication, November 27, 2009.
13   E.W. Said, *Music at the Limits* (New York: Columbia University Press, 2008), xi-xiii.
14   Mariam Said, personal communication, Amsterdam, November 30, 2009.

a configuration of pitches in time, with a distinctive profile. Obviously the term is derived from vocal polyphony, but it is used by extension for melodic profiles which are not sung, but played instrumentally. Usually polyphony rests upon the conception of equality between voices. There is typically no domination of one voice over the others, and if there is, it is usually temporary, the role of prominence switching from one voice to another.[15]

Polyphony is the result of two interacting shaping activities. One is counterpoint, the other is harmony. The *contrapuntal* activity refers to the simultaneous difference between the melodic and rhythmic profiles of the participant voices. It involves a characteristic variety of melodic relationships between those voices, like counter, oblique and parallel motions (with a preference for the former two), as well as rhythmic disparity. In polyphony in which the voices share the same melodic profile–later to be described as homogenic polyphony–, the instances of this profile are shifted to each other in time so as to become mutually contrapuntal.[16]

Yet polyphony does not imply complete independence of the participating contrapuntal voices. Counterpoint is not a matter just of antagonism. In European classical polyphony the participant voices are attuned to each other. This mutual attuning belongs largely to the *harmonic* dimension. The concept of harmony applies to the way in which the participant voices sound together in terms of pitch relationships. These relationships are subject to norms for euphony and variety, for consonance and dissonance, as valid in the particular music tradition. Harmonic is not the same as 'harmonious', for a great deal of dissonance between voices may occur. Another aspect of mutual attuning lies in ways of rhythmic complementarity and disparity between voices, as, for instance, when one voice is temporarily more active, another one may be less so.

Pierre Boulez in his *Boulez on Music Today* uses the expression 'responsibility' to characterize the ways in which the voices in polyphony relate to each other, shape each other, and contribute to the articulation of overall textures and processes.[17] He takes the word responsibility in its literal sense of 'ability to respond.' Responsibility in polyphony is thus actualized in two dimensions of ordering: the relation between one individual voice

---

15   See, however, the discussion about centered polyphony below.

16   This is an excellent instance of the frequently commented upon self-referentiality in Western classical music.

17   Pierre Boulez, *Boulez on Music Today*, ed. and transl. S. Bradshaw and R.R. Bennett (London: Faber and Faber, 1971); originally published as *Penser la musique aujourd'hui* (Geneva: Editions Gonthier, 1963).

to each of the others (contrapuntal), and the relationships within the collective of them (harmonic). Together the voices articulate the harmonic framework, and may transgress it individually as well. Boulez emphasizes that it is in the aspect of responsibility that polyphony distinguishes itself from monody, heterophony and homophony.

A consequence of this 'ability to respond' is that the voices may be perceived as transforming each other continuously. Because of their harmonic interference they elicit sonorous aspects in each other that cannot be observed if the voices were sung or played separately. Even *new* voices may be heard which are not performed as such. This happens through the interference between the acoustical fundamentals and overtones of the melodic lines. The same effect may be reached when voices cross each other in pitch position (*Stimmtausch*), thereby partly losing their original identity (at least compared with the situation in which they sound separately). In the latter instance, fresh melodic formations may be perceived, arising out of fragments of these crossing voices.

The effect of sonic interference on voices is to a large extent unpredictable, depending on the performer, the performance space, and the position of the listener. One example of such interference is *resonance*. When in a particular voice, a fundamental pitch with its overtones happens to be harmonically in agreement with pitches in other voices, these pitches may sound more emphatically than others. On the other hand, a dissonant relationship will bring out rich spectrums of overtones, with unforeseen dynamic sonic processes. Mutual responsibility is also heard in the rhythmic sense. By introducing complementarity between the voices–one being temporarily more active than another and vice versa–, these voices are given the opportunity to manifest themselves individually. This is an invitation to polyphonic listening as a practice of mutual respect, as complementarity refrains from the continuous overpowering by one voice over others.[18]

Within polyphony we may make a differentiation according to the shape of the participant voices. If all voices use the same melodic profiles we speak of *homogenic* polyphony. This is usually considered the most exacting form of polyphony. The peak of homogenic polyphony is the

---

18   See also Rokus de Groot, "Perspectives of Polyphony in Edward Said's Writings," in F.J. Ghazoul, ed., *Edward Said and Critical Decolonization* (Cairo and New York: The American University in Cairo Press, 2007), 219-40; and Groot, "Edward Said and Counterpoint," in A. Iskandar and H. Rustom, eds., *Edward Said: Emancipation and Representation* (Berkeley: University of California Press, forthcoming [2010]).

musical canon, that is the overlapping unfolding of the same melody in different voices. If, on the other hand, each of the voices displays its own melodic profile, we call this *heterogenic* polyphony.[19]

It is clear that polyphony requires considerable discipline of composing, performing and listening. Otherwise the articulation, maintenance and mutual attuning of distinctive voice profiles would not be possible.

Said and Musical Counterpoint

From the foregoing discussion of Said's fascination by music at the limits, it will be clear that he is not interested in polyphony and counterpoint just as theoretical notions, but as music's best practices of composition and performance.

Pleasure, inclusiveness, discipline, and invention are the key notions here. For Said the music of Johann Sebastian Bach is the standard of polyphony in this sense. In *Musical Elaborations, Parallels and Paradoxes* and *Music at the Limits*, Said expresses time and again his wonder about the "simultaneity of voices, preternatural control of resources, apparently endless inventiveness" of this music.[20] Said is not so much interested in notions of originality or authenticity in Bach's polyphony, as he is in invention, more particularly contrapuntal necessity and inventive freedom.[21] He emphasizes that Bach was no revolutionary or iconoclast, but used received conventions in such a way as to give them entirely new meanings. With approval he refers to the musicologist Lawrence Dreyfus, who in his book *Bach and the Patterns of Invention*, stresses the original meaning of invention as "*finding* in a phrase the possibilities for development that are there to be found."[22] Dreyfus underlines that Bach did this

> by remaining within the musical environment of his time, but so conscious and so rigorous was his power of working on a piece of music that [...] his works are a kind of musical map, a meditation on those conventions that highlights or elevates them into occasions for new reflection and analysis, thereby transforming them totally.[23]

---

19 H.W. Zimmermann, "Über homogene, heterogene und polystilistische Polyphonie," *Musik und Kirche* 41 (1971): 218-38.

20 Said, *Music at the Limits*, 5.

21 Ibid., 255.

22 Quoted in ibid., 253; see L. Dreyfus, *Bach and the Patterns of Invention* (Cambridge, MA: Harvard University Press, 1996).

23 Ibid., 254.

Therefore, Bach's works are never an affair of mechanical application of rules. As Said notes, the highest skill of the polyphonic technique never overshadows the expressive, liturgical or emotional aim of the piece.[24] On the contrary it allows "harmonic audacity, ingenious rhythmical flexibility and constant melodic inventiveness" to unfold.[25] Certainly Said must have recognized his own ideals of invention here. Dreyfus continues: what Bach's music

> embodies is a neat paradox embracing freedom and necessity, showing how one is inextricably linked to the other, how the exhilarating discovery of new thoughts brings with it severe responsibilities–in short, showing how one assumes risks and draws the appropriate consequences. This inherent respect for music demonstrates nothing less than a respect for the inherent meaningfulness of the world and every manner of *res severa* found [...] in it.[26]

It is interesting to note that Dreyfus, like Boulez, uses the notion of responsibility in polyphonic invention.

Inventio is a central notion in Said's work at least since *Beginnings* (1975). Here he orients himself by Giambattista Vico's humanism as unfolded in *La scienza nuova* (1725), adopting the term in the rhetorical sense of the finding and elaboration of arguments. To Vico, *inventio* is essentially the human competence for the construction and therefore also the understanding of history. Invention is a form of creative repetition and reliving.[27] In adopting this concept, Said underlines his own idea of secularity: "that you don't rely on some outside miracle, outside force like the divinity, but that man makes his own history."[28] This seems to tally with Bach's reported self-reflection, "what I have achieved by industry and practice, anyone with a tolerable natural gift and ability can also achieve."[29]

These observations underline the relation between invention and discipline, between freedom and necessity. Indeed, Said had the highest appreciation for Bach's total discipline in polyphony, and especially its rationalism, which relates to Said's own orientation on the humanly possible.

Yet this discipline brings the beholder to music at the limits, to the limits of the human. Said writes in *Music at the Limits*: "Counterpoint is the total ordering of sound, the complete management of time, the minute

---

24   Ibid., 252.
25   Ibid., 251.
26   Quoted in ibid., 254.
27   Ibid., 274, 286; M. Schmitz, *Kulturkritik ohne Zentrum. Edward W. Said und die Kontrapunkte kritischer Dekolonisation* (Bielefeld: Verlag, 2008), ch. 2.
28   Barenboim and Said, *Parallels and Paradoxes*, 73.
29   C. Wolff, *Johann Sebastian Bach: The Learned Musician* (New York and London: Norton, 2000), 10.

subdivision of musical space, and absolute absorption for the intellect." This earned polyphony "a particular prestige within the musical universe. For one, its sheer complexity and frequent gravity suggest a formidable refinement and finality of statement." "One cannot say more in music [...] than in a strict fugue."[30] Contrapuntal development produces "the result almost as a matter of natural logic."[31] In this way an "unusual importance is given the music. [...] Its authority is absolute."[32] All this is still within the limits of secular humanism. But Said goes on.

He typifies polyphonic discipline as the *preternatural* control of resources. In the same work he writes, "the rules of counterpoint are so demanding, so exact in their detail as to seem divinely ordained. [...] To master counterpoint is therefore in a way almost to play God."[33]

This notion is only strengthened by the striving for perfection in Western classical music, as well as by what Said calls "a contrapuntal mania for inclusiveness" in the polyphonic tradition from Palestrina through Webern. Indeed, he comments repeatedly on Bach's penchant for contrapuntal excesses. It leads him to consider that the contrapuntal mode seems connected to eschatology.[34] Again this connects Said's enchantment by polyphony with his own utopian ideas.

However, the alleged divinity of polyphonic discipline is highly ambiguous to Said. He designates the elaboration of polyphonic discipline by Bach as *fiendish*. In his essay "Cosmic ambition" about Bach's polyphonic art, Said wonders whether the composer, well aware of his creative powers, had an unconscious desire to rival God's creation in a music which seems to have assumed the outlines of a separate world altogether. He writes,

> Yet there is something unmistakably demonic and frightening about his fervor. [...] One can't help wondering whether all the piety and expressions of humility before God weren't also Bach's way of keeping something considerably darker–more exuberant, more hubristic, verging on the blasphemous– at bay, something within himself, which his music with its contrapuntal wizardry also communicates.[35]

---

30 Said, *Music at the Limits*, 5.
31 Ibid., 253.
32 Ibid., 279.
33 Ibid., 5.
34 Ibid., 5.
35 Ibid., 288.

Obviously, these considerations reinterpret the allegedly divine fundamentals and overtones in polyphony in a context of secular humanism, even though they are entertained at the border of it.

Edward Said is quite aware of the risks of converging the aesthetic with the critical and political, when musical polyphony with its inclusiveness would be transferred as a model to the domain of dialectical criticism and politics. Referring to the 'polyphonic' German artist Adrian Leverkühn in Thomas Mann's *Doktor Faustus*, he speaks of a Hitlerian version of a pact with the devil. When the composer as speculator puts himself in the position of creator, engaged in what Mann calls 'die elementa spekulieren'–to speculate the elements–, the polyphonic practice of music may fuse with theology and mold ideas about social and political processes in a totalizing, dehumanizing way.[36]

Polyphonic composition needs polyphonic performance and polyphonic listening. Edward Said found the polyphonic artist *par exellence* in Glenn Gould. The same key notions as in polyphony reappear: pleasure, inclusiveness, discipline, and invention. In *On Late Style*, Said notes: "What [his performances] consciously try to present [...] is a critical model for a type of art that is rational and pleasurable at the same time, an art that tries to show us its composition as an activity still being undertaken in its performance."[37] It is Gould who, to Said, enacts polyphony like no one else as a never-ending process of invention, that is, reinterpretation, reinventing, elaborating, rethinking, offering new modes of apprehension. I note in passing the musical reverberations in the rhythmical recurrence of the prefix 're-.' According to Said, counterpoint, when performed by Gould, "seemed to speak to you directly, intelligently, vividly, forcing you to leave your ideas and experiences in abeyance," resulting in "complexity resolved without being domesticated."[38]As an antidote to the tendency to sacralize polyphonic composition, there is something in Gould's performance which is very much to Said's taste. He observes with glee that Gould "never recoils from the comic possibility that high counterpoint may only be a parody, pure form aspiring to the role of world-historical wisdom."[39]

---

36   Ibid., 5, 285-86.
37   E.W. Said, *On Late Style* (London: Bloomsbury, 2006), 132-33.
38   Said, *Music at the Limits*, 20, 10.
39   Ibid., 6.

Said and Counterpoint as Metaphor

Having heard as a boy the famous Egyptian singer Umm Kalthoum in Cairo, Edward Said reacted by becoming acutely aware of the importance to him of counterpoint in Western classical music. In an interview conducted for Dutch television in 2000 he remembered having hungered for it more and more.[40] There are a number of testimonies that point to his special sensitivity to polyphony. He experiences identity as basically a polyphonic texture, "a set of currents, flowing currents, rather than a fixed place or a stable set of objects."[41] His *Out of Place* is quite eloquent here. He became aware of the contrapuntal potential of being a non-Western in relation to the totalizing schemes like those of Adorno's negative dialectics.[42] In fact, in *Culture and Imperialism*, he professes the idea that the global subaltern would have a privileged consciousness of counterpoint.[43] Indeed, we may point here to the mode of polyphonic listening which is typically nomadic and migratory, moving between voices, as well as constantly in-between voices.[44]

The concepts of polyphony and counterpoint are widely used by Edward Said as a metaphor in his literary and cultural criticism. Looking back on *Beginnings* in an interview in 1987, he comments: "I felt it important to work through a number of genres, critics, voices. I've always been taken with choruses, with polyphonic kinds of writing as well as singing."[45] *Beginnings* treats textualities as multi-layered forms of production and transmission.[46] Interestingly, *Orientalism* does not engage in discussions of counterpoint and polyphony, while in *Culture and Imperialism* they abound. Said's metaphorical contrapuntal readings also include musical works. A case in point is his analysis in *Culture and Imperialism* of the composition and production of *Aida* by Verdi, intended as an imperial spectacle for Cairo in 1871.[47] It is not about music or libretto, but about the conditions of its genesis, in particular its performative function

---

40   Edward Said, interview by Michael Zeeman, conducted in 2000 and broadcast by Dutch television, September 28, 2003.

41   Barenboim and Said, *Parallels and Paradoxes*, 5.

42   Said, *Musical Elaborations*, introduction.

43   See the analysis in Schmitz, *Kulturkritik ohne Zentrum*, 302.

44   Schmitz, *Kulturkritik ohne Zentrum*, 105.

45   I. Salusinszky, ed., *Criticism in Society* (London: Methuen, 1987),134, as quoted in Schmitz, *Kulturkritik ohne Zentrum*, 103.

46   Schmitz, *Kulturkritik ohne Zentrum*, 103.

47   Schmitz, *Kulturkritik ohne Zentrum*, 290.

as an instrument of imperial spatial discipline. As Said puts it: "Aida is an aesthetic of separation."[48]

It is obvious why polyphony should be so attractive to Said. It meets his basic humanistic mission of the preservation of difference without desire to dominate.[49] As polyphonic listening to polyphony is inexhaustible, it does justice to Said's orientation of being more interested in what cannot be resolved and in what is irreconcilable.[50] The polyphonic concept of mutual responsibility of voices meets his burning question of "how, beyond the ultra-individuality of existence, does one give it resonance beyond itself?"[51] Polyphony seems also an antidote against that to which Said resisted most strongly: totalizing schemes with no room for alternatives, whether in music the coercive sonata form,[52] or in critical theory 'the disciplinary society' of Foucault, or the 'inescapable historical teleology' and 'totally administered society' of Adorno in which 'no person is exempt from ideological exertion.'[53] He strongly resisted the theories of Mann, Foucault, Adorno which elevate admittedly discernible patterns in Western society of the modern period to the level of the essential and the universal.[54] To adhere to this stance would mean monophony to him, not polyphony.

We could replace the word 'secular' with 'polyphonic' when Said writes that "a secular attitude warns us to beware of transforming the complexities of a many-stranded history into one large figure, or of elevating particular moments or monuments into universals. No social system, no historical vision, no theoretical totalization, no matter how powerful, can exhaust all the alternatives or practices that exist within its domain. There is always the possibility to transgress."[55] Transgression is a key notion here: the interaction between voices enables one to develop an attitude of "moving from one domain to another, the testing and challenging of limits, the mixing and intermingling of heterogeneities, cutting across expectations [...]. Once the totalizing tendency is refused an unquestioning ascent, a whole series of transgressions both by and involving Western classical music proposes itself [...]."[56] Polyphony is also in accordance with Said's

---

48 E.W. Said, *Culture and Imperialism* (New York: Vintage Books, 1994), 129.
49 Barenboim and Said, *Parallels and Paradoxes*, 154.
50 Ibid., 168.
51 Ibid., 156.
52 Said, *Musical Elaborations*, 100.
53 Ibid., xx.
54 Ibid., 51.
55 Ibid., 55.
56 Ibid., 55.

preference for a geographical or spatial idea as "truer to the diversity and spread of human activity" than a unilinear dialectical temporal one.[57] In contrast to the classical sonata, for instance, polyphonic pieces do not impose on the listening discipline an unequivocal temporal direction.

In accordance with musical polyphony, Said's metaphorical elaboration relates to both the contrapuntal and the harmonic dimensions. This is what Said observes about counterpoint in *Culture and Imperialism*: "My point in this contrapuntal reading [of novels and operas] is to emphasize and highlight the disjunctions, not to overlook or play them down."[58] In *Parallels and Paradoxes* he adds, "So the idea of different but intertwined histories is crucial to a discussion–without necessarily resolving them into each other."[59] As to the harmonic dimension, we read: "I shall proceed on the assumption that whereas the whole of a culture is a disjunct one, many important sectors of it can be apprehended as working *contrapuntally* together."[60] In the context of the latter dimension, Said also uses the term 'integrative.' It is noteworthy that he conceives of the harmonic dimension in this metaphor as arising out of this 'working together,' and not out of an external principle. This is in agreement with his view on musical polyphony. In the same work he writes: in polyphony "there is concert and order, an organized interplay that derives from the themes, not from a rigorous melodic or formal principle outside the work."[61] I should add that this is an idealizing interpretation of musical polyphony, which does involve harmonic principles prior to, and transcending, individual compositions.

Of the four qualities of polyphony highlighted by Said–pleasure, inclusiveness, discipline, invention–it is certainly the necessity of inclusion which is underlined time and again in his polyphonic metaphor. In *Culture and Imperialism* he writes: "Instead of the partial analysis offered by the various national or systematically theoretical schools, I have been proposing the contrapuntal lines of a global analysis, in which texts and worldly institutions are seen working together [...] in which the literature of one commonwealth is involved in the literature of others."[62]

For the sake of discussion I should like to further discern two types of musical polyphony, a centered one, and a decentered one. As an example of the centered one, we may listen to a composition from Bach's

---

57 Ibid., xviii-ix.
58 Said, *Culture and Imperialism*, 146.
59 Barenboim and Said, *Parallels and Paradoxes*, 27.
60 Said, *Culture and Imperialism*, 194.
61 Ibid., 51.
62 Ibid., 318.

Orgelbüchlein on the chorale melody 'Hilf, Gott daß mir's gelinge.' It offers a complex form of heterogenic polyphony. As we have noted earlier, this means a polyphony resulting from simultaneous voices with different melodic profiles. However, in this case, one voice is usually highlighted in organ playing as a *cantus firmus*, with a prominent sonority choosing specific stops. Moreover, this prominent voice is itself played in canon in the musical sense, that is, it is 'doubled' to two versions, mutually shifted in time, as a kind of musical self-reflection and self-sufficiency. The other two voices each have entirely their own profile and timbre. The polyphony in this case is centered, as it is composed around a canonical melody-in-canon.

This is the model I should like to bring forward for certain of Said's metaphorical uses of polyphony. These uses relate to readings in which the metropolitan canon of literature occupies a certain centrality. Some examples will illustrate this point. In *Culture and Imperialism* Said proposes the rereading of the cultural archive

> not univocally but *contrapuntally*, with a simultaneous awareness both of the metropolitan history that is narrated and those of other histories against which (and together with which) the dominating discourse acts.[63]

> The point is that contrapuntal reading must take account of both processes, that of imperialism and that of resistance to it, which can be done by extending our reading of the texts to include what was once forcibly excluded [...].[64]

> We must therefore read the great canonical texts, and perhaps also the entire archive of modern and pre-modern European and American culture, with an effort to draw out, extend, give emphasis and voice to what is silent or marginally present or ideologically represented [...] in such works.[65]

From this perspective Said develops a reading of Joseph Conrad's *Heart of Darkness* and Albert Camus' *L'Étranger*. His reading in terms of a centered polyphony, with a canonical voice and contrapuntal heterogenic ones, has led Markus Schmitz to observe in *Kulturkritik ohne Zentrum* that Said does not denounce or deconstruct canonic European modern works, but completes them by means of bringing them back to the temporal-spatial background of their origin, which they deny.[66]

---

63 Ibid., 51.
64 Ibid., 66-7.
65 Ibid., 66.
66 Schmitz, *Kulturkritik ohne Zentrum*, 286.

The other model from music would be decentered heterogenic polyphony. It implies an interplay between voices with different melodic profiles with no one dominating. An excellent example is the first movement of Olivier Messiaen's *Quatuor pour la fin du temps* (1941), "Liturgie de crystal," for clarinet, violin, violoncello and piano. In this music there is no more opportunity to discern a canonical 'self' and 'other.' In *Culture and Imperialism* we meet this type of polyphony as well, as in the exhortation,

> we must be able to think through and interpret together experiences that are discrepant, each with its particular agenda and pace of development, its own internal formations, its internal coherence and system of external relationships, all of them coexisting and interacting with others.[67]

In fact, this type of polyphony is the most utopian one in Said's work, both in his musical and critical writings. He considered the elaborative style of Messiaen as an 'alternative formation' in music, a contrapuntal and dialogical mode, in which the "nonlinear, nondevelopmental uses of theme or melody dissipate and delay a disciplined organization of musical time that is principally combative as well as dominative."[68] This is a music which offers an aesthetic of "being *in* time, experiencing it together, rather than in competition, with other musics, experiences, temporalities," "another way of telling, more digressive and contemplative."[69] Katherine Fry points to the spatial and divergent temporal structure of this ideal.[70]

Utopian does not mean unattainable to Said. Contrary artists within the European classical music tradition such as Messiaen offer a perspective in which music "becomes an art not primarily or exclusively about authorial power and social authority, but a mode for thinking through or thinking with the integral variety of human cultural practices, generously, non-coercively, and, yes, in a utopian cast, if by utopian we mean worldly, possible, attainable, knowable."[71]

The metaphorical use of polyphony is deeply rooted in Said's personal life as an image of self. A striking feature here is that he emphasizes within polyphony the contrapuntal activity much more than the harmonic one. One should realize though that to observe a great deal of dissonance in

---

67   Said, *Culture and Imperialism*, 32.
68   Said, *Musical Elaborations*, 102.
69   Ibid., 100.
70   K. Fry, "Elaboration, Counterpoint, Transgression: Music and the Role of the Aesthetic in the Criticism of Edward W. Said," *Paragraph* 31 (2008): 265-80, esp. 274.
71   Said, *Musical Elaborations*, 105; in this particular case Said speaks about Richard Strauss' *Metamorphosen*.

one's life, as Said does, requires a sense of consonance, and both concepts belong to the domain of harmony:

> I occasionally experience myself as a cluster of flowing currents. I prefer this to the idea of a solid self, the identity to which so many attach so much significance. These currents, like the themes of one's life, flow along during the waking hours, and at their best, they require no reconciling, no harmonizing. They are "off" and may be out of place, but at least they are always in motion, in time, in place, in the form of all kinds of strange combinations moving about, not necessarily forward, sometimes against each other, contrapuntally yet without one central theme. A form of freedom, I'd like to think, even if I am far from being totally convinced that it is. [...] With so many dissonances in my life I have learned actually to prefer being not quite right and out of place.[72]

Concluding Observations

With polyphony and counterpoint as a metaphor, Edward Said did not offer a consistent theory or method of reading. Also, polyphony would not do as a panacea to domesticate the oft-observed contradictions, tensions and inconsistencies in his work. Yet there is such fervor in his musical and critical elaborations of polyphony as to deserve further study.

While the determination of musical practices by social processes has been amply studied, cases of the inverse effect have also been described to a certain extent. For example, the musicologist Leppert has studied music as enforcing class and gender divisions.[73] Said stresses the novelty of this approach: to think about these effects as an invasion by music into non-musical realms, rather than the other way round. He points to the significant role of music in the schooling and channeling of romantic love and religious sentiment.[74] So why not investigate the possibilities of *contrapuntal* schooling in a postcolonial world? Why not propose a *polyphonic* attitude in criticism through music?

Before entering into these questions, I should like to stress that there are no indications in Said's work of the idea that music would be *subsumed* under politics, or politics under music. Art to Said is ideally a domain of resistance. It can only function that way when it is allowed a certain distance from socio-political processes. For artists, like intellectuals,

---

72 Edward W. Said, *Out of Place. A Memoir* (1999; New York: Vintage, 2000), 295.
73 Ibid., 56-7.
74 Ibid., 56-8.

"there must always be room for dissent, for alternative views, for ways and possibilities to challenge the tyranny of the majority, and [...] to advance human enlightenment and liberty."[75] In *Parallels and Paradoxes* he emphasizes: "if every aesthetic phenomenon could be somehow recuperated to a political one, then in the end, there's no resistance; whereas I think that it's useful [...] to think of the aesthetic as an indictment of the political, and that it's a stark contrast, forcefully made, to inhumanity, to injustice." Music "is perhaps the final resistance to the acculturation and commodification of everything."[76] This thought is clearly developed in line with Adorno.

Returning to the question about the transgression of the aesthetic into the social and political, we meet daunting problems. While in music, polyphony is a highly elaborated and theorized practice, how precise a concept is polyphony as a metaphor? Can it be re-worked and re-invented with a similar kind of precision? What would count as discipline? What would be the equivalent of the harmonic dimension, and the mutual responsibility between voices? Do we have to look here to Said's universalist vision of a critically decolonized rational humanism, as a worldwide polyphony in a 'humanistic concert'? Are we, however, able to have insight into, or even have control over, the larger context of cultural voices? In music one may acquire polyphonic proficiency in creating and handling voices, since it works with a limited set of elements within homogenic systems like scales and metres. However, textualities, let alone cultural traditions, evidently offer a lot of resistance to being viewed–let alone treated– as voices in a similar way.

This is the gist of the criticism in Schmitz's *Kulturkritik ohne Zentrum*. He points to a basic ambiguity in Said's position. While his cultural criticism is part of a counterdiscourse rejecting and impeding the independence of Western systems of representation, it belongs at the same time to a global system of cultural translation of which the hegemonic center is located in the Western metropolises. Thus there is an ambivalence between the condition of production of postcolonial writing and the consummation of cultural difference. This would result from the domestication of the process of postcolonial de-exoticizing at Western or Westernized universities.[77] The basic question arises: how to decenter the space of polyphonic interaction? What would be the equivalent of Messiaen's *Quatuor pour la fin du temps*, 'the quartet for the end of time'?

---

75 Barenboim and Said, *Parallels and Paradoxes*, 181.
76 Ibid., 168; see also Said, *Musical Elaborations*, 12-17.
77 Schmitz, *Kulturkritik ohne Zentrum*, 367.

It is essential here to understand how Said's contrapuntal reading is received in the Arab political and cultural world. Kamâl Abû-Dîb's translation of *Culture and Imperialism* into Arabic is important in this respect; different literary voices are now enabled to resonate with this text, extending the corpus of reference, and transversing, transgressing, undermining the alleged independence of a Western system of reference.[78] However, Ahmad Baydûn, in his *idwârd sa'îd wa-l-baht fî-l-imbrîyâlîya*, makes us aware of the fact that Said invites the critical revision of historically generated identities while assuming a degree of freedom which the conquered do not have.[79] Apparently not all can, or want to, join the utopia of a decentered heterogenic polyphony. Referring to this, Schmitz poses the question: What are the conditions of the (im)possibility of cultural decentralization, given the tension between competitive positions and the unequal power of (self-)representation?[80]

It is important to realize here that the ideal of rational humanism is very exacting. It is music, in this case Mozart's *Così fan tutte*, which brings Said's thought to the limits, a realm beyond fixed identity. In an interview with Jacqueline Rose, in *Edward Said and the Role of the Critic* (2000), Said confessed, "I've become very, very impatient with the idea and the whole project of identity. [...] What's much more interesting is to try to reach out beyond identity to something else, whatever that is. It may be death. It may be an altered sense of consciousness that puts you in touch with others more than one normally is. It may be a state of forgetfulness [...]."[81] This may well count as an indication in the worldly domain of what would be the simile of harmonic dimension in musical polyphony.

However, even if for Said, the center remains the Western metropolises as privileged places of critical decolonization, and even if the center remains the Western canon and Western sources of doubt and resistance, as Schmitz has it, this does not invalidate the *idea* of a decentered heterogenic polyphony. Said was well aware that we are all constrained by socially and intellectually determined conventions making it impossible to go beyond certain norms, and that there is an interplay between the individuality of the reader and 'the whole history of decisions, consensus, and

78   Ibid., 295-6.
79   Quoted in ibid., 295; see A. Baydûn, *idwârd sa'îd wa-l-baht fî-l-imbrîyâlîya* (Beyrut: Dâr al-Gadîd, 1997)
80   Ibid., 363.
81   "Edward Said talks to Jacqueline Rose," in *Edward Said and the Work of the Critic: Speaking Truth to Power*, ed. P.A. Bové (Durham and London: Duke University Press, 2000), 25, as quoted in Fry, "Elaboration, Counterpoint, Transgression," 274.

transmission of a text'.[82] So in that sense, all polyphony will be centered, as it is clear in music when we listen to Bach and Gould. There is no problem here, unless a particular centering becomes dominant. This would go against the spirit of polyphony.

Another criticism leveled against Said's polyphonic metaphor is the aesthetization of the world. We are speaking of a particular kind of aesthetization, that is, musicalization, with its very strong emphasis on formal organization.[83] For one thing, how to escape the coerciveness of polyphony and counterpoint as a metaphor which Said has so eloquently analyzed in his criticism of Thomas Mann's *Doktor Faustus*? At several occasions he has criticized the perspective of making music–in particular the Austro-Germanic tradition–to represent the complete coincidence between aesthetic and socio-historical time.[84] Said has read Thomas Mann's musical narrative in *Doktor Faustus* as directly symbolic of totalitarianism. Leverkühn struck a pact with the devil, in a fable "for a musician whose technical interests replicate the parallelism possible between the least denotative and most formal of the arts, music, and life conceived in a Nietzschean mode, amorally, beyond good and evil."[85]

Would Said's concept of polyphony and counterpoint invite the same criticism as Habermas formulated against Nietzsche's recourse to the aesthetic, in particular music, as it presents "a chasm of forgetfulness against the world of philosophical knowledge and moral action, against the everyday"?[86]

Katherine Fry has amply reflected on this question. She draws the attention to Said's emphasis on the "critical potential of formal processes over representations and ideology in artworks," in particular in the case of polyphony.[87] In her view, the significance of Said's thinking on polyphony and the temporal structure of certain musical works or performances is "an aesthetic paradigm for undermining fixed identity and linear or totalizing narratives."[88] It is important to realize here that for Said polyphony did not amount to fixed structures of composition, but essentially included performance. That is why his book *Musical Elaborations* ends in a vein of both utopia and attainability. Again, invention is a central no-

---

82   Barenboim and Said, *Parallels and Paradoxes*, 117.
83   Schmitz, *Kulturkritik ohne Zentrum*, 283.
84   Said, *Musical Elaborations*,100.
85   Ibid., 46.
86   Fry, "Elaboration, Counterpoint, Transgression," 278.
87   Ibid., 277.
88   Ibid., 265.

tion in polyphonic performance: It is a "present-centered process of continually incomplete invention as a major constituent of [Said's] notion of
humanism."[89]

Edward Said makes us aware that polyphony is part of human intel-
ligence. Polyphony is a human privilege. It has been developed in a particular way in Western classical music. This music may be considered–as a
heritage to humanity–open to all. For this we need to transgress the conventional ideas about that musical tradition as elitist. At the same time,
we may explore ways to translate the concept to other musical traditions,
foremost in listening. Probably all musical traditions of the world have
polyphonic aspects.

Said, as a contrapuntal intellectual, invites us to not let our polyphonic
competence go waste, but to develop it as a basic mode of thought and
action in a post-colonial, globalizing world. If this competence has been
brilliantly proven in music, its transgression to other domains may well
be envisaged. Polyphony as a mode of thought and action would be instrumental in coping with manifold, often conflicting interests, in undermining dominant narratives, and in going beyond fixed identity. In that
sense, he considered polyphony not only as a human possibility, but also
as a possible humanism. Indeed, if music is playing such a prominent
role in the schooling of love and religion, why not in the schooling of our
multifarious existence and coexistence? Why not explore the equivalents
of polyphonic qualities here: pleasure, inclusiveness, discipline and invention? In fact, Edward Said's writings press upon us that we need our
shared polyphonic competence now more than ever. If his musical models
Bach and Gould were at the limits of thought and rationality, it was because Said realized that life itself is an extreme occasion.

---

89   Ibid., 276.

THE CANONISATION OF THE MEDIEVAL PAST: ENGLAND AND THE CONTINTENT COMPARED

PETER RAEDTS

I.

Most medieval English churches display on their walls a proud list of all the incumbents that served the parish, from the times that historical record-keeping began, usually the twelfth or thirteenth century, till the present day. In their simplicity these lists are an impressive testimony to a sense of solidarity with the whole of the past that still prevails in large parts of England. Holland, too, has its medieval churches. In these church- es lists of ministers are also displayed, but all of them, without exception, start in the year that the Reformation was introduced to that particular parish, somewhere in the 1570s or 1580s. It is as if the medieval clergy had never existed. The lists show a will to make a clean break with the me- dieval past. The inscription on the wooden beam that replaced the rood screen in the 'Old Church' in Amsterdam sums it all up: "The abuses in- troduced into God's Church bit by bit were cast off here in the year fifteen seventy eight."[1] Behind the beam the chancel is empty, no altar, no choir stalls, nothing. The pulpit in the nave has been the centre of the church from 1578 till the present day.

This example shows the difference in appreciation of the medieval past in England and on the continent. The English view of the Middle Ages is uncontroversial and untroubled. There is no doubt in the English mind that the thousand years between Rome and the Renaissance are an intrin- sic part of our past and that we owe much to the Middle Ages for which we can still be thankful: the origin of parliamentary government, the clear distinction of spiritual and temporal authority, the founding of schools and universities and the rise of literacy, and, of course, the beginnings in Italy and Flanders of a successful commercial economy that became the

---

1 The original reads: 't Misbruyck in Godes Kerck allengskens ingebracht Is hier weer afgedaen in 't jaer seventich acht–xvc. I thank Mr. J. van Zaane, chairman of the Amster- dam Reformed Church Council, for drawing my attention to this uncompromising abjura- tion of the medieval past.

foundation of Europe's dominating position in later ages. For English historians continuity between then and now needs no argument; it is taken for granted. Sandy Murray writes in the introduction to his *Reason and Society in the Middle Ages*: "In studying Europe in the central middle ages we study the first direct recognizable ancestor of the society we still live in."[2] Perhaps the most stunning proof of English belief in the continuity between the present and the medieval past is Patrick Wormald's passionate plea for the "reality of an early English nation-state," that can be traced back into Anglo-Saxon times.[3] To a scholar from the continent of Europe such a plea for continuity is incomprehensible, because it is the expression of a serene and untroubled view of the medieval past that is in the sharpest possible contrast with the acrimonious debate that has surrounded the inheritance of the Middle Ages on the continent of Europe since the days of Romanticism up till now.[4] In this contribution I would like to make some observations on this remarkable difference in approach to the medieval past between England and the continent.

II.

Until well into the eighteenth century all civilized people in England as well as on the continent would have agreed that the thousand years of the Middle Ages were a most unpleasant time. Gibbon summed up this attitude in his oft-quoted phrase that in his book he had been describing "the triumph of barbarism and religion."[5] And this was true for Catholics as well. Bossuet was just as disdainful of the Middle Ages as Gibbon was a century later. He was very critical of the medieval papacy and was convinced that the many abuses in the medieval Church had decisively contributed to the catastrophe of the Reformation.[6]

---

2 Alexander Murray, *Reason and Society in the Middle Ages* (Oxford: Clarendon Press, 1978), 5-6.

3 Patrick Wormald, "The eternal Angle," *Times Literary Supplement* (no. 5111), March 16, 2001, 3-4.

4 Although Otto Oexle, "Das entzweite Mittelalter [The Wrecked Middle Ages]," in G. Althoff, ed., *Die Deutschen und ihr Mittelalter* (Darmstadt: Wissenschaftliche Buchgesellschaft, 1992), 7-28, mainly speaks about the German debate, his conclusions are *mutatis mutandis* true for all other continental nations.

5 Edward Gibbon, *The history of the decline and fall of the Roman Empire*, ed. David Womersley, vol. 3 of 3 (1776-87; London: Penguin, 1995), 6.71 (p. 1068).

6 Jürgen Voss, *Das Mittelalter im historischen Denken Frankreichs* (München: W. Fink, 1972), 144.

The Gothic revival of the eighteenth century, that produced, besides follies, novels such as Walpole's *Castle of Otranto* and the first editions of medieval poetry (real and fake), did not alter the verdict on the Middle ages in any fundamental way. Yet, silly as the Gothic revival in many ways may have been, it was a first sign of the end of the rule of classicism and of the coming a new approach to the past. The discovery of primitive cultures in so many parts of the world raised the question if perhaps European culture had also once known a primitive stage and had, therefore, been very different from what it was now. Scottish enlightened philosophers, such as William Robertson, developed a genetic model of the sequence of societies. In that scheme the Middle Ages no longer were an unfortunate interval in history between Rome and the Renaissance; the medieval period became a painful, yet necessary stage in the growth of the states of Europe to free and enlightened nations.

An even more radical change in the view of the past occurred at the same time in Germany. It is fair to say that Scottish scholars, although sensitive to historical change, assumed that human nature, in every period of history, had always been fundamentally the same. German historians, for a variety of reasons, began to have doubts about that. If there were so many different societies and cultures both now and in the past, could they be the expression of one underlying human nature, or did one have to admit that people of different cultures were fundamentally different in their nature as well? Their conclusion was that each historical period had its individual character that could not be imitated or copied by later generations; it could only be explained. And if that was true, what authority did classical writers have now, or, indeed, the Bible, since all these literary monuments were products of totally different cultures. Johann Gottfried Herder was the first to develop a new philosophy of history that took the unique character of every culture as its starting point.

Herder's fundamental thought was that world history was the sum of the histories of all its many nations (*Völker*) and their cultures, each of which had an innate, unique and individual spirit that developed in time. Every nation and every culture deserved respect and had to be judged on its own terms, not ours. Herder openly questioned the way in which zealous Christian missionaries dealt with native cultures in Africa, Asia and America, wondering if they did not destroy more than they brought.[7] Just as each nation each historical period had its individual spirit. And

---

7 Wolfram von den Steinen, "Mittelalter und Goethezeit," in idem, *Menschen im Mittelalter* (Bern: Francke, 1967), 294.

although Herder assumed that the ultimate purpose of history was the realisation of *Humanität*, it was not the case that progress was inevitable.
Each nation had its periods of prosperity and of decline, which made it
all the more necessary to study each period in itself, without comparing
it too soon with what happened before or after.[8] But even though armed
with such an impressive array of philosophical argument, it was not easy
for Herder to be impartial about the Middle Ages. It was going to take
more than one man to remove the thick layers of three centuries of prejudice. But Herder really made an effort to discover what the Middle Ages
had contributed to the progress of Europe. Especially in his early work
(*Auch eine Philosophie der Geschichte* [1774]) he tried to show that the
medieval period saw a real advance in civilization, when compared to Roman antiquity.

What makes the work of men like Robertson and Herder so essential
in the development of new views of the Middle Ages is not the question
whether they admired the period or not. They did not.[9] What matters is
that in both their historical works the medieval period was no longer a
regrettable incident between classical antiquity and its restoration, the
sooner forgotten the better, but that it was an integral and necessary part
of the development of all nations in Europe, that it had to be studied by
everyone who wanted to make sense of the present.

III.

It was not until after the French revolution that historians, poets and philosophers began to idealise the Middle Ages in the same way that Classical Antiquity had been idealised for centuries. To the generation that saw
the Terror and the rise of Napoleon the price to be paid for freedom and
equality seemed far too high. Equality led to chaos, and freedom turned
men into beasts: that was the conclusion of the generation that grew up
after 1800. The young German poet Novalis prophesied in 1799: "Blood
will stream over Europe until the nations become aware of their extreme
madness, a madness which imprisons them, and, touched and calmed by

---

8 Wolfgang Förster, "Johann Gottfried Herder: Weltgeschichte und Humanität," in
Hans Bödeker, et al., eds., *Aufklärung und Geschichte. Studien zur deutschen Geschichtswis-
senschaft im 18. Jahrhundert* (Göttingen: Vandenhoeck and Ruprecht, 1986), 364-365.

9 William Robson-Scott, *The literary background of the Gothic revival in Germany* (Oxford: Clarendon Press, 1965), 67-72.

sacred music, they move, in colourful fusion, to previous altars."[10] Novalis identified these 'previous altars' with the Christian Middle Ages, in Novalis' eyes a society of peace, order, obedience and unity that had to be restored. Things had begun to go wrong in the era of the Reformation, and the destruction had been completed with the Revolution. Most of the German Romantics agreed with him, and although only a few drew the consequence of converting to Catholicism, the thoughts of most turned to a restoration of the medieval *Reich*. In France the influential political philosopher, Joseph de Maistre, thought that the cruelties of the Revolution clearly showed that the only way to guarantee order and peace was obedience to an authority not based on reason but drawing its legitimacy from God. Only thus could man's primitive instincts be reduced to acceptable levels. The only person who had such authority, according to de Maistre, was the pope.[11] What was needed, therefore, was a restoration of the authority of the Roman pontiff, just as it had been in the Middle Ages.

Moreover, the young generation of 1800 was no longer interested in the delights of reason and enlightened philosophy. The cult of sentiment of the Gothic revival became a glorification of the irrational, the passionate and the supernatural. "Il n'est rien de beau, de doux, de grand dans la vie, que les choses mystérieuses," said Chateaubriand in 1802 in his defence of the genius of Christianity against the enlightened citizens of the eighteenth century.[12] The great Gothic cathedrals of France gave him "une sorte de frissonnement et un sentiment vague de la divinité." Like most of his contemporaries Chateaubriand believed that Gothic architecture was natural (as opposed to the artificiality of classicism), because in its play of columns and vaults it imitated the ancient forests of Gaul. By entering a cathedral Chateaubriand felt in touch with the deepest roots of French culture, with the simple and natural religion of his ancestors.[13] The influence of the Gothic revival of the eighteenth century is obvious. But what was a play then, now became deadly serious. In order to survive European culture must return to the living source, to the naïve simplicity of its origins and most creative period, to the Middle Ages.

---

10 Novalis (Friedrich von Hardenberg), "Christenheit oder Europa," in *Schriften, 3: Das philosophische Werk II*, ed. R. Samuel (Darmstadt: W. Kohlhammer, 1968), 523.

11 Isaiah Berlin, "Joseph de Maistre and the Origins of Fascism," *The New York Review of Books*, 37, no. 14 (1990), 61-62, and no. 15, 55-56.

12 François-René de Chateaubriand, *Génie du christianisme*, ed. P. Reboul, vol. 1 of 2 (Paris: Garnier-Flammarion, 1966), 60.

13 Ibid., 400-401.

IV.

The desire for authenticity and community, for a society where everyone knew his place, where the Church was the guardian of peace and concord, for the times when people were simple and natural, those were at the root of the romantic admiration for the Middle Ages. But that is not the whole story. Despite the strong romantic reaction against the ideals of the Enlightenment, especially against rationalism and individualism, the innovative approach to the medieval period of the late eighteenth century survived. In the first half of the nineteenth century there were many historians and philosophers who did not so much consider the Middle Ages a lost civilization to be restored, but a stage in the development of modern Europe, as Herder and Robertson had done fifty years before. In France the reason for this was that many left-wing intellectuals, although they approved of the revolution in principle, agreed with their counterparts of the right that it had totally gotten out of hand with the reign of Terror under Robespierre in 1793-1794. Such a break with the past was humanly impossible and had, necessarily, led to the bloodshed of those two horrible years. Left-wing historians did not want to be seen as supporters of such radicalism and, therefore, had "to appropriate the historical field, to discover and celebrate precursors of their cause."[14] They had to show that the revolution in its first constitutional phase, with the abolition of feudalism and the establishment of a National Assembly, had not been a radical break with the past but, on the contrary, had been in continuity with the whole of French history. No one did so with more passion and conviction than Jules Michelet in his *Histoire de France*.

Michelet wanted to show that the French became a people by overcoming the confines of geography, localism and race, by forging themselves through a series of historical decisions into a united nation, in short that France was a product of history, not of nature, a triumph of will over fate, of spirit over matter: "La France voudrait devenir un monde social."[15] The Middle Ages were a crucial time in that process of forging the people. To Michelet the Crusades, which he characterises as a French enterprise, were an essential moment in overcoming the confines of race and localism. By heeding the call of Pope Urban II the French people was drawn away from local servitude: "Ils cherchèrent Jérusalem et rencontrèrent la

---

14 Ceri Crossley, *French historians and romanticism* (London: Routledge, 1993), 4.

15 Jules Michelet, *Histoire de France*, vol. 4 of *Oeuvres Complètes de Michelet* [*OCM*], ed. P. Viallaneix (1833; Paris: Flammarion,1974), 2.3 (p. 328).

liberté." He saw the revolts of the cities of northern France against their bishops as an immediate consequence of that new-found liberty.[16] The other guardian of liberty in the twelfth century was the Church, which in its struggle for freedom with the princes represented at that period the interest of all mankind. The Church by fighting for its universal claims drew mankind out of its local and geographical boundaries. All this changes with the pontificate of Innocent III. Although he seemed to triumph over all his enemies, his use of violence against the Greeks, the English and the Albigensians made his victories empty, because peace ought to be the weapon of the Church, not war. "Si l'agneau mord et déchire, si le père assassine," then it loses all claims to respect, it loses its sanctity.[17] The real victor was the king of France, who inherited the sacred role that so far had been played by the Church. It was the irony of history that the holiest of all French kings, Louis IX, by virtue of his holiness, made this historic transfer possible, and thus made an end to the Christian age of the world.[18] With Philip the Fair and his humiliation of Boniface VIII the modern age began. The Church, because of its universal mission, had contributed its share to the triumph of history over geography, but from 1300 on was no longer a historical force.[19] Nevertheless in 1833 Michelet saw the period of the Christian Middle Ages as a necessary and positive contribution to the progress and happiness of mankind in general, and of France in particular.

V.

Michelet worked on his history of France till 1844. Then the work was interrupted, and not resumed before 1855, when he published the first volume on the Renaissance period. In the introduction to that volume Michelet recanted everything that he had said about the medieval period before. He claimed that in 1833 he had been merely describing the ideal of the Middle Ages, while what he did now was describe "sa réalité, accusée par lui-même."[20] Michelet's sudden change of opinion may have had per-

---

16 Ibid., 4.2 (p. 422-23) and 4.4 (p. 444).

17 Ibid., 4.8 (p. 551).

18 Ibid., 4.8 (p. 582).

19 Michelet, *Histoire*, vol. 5 of *OCM* (Paris: Flammarion, 1975), préface (p. 39): "L'ère nationale de la France est le XIVe siècle. ... Jusqu'ici la France était moins France que chrétienté ... Aux prêtres, aux chevaliers, succèdent les légistes; après la foi, la loi."

20 Michelet, *Histoire de France au seizième siècle*, vol. 7 of *OCM* (Paris: Flammarion, 1978), 49.

sonal reasons, but it was also typical of the changing appreciation of the medieval past in the 1840s and 1850s. In the first half of the nineteenth century the Middle Ages had been universally admired, either as a place of pristine happiness, peace and justice, or as the cradle of the nation, or both. But in the 1840s, when political debate was revived and revolution was in the air once more, the debate about medieval history on the continent of Europe became a matter of contemporary politics. Michelet's change of heart about the Middle Ages had nothing to do with scholarly research, but came when in 1842 he discovered, during the debate about the monopoly of the university, that the Catholic Church, far from being a romantic remnant of the medieval past, that could now be left in peace to die gracefully, was in fact a political force to be reckoned with. Michelet voiced his anger by writing angry pamphlets about the influence of priests on women and of the Jesuits in particular.[21] After the failed revolution of 1848 things went from bad to worse in the eyes of a liberal like Michelet; the Church even regained part of the supervision of education that it had lost after 1830. That is why in 1855 he drew the bitter conclusion that the medieval world went on and on, and could not even be killed off, because it had been dead already for such a long time.

The changing appreciation of the medieval past after 1848 was a clear sign that the second half of the nineteenth century in continental Europe was very different from the first half for two reasons. First of all, the revolutions of 1848 were an abysmal failure, not only in France, but in all of continental Europe. The main consequence of this all-out victory of the forces of the right was that liberalism, belief in progress and human rights were no longer the obvious choice for thinking people. In Germany many disappointed liberal nationalists turned to Prussia to bring about the unity they so ardently desired, and they were fully prepared to abandon some of their liberal ideals of freedom to achieve it. In France under the authoritarian *Second Empire* the Church tightened its grip on the nation, as Michelet found out to his own dismay, and that met with remarkably little protest.

An even more important development was that, almost a hundred years after Britain, continental countries began to industrialise as well, with all the harsh consequences that had for traditional social bonds. Liberalism may have been all right for the rich and privileged who could fend

---

21 For an extensive discussion of Michelet's struggle against the Church, see Laurens van der Heijden, *De schaduw van de jezuïet. Een pathologie van de Franse publieke opinie tijdens de schoolstrijd van 1841-1845*, 4 vols. (PhD diss., University of Amsterdam, 2004) 1: 151-189, 2: 365-378, 3: 445-478, 667-717.

for themselves, but what the new industrial proletariat needed were new forms of community which could give them the feeling, or rather the certainty, that they were not left to fight for themselves. In that conflict the Middle Ages became an instrument in the hands of the forces that began to react against liberalism, individualism and rationalism. The vague romantic nostalgia for the lost ages of faith, community and order, that had been so characteristic of the first half of the nineteenth century, now was forged into a political programme on the right and the left, in which a return to the values of community, interdependence, solidarity, paternal authority, and religion stood at the top of the list.

VI.

Nowhere was that legitimating use of the medieval past as successful as in the Catholic Church. Up to 1848 Church authorities had been very sceptical about the romantic dreams of a revival of the medieval Church. It was altogether too mystical and too radical for their taste. The condemnation of Lamennais in 1832 showed clearly that the Church had no use for romantic hotheads, even if they ranted on about the authority of the Pope. But after 1848 the romantic picture of the Christian Middle Ages with its emphasis on strong leadership of the pope and the unquestioning obedience of the laity became a powerful historical image in the hands of the Church during the strong centralisation and the rallying of the Catholics around the papacy that took place in the period between 1850 and 1900. What in fact was perhaps one of the most thoroughgoing reorganisations that the Catholic Church had witnessed for many centuries was presented as a return to the halcyon days of Gregory VII and Innocent III.[22]

The cult around the person of Joan of Arc in France provides an excellent example of the monopolisation of medieval history by the Church. In 1803 Napoleon had restored the commemoration of Joan of Arc in Orléans cathedral, because her actions, as he said, proved that French genius was at its best when national independence was threatened. Once again it was Michelet who canonised Joan of Arc as a heroine of the people. For him Joan personified the French people at the moment of its greatest ordeal in history, the occupation of half of France by the English. Her decisive victory at the siege of Orléans obliged France to become "la France

---

22 Peter Raedts, "Prosper Guéranger O.S.B. (1805-1875) and the struggle for liturgical unity," in R.N. Swanson, ed., *Continuity and change in Christian worship*, Studies in Church History 35 (Woodbridge: Boydell Press, 1999), 333-344.

consciente et libre."[23] But in 1869 the Church moved in, when Bishop Dupanloup during the annual commemoration of the siege of Orléans announced that he had requested the Pope to canonize Joan. It proved an immensely popular move, all the more since it happened on the eve of the defeat against Prussia in 1870. After that Catholics could hold up the example of Joan to prove that France could only be victorious if it honoured the Church and the King. On May 30, 1878, the anniversary of the death of both Voltaire (centenary) and Joan of Arc, the victory of the republic was celebrated at the *Théâtre de la Gaieté* in Paris, the fall of the monarchy in the fields of Domrémy, where Joan had heard the voices of her saints. Joan and the Middle Ages had become the property of the anti-liberal forces in the new French Republic, as Pope Leo XIII confidently stated in 1894: "Joanna est nostra."[24]

In German lands much the same thing happened, although it was the struggle for unification and the process of industrialisation more than the role of the Church that was decisive for the politicisation of the medieval past. Two powerful alternatives to a liberal society were developed in Germany, although one of them, Marxism, was thought out in the reading room of the British Museum in London. But before speaking of Marx and the Middle Ages attention must be paid to the development of another answer to the challenges of industrial society, social Catholicism. Catholics everywhere were very much aware of the poverty and misery of the new proletariat. In France Frédéric Ozanam founded the justly celebrated Societies of Saint Vincent de Paul to bring working people together and promote their interests.[25] But the case of Germany was different in the sense that industrialisation began in two deeply Catholic regions, Upper Silesia and the Ruhr, so that Catholics were among the first in Germany to be confronted with the disastrous social consequences of industrialism. And they proved up to the challenge, mainly guided by one of the most forceful personalities in the nineteenth-century German Church, Wilhelm Emmanuel von Ketteler, from 1850 bishop of Mainz. Ketteler became famous as one of the leading Catholic participants in the National Assembly of Frankfort in 1848, where he surprised many when he told his audience in one of his speeches that not the New German Constitution

---

23   Gerd Krumeich, *Jeanne d' Arc in der Geschichte* (Sigmaringen: J. Thorbecke, 1989), 61, 64.

24   Michel Winock, "Jeanne d' Arc," in Pierre Nora, ed., *Les lieux de mémoire*, vol. 3: *Les France*, 3: *De l'archive à l' emblème* (Paris: Gallimard, 1992), 708.

25   Jacques le Goff and René Rémond, eds., *Histoire de la France religieuse*, vol. 3 : *Du roi Très Chrétien à la laïcité républicaine* (Paris: Seuil, 1991), 285-291.

but the Social Question was the main problem of the age.[26] Later on in the same year he preached a series of sermons in Mainz cathedral in which he condemned both liberal and socialist concepts of property. He showed that Thomas Aquinas six centuries earlier had come up with the right solution, when he posited that the absolute right of property belongs to God only (and not to man as the liberals said), and that man has received all his possessions from God as a temporary gift that should be shared freely with the less fortunate.[27]

But quite soon he realised that generosity of rich Catholics was not enough to solve the problem. The situation demanded structural solutions. Like most other Catholics in Germany Ketteler did not really trust the state, and after 1870 his suspicions turned out to be well-founded. Invoking Aristotle he maintained that the state could become a threat to man's freedom, if there were no intermediate institutions (*Genossenschaften*) which could give voice to man's social, economic and religious aspirations.[28] Medieval society had been organised that way. All social classes and all human activities had formed their own associations that had protected the personal liberty of their members against the capriciousness of the state and the blows of fate. That richly textured society had been torn apart by absolutism first and then by liberalism, so that now the weak and poor had no longer anyone to turn to.[29] What Ketteler wanted were new associations for the working class, modelled on the medieval guilds, associations in which the relations between employer and worker would be like that of medieval guildsmen, one of equal responsibility and co-ownership, so that the working man once more could be the master of his own fate.[30] With his ceaseless hammering on the social responsibility of Catholics Ketteler became the founding father of what later became known as the Rhineland model that has been very influential in the organisation of labour relations in Germany up till now.

---

26 Wilhelm Emmanuel von Ketteler, "Rede vor der ersten Versammlung des katholischen Vereines Deutschlands," in *Sämtliche Werke und Briefe*, ed. Erwin Iserloh, 2 vols. of 11 parts (Mainz: von Hase und Koehler, 1977-2001), 1.1: 18-20.

27 Ketteler, "Die großen socialen Fragen der Gegenwart" (1848), in *Sämtliche Werke und Briefe*, 1.1: 22-87, 26-31.

28 Ketteler, "Die Katholiken im deutschen Reiche" (1873), in *Sämtliche Werke und Briefe*, 1.4: 187-262, 214-215.

29 Ketteler, "Katholiken," 1.4: 206; see also, "Freiheit, Autorität und Kirche" (1862), in *Sämtliche Werke und Briefe*, 1.1: 225-364, 262-263.

30 Ketteler, "Die Arbeiterfrage und das Christenthum" (1864), in *Sämtliche Werke und Briefe*, 1.1: 368-515, 380-386, 399-402, 447-449; "Ansprache," 1.1: 687.

That Catholics looked back to the Middle Ages to find solutions for contemporary problems will cause no surprise: it was their age of glory. That socialists could be seduced by the Middle Ages requires more of an explanation. In the *Communist Manifesto* (1848) Karl Marx called the "feudal socialists" who wanted to escape from industrial society by reviving the Middle Ages idiots who wanted no more than exchanging one form of exploitation for another.[31] But in his main work *Capital* he spoke about the Middle Ages with much more respect, even warmth. Objectively it was an era of ruthless exploitation by feudal landowners, but at the same time Marx saw much that he liked and that disappeared with the rise of capitalism at the end of the fifteenth century. It is a contradiction in Marx's work that Edmund Wilson commented upon in his classic study of socialism *To the Finland Station*. Wilson sees Marx on the one hand as a philosopher trying to uncover the inexorable laws of history. On the other hand he sees him as a prophet who could not suppress his wrath about the terrible injustice done the poor and powerless then and now.[32] That anger comes very much to the fore when Marx explains how the independence of medieval peasants was destroyed when agriculture was subjected to the forces of the market.

Officially medieval peasants were serfs who were forced to work for their lords. But they also possessed (not owned) their own houses, they had small plots of land where they could grow their own food, and most important of all, in fact, they possessed their own means of production. That was sufficient for a simple, yet dignified and independent way of life.[33] The same applied to craftsmen in towns, who had the additional advantage of being protected by their guilds. All this came to an end when in the later Middle Ages a market economy began to grow that needed free and cheap labour. That became quickly available, because landowners in countries such as England discovered at the same time that sheep farming was much more profitable than traditional agriculture. So they robbed the peasants of their ancient rights and of their land (*enclosure*) and pulled down their houses to clear the land for sheep. The victims of this ruth-

---

31 Karl Marx, "Manifest der kommunistischen Partei," in Karl Marx and Friedrich Engels, *Werke*, Band 4 (Berlin: Dietz Verlag, 1959), 459-493, 482-484.

32 Edmund Wilson, *To the Finland Station* (1940; New York: Farrar, Straus and Giroux, 1953), 294-295.

33 Stephen Rigby, "Historical materialism: social structure and social change in the Middle Ages," *Journal of medieval and modern studies* 34 (2004): 473-522, 477 (reprinted as "Marx, Engels, and the Middle Ages," in Natalie Fryde, et al., eds., *Die Deutung der mittelalterlichen gesellschaft in der Moderne*, Veröffentlichungen des Max-Planck-Instituts für Geschichte 217 [Göttingen: Vandenhoeck and Ruprecht, 2006], 147-180).

less rationalisation lost their own means of productions with their houses and land and now became completely dependent on the exploitative force of the market. The supreme irony was that the whole process of enslavement was described as liberation from feudal dues.[34] What is very striking is that the way Marx pictures the life of medieval peasants and craftsmen reminds the reader very much of his images of life after the proletarian revolution. That is perhaps also the reason why he grows so indignant when he describes how this peaceful age of independence for the working man came to an end after 1400. What Marx clearly admired in medieval society was its sense of community, solidarity, and cooperation.

But the feeling that the Middle Ages presented an example of social life that could be held up as a mirror to modern man, was, at least in Germany, not restricted to Catholics and socialists. After 1870 a sense of loss and pessimism seemed to pervade all of German society except for the few liberals that remained. It is an interesting question, though not for this essay, why a society that was so immensely successful and prosperous, generated a culture that was so pessimistic, inward-looking and nostalgic. But that was what happened. In 1887 the founding father of sociology Ferdinand Tönnies published his classic *Gemeinschaft und Gesellschaft*. In that work Tönnies roundly condemned modern society for its cold and calculating rationality and presented the Middle Ages as a viable alternative, a time of organic order (*Ordnung*), a time when community took priority over the individual, and freedom was wisely limited by benevolent authority. It became a commonplace in Germany to compare the German *Kultur*, founded in the Middle Ages and restored in the nineteenth century, with the superficial and ahistorical *Zivilisation* of the West, where the only things that counted were ruthless competition and rampant individualism. For the vast majority of German intellectuals that was sufficient reason to go to war with the West in 1914. The Republic of Weimar for most Germans was nothing but a victory of *Zivilisation* over *Kultur*. The call for a return to the Middle Ages, a return to community, obedience and strong leadership, became even stronger in the 1920s than it had been before 1914. What the new leader of Germany could look like was described by Ernst Kantorowicz in his biography of the emperor Frederick II (1927). Kantorowicz idealised the era of the Hohenstaufen as Germany's heyday, and Frederick II as the messianic leader who in his person had united the German people. It was Kantorowicz's express intention with his biography not

---

34 Karl Marx, *Das Kapital, i: Der Produktionsprozeß des Kapitals*, in Marx and Engels, *Werke*, Band 23 (Berlin: Dietz Verlag, 1962), 744-753.

only to paint a picture of the past, but to present an alternative for the future. He did not have to wait long before the alternative presented itself.[35]

VII.

At the same time that on the continent of Europe the Middle Ages became the object of bitter political controversy between liberals and communitarians of the left and the right, the opposite happened in England: a shared, uncontroversial image of the medieval past became part of the historical inheritance of all Englishmen. This had not always been so. In the seventeenth century and well into the eighteenth century the medieval past had been as much a matter of public, political debate in Britain as it became in continental Europe in the later nineteenth and twentieth centuries. Whigs and Tories had argued about the prerogative of the King, the antiquity of Parliament, and the status of Magna Carta, and historical discussion about these issues had always had a sharply contemporary political angle. But that changed after the Settlement of 1688. Perhaps David Hume was the last historian of the English Middle Ages who caused a serious political controversy when he argued in his *History of England* that liberty was something that was established in the seventeenth century and not restored from some medieval precedent. Hume showed that the Anglo-Saxons were not free warriors, but the clients of their lords. Postconquest England was in many ways a despotic society, and under the Tudors the English enjoyed about as much liberty as the subjects of the Grand Turk. The arguments of the Whigs about the ancient English Constitution were historical nonsense; royalists such as Henry Spelman and Robert Brady had been much the better historians.[36] Hume was no supporter of Stuart absolutism. The point he wanted to make was that to understand the English political present, one need go back no further than the seventeenth century. The Middle Ages were irrelevant, everything had changed since then. Not everyone understood that. Many Whigs thought that for the constitution of 1688 to be legal, it had to be the same as that

---

35 Otto Oexle, "Das Mittelalter als Waffe. Ernst H. Kantorowicz' 'Kaiser Friedrich der Zweite' in den politischen Kontroversen der Weimarer Republik," in Oexle, *Geschichtswissenchaft im Zeichen des Historismus* (Göttingen: Vandenhoeck and Ruprecht, 1996), 163-215.

36 John Burrow, *A liberal descent. Victorian historians and the English past* (Cambridge: Cambridge University Press, 1981), 25-27; Smith, *Gothic bequest*, 77-81.

of medieval England. In their view Hume was undermining the historical foundations of the Glorious Revolution by denying its medieval roots. But what could have become a source of bitter controversy between the advocates of historical change and those of an unchanging past, was in fact defused by Edmund Burke. He showed that such a choice between continuity and change was not necessary; continuity with the past was possible, even while all was changing.

Burke expressed his views on England's unique history most succinctly in his *Reflections on the revolution in France* (1790). The purpose of that book was to show that a clean break with the past, as had now happened in France, was the end of civilisation and freedom, that it must lead to "a ferocious dissoluteness in manner, and of an insolent irreligion in opinions and practices."[37] True freedom was only possible, if it was tempered by a sense of obligation to the past, in Burke's words: "Always acting as if in the presence of canonized forefathers, the spirit of freedom, leading in itself to misrule and excess, is tempered with an awful gravity."[38] Burke does not say that we should now act 'as' our forefathers, but only 'as if in the presence of' our forefathers. The difference is crucial, as can be seen from his discussion of the theory of the Ancient Constitution. Burke explicitly refers to the work of Henry Coke, perhaps the most uncompromising supporter of that theory. But the important thing to Burke is not whether Coke and other Parliamentarians were right in maintaining the unchanging nature of England's laws, but rather the fact that they wanted to consider England's past as part of their present: "From Magna Charta to the Declaration of Right, it has been the uniform policy of our constitution to claim and assert our liberties, as an entailed inheritance derived to us from our forefathers, and to be transmitted to our posterity."[39] Continuity in Burke's eyes is not an objective property of history. It is a way in which the present generation looks upon history, it is the will of the living to respect the authority of the dead. From there it follows that continuity does not exclude change. The English political system is not a dead weight: it is a living organism.

Burke's influence on England's way of dealing with its past was decisive. Burke himself was only talking about the English Constitution as a living organism, but in the course of the nineteenth century his model of conti-

---

37   Edmund Burke, *Reflections on the revolution in France*, ed. Conor Cruise O' Brien (London: Penguin, 1986), 125.

38   Burke, *Reflections*, 121.

39   Burke, *Reflections*, 119.

nuity and change, was transferred from strictly constitutional history to the history of England as a nation.[40] In its finished form this Whig interpretation of history ran somewhat like this: Contrary to the unfortunate nations on the other side of the Channel it was England's great and unique privilege to have, since the invasion of the Anglo-Saxons at least, a history of unbroken continuity, where change only affirmed that continuity and strengthened it. It was a history of growing freedom, prosperity and success, the medieval stage of which was marked by Magna Carta and the beginning of Parliament. There was nothing in that past that an Englishman needed to be ashamed of. Every period had made its own invaluable contribution to the nation's glorious progress in time, in Freeman's words: "Our ancient history is the possession of the liberal."[41] In the course of the nineteenth century it became a vision shared by all Englishmen of every political conviction.[42]

There are two reasons, I think, why the image of the medieval past could become such a common inheritance. The first is political and social. In Continental Europe the medieval past became controversial, because Europe was the stage of bitter political and social struggle all through the nineteenth century. England had fought its constitutional battles in the seventeenth century and had reached a consensus on essential matters by 1688, a Settlement that has been interpreted and developed, but that has never really been challenged since. Moreover, industrialisation had started in the late eighteenth century, and by the mid-nineteenth century, when continental Europe first began to realise the terrible social consequences of industrialisation, the British began to take the first measures to improve the fate of the proletarian working classes within the liberal consensus. Hume was right, of course, when he argued that the Act of Settlement was modern and had no real medieval precedent, but the appearance of continuity with the medieval past was preserved and religiously believed in by most. Because this partly real, partly imaginary link with the medieval past was so woven into the constitutional consensus in England by 1800, it became a natural, unchallenged part of the success story of England as a nation when it was written up by the great historians of the nineteenth century.

The second reason has to do with the Church. In the nineteenth century everyone saw the medieval past as a Catholic past, in fact the most

---

40 Burrow, *Liberal descent*, 106.
41 Ibid., 3.
42 Ibid., 2, 241.

glorious part of the Catholic past. Claiming the medieval past, therefore, implied in some way heeding the claims of the Church of Rome. In Europe that proved a decisive stumbling block in accepting the whole of the medieval past as the nation's past, in the first place in Protestant countries, but perhaps even more so in Catholic countries where the Church remained a powerful political presence claiming an allegiance that, in an age of nationalism, rightly seemed to belong to the nation, as we saw from the example of Michelet. The amazing thing that happened in England was that the Established Church, although it was Protestant, managed to reclaim the medieval past as part of its inalienable inheritance. That was, of course, the work of the Oxford Movement, a religious revival unparalleled in the rest of Protestant Europe. In almost all Protestant Churches there was an orthodox revival in the nineteenth century to stem the tide of liberalism and state interference. What made England special was that the call for a purer and more independent Christianity took the form of a Catholic revival, a return to the doctrine of the Church Fathers and the authority of the medieval Church. The opposition against the Tractarians was massive, but in the end the Oxford movement changed the face of the Church of England completely, not so much in its doctrine, but where it mattered most, in its rituals and its church interiors. By the end of the nineteenth century the Church of England was as much in possession of its medieval past as the nation, whose Church she was. The whole of the Middle Ages had been absorbed into the story of England's growth to prosperity and freedom.

Burke was quite right when he said that continuity is not a property of history but the will of the living to stay in communication with the dead. In that sense the English story of the medieval past as the beginning of the modern is just as much a construction as the continental myth of the Middle Ages as the days of community and authenticity. In both constructions important parts of the medieval past tend to disappear from sight. English historians rarely emphasise the barbarous and violent character of medieval society, continental historians usually forget to say that rationalism, individualism and even scepticism were as much part of the Middle Ages as faith, community and obedience. In the writing of history we need constructions, but we must always stay aware of the facts, so that we do use them to tell our stories. Even more important is the need to be aware that in using those constructions we help to shape the present as much as we try to re-create the past. And it is precisely on this point that it is my 'melancholy duty,' as Gibbon would have said, to conclude that continental medievalists have failed to see that truth. By presenting the Middle Ages as the prototype of a communitarian, homogeneous society, medieval historians have played into the hands of political and social reformers who wanted to limit or even abolish individual freedom, who preferred instinct and irrational passion to critical reason, and who put the ties of blood, race and class above those of citizenship. The English story of the medieval past may be a myth as well, but it can certainly help continental historians to take leave of the destructive nostalgia, that has for so long characterised their work, and to make them aware of the fact that the Middle Ages are not an alternative to but a part of the history of modern Europe.

SCHOLARSHIP OF LITERATURE AND LIFE: LEOPOLD ZUNZ AND THE INVENTION OF JEWISH CULTURE

IRENE ZWIEP

Around 1820, a group of Berlin students assembled to found Europe's first Jewish historical society. The various stages in the society's brief history neatly mirror the turbulent intellectual *Werdegang* of its members. The studious, typically Humboldian *Wissenschaftszirkel* they established in 1816 was changed into the more political Verein zur Verbesserung des Zustandes der Juden im deutschen Bundesstaate in the wake of the HEP!HEP! pogroms of 1819, only to be relabelled the Verein für Cultur und Wissenschaft der Juden two years later, in November 1821. In January 1824, in a session attended by a mere three members, the society's meetings were again suspended. Thus, within less than five years, its ambitious attempts at building an alternative, modern scholarly infrastructure had come to a halt. The new Institut für die Wissenschaft des Judentums that was to serve as the Verein's headquarters never materialized. Its relentlessly academic *Zeitschrift für die Wissenschaft des Judentums* (1822/23) did not survive its first issue. And when trying to strengthen their position within German society, many of its supporters, including first president Eduard Gans (1797-1839) and the ever-ambivalent Heinrich Heine, seem to have preferred smooth conversion to Lutheranism to a prolonged career in Jewish activism.[1]

Yet if the Verein's attempts at establishing a new, comprehensive infrastructure remained without immediate success, its overall agenda had a lasting impact on modern Jewish discourse. In the early 1820s, Wissenschaft des Judentums as a form of shared political activism had been doomed to fail; during the following decades, however, a whole genera-

---

1 For a short history of the Verein, see I. Schorsch, "Breakthrough into the Past. The Verein für Cultur und Wissenschaft der Juden," *Yearbook of the Leo Baeck Institute* 33 (1988): 3-28, and M. Graetz, "Renaissance des Judentums im 19. Jahrhundert. Der 'Verein für Cultur und Wissenschaft der Juden', 1819-1824," in M. Awerbuch and S. Jersch-Wenzel, eds., *Bild und Selbstbild der Juden Berlins zwischen Aufklärung und Romantik* (Berlin: Colloquium Verlag, 1992), 211-227. On Gans, see esp. N. Waszek, ed., *Eduard Gans (1797-1839). Hegelianer – Jude – Europäer. Texte und Documente* (Frankfurt a.M.: P. Lang, 1991).

tion of *Wissenschaftler* arose, who continued to put the historical scrutiny of Judaism at the service of joint emancipation, religious reform and, increasingly, private intellectual reorientation. By admitting Western codes and categories (most notably the apparatus of the German *Altertumswissenschaft* and *Idealismus*) into Jewish thinking and applying them to the Jewish cultural heritage, they wrought a fundamental change in modern Jewish self-perception.[2] In the hands of literary historian Leopold Zunz, social historian Isaac Marcus Jost and Reform rabbi Abraham Geiger, timeless Jewish tradition was transformed into time-bound national history. Accumulative exegesis was traded for contextual research, hoary myth replaced by nineteenth-century fact and, perhaps the greatest achievement of all: the Jews now had the means to become the authors of their own history.[3] No longer subject to Christian curiosity, they were now able to freely explore their past and, in doing so, to construct and articulate their own essential *Volkstümlichkeit*.

In their reliance on German historicism, the founders of the Wissenschaft des Judentums are often said to have paved the way for the-much more diverse, though generally no less political-modern academic study of Judaism.[4] As if to acknowledge this indebtedness, Jewish scholarship has produced a vast library of studies on the movement's heroes and critics, its journals and institutions, its adaptations in other national contexts, its scholarly models and monuments, its political implications and impact on Jewish identity. Yet despite this intense and wide-ranging interest, research into the Wissenschaft still has its blind spots. In this brief contribution, I wish to draw attention to one such hitherto neglected detail: the introduction, by the movement's earliest exponents, of the concept of

---

2   For the Jewish appropriation of the tools of the contemporary Altertumswissenschaft, see, e.g., G. Veltri, "Altertumswissenschaft und Wissenschaft des Judentums. Leopold Zunz und seine Lehrer F.A. Wolf und A. Böckh," in R. Markner and G. Veltri, eds., *Friedrich August Wolf. Studien, Dokumente, Biographie* (Stuttgart: Franz Steiner, 1999), 32-47. On the Wissenschaft's dependence on German Idealism and Hegelian dialectics, see R. Schäffler, "Die Wissenschaft des Judentums in ihrer Beziehung zur allgemeinen Geistesgeschichte in Deutschland des 19. Jahrhunderts," in J. Carlebach, ed., *Wissenschaft des Judentums. Die Anfänge der Judaistik in Europa* (Darmstadt: Wissenschaftliche Buchgesellschaft, 1992), 113-131.

3   The process is best described in I. Schorsch, *From Text to Context. The Turn to History in Modern Judaism* (Hanover, NH: University Press of New England, 1994), 151-76 (chapters 8-9, "*Wissenschaft* and Values" and "The Ethos of Modern Scholarship").

4   Cf. N.N. Glatzer, "The Beginnings of Modern Jewish Studies," in A. Altmann, ed., *Studies in Nineteenth-Century Jewish Intellectual History* (Cambridge, MA: Harvard University Press, 1964), 27-45, and, more recently, R. Livneh-Freudenthal, "Jewish Studies. The Paradigm and Initial Patrons," in. M.F. Mach and Y. Jacobson, eds., *Historiography and the Science of Judaism* [in Hebrew] (Tel Aviv: University of Tel Aviv, 2005), 187-214.

'culture' into Jewish discourse, and the persistent echoes of its initial over-tones in later nineteenth- and early twentieth-century texts.

No doubt misled by the omnipresence of the term in contemporary historical writing, modern scholars have unanimously understood the 1821 Verein für *Cultur* und Wissenschaft der Juden as an essentially mod-ern *Culturverein*. Both implicitly and explicitly they have portrayed it as a society whose goal had been to promote *general* culture, to validate Jew-ish *secular* culture, or to instigate an extensive Jewish cultural *reform*.[5] In the following, I will suggest a slightly different, less anachronistic read-ing. If anything, this more contemporaneous interpretation should help us explain how the 'Verein zur Verbesserung des Zustandes der Juden' could have changed into a 'Verein für Cultur and Wissenschaft' without betraying much of its original agenda. More in particular, I hope to find out what sense of culture the Jewish students of Hegel, Böckh and Wolf had in mind when including the concept in the title of their learned circle, and how they envisaged the relation between Cultur and Wissenschaft in their struggle for Jewish knowledge and emancipation.

* * *

In adopting the term Cultur, at the time a relative novelty in the German lexicon, the Jewish scholars showed themselves very much *au courant* with recent linguistic and conceptual developments.[6] In fact, when they turned to the government and applied for official incorporation of their society, a prejudiced official misread 'Cultur' for 'Cultus' and, suspect-ing yet another unwelcome attempt at Jewish religious reform, promptly

---

5 Examples are too numerous to be listed here. A telling case in point is the entry by G. Deutsch and E. Cohn in the *The Jewish Encyclopedia* (New York: Funk and Wagnalls, 1901-1906), 3: 383, where we find: "Culturverein der Juden. See Verein für Cultur und Wis-senschaft des Judentums."

6 The word had been introduced into German by J.C. Adelung in his *Versuch einer Ge-schichte der Cultur des menschlichen Geslechts* (1782); cf. I. Baur, *Die Geschichte des Wortes 'Kultur' und seiner Zusammensetzungen* (PhD thesis, Munich, 1951), 75ff. NB: Even had they wished to, Zunz c.s. could not have relied on an indigenous Jewish precedent. From late antiquity onwards, Hebrew texts feature the term *tarbut*. Roughly equivalent to the Lat-in *cultura*, the term had strong agricultural connotations and was used primarily for badly domesticated animals and children (*tarbut ra'ah*). Medieval texts show a continued empha-sis on (good) behaviour, both individual (as in *torah melammedet tarbut*, 'Torah teaches *mores*') and national (as in *tarbut parsiim she-tzenu'im*, 'the *mores* of the Persians, who are chaste'). No pre-modern Jewish author, however, had ever tried to identify certain traits as defining the *tarbut yisrael* or Jewish culture.

denied the request.[7] In texts relating to the Verein, the word still occurs only sporadically and with little explicit qualification, which makes it difficult to gauge its exact connotations. A closer look at its immediate contexts, however, and at such relevant epitexts as the authors' biographies and overall agenda should help us reconstruct both the meaning and the significance attributed to 'Cultur' by the first generation of Jewish *Wissenschaftler*.

The first to embrace the concept and apply it to the 'Jewish condition' was the movement's acknowledged founding father Leopold Zunz (Detmold 1794-Berlin 1886). Classical philologist by training, Jewish philologist by vocation, Zunz began his career at the age of twenty-four by publishing a concise treatise named *Etwas über die rabbinische Literatur*.[8] Behind the inconspicuous title a grand new programme lay hidden. In fifty typo-ridden octavo pages, Zunz proposed an integral adjustment of the entire Jewish curriculum to modernity, a grand-scale revision that favoured historical enquiry *unter der Aegide der Kritik*[9] over cumulative interpretation, and preferred to rely on a broad selection of modern academic disciplines rather than on casuistry and wit.[10] Zunz's revolutionary scheme necessarily implied a redefining of the traditional Jewish corpus in foreign, modern terms, first and foremost as 'literature.' For all his scholarly aplomb, however, Zunz still had one preliminary detail to explain to his readers. For why should they aspire to become historians and devote themselves to the critical examination of their ancestors' literary legacy?

Against the background of Hegelian philosophy and early nineteenth-century cultural nationalism, the answer was quickly formulated: the critical study of centuries of Jewish books and manuscripts would equip

---

7 Schorsch, "Breakthrough into the Past," 5.

8 L. Zunz, *Etwas über die rabbinische Literatur. Nebst Nachrichten über ein altes bis jetzt ungedrucktes hebräisches Werk* (Berlin: Maurersche Buchhandlung, 1818). Zunz would have preferred the term 'neuhebräische' or even 'jüdische Literatur,' as he himself acknowledges in a footnote (p. 5). We may assume that he ultimately opted for the adjective 'rabbinic' in order to explicitly 'reappropriate' the study of Judaism from Christian theology and liberate it from centuries of Christian scholarly bias.

9 Ibid., 8.

10 As subdisciplines, Zunz distinguished theology (including the study of liturgy, to which he soon was to devote much time and effort), law, ethics, physics (both theoretical and applied, encompassing such widely diverging fields as commerce and music), history and antiquity, language, and booklore (which should culminate in the writing of a comprehensive history of Jewish literature); ibid., 9-34. Being a universal rather than a particular, national achievement, philosophy was mentioned *hors catégorie*: "...über den ganzen Tummelplatz menschlicher Thätigkeit herrscht mit ausschließender Majestät die Philolophie, überall unsichtbar..." (42).

his readers to know themselves, as members of the Jewish nation. In one anacoluthic sentence Zunz explained that to study a nation's literature allowed one to fully know and comprehend that nation, since literature provided the main entrance to grasping *the course of a nation's culture* through the ages:

> Wie die Litteratur einer Nation als den Eingang betrachtet zur *Gesammt-kenntnis ihres Culturganges* durch alle Zeiten hindurch,–wie in jedem Moment ihr Wesen aus dem gegebenen und hinzukommenden, d.i. aus dem Inneren und dem Äußern sich gestaltet,–wie Schicksal, Clima, Sitten, Religion und Zufall freundschaftlich oder feindlich ineinander greifen,–und wie endlich die Gegenwart, aller dagewesenen Erscheinungen als nothwendiges Resultat dasteht.[11]

Zunz' portrayal of *die Gegenwart* as the 'sum of culture past and present,' of culture as the nexus of a nation's *Geist* and various internal as well as external factors, and of literature as the prime key to decoding and analyzing that intricate ensemble, may strike us as a typical example of nineteenth-century German epistemology. In the hands of a young Jewish scholar, however, that epistemology soon acquired a distinctive political potential. The Verein's decision, in 1821, to devote itself henceforth to the *Cultur der Juden* did not imply a move away from politics towards promoting general or secular culture. Rather, it allowed Zunz and his fellow members to continue advocating the cause of Jewish civic emancipation with even more cutting-edge concepts and strategies: Cultur und Wissenschaft. Culture being the sum of past and present and of *Litteratur* and *bürgerliche Existenz*, the act of reconstructing the Cultur der Juden was at once more sophisticated than, *and* fully synonymous to, working towards the 'Verbesserung des Zustandes' of the Jews currently living in the German *Bundesstaat*.[12]

The conviction that to study Cultur meant to retrieve historical facts as well as to address and improve contemporary life echoed through the pages of the only issue of the society's *Zeitschrift für die Wissenschaft des Judentums*. In the Verein's most elaborate manifesto, drawn up by Im-

---

11 Ibid., 7 (emphasis mine).
12 Cf. ibid., 4, where Zunz writes: "Nicht um einen Knäuel zu entwirren, an der geschicktere Finger sich versuchen mögen, sind wir von der Litteratur eines Volkes in seine Existenz abgeschweift. Wir kehren vielmehr, nach dem wir *beider Wechselwirkung aufeinander* mit einem Paar zügen gezeichnet…" (emphasis mine). NB: *Pace* Schorsch, who in his excellent article "Breakthrough into the Past" (11) translates *bürgerliche Kultur* as 'secular culture,' I would prefer the term 'civic'; cf. J. and W. Grimm, *Deutsches Wörterbuch* (Leipzig: Hirzel, 1854-1860; also located at http://germazope.uni-trier.de/projects/DWB), *s.v.* '*Bürgerlich*,' which among others is related to concepts such as 'state' and 'public.'

manuel Wolf (one of Hegel's many Jewish disciples who eventually converted to Christianity), we read again that the religious idea of Judaism
had revealed itself "in einer doppelten Gestaltung, einmal enthalten in
historisch-litterarischen Documenten... zweitens, als noch lebendes Prin-
zip." Both manifestations, Wolf argued, were "an und für sich der wissen-
schaftlichen Behandlung fähig und bedürftig" and should be approached
with the help of, on the one hand, literary history and, on the other, exhaustive statistical enquiry ("[die] statistische Judenthumskunde in Beziehung auf die heutigen Juden in allen Ländern der Erde").[13] In the final
pages of the first issue, the productive Leopold Zunz punctually provided
a rudimentary outline for this branch of research, which, we should add,
was never properly followed up by later generations of Jewish historians.[14]

If anything, the Verein's speedy appropriation of the new German
concept Cultur and its programmatic exploitation of the term's political
potential effectively illustrate David Ruderman's recent claim that the difference between the early-modern and modern periods lies in the introduction of 'the political' into Jewish life and discourse.[15] This becomes
particularly clear when we compare Zunz's rather couched definition of
Cultur with the slightly more systematic characterization offered by Moses Mendelssohn (1729-1786) in a famous article on Enlightenment published two years prior to his death–one of the first occurrences of the
word 'Kultur' in German literature *per se*:

> Bildung zerfällt in Kultur und Aufklärung. Jene scheint mehr aus das
> *Praktische* zu gehen... Aufklärung hingegen scheinet sich mehr auf das
> Theoretische zu beziehen... Eine Sprache erlanget Aufklärung durch die
> Wissenschaften, und erlanget Kultur durch *gesellschaftlichen Umgang, Poesie
> und Beredtsamkeit.*[16]

Here we encounter 'Kultur' alongside 'Aufklärung' as one of the two components of that other virtually untranslatable German concept: *Bildung*.
Where Aufklärung was primarily associated with the field of theory, Kultur according to Mendelssohn always had more practical implications.

---

13 I. Wolf, "Über den Begriff einer Wissenschaft des Judenthums," *ZWJ* 1 (1822): 1-24,
esp. 15-18.

14 L. Zunz, "Grundlinien zu einer künftigen Statistik der Juden," *ZWJ* 1 (1822): 523-532.

15 D. Ruderman, "Why Periodization Matters. On Early Modern Jewish Culture and
Haskalah," *Simon Dubnow Institute Yearbook* 6 (2007): 23-32.

16 M. Mendelssohn, "Über die Frage: was heißt Aufklären?" *Berlinische Monatsschrift*
4 (1784): 193-200; the passage is quoted from N. Hinske, ed., *Was ist Aufklärung? Beiträge
aus der Berlinischen Monatsschrift* (Darmstadt: Wissenschaftliche Buchgesellschaft, 1977),
445ff. (emphasis mine).

When put into language, Aufklärung would express itself through the sciences, while Kultur would find expression in social exchange as well as in the arts, most conspicuously in poetry and rhetoric. Offering a slightly more interpretative recapitulation of these lines, one might say that for Mendelssohn too, culture, as perceived through language, was the sum of *gesellschaftlichen Umgang* and *Poesie*, of life and literature. Writing in 1784, however, he did not yet view it as a central concept in the struggle for *improving* Jewish life, as the earliest exponents of the Wissenschaft des Judentums would less than half a century later.

* * *

Having arrived at the conclusion of this brief essay, we should remember that, the very idea of culture being firmly rooted in life itself, scholars like Zunz and Gans never contemplated the possibility of an abstract *Jewish* culture, but remained attached to studying the actual, tangible culture *of the Jews*. Besides the political, civic aspect, there may well have been an additional personal dimension to this particular bias. By entering university, the first generation of Jewish academics had almost literally 'come out of the ghetto' or, more precisely, had left the *kehillah*, the autonomous community that had constituted the social, religious and cultural horizon of every Jew in the Diaspora.[17] In their youth, they had experienced the totality of pre-modern Jewish Cultur in the broadest sense. In their adult lives, they wished to preserve that experience, which to a large extent continued to define their Jewishness.[18] As children of the *kehillah*, they had been endowed with an obvious sense of 'Jewish life'; as alumni of the

---

17 Zunz's own biography is exemplary for this intellectual exodus. In 1799, at the age of five, he was sent to the maskilic (i.e., Jewish enlightened) Samsonsche Freyschule in Wolfenbüttel, which in his view had still resembled the traditional, 'backward' cheder. With much relief he had entered the local Gymnasium in 1809, where he developed a penchant for algebra. In 1815 he left for Berlin, where he took up classics and soon developed his own concept of *jüdische Philologie*; cf. M.A. Meyer, *The Origins of the Modern Jew. Jewish Identity and European Culture in Germany, 1749-1824* (Detroit: Wayne State University Press, 1967), ch. 6 ('Leopold Zunz'), and more recently C. Trautmann-Waller, *Philologie allemande et tradition juive. Le parcours intellectuel de Leopold Zunz* (Paris: Cerf, 1998).

18 In his empathetic portrait of Zunz and the other members of the Verein, Michael Meyer convincingly depicts a generation whose self-conception as Jews had changed from a social and *theological* self-definition to a predominantly *psychological*, nostalgic one (witness Heinrich Heine's otherwise inexplicable fondness of a traditional dish like *tshulnt*); Meyer, *The Origins*, ch. 6; cf. also D. Bourel, "Nostalgie et 'Wissenschaft': note sur l'étude du judaïsme allemand," *Pardès* 5 (1987): 187-194.

new academy, they had come to believe that critical historical study was
enough to keep that sense alive.

In the eyes of the first, transitional generation, for whom collective Jewish experience would always be a (distant) reality, the Wissenschaft des
Judentums thus became an ideal strategy for combining cultural memory
and political activism. The following generations, however, soon lost touch
with the self-evidence of pre-modern Jewish life, and thus with an important part of the culture they were studying. When nostalgia waned and social urgency faded, the Wissenschaft became a goal in itself, and its prime
object 'Cultur' was reduced to an abstract conjunction of the supposed
Jewish *Geist* and the carefully reconstructed history of its manifestations
through the ages.[19]

Few scholars were ready to accept the rupture between scholarship and
life, as for example Moritz Steinschneider (1816-1907), the indefatigable
bibliographer who is often quoted for having said that Jewish scholarship
merely served to provide what was left of Judaism with a decent burial.[20]
In the course of the nineteenth and twentieth centuries, however, a mixed
choir of critics arose, who each voiced their frustration with the Wissenschaft's increasingly antiquarian, 'archaeological' orientation. Whether
neo-orthodox, Reform, assimilated or Zionist, they all emphasized that
Wissenschaft should never be pursued "als Selbstzweck, nicht, um vergan-
gene Zeiten und tote Schriftdenkmäler wieder erstehen zu lassen, sondern
um die Fundamente zu erschließen, auf denen *die Gegenwart* sich auf-
baut. Ihr Ziel ist und bleibt das *lebendige Judentum...*"[21]

19 Cf. the following characterization of the Wissenschaft by Reform preacher and editor Ludwig Philippson (in *Allgemeine Zeitung des Judentums* 43 [1879]: 6-7): "Sehen wir
uns ihren Entwicklungsgang bis heute genauer an, so müssen wir uns eingestehen, daß sie
eigentlich nur Geschichtsforschung geworden und wiederum diese Geschichtsforschung
zur Geschichtsmikroskopie"; quoted in M.A. Meyer, "Jüdische Wissenschaft und jüdische
Identität," in Carlebach, ed., *Wissenschaft des Judentums*, 13.

20 "Wir haben nur noch die Aufgabe die Überreste des Judentums ehrenvoll zu be-
statten"; quoted ibid., 15. Steinschneider's own conception of Kultur was emphatically free
of political overtones; witness his definition in *Allgemeine Einleitung in die jüdische Literatur des Mittelalters* (Jerusalem: Bamberger and Wahrmann, 1938), 10-11: "Die Kultur is die
Thätigkeit des Geistes selbst...Kulturgeschichte is das eigentliche Ziel der Weltgeschichte...
Die Geschichte ist nicht philosophischer Schematismus (Hegel) oder politischer Pragma-
tismus..."

21 Thus Ismar Ellbogen in his call for a 'Neuorientierung unserer Wissenschaft' in
"Ein Jahrhundert Wissenschaft des Judentums," in *Festschrift zum 50-jährigen Bestehen der
Hochschule für die Wissenschaft des Judentums in Berlin* (Berlin: Philo Verlag, 1922), 142
(emphasis mine). Other important publications were Samson Raphael Hirsch's neo-ortho-
dox plea "Wie gewinnen wir das Leben für unsere Wissenschaft?" *Jeschurun* 8 (1862), and
Gershom Scholem's famous Zionist critique in "The Science of Judaism: Then and Now,"
published in Scholem, *The Messianic Idea in Judaism and Other Essays on Jewish Spirituality*
(New York: Schocken Books, 1971), 304-314.

For Leopold Zunz and his immediate followers, culture was found and scholarship was to be pursued whenever Jewish literature met Jewish life.[22] Yet we do observe that, in the course of modern history, Jewish life became an increasingly vague and artificial concept. Working in the United States in the early 1930s, Reconstructionist rabbi Mordecai Kaplan (1881-1983) noted that it was "not only Judaism, the religion, that is threatened, but Judaism, the civilization... [due to] the *irrelevance, remoteness and vacuity of Jewish life...*"[23] Over the years, Kaplan's subsequent, comprehensive rescue plan for Jewish civilization has turned out a most "satisfactory ideology for the modern Jew."[24] Today, the majority of American Jews define themselves as 'cultural Jews' and claim to have no affinity with religion.[25] Since 2003, New York even has its own Center for Cultural Judaism, a deeply ideological institution that wishes to provide a platform of shared experience for secular Jews in the US and beyond.[26] And in post-Holocaust Europe, where vacuity and remoteness are felt even more acutely, Jewish culture is present even where Jewish life is not, as many things Jewish-religion, music, theatre, history-are being appropriated, and jointly celebrated, by a substantial non-Jewish audience.[27] In a sense we might say that post-modern society has thus restored the pre-modern *kehillah*. It has succeeded in reconstructing at least some form of shared Jewish horizon, often without religion, occasionally without Jews, but always inspired by that other, most abstract and elusive component: Jewish culture.

---

22   Cf. Abraham Geiger, *Allgemeine Einleitung in die Wissenschaft des Judentums* (Berlin: Louis Gerschel, 1875), 10: "...und hierbei ist Literatur und Leben, also Cultur, gleichmässig zu berücksichtigen."

23   M. Kaplan, *Judaism as Civilization. Towards a Reconstruction of American Jewish Life* (New York: Macmillan, 1934), 178 (emphasis mine).

24   Ibid., xiii.

25   Cf. E. Mayer, Barry A. Kosmin and Ariela Keysar, eds., *American Jewish Identity Survey. An Exploration in the Demography and Outlook of a People* (New York: Center for Cultural Judaism, 2001).

26   The Center can be accessed through its website http://www.culturaljudaism.org/.

27   Thus, polemically, R.E. Gruber, *Virtually Jewish. Reinventing Jewish Culture in Europe* (Berkeley: University of California Press, 2002).

CENSORSHIP AND CANON: A NOTE ON SOME MEDIEVAL WORKS AND AUTHORS

LEEN SPRUIT

Until recently systematic research into Catholic censorship was blocked by the enduring closure of the archives of the Roman Index and Inquisition.[1] Only the opening in 1998 of the archives of the Congregation for the Doctrine of Faith, which includes the historical records of the Holy Office (or Inquisition, founded in 1542) and the Index (founded in 1572),[2] removed the barrier to detailed study of censorship and made it possible to assess the structure and inner mechanics of Roman censorship in the early modern era. What was revealed by the first studies was an extremely complex picture of the activities of the two Congregations.[3] In this essay I discuss some issues regarding early modern Catholic censorship of medieval works and authors, with particular attention to theological and philosophical works.[4] Some preliminary remarks and caveats are due.

First, in view of the well-known thorny problems of periodization a neat distinction between medieval and early modern authors and works is problematic. As far as ecclesiastical censorship is concerned, however, the rise of the printing press and of the Protestant Reform seems a more sensible caesura than any watershed in epochs. Thus, for present purposes, I

---

1 Now held in the Archivio della Congregazione per la Dottrina della Fede (from now on: ACDF) in Rome.

2 It must be noted that, unlike the archives of the Holy Office, the records of the Index are relatively intact. The Inquisition holdings suffered many and serious losses. For example, the burning of the Inquisition palace in 1559 on the death of pope Paul IV; then the removal of the archival records by Napoleon after his occupation of Rome. For discussion of the latter, see R. Ritzler, "Die Verschleppung der päpstlichen Archive nach Paris unter Napoleon I. und deren Rückführung nach Rom in den Jahren 1815 bis 1817," *Römische Historische Mitteilungen* 6-7 (1962-1964): 144-90.

3 C. Stango, ed., *Censura ecclesiastica e censura politica in Italia tra Cinquecento e Seicento*. VI giornata Luigi Firpo. Atti del Convegno 5 marzo 1999 (Firenze: Leo S. Olschki, 2001); G. Fragnito, ed., *Church, Censorship, and Culture in Early Modern Italy* (Cambridge: Cambridge University Press, 2001); A. Borromeo, ed., *L'Inquisizione*. Atti del Simposio internazionale, Città del Vaticano, 29-31 ottobre 1998 (Città del Vaticano: Biblioteca Apostolica Vaticana, 2003).

4 For medieval censorship, see P. Godman, *The Silent Masters. Latin Literature and its Censors in the High Middle Ages* (Princeton: Princeton University Press, 2000).

intend by the term medieval authors those active, *grosso modo*, till the end of the fifteenth century.

Second, Roman censorship, as organized in the Congregations of the Holy Office and the Index, concentrated on living persons and recently published books. Thus, in addition to older prohibitions and condemnations of notorious heretical or suspect authors (among whom Abelard, Joachim of Fiore, Michael of Cesena, William Ockham, John Wycliffe, and Marsilius of Padua), most medieval authors were examined only when their works appeared in print.[5] Now, several distinct cases can be distinguished. Often, works of orthodox Fathers and medieval doctors were examined and/or prohibited simply because they appeared in editions published by Protestants or suspect authors and printers, active for the most part in Switzerland and Germany.[6] By contrast, many suspect or heretical authors were never placed on the Index, because their works had already been condemned by ancient or medieval councils.[7] Origen is a case in point. Many authors, among whom Ockham and Michael of Cesena, probably appeared for the same reason on early indexes, and were tacitly removed in the later sixteenth-century indexes. Other suspect medieval authors were examined in the sixteenth century by the Congregation for the Index when their works appeared in print. They were condemned on some local list or prohibited in one of the Roman Indexes, but they were tacitly removed at the end of the century. Cusanus is a case in point.[8] Many works on astrology and divination by Arab authors (Avenaris, Albubather, Albumasar, Alchibitius), who

---

5 For example, editions of Alain de Lille, Cyprianus, and Lactantius were examined and prohibited in the late seventeenth century. Cf. *Index des livres interdits* (from now on: ILI), eds. J.M. De Bujanda et al., 11 vols. (Sherbrooke-Genève: Éditions de l'Université de Sherbrooke-Droz, 1980-2002), 11: 55, 261-2, and 496.

6 Examples are Augustine, Epiphanius, Eusebius, Gaudentius, Irenaeus, John Chrysostom, Bede, Hilary. See ILI, 10, under the respective entries. The same holds for editions of Aristotle, Ovid, Stobaeus, Trentius, Apuleius, Lucian, Epictetus, Dioscorides, Hermes Trismegistus, Flavius Josephus, Macrobius, and Pliny.

7 For the general prohibition of works condemned before 1515, see Rule I of the Tridentine Index, also adopted in the Clementine Index; cf. ILI, 9: 920.

8 From 1574 it was not permitted to sell the works of Nicolaus Cusanus (Nikolaus von Kues, 1401-1464) in the Ecclesiastical State without explicit permission from the authorities; see the "Aviso alli librari" of the Master of the Sacred Palace (22 May 1574), published in ILI, 9: 746-7, 757. Since 1577, *De concordia catholica* (reprint: Basel 1565) was prohibited in Rome; ILI, 9: 750, 755, 766; cf. ACDF, Index, *Diari*, 1, f. 8r. Later, Cusanus' works were mentioned in a list of works "extra Indicem prohibiti" (ILI, 9: 770, 776), and were placed in the so-called Index of Parma (1580); ILI, 9: 159. They came again under examination of the Congregation for the Index from 26 November 1587; see ACDF, Index, *Diari*, 1, fols. 28v-29r. Cusanus was placed in the Sixtine Index (ILI, 9: 390, 835), but not in later Roman Indexes (1593, 1596). On 7 August 1594, the correction of his works was commissioned to the second class of Consultors, but ACDF does not hold these corrections; cf. *Diari*, 1, f. 80v.

formally could not be marked as heretical,[9] were prohibited because they treated subject matters that attracted the attention of the bodies of ecclesiastical doctrinal control. For similar reasons, several indexes prohibited the works of Guido Bonatti, John Estwood, and Marsilio Ficino.

Third, although the two Roman Congregations were intended as universal bodies of doctrinal control, in actual fact their jurisdiction only extended to the Ecclesiastical state (including Avignon), to the majority of other Italian states and to Malta. The Index was only formally accepted within the borders of the Italian peninsula. Elsewhere, it was often seen as a list of fascinating works, and soon it became a reader's guide to the essential literature of protest.[10] It provided Protestant printers with a list of profit making titles and free advertising while alerting potential Catholic purchasers to the existence of forbidden fruit.[11]

In order to duly assess the issue under scrutiny, the distinction between heresy and other forms of heterodoxy (section 1) and the two types of ecclesiastical *censura* (section 2) are outlined. Then, in section 3, proceedings concerning Arnaldus of Villanova, Ramon Lull, and John the Scot Eriugena are discussed, as these individual cases of early modern censorship exemplify the inconsistency and fluctuation between overall prohibitions and a more relaxed interpretation of ecclesiastical restrictions concerning medieval authors. It has been stated recently that the early modern period is generally characterized by the dialectics of censorship and canon.[12] In the final sections, however, it will be shown that as a rule censorship only marginally affected the fortune of medieval authors and works.

1. Heresy and heterodoxy

The Inquisition opposed heresy, which was generally defined as the voluntary adhesion of the intellect to a proposition that contradicted Catho-

---

9 See section 1.

10 See Thomas James, *A Treatise on the Corruption of Scripture, Councils, and Fathers by the Prelates, Pastors, and Pillars of the Church of Rome, for the Maintenance of Popery and Irreligion* (London: printed by H[umphrey] L[ownes] for Mathew Lownes, 1611); and for discussion, cf. L. Balsamo, "How to doctor a bibliography: Antonio Possevino's practice," in G. Fragnito, ed., *Church, Censorship, and Culture in Early Modern Italy*, 71, 77-78.

11 E.L. Eisenstein, *The Printing Press as an Agent of Change. Communications and Cultural Transformations in Early-Modern Europe*, 2 vols. (Cambridge: Cambridge University Press, 1997), 145.

12 W. Schulze, "Kanon und Pluralisierung in der Frühen Neuzeit," in A. and J. Assmann, eds., *Kanon und Zensur: Beiträge zur Archäologie der literarischen Kommunikation II* (München: Fink, 1987), 317-25, at 317-18.

lic doctrine.[13] Thus, heresy had a substantial aspect, namely that of being a proposition–or a set of propositions–which somehow contradicted the dogmatic view as defined by the Church,[14] and a psychological aspect, insofar as the person who maintained that proposition was fully aware of this contradiction. In addition to manifest heresy, schisms, and apostasy, the Inquisition was also supposed to prosecute magic, *sortilegia*, divination, abuse of sacraments and whatever else could be construed as heresy. As a matter of fact, later sixteenth-century trials show a tendency to extend the notion of heresy also to propositions that contradicted broader theological beliefs which had not (yet) been defined as dogmas.

A distinction should be drawn between openly professing a view, on the one hand, and simply entertaining an idea, on the other. In the latter case, heresy was considered a sin and had to be confessed in order to obtain absolution. By contrast, explicit adhesion to heretical views was a serious crime and put on a par with high treason ("crimen laesae maiestatis"),[15] to be judged by the Tribunal of the Inquisition that could decree sanctions, penalties and abjurations.[16]

A charge of heresy presupposed that one had been educated in the true faith. It therefore followed that the ancient philosophers, children educated in Protestant countries, Muslims and Jews could not strictly be viewed as heretics,[17] nor be brought to trial as such. Furthermore, heresy distin-

---

13   See, for example, Alfonso de Castro, *De iusta haereticorum punitione* (Venetiis: Ad signum spei, 1549; first edition: Salamanca 1547), f. 5r-v. Cf. Roberto Bellarmino in his 1587 pronouncement on Erasmus, in ACDF, Index, *Protocolli*, B (II.a.2), f. 406r: "Nam, ut quis hereticus dici possit, requiruntur duo: error fidei contrarius, et pertinacia, ita ut ex electione oppugnet id quod scit ab Ecclesia definitum vel doceat quod scit ab Ecclesia condemnatum." For discussion of the historical development of the concept of heresy, see N. Brox, "Häresie", in *Reallexicon für Antike und Christentum*, vol. 13 (Stuttgart: Hiersemann, 1986), 248-96; M.-D. Chenu, "Orthodoxie et hérésie. Le point de vue du théologien," in *Hérésies et sociétés dans l'Europe pré-industrielle*, ed. J. Le Goff, (Paris-La Haye: Mouton, 1968), 9-17; O. Hageneder, "Das Häresiebegriff dei den Juristen des 12. und 13. Jahrhunderts," in W. Lourdaux and D. Verhelst, eds., *The Concept of Heresy in the Middle Ages (11th-13th c.)*, (Louvain: Leuven University Press, 1976), 42-103; J. Koch, "Philosophische und theologische Irrtumslisten von 1270-1329. Ein Beitrag zur Entwickelung der theologischen Zensuren," in *Mélanges Mandonnet. Études d'histoire littéraire et doctrinale du Moyen Age*, vol. 2 (Paris: Vrin, 1930), 305-29.

14   Heresy did not consist in contradicting a generic religious belief, but one that was well-defined by the *magisterium* of the Church, because a proposition that disputed only traditional views was not a formal heresy.

15   Hageneder, "Das Häresiebegriff," 88, 100-101.

16   F. Beretta, *Galilée devant le Tribunal de l'Inquisition. Une relecture des sources* (Fribourg: s.i., 1998), 140.

17   Alfonso de Castro, *Adversus omnes haereses libri quatuordecim. Opus nunc denuo ab auctore ipso recognitum est* (...) (Lugduni: apud J. Frellonius, typis Mich. Sylvii, 1555; first edition: Paris 1534), f. 42v.

guished itself clearly from other types of doctrinal deviation, namely, the endorsement of propositions which Catholic theology qualified as "erronea," "sapiens haeresim," "male sonans," "temeraria," or "scandalosa."[18]

To establish the heretical nature of an opinion or a proposition required that one first had to discern a "propositio de fide definita."[19] The criteria developed by Alfonso de Castro in De iusta haereticorum punitione were certainly of some help: [20] (1) the Holy Scripture as long as its sense was clear, that is "apertus et indubitatus,"[21] (2) the conciliar decrees, given that the content of several articles of faith is not explicitly given in Scripture,[22] (3) the "consensus universalis Ecclesiae," and (4) the opinion of the Holy See and the views of the doctores.[23]

---

18 See Castro, De iusta haereticorum punitione, fols. 12r-16v. An erroneous proposition was one that contradicted a "veritas aliqua ab Ecclesia non definita." An example of a "sapiens haeresim" proposition is that 'the Bible contains errors,' because the Holy Writ is the supreme truth, but individual (printed) Bibles may contain misprints. An example of "propositio male sonans" was an orthodox doctrine that had been wrongly expressed. For example, "fides iustificat" was not a heretical view, but when proclaimed by a Protestant it did not 'sound good.' "Temeraria" was a proposition expressing an unjustified truth, such as "Dies iudicij erit infra annum." Other kinds of propositions were qualified as "schismatica" (undermining the unity of the Church), "blasphema," and "iniuriosa."

19 The medieval background is discussed in A. Lang, Die theologische Prinzipienlehre der mittelalterliche Scholastik (Freiburg: Herder, 1964).

20 Castro, De iusta haereticorum punitione, fols. 17r-22v. For discussion of the views of Melchior Cano and Domingo Bañez, see A. Lang, "Die Gliederung und die Reichweite des Glaubens nach Thomas von Aquin und den Thomisten. Ein Beitrag zur Klärung der scholastische Begriffe: fides, haeresis, und conclusio theologica," Divus Thomas 21 (1943), 79-97. For medieval origins, see Ch.H. Lohr, "Modelle für die Überlieferung theologischer Doktrin: Von Thomas von Aquin bis Melchior Cano," in W. Löser, K. Lehmann and M. Lutz-Bachmann, eds., Dogmengeschichte und katholische Theologie (Würzburg: Echter, 1988), 148-66.

21 Generally, the literal sense prevailed over the mystical sense.

22 The formulation of this criterion was inspired by the conviction that the works of ancient philosophers, in particular Plato and Aristotle, even though not being formally heretical, contained many doctrines that were extremely dangerous to the Catholic faith. However, the possibly heretical outcomes of the interpretation of ancient philosophy were controversial. Antonio Possevino, Bibliotheca selecta qua agitur de ratione studiorum in Historia, in Disciplinis, in Salute omnium procuranda, 2 vols. (Rome: Ex typographia Apostolica Vaticana, 1593), 42, argued that ancient philosophers cannot be viewed as heretics. A well known example was the dogma on the human soul which the Council of Vienna (1311-12) explicitly defined as "forma corporis."

23 The latter was controversial. Peña made a clear distinction between the opinions of the Fathers and those of scholastic theologians in order to safeguard the distinction between heretical and erroneous propositions. For example, from a doctrinal point of view, to deny the Immaculate Conception of Mary was to be regarded as an error, but not a heresy. As to the former, it should be borne in mind that since the pontificate of Sixtus V the authority of the Holy See had been substantially strengthened, the pope becoming the supreme judge in doctrinal controversies. The origin of the pope's primacy, as to doctrinal matters, is in the period preceding the Fifth Lateran Council; see Lohr, "Modelle für die Überlieferung theologischer Doktrin," 163-65.

2. Censura: *assessment and expurgation*

The *censura* was a central element in the practice of the Roman Congregations, consisting in the valuation of the congruence of a view, doctrine or
work with Catholic orthodoxy. *Censurae* were of two kinds:[24] assessments
containing a critical examination of a view or of the content of a work,[25]
on the one hand, and expurgations, that is, proposals for correction, on
the other.[26] Now, in the case of a prohibition by the Index, a work could be
condemned *tout court* or else with the stipulation of "donec corrigatur" or
"donec expurgetur." Expurgation, as suggested in Michele Ghislieri's 1559
Instructio, was a remarkable innovation of the Tridentine Index (1564)
and regarded books "quorum principale argumentum bonum est, in quibus obiter aliqua inserta sunt, quae ad haeresim seu impietatem, divina-
tionem aut superstitionem spectant."[27] Works prohibited with the proviso
"donec corrigatur" could be reprinted in an emended edition, or else local bishops or inquisitors could grant reading permits on condition that
the work was corrected according to the instructions of the Congregation
for the Index. Italian libraries contain many works that bear the signs of
several kinds of intervention: the cancellation of names and lines, the cov-
ering or physical elimination of individual passages or entire pages and
sections. Forbidden books that were not corrected, neither officially nor
privately, were destined to a clandestine circulation.

Expurgation could be asked for by the author, but most of the time it
was required by the representatives of the legal and medical professions,
printers and publishers,[28] as well as by relatives and scientific or cultur-

---

24   For the broader cultural background to the phenomenon, see P. Godman, *The
Saint as Censor. Robert Bellarmine Between Inquisition and Index* (Leiden: Brill, 2000), 130:
"Censorship was not only an expression of those strivings [i.e. to grapple with the issues
of authority and control]; it was more. A method of discussion, a vehicle of debate, a form
of thought: so commonly practised and so widely diffused was *censura* that any problem–
theological, political, or moral–was able to be condensed into propositions and submitted
to the judgement of peers, colleagues, or superiors."

25   As is well known, censorship could be exercised in two ways: before the printing or
publishing of a work (*censura praevia*), and after the printing or publishing, by prohibiting
it (*censura repressiva*). The bull *Inter sollicitudines* (1515) and the Tridentine Index (1564)
had established preventive censorship and approbation, which pertained to other Church
officials (the local inquisitors and the Master of the Sacred Palace), while the Roman Congregations investigated works printed without an *imprimatur* or which circulated in manuscript form.

26   When the correction was carried out, the print and reading of the work could be
permitted again.

27   ILI, 8: 817.

28   Jean Bodin's Venetian printer Nicola Manassi is a case in point.

al academies.[29] As a rule, it regarded works prohibited with the proviso "donec corrigatur," but frequently totally prohibited works were also corrected if they were regarded as useful. Even some books that had never been condemned or prohibited were corrected if they were considered in some way or another to be suspect. In general, expurgation was presumed to be carried out according to the Index Rules, or else it had to be based upon pre-existent *censurae*, with a preference for those kept in the archive of the Congregation for the Index in Rome. However, expurgation was not centralized until 1587,[30] and before this date there was a proliferation of local correctors, partly experts (inquisitors and their assistants and consultors) and partly common readers requested to correct the books they were allowed to read.[31] After the promulgation of the Clementine Index in 1596, the Congregation decided to set up local commissions for the correction of books prohibited in the second class,[32] but this attempt did not furnish the desired results. After the publication of Guanzelli's Expurgatory Index in 1607, the Congregation for the Index abandoned the large-scale project of composing corrections for the works listed in the second class.[33]

The reasons motivating correction were multifarious: obscenity, mixing up profane and holy, derision of rites and devotion, irreverence to clergy, attribution of divine aspects to common people, etc. The fundamental problem in expurgation regarded the criteria underlying an adequate correction. Rule VIII of the Tridentine Index concerned those heretical or suspect statements in books which occurred occasionally (*obiter*), and this suggested that they could be easily isolated. And indeed, until only names or clearly distinct passages were to be eliminated things were rel-

---

29 The expurgation of Castiglione's *Cortegiano* was supported by his son Camillo, that of Machiavelli by the Florentine academy and his relatives; similar cases are those of Boccaccio and Bernardino Telesio. The expurgation of the Talmud was requested by the Jewish community. See V. Frajese, *Nascita dell'Indice. La censura ecclesiastica dal Rinascimento alla Controriforma* (Brescia: Morcelliana, 2006), 307-8.

30 ACDF, Index, *Diari*, 1, f. 17v. The very term is used for the first time on 12 November 1587; cf. ACDF, Index, *Diari*, 1, f. 28r.

31 The correction of prohibited or suspect works was initially seen as the aim of the grant of reading permits. Later, by contrast, it often became a condition of the latter.

32 The distinction in three classes was introduced in the Tridentine Index: one category contained all the works of heretical authors, a second category contained individual works by authors not included in the first category, and a third category contained works by authors *incerti nominis*.

33 A detailed reconstruction for the period 1559-1753 is in ACDF, Index, *Protocolli*, II.a.84, fols. 368r, 369r-377v.

atively simple.[34] The situation got quite complicated when the book was placed on the Index because the author put forth views in open or veiled conflict with Catholic doctrine, and in particular when the censor had to tackle erroneous propositions that were intimately rooted in complex theoretical systems.[35]

The censor was presumed to take into consideration any possible kind of peril, but first of all the title page, the name of the author or editor, and the place of edition.[36] Then, he should examine the text, and formulate his proposals for correction.[37] Often, however, the censor could also operate at a substantially different level: connect the mutilated parts and/or rewrite entire sections,[38] and thus insinuating orthodoxy. As a consequence, works could assume an outlook strongly deviating from the author's original intentions.[39] Thus, while some corrections were visible or traceable, others were completely invisible. As to the latter, they were probably more damaging than a downright prohibition.[40]

3. Arnaldus of Villanova, Ramon Lull, and John the Scot Eriugena

Arnaldus of Villanova (1235–1311) was celebrated in his day as a physician, pharmacist, and alchemist. Although a layman he wrote much on theology, and his heterodox opinions concerning crucial dogmatic issues

---

34 Around 1587, Vincenzo Bonardi composed a *Modus et ratio expurgandi vel corrigendi libros*; the text is in ACDF, Index, *Protocolli*, M (II.a.10), fols. 124r-125r. See also ACDF, Index, *Diari*, 1, f. 20v. Comments by Ruggiero, Peña, Allen, Morin, and an anonymous author are in ACDF, Index, *Protocolli*, B (II.a.2), fols. 528r-537v. On 8 October 1594, Marcantonio Colonna handed over to his censors a printed *Instructio pro expurgatione et impressione librorum*; cf. ACDF, Index, *Diari*, 1, f. 81r. This text was probably the basis for the *Instructio* printed in the Clementine Index; ILI, 9: 859-62.

35 Examples are the works by Francesco Giorgio and Francesco Patrizi, which did not directly contradict Catholic doctrine, but which contained many views with pernicious potentialities.

36 For general rules, see ILI, 9: 859-62.

37 In general, the censors should prefer correction to cancellation. On 19 September 1592, the Congregation exhorted its consultors to follow the pope's intention in this sense: "Disputatum inter hos Consultores et de mente Sanctissimi conclusum quod expurgatio Librorum fiat non delendo sed solum notando errores" (ACDF, Index, *Diari*, 1, f. 52v).

38 Ambrogio da Asola's corrections of Levinus Lemnius are an illustrative example; cf. ACDF, Index, *Protocolli*, O (II.a.13), fols. 279r-296r.

39 A clamorous case of the wrenching of a literary work was Girolamo Malipiero's transformation of Petrarca's *Canzoniere* (published in 1536); cf. A. Del Col, *L'inquisizione in Italia dal XII al XXI secolo* (Milan: Oscar Mondadori, 2006), 530-31.

40 Paolo Sarpi considered altering the thought of an author to be a greater offence than its absolute prohibition. See Balsamo, "How to doctor a bibliography: Antonio Possevino's practice," 50.

(the Mass, the Antichrist, the end of the world, the person of Christ) repeatedly forced him to wander from place to place as Inquisitors in Spain
and France had sentenced him to banishment.[41] A large number of ACDF
documents attests an almost unremitting attention by the Congregation
for the Index to Arnaldus' works and his commentary on *Regimen sanitatis* or *Schola salernitana*. Furthermore, this documentation shows that it
took a fairly long time for the Congregation to reach a definite view of the
author and his works.

The condemnation of thirteen treatises in 1316 by the Archbishop of
Tarragona (Catalonia) laid the groundwork for Arnaldus' first sixteenth-
century prohibition: in 1554 the Venetian Index adopted the Bishop's decree.[42] Arnaldus' works probably caught the attention of the Roman bodies
of doctrinal control as early as the late 1550s, when an anonymous censor
of the Holy Office recommended his condemnation as a heretic,[43] which
eventually took place in 1559.[44] Two years later, he was included among
the authors of the first class on the Index of Portugal.[45] Subsequently, Arnaldus was mentioned several times in Giovanni Dei's catalogue of heretical and suspect books (1576).[46] Then his works were prohibited by the
Master of the Sacred Palace in 1576[47] and mentioned in local lists of forbidden books in Turin (ca. 1580)[48] and Rome (ca. 1583).[49] Contemporar-
ily, Arnaldus was condemned in the so-called Index of Parma (1580), and
in those of Portugal (1581) and Spain (1583).[50] In the Spanish Expurgatory Index of 1584 only seven treatises from the *Opera* were condemned.[51]

---

41   For a summary of the heresies that Arnaldus was usually accused of, see Matthias
Flacius Illyricus et al., *Ecclesiastica historia, (...) perspicuo ordine complectens: singulari dili-
gentia et fide ex vetustissimis et optimis historicis, patribus, et alijs scriptoribus congesta*, 13
parts in 8 vols. (Basileae: per Ioannem Oporinum [et Hervagium], 1560-1574), VIII, cols.
571-572. This list was probably based upon Nicolao Eymeric's *Directorium inquisitorum*.

42   On 8 November 1316 the Bishop of Tarragona prohibited the following works: *De
humilitate et patientia Iesu Christo, De fine mundi, Informatio Beguinorum, Ad Priorissam
vel de caritate, Apologia*, inc. "Domino carissimo", *Denunciatio facta coram Domino Episcopo
Gerundensi, De elemosina et sacrifitio*, inc. "Per ço molts desiguen saber", *Alia informatio Beguinorum*, inc. "Devant vos senyor", inc. "Cant fuy Avinió", and *Responsio contra Bernardum
Ricardi*. It should be kept in mind that some of these works have been lost, while others survive only in Latin, Catalan, Italian or Greek translations; see ILI, 3: 222-25.

43   See Bibliotheca Apostolica Vaticana (from now on: BAV), *Vat. Lat.* 6207, f. 221r.

44   ILI, 8: 262.

45   ILI, 4: 352.

46   ACDF, Index, XIV.1, f. 9v.

47   ILI, 10: 829-30.

48   ILI, 9: 758.

49   ILI, 9: 770, 774, 775.

50   ILI, 9: 80; 4: 352; 6: 180.

51   See ILI, 6: 985.

The total prohibition of the author did not prevent the Congregation from pondering on the possibility of a conditional permission for (some of) his works.[52] Thus, on 5 November and 3 December of 1587, Silvio Antoniano presented *censurae* of Arnaldus' works in the Congregation.[53] And by the end of the 1580s, Arnaldus and *Regimen sanitatis Salernitanum*, although inserted into lists of books that were retracted from sale, were frequently mentioned in general lists of books to be examined, and in lists of books already corrected. In the Roman Index of 1590, Arnaldus was again included among the authors of the first class.[54] However, between the end of the 1580s and the early 1590s the Congregation received urgent requests for expurgating his works. By March 1593, the Congregation commissioned an expurgatory *censura* to Salamanca. Arnaldus was again condemned for heresy in the later Indexes of Rome (1593, 1596).[55] Nonetheless, in ACDF documents his books were again listed as having been already corrected. In his 1607 Expurgatory Index, Guanzelli merely adopted the prohibition of the seven treatises by the 1584 Spanish Expurgatory Index.[56]

Almost immediately after Ramon Lull's death, a long and intricate debate evolved concerning his doctrines.[57] As is well-known, these doctrines were greatly influenced by a then flourishing pseudepigraphal literature, or rather, the rapidly expanding corpus of mnemotechnic and theological works composed by Lull's disciples under his name shortly after his death. During the second half of the fourteenth century, the Faculty of Theology in Paris censured several propositions as well as the terminology of

---

52 Most probably, the Congregation was urged by librarians and physicians; see, for example, the request of twenty-one Bolognese librarians who in a letter dated 10 August 1577 asked Card. Sirleto for the correction of his works in order to make them available for sale. See BAV, *Vat. Lat.* 6417, fols. 365r-366v.

53 ACDF, Index, *Diari*, 1, fols. 27r, 28r, 29v.

54 ILI, 9: 802.

55 ILI, 9: 465-6, 864, 933.

56 See Giovanni Maria Guanzelli da Brisighella (Brasichellensis), *Indicis librorum expurgandorum in studiosorum gratiam confecti tomus primus* (Romae: ex Typographia R. Cam. Apost., 1607), 36. For specifications and extensive references, see U. Baldini and L. Spruit, eds., *Catholic Church and Modern Science. Documents from the Archives of the Roman Congregations of the Holy Office and the Index*, vol. I: *Sixteenth-Century Documents*, 4 vols. (Città del Vaticano: Libreria Editrice Vaticana, 2009), chapter on Arnaldus of Villanova, introduction.

57 For a reconstruction, see *Dictionnaire de théologie catholique*, 33 vols. (Paris: Librairie Letouzey et Ane, 1909-1960), 9: 1135-40; cf. L. Pérez Martínez, "Intervención de la Santa Sede en la causa luliana," *Estudios Lulianos* 6 (1962): 151-78, and A. Madre, *Die theologische Polemik gegen Raimundus Lullus. Eine Untersuchung zu den* Elenchi auctorum de Raimundo male sentientium (Münster: Aschendorff, 1973). ACDF preserves several eighteenth-century reconstructions, among which *Protocolli*, I (II.a.8), fols. 174r-179r, is worth mentioning.

Ars magna. In Spain, the controversy was fueled by the pursuits of the Dominican monk Nicolau Eymeric (ca. 1320-1399), inquisitor and subsequently procurator of the Order in Aragon, who from 1371 raised the Lullist issue in lasting controversies with King Pedro IV. As chaplain to Gregory XI, Eymeric probably urged the pope to issue the bull *Nuper dilecto* (5 June 1372), which ordered the Archbishop of Tarazona (Aragon) to examine Lull's works and to burn any part containing errors. Moreover, on 29 September 1374, the pontiff ordered the shipment to Avignon of a book written by Lull in Catalan (*Liber de philosophia amoris*). Irritated by these pontifical actions, Pedro IV expelled Eymeric on 11 March 1375 from all his dominions. After less than a year, the reputed bull *Conservationi puritatis* (dated 25 January 1376) was distributed, condemning twenty of Lull's books,[58] including apocryphal and now lost works. This bull also identified two hundred heretical propositions extracted from the latter and ordered a close examination of the rest of Lull's works. It is in this bull that the eternal Lull case originates. The authenticity of the bull, generally taken for granted by the Dominicans but challenged by the Franciscans, was never proved and its apocryphal character is now solidly established.[59]

---

58 Nicolau Eymeric, *Directorium inquisitorum* (…) *cum commentariis Francisci Pegnae* (…) *in hac postrema editione iterum emendatum et auctum, et multis litteris Apostolicis locupletatum* (Romae: in Aedibus Populi Romani, 1585), 272-77, mentions the following works: *Liber de philosophia amoris, Liber de centum Dei nominibus, Liber contemplationum, Liber de septem arboribus, Liber de trecentis proverbiis, Liber de confessione, contritione, satisfactione et oratione, Liber de orationibus, Liber amati et amici, Liber de Benedicta tu, Liber de articulis fidei, Liber de doctrina puerili, Liber de planctu Raymundi, Liber de intentionibus, Liber de arte amativa, Liber de temptatione, Liber de oratione et alius a praedicto, Liber de anima, Liber sententiarum*, and *Liber apostolicon*.

59 The following points may be considered. First, more than a year after its 'promulgation,' King Pedro IV, one of the major participants in the debate, was still not acquainted with the bull, as appears from his letter of 7 January 1377, in which he demanded that the pope should give permission for the examination of the aforementioned Catalan book (*Liber de philosophia amoris*) in Barcelona. Now, if this book had been condemned for more than a year, as for example was maintained by Eymeric in his *Directorium Inquisitorum*, when referring to the 1376 bull, such a request would not have made any sense. Second, the condemnation of twenty books and two hundred propositions without any indication either of the titles to the works or the nature of the propositions was in gross contrast to the style employed by the Roman Curia. Third, the bull was not recorded in Gregory XI's registers, as is revealed by some 1395 research carried out at the request of Antonio Riera. Fourth, due to his obvious bias, Eymeric's testimony turned out to be anything but trustworthy. As early as 1386 a Joint Commission of Dominicans and Franciscans established that three of the propositions extracted from the *Philosophia amoris* and condemned as heretical by Eymeric were not to be found in this work at all. Eventually, the Holy See itself challenged the authenticity of the 'bull.' After decades of continuing controversy, Martin V demanded a definite judgment from Card. Alamanno Adimari. The latter, legate in Aragon, appointed Bernardo Bartolomei, Bishop of Città di Castello, who on 24 March 1419 after due research declared the 'bull' to be apocryphal and without any value.

Under the pontificate of Sixtus IV (1471-1484), the issue was again raised when Pedro Dagui, first professor of the Lullist *Studium* in Palma de Maiorca, was accused by the Dominicans. When Degui successfully defended himself against these attacks, the Inquisitor of Majorca proceeded to print Eymeric's *Directorium*, including Gregory XI's 'Bull' and a hundred errors and heresies attributed to Lull.[60] This laid the groundwork for Lull's inclusion in the Roman Index of 1557,[61] which was not promulgated, and in the 1559 Index, which condemned "Raimundi Lulli opera per Gregorium XI damnata".[62] However, at the Council of Trent some of Lull's followers, among whom Juan Luis Vileta, Dimas de Miguel, and Juan Arce de Herrera, had the decision revoked. On 1 September 1563, the Council decreed that Lull's works were to be removed from the Index, and this decision was recorded in the 1564 Index.[63] Nonetheless, in 1576 the Master of the Sacred Palace prohibited his "opera alias damnata."[64] In 1578, Francisco Peña published a new edition of Eymeric's *Directorium*, being the likely cause of a new change in the history of the Church: by decree of 9 February 1583[65] the Congregation for the Index again prohibited Lull's works. This decision in turn prompted the reaction of the Lullist faction and in the long run the intervention by King Philip II of Spain, which inspired the Index decrees of 3 June 1593 and of 16 July 1594, ratifying in effect a return to the decision taken by the Council of Trent.[66]

In the context of this long and peculiar succession of surprising changes, quite unique in the history of the Roman Index, prohibitions recorded in other sixteenth-century Indexes are to be considered. The condemnation of twenty treatises on account of Gregory XI's 'Bull' was accepted by the Indexes of Venice (1554), Rome (1559, 1593) and Parma (1580).[67] *Phi-*

60 For the text, see Madre, *Die theologische Polemik gegen Raimundus Lullus*, 147-57.

61 ILI, 8: 744 and 302-3.

62 See BAV, *Vat. Lat.* 6207, f. 236r: "Raimundi Luli opera. 20 opera sunt in quibus 500 [sic] errores offenduntur." The number of 100 errors goes back to Nicolau Eymeric's *Directorium Inquisitorum*; see Eymeric, *Directorium Inquisitorum*, 272-77; cf. 277-78, for the errors of his followers.

63 Notice, however, that the first Rule of this Index prohibited all books "quos ante annum MDXV aut summi Pontifices, aut Concilia oecumenica damnarunt."

64 ILI, 10: 837.

65 ACDF, Index, *Diari*, 1, f. 11v.

66 In ACDF, Index, *Protocolli*, S (II.a.17), f. 521v, Lull's cause is summarized in the following way: "Raimundi Lulli doctrina instante Procuratore Regni Aragoniae, examinanda per deputatos consultores 6. Aug. 1589. et Cardinales 16 Iunij 1590. et expeditae literae compulsoriales instante Oratore Regis Catholici 4 Martij 1595., et iam sublatus fuerat ex Indice 3 Iunij 1593."

67 ILI, 3: 349-51; 8: 302-3; 9: 423, 168. There are slight differences with Eymeric's list (see *supra*): *Liber de Benedicta tu* is lacking, while *Liber de contemplatione* substituted *Liber de temptatione*.

losophia amoris, already prohibited in the Indexes of Venice (1554), Portugal (1581) and Spain (1583), was also prohibited in the later Roman Indexes (1590, 1593, 1596).[68]

Undoubtedly, the inclusion and removal of the same author on more than one occasion from the Index of Forbidden Books flew in the face of the *stylus* of the Roman Congregation which had great difficulty in explaining the exact reasons for its continuous changes.[69] Some documents testify to the Congregation's fundamentally uncertain attitude and the perplexity of its collaborators with respect to the person and the works of Ramon Lull. In 1576, Giovanni Dei put Lull in the category of suspect authors, having been condemned previously and included in other Indexes.[70] A similar motivation probably inspired the authors of local lists (issued in the 1570s and 1580s)[71] and consultors of the Index.[72] However, the legitimacy of this motivation was generally challenged, and doubted even by the Dominican Bartolomé de Miranda, Master of the Sacred Palace.[73] Some consultors advised that the works be expurgated as they considered them useful to scholars in natural science and medicine,[74] while others,

---

68   ILI, 3: 349; 4: 458-59; 6: 508; 9: 696, 838, 898.

69   See ACDF, Index, *Protocolli*, R (II.a.16), f. 15v: "Ad quintum caput. Non est novum Pontifices successores Predecessorum constitutiones, decreta, et prohibitiones in melius commutare et ob causas non minus graves, quod per posteriores constitutiones antiquatum fuerat renovare prout in novo Indice de Raymundo Lullo factum est, presertim cum Pij Quarti Index Pio Quinto successori et Inquisitoribus non plane satisfecerit ob hanc potissimam causam quod nonnullos auctores et libros in Indice Pauli IV. vetitos, iterum legendos concesserit, praeterea censores in hoc eodem Censurae capite modo pugnant pro Indice, et regulis Pij IV, modò tacitè reprehendunt, et nuncupatim exprimendum ducunt in novo Indice quod in ipso priore generatim de libris Geomantiae tradebatur."

70   See ACDF, Index, XIV.1, f. 44r.

71   Lists composed in Vercelli (1574), Turin (ca. 1580), and Rome (ca. 1583) refer to Eymeric and Gregory XI's bull; see ILI, 9: 757, 767, 777. See also the lists issued in Alessandria (ca. 1575) and Asti (1576); cf. *Scriniolum Sanctae Inquisitionis Astensis: In quo quaecunque ad id muneris obeundum spectare visa sunt, (...), quaeve hucusque in partes veluti frustratim concisa, atque distracta sparsim ibant, nunc in unum collecta, (...) repositaque sunt* (Astae: apud Virgilium de Zangrandis, 1610 [but: at least 1612]), 88-89.

72   See Giambattista Lanci's list (17 November 1580), in ACDF, Index, *Protocolli*, A (II.a.1), fasc. 87, 11v.

73   See ACDF, Index, *Protocolli*, P (II.a.14), f. 22r: "Posset aliquis dubitare non omnes libros in Indicem coniectos iure esse damnatos, cum in eorum censuris nihil certe, quod sit magni momenti deprehendatur. Hi vero sunt qui sequuntur"; cf. on f. 23r: "Raymundi Lulli opera per Gregorium IX.[sic] Damnata [in the margin: deleatur ab Indice]."

74   See ACDF, Index, *Protocolli*, B (II.a.2), f. 232v. In a letter dated 10 August 1577 a group of twenty-one Bolognese librarians asked Card. Sirleto for the correction of Lull's works in order to make them available for sale, stating explicitly: "volessimo sapere quali opere siano cative." See BAV, *Vat. Lat.* 6417, fols. 365r-366v.

such as Vincenzo Bonardi, regarded this expurgation as rather complex.[75] This set the frame for intricate discussion in the 1590s concerning Lull's possible inclusion in the Index.[76] The decision to place the books condemned by Gregory XI on the 1593 Index was taken in mutual consent with the Holy Office, but later challenged by Clement VIII and subsequently revoked in the 1596 Index.[77] The case of Lull continued to drag on in the centuries to come.[78]

Although John Scottus Eriugena's doctrines of predestination and of the Eucharist were condemned at the Councils of Valencia (855), Langres (859), and Vercelli (1050), it was not until the beginning of the thirteenth century that the pantheism of *De divisione naturae* was formally condemned. The Council of Paris (1225) coupled the condemnation of Eriugena's work with the previous condemnations (1210) of the doctrines of Amalric of Bene and David of Dinant. Yet, the major scholastic doctors apparently were unacquainted with Eriugena's work. After Scottus had been almost forgotten for many centuries, he was again discovered in 1681, when Thomas Gale issued *De divisione naturae* in Oxford.[79] The Roman Church was informed, and on 11 July 1684 the Congregation for the Index commissioned friar Giovanni Antonio of Palermo to examine the book. On the basis of his *censura* the Congregation decided on 5 September of that year to prohibit the book, "sine alia," that is without any

---

75   See ACDF, Index, *Protocolli*, B (II.a.2), f. 502v: "Per la terza parte dell'espurgazione, sono moltissimi, i, libri da espurgarsi, et darà non poco fastidio il negotio di Raimondo Lullo, che da Paolo quarto fu prohibito, et da Pio quarto nell'Indice del Concilio fu lasciato, à, dietro."

76   See *infra*. Discussing the Index Rules in his 1588 *Enchiridion*, Gregorio di Napoli argued that Lull's removal from the Tridentine Index did not entail that he was to be regarded as an author "approbatus," because Rule I of this Index banned all works prohibited before 1515, and thus also Lull's works condemned by Gregory XI. Gregorio also recalled Eymeric's list of 100 errors and the 200 errors that contemporary theologians identified in Lull's works. Furthermore, arch-heretics, among whom Agrippa, wrote commentaries to his works. See Gregorio di Napoli, *Enchiridion ecclesiasticum, Sive praeparatio pertinens ad sacramentum Poenitentiae et sacri Ordinis (…), nunc denuo auctum, et amplificatum ab eodem Auctore, et tandem typis chalcographis traditum* (Venetiis: sumptibus Iaco. Anelli de Maria Bibliopolae Neapolitani, Hieronymo Polo Typographo Veneto imprimente, 1588), fols. 215v-219v.

77   ACDF, Index, *Protocolli*, M (II.a.11), f. 245r: "De Raymundo quidem non erat idem omnium sensus, sed tandem sequuta est Congregatio voluntatem Sancti officij."

78   For example, in the seventeenth century (probably during the 1620s) the Congregation for the Index informed the Inquisitor of Bologna in an extended file of eighteen pages (kept in the Biblioteca dell'Arciginnasio di Bologna) about the several phases of the case, summarizing and mentioning decrees and *censurae* concerning his works.

79   Johannes Scotus Eriugena, *De divisione naturae libri quinque, diu desiderati. Accedit appendix ex Ambiguis S. Maximi Graece et Latine* (Oxonii: E Theatro Sheldoniano, 1681; reprint: Frankfurt am Main, 1964).

possibility of correction. The decree of prohibition was promulgated on 3 April 1685.[80]

In his *censura*,[81] Giovanni Antonio of Palermo first recalls the condemnations of Scottus' doctrines of the Eucharist and of predestination, as well as those of his *De divisione naturae*. Then, he challenges some specific, related issues: sexual distinction as an effect of original sin (which by consequence will disappear after the resurrection); the view that man preserves the divine image also after the fall; that Christ's body when he appeared to the disciples cannot be referred to any time or place; that the universal judgment will not take place in any material location; that no time elapsed between Christ's resurrection and his ascension to heaven; that Paradise and Hell are not to be identified as material places; that the eternal punishment is similar to some sort of sadness, as the human soul cannot undergo 'real' pains; the universal election of man; beatitude as theophany rather than as vision of God; and the 'ubiquity' of Christ's body.

4. Censorship and canon

One part of the fascination that censorship exercises is that it does not readily lend itself to definition. Yet, or probably for this very reason, any discussion of censorship easily generates well-known commonplaces. For example, the Roman Congregations of the Holy Office and the Index are usually seen as obscurantist, repressive bodies, hostile to any expression of rationalism, science and cultural innovation. Now, it cannot be denied that the effect early modern censorship produced on the ecclesiastical attitude towards new intellectual or scientific ideas not in themselves directly concerned with or resulting from religious heresy, could not but be constrictive, and the quasi-tolerance of philosophical and other novelties which marked the Church of the Italian Renaissance came necessarily to be heavily modified in the course of the second half of the sixteenth century. Not only were the obvious texts of religious heterodoxy prohibited entirely, the Indexes also prohibited or expurgated literary works of major Italian authors, including Boccaccio, Franco, Sansovino, Bandello, Gelli and others. Moreover, also books with no religious content written by known Protestants (including legal, scientific and medical texts) were banned and made unavailable to Italian readers. Yet, the cases discussed

---

80 See ACDF, Index, *Diari*, 8, fols. 10r, 17r, and 18v (modern numeration).
81 ACDF, Index, *Protocolli*, TT (II.a.43), fols. 138r-142r.

in the previous section show the wavering of Catholic censorship between rigor and relaxation. And moreover, in attempting to enforce its authority, the Index helped consolidate forces in opposition.[82] As a result, book censorship was attenuated in several ways.

Many works were prohibited with the so-called "donec corrigatur" stipulation, and thus were available on condition that they were corrected, that is, readers were supposed to skip or cover some passages, or else to replace them by alternative readings. Sometimes the prescribed corrections were minimal, while at other times the censors attempted to rewrite the incriminated books in part or almost entirely.[83]

The conditioned availability of many works was intimately linked to the system of licences to read forbidden books, granted in Italy by the Inquisition, the Index, and the Master of the Sacred Palace. The grant of reading licences, which makes it possible to assess the difference between the hypothetical and the real efficacy of ecclesiastical censorship, also reveals the interaction of essentially religious and cultural criteria with the practical requirements of contemporary society which the Church could not completely ignore or suppress.

Finally, censorship had a repressive, but also an emancipatory element, that is, as a rule-embedded phenomenon, it was constitutive and regulative.[84] The assessment of Hebrew literature is an example of the constitutive role of censorship. Recent studies have indeed demonstrated that Roman censors of Hebrew works (for the most part converts) participated, unintentionally, in the extensive redefinition of the boundaries of reading, in partial accord with contemporary Jewish trends. The explicit intention of the censors was to prevent forbidden contents; the practice of censorship, however, resulted in the authorization of what the Church considered to be permissible knowledge. Thus, the control of Hebrew print led to the Church's official recognition of Hebrew literature, and consequently of Jewish practice.[85]

Now, considering that the availability of medieval works was only marginally conditioned by prohibitions, what can be said about the effects of censorship on the fortune of medieval books and authors? More specifi-

---

82　S.C. Jansen, *Censorship. The Knot that Binds Power and Knowledge* (New York-Oxford: Oxford University Press, 1988), 64.

83　See above section 2.

84　For discussion, see Schulze, "Kanon und Pluralisierung in der Frühen Neuzeit."

85　See, for example, A. Raz-Krakotzkin, *The Censor, the Editor, and the Text. The Catholic Church and the Shaping of the Jewish Canon in the Sixteenth Century* (Philadelphia: University of Pennsylvania Press, 2007). See also St. Wendehorst, *The Roman Inquisition, the Index and the Jews. Contexts, Sources and Perspectives* (Leiden: Brill, 2004).

cally, did Roman censorship influence in any sense the canon of medieval doctrinal works? Before tackling this question, still another issue should be raised: did there exist any canon of medieval authors and books in early modern times?

Canon, like censorship as was seen above, is a plurisignificant and multifunctional phenomenon. 'Canon' can become a focus for debate in any period in which artists, critics, philosophers and theologians try to match an inherited body of texts, practices or ideas to their perceived present and future cultural needs. Canons of medieval books and authors developed in different circles and at different levels. Thus, one should consider the circulation and function of actual historical canons in specific communities, institutions, and individual careers in order to arrive at a realistic appraisal of both the imaginative possibilities and the cultural limitations presented by past canons.[86] For the issue under scrutiny a glance at sixteenth-century bibliographies that certainly played a role in the rise of early modern canons may be of some help.

5. Bibliotheca universalis–Bibliotheca selecta

The abbot Johann Tritheim (1462-1516) was the first to devote himself professionally to the compilation of bio-bibliographic repertoria, but it was Conrad Gessner who published the first modern universal bibliography.[87] His extensive *Bibliotheca universalis* (Zurich 1545) listed more than 3000 authors and over 15,000 works (including the 1555 *Appendix*), based on libraries in Rome (among which the Vatican Library), Florence, Bologna and Venice, on inventories of libraries in German countries, private collections (Erasmus and Peutinger), on *catalogi typographorum*, and on citations and lists in ancient works.[88] In 1548 he published a second part, entitled *Pandectae*, presenting a systematic classification of the works listed in the first part and inspired by the view of philosophy as the mother of all sciences. The third section, which was to contain the *loci communes* from the works given in the *Bibliotheca*, was replaced by a comprehensive alphabetical index at the close of the *Pandectae*.

---

86   J. Gorak, *The Making of the Modern Canon. Genesis and Crisis of a Literary Idea* (London: Athlone, 1991), introduction.

87   For earlier bibliographies on specific disciplinary fields, see L. Balsamo, *La bibliografia: storia di una tradizione*, (Firenze: Sansoni, 1984; English trans. Berkeley, 1990), 24-28.

88   For discussion, see H. Fisher, "Conrad Gesner (1516-1565) as bibliographer and encyclopedist," *The Library*, fifth series, 21 (1966): 269-81.

Gessner's work had an extraordinary success, thus triggering the attention of Catholic censors.[89] It gave a detailed picture of the works published in Germany, and thus was seen as a dangerous instrument for the spread of Protestant views. ACDF documents testify that his *Bibliotheca* was frequently used for the composition of new indexes.[90] Moreover, several *censurae* were composed of this work.[91] Gessner was condemned as a heretic in early Roman indexes (1559 and 1564). However, he is not even mentioned in many lists composed by Roman censors during the 1570s and 1580s, including Giovanni Dei's detailed catalogue of heretical and suspect books.[92] Remarkably, the total prohibition was revoked in later sixteenth-century indexes (1593, 1596).[93]

Gessner's work also triggered another kind of Catholic reaction, Antonio Possevino's *Bibliotheca selecta* (first edition 1593), composed as an encyclopedic dictionary and meant to contrast the *Pandectae*. Now, while Gessner catalogued all the works he was able to find and furnished ample information to assist the reader in making a reasoned choice in his personal quest for knowledge, Possevino, by contrast, relieved readers of this responsibility and protected them against possible dangers, taking pains to list only 'good' books which complied with the principles of Catholic morality.[94] The second part, entitled *Apparatus sacer* (published in 1603), was intended to countervail the first part of Gessner's *Bibliotheca*. Again, the authors were 'selected' by virtue of their accordance with Catholic doctrine. In effect, it was a complement to the Index of forbidden books, as it set out a list of indubitably orthodox authors and works that could be read on the Church's advice. Finally, Possevino gave practical instructions

---

89   It was prohibited in indexes issued in Portugal, Paris, Louvain, and Venice. See ILI, 10: 199.

90   See, for example, Alfonso Chacón's pronouncement for the new index in ACDF, Index, *Protocolli*, B (II.a.2), f. 246r-v (autumn 1587). For the use of Gessner's *Bibliotheca* as a catalogue of works written by a garden variety of Protestant authors, ever since the preparation of the 1559 Index, see ILI, 8: 36, 119-20.

91   See, for example, ACDF, Index, *Protocolli*, F (II.a.5), fols. 45v-47v; *Protocolli*, X (II.a.20) fols. 145r-156r, 162r-163r.

92   See ACDF, Index, XIV.1. The only significant exception is a rather permissive expurgatory *censura*, published in the proceedings of the Inquisition in Asti, in the appendix of a 1576 list of authors prohibited in the diocesis; see *Scriniolum*, 104.

93   ILI, 10: 199.

94   Possevino also published numerous offprints of parts of the book. In particular those relating to history and philosophy were printed as independent texts, so that they could be used as school texts by preachers, confessors, catechists, and teachers.

for "correcting, emending, expurgating books".[95] Thus, Possevino's work, which was meant to circulate internationally in place of Gessner's bibliography, was not a merely bibliographical work, it was a vademecum that faithfully mirrored the doctrine of the Catholic Church.

* * *

In the process of 'canonization' of medieval works and authors the role of Index and Inquisition was quite marginal. At least till the early seventeenth century, other factors had a greater impact, among which surely the influence of Gessner's and Possevino's bibliographies has to be mentioned. In addition, it goes without saying that also the numerous contemporary scholastic manuals and commentaries played a crucial role in shaping a canon of authoritative medieval authors and views. These works influenced both Catholic and Protestant scholars and in general they substituted the texts they were based on, that is, Aristotle, his commentators, and the major schoolmen, including suspect (or heretical) authors, such as Peter John Olivi and William of Ockham.

As a matter of fact, medieval works did not present the principal threat to the Roman Church. Therefore, most medieval canons arose independently of prohibition and expurgation, while the only significant exception is the canon related to Jewish literature. Let us now return to the three authors discussed in section 3.

The anonymous *censurae* on Arnaldus' works held in ACDF call attention to the pernicious implications of his astrology.[96] The *censura* presented to the Roman Congregation by Girolamo Pallantieri on behalf of the Paduan commission for the correction of philosophical and medical works stressed that all astrology without any clear link with medicine was illegitimate and therefore simply to be condemned.[97] Thus, the Paduan censors recommended the unconditional prohibition of four of Arnaldus' astrological and divinatory treatises because they lacked any medical purpose, and merely aimed at predicting the future. Arnaldus was not removed from the Index's first class which listed heretical authors. Yet, the Congregation labored to make at least some of his works available for

---

95 Here it is worth mentioning that, in the 1590s, Possevino presented a note on books that require correction to the Congregation for the Index. ACDF, Index, *Protocolli*, O (II.a.13), fols. 509r-510v.

96 ACDF, Index, *Protocolli*, H (II.a.7), fols. 428r, 429v, 430r-v.

97 ACDF, Index, *Protocolli*, N (II.a.12), fols. 75r-78r.

Catholic readers. Like many other authors on magic, secrets and the like, his fame rapidly declined after the rise of modern science.

Ramon Lull, definitively removed from the Index in 1593, is a particular case. He became object of a local cult in Catalonia and in the Kingdom of Majorca. Chairs for the propagation of the theories of Lull were set up at the University of Barcelona and the University of Valencia. Therefore, during the seventeenth and eighteenth centuries the Congregations of the Inquisition and the Index continued to examine his case.[98] Later, the Catholic Church beatified Lull, when Pius IX confirmed his cult in 1858. He is called Doctor Illuminatus, but he has not been canonized.

Scottus's case represents the most rigorous intervention. At the end of the eighteenth century, he was rediscovered by German idealism, like his 'fellow pantheists' Giordano Bruno and Spinoza, and this probably explains the fact that he remained on the Index until the latter was abolished in 1966.

---

98   See, for example, ACDF, SO, *St. st.*, UV 46, fasc. 32 (after 1627), on the question whether Ramon Lull was a heresiarch and for his defence.

DOES THE CANON NEED CONVERTING? A MEDITATION ON AUGUSTINE'S *SOLILOQUIES*, ERIUGENA'S *PERIPHYSEON*, AND THE DIALOGUE WITH THE RELIGIOUS PAST

WILLEMIEN OTTEN

Canon, Culture, and Conversion

Augustine's early work the *Soliloquies* has played an important role throughout my scholarly career. Reading this work marked my first serious encounter with Augustine, and the work became the topic for what I still consider my most successful graduate student paper, written at the University of Toronto for a classics seminar taught by John Rist in 1983-84.[1] Ever since I have kept a remarkable fondness for this work, even though it is often relegated to the category of Augustine's early Neoplatonic writings and its Christian identity sometimes questioned. In that respect the work is not unlike Boethius' *Consolation of Philosophy*, whose Christian character likewise does not jump out at its readers from every page.[2] Like that work it was translated by Alfred the Great into English already in the ninth century and survived the entire Middle Ages without much criticism. Still, in the modern age the *Soliloquies* never enjoyed the same degree of attention, overshadowed as it has been by Augustine's own superior follow-up, the prayer-like *Confessions*.[3]

---

1 At the time of this seminar Rist was working on his book *Augustine. Ancient Thought Baptized* (Cambridge: Cambridge University Press, 1996). My Dutch article "Het 'redelijk' geheim van Augustinus' vroege dialoog, de *Soliloquia*," in H.J. Lam, P.J. Vergunst, and L. Wüllschleger, eds., *Kerk rond het heilgeheim. Opstellen aangeboden aan prof.dr. A. de Reuver* (Zoetermeer: Boekencentrum, 2007), 36-49, goes back to work done initially for that paper.

2 See the classic and still interesting study by Edward K. Rand, *Founders of the Middle Ages* (Cambridge, MA: Harvard University Press, 1928), 85-135.

3 For the influence of Augustine's *Soliloquies* followed by his *Confessions* in the culture of the western Middle Ages and the Renaissance, see Brian Stock, *Ethics Through Literature. Ascetic and Aesthetic Reading in Western Culture. The Menahem Stern Jerusalem Lectures* (Hanover and London: University Press of New England, 2007), 1-46 ("The Reader's Dilemma") and 47-92 ("The Ascetic Reader"). Stock's own work has consistently foregrounded the meditative, *Soliloquies*-like moment in Augustine's approach to reading and text; see his *Augustine the Reader. Meditation, Self-Knowledge, and the Ethics of Interpretation* (Cambridge, MA: Harvard University Press, 1996).

As if to remedy this neglect as well as to counter the criticism that Augustine was capable of writing something that would not be truly and thoroughly Christian, scholars like Carol Harrison have pointed out how Christian the work, and Augustine's early thought in general, really is.[4] Her take on Augustine forms an interesting contrast with the classic study by Henri-Irénée Marrou, *St Augustin et la fin de la culture antique*.[5] If we evaluate their respective approaches, it seems that for Harrison, Augustine's Christianity somehow needs to be purified from secular taints, or at least elevated above them, as if they detract from his iconic status as the patriarch of western Christianity. For Marrou, by contrast, Augustine's early dialogues show us a late-antique mind in action, keen on searching and investigating the truth even if he does not yet find what he is after. If the Christian nature of Augustine's truth troubles Marrou, it is not for any doctrinal content, but rather for its entailment of decline by the standards of ancient rhetorical culture. In the eyes of Marrou Augustine's works do not just echo but precipitate this decline, as if his personal embrace of Christianity put western culture on an irreversible course to a complete Christian takeover.

Rather than following in Harrison's footsteps and raking up the debate on the early Augustine or on Augustine's Platonism, which has recently been done by Phillip Cary to mixed results,[6] in this essay I want to pursue another line of argument. My aim is to ponder why contemporary scholars fixate on and feel such a need to define Augustine's Christian identity.[7]

---

4 See Carol Harrison, *Rethinking Augustine's Early Theology. An Argument for Continuity* (Oxford: Oxford University Press, 2006). In her discussion of the so-called two Augustines-controversy on pp. 15-19, she argues convincingly that there are good reasons not to separate the early Augustine from the late Augustine based solely on his watershed thinking about original sin and grace.

5 After publishing his doctoral thesis in 1938, Marrou published a *Retractatio* in 1949. I have used the edition of 1983 (Paris: Editions de Boccard, 1983), which is a reprint of the fourth edition of 1958 containing both texts.

6 See his trilogy *Augustine's Invention of the Inner Self: The Legacy of a Christian Platonist* (Oxford: Oxford University Press, 2000), followed by *Outward Signs: The Powerlessness of External Things in Augustine's Thought* (Oxford: Oxford University Press, 2008) and *Inner Grace: Augustine in the Traditions of Plato and Paul* (Oxford: Oxford University Press, 2008). While Cary rightly pays attention to Augustine's Platonism, his schematic reading of it undercuts the timeliness of his work.

7 Obviously the most important historical contribution in this regard is made by James J. O'Donnell, *Augustine: A New Biography* (New York: Harper Collins, 2005), who argues that Augustine (and other Fathers of the Church) invented Christianity in a way (pp. 190-202, esp. 194), wiping out indigenous North African Christianity in the process by rallying behind its Roman, papal form. But I also want to call attention to Paula Fredriksen's unexpected and rather explicit defense of Augustine's Christian view of Judaism; see her *Augustine and the Jews: A Christian Defense of Jews and Judaism* (New York: Doubleday, 2008).

As I oversee the scholarly landscape, the answer appears to lie in part in a kind of cultural gap that increasingly severs our contemporary understanding of past Christian culture from that culture as itself conceived and constructed as Christian in the past. Our contemporary understanding seems marked by a clear lack of knowledge about and interest in the specific solutions found in earlier, so-called Christian eras of our culture. It is almost as if for us these could somehow not be simultaneously cultural and Christian in an integrated way. In what follows I will draw on examples from both early-Christian and medieval culture, arguably among the most religious of historical eras in the West, to explain how I see this.[8]

While this gap has not always been there, it seems rapidly growing in recent decades. Not only do we find any notion of cultural Christianity frowned upon in the current toxic climate where increased secularization faces off with theological reconfessionalization, but the categories of culture and Christianity seem to have grown so alienated that they are almost by definition considered incompatible. This may explain why just a few years ago church historians and other religious professionals in the Netherlands felt it necessary to draft their own canon in addition to the canon that had already been put out by the official Committee for the Development of a Canon convened by the Dutch minister of education.[9] Elsewhere in this volume Piet de Rooy has sketched the genesis of that national canon and the misunderstandings that surrounded its function and purpose from the start.[10]

It is not only confessional voices that try to reassert themselves in our modern-day culture, which is increasingly perceived as non-religious, if not anti-Christian. There are also those who see our society's structural lack of religious appreciation as potentially undermining the values of

---

8 As I make this statement, I am not unaware that the idea of the Middle Ages as a Christian culture is to some extent a nineteenth-century ideology. On the historiography of the Middle Ages in the nineteenth century, see the contribution to this volume by Peter Raedts, "The Canonisation of the Medieval Past: England and the Continent Compared," pp. 147-64.

9 The Dutch canon as devised by the government committee chaired by Frits van Oostrom and published in 2006 contains fifty windows connected by fourteen so-called main lines of the canon. For an English explanation, see http://entoen.nu/en. In reaction to the perceived lack of attention for religion a number of Dutch (church) historians amended the canon. Soon after the magazine *Volzin* published a so-called relicanon (http://www.opinie-bladvolzin.nl/relicanon.html). A more extensive, published version of the twenty five windows of this relicanon can be found in: Willem van der Meiden, *Beeldenstormers en bruggenbouwers. Canon van de Nederlandse religiegeschiedenis* (Zoetermeer: Meinema, 2008).

10 See Piet de Rooy, "The Search for the Canon and the Problem of Body and Soul," pp. 119-25.

western politics and democracy that have made religious emancipation possible, including the emancipation from religion. This may explain why Hent de Vries, a well-known philosopher of religion whose work can hardly be aligned with that of the average Dutch church historian, has recently advocated a religious canon in various Dutch newspapers.[11] Obviously not content just to highlight church-historical events, episodes, or persons, he would want his canon to include foundational texts from all major religions, possibly atheism among them. Its purpose can best be described as the promotion of religious literacy, the continued access to which he deems necessary to defend western democratic values against a possible clash of civilizations.

A friend of western democracy myself, I doubt very much whether prescribing such a canon, even if doing so in sober fashion without evoking the utopian fallacy of a Thomas More or the Orwellian specter of Big Brother, can bring the entities of religion and culture in the West back together. However sympathetic I am towards the idea put forth by Job Cohen, current mayor of Amsterdam, that religion need not merely be seen as a source of distrust and fragmentation but can be a cohesive factor in society,[12] such cohesion can only come about if religious people fully contribute to the culture of the society in which they live and are educated. For that development to bear fruit, however, we need to operate on an idea of religion seen as integral to the culture of society, not a forensic addition to be embraced or shunned as society sees fit. Religion is like race, gender, and class: it is there, and as much as we can try to prevent discrimination, promote literacy, and generally heighten awareness, in the end we are unable to pass a verdict about whether it is to be seen as a good or a bad thing.

---

11 De Vries' plea for a religious canon was published in the Dutch newspaper *Trouw* of June 16, 2009. The point of such a canon for De Vries is clearly not normative, as was implied by the emendation of Van Oostroms' original canon by a group of (church) historians, but rather practical, as the canon aims to point out what a Dutch citizen at the beginning of the twenty-first century needs to know about religion. In that sense there is an interesting link with the practicality of Augustine's use of the liberal arts. On this, see Catherine Conybeare, "The Duty of a Teacher: Liminality and *disciplina* in Augustine's *De Ordine*," in Karla Pollmann and Mark Vessey, eds., *Augustine and the Disciplines. From Cassiciacum to Confessions* (Oxford: Oxford University Press, 2005), 49-65.

12 This is the view that Cohen first put forth in his famous Cleveringa-lecture, University of Leiden, 2002. See also Job Cohen, "Can a Minority Retain Its Identity in Law," in Hent de Vries and Lawrence E. Sullivan, eds., *Political Theologies. Public Religions in a Post-Secular World* (New York: Fordham University Press, 2006), 539-56.

Coming back to the study of Augustine now, a matter dear to Burcht Pranger in ways that far surpass my interest in the *Soliloquies*, I would like to revisit Marrou's question of how Augustine transformed ancient rhetorical culture, and link it to the problem of his Christian identity. As hinted above, I want to do so by using particular insights from the resulting product of this transformation, i.e., the culture of early Christianity and the Middle Ages, rather than taking off from ancient culture as Augustine's immutably fixed starting position. For while the notion that Augustine "baptized ancient thought," to quote the title of the wonderful book by John Rist,[13] may have been the path that Marrou initially set out to follow, as Augustine supplanted the truths of a fading ancient culture with revealed Christian wisdom (*sapientia*),[14] in the end, that is to say in the retractation which he–like Augustine–wrote to correct his earlier assessment, that is not what he considered Augustine's lasting accomplishment. Rather than being a failed Rembrandt, in Marrou's eyes Augustine had developed into a Picasso or Braque, a painter using an improvised new technique to project reality in ways that may have been at variance with the norms of his age but that captured its dynamic both with greater power and more precision than existing stylistic means.[15] It may not be irrelevant that Marrou wrote his retraction after the Second World War, which would have

---

13 See above n. 1.

14 Marrou does not think that Augustine's embrace of Christianity is at fault for the decline of ancient culture. See his *Retractatio*, 682: "Je ne vois pas qu'il y a eu, d'un point de vue épistémologique, régression, dimunition de qualité dans la culture chrétienne et spécialement dans celle d'Augustin; car enfin s'il a préféré la cosmogonie de la Génèse à celle du Timée (en fait c'est très précisément de cela qu'il s'agit), il n'a pas, ce faisant, abandonné une vision scientifique du monde pour une autre de caractère prélogique ou folklorique: il a choisi entre deux formes de « science », aussi étrangères l'une et l'autre à notre propre ideal, la grecque et l'orientale.....; méthodologiquement elles se valaient: saint Augustin a eu à choisir entre deux livres, entre deux autorités." It is interesting to contrast Marrou's subtlety with the sledgehammer approach of Charles Freeman, *The Closing of the Western Mind. The Rise and the Fall of Reason* (New York: Alfred Knopf, 2003), which is premised on the idea that the fourth and fifth centuries CE saw the triumph of faith and the end of scientific thinking, with Augustine in a leading role.

15 See Marrou, *Retractatio*, 665-66: "Reprocher au rhéteur Augustin « de ne pas savoir composer », c'est prétendre que Braque ou Picasso n'étaient pas capables de dessiner une guitare selon les lois de la perspective. Ces lois, ils les connaissent aussi bien que nous les connaissons; seulement elles n'ont plus pour nous la saveur, la richesse expressive qu'elles possédaient pour les contemporains de Mantegna: nos nerfs blasés exigent des effets moins attendus, des combinaisons plus nouvelles, et qui sentent moins l'école des Beaux-Arts."

given him a new view of western culture as not just about symmetry and balance, but with room for caricature and the grotesque.[16]

Yet Marrou's shift of position cannot be attributed to a recalibration of literary standards alone, as if one can just swap one painting technique for another. A contributing factor to why Marrou was able to gain a new appreciation of Augustine, despite the latter's sacrifice of his beloved ancient rhetorical standards, is because his analysis projects a sense of cultural continuity that prevented the decline of Augustine's age from becoming his leading question.[17] Such awareness of cultural continuity presupposes an openness to new repertoires of knowledge and new cultural goals. This may explain how it is that despite his attachment to classical standards Marrou yet understood why Augustine–in contrast to Jerome[18]–no longer regarded the survival of Christianity as exclusively dependent on the well being of the Roman Empire. In this concrete sense Marrou's Augustine ushers in the Middle Ages as much as he closes the book on antiquity.[19] Also, it is worth underscoring the enormous trust that is required on the part of the humanist scholar, in this case Marrou, to assume that such important enigmas in the history of culture can be solved merely by reflecting

---

16   While Marrou does not mention the war but rather the saturation with the esthetic scholasticism either of the beaux-arts or ancient literary composition, one cannot help but wonder whether it does not play a role in his re-evaluation of Augustine. The war is in the background of his *L'Ambivalence du temps de l'histoire chez Saint Augustin* (Montreal: Institut d'Études médiévales Albert le Grand, 1950), 32-33: "Comment pourrions-nous fermer les yeux sur ce qu'on pourrait appeler l'aspect sinistre de l'histoire? Elle n'est pas qu'une série d'heureuses réussites, de pas en avant sur la voie du triomphe: qui peut oublier de quel prix sont payées ses conquêtes? Tant de sang versé, de souffrances et d'horreurs. Il fallait aux philosophies issues de l'*Aufklärung* une belle dose d'aveuglement pour oublier tout ce passif."

17   See his implied opposition to the fact that his story would reflect the narrative of Gibbon's *Decline and Fall of the Roman Empire*, at *Retractatio*, 663ff.

18   See Peter Brown, *Augustine of Hippo. A Biography* (London: Faber and Faber, 1967), 287-298, on Augustine's reaction to the sack of Rome contrasted with, among others, Jerome's, with reference to the latter's *Ep.* 123.16: "If Rome can perish, what can be safe?" (cited at 289).

19   See Marrou, *Retractatio*, 663-77. Marrou does not state in so many words that Augustine was the first medieval author but he distances himself explicitly from earlier judgments about Augustine as a man of the dying and declining culture of late antiquity, viewing him more as starting something new. See also the conclusion of his *Retractatio*, 689: "La civilisation du Bas-Empire, telle qu'elle se réflète dans la culture d'Augustin est un organisme vigoureux, en pleine évolution; il pouvait avoir à connaître bien de vicissitudes, des hauts et des bas: rien ne le condamnait *a priori* à périr. Le titre auquel après bien des hesitations je m'étais arrêté [*Saint Augustin et la fin de la culture antique*] implique, dans son laconisme, une grave erreur de jugement: saint Augustin ne nous fait pas assister à la fin de la culture antique. Ou plutôt si, mais elle n'est pas chez lui en voie d'épuisement: elle est *déjà* devenue tout autre chose."

and ruminating upon them, without any attempt to forego discussion or resort to stereotypes and familiar imaging techniques.

In terms of canon and conversion, however, Marrou's problem was not whether Augustine would fall outside the canon, proportionate to his deviation from classical norms. The canon was not yet a problem for him and the importance of Augustine such that he towered unassailably above any known canon anyway. Marrou's problem was rather whether Augustine's oeuvre embodied the best or the worst, not of classical literature, but of literature *tout court*. It is evident that his judgment of Augustine in the end was positive. Yet it must have taken great moral courage for Marrou not only to revise his original position but, especially, to embrace a view of literature to which the religious component was intrinsic without thereby detracting from either its aesthetic value or its effective conveyance of truth.[20]

This may well be the best starting-point for any meaningful discussion on canon and religion then. If there is a canon, religion should be integrated with it, as I hold any attempts either to convert the canon or to have a religious canon in the end as self-defeating. In the first case one simply risks not achieving one's stated goal, while in the second one may well end up preaching only to the converted. Threatening the impending derailment of both scenarios, moreover, is the ever-lurking danger of the tail wagging the dog, which situation seems to occur when the meaning of canon becomes narrowed to a rule to be (mechanically) imposed, pushing out all reflection about the cultural construct that it–at least also–is.

Inverting History: On Theodulf, Augustine, and Abraham Lincoln

Rather than prescribing any canon, it seems more important to foster a sense of cultural continuity in education, of the kind Marrou seems still to have possessed. In terms of the religious past this would mean that one tries to avoid sharp breaks in appreciation between the different historical eras of western culture, as happens with the current overemphasis of the Enlightenment, which has inaugurated an irreversible parting of the ways

---

20 Although Marrou does not discuss this point as such, it seems an important aspect of the reign of classical culture that it was more philosophical than Christian.

between believers and non-believers.[21] If there is one fact that the various canons being drawn up today make clear collectively, it is that there is not much cultural continuity left, as the basic sense of trust once sustaining it has largely eroded. While this shines through, for example, in the fragmented and confessionally polarized nature of the academic study of religion in the Netherlands today, in the long run it may well be a problem haunting the humanities more broadly. To the extent that there is any material value to the current cascade of canons, we do best to cultivate them as a shorthand substitute for what decades ago–if we hark back to Marrou's intellectual and cultural openness–was still an active mindset. With that idea in mind, canons are in my view most valuable, that is, as long as they are drafted to open rather than close off any minds, as a way to inject the imagination back into our cultural discussions.

Let us use our imagination then, leaving the hard notion of a prescriptive canon behind, and turn to the soft notion of an active and open mind, one which is not adverse to the idea of cultural continuity by either despising or exaggerating the unique importance of one particular era. The advantage of embracing a supple sense of cultural continuity is that it allows for a vision of *longue durée*, of the kind demonstrated by Marrou when he made room for Augustine as in effect preparing the way for medieval culture. While long-term visions at first sight seem to invoke a relativist historiography, their result may actually be the reverse. On a deeper level a long-term vision can have two interlocking effects. On the one hand it allows us to approach history as made out of whole cloth, i.e., the whole cloth from which cultures are ultimately sewn and patched together, rather than forcing us to detect individual patterns without ever setting an eye on the resulting tapestry. On the other hand, and in a fundamental twist on standard historiography, long-term visions open us up to temporality, as they invite us to break free from the constraints of historical chronology altogether. While the fleeting nature of temporality may seem to undermine the fixed rhythm of chronology, in fact it anchors us deeper in reality by tying history to the present as the only realistic position from which historical judgments can and ought to be made.

---

21 In addition, the Enlightenment has radically changed the meaning of belief. See on this and on Schleiermacher's role in equating religion with feeling W. Otten, "Religion as *Exercitatio Mentis*: A Case for Theology as a Humanist Discipline," in Alasdair A. MacDonald, Zweder R.W.M. von Martels, and Jan R. Veenstra, eds., *Christian Humanism. Essays in Honour of Arjo Vanderjagt* (Leiden: Brill, 2009), 59-73. See also M.B. Pranger, "Religious Indifference. On the Nature of Medieval Christianity," in H. de Vries, ed., *Religion: Beyond a Concept* (New York: Fordham University Press, 2008), 513-23.

Rather than converting the canon, therefore, I favor that we entrust ourselves to a vision of *longue durée*. In various medieval authors, to an example of which I will now turn, such trust can result in a more creative approach to history, pushing us even to subvert or invert its sequential order as a more powerful and effective way to affirm it. Let me explain this with an interesting passage from the so-called *Opus Caroli* (formerly known as the *Libri Carolini*), commissioned by Charlemagne at the end of the eighth century.[22] In it the Spanish theologian Theodulf of Orleans refutes the image-worship of the Greeks, which the king had asked him to do and which thus defined his intellectual mission. In doing so Theodulf is prepared to launch the West for the first time ever into a position of leadership over the whole of Christianity.[23] Going to great lengths to explain why the Greek position on icon-worship is untenable, he repeats time and again how the Carolingians have the support of the entire Christian tradition, including the apostles and the Church Fathers.[24] The impact of his mantric statements reaches much further than a mere reiteration of the assertion that the Greek position is seriously mistaken. By condemning the moral depravity of the East, Theodulf substantially boosts the self-confidence of the West. In what may best be termed as a movement of *translatio ecclesiae*,[25] analogous to the notion of *translatio studii* as an accepted theorem of western cultural history[26]–one on which Marrou may

---

22 The text of the work is found in *Opus Caroli Regis Contra Synodum (Libri Carolini)*, ed. Ann Freeman with the cooperation of Paul Meyvaert, Monumenta Germaniae Historica [=MGH], Concilia, vol. 2, supplement 1 (Hannover: Hahnsche Buchhandlung, 1998), 97-558. A summary of the work's arguments can be found in Thomas F.X. Noble, *Images, Iconoclasm, and the Carolingians* (Philadelphia: University of Pennsylvania Press, 2009), 180-206.

23 For an analysis of Theodulf's rhetorical and theological strategy in the *Opus Caroli*, see W. Otten, "The Texture of Tradition: The Role of the Church Fathers in Carolingian Theology," in Irena Backus, ed., *The Reception of the Church Fathers in the West from the Carolingians to the Maurists* (Leiden: Brill, 1997), 3-51, esp. 9-24.

24 See Otten, "Texture of Tradition," 9-24. See also Noble, *Images, Iconoclasm, and the Carolingians*, 179.

25 See on this my article "Identiteit en triniteit: de controverse rond het *filioque*," in W. Otten and W.J. van Asselt, eds., *Kerk en conflict. Identiteitskwesties in de geschiedenis van het christendom* (Zoetermeer: Meinema, 2002), 37-54 passim. Noble's take on this is that the Carolingians indeed claimed to be in charge of the 'vertical' tradition, while in *Opus Caroli* IV.28 they also relaxed the criteria for horizontal unanimity to enable local, presumably western, synods to promote the catholic faith. See Noble, *Images, Iconoclasm, and the Carolingians*, 179-80.

26 See on this E. Jeauneau, "*Translatio studii*. The Transmission of Learning: A Gilsonian Theme," Gilson lecture, Pontifical Institute of Medieval Studies, Toronto, Canada, published under the same title (Toronto: Pontifical Institute of Mediaeval Studies, 1995), repr. in E. Jeauneau, "*Tendenda Vela.*" *Excursions littéraires et digressions philosophiques à travers le Moyen Âge* (Leuven: Brepols, 2007), 1-58.

invoke

well have tacitly relied for his view of Augustine-, the *Opus Caroli* shows us the Latin church finally coming into its own through the taking of theological control. Theodulf's strategy in executing his *translatio ecclesiae* is to make the wavering position of the Greeks–did they not favor icon worship before they were against it, only to switch positions again?–a *de facto* disqualification of their capacity to direct a unified church, which role should henceforth fall to the West. Once Theodulf has reached this conclusion, however, which seems to have animated his work from the start, it so permeates the rhetorical expression of his convictions that he is willing to sacrifice standard historical protocol to drive his point home.

A case in point is *Opus Caroli* II.16,[27] where Theodulf's moral condemnation of the Greeks pivots–not coincidentally–around the position of Augustine, whose support the Greeks had dared to evoke in defense of their iconolatry. In what amounts to an a-chronological but not thereby ahistorical refutation of the Greeks, and a very effective one at that, Theodulf crushes their appeal to Augustine whose authority he wants to claim and preserve for the West at all cost. In going about his goal he first sets up Scripture as the ultimate authority by citing Col. 1:12-15 in which Christ is depicted as the true *imago dei*, thereby disqualifying all material images. For Theodulf it is obvious that Augustine faithfully supports this scriptural position, which he assumes to be genuinely Pauline and puts in sharp contrast with the mere substitute image-cult of Greek icon-worship. Reversing historical chronology, Theodulf next summons Ambrose, a theological authority in his own right but writing decades *before* Augustine, to assist him in defending what he now labels the latter's 'middle position', which is theologically positioned between the truth of Scripture and Ambrose's own view.

> Say you then also, most holy Ambrose, what it is certain to think about this image. Defend blessed Augustine who through you, with the help of God, was converted to the basics of the faith, and whom you now see unjustly accused by the worshippers of images. Give him a little support, so that he who through your intervention divested himself once from the error of he-

---

27 See *Opus Caroli* II.16 (pp. 263-67): "Quod non pro materialibus imaginibus ut illi aiunt beatus Augustinus dixerit: *Quid est imago Dei, nisi vultus Dei, in quo signatus est populus Dei?*"

retical doctrine may now be divested from the weight of such a great of-fense.[28]

Augustine's avowed middle position between Scripture and Ambrose, while clearly out of step with chronological order, dovetails nicely with the *via media* which Theodulf claims the West generally to follow,[29] form-ing thus an appealing and solid alternative to the Greek extremes of both iconoclasm and iconolatry. With the *via media* shored up by Augustine's balanced position, and conveniently aligned with Charlemagne's politics of the *via regia*, Theodulf is ready to launch the new western theology of images as the only logical conclusion.[30] Central to it is the shift of em-phasis away from the materiality of icons and closer to a Christological-anthropological interpretation of the notion of image.

I have chosen to highlight the rhetorical ingenuity with which the Carolingians managed to forge cultural continuity (here with the biblical and patristic past) where none was readily available as a way to exhort us to muster our own resources and do likewise. Finding ways to create cultural continuities and connections is both a more effective and a more integral way of facing religion's declining cultural status without losing contact with its past than embracing a religious canon that will always be more 'separate than equal.'

Let me give an example how this might work by returning once again to Augustine, this time to his ecclesiology and his theology of empire, for an attempt at a modern connection. While contemporary scholars across a broad confessional spectrum and beyond have replaced the mechanics of his double-predestinarian grace with an openness towards his theory

---

28 See *Opus Caroli* II.16 (p. 265): "Dic itaque etiam tu, sanctissime Ambrosi, quid de hac imagine sentire te constet. Defende beatum Augustinum per te favente Deo ad fidei rudimenta conversum, quem vides nunc ab imaginum adoratoribus infauste criminatum. Prębe ei adminiculum, ut exuatur tanti criminis mole, qui quondam per te exutus est he-retici dogmatis errore." See Otten, "Texture of Tradition," 20, n. 49, on the dramatic appeal that Theodulf makes to Ambrose. Theodulf cites from Augustine's *De diversis quaestionibus* 74 (about the fact that the Father's generation of the Son is not a temporal one) and from Ambrose's *De fide ad Gratianum* I.7.49-50.

29 See the end of Theodulf's preface to the *Opus Caroli*, 102 and n. 28, where he quotes Is. 30:12 about walking in the way and not straying to the right or the left, and links this with the Carolingian principled view on images as the royal way (*via regia*). Apparently the connection between not straying from the path and the *via regia* predates Theodulf. Free-man also lists other biblical passages that may have led Theodulf to this connection (Hebr. 12:13, 2 Cor. 6:7, 1 Tim. 5:21). See also Otten, "Texture and Tradition," 12, n. 20.

30 Citing recent scholarship, Noble argues that Theodulf was not only aware of the Greek position but quite capable in refuting it, making him superior to his Byzantine col-leagues; see Noble, *Images, Iconoclasm, and the Carolingians*, 182-83.

of will and the moral life,[31] and are equally interested in Augustine as the author of authentic selfhood, it seems that no redemption can be found for Augustine's endorsement of a universal church, one that was not just coextensive with the Roman Empire but condoned the use of force when convenient. Elaine Pagels sees Augustine moving towards such unity at the expense not just of the doctrinal plurality of early Christianity, but also of its social diversity, with Gnostic believers and women targeted especially for submission and/or exclusion.[32] In a similar vein O'Donnell holds Augustine responsible for wiping out the indigenous Christianity of North Africa, if not North African Christianity *per se*.[33]

Less to counter these accusations than to continue an open discussion on Augustine as the theologian of empire,[34] I intend to follow a different path. I am guided in this by Barack Obama's frequent use of Abraham Lincoln as the model for pragmatic American statesmanship and his quite formative influence as he tries to overcome the partisan differences that riddle contemporary American politics. The antagonism between Democrats and Republicans has reached such extremes that it thwarts political progress on issues of national importance, ranging from healthcare to homeland security. This stalemate is not unlike the way in which the North and the South were facing off at the time of the Civil War, with the South threatening to break up the union, turning the United States in effect into two different countries (not counting Canada and Mexico) on a single continent. The foresight and shrewd maneuvering of Abraham Lincoln, who thereby prepared America for a leading role on the world stage in the next century, prevented this breakup. Because of this he is considered the patriarch of the nation in a way that no other president may ever

---

31   See on this especially James Wetzel's forthcoming *Augustine: A Guide for the Perplexed* (New York: Continuum, 2010); in ch. 1 Wetzel puts Augustine in conversation with Cicero on this issue. See also his earlier *Augustine and the Limits of Virtue* (Cambridge: Cambridge University Press, 1992).

32   See her classic *Adam, Eve, and the Serpent* (New York: Random House, 1988), esp. 98-126 (ch. 5: "The Politics of Paradise").

33   This is the price of Augustine's opposition to Donatism; see O'Donnell, *Augustine*, 209-243, with the telling chapter title "The Augustinian Putsch in Africa."

34   Obviously there is the issue that Augustine endorsed slavery, legitimated force against the Donatists under the gospel motto 'force them to go in' (*compelle intrare*; Luke 14:16-24 in Letter 173, written 411-14 to the Donatist priest Donatus), and theorized about just war. In twentieth-century debates the subject of Augustinian politics has been taken in many different, even contradictory directions, as can be seen by the studies of respectively Hannah Arendt, *Love and Saint Augustine* (1929; Chicago: University of Chicago Press, 1996); Jean Bethke Elshtain, *Augustine and the Limits of Politics* (Notre Dame: Notre Dame University Press, 1995); and Eric Gregory, *Politics and the Order of Love. An Augustinian Ethic of Democratic Citizenship* (Chicago: University of Chicago Press, 2009).

be. It is to that presidential status of national unity over bipartisan conflict that Obama also aspires.

As Lincoln would simply not tolerate secession, he steadfastly refused as president of the United States to let the South break away from the union, even though the country was a voluntary union of states. When he backed up his leadership position by proclaiming the emancipation of slaves on January 1, 1863, a sore point for the South whose identity was closely tied to slavery, he exacerbated the country's division that had already ignited the civil war. Having launched the Emancipation proclamation ostensibly as a military measure only, out of his authority as commander in chief so as not to infringe on the political sovereignty of the (southern) states, Lincoln was fully aware of its long-term political consequences. His proclamation was bound to demoralize the South, as it would conversely invigorate the North, where northern slaves could fight for their freedom alongside the whites who welcomed this political endorsement by the president of the union. That Lincoln meant his actions, however much causing turmoil and strife, to strengthen the quality of the union is best summed up in his Gettysburg address, in which he famously commemorated the dead on the battlefield of what was one of the worst battles in the Civil War.

According to Garry Wills' magnificent analysis in *Lincoln at Gettysburg*,[35] it is as if history contracts to a point here in the sense that with this little address of just over 200 words Lincoln changed the United States from a plural noun to a singular.[36] For in his address he consecrates a new concept of nation, one forever elevated above the alliance of individual states. According to Lincoln's view of the American nation, the living see themselves not just in 'vertical' continuity with their genealogical forebears (Southerners with Southerners, and Northerners with Northerners) but in 'horizontal' community with all their contemporary dead. This places a new burden on the entire nation that has to follow in their footsteps but also breathes enormous inclusive trust. Here is the end of the Gettysburg address where Lincoln makes that point:

> It is rather for us to be here dedicated to the great task remaining before us-
> that from these honored dead we take increased devotion to that cause for
> which they gave the last full measure of devotion-that we here highly resolve
> that these dead shall not have died in vain-that this nation, under God, shall

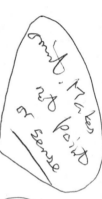

---

35 My account of this formative historical episode of American history relies heavily on Garry Wills, *Lincoln at Gettysburg. The Words That Remade America* (New York: Touchstone, 1992), esp. 121-47 ("Revolution in Thought").
36 See Wills, *Lincoln at Gettysburg*, 145.

have a new birth of freedom-and that government of the people, by the people, for the people, shall not perish from the earth.[37]

Lincoln's declaration of a new birth of freedom is a far distance from
Carolingian times, but one can ask if, in spirit, his claim is really so different from the confidence with which Alcuin pledges that the Carolingian school, however primitive, has come to replace the glory of the
Platonic academy.[38] There we had a medieval case of *translatio studii*, giving rise soon to the *translatio ecclesiae* which Theodulf effectively put in
place. What we witness in Lincoln is not just a new birth of freedom in
the United States but, given its wider ramifications, especially in the twentieth century, also the single-handed transference of power, or *translatio
imperii*,[39] from the European to the North American continent.

What remains intriguing when one compares Lincoln with Augustine,
however, is the contrast between the starkly divergent moral evaluations
of their univocal ambition for unity and universality. While Lincoln is
generally eulogized for the foresight with which he treated the separatism
of the Southern states as a case of insurrection,[40] even sanctioning the use
of force to reach his goal of a unified nation, Augustine is widely maligned
for his suppression of Donatism in favor of ecclesial unity and a universal
church.[41] It is almost as if Augustine had built up the western church sin-
gle-handedly into such a hegemony of stifling suppression over community that it simply could not fail to initiate its own undoing in modernity. I
cannot help but think that it is as much the contemporary aversion to the
institutional church, especially perhaps to Roman Catholicism, construed
as the opposite of religious pluralism, moral responsibility, and intellectual tolerance, that drives this vision not just of *longue* but of perennial
durée as it is the full-scale analysis of Augustine's ecclesiology.

---

37 I follow the final text of the address found in Wills, *Lincoln at Gettysburg*, 263.

38 See Otten, "Texture of Tradition," 3, n.1, with reference to Alcuin, Epistle 170 (MGH
Epistulae 4: 279). See also, Jeauneau, "*Translatio Studii*," 9-10 on the fact that Gilson, who
was the first to draw attention to this theme, assigned Alcuin an important place in the historical transmission of learning, even dedicating his famous *La philosophie au Moyen Âge* to
the memory of Alcuin of York, *praeceptor* of Gaul ("*Translatio Studii*," 14). Gilson continued
in Alcuin's footsteps by founding the Pontifical Institute of Mediaeval Studies in Toronto,
Canada, in 1929. Burcht Pranger studied there in 1969-70 and I followed suit in 1983-84.

39 On *translatio imperii*, see S. de Boer, "Welk dier was Rome? De *translatio imperii* en
de vroeg-christelijke interpretatie van Daniël 2 en 7," in S. de Boer and M.B. Pranger, eds.,
Saecula saeculorum. Opstellen aangeboden aan C.W. Mönnich (Amsterdam: Polak & Van Gennep, 1982), 98-141, and J. Le Goff, *La civilisation de l'Occident médiéval* (1977; Paris: Arthaud,
1984), 190-200. See the link between *translatio imperii* and *translatio studii* on p. 194.

40 Both Wills and Obama, each in their own way, form an interesting case in point.

41 Here the case is most forcefully made by O'Donnell (n. 5 above).

Dialogue as Discipline: Augustine and Eriugena

Leaving Augustine's ecclesiology aside for now, let us return to the dialogue of the *Soliloquies* and the problem of canon and conversion, approaching it this time from the medieval side. Two things seem to make
Augustine's *Soliloquies* particularly difficult for us to understand: the first
is that in it this torchbearer of Christianity does not carry his religion
on his sleeve, and the second that the dialogue seems somehow to have
failed, to the extent that Augustine does not reach his stated goal of attaining God. As to the first point, it has already been noted that the Christianity of this work was never questioned in the Middle Ages. Neither was
Boethius' *Consolation*. Leaving Augustine's Christian identity aside for a
moment, I want to shift focus to the latter point, i.e., the work's asserted
failure, which seems to have puzzled Marrou as well.[42] I will concentrate
on Augustine's use of genre, i.e., the Platonic dialogue-form which he
probably encountered through Cicero.

Its shortcomings notwithstanding there is something unique about
the *Soliloquies*, as a certain intimacy seems to interfere with its straight-
forward unfolding. Augustine did not dictate this work to his secretaries,
as he did the other Cassiciacum-dialogues, thus emphasizing its almost
private character.[43] After all, what is at stake in the text is not just the
measuring of scientific progress but the baring of Augustine's soul whose
potential failure to reach his goal he may have felt compelled to shield
from view. This hypothesis of an atmosphere of protective intimacy corresponds well with the argument Augustine gives us for calling it a *soliloquia*, a 'harsh' neologism to indicate what happens in this work. Reason,
who is Augustine's interlocutor in the work, explains how he adopted the
familiar format of a dialogue as most conducive to intellectual progress,
and so rejected writing a monologue. Cautious not to impose shame on a

---

42   See Marrou, *St Augustin et la fin de la culture antique*, 314-15. Marrou discusses
the *Soliloquies* in the context of a wider discussion of the liberal arts, especially dialectics,
in Augustine, seeing him in light of his arts-program effectively as the connecting link between Hellenistic philosophy and the ideals of medieval *paideia*. See Danuta R. Shanzer,
"Augustine's Disciplines. *Silent diutius Musae Varronis*?," in Pollmann and Vessey, eds., *Augustine and the Disciplines* (above n. 11), 69-112, for a more nuanced discussion of the arts'
transmission into the Middle Ages.

43   See Robin Lane Fox, "Augustine's *Soliloquies* and the Historian," in F. Young, M. Ed-
wards, and P. Parvis, eds., *Studia Patristica*, vol. 43: *Augustine, Other Latin Writers* (Leuven:
Peeters, 2006), 173-189, esp. 177. Lane Fox connects this private character to Augustine's
interest in finding wisdom.

discussion partner who might be proven wrong, Augustine opted for an unusual self-discussion without onlookers.[44]

Aside from his desire to ward off strange and impertinent glances, Augustine's choice for a soliloquy to keep an opponent from being proven wrong strikes me nevertheless as odd. For would the acting as one's own discussion partner and potentially failing at it, not cause *more* rather than *less* distress? Given that we are dealing with a constructed-*cum*-constructive dialogue here, Augustine has no one else but himself to blame for any perceived lack of progress. Such arguments may well lead us to reconsider the stated intimacy of the work, for are the *Soliloquies* really the best case for that? Remembering that the one choosing dialogue over monologue is not Augustine but Reason (*ratio*), we have perhaps all too easily assumed him to be Augustine's *alter ego*.[45] But does Augustine not state early on in the dialogue that he did not know where this voice came from: from inside or outside? Marrou rightly pointed out how Reason plays the same tricks here on Augustine that Augustine plays on his friends in the other *Cassiciacum*-dialogues,[46] which should make us careful not to interpret this work's supposed intimacy too quickly as a mere prequel to the *Confessions*.[47] Marrou's own conclusion, which I am inclined to follow, was to regard this dialogue as a case study of *exercitatio mentis*, a literal training of the mind, both of the reader and of the author. This may go far to explain the trial character that the work breathes throughout, allowing for false beginnings and incomplete endings, and disappointing most modern readers of Augustine in the process. Emphasizing the work's experimental character can also mitigate any perceived conflict between Augustine's Christian versus his Neoplatonic identity, which is sometimes taken as the work's main point. On a more literary note, it invites us to appreciate the craft

---

44 See *Solil.* II.7.14. The standard edition of the *Soliloquies* by W. Hoermann is found in *Corpus Scriptorum Ecclesiasticorum Latinorum* 89 (Vienna: Hölder-Pichler-Tempsky, 1986). I will henceforth refer to page numbers of text and translation in *Saint Augustine. Soliloquies and Immortality of the Soul*, with an introduction, translation and commentary by Gerard Watson (Warminster: Arris & Phillips, 1990), which contains the CSEL-text.

45 It is worth stressing that Augustine as the author of the dialogue has Reason making this comment, which to some extent does allow him to blame someone else. Neither Lane Fox, "Augustine's *Soliloquies* and the Historian," nor Peter Brown, *Augustine of Hippo*, 115-16, comment on this fact.

46 See Marrou, *St Augustin et la fin de la culture antique*, 314. Marrou calls the *Soliloquies* "un livre composé à tête reposée, où tout est disposé en fonction du lecteur," and contrasts it with *De immortalitate animae*, which he thinks Augustine wrote just for himself.

47 In that regard this article has made me change my mind on the relation between the *Soliloquies* and the *Confessions* compared to my earlier article "Het redelijk geheim van Augustinus' vroege dialoog de *Soliloquia*" (above n. 1).

and skill that Augustine applied to his writing, sensitizing us especially to the notion of dialogue as rooted in *disciplina*. Could not the awareness that his craft was to some extent unpolished be as plausible an explanation for Augustine's reticence in having others taking it down for him, as the vicarious prevention of any discussant's anticipated shame?[48]

While Marrou seized on the notion of *exercitatio mentis* to explain–and perhaps explain away–his frustration in reading the *Soliloquies*,[49] he was simultaneously operating on a fixed epistemological hierarchy, with any Augustinian project involving *scientia* relegated to second place behind works fostering the search for *sapientia*.[50] If one adopts Augustine's perspective in *On Christian Doctrine*, which is one of Marrou's key texts in interpreting him, there is indeed reason to accept such a hierarchy. Yet in my mind it is precisely the failure to distinguish clearly between *scientia* and *sapientia* that makes the *Soliloquies* so puzzling but also so interesting. After all, Augustine is not just involved in the quest for knowledge about God and the soul, which would be a bona fide 'scientific' (in the sense of *scientia*-like) project that any modern-day philosopher could assent to, but crosses over into the domain of the 'sapiential.'[51] This is the case, for example, when he exclaims in *Solil.* II.1.1: *Noverim me, noverim te* ('That I may know myself, that I may know you'),[52] which reminds us

---

48 The reason that Augustine wrote this dialogue down himself may then be only gradually, but not substantially different from why he did not finish his entire liberal arts project. This explanation would also correspond with the idea of wisdom as superior to science (see below n. 51). Augustine's project in the *Soliloquies*, with its insight into the role of the teacher, may in the end not have been that different from what happens in *De ordine* (see Conybeare, above n. 11) or in *De magistro*, in that it leads him to reconceptualize the meaning of teaching as rooted in exegesis and (self-)reflection in *On Christian Doctrine*.

49 I have followed this 'other' interpretation (which I admittedly did not think of as so different at the time) in Otten, "Religion as *Exercitatio Mentis*: A Case for Theology as a Humanist Discipline," 61-64 (as at n. 21). This article goes back to my address on the occasion of the *dies natalis* of Utrecht University on March 26, 2007, entitled "*Exercitatio mentis*: religie als denkoefening" (Utrecht: Utrecht University, 2007), 3-14. I am grateful to Burcht Pranger for supplying me with the title.

50 The difference between *scientia* and *sapientia* is not a case of simple hierarchy, however, as testified by Marrou, *St Augustin et la fin de la culture antique*, 357-467. While generally seeing Augustine holding *sapientia* in higher esteem than *scientia*, Marrou sees *On Christian Doctrine* with its emphasis on exegesis to some extent as replacing philosophical *sapientia* with a Christian form of *scientia*. This has much to do with his stress on the fact that the work lays out a cultural rather than an ecclesiastical program (381). See also Marrou's Appendix on *scientia* and *sapientia* in the language of Augustine, 561-69.

51 This also opens up an interesting comparison between the *Soliloquies* and the *Proslogion* of Anselm of Canterbury, where a prayer precedes a hyper-logical argument.

52 See Watson (transl.), *Solil.* II.1.1, 68-69. Interestingly, Augustine calls this exclamation explicitly a prayer: *Oratum est*.

more of the prayer-like language of the *Confessions* than of comparable early dialogues.[53] What the above example shows us is that Augustine's direction of thought in the dialogue does not follow any preconceived intellectual scheme, since he never marks his boundaries.

Rather than concluding to a hierarchy between lower (*scientia*) and higher (*sapientia*), therefore, what we witness instead is a kind of intuitive reciprocity between the outer (rational) quest and a more intimate, inner–more contemplative than mystical–quest, prompting a constant pendulum switch between the objective and the subjective voice, or the discursive and the reflective narrative. While Augustine does not demonstrate that he has a preconceived way of how the one ought to relate to the other, there is a clear sense that they mutually help to propel his inquiry. This becomes especially clear when in *Solil.* I.6.12-7.14 Augustine compares the quest for God with the mechanics of eyesight, explaining how one can strive to see the divine only once the eyes are purified.[54] Yet the actual mental ascent, however much the *Soliloquies* may try to prepare us for it, will only culminate in beatific vision after this life. In the end attaining the pinnacle depends solely on the gift of divine grace, which can be neither calculated nor counted on.

A more satisfactory, for complete, way to comment on the dialogue's inbuilt dynamic tensions perhaps is to see them as typical of what Pierre Hadot has called the idea of 'philosophy as a way of life,' which he regards as central to the development of ancient thought. Hadot refers to the fact that ancient interest in speculative thought was far from an idle matter, its progress measured carefully according to the degree that it allowed one to master the art of life, which was at the same time its ultimate goal.[55] While it may not be easy to see Augustine in the *Soliloquies* involved in any practical matters, at various times the dialogue gives us little clues about Augustine's wavering confidence that point in a personal, less abstract direc-

---

53 Cf. the passage about the restless heart (*cor inquietum*) that will only rest in God in *Conf.* 1.1.1 or the *sero te amavi* passage in *Conf.* 10.27.38 ('Late have I loved you, Beauty so old and so new').

54 See *Solil.* I.6.12-7.14 (trans. Watson, 40-45). See esp. I.6.12: "'Healthy eyes' (*oculi sani*) means a mind which is free from all stain of the body (*mens ab omni labe corporis pura*), that is, far removed and cleansed (*iam remota atque purgata*) from all longings for mortal things. And it is nothing other than faith (*fides*) which grants it that in the first place."

55 See Pierre Hadot, *Philosophy as a Way of Life. Spiritual Exercises from Socrates to Foucault*, ed. Arnold I. Davidson (Oxford: Blackwell Publishing, 1995), 47-144. See also his *The Present Alone is Our Happiness. Conversations with Jeannie Carlier and Arnold I. Davidson* (Stanford: Stanford University Press, 2009), 87-120.

tion.[56] Where the notion of philosophy as a way of life may be especially useful is in helping to explain all the frustrating detours that Augustine and Reason go through in their discussion, with the frustration serving both as a sign of discouragement and an implicit incentive to move on and try even harder.

It is here that the dialogical format in general, but the dialogue of the *Soliloquies* in particular, shows us how philosophy as a way of life became for Augustine a discipline to be practiced. By this I refer concretely to discipline as the mental *askēsis* or persistence to continue on a potentially circular path and to keep doing so even in the absence of a clear beacon to orient one's thought. What the *Soliloquies* demonstrates by having Augustine *not* achieve his goal of union with God is neither the more exegetical *disciplina* of signs and things, which he would come to elaborate in *De doctrina christiana*, nor the moral perseverance by which divine providence, masking as predestination, works its mysterious ways in human lives, which became the subject of his anti-Pelagian works. But it is *disciplina* nonetheless, the more heuristically so, the less it seems to be under the author's control.

To underline this last point I want to compare Augustine's *Soliloquies* with the medieval work *Periphyseon* ('On the Division of Nature') by John Scottus Eriugena, written around 864-866. My aim in doing so is to shed a different light on Augustine's early dialogue and the kind of *disciplina* which it involves on two counts. First, I want to make clear that the apparently aimless detours of the *Soliloquies* need not by definition be seen as thwarting intellectual progress, a view that prompted Marrou to continue Augustine's pessimism in this dialogue merely by observing it, but may represent a particular form of slow and meandering but not thereby ineffectual learning. In that sense the *Soliloquies* foreshadows the tradition of exegetical commentaries in which medieval monasteries would excel for centuries. We may add that it was this same *disciplina* of free-ranging thought, rooted in the liberal arts that, beginning with Anselm in the eleventh century, would suddenly unleash new intellectual projects, as demonstrated by the latter's proof for the existence of God or his analysis of the incarnation.[57] Serving as a catalyst for new and exciting perspectives, soon after also impacting the quadrivium, what had been an apparent standstill

---

56 See e.g. *Solil.* I.15.27 on Reason's divinely inspired role, somewhat unclear to himself, as he leads Augustine; *Solil.* I.15.30 where Reason admonishes Augustine to put his trust in God and *Solil.* II.1.1 where Reason even urges him to pray.

57 On Anselm, see M.B. Pranger, *The Artificiality of Christianity. Essays on the Poetics of Monasticism* (Stanford: Stanford University Press, 2003), 97-190.

for centuries now fed into the twelfth-century renaissance.[58] Insofar as with Eriugena we find ourselves back in the world of Carolingian culture and learning, it is worth pointing out that Eriugena's reasoning in the *Periphyseon* mirrors that of Theodulf's *Opus Caroli* both in scope and in stylistic flair, even though their subject matter was completely different.

The second count on which the *disciplina* of the *Soliloquies* may be fruitfully compared with Eriugena's *Periphyseon* has to do not with its lack of progress but with its failed outcome. In the end Augustine proves unable to overcome the limitations of his wooden dialogue and converse with God in the intimate and effective way of prayer that would mark the later *Confessions*. Matters start to look very differently, however, if we change the terms of this skewed and hence self-defeating comparison by seeing the *Soliloquies* not just as a work about the self, or about the self and God, but also about the cosmos, as a kind of natural extension of self from which it cannot be distinguished by hard and fast boundaries.[59] Drawing a comparison with the *Soliloquies* on this point can be very beneficial for the reading of the *Periphyseon* as well, to the extent that this work has suffered from the opposite problem in that it is generally read as a work about the universe alone without involving the self.[60] Yet there is a way in which Eriugena's cosmic detours can productively be read not just as revealing the voice of a hidden self, but as testing how far the exploration of self can actually be stretched.

The famous opening exchange between the Master (*Nutritor*) and the Student (*Alumnus*) may serve as an example of this stretching of self:

> M. Often as I *ponder and investigate*, to the best of my ability, with ever greater care the fact that the first and foremost division of all things that can either be *perceived by the mind or transcend its grasp* is into things that are and things that are not, a general name for all these things suggests itself which is ΦΥCIC in Greek or *natura* in Latin. Or do you have another opinion?
>
> S. No, I definitely agree. For when entering upon the path of reasoning, I also find that this is so.
>
> M. Is nature then a general name, as we have said, of all the things that are and that are not?

---

58 See W. Otten, *From Paradise to Paradigm. A Study of Twelfth-Century Humanism* (Leiden: Brill, 2004), 9-44 and 256-85, on the 'theologizing' dimension of this very renaissance and its ultimate demise.

59 This is another similarity to the *De ordine* and another difference with the *Confessions*, where the cosmos is much more the theater of God's glory and the reason to praise the divine majesty in a non-Manichaean way.

60 The exception is the idealist reading of Eriugena which foregrounds the mind but risks phasing out the reality of nature and the world. See below n. 62.

S. That is true. For nothing at all can occur *in our thoughts* that could fall outside this name.[61]

What is unique about the *Periphyseon*'s project as here introduced, and not unlike Augustine's approach in the *Soliloquies*, is that we are dealing with a balance between the discursive (the division of nature into being and non-being, based on what can be perceived by the mind or transcends it) and the reflective ('often when I ponder….'). Instead of being hamstrung by this division, however, as seems to be the problem with Augustine's more personalized dialogue in the *Soliloquies*, Eriugena seizes on this tension as his very point of departure, one that allows him to set up the five books of dialogue that will follow. The opening paragraph of the work shows him engaged in a kind of complex double backing, as he locks the medieval paradigm of *disciplina* into place by firmly wrapping the discursive inside of the reflective.

Instead of declaring Eriugena's division into being and non-being to be an expression of the author's idealist mind, however, which is the view of a fertile new strand of Eriugena-interpretations in the wake of the demise of the onto-theological synthesis of western culture,[62] I cannot help but see this so-called idealism preceded–and trumped–by the *Periphyseon*'s rhetorical opening phrase, one that is not less powerful because it is medieval.[63] In my view Eriugena's aim in insisting not just on the use of the human mind as his sole arbiter in mapping out the order of reality but in seeing the entire project built on this division ultimately as a trope or a mental exercise (*saepe mihi cogitanti….*) is to protect the self against idealism, not unlike how Augustine's *cogito* in *Solil.* II.1.1 and elsewhere pro-

---

61 See *Iohannis Scotti seu Eriugenae Periphyseon* I.441A, Corpus Christianorum Continuatio Mediaevalis 161, ed. E. Jeauneau (Turnhout: Brepols, 1996), 3: "N. *Saepe mihi cogitanti* diligentiusque quantum uires suppetunt *inquirenti* rerum omnium *quae uel animo percipi possunt uel intentionem eius superant* primam summamque diuisionem esse in ea quae sunt et in ea quae non sunt horum omnium generale uocabulum occurrit quod graece ΦΥCIC, latine uero natura uocitatur. An tibi aliter uidetur? A. Immo consentio. Nam et ego, *dum ratiocinandi uiam ingredior*, haec ita fieri reperio." The translation is taken from W. Otten, *The Anthropology of Johannes Scottus Eriugena* (Leiden: Brill, 1991), 7; the italics in the Latin and the English are mine.

62 This approach is exemplified by a range of studies contained in Stephen Gersh and Dermot Moran, eds., *Eriugena, Berkeley, and the Idealist Tradition* (Notre Dame: University of Notre Dame Press, 2006). See especially Dermot Moran, "*Spiritualis Incrassatio*: Eriugena's Intellectualist Immaterialism. Is It an Idealism?," 123-50.

63 In fact, the opening words *saepe mihi cogitanti* are a Ciceronian borrowing, as identified by Eriugena's first modern biographer M. Cappuyns. Jeauneau's edition lists *De oratore* I.1, *De diuinatione* II.1, and *De amicitia* VIII.1.

tects the latter against skepticism.[64] If we take the *Periphyseon*'s opening words to heart ('often when I ponder....'), it seems as if Eriugena needs this Ciceronian moment of concentration to help his readers prepare for the heavyweight metaphysical lifting that follows. For that reason he summons them from the start to treat his display of dialectics, metaphysics, and exegesis at least in part as casual conversation.

In my opinion the kind of casual conversation that the *Periphyseon* stands for, even if the dialogue is so reified at times that it is extremely difficult to retrieve what exactly is being discussed and even more why, is not unlike what more than a millennium later Stanley Cavell would come to detect especially in the thought of Ralph Waldo Emerson, namely the attempt to make philosophy inhabit the domain of the ordinary and see the final aim of one's thought as conveying an intimacy with existence itself.[65] Furthermore, it is precisely in its casualness that the *Periphyseon* seems more successful than Augustine's *Soliloquies* (or Boethius' *Consolation of Philosophy*)–both of which attempt to strike up a conversation but do not completely follow it through, hampered as they were by the weight of the artful and artificial prosopopoietic form–making this Carolingian work in some aspects suddenly edge closer to the *Confessions*.[66]

Canon, Conversion, and the Phenomenology of Dialogue: Marrou, Marion, and Cavell

If I see any value for the instrument of a canon at all–and despite some criticism I cannot say that I do not–in line with the above it is not to distribute privileged knowledge but to highlight and celebrate the impor-

---

64   See *Solil.* II.1.1 (ed. and transl. Watson, 68-69). Augustine states there that he knows that he thinks, whereupon Reason concludes: *Ergo verum est cogitare te.*

65   See Stanley Cavell, *The Senses of Walden. An Expanded Edition* (1972; Chicago: University of Chicago Press, 1981), 121-60, and especially *Emerson's Transcendental Etudes* (Stanford: Stanford University Press, 2003). I have elaborated the 'Cavellian' connection between Eriugena and Emerson in W. Otten, "Eriugena, Emerson, and the Poetics of Universal Nature," in R. Berchman and J. Finamore, eds., *Metaphysical Patterns in Platonism: Ancient, Medieval, Renaissance, and Modern Times* (New Orleans: University Press of the South, 2007), 147-63 and in "Nature as Religious Force in Eriugena and Emerson," in H. de Vries, ed., *Religion: Beyond a Concept*, 354-67 (as in n. 21).

66   A better way of explaining what I mean here is to say that, while the *Confessions* is indeed a different work altogether than the *Soliloquies*, the fact that the former lacks the dialogue form is not central to its changed outlook.

tance of knowledge that is already shared.[67] Accessing this shared knowledge and transmitting it will probably go the way of all sharing: it relies predominantly on voluntary acceptance and distribution. Hence there is no room for a 'canonized canon,' as canon and canonization are in my view mutually exclusive categories. Whereas cultural figures and developments can be canonized to underscore that they are deserving of constant study and recognition, inherent in the notion of canon is that it can never aspire to such transcendent status itself.[68] The current confusion about whether or not any Dutch canon should be prescribed in teaching makes clear how it is the canon itself that is the problem, with every attempt to fixate it generating its own discontent.

While doing without a canon altogether may allow us to avoid certain tensions, there is the counter-risk that a great many will not be able to reap its educational benefits, or that relevant knowledge will either be ignored or suppressed, as is the case with religious knowledge in the current secular climate. But even if advocating maximum breadth, one should not turn the canon into an elevated and lofty construct, thereby bestowing on it the ethereal quality of a Gothic cathedral with compartmentalized chambers on all levels. Canon has to do with community in an organic, not a prescriptive sense. Since communities are by nature time-bound, they are by definition always involved in *translatio studii*. While the concept of *translatio studii* originally appears to have had a strong spatial dimension,[69] I here want to particularly highlight its temporal and diachronic aspect, involving a process that is not only temporal in nature but also takes 'time' to work out. It may be self-evident at this point that more im-

---

67 The most recent classic formulation is Harold Bloom, *The Western Canon. The Books and School of the Ages* (New York: Riverhead, 1995). The most famous case where the role of the canon is mistakenly seen as normative is Allan Bloom, *The Closing of the American Mind. How Higher Education Has Failed Democracy and Impoverished the Souls of Today's Students* (New York: Simon and Schuster, 1987).

68 It is a misconception to assign such a transcendent status even to the canon of Scripture. One of the most puzzling experiences of my career in this regard was when as dean of the Utrecht University Faculty of Theology I was confronted by the church professors of the soon to be founded Dutch Protestant Theological University (PThU), refusing to accept the study of extra-canonical literature as part of a New Testament studies requirement. On the canon as the product of rather than the divine norm for the church, see Garry Wills, *Why I Am A Catholic* (New York: Mariner, 2003), 64: "Protestants who would later say that only the Bible should be trusted, not the church, forgot how the Bible was created *by* the church during this time of sifting, to reach apostolic consensus. The Bible was what the church (the six apostolic communities) said it was."

69 See Jeauneau's comments on the wanderings of Alcuin and other medieval masters, "*Translatio studii*," 5-13.

portant for me than what we include in or exclude from our canon(s)–and I reiterate that I regard neither the conversion of the canon, nor its compartmentalization, nor its canonization as viable options–is the fact that as a reflection of their dynamic cultural character any and all canons should invite us to engage in dialogue. By this I do not just mean to further contemporary debate but to point especially to the importance of a dialogue with the past, as I see the attempt to shuttle the past towards the future as integral to the principle of canon. But how ought such a dialogue with the past, including the religious past, be conducted?

In his recent book on Augustine,[70] Jean-Luc Marion takes what may be called Augustine's canonical status as the point of departure for phenomenological analysis, with his project as much a solid exposition of Augustine's thought as a promulgation of Marion's own contemporary theological project on self, love, and eroticism. In one sense this is ideally what can and should be done with many canonical figures, who can thus become valuable discussants as we sort through our need for cultural transformation in the present secular age. But why the need to turn anew to Augustine? Writing almost seventy-five years after Marrou, Marion has a rather different set of issues to grapple with concerning the relation between culture and catholicity. No longer worried about Augustine's deviation from classical rhetorical standards, Marion may have wanted to rescue Augustine's *Confessions*, as the central Augustinian text to which he will always come back, both from a narrow confessional-theological analysis and from a postmodern secular reading. What is unmistakably clear–even if no less legitimate for that–is that Augustine allows Marion to unfold his own theological project, under which he subsumes a broad set of philosophical issues associated with the malaise of modernity, all of which requiring strict analysis before western culture can move forward. Notwithstanding their differences, this is in the end where Marrou and Marion meet, as for both Augustine's canonical status contracts to his role as mediating truthful and trustworthy cultural vision.

But this is at the same time where Marrou and Marion part ways. Having already discussed Marrou's view at length, let me try to draw some conclusions from Marion's discussion of Augustine.[71] For Marion, the problem with Augustine is not the mediation of ancient culture but the

---

70 Jean-Luc Marion, *Au lieu de soi. L'approche de Saint Augustin* (Paris: Presses Universitaires de France, 2008).

71 See my review of Marion's book in the *Continental Philosophy Review*, 2010, DOI 10.1007/s11007-009-9117-x.

mediation of secular culture as it has turned away from God and as a consequence appears to be out of touch with self. This may be why Marion
identifies so strongly with Augustine's self-confrontation in *Conf.* IV.4.9:
Factus eram ipse mihi magna quaestio ("I have become a major problem
to myself"), a phrase which he considers to lie at the heart of the bishop's
thought in books I-X.[72] Zooming in on this phrase Marion applies it not
just to the situation of the fourth-century historical Augustine of Hippo
but seems to take it as a synecdoche for the predicament of western culture, which after the eclipse of traditional metaphysics and classical the-
ism finds itself in the throes of postmodernism. So far so good, as one can
only praise Marion's careful and original reading of Augustine's thought.
Yet however noteworthy, his interpretation does not constitute the kind
of reading that fosters dialogue with the religious past in the sense which
this essay has wanted to propagate, precisely because it appears to fore-
shorten discussion whereas the point of including Augustine in any canon
as I have laid out would be to open it up.

The result is that Augustine slips through the mazes of Marion's analytical net both from a historical viewpoint and from the perspective of
the phenomenology of dialogue. Let me conclude this article by discussing
both points. First, it is clear that Marion invites us along on his life's journey of reading Augustine in part to counter and cure our culture's secular-
ism. To bring the thought of the fourth-century bishop home to a wider
audience no longer familiar with the Christian tradition and beyond the
tradition of western metaphysics, Marion describes him as our utopian
contemporary,[73] for which the aforementioned phrase from *Conf.* IV.4.9:
Factus eram ipse mihi magna quaestio ("I have become a major problem
to myself") seems to serve as a guiding motto. But while the advantage of
seeing Augustine as such is that he shares our problems and we may thus
consult him for a solution, the inevitable consequence is that in the process he loses status as our *historical* conversation partner. This occurs when
Marion treats *factus eram ipse mihi magna quaestio*, however much uttered
as a biographical outcry by Augustine, not as the methodological equivalent of Eriugena's *saepe mihi cogitanti*, even if uttered far more passionately,
i.e., as an intellectual opening and a demonstration of his willingness to engage in dialogue with God, wherever that may lead him, but as its exact opposite, namely as a way to set Augustine on the privileged road of finding
rather than seeking God. In a few little instances Marion reveals that this is

---

72 See Marion, *Au lieu de soi*, 66.
73 See ibid., 28.

indeed his intention, thereby running the risk of turning a privileged road into an exclusive shortcut. Thus he concludes too quickly that the mysterious voice in the opening of the *Soliloquies* whose origin Augustine proclaimed not to know (*nescio*) can only be God's.[74] He sees the same *nescio* re-emerging in the famous conversion scene in *Conf.* VIII.12.29, where Augustine professes his ignorance as to whether the voice singing "pick up and read" (*tolle, lege*) is a boy's or a girl's.[75] Whatever the wealth of Marion's analysis, and his contrast between Descartes' and Augustine's *cogito* is a major accomplishment–but not surprisingly one from a historical rather than a utopian viewpoint–, I want to counsel contemporary interpreters like him not to lose sight of the historical otherness of Augustine as one extending also to his religion and to his (view of) God.[76]

In terms of a phenomenology of dialogue one may try to tackle the above problem differently by borrowing terms from John L. Austin's *How to Do Things with Words*, which I will read in tandem here with Stanley Cavell's perceptive interpretation and augmentation in his chapter "Performative and Passionate Utterance."[77] Upon reading Austin, the following picture of Augustine's search for God begins to emerge, which not only sheds more light on the difference between the Augustine of the *Confessions* and Eriugena, but even more on that between Marion's interpretation of Augustine and Augustine himself. It may be argued that in Austin's view both Augustine's *factus mihi magna quaestio* and Eriugena's *saepe mihi cogitanti* should be seen as so-called illocutionary acts, comparable to utterances like 'I promise' and 'I argue', whose distinguishing characteristic is that the consequence of the saying is contained in the very saying itself. That is indeed the move that I had in mind when first setting up the comparison between Augustine and Eriugena, ready as I was to see the Augustine of the *Soliloquies* as a straight precursor to the Augustine of the *Confessions*, which position this essay has since tried to modify,[78] and ready as I generally am to counsel against an emotive reading of premodern texts.

---

74 See ibid., 46 with reference to *Solil.* I.1.1 (transl. Watson, 23): "When I had been pondering many different things to myself for a long time…, there suddenly spoke to me –what was it? I myself or someone else, inside me or outside me? (this is the very thing I would love to know but don't (*nescio*)…."

75 See Marion, *Au lieu de soi*, 48, n. 2.

76 For a demonstration of Augustine's historical otherness, see Burcht Pranger's perceptive analysis of Augustinian emotion in "Tranen in het antieke christendom. Augustinus en de dood," in R.E.V. Stuip and C. Vellekoop, eds., *Emoties in de Middeleeuwen* (Hilversum: Verloren, 1998), 29-47.

77 Stanley Cavell, "Performative and Passionate Utterance," in *Philosophy the Day After Tomorrow* (Cambridge: Harvard University Press, 2005), 155-191 with reference to J.L. Austin, *How to Do Things with Words* (1962; Cambridge: Harvard University Press, 1975).

78 See above n. 48.

Having read Cavell's commentary on and addition to Austin, however, I think that another and more powerful reading is possible as well. For could it not be the case that for both Augustine and Eriugena the quoted statements have what Austin called a perlocutionary value, in his sense that what is entailed in the act, the consequences that inevitably follow it, are in fact indicated with the statements made? If we apply this notion of perlocutionary act to Eriugena's opening statement, his *saepe mihi cogitanti* would no longer just foreshadow the full scope of the division of nature, as I argued above, but truly contain it, with the motto and size of the work relating to each other as the center and the circumference of a circle. In the case of Augustine, reading the statement that he has become a problem to himself as a perlocutionary rather than an illocutionary act would not merely foreshadow his conversion in *Conf.* VIII, but contains the potential of actually bringing it about, comparable to how God's words in Genesis do not announce the birth of creation but realize it.

But that kind of interpretation, however rhetorically and theologically appealing, seems to carry a substantial risk in that it telescopes the levels of human and divine authorship in a way which Marion seems eager to embrace but I have felt myself keen to avoid. It is precisely on the point of this stalemate that Cavell's new and sophisticated interpretation of Austin's perlocutionary acts, continuing where the latter left off from a deep desire to make philosophical sense of so-called passionate utterances, seems to open up a potentially new avenue for reading Augustine's *Confessions*, one which avoids the kind of shortcut that I flagged in Marion's interpretation, while enabling the contemporary dialogue with the religious past without either usurping or unduly alienating that past.

Adding his own newly designed six parallel perlocutionary acts to the six illocutionary acts already mentioned by Austin, Cavell has completed a task that Austin never finished. But he adds a seventh act, to which I would like to draw attention here. This seventh perlocutionary act concerning passionate utterance runs as follows:

> You may contest my invitation to exchange, at any or all of the points marked by the list of conditions for the successful perlocutionary act, for example, deny that I have that standing with you, or question my consciousness of my passion, or dismiss the demand for the kind of response I seek, or ask to postpone it, or worse, I may or may not have further means of response. (We may understand such exchanges as instances of, or attempts at, moral education.)[79]

---

79 See Cavell, "Performative and passionate utterance," 182.

When Augustine utters his famous phrase *factus mihi magna quaestio*, he is in my view not offering us any shortcut, not even secretly, to the Christian God, but rather working out the relational dynamics which Cavell has subsumed here under the rubric of "I may or may not have further means of response." Cavell goes on to argue how passionate utterances deserve indeed a place as a subspecies of perlocutionary acts, improving on Austin and turning to the literature of Jane Austen's *Emma* for a telling example. Turning back to Augustine for a final time, it seems to me that much of what he is doing in the *Confessions*, his peculiar brand of dialogue as antiphonal discourse, can best be explained as the engagement in a kind of proto-perlocutionary acts, poised on the narrow ledge that separates *I may* from *I may not* in Cavell's phrase "I may or may not have a further means of response." For is it not true that when Augustine states that he has become a problem to himself, it is in the nature of that problem not that he find a solution but that he may or may not decide to involve God and open up a dialogue (with himself, with God, with his readers) in making his choice. In that sense this phrase entails indeed the outcome: not by bringing about a solution, let alone by dictating the content of what that solution might be, but by explicitly holding forth simultaneous possibilities. In other words, reading Augustine's passionate utterance "I have become a major problem to myself" as a proto-perlocutionary act underscores how the human condition is intensified rather than resolved by bringing divine grace into the conversation.

A further connection between the *Confessions* and the *Soliloquies* opens up now too, especially if we think back of Augustine's statement that he does not know whether the voice that speaks to him comes from within or without. As Cavell goes on to say in his attempt to move Austin beyond the identification of performance with ritual: "a passionate utterance is an invitation to improvisation in the disorders of desire."[80] Putting Augustine on too straight a path to the Catholic God sacrifices in my view the performative quality of his language, what Austin calls 'our word is our bond,' with accuracy, meaning the faithful expression of the inward situation, and morality as joint–not opposed–allies here,[81] in favor of a moralism and a confessionalism that are not only separable but ultimately risk drowning out Augustine's own voice as quintessentially human and as such by definition fragile. This is the essence of my problem with Marion's reading of this phrase, and sketches at the same time the contours of my alternative.

---

80 See ibid., 185.
81 See Austin, *How to Do Things with Words*, 9-10.

The reading of *factus mihi magna quaestio* which I have here presented also applies to the way in which I want to approach the canon as a performative instantiation of the phenomenology of dialogue, including the dialogue with the religious past. The canon should be taken as performative not in a ritualistic but in a passionate way, with the seat of passion not located in the emotive or devotional quality of the texts it contains but tied to their capacity to create an anti-morality as the only way to preserve the bond between accuracy and morality and refuse moralism.[82]

The above view could entail doing without or refusing to accept a canon altogether, for "I may or may not have further means of response." Rather than having *factus eram ipse mihi magna quaestio* misguide us as a question that demands an answer, perhaps the best advice both in the contemporary discussion on canon and conversion and in the dialogue with the religious past is to hear the words spoken by the child in Augustine's *Confessions*, whatever its sex, as a call to ensure that future generations continue to have educational access to the treasures of the religious past: *Tolle, lege* ("pick up and read"). Whatever canon can succeed in helping us to achieve that goal will have proved itself to be already a converted one.

---

82 See Cavell, "Performative and passionate utterance," 187 and 191.

BETWEEN PEDAGOGY AND DEMOCRACY:
ON CANONS AND AVERSION TO CONFORMITY IN
ORDINARY LANGUAGE PHILOSOPHY

ASJA SZAFRANIEC

> The particular disdain for official culture ... is itself an expression of democ-
> racy and commitment to it.
> *Stanley Cavell*

When does pedagogy end? I take this question to name the real stakes of
canon debates: where is the point at which we are self-reliant enough not
to need to take recourse to ready-made standards with which we are continuously presented? The contemporary debate about the canon is after
all only a small fragment of what has been over the ages one of the most
continuous preoccupations of human beings–seeking standards and seeking to transcend them–and it might gain in explicitness by placing itself in
this context. A canon, etymologically referring to a reed or a rod, is primarily an instrument of measurement (hence an instrument in support of
judgment) and the debate is thereby one of seeking, questioning and accepting or rejecting standards, conceived as conditions of understanding,
reading, thinking and of judgment: scientific, legal, religious, aesthetic
and ethical.

Burcht Pranger's work testifies to the desire to approach texts with
ever greater precision, without concessions to pre-given measuring tools,
even if this means having to acknowledge hesitation and admit the perplexities riddling the discourses of his major historical personas: Bernard
of Clairvaux, Anselm of Canterbury, Augustine of Hippo. He employs to
this end two strategies: on the one hand, relaxing the grip of periodization, suspending any standard temporal presuppositions, so as to uncover
the unique voice emitted by the given work; on the other hand, measuring
the resonances of thought across time: between Johannes Scottus Eriugena
and James Joyce; Augustine and John Henry Newman and Cavell; Pseudo-
Dionysius and Ignatius Loyola; Bernard of Clairvaux and Schleiermacher.
It is this double gesture of declining recourse to standards in our approaches to history that allowed him to discover and explore those most difficult
and problematic features of the early Christian manifestations of thought,

its central points of obscurity: the indeterminacy and artificiality of the "properly" religious, the unfathomability of the sincerity of faith, the indifference–and what he calls the "facelessness"–of devotional practices.

Another focus of Pranger's work, closely related to this, is the question of the seriousness of texts, their being meant by the author, the author's taking responsibility for them–all ways of referring us to some core property that would guarantee that the sound they emit from the distant past comes from trustworthy sources. Significantly, Pranger qualifies this core property as "unfathomable," which is to say, unstandardizable, immeasurable (fathom, just like "canon," was originally a standard of measurement). This resistance to judgment at the heart of texts is one reason to be suspicious of canons. Another is a common intuition, defended among others by Nietzsche, that to give a work its due, both to find such a work and to judge it on its merit, one should not need a canon: a good ear should suffice. But then the ear itself becomes a standard of measurement and the problem of unfathomability returns: what is it about an ear that can be trusted?[1] Here the core of the canon debates reveals itself as responding to the problems of skepticism: if skepticism always returns to the formula of "how can we be sure that...", then in this particular case it takes the form of the question of how can we be sure that we know how to judge the work of others and how to judge our own judgment (how can we be sure that our judgments are transmittable, shareable). Then skepticism about canons is the skepticism about the precise interrelation of three sources of our criteria: inheritance (i.e., teaching, pedagogy), individual expression (the inner ear) and the critical evaluation in the public cultural space.

When we consider this, it becomes clear that Pranger's pursuit and strategies for realizing it bring with themselves the questioning of the canon in its very principle, as the problem of measuring, or in other words,

---

1 One might say, these texts are in themselves the sources (or the guardians) of their standards, and it is solely by surveying them that we find the measure against which they are to be read. The idea that each text contains an access to its own law was expressed by the readings of literature performed by Jacques Derrida, for example in his reading of Kafka's "Before the Law." On that account each literary work produces its own law, instantiates it by internal repetitions to be uncovered in the process of reading; it is those repetitions that present themselves to us as measurement instruments: they are so to speak the rhythms of perspective guiding the reader's eyes towards the horizon of its law. But even Derrida had to concede that no such intrinsic standard of judgment can exist in isolation, that always at least one other work is needed to confirm, co-sign it, so that we always have to begin with at least two works, a minimal canon. The idea of a canon as a set of points in a particular configuration replaces here the single work viewed as a unique Archimedean point of its own suspension.

the problem of being able to trust any pre-given constellation of points as a focus of approach, but perhaps equally of being able to trust one's own. In this his questions regard not only the canon debate but are also close to the concerns of that strain of philosophy associated with Ludwig Wittgenstein, J.L. Austin and, more recently, Stanley Cavell, which might arguably be called a philosophy of standards. There is something about Wittgenstein's work that reaches back to the classical Greek origins of not only philosophical but also artistic reflection, to the classical period, in which "canons govern practical activities such as building a temple, and artistic pursuits such as decorating it; contemplative pursuits such as moral philosophy, and early scientific accounts of the laws of nature."[2] It should suffice to evoke Wittgenstein's continuous preoccupation with the metaphor of a measuring rod (or the standard meter in Paris), including the formulation of his major ideas with help of that metaphor: the definition of propositions, systems of propositions and later language games as yardsticks (initially projected against reality, later, with language games, projected against one another).[3] Another case in point is Cavell's later attention to the established centers of the Western canon such as the Bible and Shakespeare, or to the equally canonical set of films of early Hollywood cinema, always accompanied by attention to notions of measurement, counting and re-counting. It is true that the meaning of canon in the earliest Greek thought gradually moved "from mensuration to evaluation,"[4] (and it is interesting to note that the shift of focus in Wittgenstein's work went, mutatis mutandis, in a similar direction–from problems of representation to problems of normativity) but the ordinary language philosophy does not want to forget the origins of the term: the yardstick metaphor (just as the staff of the Kouroo artist in Thoreau's final paragraphs of *Walden* and Cavell's reading of it) is applied to discuss practices, aesthetic and ethical norms *and* the perception of reality, similarly as it was done by Plato or Aristotle.

---

2 Jan Gorak, *The Making of the Modern Canon* (London: Athlone, 1991), 9.

3 Ludwig Wittgenstein, *Philosophical Remarks*, trans. Rush Rhees (Oxford: Basil Blackwell, 1975), 317: "I once wrote 'a proposition is laid like a yardstick against reality. Only the outermost tips of the graduation marks touch the object to be measured.' I should now prefer to say: a system of propositions is laid like a yardstick against reality. What I mean by this is: when I lay a yardstick against a spatial object, I apply all the graduation marks simultaneously."

4 Gorak, *The Making of the Modern Canon*, 10.

Relying on that strain of philosophy, John Gibson, in his "Reading for Life,"[5] argues that the value of literature resides in its offering a secure, unchangeable context for preservation of standards–from which one may conclude that the value of the literary canon resides in its gathering and protecting archives that in themselves contain another order of standards. Gibson bases his argument on the following remark by Wittgenstein:

> there is *one* thing, of which one can say neither that it is one metre long, nor that it is not one metre long, and that is the standard metre in Paris.–But this is, of course, not to ascribe any extraordinary property to it, but only to mark its peculiar role in the language-game of measuring with a metre-rule.–Let us imagine samples of colour being preserved in Paris like the standard metre. We define: "sepia" means the colour of the standard sepia which is there kept hermetically sealed. Then it will make no sense to say of this sample either that it is of this colour or that it is not. We can put it like this: This sample is an instrument of the language used in ascriptions of colour. In this language-game it is not something that is represented, but is an instrument of representation… It is a standard in our language game, something with which a comparison is made. And this may be an important observation, but it is nonetheless an observation concerning our language game–our method of representation.[6]

Gibson claims that our canon of literary works performs a function analogous to the Paris archive in which the standard meter is kept. In it we find preserved "Medea's madness, Othello's jealousy, Baldwin's depiction of a lynching" as well as standard representations of "love, suffering, exploitation or devotion,"[7] all of them "hermetically sealed" samples that function for us as instruments of representation rather than as representations themselves. Gibson's argument significantly extends the already wide scope of the yardstick metaphor in Wittgenstein with the consequence of becoming vulnerable to the question of the legitimacy of such an extension. As already mentioned, Wittgenstein himself extended its scope throughout his working career, assigning the status of "measuring rods" first to propositions, then to whole systems of them, still later to language games (suggesting that there is something like a canon of promising, and

---

5 John Gibson, "Reading for Life," in John Gibson and Wolfgang Huemer, eds., *The Literary Wittgenstein*, (London, Routledge: 2004), 109-124.

6 Ludwig Wittgenstein, *Philosophical Investigations*, trans. G.E.M. Anscombe (Oxford: Basil Blackwell, 1967), par. 50. Cf. also Cora Diamond, "How Long is the Standard Metre in Paris?" in Timothy G. McCarthy and Sean C. Stidd, eds., *Wittgenstein in America* (Oxford: Clarendon, 2001).

7 Gibson, "Reading for Life," 115, 121.

that this canon can be compared with the canon of joking, of apology, of excuses, of saying good-bye).[8] It is not certain that this permits extending this status to literary representations of, e.g., complex psychological concepts (Othello as the standard of jealousy). In particular, temporal problems arise: there is something questionable about the aligning of the status of devotion of a given literary character as a standard sample of such a human attitude in general, with the status of the standard meter in Paris. Is the meaning of "devotion" really set apart and preserved from change for centuries in the same way, or does it evolve with the way the "game" of devotion evolves? While the meaning (the grammar) of devotion may be "deposited" in a work of literature, it is far from clear that it assures this meaning's permanence in culture. Perhaps "jealousy" is still for us what it was for Othello, but surely questions can be raised about the permanence of, say, Homeric "hubris." (Perhaps a distinction could be made between "properly" psychological states like jealousy or madness and more codified forms of behavior like devotion. It might be argued that while the former share their expression with pain and so are not prone to evolve with time, this cannot be said about devotion. But even then the expression of pain may turn out not be free from a grammatical component.)

It is in the context of this question of the possibility of preserving the meaning of all words that have a life in our ordinary language "hermetically sealed," analogously to the "standard meter" and "sepia," that the question arises whether indeed, as Gibson puts it, Wittgenstein's remark on the standard meter in Paris offers a "totally demystified picture."[9] There is a strange undecidability here between a standard of measurement perceived as something that is set beyond the ordinary and the same standard being relentlessly chiseled by the ordinary. While the concepts of measurement conform to the former view of the canon (as hermetically sealed), it might be argued that the names of complex psychological concepts and the names of colors, like sepia are closer to the latter view (as

---

8 Ludwig Wittgenstein, *Philosophical Investigations*, par. 130-131: "Our clear and simple language-games are not preparatory studies for a future regimentation of language–as it were first approximations, ignoring friction and air-resistance. The language-games are rather set up as *objects of comparison* which are meant to throw light on the facts of our language by way not only of similarities, but also of dissimilarities. For we can avoid ineptness or emptiness in our assertions only be presenting the model as what it is, as an object of comparison–as, so to speak, a measuring-rod; not as a preconceived idea to which reality must correspond."

9 Gibson, "Reading for Life," 119.

a standard constantly chiseled by the ordinary).[10] Has our temptation to metaphysics been successfully appeased or exorcised here? Can our notion of the canon, whether it is a list of works or one particular work (as was the case with the sculptures by Polycleitus that became the canon of the beauty of the human body) or a sample of color or of a psychological state be presented, in view of the life of culture and of the flow of time, in a totally demystified way? (Of course, such a question must inevitably betray a metaphysician in the one who poses it, but then it is the advantage of Cavell's interpretation of Wittgenstein that metaphysics, like the condition of skepticism, is not there to be eradicated but to be lived.)

As Jan Gorak observes in his *Making of the Modern Canon*, many of the problems of the canon controversy should be traced back to the failure to acknowledge the specificity of distinct conceptions of a canon and the coexistence of a plurality of canons. Indeed, the controversy, when it started in the early eighties, was only superficially directed against any particular fault or penchant of the canon (western, white, male, etc.), and more profoundly against the idea of the canon as such, against the "canonical disposition"[11] and against the idea of the constancy of the canons, associated with Marcuse's thesis that "throughout the long history of art, and in spite of changes of taste, there is a standard which remains constant."[12] But it is not the intention of the present paper to repeat here Gorak's work, discussing the most prominent attitudes to the Western Canon in the last century (both those he takes to be endorsing it, in the work of Sir Ernst Gombrich and Northrop Frye, and those remaining critical towards it without rejecting it altogether, as Frank Kermode and Edward Said[13]). Rather, I choose to focus on the ambiguous attitude of certain thinkers towards the already mentioned "canonical disposition" in general, even while they do acknowledge the existence of both the multiple forms of canonicity (with at the one extreme canon conceived as simply a practical blueprint, and at the other as partaking in the realm of Platonic Ideas) and of the plurality of canons (aesthetic, moral, literary, philosophical, theological, etc.). Undeniably, the canon has been blamed many times for propagating ideologies and for being a tool of discrimination, with

---

10   In the latter case the canon's reshaping or adjustment is not due to some change in a given aspect of reality it represents but in the slow transformation of our grammar of colors.

11   Gorak, *The Making of Modern Canon*, 186.

12   Herbert Marcuse, *The Aesthetic Dimension: Towards a Critique of Marxist Aesthetics* (London: Macmillan, 1977), x.

13   Gorak, *The Making of Modern Canon*, 7.

its proneness to exclusions dictated by the discourses and institutions in power.[14] But more fundamentally, even before the critique of the canon motivated by the defense of variously conceived "otherness," the canon was vulnerable to criticism for reasons more Nietzschean (or Hegelian, or generally more romantic) in character: already from the thirties on one notes the emergence of writers such as Albert Cohen and Witold Gombrowicz who criticized its pedagogy of servitude, present in the very idea of the unquestionable worthiness of certain texts and authors and in fact present in the very idea of being instructed about worth *tout court*.[15] The canon would lead to (at least temporary) alienation of our right to proffer a judgment of value, hence of a vital part of our autonomy; in the worst case it would even encourage such alienation. At the same time, it was difficult to deny that we cannot do without canon and pedagogy. While various postmodernisms accepted the status quo of the necessity of such temporary alienation of autonomy they focused on denouncing the pervertibility of canon as an instrument. Recently again the notion of the impossibility to dismiss such an instrument has become more prominent, raising again the question of reconciling the obvious need to trust canons with that which, according to Cavell, expresses our commitment to nothing less than democracy, called by him, after Emerson, "aversion to conformity."

Let us return to Gibson's claim that Wittgenstein's notion of the standard meter, making it possible to understand a canon as a sample lifted out of the everyday world (the specificity of which consists only in the very fact of its being picked out, put aside, archived), offers a demystified picture. Indeed, the measuring instrument that is simply lifted from real life, like a mason's rule, has nothing mystifying about it. But then an analogy is proposed between its status of a sample and the similar status of the criteria to which our language games constantly appeal, suggesting that the latter are lifted from the ordinary in a similar fashion. This is the sense of

---

14   Jane Tompkins, *Sensational Designs: The Cultural work of American Fiction 1790-1860* (New York: Oxford University Press, 1985).

15   Gombrowicz's oeuvre was, from 1937 on, such a vitriolic and exemplary attack on the canon (in fact on any standards in general; and not only, as might be expected, on the easy targets like the standards adhered to by the bourgeoisie, or the pre-war ideals of education, and, precisely, on the sanctities of national literary canon, but also on the standards of "modernity" and–for Gombrowicz a separate category–those employed by the very dissidents themselves) that I was surprised to find it included in Bloom's *Western Canon*. Cf. Witold Gombrowicz, *Ferdydurke*, trans. Eric Mosbacher (London: Marion Boyars Publishers, 2005); Harold Bloom, *The Western Canon: The Books and School of the Ages* (New York: Harcourt, 1994), 558.

the canon to which Gibson appeals: just as when Pliny said of Polycleitus that he "made what artists call a canon, or model statue, from which they draw their artistic proportions, as from a sort of standard,"[16] Gibson says about Shakespeare that he provided us with a model of jealousy that became canonical and infused the whole western culture. Analogously, we might say that Augustine provides us with the model of confession and of conversion.

Should we wish to pursue this idea of the canonical works of literature as preserving for us the standards of the more complex entities of meaning to which we constantly refer, we need also to take into account Wittgenstein's claim that the language games are measuring rods to be compared with one another, hence to be measured *by* one another. Wittgenstein did not specify whether he had in mind types of language games or their occurrences. In the latter case the language game of confession as played by Augustine is liable to revision each time the game is played by someone else, say, Rousseau. This is a motif in Wittgenstein of which Stanley Cavell's work has derived the ultimate consequences: that our standards undergo a constant process of measuring and being measured in turn.[17] In view of this process, while a measuring rod with the length of one meter arguably can have a stable status, the complex cultural or psychological concepts cannot have it, or at least the degree to which they may have it is limited. Every single public utterance and every literary work may turn out to be the limiting or modifying case for a given standard. When it is used to measure, it is admittedly lifted out of reality, temporarily beyond questioning; but as soon as it is itself measured, put alongside another standard, it returns to reality and can be questioned again. Perhaps it is true that the measuring instrument that is lifted from real life has nothing mystifying about it; but our condition as readers, thinkers and authors of judgment, where the criteria at our disposal constantly oscillate between the condition of being the tool of criticism and its object, still remains, if not mystifying, then at least dizzying. It is my contention that the function

---

16 Pliny, *Natural History*, vol. 9 of 10, Loeb Classical Library, trans. H. Rackham (London: William Heinemann, 1961), 168-9 (translation modified).

17 I am not unaware of the distinction Cavell makes both between the notion of 'standards' and 'criteria' and, within the latter, between the ordinary and the Wittgensteinian notion of criteria. By connecting them all I give expression to the conviction of a (still unexplored) rapport existing between Wittgenstein's reflections focusing around the metaphor of the yardstick and his notion of the criterion. Cf. Stanley Cavell, "Criteria and Judgment," in Cavell, *The Claim of Reason. Wittgenstein, Skepticism, Morality and Tragedy* (Oxford: Oxford University Press, 1979), 3-37.

of the canon in ordinary language philosophy is continuously threatened by a resurgence of a certain temporal vertigo, hence, of metaphysics.

It is in my view as a result of having to deal with this dizzying condition of play between stability and dismantling of standards that a certain tension is ineradicable from ordinary language philosophy. This tension can be expressed in the following question: how to avoid bringing together two conflicting attitudes towards the self within this philosophy. On the one hand, the ordinary language philosophy endorses the Nietzschean (or Emersonian) perception of the self as the supreme measure of things and the origin of judgment supervening on any canon. In his "Aversive Thinking," for example, Cavell explicitly promotes aversion to canons as standards of judgment because the only reliable, valid and morally acceptable standard is the individual voice.[18] On the other hand, the very recourse to the ordinary, typical for that strain of philosophy, makes the self appear negligible in the vast play of existing grammars and conventions: especially when it comes to the issue of sincerity of intentions, the contingencies of the self are merely excuses, invalid in the public game of morality. It is enough to remember J.L. Austin's aversion to any reference to the inner self as the standard against which to measure the truth of intention or sincerity, with his credo, "my word is my bond" aimed to combat what Austin called "the metaphysics of excuses." Can the inner sense of judgment defended by Cavell via Nietzsche and Emerson be divorced from the inner ear for the truth of intention attacked by him together with Austin? Admittedly, Cavell does not follow Austin on this latter point but the very path he takes to avoid what he perceives as Austin's bondage to the performative consequences of the spoken word is illuminating.

In another of his texts, "The Politics of Interpretation," Cavell called Austin's way of dealing with his aversion to the conception of the inner as a standard of sincerity "a politics of superficiality, directed accordingly against what Austin would have seen as a politics of profundity and mystification."[19] It might then be said for the purposes of the present context that Austin was the thinker of an outward canon, of public standards: he embraced the guidance of "my word is my bond" as the "standard meter," against the mystifying idea of the primacy of the self. And the

---

18 Stanley Cavell, "Aversive Thinking; Emersonian Representations in Heidegger and Nietzsche," in *Conditions Handsome and Unhandsome* (Chicago: University of Chicago Press, 1990), 33-63.

19 Cavell recognized this politics of superficiality as "an element of what I understand the ordinary to be in ordinary language philosophy." See Stanley Cavell, *Themes Out of School: Effects and Causes* (Chicago: University of Chicago Press, 1984), 29.

choice, as Cavell underlined, was not ontological (the denial that there is something like the private inner self) but political (refusing to allow this private inner self to serve as an excuse). But this 'political' choice of approach makes the idea of the self as the supreme measure of things also seem merely political, politically opportune. Is this what our individuality boils down to, the fact that we live in democracy, the form of life relying formally on contributions of every individual?

As a result of this tension between two different heritages, Cavell has to find a resolution for those two recourses to the inner, one of which is deemed by him legitimate, the other illegitimate. His resolution is to broaden the scope of what Austin considered to be the "metaphysics of excuses" to all kinds of bondage to standards, both inner and outer: for Cavell, metaphysics (the mystification) is not in the inner as opposed to the outer (the unutterable privacy of the self), or in the outer as opposed to inner (the ideology, the form, the official canon), but in their very separation. Consequently, Cavell must question the separation between the politics of superficiality and the politics of profundity: the inner must express itself on the surface of our shared language, but this expression must remain open for future modifications–so that the inner and the superficial are shown to be intimately interconnected. It is for this reason that in his *Claim of Reason* he undertakes a reexamination of the idea that Wittgenstein criticizes the inner. "What gives the impression that Wittgenstein wishes to deny that the soul is private?"[20]

And yet, the uneasiness remains. At the end of the day, Cavell insists, with Austin and against Emerson and Nietzsche, that the politics of superficiality is "an element of what I understand the ordinary to be in ordinary language philosophy; "[21] while he also insists, against Austin, that such superficial adherence to visible standards leads to exchanging one kind of bondage for another, and (with Emerson this time) that "the *particular disdain for official culture* taken in Emerson and in Nietzsche ... *is itself an expression of democracy and commitment to it.*"[22] What weighs heavier, the praise of the canonical ordinary or the individualist call for disdain for official culture? What Cavell rejects, together with Austin–the private inner canon as an organ of judgment (metaphysics of excuses)–turns out to be surprisingly close to what he wants, with Emerson, to defend: the projection of the inner defined as pure aversion to all existing canons, to

---

20 Stanley Cavell, *The Claim of Reason*, 329.
21 Stanley Cavell, *Themes Out of School*, 29.
22 Stanley Cavell, *Conditions Handsome and Unhandsome*, 50 (emphasis mine).

the canonical disposition (the precondition of democracy). This tension becomes particularly palpable in the conjunction of Cavell's interest in democracy with his investment in the idea of pedagogy. And despite Cavell's insisting on the distinction between the phases of childhood, adolescence and adulthood in human life, his conception of philosophy as the "education of grown-ups" (Cavell's recent title *Pedagogical Letters on the Register of Moral Life* confirmed Hilary Putnam's characterization of Cavell's philosophy[23]) makes it clear that pedagogy cannot be seen as limited to a particular age group, that rather it must be seen as an integral part of human culture. The more so, since it is clear, also in Wittgenstein's work, that human culture, and hence also democracy, is not possible without untouchable standards–thereby that it depends on our ability to project and protect canons even while we contest them. Pedagogy requires an emulation of standards (we do not question the table of multiplication) while democracy relies on an aversion to standards.

This unresolved tension between pedagogy and democracy is ultimately the reason for Cavell's often stated propensity to speak without offering a final standard that he motivates by a 'pedagogical patience.' Cavell's intention here seems to be to seek primarily an acknowledgment concerning an agreement on criteria as grounding, in a decisive way, the possibility of our agreement in judgment. Since only via shared criteria is agreement in thesis possible, failing agreement in criteria, it would be absurd to seek agreement in judgment. "Belief is not enough. Either the suggestion penetrates past assessment and becomes part of the sensibility from which assessment proceeds, or it is philosophically useless."[24] But there must be an interdependence of criteria and judgments, since our criteria have not fallen from the sky–they are in turn dependent on agreement in judgments. We might say that criteria in Cavell function as sensible intuitions do in Kant: criteria without judgments are blind, judgments without criteria are empty.

While Cavell combats the separation of the domains of the private and the public as the sources of our normativity, he does separate between judgments and criteria, placing them, the reference to them, in two distinct temporal, or transcendental dimensions: when a judgment is proffered, the criteria are only mutely presupposed (we only ask about the

---

23   Cf. James Conant and Hilary Putnam, eds., *Realism with a Human Face* (Cambridge: Harvard University Press, 1990), lvii.

24   Stanley Cavell, *Must We Mean What We Say* (Cambridge: Cambridge University Press, 1976), 71.

criteria when something in the judgment fails); and in turn the influence of the given utterance on the criteria can only be *nachträglich*, formed on the condition of that judgment. Individual judgments and the criteria on which they are founded never function as measures of one another at the same moment. They always and endlessly refer to one another. If they seem to us to appear together, one should consider that in order for a judgment to be meaningfully questioned, the agreement in criteria it presupposes must be fixed: the criteria and the judgment cannot be questioned at the same time, just as the criteria cannot come to existence simultaneously with a single judgment. Wittgenstein's solution to this problem was similar: that of distributing the gestures of protecting and contesting of standards among different temporal or transcendental realities ("If there's no room here, there is room in another dimension"[25]). Nothing can be a standard and an object of judgment at the same time.

If we are to trust Wittgenstein's and Cavell's accounts of the interaction between standards and judgments, then the historical shifts in attitudes to canons are transcendentally motivated: they reflect the necessary oscillation between the perception of any canon as a tool for judging reality (its status of the tool makes it untouchable) and a set of texts that is an object of judgment. It is only in the second case that we will take the canon to be a tool for preserving orthodoxy. In the first case we will have to take it as it is.

But if metaphysics is defined as neither the inner as opposed to the outer nor the outer as opposed to the inner, but as their very separation itself, one might legitimately ask why the separation between two (temporal or transcendental) dimensions (one in which we are allowed to perceive standards as susceptible to judgment–hence no longer as standards but merely as the things measured–another one in which we are not allowed to do so), is less "metaphysical" than the criticized separation between two (social) dimensions of the inner and the outer. In both cases there is "room in another dimension." It might be argued that the stable separation is replaced in ordinary language philosophy by an unstable one, an oscillation between the two dimensions. (But then the separation in traditional metaphysics, say in Hegelian dialectics, is also one of oscillation.)

I have until now dealt with the problems of the critique of the "canonical disposition" in the name of individual emancipation of readers. In the concluding paragraph of this paper I'd like to address a possible response to this discussion. The major line of response from the defenders of the canon, the accusation that the canon's detractors represent a "school of

---

25 Wittgenstein, *Philosophical Investigations*, part II, xi (pp. 193-229).

resentment,"[26] presents the case differently. According to Harold Bloom, the critique of the canon does not promote individual emancipation but merely ventilates resentment in its classical Nietzschean version. It represents the revolt of the slaves and a slave system of values, solely based on the principle of negation. As Nietzsche puts it himself, the major feature of *ressentiment* is the "reversal of the evaluating glance ... in order to come about, slave morality first has to have an opposing, external world ... its action is based on reaction."[27] On Bloom's reading it is not the adherence to the canonical disposition that is slavish (in its emulation of the pre-given standards), but the (post-colonialist, feminist, etc.) arguments for the rejection of the canon. Bloom attempts to connect the idea of the canon precisely to that to which it was opposed, the individual emancipation: "the Canon, once we view it as the relation of an individual reader and writer to what has been preserved out of what has been written, and forget the canon as a list of books for required study, will be seen as identical with the literary Art of Memory, not with the religious sense of canon."[28] As a result Bloom can reverse the argument about standards–it is not the literary canon that is to be seen as a standard to be suspicious of but the various critical discourses against it–and propose a different perception of the detractors of the canon in terms of an image of resentment.

It seems at first sight that to mobilize Nietzsche in this way against the critics of the canon is fully legitimate and convincing: the really great works cannot be criticized by pointing out that they fail to be something they are not, in the way in Nietzsche that the eagle fails to represent the values of the lamb. But Cavell's "Aversive Thinking" employs Nietzsche (or rather Nietzsche's master, Emerson) for an argument precisely opposed to this one. The rejection of standards (aversive thinking) is not a sign of adherence to a "school of resentment," but a token of an activity that, as Cavell argues, characterizes democracy. On this reading it is precisely disdain for the canon that is a mark of democracy. Emerson gives proof of aversive thinking when he says, "every word they say chagrins us," and when he presents his own life and work as an alternative standard.

The question that haunts ordinary language philosophy is, when have we read enough, when have we absorbed standards sufficiently so as to

---

26 Harold Bloom, *The Western Canon*, 25ff.

27 Friedrich Nietzsche, *On the Genealogy of Morals*, I, 10. I quote from *The Nietzsche Reader*, ed. Keith Ansell Pearson (London: Blackwell, 2006), 400.

28 *The Western Canon*, 17. It should be noted that one of the characteristics of the spirit of resentment in Nietzsche was a prodigious memory.

be justified in pronouncing our aversion? There is a tension between, on the one hand, an anti-metaphysical (i.e., anti-authoritarian) rejection of canons (just like there are no beaux-arts, just paintings, so there cannot be canon, just works) and, on the other, the pedagogical, normative, political (not just expediency but) necessity of acknowledging the grounds we share.

ON THE SIGNIFICANCE OF DISAGREEMENT:
STANLEY CAVELL AND
ORDINARY LANGUAGE PHILOSOPHY

PAOLA MARRATI

One of Cavell's constant preoccupations is to address the sentiment often voiced by critics of ordinary language philosophy that its methods and its very inspiration are conservative in nature. Those who express such a concern or criticism see in Austin's analysis and in the procedures of Wittgenstein in the *Philosophical Investigations* the attempt to deny any relevance to the traditional practice of philosophy–with its sets of questions, problems, and specific terminology–in the name of nothing else, or nothing better, than the defense of common sense and of the supposed beliefs of ordinary people, that is to say in the last resort in the name of the blessing given to things as they are. As if the world, in its present state, were perfectly in order and no one–and particularly not philosophers–should feel entitled, let alone called upon, to raise the slightest objection about it. In other terms–which are not exactly those used by Cavell, but that strongly resonate, I believe, with his–this brand of criticism addressed to Austin and Wittgenstein sees in their methods the betrayal of what Plato considered the original vocation of philosophy: namely, the vocation to break with the power of opinions and the tyranny of *doxa* in favor of an altogether different conception, and practice, of knowledge.

To such a criticism Cavell answers along several different though related lines, without avoiding the question of what in Austin's and Wittgenstein's approach to philosophy creates the sense of a certain conservatism, and indeed produces the impression that they aim at a defense of 'ordinary beliefs'–of what others would call dominant opinions. One line of response consists in emphasizing that ordinary language philosophy rather than being a repudiation of philosophy is a revolution internal to it, a new way of thinking philosophically. Another line of response that Cavell finds particularly important highlights that the philosophy of the ordinary, when it comes to politics, leaves the question totally open of knowing whether what is at stake is the consent given to things as they are or, to the contrary, the need for a thorough criticism of culture and society.[1] The constant reference to the figure of Socrates is, I believe, yet another way for Cavell to foreground a vision of philosophy as a practice of knowledge and self-knowledge rooted in the moral and political realm of the city that is hardly compatible with any form of submission to the powers of the day, or of uncritical conformism.[2]

In the last instance, however, the most complete rejection Cavell offers of this kind of criticism of ordinary language philosophy is to be found in his own interpretation of what is at stake in Austin's and Wittgenstein's appeal to ordinary language. It is obviously impossible to discuss all these different threads in the present essay and in what follows I will limit myself to certain aspects of Cavell's understanding of ordinary language that can be found in *Must We Mean What We Say?* and in the *Claim of Reason*–the two works in which Cavell arguably lays out the general framework of his philosophy. I will particularly focus on Cavell's remarks about Kant's analysis of aesthetic judgments and on the connections he establishes with Wittgenstein's use in the *Philosophical Investigations* of the first person plural, of the 'we,' as the only source of authority for the elucidation of the grammar of our language. My hope is to clarify why the appeal to the ordinary in Cavell cannot be understood as a call for the acceptance of the present state of society, or as a demand for renouncing the critical task of philosophy.

1. The Universal Voice

In "Aesthetic Problems of Modern Philosophy," one of the essays collected in *Must We Mean What We Say?*, Cavell discusses what he finds most relevant in Kant's famous analysis of the nature of aesthetic judgments and draws some comparisons with the inspiration that guides ordinary language philosophy. In the *Critique of Judgment*, Kant singles out aesthetic judgments for being essentially *subjective* rather than logical or objective and thus for following their own specific rules. He further distinguishes between two kinds of aesthetic judgment: on the one hand, those that

---

1 See Stanley Cavell, *Must We Mean What We Say?* (Cambridge: Cambridge University Press, 1976), xviii, xxxix.

2 See ibid., 39-40. If the reference to Socrates expresses Cavell's own understanding of the task of philosophy more than it is an interpretation of Austin' and Wittgenstein's methods, it is nevertheless quite central to what he takes the appeal to ordinary language to be and mean.

concern what he calls the 'taste of sense' and deal with what we find pleasant and, on the other hand, those that concern 'the taste of reflection' by
which he means our assessments of beauty in the realms of nature and
art alike.[3] This distinction is important because it underlines that beauty,
for not being an intrinsic property of objects but a subjectively recognized
feature, is nevertheless more than what we happen to find pleasant and
thus opens the space for the specificity of conversations about the beautiful and the peculiar nature of judgments pertaining to it.

The irreducibility of beauty to the merely pleasant is expressed by the
fact that judgments of reflection, contrary to judgments of taste, postulate
the assent of everyone, demand general validity and universal agreement.
To say it in another way, when we claim the beauty of something, our
judgment is accompanied by the feeling or the belief that we are speaking–as Cavell has it–with a 'universal voice,' that what we express is or
should be the *sensus communis* of humans, and that this demand holds
regardless of the factual agreement of others.

Cavell is mainly interested in two aspects of Kant's position: first, he
aims at understanding the specific nature of the differences at stake and
of the analysis that foreground them; and, second, he gives considerable
attention to the notion of the universal voice (*sensus communis*) and to its
implications for a conception of reason at large. In his discussion of these
two points, Cavell develops a line of inquiry that explores a certain affinity
between Kant and the philosophy of ordinary language in general, and of
Wittgenstein in particular, that is decisive for his innovative interpretation
of the *Philosophical Investigations* as well as for his own understanding of
what is at stake for philosophy in taking ordinary language as its focus.
Let me begin with the first issue, that of the nature of the differences in
kinds of judgment, before turning to the question of the universal voice.

Rather than focusing on the most explicit assumptions of Kant's argument, Cavell carefully considers the logic of the examples Kant uses to develop the difference between what we judge pleasant, and are content if it
turns out that it pleases us only, and what we judge beautiful, for which,
in contrast, we require general assent. He notices that differences emerge
concerning the ways in which our conversations about these matters can
or cannot be pursued, and concerning the consequences that these cases
have for our relations to one another. Cavell quotes the following passage
from the *Critique of Judgment*:

---

3 Kant develops these points in sections 7 and 8 of *The Critique of Judgment*. From
now on I will refer to them respectively as judgment of taste and judgment of reflection.

...someone is quite content that if he says, 'Canary wine is pleasant,' another man may correct his expression and remind him that he ought to say, 'It is pleasant *to me*.' And this is the case not only as regard the taste of the tongue, the palate, and the throat, but for whatever is pleasant to anyone's eyes and ears...To strive here with the design of reproving as incorrect another's man judgment which is different from our own, as if the judgments were logically opposed, would be folly (...) The case is quite different with the beautiful. It would (on the contrary) be laughable if a man who imagined anything to his own taste thought to justify himself by saying: 'This object (...) is beautiful *for me*.' For it must not call it *beautiful* if it merely pleases him...[4]

What the examples show, in Cavell's view, is that using an expression like 'it is pleasant to me' makes perfect sense in certain contexts, but not in others, and that its 'correct' or 'incorrect' use is not a matter of factual rectitude or formal logic, but rather of the responses it provokes: it is a matter, as Kant writes, of saying something 'laughable' or 'foolish.' In order to further emphasize the internal coherence between the expressions we use in certain conversations and the emotional responses they cannot fail to produce, Cavell gives his own version of the Kantian examples and, significantly, adds a new one:

1.   A: Canary wine is pleasant
     B: How can you say that? It tastes like canary droppings.
     A: Well, I like it.
2.   A: He plays beautifully doesn't he?
     B: Yes; too beautifully. Beethoven is not Chopin.
Or he may answer:
     B: How can you say that? There was no line, no structure, no idea what the music was about. He's simply an impressive colorist.

[...]

3.   A: There is a goldfinch in the garden.
     B: How do you know?
     A: From the color of its head.
     B: But goldcrests also have heads that color.
     A: Well, *I* think it's a goldfinch (it's a goldfinch to me).[5]

What these fragments of possible conversations highlight is that, depending on the context, different argumentative patterns are required: they can unfold along a variety of lines, but they are not arbitrary as it is shown by the response that an inappropriate reply inevitably provokes. No one is going to seriously object to the fact that I like this wine and say so: no

---

4   Cavell, *Must We Mean What We Say?*, 90.
5   Ibid., 91-92.

matter how undrinkable you may find it, you are not going to write me off as a conversational partner; at most you will conclude that when it comes to wine I am hopeless. Things are different with the judgment of a musical performance: your arguments are pertinent and if I don't answer them with equally pertinent remarks then I exclude myself–at least for the time being–from the realm of conversation about music. Simply replying 'Well, I liked it' is not a way of continuing the argument but of withdrawing from it. And things are different still with the example of the goldfinch: in this case, claiming that 'it is a goldfinch *to me*' is not just a retreat from a conversation that I may be unable or unwilling to pursue (as with Beethoven), but expresses a lack of knowledge about knowledge itself. Knowing what something is, identifying objects, is by necessity a shared enterprise: knowledge by identification cannot be 'for me' only, and if you say that it is, the inevitable outcome is that I can no longer understand you. Cavell insists on the fact that what we say has consequences that are not arbitrary:

> This ['It is a goldfinch to me'] is no longer a feeble rejoinder, a retreat to per
> sonal opinion: and the price that would be paid here is not, as it would be in
> the former case, that he is not very articulate, or not discriminating, or has
> perverse tastes: the price here is that he is either mad, or doesn't know what
> the word 'know' means, or is in some other ways unintelligible to us. That is,
> we *rule him out* as a competent interlocutor in matters of knowledge (about
> birds?): whatever is going on, he *doesn't* know there is a goldfinch in the gar
> den, whatever else he thinks he 'knows.' But we do not, at least not with the
> same flatness and good consciousness, and not with the same consequences,
> rule out the person who liked the performance of Beethoven [...]. [6]

If we can distinguish different kinds of judgment, it is because both the patterns of argumentation and the affective reactions that accompany them are neither interchangeable nor arbitrary. We see, as Kant did, the necessity that underlies them. But what kind of necessity is this? Traditionally, philosophy recognizes necessity in the domain of logic, but most philosophers, particularly in the positivist tradition, would strongly object to granting logical status to arguments such as the ones in question on the grounds that they show no formal rigor and carry strong emotional weight.[7] The realm of feelings and affects, and of the conversations that

---

6 Ibid., 92.
7 In this essay Cavell is explicitly addressing the divide in analytic philosophy between positivist and post-positivist stances, but his remarks are pertinent beyond that specific context.

express these subjective responses, seems to belong to psychology rather than to logic. As Cavell underlines, however, the traditional conception of psychology knows nothing about necessity, as if the life of the soul would be almost by definition the domain of the contingent. Hence, philosophers inspired by the analysis of ordinary language, Cavell argues, resist the idea that the differences in types of judgment here described are merely psychological.

The traditional alternative between logic and psychology thus seems to fall short of providing a convincing account of 'what we say when,' and of the 'price' attached to our words, of the consequences our words bring about. But if this is case, it is because of assumptions about both logic and psychology that, in Cavell's view, need to be called into question. Namely, the assumptions that psychology knows no necessity and the assumption that logic as such leads to agreement. Cavell remarks, and it is an important point, that most of the time one thinks of logic as a set of argumentative procedures that, if followed correctly by reasonable interlocutors, reach by necessity one and the same conclusion, as in a valid syllogism. But if such an understanding may be accurate for formal logic, it has the undesirable consequence of excluding from the realm of rationality domains like aesthetics, morality, and politics where–obviously–arguments are rarely conclusive. Conversely, it has the consequence of measuring the rationality of arguments by the possibility of agreement. In such a conception, there is no legitimate place for something like a reasonable disagreement: reason *entails* agreement, and the lack thereof is the sure sign of an impaired rationality, or of its absence altogether.[8]

The judgments we have discussed, however, do not fit such an alternative: on the one hand they display *some kind* of necessity–both in the argumentative patterns they follow and in the emotional responses they elicit–and cannot therefore be considered 'merely psychological'–while, on the other hand, they do not guarantee the agreement that a certain conception of logic deems necessary. Cavell suggests that we could call the differences in judging wine, music, birds, etc., logical differences, on the condition of disentangling in the concept of logic the idea of argumentative patterns from that of the final agreement they should lead us to. Alternatively, we could call them psychological, but on the condition of freeing psychology from the idea that in the life of the soul everything is possible. Either way, what truly matters is to recognize that in this domain

---

8 On this point see also, Stanley Cavell, *The Claim of Reason* (Oxford: Oxford University Press, 1979), 254.

there is a necessity that links together the 'logic' of arguments and the 'psychology' of emotions and that to understand the nature of this specific necessity we need to rethink logic, psychology, or both.

Kant who is the first to highlight all these aspects and their internal consistency calls the difference in question 'transcendental,' thus aiming at transforming the traditional concept of logic; Wittgenstein, Cavell further suggests, would have called it 'grammatical,' thus aiming at transforming our conception of psychology. In Cavell's account, Wittgenstein's effort in the *Philosophical Investigations* to elucidate the grammar and criteria of our language should indeed be understood as an attempt at undoing the 'psychologizing of psychology' in a gesture analogous to, and complementary to, Frege's and Husserl's attempts to undo the 'psychologizing of logic.'[9] In other words, grammar discloses the necessity that guides the application of our psychological and behavioral categories, the logic that sustains human actions and passions, but it equally shows that such a necessity lies in a human form of life and, as a consequence, has no metaphysical or transcendental foundation.[10] Cavell expresses this idea in a particularly clear manner in his seminal essay "Knowing and Acknowledging," also printed in *Must We Mean What We Say?*, where he addresses the question of what kind of force Wittgenstein's remarks–those, for instance, that concern the impossibility of having someone else's pain–carry. He suggests that while their force consists precisely in describing some general facts of human life, we should be careful not to think human nature itself as endowed with some metaphysical necessity:

> Why is 'being unable to feel another's sensation' not a circumstance? Because, I take it, it is not something that can coherently be imagined other than it is; it does not describe an inability of ours, but a general fact of (human) nature. (This is, one assumes, the force of saying 'the difference resides in the language game itself'.) But why can't a general fact of nature be thought of, accurately, as a circumstance?[11]

In other terms, if Wittgenstein's grammar is a 'depsychologizing of psychology,' it is because it uncovers the logic proper to human actions and passions while calling attention to the fact that such a logic has no absolute autonomy, but depends on the more or less permanent circumstances of a given form of life.

---

9 Cavell, *Must We Mean What We Say?*, 91.
10 Ibid., 188; Wittgenstein, *Philosophical Investigations* §583.
11 Cavell, *Must We Mean What We Say?*, 260.

Against the backdrop of such an understanding of the logic of our judgments, Cavell turns his attention to what is at stake in the Kantian idea of the universal voice. I would like to discuss now the convergence that Cavell sees between Kant's peculiar claim to universality and Wittgenstein's conception of grammar and criteria.

What makes judgments about beauty what they are is according to Kant (and to Cavell) precisely their claim to universality. When I make a judgment about the aesthetic value of an object, I speak in the first person, but I am not affirming something about myself: I am speaking on the contrary with the belief or the conviction that my voice is a universal one, that my judgment reflects yours. Such a demand for universality is a necessary aspect of judgments of reflection, a logical property–in the sense discussed–of what we mean when we say the beauty of things, regardless of the existence of any factual agreement or, we could also say, regardless of any achieved universality. The significance of Kant's remarks may be fully grasped, in Cavell's view, if one takes into account some consequences of this line of thought that often go unnoticed.

According to Cavell, the logic of Kant's claim to universality not only does not depend for its validity on the fact of some actual agreement, but further implies that the very *possibility* of agreement *should not* be taken for granted. All the patterns of argument proper to aesthetic conversations presuppose precisely the *uncertainty* about the agreement, hence the need to justify and articulate our sense of beauty as we do in art criticism, or simply our search for the right words to express to ourselves and to one another the beauty of things. If agreement were necessary, in principle if not in fact, there would be no need for words to convey the relevance of our judgments, and no such a thing as the realm of 'aesthetic reason.'

Let us imagine, Cavell suggests, that there would indeed be universal consensus about the value of a specific object: such a factual agreement would not dispense with the need to make our aesthetic judgments intelligible, to pursue our conversation on beauty according to its own logic, which is one that calls for agreement precisely because it knows that nothing can guarantee its existence.

For Cavell, this is exactly what Kant means when he affirms that reflective judgments are essentially *subjective*, that is to say that their specific rationality appears in the quest for a universality that is not given either in principle or in fact. Or, to put it another way, the heart of the matter is that the universal voice *is and remains a singular voice*: mine, or yours, in the pursuit of the possibility of a shared conversation. This bring us to a crucial point of Cavell's philosophy, namely, his idea that subjectivity neither can nor should be erased from the space of reason, contrary to what he sees as the unfortunate effort of a dominant strand in modern philosophy to get rid of the subject altogether.

What Kant highlights for aesthetics judgments thus has, for Cavell, broader consequences and should bring us to acknowledge that if we are guided by the desire for agreement, disagreement has nothing intrinsically irrational about it: it is not necessarily the result of prejudice or error, it is not the fatal outcome of passions that mislead us. Rather, it is a constitutive possibility of reason as such when it ventures in the regions of aesthetics, politics, and morality. In Cavell's philosophy, the wish and search for agreement or community cannot be separated from the acknowledgment of the importance of disagreement or, more precisely, from a conception of reason–and of the human–that does not make of consensus the ultimate foundation of rationality.

2. Wittgenstein's 'We'

Cavell sees an important connection between the Kantian notion of a universal voice and the voice that in the *Philosophical Investigations* elucidates the criteria or the grammar of what 'we' say. In the *Claim of Reason* Cavell gives considerable attention to what exactly Wittgenstein means by 'grammar' and 'criteria,' two related notions that sustain Wittgenstein's vision of language and of the task of philosophy, and therefore constitute the crucial point of any interpretation of his later work. I cannot in this context fully discuss Cavell's important analysis of the nature and function of criteria, but would like to briefly recall some aspects that are relevant for my present purpose.

Cavell takes as the starting point of his analysis a comparison between the ordinary use of the term criteria and the one Wittgenstein makes in the *Investigations*. The comparison highlights that, in both cases, criteria function as means by which certain persons or groups provide a 'kind of definition,' or show what 'count as' something, or what something 'consists in,' that is to say that, be it in ordinary language or in the *Investigations*, criteria are a set of specifications by means of which we can judge whether an object belongs to a certain category.[12] There are, however, im-

---

12 See Cavell, *The Claim of Reason*, 8-11. For an extensive discussion of criteria in Wittgenstein and Cavell, see Stephen Mulhall, *Stanley Cavell: Philosophy's Recounting of the Ordinary* (Oxford: Oxford University Press, 1994).

portant differences between ordinary criteria and Wittgenstein's when it comes to the objects they are applied to and to the source of authority that establishes them, and it is this second difference I would like to discuss in more detail.

Ordinary criteria are used to evaluate very specific objects and situations: what counts as a stable government for the American army, for instance, or what counts as neurotic behavior in children according to Anna Freud.[13] As Cavell remarks, to the specificity of such objects corresponds the specificity of the source of authority that determines the appropriate criteria of evaluation: not anyone is in the position to assess the stability of a foreign government or the play of a child, for which some specialized training or knowledge is required. In other words, in ordinary cases criteria are applied to objects whose status or ranking clearly require evaluation, and the point of establishing criteria is precisely to help to come to a judgment that is as rational and objective as possible. It is because the value of some objects is manifestly difficult to assess that we set up criteria. But Wittgenstein's objects are not of this kind at all: Wittgenstein appeals to criteria to determine things such as "whether someone has a toothache, is sitting on a chair, is of an opinion, whether it's raining."[14] The overall range of familiar activities, from reading to following a rule, from thinking to expecting someone, are the 'objects' that Wittgensteinian criteria are meant to determine.[15] Cavell calls Wittgenstein's objects 'generic' in order to better contrast them with the objects of ordinary criteria and emphasizes that to the difference in kinds of objects corresponds the difference in the source of authority.[16] Rather than being set up by a person or a group with specific competences, Wittgenstein's source of authority is always 'we,' criteria are always 'ours,' and nowhere in the *Investigations* is the appeal to 'what we say' supported or justified by some specific competence or specialized knowledge.

The question thus obviously arises of is the identity of 'us.' Wittgenstein seems to speak in the name of the human group as such, as a 'representative human,' but what gives him, and the philosopher of ordinary language in general, the right to voice what humans say, the right to take

---

13   See Cavell, *The Claim of Reason*, 8-9. Cavell uses a list of examples that ranges from criteria for the stability of a government set up by American officials to Anna Freud's evaluation of infantile neurosis, or to Radcliffe's criteria of excellence for freshman admissions.

14   See ibid., 14.

15   See ibid., 72-77.

16   It should be noticed that the distinction is not so much about different *kinds* of objects, but about different *problems* of knowledge that may arise depending on the context.

himself or herself as representative of humanity at large? As Cavell notices, the situation creates–understandably–a sense of dogmatism which
is only reinforced by the apparent normativity of the methods of ordinary
language philosophy that seem not only to describe what we say, but also
to dictate what we can or cannot, should or should not, say.[17]

For Cavell the charge of dogmatism would be absolutely accurate if
Wittgenstein would proceed by generalization from what *he* says to what
we all say, but that is not the case. If Wittgenstein describes what we say,
he is also constantly aware that someone else, a different human group, a
'tribe', may disagree and not say at all what we say. In other words, Wittgenstein's effort to elucidate our criteria cannot be dissociated from his
awareness that criteria may not be shared, that human beings may always
disagree and be an enigma to one another, as Cavell writes: "Disagreement
about the possibility of our criteria, or the possibility of disagreement, is
as fundamental a topic of the *Investigations* as the eliciting of criteria itself
is."[18]

The emphasis on disagreement rules out the idea that Wittgenstein
proceeds by generalization and shows rather that he is producing an *instance*, a sample, of what we say. In Cavell's reading, rather than describing
supposed norms, Wittgenstein invites us to see whether we have the same
sample, whether we do indeed say what he says, or can accept what he
says as a meaningful projection of what we say. But when the invitation
cannot be followed, when criteria are not shared, the consequence is that
there is no 'us', that I cannot speak for you or you for me, at least not yet.
This need for an invitation and the constant possibility of its failure show
that the only source of authority for criteria is ourselves, each and everyone of us, or, to put it another way, that the grammar of our language has
no external foundation:

> We learn and teach words in certain contexts, and then we are expected and
> expect others, to be able to project them in further contexts. Nothing insures
> that this projection will take place (in particular, not the grasping of univer-
> sals nor the grasping of books of rules), just as nothing insures that we will
> make, and understand, the same projections. That on the whole we do is a
> matter of our sharing routes of interest and feeling, modes of response, sens-
> es of humor and of significance and of fulfillment, of what is outrageous,
> of what is similar to what else, what a rebuke, what forgiveness, of when an
> utterance is an assertion, when an appeal, when an explanation–all the whirl
> of organism Wittgenstein calls "forms of life." Human speech and activity,

---

17 See Cavell, *The Claim of Reason*, 18.
18 Cavell, *The Claim of Reason*, 18.

sanity and community, rest upon nothing more, but nothing less, than this. It is a vision as simple as terrifying.[19]

Against the backdrop of this vision of language, Wittgenstein cannot be held accountable of any dogmatism: the 'we' he constantly uses in the *Investigations* is representative of humanity as one of its instances in a situation in which no instance is more authoritative than any other; rather than pretending to a false generalization, it exposes the 'simple and terrifying' fact that there may be no 'we.' In this sense, Cavell understands the methods of ordinary language philosophy in its appeal to 'what we say' as the search and wish for community, rather than the dogmatic affirmation of a 'human nature' that 'we' would supposedly represent better than any other 'tribe.' He, in fact, very much echoes Kant's voice, expressing its singularity precisely in the quest for universality:

> The philosophical appeal to what we say, and the search for our criteria on the basis of which we say what we say, are claims to community. And the claim to community is always a search for the basis upon which it can or has been established. I have nothing more to go on than my conviction, my sense that I make sense. It may prove to be the case that I am wrong, that my conviction isolates me, from all others, from myself. That will not be the same as a discovery that I am dogmatic or egomaniacal. The wish and search for community are the wish and search for reason.[20]

For Cavell, reason is defined by the search for community and society (in its attempt to avoid madness) and, as a consequence, community and society are not the foundation for the intersubjectivity of reason. The difference is crucial: in Cavell's reading of the *Investigations*, community or social conventions do not play the role previously attributed to metaphysical or transcendental categories as the guarantors of language and rationality; they do not replace the supposed universals of language with the equally supposed universals of communication.[21] No social norm, established value, or 'ordinary beliefs' can play the role of the judge in the Kantian tribunal of reason. Needless to say, Cavell is perfectly aware of the power of social norms to define what counts as 'reason' and 'normality' and of their power of exclusion–or worse–of those who 'disagree' or don't say what 'we' say, but his claim is that this is not the lesson to be drawn from the *Investigations* or from Wittgenstein's teaching in general.

---

19 Cavell, *Must We Mean What We Say?*, 52.

20 Cavell, *The Claim of Reason*, 20.

21 On this set of issues, see also "The Argument of the Ordinary. Scenes of Instructions in Wittgenstein and Kripke," in Stanley Cavell, *Condition Handsome and Unhandsome* (Chicago: Chicago University Press, 1990), 64-100.

In Cavell's view, the lesson to be learned from Wittgenstein's use of 'we' is quite different: it is that community and reason are more a task than a given, that the paths that lead to the one and the other have to be re-opened ever again, and that the search for reason cannot be pursued in the metaphysical isolation that skepticism presupposes and by which it is haunted.

It is particularly significant in this regard that Cavell introduces in his discussion of the 'we' as source of authority of Wittgensteinian criteria an excursus on what he considers to be the function of social contract theo-ries, particularly in Rousseau's version and later in Rawls'. I would like to turn to this discussion to make my conclusions.

3. Social Contract and Consent

One of the important questions raised by Wittgenstein's use of 'we' as the source of elucidation of criteria is the question of how to explain the fact that, if I am indeed a member of the group that establishes 'our' criteria, I may not truly know them, that I may need to elicit them over again, or that I may not even be aware of having taken part in such an enterprise. In other words, if criteria are ours, how does it come about that I do not or no longer know them, or no longer recognize them as mine? How does it come about that criteria need to be elucidated in the first place? Phrased in such a way, the question is obviously reminiscent of one of the main problems of social contract theories, namely the problem of how to ex-plain the fact that if consent is at the origin of society I may be unaware or forgetful of my consenting to it or may not even recognize myself as a member of (my) society.[22]

Cavell sees an answer to this problem, or rather a better way to state it, in the idea that the purpose of social contract theories is not to look for some mythical fact that would be at the origin of society–like ordinary language philosophy the purpose of which is not to collect some new facts about language–, but to provide instead some guidance for the kind of so-ciety we aim at creating and consider worth consenting to, as well as to address the question of those with whom are we in community. To put it another way, the idea of the social contract gives criteria about a specific notion of society: in the first place it recognizes the principle of consent

---

22 See Cavell, *The Claim of Reason*, 23-24. On the importance of the idea of the so-cial contract for Cavell's political philosophy, see Andrew Norris' forthcoming book with Stanford University Press entitled *Publicity and Partiality: Political Reflection in the Work of Stanley Cavell*.

itself, that is to say the principle of political equality; in the second place it underscores the fact that each member of society is not only responsible *to* it but also *for* it, because society is his or her own, and with membership comes responsibility.[23]

From such a perspective, the question raised by social contract theories has an essentially critical function that Cavell sums up along these lines: given that my responsibility is always already engaged in the society I live in, that I am compromised in it and by it, asking what I am consenting to is a way of evaluating whether my society in its current state, with its lot of injustice and inequality, is nevertheless still such as I should continue to consent to it.[24] Social contract theories thus aim at keeping the question open of what exactly I am consenting to, of the consequences of the renewal or withdrawal of my consent, and of those with whom I am in society.

The question of consent, therefore, like that of agreement in criteria, cannot be separated from the ever open possibility of dissent and disagreement. The exercise of citizenship, like the practice of reason, simultaneously demands the expression of my voice and the search for community. Neither singularity nor true companionship come, for Cavell, without the effort necessary to understand ourselves and one another, what our true needs and wishes are. Such efforts are pursued with the words we have, with our 'ordinary language,' if we take it to be, as Cavell does, not a specific set of the linguistic realm to the exclusion of others, but just the language we do in fact speak, and if we take language, as Cavell also does, to be necessarily intertwined with the world, the knowledge of the one always shaping the knowledge of the other and vice versa: "We learn language and learn the world together, they become elaborated and distorted together, and in the same places."[25]

It should not be surprising therefore to see the question of the 'we' as the source of authority for criteria to converge with that of the social contract: in one case as in the other what is ultimately at stake is a claim to community (and reason) that has no ground or justification outside the agreement we may reach in a form of life.

Likewise it should not be surprising to see a convergence between the task of philosophy as the critique of culture (one of the repeated defini-

---

23   Ibid., 23.
24   See also Cavell's essay on Rawls in *Cities of Words* (Cambridge: Harvard University Press, 2004), 169-170.
25   Cavell, *Must We Mean What We Say?*, 19.

tions of philosophy Cavell provides) and its clinical or therapeutic task as care of the self.[26] The part of the world and of language that is distorted needs to be addressed over again in ourselves and in society. Knowledge and self-knowledge cannot avoid each other in some domains, as the quest to express myself is hardly conceivable without the willingness to acknowledge the expression of others. What sustains my own voice, included in my solitude, in the essential separation that Cavell takes finitude to mean, is after all the hope of an eventual conversation. Conversely, what conversation can I hope to engage in if I do not even know my words, if I cannot mean what I say? The true aim of the procedures of ordinary language philosophy is to make us conscious of our words, hence, for Cavell, of our lives, and in this regard such an understanding of philosophy is revolutionary rather than conservative, because it renews in its own way a quest for truth that cannot be separated from the quest of bringing truth into this world:

> But then wherever there really is a love of wisdom–or call it the passion for truth–it is inherently, if usually ineffectively, revolutionary; because it is the same as a hatred of the falseness in one's character and of the needles and unnatural compromises in our institutions.[27]

Probably not everyone would agree with such an understanding of what a 'revolutionary' attitude is or means, but this only underlines the pertinence of Cavell's idea that much is at stake in our use of words and that the attention we should pay to them is the opposite of the inclination toward conformity.

---

26 See ibid., xix.
27 Ibid., xxxix.

FAST FORWARD, OR: THE THEOLOGICO-POLITICAL EVENT IN QUICK MOTION (MIRACLES, MEDIA, AND MULTITUDES IN ST. AUGUSTINE)

HENT DE VRIES

No better starting point than St. Augustine's views can be found to obtain a summary–albeit contradictory and evolving, exemplary as well as speculatively deeply appealing–understanding of the early and medieval Church's now exuberant, then more reluctant, but always extensive and intensive, dealings with miracles and marvels and the claims, true and false, that were made in their name by the faithful and imposters alike. More than St. Paul or any other of the Fathers of the Church, Augustine sets out the parameters for reconceiving the theology of miracles and miracle belief, together with their epistemological and moral, spiritual and ecclesial presuppositions and ramifications. In spite of his initial reluctance to give miracles and miracle belief their philosophical no less than theological or pastoral due, Augustine's final statements on the subject arguably remain the most important point of departure and overall frame of reference for all subsequent considerations of their force and signification, event and effect. From St. Thomas Aquinas through the Reformation, and from Blaise Pascal up to Ludwig Wittgenstein, but also in the writings of Alain Badiou no less than those of Jean-Luc Marion, to name just a few examples, the Augustinian legacy of conceptualizing miracles and miracle belief has left a lasting impact on the Western theological and philosophical imagination. It may even offer some of the most suggestive ingredients of any account of the contemporary postsecular world in which religion and media and, I would venture to add, miracles and special effects inform and transform the ways in which current affairs and especially political events present themselves in a variety of generalizing–universalizing, yet also equally intensifying and trivializing–ways.

In so-called everyday life, what is considered extraordinary is given ever newer opportunities to graft itself upon the ordinary, lifting it out of habitual patterns of perception and expectation. Yet in so doing, it exposes the everyday and the ordinary simultaneously–but also, with increasing intensity and at an exponentially growing scale and pace–to possible sublimity *and* banality, thus amplifying a risk that was always inherent in the proliferation or, more precisely, dissemination of religious notions and sensibilities, discourses and regimes. Paradoxically, the expansion and phenomenal success of the extraordinary in the ordinary implied a diminished, if remaining, significance of things–indeed, a becoming ordinary of the extraordinary–as well.

This paradoxical logic may surprise us, but it is exactly how the Western canon (and pretty much anything else of significance, elsewhere in the world) was won and, inevitably and immediately, lost again. No one among the Fathers of the Church seemed more acutely aware of this chance and risk–including its political scansion and reverberations–than Augustine. And this is precisely why his writings have remained a standing reference for contemporary political thinking or have regained more and more relevance in the political actuality of everyday as the inner contradictions of modern society and the so-called secular age have become more and more apparent.

While suspicious of the abundant expressions of popular religion such as magic and exorcism, healings and relics, Augustine entertains a complex relationship with the domain of what, traditionally, is conceived as the supernatural. It is this complicated relationship that I wish to bring out in a few broad strokes, mindful of the complexity of the matter and mostly concerned with three or four striking traits of his conception, namely the miracle belief's *publicness and publicity*, on the one hand, and the miracle's presumed *acceleration and fastforwarding* of natural processes and, hence, *special effect* on us, on the other. These are two motifs and motivations that, to my knowledge, have not yet found the attention they deserve.

Moreover, Augustine's argument also relies, thirdly, on a conception of *multitude* and *catholicity*–indeed, *universality* or *globality*–that is not without implications for the philosophical and theologico-political work that his writings continue to inspire and that, anachronistically speaking, they seem to have anticipated all along, not least in their nuanced dealing with and theorization of miracles, their strategic and pragmatic use and momentum, their political but also more generally persuasive and perlocutionary aspect.

A final, fourth, motif, not explicitly mentioned but deployed throughout his later thought on miracles, martyrs and healings, combines, as Peter Brown has suggested in his study of the lives of the saints, a figure of "inversed magnitudes"[1] to link a heavenly and earthly aspect of things (often fragmented objects, relics, and the like). In so doing, it enables what I would like to call a specimen of *counterfactual thinking* that at once liberates and burdens human agency–and, again, politics–in a truly innovative way. Swapping the minimal and the maximal, the particular and the general, singular and universal, the logic of the miracle and of miracle belief holds the key to our understanding of what (in modern terms) we call events, just as it allows us to unlock the contemporary reality and virtuality of so-called special effects (of visual and sensory shock and awe, absorption and immersion, spin and the political affect). Both operate on a less than fully conscious level according to a systematics and rhythm that the documented as well as immemorial archive of religious tradition–again, notably of miracles and miracle belief–is best equipped to make us see (hear, feel) and, indeed, analyze and think through.

As in the immense and infinite spaces of Augustine's *memoria* as well as in the infinite spaces within and without of which Pascal speaks no less suggestively, the religious archive of miracles and their testimony holds more in stock than is present, represented or presentable, at any given moment at time. Yet at each of its unique instantiations it makes the virtual totality–and, indeed, total social fact–of its resources and repository felt in the most acute and pressing of manners. As Wittgenstein may have intimated with so many words, religion's (or, for that matter, the miracle's) "essence" is the sheer ontological weight with which our human need and custom seems to continually call for these motifs' and motivations' reinstantiations, as if there were nothing outside of the very "metaphysics" that our language espouses whenever and wherever it "goes on a holiday" (that is to say, potentially anytime and anywhere).

For reasons that I cannot develop here in all necessary detail, the four aforementioned traits may well be Augustine's proleptic intuition–and strikingly original interpretation *avant la lettre*–of the ways in which the phenomena of public and global religion present themselves in the current day and age, propelled and filtered as they now increasingly are by technologies of communication, that is to say, of networks and new media. This already would be sufficient ground to consider Augustine's thought of continued and renewed interest in the debates concerning the prominent–now salutary, then again disturbing–political theologies in the contemporary, so-called postsecular, world.

---

1 Peter Brown, *The Cult of the Saints: Its Rise and Function in Latin Christianity* (Chicago and London: University of Chicago Press, 1981), 79.

Augustine's Initial Views

Augustine's early definition of miracles is far from rigid, but it has a re-markable precision of its own that is not really affected by its later devel-opment, which is marked by revision no less than retraction, attuned as it increasingly is to pragmatic circumstances and perlocutionary effects more than anything else. But then, all these aspects can already be gleaned from the definition that *De utilitate credendi* (*The Usefulness of Belief*) (xvi, 34) introduces as follows:

> By 'miracle' I mean something strange and difficult which exceeds the ex-pectation and capacity of him who marvels at it. Among events of this kind there is nothing more suited to the populace, and to foolish men generally, than what appeals to the senses. But... there are two kinds of miracle. Some there are which merely cause wonder; others produce great gratitude and good will. If one sees a man flying one merely marvels, for such a thing brings no advantage to the spectator beyond the spectacle itself. But if one is affected by some grave and desperate disease and at a word of command im-mediately gets better, love of one's healer will surpass wonder at one's heal-ing. Such things were done when God appeared to men as true Man, as far as was necessary. The sick were healed. Lepers were cleansed. To the lame the power to walk was restored; to the blind, sight; to the deaf, hearing. The men of that time saw water turned into wine, five thousand satisfied with five loaves of bread, waters walked upon, the dead raised.[2]

One crucial element in this definition and its several characterizations is that the miracle presents an 'authority' that is needed by the man who ei-ther lacks reason or is unable to follow its reasonings in full rigor and thus does not succeed in beholding eternal truths in any clear and steadfast manner. This view is intimately connected with the assumption that mira-cles have, first of all, a *deeply pragmatic* function and meaning, which, of course, raises the question what, exactly, is wrong with phenomena that are 'merely marvels' or that bring 'no advantage to the spectator beyond the spectacle itself.' After all, could such uselessness not rather be an in-dication of some inner worth, some intrinsic and objective value, inde-pendent from any spectator's subjective appreciation? Alternatively, could not the useless, at certain times and in special contexts, be precisely the most effective and productive, creative or subversive of qualities as the, as it were, aneconomic–or otherwise unmediated or non-mediatized–end in itself that does not let itself be appropriated as a means to an ulterior end

---

2   Augustine, *The Usefulness of Belief*, in idem, *Earlier Writings*, trans. John H.S. Bur-leigh (Philadelphia: Westminster Press, 1979), 291-323, at 320.

(thus echoing a definition of what Kant coined the very categoricalness of moral imperatives)? In other words, is there not some pragmatic value in things that shun any such value or evaluation? Augustine doesn't think so or, at least, does not consider miracles and miracle belief in merely meditative, contemplative terms. If miracles matter, then their effective use or abuse is what primarily characterizes the witnesses and the multitudes they generate.

Unlike Pascal, in his *Pensées*, Augustine does not suggest that reason is feeble and fickle *per se* (and, hence, more on the side of the external senses than of, say, the heart and its immediate and intuitive feelings). But it cannot provide the required authority for all possible situations (or at all times), nor does it offer pragmatic orientation on the concrete perils and chances with which life presents us. Most people, most of the time, need means and avenues for their purification of which Augustine mentions two, adding that each one of them has a partial contribution to make. No one really doubts, he claims, that the occurrence of miracles had and has to go hand in hand with the emergence of multitudes of those who accept and attach to them man's sole appeal to find or stay his course.[3]

Of the miracle stories cited above, Augustine goes on to say that,

> some looked to the body, conferring on it an obvious benefit, others looked to the mind, conveying to it a hidden signal. But all of them had regard to men, bearing testimony to them of the majesty of Christ. So at that time divine authority drew the erring minds of mortal men towards itself. But why, you say, do such things not happen now? Because they would not affect us unless they were marvellous, and they would not be marvellous if they were familiar. Take the alternation of day and night, the unvarying order of the heavenly bodies, the annual return of the four seasons, the leaves falling and returning to the trees, the endless vitality of seeds, the beauty of light, colour, sounds, odours, the varieties of flavours. If we could speak to someone who saw and sensed these things for the first time, we should find that he was overwhelmed and dizzy at such miracles. But we make light of all these things, not because they are easy to understand–for what is more obscure than their causes?–but because we are continually aware of them. Christ's miracles, therefore, were done at the most opportune moment so that a multitude of believers might be drawn together, and that authority might be turned to profitable account in the interest of good morals.[4]

In other words, the pragmatic element and purpose that marks, if not motivates, miracles comes out only by value of its contrast to habitualized

---

3 Ibid., 319, 320.
4 Ibid., 320-321.

perceptions and patterns of behaviour. This is why miracles may not always be needed or opportune and effective (but were–or could again be–
indispensable at other times, in different situations, for alternative audiences). Indeed, their very success at bringing something radically novel
and memorable, creating a 'multitude' that adheres to its principle and
practices fidelity to their event, makes us 'continually aware' of them and
causes us to forget the extraordinary origin and significance of what has
now become a mere ordinary–near-natural, and automatic, conventional
or normative–given (but was not always quite like that).

It has been suggested that Augustine's definition extends to, perhaps,
too broad a variety of natural and supranatural phenomena and events.
One interpreter summarizes this tendency as follows: "scattered through
his writings the term *miraculum* has at least five different meanings; angelic prodigy, diabolical *mirum*, magical legerdemain, a phenomenon attributed to pagan deities, and in general anything strange or marvelous."[5]
Does this mean that the term miracle, far from being a *terminus techni-
cus* with definite description or clear reference, designates "merely an extraordinary event"[6] of any nature (the *supra naturam* included), directed
to man's 'body' or 'mind' with a specific pragmatic purpose in mind? If
something more or else–different also from a 'hidden signal'–is implied in
Augustinian miracles and the belief that they install or recreate in multitudes, what exactly, then, could it be?

To answer these questions we must first determine what it would mean
for a miracle to appear as arduous or unusual and thereby to exceed the
expectation or ability of the one who witnesses it or who subsequently–
having first been present as an eyewitness–becomes a martyr for it, thus
inspiring or constituting a multitude as things happen. For one thing, it
cannot mean that the miracle, for all its supranatural quality and aura,
can be believed to have violated or interrupted a natural law in any strict,
modern-mechanistic or causalistic sense of the word 'law.' Even if God is
the free, uncaused 'cause' of the universe, His world is not that of a chain
of being, of things and events, in which causes determine effects in exclusively proportionate ways.

In *Contra Faustum Manichaeum* (*Answer to Faustus, a Manichean*)
(26.3), Augustine notes explicitly that miracles cannot counteract the di-

---

5 John Hardon, "The Concept of Miracle from St. Augustine to Modern Apologetics,"
Theological Studies 15 (1954): 229-257, at 230.

6 R.M. Grant, *Miracle and Natural Law in Graeco-Roman and Early Christian Thought*
(Amsterdam: North Holland Publishing Company, 1952), 217, cited also by Hardon, "The
Concept of Miracle from St. Augustine to Modern Apologetics," 230, n. 2.

vinely established and universal order of things and events, since not even God can act against Himself and the laws of created nature He Himself ordained. All things created follow God's command and general or special providence, and so do the occurrences or happenings we experience (witness and baptize) as miracles and that seem to contravene our habitual patterns of perception and expectation and that, hence, exceed the far from adequate knowledge that we human creatures (as finite, i.e., mortal, sinful and 'still weak' beings) base upon them:

> God, the creator and maker of all natures,... does nothing contrary to nature. For what he–who is the source of all the measure, number, and order of nature–does will be natural to each thing. But human beings do not do anything contrary to nature except when they sin, but they are restored to their nature by punishment.... But it is not wrong for us to say that God does contrary to nature what he does contrary to what we know of nature. For we also call nature the usual course of nature known to us, and, when God does something contrary to it, these actions are called marvelous and miraculous. But God does nothing contrary to that supreme law of nature which is removed from the knowledge of those who are wicked and still weak, just as he does nothing contrary to himself. But a spiritual and also rational creature, to which class the human soul belongs, sees better what is possible or what is impossible the more it partakes of that immutable law and light. But the more it is removed from it, the more amazed it is at what is unfamiliar and the less it discerns what the future holds.[7]

Such an explanation would seem to suggest that the belief in miracles must, first of all, be attributed to a subjective stance and has, therefore, no objective ground, correlate, or–in terms of the later medieval controversy concerning so-called universals–no so-called *fundamentum in re*. Miracles, on this view, do not contradict a divinely instituted and universal natural rule or regularity, which, after all, is inviolable, but only the limited interpretation that we–again, as finite, sinful and weak creatures–are given (or give ourselves) of it.

Does this mean, as has been suggested, that "the only difference between miracle and non-miracle is that miracle, being unusual, is assigned to a different mode of causation from ordinary events" and that it springs from so-called "*semina seminum* implanted in the world at creation," whereas non-miracles or false miracles have no such seminal ground to

---

7 Augustine, *Answer to Faustus, a Manichean* (*Contra Faustum Manichaeum*), The Works of Augustine, A Translation for the 21st Century, vol. I/20, trans. Roland Teske, ed. Boniface Ramsey (Hyde Park, New York: New City Press, 2007), 389-390; cf. also Michael E. Goodich, *Miracles and Wonders: The Development of the Concept of Miracle, 1150-1350* (Hampshire, Butlington: Ashgate, 2007), 13, n. 31.

explain and justify them?[8] In other words, do miracles, non-miracles, and false miracles, simply belong to different "classes of events," all of them thoroughly "natural,"[9] since there is nothing else they ever could be (there being nothing but one, single created universe, for us, mortal beings)? Or is the naturalness of miracles also–or, perhaps, first of all–supranatural in the precise sense that "besides their natural constituents creatures also possess certain seminal elements (*seminales rationes*) which God can stimulate into operation, contrary to the creature's ordinary mode of activity"?[10] In the latter scenario, the meaning of 'supranatural' would be that of something in and of "nature" which "only a direct intervention of God can actuate."[11] Put differently, as the Scholastics would come to call it, the miraculous quality would thus signal an 'obedential potency' that lies dormant in nature waiting only for God to be triggered.

We need not consider the details of these views here, but this much is clear: if we can reconstruct matters along these lines, a traditional distinction throughout the history of medieval and early modern thought, namely between the *secundum naturam* ("according to nature") and *supra naturam* ("above nature") is already preempted by Augustine's more subtle–i.e., neither naturalist nor supranaturalist–interpretation of the phenomena in question.

Augustine's stroke of genius comes at a price, albeit it one that no historical or contemporary conception of miracles and miracle belief seems to be able avoid paying. After all, if the world of creation is as such a miracle (an "absolute" miracle, as Wittgenstein will come to suggest in his famous "Lecture on Ethics"), then the smaller, "relative" miracles are, strictly speaking, superfluous or, in any case, not quite up to their concept of eminent–more precisely, divine, if not necessarily exclusive, exceptional–signs. Relative miracles, compared to the absolute miracle that alone is consistent with its concept, would, on this view, be impossible, that is to say, unable to demarcate or otherwise distinguish themselves from the wonder of wonders that the world as such (as a created cosmos or universe) already signals in every single one of its aspects.

Yet, conversely, the modern view that would seek to avoid such contradictions of assuming the presence of relative miracles in the presence of a single absolute one, in the end, fares no better. For if the world is in-

8 Grant, *Miracle and Natural Law in Graeco-Roman and Early Christian Thought*, 218-219.
9 Ibid.
10 Hardon, "The Concept of Miracle From St. Augustine to Modern Apologetics," 213.
11 Ibid.

terpreted, not as a grand miracle, but in naturalistic-causal-mechanical terms, then there is no room for separate–relative–miracles either (unless, of course, they are defined as exceptions from and violations of the principle of sufficient reason and natural law, which is, precisely, what renders them unintelligible and a matter of perspectival illusion, superstition or projective, in any case subjective, whim, alone). Against this foil, miracles would likewise represent the impossible par excellence (and an impossibility that not even God, let alone some Deist World-architect, could want or pull off).

Whereas in the classical view the concept of relative miracle does not come off the ground or acquire any distinction since it cannot mark itself off from a creation that is miraculous as such or *in toto*, in the modern view the miracle (whether relative or absolute, the difference matters little) cannot be thought or experienced since it contravenes the bounds of sense or any horizon of possible phenomenologization in principle. Wittgenstein is only consequent, then, to call it nonsensical or absurd. "Saturated" as the phenomenon of the miracle in its own way may be in either (relative or absolute) case, it is fully absorbed in the order and fabric of things (the "great chain of Being," as Arthur Lovejoy called it) in the first, traditional, interpretation and fully excluded–again, impossible or one form of so-called nonsense–in the second, modern one.

And yet, it is no accident that it is, precisely, in these two–historical no less than different systematic (i.e., conceptual and analytical)–contexts that miracles and miracle belief have been most intensively debated and, paradoxically, succeeded in making themselves somehow, if not perceived, then at least *felt*. They did so even there wherever they presented or represented the unthinkable and impossible as that which eludes all possible forms and categorizations of experience (and, hence, remained "our call," indeed, for us, in faith and good faith, to decide and live up to).

The Pretext of the World

In *The City of God*, Augustine writes that "God made a world full of innumerable miracles, in sky, earth, airs, and waters, while the earth itself is beyond doubt a miracle greater and more excellent than all the wonders with which it is filled."[12] This theological, indeed, Scriptural claim–in tune

---

12 Augustine, *The City of God Against the Pagans*, ed. and trans. by R.W. Dyson (Cambridge and New York: Cambridge University Press, 1998), XXI: 7 (p. 1057).

with the final books of the *Confessions*, which offer an at once exegetical and philosophical meditation on the book of *Genesis*–preempts any accusation that Augustine's conception of miracles and miracle belief is *either* all too inclusive (and, hence, unable to ward off any confusion between miracles and phenomena and events which may well appear to us as wondrous or true at first glance, but which turn out to be impositions, on second reflection) *or* too stringent (and, therefore, too limiting, allowing no miracle but the one of creation as such or *in toto* to deserve the name). There is a fine balance, then, between the global and minimal presentations of the wondrous that precedes the further differentiation between *miracula* and *mirabilia*. What the references to these extremes make clear is that Augustine hovers in between them, elevating both to a mere moment of a grander vision, albeit one whose theological or ontological prize the moderns and our contemporaries may no longer be willing to pay.

The contemporary interest in so-called *generic* miracles and forms of miracle belief–in terms of the "extraordinariness of the ordinary" (Stanley Cavell), "secular faith" (Sari Nusseibeh) or "laicized grace" (Alain Badiou)–likewise can be seen as the endeavor to circumvent the historical and systematic bifurcation between the miracle as special (*mirabilia*) and exceptional (*miracula*), together with the conceptual difficulties each of them entails, *without* fully escaping their shadows (to begin with an inherited terminology that is here to stay, for at least some time still to come, and loaded with a host of theological and theologico-political presuppositions that are neither easily forgotten nor overcome). What these thinkers have in common is the articulation of the subtle balance between the objective and subjective aspect of miracles and miracle belief in ways that surpasses both. This new perspective is one that both Augustine and the thinkers of the generic miracle share.

This said, miracles and the belief in them may well be my call, but one needs a *pretext* in the phenomenal world for calling it so. In other words, the value of miracles and miracle belief in even the most pragmatic (rhetorical, perlocutionary, and strategic-militant) of its guises needs at least the *semblance* of an objective cause–whether divine or natural–that triggers, if not explains or justifies, the effect as it affects a specific addressee or audience in special ways.

The view *that the world as such is* the miracle, more than any particular fact or event *in* it, finds a remarkable echo in a twentieth century thinker for whom Augustine became an important reference, namely Ludwig Wittgenstein. True enough, Augustine often serves as negative foil against which Wittgenstein's own thinking (on language, time, etc.) receives its distinctive profile (in the opening sections of the *Philosophical Investigations*, in the *Blue and Brown Books*, and elsewhere). Yet for Wittgenstein, as for Augustine, it is the world itself which is the most miraculous miracle, the wonder of wonders, leading him to suggest that, for those whose belief is a profound sense of safety, there is nothing, really–nothing that exists, nothing that is the case–that could possibly contradict the wonder that things are.

As Burnyeat notes with reference to Wittgenstein's post-Tractarian engagement in the opening sections of the *Philosophical Investigations* with the so-called scene of instruction in Augustine's philosophy of language and its acquisition in children:

> Augustine shares with Wittgenstein a strong sense that nothing other people may do or say and no fact about the world around me, can determine me to respond in the right way. No one can achieve my understanding for me, not for the trivial reason that it is mine, but because to internalize the requisite connections is to go beyond what is presented on any occasion of so-called teaching.[13]

Mutatis mutandis, miracles and miracle belief cannot be taught, nor do they, strictly speaking, teach us anything in turn! The example they set needs to be emulated–as Burnyeat says, "internalized"–or faithfully adhered to and followed up on in an altogether different way.

While miracles have thus an objective component (locating whatever happens in the realm of things, objects, bodies, or other bits of finite matter), just as they have also subjective component (requiring us to see and judge things for what they are), they do not find the ground of their legitimation in either of these objective or subjective elements and forms, and reconstellate themselves in any number of ways. Just as according to Augustine only God can teach us, so only God–or whatever name we wish to give the instance that, in modernity and beyond, takes His place–does miracles and makes us believe them. To see or experience a miracle is already to believe, and not just this very event in isolation. Indeed, every miracle calls for at least one other and conjures up whole sets of beliefs and acts, perceptions and judgments, affects and effects; in other words, whole universes of different possible worlds.

---

13 M.F. Burnyeat, "Wittgenstein and Augustine's *De Magistro*," in Gareth B. Matthews, ed., *The Augustinian Tradition* (Berkeley and Los Angeles: University of California Press, 1999), 286-303, at 300. Cf. also Herbert Spiegelberg, "Augustine in Wittgenstein: A Case Study in Philosophical Stimulation," *Journal of the History of Philosophy* 17 (1979): 319-326.

But if this is the case, is Burnyeat's view in the end not just another example of the subjective stance which we discussed earlier, according to which justified miracles are always merely *relative to us*? We need not draw this conclusion, even though a fine line of nuance separates the two possible readings that interest us here. Suffice it to note that we can also say that miracle belief is nothing outside a certain 'fidelity to the event' that requires a certain structure of iterability, that is to say, more than one miracle, yet another belief.

The Classical View

Augustine inaugurates a line of argument whose multiple motifs and motivations extend all the way through the Middle Ages and up to modern philosophy. As one scholar remarks, he "lays the groundwork for the later medieval concern to eliminate through judicial or scientific means those alleged miracles which, despite the gullibility and ignorance of the untrained observer, could be rationally understood."[14] Indeed, when Augustine states that "nature is the will of God (*Dei voluntas rerum natura est*)," implying that "a portent is not contrary to nature, but contrary to our knowledge of nature (*Portentum ergo fit non contra naturem, sed contra quam est nota natura*),"[15] then he anticipates almost verbatim the modern scientific view, according to which miracles must be attributed to a subjective evaluative expression that has no objective correlate *per se*.

Paradoxically, it is this modern view which, in turn, will trigger the 'great debate of miracles' in which the latter are seen as–irrational and superstitious, implausible, in any case, unverifiable–attempts to exempt events from the order of reasons, to sever the natural connection between cause and effect, and to break through habitualized or conventional patterns of expectation. Miracles are now portrayed as violations or infringements of a natural or social and psychological rule and general sense of lawfulness, whose testimony, let alone proof, is inconclusive at best. From Spinoza to Hume–and, more obliquely, Locke–and from Feuerbach up to Schopenhauer this seems the accepted view. With the exception of Pascal, we have to wait until the nineteenth and twentieth centuries before an oblique return to the more subtle Augustinian position in thinkers as diverse as Walt Whitman, Wittgenstein, Hannah Arendt, Cavell, Emmanuel Levinas

---

14 Goodich, *Miracles and Wonders*, 13.
15 Augustine, *City of God*, XXI.8.

and Jacques Derrida becomes apparent (albeit mostly without explicit reference to the philosophical depth of the Church Father's theological archive, not to mention its political edge).

It would go too far here to speculate about the reasons for this resurgence and renewed relevance of the Augustinian conception of the miracle and of miracle belief. But the current trends in public and global religion, together with their politically mediated and, especially, technologically mediatized elements and forms (or ways) of modern and postsecular life would have to be part of any explanation of this phenomenon and the overall impression it leaves well beyond strictly theological or philosophical debates. As I suggested earlier, with his interest in publicness and acceleration, multitudes and catholicity–and, especially, in his adoption of the principle or heuristics of "inverse magnitudes"–Augustine has, in a sense, anticipated much of this trend by outlining some of its operating principles and doing so in a spiritual and political world which is no longer our own even though it determined to no small extent how the West established its intellectual canons and was eventually won.

No miracle, for Augustine, can be unnatural or *contra naturam*, since nature is in its ultimate reality and structure God's providential design which from the very outset "provides all natural history with all kinds of exceptional events."[16] Such events merely form a stark contrast with the "observational regularities" that alone are available to us, human creatures: "They are incomprehensible to men and function to demonstrate God's sovereignty to believers."[17] But that does not make them supranatural, let alone violations or infringements of natural law and therefore impossible, as many moderns–with their more stringent conception of cause and effect–would eventually come to believe. Nor is miracle belief, therefore, *ipso facto* irrational, based on a form of religiosity that Spinoza, following Lucretius, called *superstitio* or that philosophical anthropologists like Feuerbach and Fokke Sierksma identified with a projective mechanism, of sorts.

There is far more continuity between the different categories of natural and wondrous–and, in that sense, divinely ordained and supernatural–events that interest Augustine (marvels and miracles being the most prominent among them). As Lorraine Daston observes:

---

16 Simo Knuuttila, "Time and Creation in Augustine," in Eleonore Stump and Norman Kretzmann, eds., *The Cambridge Companion to Augustine* (Cambridge and New York: Cambridge University Press, 2001), 103-115, 107.

17 Ibid.

> Marvels shaded into miracles without a sharp break for Augustine, for both
> testified to how far the power exceeded that of human understanding. This
> is why Augustine parried the objections of the pagan philosophers to Chris-
> tian miracles like the resurrection by listing natural wonders–the wood of a
> certain Egyptian fig tree that sinks rather than floats, the Persian stone that
> waxes and wanes with the moon, the incorruptible flesh of the dead pea-
> cock–that also defied explanation: "Now let those unbelievers who refuse to
> accept the divine writings give an explanation for these marvels, if they can."
> However, certain events deserved to be singled out from the perpetual won-
> der of nature as true miracles because of the message they bore. The mira-
> cles of the early Christian church were of this sort, consolidating faith and
> unity by a wave of conversions...[18]

During his early career Augustine had been convinced that the time of
miracles was over and that the extensive appeal to so-called *memoriae*,
which contained supposed remnants of martyrs and saints, needed to be
condemned if the Church and ecclesiastical authority were not to expose
themselves to pagan practice and philosophical scorn. He feared that the
early church would drown out its claims in the increasing number of un-
controllable and often implausible claims that popular culture seemed to
yearn and rely on. "They worship every bit of dust from the Holy Land,"[19]
Augustine complained as he started to look out for a means to bring
structure and some reason in the plethora of demands for salvation and
the immediate gratification of religious desires.

Yet while from his extensive discussion of wondrous events and miracles in *De civitate Dei* as well as his more fleeting remarks in the *Confessiones* on the vice of "curiosity," it is thus clear that, in Augustine's eyes,
the time of miracles–which were necessary during Biblical and apostolic
times–is largely over, there is no doubt that the older Augustine radically
shifted his perspective as he became not only more attuned to the devotion of his flock, but also intent on solving an important conceptual problem: Why or in what sense do miracles persist? And how do they (still,
once again, and, perhaps, on an even greater scale and with more fervor
than ever before) speak to us, spectators and witnesses–in French, *mirac-
ulés*–of later generations? To answer these questions, we must briefly map
out the evolution of Augustine's later thought and the *retractationes*–not

---

18   Lorraine Daston, "Marvelous Facts and Miraculous Evidence in Early Modern Europe," *Critical Inquiry*, 18.1 (1991): 93-124, at 95-96.

19   Cited after Peter Brown, *Augustine of Hippo: A Biography, A New Edition with an
Epilogue* (Berkeley and London: University of California Press, 2000), 417. Cf. D.P. de Vooght,
"Les miracles dans la vie de Saint Augustin," *Recherches de théologie ancienne et médiévale*
11 (1939): 5-16.

least on the subject matter of miracles and miracle belief–it entails and bequeathed to an emerging and receptive Western canon.

While in the early work *De vera religione* (*Of True Religion*), Augustine had claimed that the miracles that occurred in New Testament times were now superfluous, a radical view he would reiterate with so many words in later books and sermons, he gave these phenomena further thought and a much more prominent place in later life as he reassessed basic tenets of his theology and especially its ecclesial and pastoral implications. The later view of miracles and miracle belief, I would claim, also contains important elements of a complete philosophy of history and of politics. This is hardly surprising when one considers that miracles are not an afterthought, but concern precisely the–tangential yet consequential–points of contact where divine agency touches upon the human, earthly realm and lifts it out of its habitualizations, freeing it up for meanings and acts that enable it to militate for a heavenly city. Indeed, there is a curious logic of "inverse magnitudes" that allows the most minimal events to obtain special–indeed, maximal–effect, just as there is a sense that the infinitesimally small acts bring down the greatest of powers (if only by mocking their presumed totality, rendering them obsolete and overcoming them by one single–and, often, idiosyncratic–stroke of fate, that is to say, of providence).

Before discussing these matters further, it is useful, though, to consider the careful reasoning that surrounds Augustine's earlier view, before moving to its later revocation or, rather, reinterpretation. The full quote from *Of True Religion,* xxv, 47, leaves no doubt as to the complexity of Augustine's early position as it relies on the emergence of a certain catholicity–a universal multitude, as it were–that is seen a resituating the place of miracles and miracle belief:

> We have heard that our predecessors, at a stage of faith on the way from temporal things up to eternal things, followed visible miracles. They could do nothing else. And they did so in such a way that it should not be necessary for those who came after them. When the Catholic Church had been founded and diffused throughout the world, on the one hand miracles were not allowed to continue till our time, lest the mind should always seek visible things, and the human race should grow cold by becoming accustomed to things which when they were novelties kindled its faith. On the other hand we must not doubt that those are to be believed who proclaimed miracles, which only a few had actually seen, and yet were able to persuade whole peoples to follow them. At that time the problem was to get people to believe before anyone was fit to reason about divine and invisible things. No human authority is set over the reason of a purified soul, for it is able to arrive at clear truth. But pride does not lead to the perception of truth. If there

were no pride there would be no heretics, no schismatics, no circumcised, no worshippers of creatures of images. If there had not been such cases of opponents before the people was made perfect as promised, truth would be sought much less eagerly.[20]

True, Augustine never seems to fully repudiate his insight that "[i]f we look for a cause of awe and wonder now, we should contemplate nature" (*de utilitate credendi*, xvi, 34), nor does he ever forget that the "daily miracles of creation are as great as those of the incarnate Lord" (*Tractatus in Johannis Evangelium*, 9.1), arguing further that the "material miracles," such as the healing of "blind eyes," worked by Christ according to the Gospel stand in no comparison to the "miracles of inward moral conversion" of the faithful, which signal the opening of "blind hearts," just as charity by far outweighs the miracle workings that may have been opportune or necessary at earlier moments in time (*Tractatus in Johannis Evangelium*, 17.1).[21] Last but not least, throughout his writings Augustine maintains that the miracles from New Testament and apostolic times symbolized first of all the later sacraments of the Church and should, hence, be taken figuratively more than anything else.

Yet Augustine also softens his assessment of the many popular religious claims with which he was confronted as a bishop in his own congregation and those of his colleagues. Chadwick speaks of a "shift" from the earlier position which becomes clear by 426 when Augustine is composing the final book of the *City of God* as well as from what he says in the *Rectractationes*, where he notes that pagans are wrong to dismiss the claim that miracles take place at the tombs of the saints. True, he acknowledges, there are "not such notable wonders as in apostolic days, but not none at all" (*Rectractationes*, 1. 14.5). The question thus becomes: what may these latter day miracles still or yet again mean? How could what were once conceived as unique–once-upon-a-time-only–events now come to be re-iterated (i.e., repeated and displaced or disseminated) beyond their original *Sitz im Leben* and burst onto the scene with newly defined pragmatic, perlocutionary purposes in view? Further, how do contemporary miracles constitute alternative multitudes, whose public and political claims require the formation of a newly conceived universality or, rather, catholicity? In other words, what makes miracles into more than mere metaphors for a

---

20 Augustine, *Of True Religion*, in idem, *Earlier Writings*, 225-283, at 248; cf. Brown, *Augustine of Hippo*, 419.

21 These references I take from Henry Chadwick, *Augustine of Hippo: A Life* (Oxford: Oxford University Press, 2009), 77.

spiritual transformation that is reported starting from one soul and its confession alone?

As Chadwick notes in his beautiful rendering of the *Confessiones*: "In his own time Augustine stressed the sacraments as God's present means of special grace, and saw in conversion the greatest of miracles. Like miracles, however, the sacraments are a visible ladder to reach spiritual and invisible things."[22] Or again: "Visible signs and sacraments are a necessity because of the fallen nature of humanity. Signs are required by sinful people, but truly spiritual Christians look higher, beyond material means."[23] In other words, for all their transformational power, they are not ends in themselves and as "special providences" they do not contravene the "primary marks" of divine Creation which, Chadwick explains, are "mathematical order and reason," meaning, once again, that miracles are "contrary not to nature but to what we know of nature."[24]

Thus, the *Confessiones* claim that it is often merely a symptom of "curiosity" when people

> study the operations of nature which lie beyond our grasp, when there is no advantage in knowing and the investigators simply desire knowledge for its own sake. This motive is again at work if, using a perverted science for the same end, people try to achieve things by magical acts. Even in religion itself the motive is seen when God is 'tempted' by demands for 'signs and wonders' (John 4:48) desired not for any salvific end but only for the thrill.[25]

Interpreting biblical Scripture and inferring that the created earth "does not ask for great miracles to bring faith into being"–and immediately adding: "Nor does it refuse to believe unless it sees signs and wonders (John 4:48)"[26]–Augustine here takes all references to wonder and wonders to be signs of ignorance, gestured not so much to those who believe, but to those who do not. In post-biblical times, he goes on to implore, a different register may be called for. And the allegorical reading of the opening chapters of Genesis suggests as much, indicating that we have come a long way since the prophetic and apostolic times of old:

> May your ministers now do their work on 'earth,' not as they did on the waters of unbelief when their preaching and proclamation used miracles and

---

22 Saint Augustine, *Confessions: A New Translation by Henry Chadwick* (Oxford: Oxford University Press, 1991), 290, n. 27.

23 Ibid., 289, n. 24.

24 Ibid., 290, n. 27.

25 Augustine, *Confessiones* 10.55.

26 Ibid., 13.21.

sacred rites and mystical prayers to attract the attention of ignorance, the mother of wonder (*mater admirationis*), inducing the awe around by secret symbols. That is the entrance to faith for the sons of Adam who forget you, who hide from your face (Gen. 3:8) and become an 'abyss.' May they now do their work as on dry land separated from the whirlpools of the abyss. May they be an example to the faithful by the life they live before them and by arousing them to imitation (I Thess. 1:7).[27]

In other words–and this motif becomes something like a refrain for his thoughts on the matter, for Augustine, the "sacraments of initiation and miraculous wonders" are merely "necessary to initiate and convert 'uninstructed and unbelieving people' (I Cor. 14:23)."[28] They add nothing decisive for those who live a genuine life in faith already and who see–if not face to face, no longer as if through a mirror–then at least more directly and clearly.

Augustine's initial view on miracles and miracle belief is thus not so far removed from Pascal's later insight that the phenomena are mostly "momentary [*ponctuel*] and ephemeral," with as its inevitable consequence that the testimony of miracles speaks to relatively few people (and first and foremost the direct witnesses who were right there or who heard of these events from those who had seen or heard them first hand). It is an insight that may well have convinced Pascal to remove the "dossier" with extensive, if somewhat loose, observations on miracles from the apologetics for the Christian faith he had originally planned and to insist instead on the single argument of the *miracle subsistant*, that to say, the fact, revealed by Scripture, that the unique creation is itself the miracle that matters and remains, for all eyes to see and every heart to rejoice in.[29]

Several fragments make this argument in succinct terms, emphasizing the provisional and anticipatory, proleptic–and, hence, already *counterfactual*–claim or usage of miracles in biblical, apostolic, and patristic times, while explaining their relative obsolescence in the times that followed the prophesied 'conversion of nations,' the decisive geopolitical event that turned the need for special effects tailored to special audiences into the global awe, the 'final effect,' that the 'subsistent miracle' inspires.

Miracles and their belief, then, belong neither to the abstract metaphysical proofs of 'reason' as it determines and uses 'principles' that are structurally limited and that all too easily and quickly elude us, nor to the

---

27   Ibid.

28   Ibid., 13.27.

29   As is suggested by Philippe Sellier in his edition of the *Pensées: Édition établie d'après l'"ordre" pascalien* (Paris: Agora Pocket, 2003), 451.

directness of 'inspiration' of the 'heart' and of 'feeling.' If anything, Pascal suggests, with a turn to the realm of what we would now call the ordinary, that miracles and miracle belief form an integral part of the world of 'custom.' In this everyday world they, paradoxically and pragmatically, represent and present the possibility of new, unexpected habitualizations (having first enabled us to break with old ones), based as these are on "instinct" and "automatism," without therefore having the instantaneousness of the very "feeling" in which, Pascal says, we should put all our "faith," given that reason and the intellect are such that they must "always waver."[30] Indeed, Pascal writes: "It is the heart that feels God, not reason: that is what faith is. God felt by the heart, not by reason. The heart has its reasons which reason itself does not know: we know that through countless things."[31] We do not so much constate or infer, observe or demonstrate, miracles, therefore, but "know" and acknowledge them differently, with a faculty that is neither that of the senses nor the intellect, but one of feeling, that is to say, the heart. And, in this, Pascal once more echoes an Augustinian view that gives "love" prevalence over any and all human faculties, since precisely it alone gives the "restless heart"—the *cor inquietum*—the peace it seeks but finds nowhere but in God.

Retractationes

What makes for the shift in Augustine's appreciation of miracles, especially the healings or reports thereof, that he encounters in his days as a bishop in Northern Africa, where the cults of the saints and the practices of popular belief were widespread? As to the diffusion of so-called *memoriae* Brown comments that

> Africa had always been full of such holy bodies. What was new, however, was the sudden wave of miraculous cures associated with them: seventy would take place in Hippo within the space of two years.... Miracles had remained a matter of vague popular feeling: those who experienced them, treated them as intimate, personal revelations [e.g., *de civ. Dei*, XXII, 8, 164-168]; those who heard them, quickly forgot or garbled their accounts [*de civ. Dei*, XXII, 8, 400]; Augustine decided both to examine and record each instance, and to give verified cures a maximum of publicity. In Hippo,

---

30 The tripartition of heart, instinct, and principles is mentioned in Blaise Pascal, *Pensées, and Other Writings*, trans. Honor Levi (Oxford and New York: Oxford University Press, 1999), 58; the correlative distinction between inspiration, custom, and reason is made in ibid., 147.

31 Ibid., 157-158.

he insisted on receiving a written report from the healed person, a *libellus*; and this document would then be read out in church, in the presence of the writer, and later would be stored in the bishop's library.... His aim was to draw together these scattered incidents, until they formed a single corpus, as compact and compelling as the miracles that had assisted the growth of the Early Church [*de civ. Dei*, XXII, 8, 350-353]. It is not the first time that Augustine had appealed to the 'facts' of popular belief.... The aim of this new campaign, as it is applied in the last book of the *City of God*, is also to 'bend' the 'shocking hardness' of the reasonable pagans, many of whom were eminent doctors, by a direct appeal to the astonishing things happening in the Christian communities all around them.[32]

In the "unwieldy and picturesque catalogue of strange occurrences in Hippo, Carthage,"[33] documented in Book XXII of *De Civitate Dei* but also in Book IX (vii, 16) of the *Confessions* as well as in the *libelli* or pamphlets destined "for public reading and circulation"[34] that the later Augustine authorized as a pastor and bishop, we find a host of miracle stories, all of which relate a profound sense of the continued role of divine intervention. In Augustine's view, as expressed in *The City of God*, they record, "in our times, frequent signs of divine powers similar to those of old"; in other words, they present as many signs of the "eloquence of God, as it were, evinced in this divine work":

> [e]ven now... many miracles are wrought by the same God Who wrought those of which we read, acting by whom He will and as He wills. But they are not as well known as the former ones, nor are they beaten into the memory by frequent reading, like gravel into a path, so that they cannot pass out of the mind. Even where care is taken to read to the people the written accounts of those who receive such blessings–and we have now begun to do this at Hippo–those who are present hear the story only once, and many are not present. In any case, those who were present do not retain in their minds what they have heard for more than a few days, and scarcely anyone is found who can tell what he has heard to one he knows to have been absent.[35]

Yet, as Brown explains, this shift in appreciation and explanation had not only to do with the increasing popularity of the *memoriae* and the need for careful public monitoring–and, indeed, "maximum publicity"–it re-

---

32 Brown, *Augustine of Hippo*, 417-418.

33 Ibid., 422.

34 James J. O'Donnell, *Augustine: A New Biography* (New York: Harper Collins Publishers, 2005), 177. Cf. H. Delehaye, "Les premiers 'libelli miraculorum,'" *Analecta Bollandiana* 29 (1910): 427-434, and idem, "Les recueils antiques de miracles des Saints," *Analecta Bollandiana* 43 (1925): 5-85 and 305-325.

35 Augustine, *The City of God*, 22.8 (pp. 1131-1132).

quired in the bishop's eyes. Nor did it result from pragmatic and apolo-
getic considerations alone (the need to contain unruly popular belief and
to respond to the skeptical attitude of non-Christian Romans with a host
of tangible proofs for the truth of ecclesial faith):

> Augustine's sudden decision to give a maximum publicity to miraculous
> cures in Africa should not be regarded as a sudden and unprepared surren-
> der to popular credulity. It is, rather, that, within the immensely complex
> structure of Augustine's thought, the centre of gravity had shifted; modern
> miracles, which once had been peripheral, now become urgently important
> as supports to faith.
>
> In this evolution, indeed, we have a microcosm of the deep change that
> separates the religion of the young Augustine from that of the old. Like most
> late Antique men, Augustine was credulous without necessarily being su-
> perstitious. When remarkable events happened at holy places, he was thor-
> oughly well-armed, as a philosopher, against crude interpretations of the
> event, but not against the event itself. He was not prepared to deny what
> reliable men told him; but he would tenaciously criticize any explanation
> of such events, or any religious practice, that seemed unworthy of a correct
> view of God and the soul.
>
> Even the natural world was full of unique and surprising happenings....
> The wise men of the ancient world had failed to map out the whole world of
> nature.[36]

In this vein, Augustine's perspective and language have all the characteristics of a reorientated and reconstructed Neoplatonism, rather than showing any remnants of the Manicheism of old, as he struggles to come to
terms with the polytheism, mysteries, and popular religion of the Graeco-Roman pagan world, which found itself at the mercy of the barbar-
ian tribes that ransacked Rome in 410. It was this major political event
that triggered a new round of accusations at the address of a Christendom
now held responsible for the disintegration and demise of the empire as
it had hollowed out its cultural traditions and, hence, moral substance.
Augustine's conception of history and God's hand in the larger scheme
of things as well as in special acts of divine intervention–two conjoined
themes which weave a central thread of argument in the lengthy exposi-
tions in his *City of God*–can be seen as a theological and philosophical
riposte to this claim of Christianity's supposed subversion of the political
powers that be. Augustine had too fine a political mind to let the accusation stand and offers a subtle rebuke, point by point, addressing himself to
the intellectual elites of his day. As in his more occasional writings, mostly

---

36 Brown, *Augustine of Hippo*, 419.

letters, on internal affairs of the Church, he shows himself a master in the art of pacifying the contrary view, without ceding anything of doctrinal substance in turn.

"In Quick Motion": Token Reminders of Our Limitation By Habit

With reference to Henri-Irénée Marrou's classic study *Saint Augustin et la fin de la culture antique*, Brown makes much of the fact that, for Augustine, miracles, more than supports to faith are, first of all, token reminders of the fact that, as Shakespeare's *Hamlet* has it, "There are more things in heaven and earth, Horatio,/Than are dreamt of in your philosophy."[37] In Brown's words:

> A 'miracle' for Augustine was just such a reminder of the bounds imposed on the mind by habit. In a universe in which all processes happen by the will of God, there need be nothing less remarkable in the slow, habitual process-es of nature. We take for granted the slow miracle by which water in the irri-gation of the vineyard becomes wine: it is only when Christ turns water into wine, 'in quick motion' as it were, that we are amazed. [cf. *Ep.* 137, iii, 10][38]

What is central to the miracle is, on this reading, a certain *intensification*– and, in this case, *dramatization* and *acceleration*–of the ordinary and the everyday, even the habitual, which reminds us of their principle extraordi-nariness, that is to say, of the fact that they ultimately express a world of wonder, the wonder of the world, which is, after all, the 'miracle of miracles':

> Augustine essentially regarded miracles as an acceleration of the normal processes of nature whereby the seeds (*semina seminum*) inherent in nature are activated. These phenomena occurred in such an unusual way that they are termed miracles and are intended to teach us a lesson. The ultimate aim is to console and bring the faithful to God, or to confound the non-believer or heretic.[39]

With the remarkable hypothesis motif of "acceleration" we stumble upon a trope that enables us to connect Augustine's meditation in his *City of God* with twentieth and twenty-first century observations regarding the pacing of technological invention and its repercussions for our sense of time and space or place. We might wager a speculative leap and blatant anachronicity and suggest that just as the miracle, for Augustine, is God's

---

37   Cited after Henri-Irénée Marrou, *Saint Augustin et la fin de la culture antique* (Paris: Éditions de Boccard, 1983), 154.
38   Brown, *Augustine of Hippo*, 420.
39   Goodich, *Miracles and Wonders*, 14.

tending to things natural and created according to the providential order of divine laws, but this time "in quick motion," so also the contemporary global increase in the pace no less than in the scale of things and trends produces perceptions and sensations that predispose toward–and, indeed, border upon–the miraculous. The sheer quantity of proliferated images and their ever faster movement reverts into a qualitative leap to which we can adhere in faith or pay no attention. But belief and disbelief, the suspension of disbelief or belief, are merely two sides of the same phenomenon.

Also the question of agency and embodiment is important here. In the many wondrous stories which Augustine relates, the way in which the memory and presence of saints and martyrs, their shrines and relics, are recorded and rendered–mediated or mediatized–is crucial, even if "[t]he idea that such tokens of the dead could be powerful and worthy of special treatment grew on him slowly."[40] In *The Cult of the Saints* Brown argues as much when he says that Augustine's

> accounts of the miracles at the shrine of Saint Stephen, in the last book of the *City of God*, were far from being a capitulation to the "silly stories" current among the "common herd." For Augustine they are surreal rather than "silly." They betray the effort by which Augustine, a man formed in the austerely immaterialist current of Neo-Platonic thought available to an educated man of his age, had come to think of a future integration of flesh and spirit. The recorded miracles of healing at the shrines show God's power and his abiding concern for the flesh. And this power, Augustine now believes, is shown most appropriately at the places where those dead now lie, who had been prepared to lose their close-knit bodies in the faith of the unimaginable mercy of the resurrection. Miracles that had once struck Augustine, the contemplative, as of little significance, as so many lights dimmed by the sun of God's harmonious order, now take on a warmth and a glow of their own, as Augustine pays more heed to the instinctive fears and yearnings of the once-neglected body.[41]

The "local miracles," Brown suggests, represent mostly "physical cures" and, as such, indicate an aspect of religion that Augustine had, perhaps, neglected at an earlier age, namely the fact that the body and its health form just as much part and parcel of the essence of faith as the mind and the injunction "to heal the eyes of the heart." In Brown's words:

> A God Whose generosity had scattered so much purely physical beauty on the earth, could not neglect physical illness.... These miracles had sprouted from the desperation of men afflicted by 'more diseases than any book of

---

40 O'Donnell, *Augustine*, 175.
41 Brown, *The Cult of the Saints*, 77.

medicine could hold.' The evident horrors of human existence, its *miseria*, assumed an urgent need for some relief, for some few *solacia*. These reliefs were some slight hint, like thin rays of sunshine entering a darkened room, of the final transformation, the glorious resurrection, of the bodies of the elect.[42]

Local miracles thus come to supplement–but not substitute for–the "global" one which is the miracle of creation, of the world, or, as Pascal will say, the "continuous" or "subsistent" miracle (*miracle subsistant*) as such. But this much is clear, one cannot think, believe, or act on one without assuming the other. In a sense, Augustine's later development–and apparent *retractatio*–in matters miraculous is thus, first of all, that of a theological, if not philosophical or logical, consequence. The later view need not be seen as rebuking the earlier one, but is inscribed in a larger perspective on the question of eternity and immortality that we need not develop here. More precisely, Brown notes,

> an intellectual breakthrough of the first order lies behind what is too often presented as a belated concession to the mindless weight of 'popular belief.'
>
> Yet Augustine's formulation of his later views, and his decision to add the records of local cases of healing to his final cannonade against all the unquestioned assumptions of the pagan philosophical world view, are only special cases in the working out of the imaginative dialectic surrounding the very special dead. The result of this dialectic has been not merely to block out the negative associations of physical death with all the resources of an imaginary of paradise, but to raise the physical remains of the saints above the normal associations of place and time.... The relic is a detached fragment of a whole body... But it is precisely the detachment of the relic from its physical association that summed up most convincingly the imaginative dialectic... For how better to suppress the fact of death, than to remove part of the dead from its original context in the all too cluttered grave? How better to symbolize the abolition of time in such dead, than to add to that an indeterminacy of space? Furthermore, how better to express the paradox of the linking of Heaven and Earth than by an effect of "inverted magnitudes," by which the object around which boundless associations clustered should be tiny and compact? Detached fragments of the saints in gold and silver caskets, or in their miniature marble shrines, had some of the measureless quality of an *objet trouvé*.... Yet, in detaching the relic from direct association with physical death, the imaginative dialectic was, if anything, heightened. For what was being brought were tiny fragments around which the imaginative associations of a very special kind of death could cluster undisturbed. And this very special kind of death had been almost invariably unpleasant.... At the root of every miracle of healing at a martyr's shrine of late antiquity

---

42 Brown, *Augustine of Hippo*, 421.

there lay a miracle of pain.... For the sufferings of the martyrs were miracles in themselves.[43]

Brown's illuminating picture of the "inverted magnitudes" animating the "imaginative dialectic" of the popular belief as well as its most subtle re-formulation in Augustine's later writings also suggests that the miracle of miracles, the miracle of Creation, of the world as a whole and as such, re-quires *at least* one more miracle. There simply cannot be just *one* miracle. One miracle calls for another, for, at least, one other. Indeed, it is as if the miracle presented nothing short of a question calling out for a response, which could be nothing less than a miracle, in turn. One miraculous act solicits another, depends on another. And our very testimony of the effect of this iteration will be all the more miraculous the less this following up and following through–like the "going on" of which Wittgenstein, in his discussion of rule following speaks in his *Philosophical Investigations*–is warranted by the facts or states of affair of the world, as we know it (or thought we did). In sum, miracles and miracle belief are not governed by criteria. Put differently, all the criteria (concepts, definitions, rules, etc.) we ascribe to them will necessarily disappoint us.

Conclusion

One is struck by the twofold observation in Augustine's later writing that miracles and miracle belief are tied to a certain notion of *the publicness and even publicity of faith*, just as they are said to consist in a *special per-ception*, caused or effected, triggered or invited, by no one but God. Ac-cording to the first view, miracles find their meaning and confirmation in a specific medium, of *memoriae* or *libelli*, and their communal pres-entation and declamation in a public forum or square, of sorts, ritualized events which, Augustine insists, must be properly processed and archived so as to avoid giving a wrong impression (to believers and unbelievers alike).

According to the special perception view, natural processes can, on certain unexpected and rare occasions, appear *as if under an optical illu-sion* that makes their event altogether special. In other words, they can be presented in what we might call a charitable light, which only a charitable disposition, itself an effect of divine grace, is able to reveal to us in the first place. That this is possible should not surprise us. After all, all natural

---

43   Brown, *The Cult of the Saints*, 78, 79.

processes are based on the very laws that govern God's creation by His own divine decree and providence and, indeed, reveal "all of nature as a miracle," that is to say, as "the will of God realized."[44]

The two aspects, taken together, offer important conceptual tools for the study of religion in the present day and age. Yet why and how, exactly, this should be the case will require further investigation.

---

44 Daston, "Marvelous Facts and Miraculous Evidence in Early Modern Europe," 95.

THE CHRISTIAN MIDDLE AGES

TANGERE AUTEM CORDE, HOC EST CREDERE: AUGUSTINE ON 'TOUCHING' THE NUMINOUS

In his insightful article "Augustine and the return of the senses" Burcht Pranger explores, among other things, the Church Father's allusions in his *Confessions* to a quandary: the perceived discontinuity between the sensory experience of the material world and the non-sensory, in his view more truly real, experience of the divinely numinous.[1] If I understand him correctly, he points to Augustine's use of sensory metaphors and analogies  to describe spiritual experience as an indication that, for him, the physical senses are to a certain extent models for apprehending this spiritual experience.[2] What he qualifies as Augustine's aporetic thinking about this issue, he explains, cannot be understood through an underlying neoplatonic or a biblical structure of ideas, but is determined by his attitude of continuous attentive openness to intermittent and unfathomable perceptions and momentary theophanies, which—as in *poesis*—can in part be described in terms of sensory analogies.

Thus although Augustine describes the theophanic moment of ecstasy at Ostia as having come forth out of a conversation with his mother about the saints' heavenly non-sensory perception of God, he describes this speaking-while-projectively-imagining with metaphors of sense experience as: "we were panting after the heavenly flowing of your fount, the fount of life, with the mouth of our heart (*inhiabamus ore cordis in superna fluenta fontis tui, fontis vitae*)."[3] It was during this dreaming-wishing, as he describes it, "to attain/touch the region of never-ending bountifulness (*ut attingeremus regionem ubertatis indeficientis*)" of "the life that is the Wisdom through which everything is being made" (*vita sapientia est,*

---

1 In Giselle de Nie, Karl F. Morrison and Marco Mostert, eds., *Seeing the Invisible in Late Antiquity and the Early Middle Ages*, Utrecht Studies in Medieval Literacy 14 (Turnhout: Brepols, 2005), 53-67.

2 Pranger, "Return," 65 and 67.

3 Augustine, *Confessionum libri XIII*, ed. Martin Skutella and Lucas Verheijen, Corpus Christianorum Series Latina [CCSL] 27 (Turnhout: Brepols, 1981), IX.x.23 (p. 147). Quotations of the *Confessions* are from this edition; the translations are my own unless otherwise indicated, and differ somewhat from those given in Burcht Pranger's article.

per quam fiunt omnia)"–in other words, the continuously creating "Being itself, [which] is eternal (*esse solum, ... aeterna est)*"[4]–that an interior encounter suddenly takes place. Having left the experience of the sensible world behind as they entered into the awareness of their own souls, Augustine says, and then going beyond it, "while we talked and panted after it, we touched it lightly with a total shock/upheaval of the heart (*dum loquimur et inhiamus illi, attingimus eam modice toto ictu cordis)*."[5] Exactly what this means is of course very difficult to determine.[6] I would add here, however, that it looks as though what is described as the act of panting, as it were trying to "inhale" and become part of the imagined divine creative movement pointed to by the words, may also have been instrumental in leading to the spiritual sensing of actually coming into "contact" with it. Also, it would seem that the abstract notions preceding this contact allow the Latin verb *tangere* here to mean the more cerebral "attain" as well as the affective "touch".[7] The shock effect, however, seems to point to the predominance of an interior, affective kind of apprehending that nevertheless can be conceptualized as analogous to a sensory touch. Burcht Pranger points out that Augustine seems to have experienced this sudden leap between sensory and spiritual experience as a rare divine gift which cannot be humanly brought about or even initiated, and must simply be awaited in a state of constant attentive receptiveness to the present moment, because it is in this that time and eternity mutually embrace each other.[8]

Many references to "seeing" God and "hearing" his messages through what Augustine often describes as the "eyes" and "ears" of the heart[9] may be found in his writing after the *Confessions* had been written (in 397/401). The notion of touching with the heart, an expression that does not occur in any other contemporary writer,[10] occurs as well, and now not

---

4 *Conf.* IX.x.24 (p. 147).

5 *Conf.* IX.x.24 (p. 147). Pierre Courcelle, *Recherches sur les Confessions de saint Augustin* (Paris: de Boccard, 1968), 222-26, points to parallels with Plotinian ecstasy.

6 Pranger, "Return," 62, gives the translation "a moment of total concentration of the heart" (from Henry Chadwick, *Confessions* [Oxford: Oxford University Press, 1992], 171).

7 Albert Blaise, *Dictionnaire latin-français des auteurs chrétiens* (Turnhout: Brepols, 1954), 61.

8 Pranger, "Return," 65.

9 More substantially, on seeing God, see *Epistulae* 147 and 148 in *Epistulae 124-184*, ed. Almut Goldbacher, Corpus Scriptorum Ecclesiasticorum Latinorum [CSEL] 44 (Vienna: Tempsky, 1904), 274-347 (this edition in what follows); on hearing his voice, see *Conf.* IX.x.25 (p. 148).

10 Ambrose, however, speaks similarly of the effect of Absalom's kind acts: *intimorum tangunt viscerum sensum* (*De officiis ministrorum*, Patrologia Latina [PL] 16 (Paris: Migne, 1844-55), 2.22.114 [col. 142B]).

only as a metaphor of but also as a *model for* spiritual experience.[11] For whereas, in the *Confessions*, it functions as an analogy to facilitate the cognitive apprehending of what he there describes as a passively experienced spiritual sensing, certain passages in the sermons–especially of the long period in which Augustine believed that miracles had ceased to happen after apostolic times[12]–use the act of physical touching in a well-known Gospel miracle to construct and encourage a self-initiated mode of spiritual "touching" of the divine Christ. Finally, touching becomes physical in Augustine's brief descriptions in 426 of cures through relics happening in his own city.[13]

If not in the *Confessions*, then, he must later have assumed–if not verbalized–some kind of closing of the "gap" between sensory and super-sensory experience to take place. To find out how he may have understood this to happen, I shall look at some of his thoughts about accessing Truth in the human mind-heart as they appear in the *Confessions*. With these in mind I shall examine, first, his later encouragements of spiritually "touching" a mentally-imaged Christ in the sermons, and then his still later brief descriptions in the last book of the *City of God* of the incontrovertible facts whose mere concrete existence must have made his philosophical problem evaporate. Extending Burcht Pranger's notion of Augustine's indicating a certain "return of the senses" through his descriptions of his purely spiritual experience in terms of sensory metaphors, one could thus regard the Church Father's subsequent descriptions of these miracles as showing his ultimate acceptance of a *de facto* continuity of some kind between sensory and spiritual experience.[14] Stronger still, these miracles could qualify as *incarnated* versions of what Burcht Pranger refers to as the intermittent "hard-core moments" and "epiphanic time-cells" of spiritual "real hearing, seeing and touching" for which Augustine was always looking and hoping.[15]

---

11 On the notion of "model for," see Clifford Geertz, "Religion as a cultural system," in idem, *The Interpretation of Cultures* (New York: Basic Books, 1973), 87-125, at 93.

12 See on this, D.P. de Vooght, "Les miracles dans la vie de saint Augustin," *Recherches de théologie ancienne et médiévale* 11 (1939): 5-16, and, more recently, Leopold Tanganagba, *Miracle comme* argumentum fidei *chez saint Augustin*, Hereditas. Studien zur alten Kirchengeschichte 21 (Bonn: Borengässer, 2002), 20-62. My own study of Augustine's changing view of miracle will appear in my *Poetics of Wonder. Discovering and Imaging the New Christian Miracles in Late Antiquity* (Turnhout: Brepols, 2011).

13 On these miracles see Serge Lancel, "Saint Augustin et le miracle," in Jean Meyers, ed., *Les miracles de saint Étienne. Recherches sur le recueil pseudo-augustinien (BHL 7860-7661)*, Hagiologia 5 (Turnhout: Brepols, 2006), 69-77.

14 Elsewhere in this volume Hent de Vries also points to Augustine's later view of the integration of flesh and spirit, p. ##.

15 Pranger, "Return," 67.

I. Ictus cordis *as* momentum intellegentiae: *sensory impressions, mental images, interior sensing and the innate divine image*

Many passages in the *Confessions* make clear that Augustine was acutely sensitive to the delights of the physical senses.[16] His conception of their relation to spiritual experience appears when he says that the beauty that can be discerned as implied in all created things is the shining-through (a visual metaphor) or voice (an aural one) of the divine Wisdom, who is Christ: [17] "He indeed speaks to all, but only those understand it who bring his voice as it is received from without [through the senses] together with the truth which is within" (*immo vero omnibus loquitur, sed illi intel-legunt, qui eius vocem acceptam foris intus cum veritate conferunt*).[18] What kind of 'bringing-together' is this? Although this apprehending involves aesthetic judgment and therefore a kind of affective cognition, Augustine's rhetorical past makes him sometimes speak of this process as "reading": apprehending the shape or configuration of the visible event as the equiv-alent of a written "word" communicating a divine message.[19] For him, the sensory sign's truth value is thus assessed by the mind by matching it with its innate exemplars of truth, divinely inserted when, as the book of Genesis states, it was created according to the image of God.[20] For it "presid[es] over and judg[es] the responses of the sky and of the earth and of all things that are in them saying: 'we are not God' and 'He made us'" (*praesidenti et iudicanti de responsionibus caeli et terrae et omnium, quae in eis sunt, dicentium: 'non sumus deus' et: 'ipse fecit nos'*)."[21]

For Augustine, however–and this is a crucial part of the "gap" to which Burcht Pranger refers[22]–it is not the raw impressions received by the sense organs that themselves reach the mind because, crucially, the latter was then regarded as being inaccessible to direct influences deriving from the body. Influenced by the Stoic philosophical tradition, Augustine held that these impressions were relayed there in the form of representational sy-naesthetic images fashioned by the human spirit or imagination; it is these

---

16   As also Pranger, "Return," 65, quoting Augustine, *Conf.* X.vi.8 (p. 159).

17   Cf. Carol Harrison, *Beauty and Revelation in the Thought of Saint Augustine* (Oxford: Clarendon Press, 1992).

18   *Conf.* X.vi.10 (p. 160). I am grateful to Catherine Conybeare for this and other translations of *conferunt*.

19   As in Augustine, *In Iohannis Evangelium Tractatus*, ed. Radbodus Willem, CCSL 36 (Turnhout: Brepols, 1954), XXIV.6 (p. 246).

20   Gn 1:26.

21   *Conf.* X.vi.9 (p. 160).

22   Pranger, "Return," 55.

images or *species* that are perceived by the mind's *inner senses*, as differentiated from the body's *sensory organs*.[23] He is ambivalent, however, about the ontological status of these representational images, sometimes indicating that they form a continuous self-generating chain from sensible objects to the mind's images, at other times saying that these images are formed by the spirit or imagination itself according to the impression presented.[24] The latter view appears when he says that the things he has perceived in the physical world "are not within me, but their images [only], and I know through which bodily sense each was impressed upon me (*nec ipsa sunt apud me, sed imagines eorum, et novi: quid ex quo sensus corporis impressum sit mihi*)."[25]

By contrast, he says of the innate intra-mental exemplars of Truth, with which the mind compares these images or *species*, that they are "not images but the very things themselves (*non imagines earum, sed ipsas*)"[26] and that the mind perceives them "without images, just as they are, we see them through themselves within us (*sine imaginibus, sicuti sunt, per se ipsa intus cernimus*)."[27] Moreover, he says that "when I learned about them I did not believe someone else's heart, but recognized them in my own and approved them as being true [...] for they were there before I had learned about them, but they were not in my memory (*cum ea didici, non credidi alieno cordi sed in meo recognovi, et vera esse approbavi [...] ibi ergo erant et antequam ea didicissem, sed in memoria non erant*)."[28] These invisible forms or patterns of truth, he indicates, can be accessed by sustained mental effort, that is: "by thinking [meditating?], as it were gathering [them] (*cogitando quasi colligere*)"[29] from their hidden places. In this passage Augustine appears to think of these exemplars as more or less abstract cognitive principles and to approach them accordingly in a somewhat distanced, analytical manner. As we saw, this is in contrast to

---

23　See on this subject Leen Spruit, *Species Intelligibilis. From Perception to Knowledge*, Brill's Studies in Intellectual History 48, 2 vols. (Leiden: Brill, 1994), 1: 179-86; on the distinction between senses and sensory organs, see ibid., 180, n. 19. Modern psychology has confirmed this insight, as in: "What is consciously perceived is imagery which is created by the organism itself" (Silvan S. Tomkins, *Affect, Imagery and Consciousness*, vol. 1 (New York: Springer, 1962), 13.

24　Spruit, *Species*, 185.

25　*Conf.* X.viii.15 (p. 163).

26　*Conf.* X.x.17 (p. 163).

27　*Conf.* X.xi.18 (p. 164).

28　*Conf.* X.x.17 (p. 164).

29　*Conf.* X.xi.18 (p. 164). A modern form of this notion is that of universal innate psychological patterns or "archetypes": Carl G. Jung, *The Archetypes and the Collective Unconscious* (London: Routledge and Kegan Paul, 1975).

what he describes in the Ostia experience as leaving this mental process-
ing behind to access *affectively* what he experiences as the comprehensive
living, creating invisible divine Wisdom–that nevertheless encompasses
these (more or less immobile?) exemplars.

Thus when he remembers the Ostia experience a second time, he indeed speaks of having strained his ear to hear the Creator, not as mediated
(and thus mentally processed) through angelic voices or thunder or the
mysteries of symbols, but directly, through his own voice: "himself, whom
we love in these things, we hear him without these things, just as we now
we reached out and with a leap of the mind touched/attained the eternal Wisdom remaining above all things (*sed ipsum, quem in his amamus,
ipsum sine his audiamus, sicut nunc extendimus nos et rapida cogitatione
attingimus aeternam sapientiam super omnia manentem*)."[30] While the experience is thus again described as a direct "hearing" that followed upon
a mental-affective reaching-out beyond ordinary sensory experiences, it
must this time be a leap of the mind (over the "gap") that–somehow–attained the interior hearing and touching of a spiritual dimension that
had first been mentally-affectively distilled from the information in sensory phenomena.[31] Augustine here clearly feels this affective experience of
sudden access to the discerned divine essence itself to have occurred in a
mysterious way, outside his conscious mental activity. At the very beginning of the *Confessions*, however, he had realized that notwithstanding his
painful seeming absence, God was also already in him, saying: "Why do
I seek that you should come into me, who would not be unless you were
in me? (*quid peto ut venias in me, qui non essem nisi esses in me?*)."[32] His
reaching out, then, is at the same time an attempt to enter into the hidden place in himself and connect with the living God himself who resides
there through his reflected "image" and radiates the invisible patterns,
forms or exemplars of his Truth. As Burcht Pranger indicates, in the *Confessions* Augustine seems to feel that he does not know how this connection is made and attributes it to God's initiative.

---

30 *Conf.* IX.x.25 (p. 148). Pranger, "Return," 62, has "a flash of mental energy" (perhaps
also from Chadwick, *Confessions*, but without page reference).

31 The words in the preceding conversation are here not explicitly pointed to as a way
to God. Later, Augustine would develop a notion that Christ as the divine Word becomes
embodied in the human word about divine things and might in this way enter the heart; see
on this Marcia Colish, *The Mirror of Language. A Study in the Medieval Theory of Knowledge*
(Lincoln: University of Nebraska Press, 1983), 26.

32 *Conf.* I.ii.2 (pp. 1-2); translation by Catherine Conybeare in her "Beyond Word and
Image: Aural Patterning in Augustine's *Confessions*," to be published in Giselle de Nie and
Thomas F.X. Noble, eds., *Dynamic Patterns in Images and Texts* (Notre Dame: Notre Dame
Press, 2011).

Concluding the second remembering of his Ostia experience, Augustine then regrets the rapid passing of this "moment of understanding, for which we [now] sigh (*momentum intellegentiae, cui suspiravimus*)," wondering whether it will perhaps return and be eternal at the resurrection.[33] Here again, significantly, breathing appears to be a sensory experience that is intimately associated with access to the spiritual-affective one. When Augustine speaks of his enhanced spiritual state just after baptism, it is likewise in terms of breathing: "having formerly sighed for you and now finally breathing in you (*olim suspirans tibi et tandem respirans*)."[34] The unitive experience of a "touching with a total shock/upheaval of the heart" is thus at the same time an "understanding through a leap of the mind."[35] I suggest that the conflation of heart and mind which we see here reveals Augustine's understanding that the intermittent and unpredictable leaps over the gap between the sensory impression as represented in its mental image on the one hand, and the interiorly sensed image-reflection-presence of a purely spiritual Being on the other, take place in an *involuntary affective mode of cognition* that–as he himself clearly indicates–differs from the voluntary process of mental matching with the interior exemplars of Truth.

II. Utinam discat tangere! *Imaginatively "touching" the divine Christ in the sermons*

What Augustine's later sermons say, however, about the self-initiated affective act of trusting-believing through interiorly enacting a "touching" of the mentally imaged divine person of Christ as precipitating an interior miracle–also likely a moment of shock–appears to be a much more easily accessible experience. He knew, of course, that in the Gospels Jesus' personal touch–in combination with his words–transmitted a divine power that purified the interior as well as the exterior person from an evil that debilitates.[36] As the Gospel reports, this happened so frequently that the men of Gennesaret brought him all that were sick, that they might only

---

33 *Conf.* IX.x.25 (p. 148).
34 *Conf.* IX.vii.16 (p. 142).
35 Elsewhere in his writings too, true understanding is for him not a distanced appraisal but, quite on the contrary, an affective-cognitive becoming-one with the quality or pattern of whatever is understood; e.g. *Epist.* 147.xvii.44, (CSEL 44, p. 318).
36 Cf. "Touch," *International Dictionary of New Testament Theology*, vol. 3 (Grand Rapids: Zondervan, 1976), 860.

touch the fringe of his garment, and "as many as touched it were made well" (*Et quicumque tetigerunt, salvi facti sunt*).[37]

In Augustine's sermons, the most elaborate treatment of spiritual touching, not surprisingly, is found in his explanations of the story of the woman with the issue of blood who was healed by touching the fringe of Jesus's garment (Mt 9:20-22; Mk 5:25-34). A sermon that has been dated to 402-404[38] and seems addressed (also) to non-believers, designates the woman as a figure of the then still invisible future Gentile Church bleeding with her martyrs. And Christ's noticing the difference between her and the crowd jostling around him is described as: "The Lord said, 'Someone touched me', [meaning:] I feel the one touching me more strongly than the whole pressing crowd. The crowd knows how to do the easy pressing: would that it learned how to touch! (*Ait dominus:* TETIGIT ME ALIQUIS: *magis sensi unam tangentem, quam turbam prementem. Turba facile novit premere: utinam discat tangere!*)."[39] What kind of touching is this? In another early sermon, Augustine says:

> We do not run to Christ by walking, but by believing; we reach him not by the motion of the body, but by the wish of our heart. Thus the woman who touched the fringe [of his clothing] more truly touched him than the crowd that pressed upon him. [...] What is 'touched' if not 'believed'?[40]

The "wish of the heart"–which we also saw preceding the Ostia experience–then as it were opens it to the experience, and the decision to reach out and actually touch, imaginatively, is the decision to *trust* that one will find what one seeks. In another sermon, dated to the year 428,[41] Augustine similarly explains that "touching with the heart: that is believing; for the woman who had touched the fringe, touched with her heart, because she believed (*Tangere autem corde, hoc est credere; nam et illa mulier, quae fimbriam tetigit, corde tetigit, quia credidit*)."[42]

---

37 Mt 14:36; similarly, Mk 6:56.

38 A. Kunzelmann, "Die Chronologie der Sermones des hl. Augustinus," in *Studi Agostiniani, Miscellanea Agostiniana*, vol. 2 (Rome: Tipografia Poliglotta Vaticana, 1931), 417-520, at 434, 515.

39 *Sermo* Mai XCV.6.24-5, in *Miscellanea Agostiniana*, vol. 1 (Rome: Tipografia Poliglotta Vaticana, 1930), 345. Cf. Ambrose, *Expositio evangelii secundum Lucam*, ed. Marcus Adriaen and P. A. Ballerini, CCSL 14 (Turnhout: Brepols, 1957), VI.6.57 (p. 194, ll. 581-2).

40 *Tract.* XXVI.3.2-5, 8-9 (CCSL 36, p. 261): *Non enim ad Christum ambulando currimus, sed credendo, nec motu corporis, sed voluntate cordis accedimus. Ideo illa mulier quae fimbriam tetigit magis tetigit quam turba quae pressit. [...] Quid est tetigit nisi credidit?* For Ambrose, however, "touching" Christ could also be effected through self-mortification: *Exp. ev. sec. Luc.* X.164.1563 (CCSL 14, p. 393).

41 Kunzelmann, "Chronologie," 428, 516.

42 *Sermo* Guelferbitanus XIV.2.28-30 (*Misc. Agost.*, 1: 487).

Believing, then, means an inner movement of affective surrender in absolute trust. In another sermon, however, we see that there is also a cognitive element. Explaining the risen Christ's saying to Mary Magdalene at
the empty tomb that she should *not* touch him because he had not yet
gone up to the Father, Augustine lets Christ say: "You see me, humble, on
earth: touch me [now], and you will remain on earth. Touch me [later]
as a higher one, believe me to be in heaven, believe in [me as] the only
Son and co-equal of the Father; for when you understand me to be equal,
then I will ascend for you to the Father (*Vides me humilem in terra: tangis
me, et remanes in terra. Altiorem me tange, in altiorem me crede, in uni-
genitum Patri aequalem crede; quando enim me intellexeris aequalem,
tunc tibi ascendi ad Patrem*)."[43] Augustine concludes this sermon saying:
"Christ will therefore ascend for us and we shall touch him if we believe
in him [as divine], for he is the Son of God [...] Believe [this], and you
will have touched [him]. [And] touch [him] in this way, so that you may
stay close [to him] (*Ascendat ergo nobis Christus, et tangamus eum, si credamus in eum, quia Filius dei est [...] Sic credite, et tetigistis. Sic tangite, ut
haereatis*)."[44] "Touching", then, can now be more or less continuous.

The fact that, in Augustine's view, only the holding in the heart of a *true*
representation or image of Christ as divine and all-powerful would make it
possible for the heart to "touch" or connect to his nature itself indicates and
assumes that it is the essential *resemblance* of this mental representation
(*species*) to the corresponding invisible affective-spiritual image-pattern of
his presence in the mind-heart that connects them. The unexpressed principle underlying this crucial supposition, I suggest, must be another late
antique notion, everywhere taken for granted: that "like attracts like" and
spontaneously merges with it.[45] Modern psychology, speaking in more secular language about meditation and the insight that "images are the con-
cretizations of emotions,"[46] has described this psychological process as the
well-attested assimilation–through involuntary *mimesis*–by the seer of the

---

43 *Sermo* Guelf. XIV.2.25-28 (*Misc. Agost.*, 1: 487).

44 *Sermo* Guelf. XIV.2.34; 1, 5-6 (*Misc. Agost.*, 1: 187, 488); similarly, *Sermo* 243.II.2
and 245.II.2 in PL 38, col. 1144C and 1152D.

45 It was the basis of the practice of divination and of magic; see "Mageia," *Paulys
Realencyclopädie der classischen Altertumswissenschaft*, vol. 27, rev. ed. by Georg Wissowa,
(Stuttgart: Druckenmüller, 1928), cols. 314-15.

46 Gerald Epstein, *Waking Dream Therapy: Dream Process as Imagination* (New York:
Human Sciences Press, 1981), 18.

affective pattern made visible in the seen.[47] Formulated in somewhat more modern terms, then, what Augustine's advice presupposes is that the belief in this, for ordinary people almost certainly imaged, representation of the divine Christ, inducing an affective surrender to a mental representation of the *living* pattern of all-powerful love which it makes visible, will–through the mutual resemblance–*affectively* connect and merge with the *living* image-pattern itself of Christ's love, already deep within the believing subject, that is waiting to be found, recognized and "touched." Mentally imaging a smiling Christ, then, could lead to an interior sensing of his invisible Love.

Augustine's advice to his community here points to a less ecstatic kind of interior "touching" than that experienced in Ostia, one that gives a greater role to human initiative and promises a great deal more hope of repeatability and continuance than his reflections in the *Confessions* about the usual inaccessibility of God.[48] It is no longer an impotent, if attentive, waiting for the abstract, divine, continuously creating Wisdom to allow an unpredictable and extremely infrequent opportunity for the ecstatic shock of a tremulous "touching/attaining". Now it is one's own initiative and responsibility to reach out and "touch" the–mentally visualizable–person of Christ in a model of interiorized movement which ordinary, non-philosophical, people could imaginatively imitate and hope to achieve. Crucially, too, the heart-mind now does not leave the images of the sensible world behind but embraces and experiences these as it were as leg-ups to sensing-apprehending analogous noniconic divine patterns of Truth.

The miracle of the woman with the issue of blood, however, showed that her trust, combined with her touch, could also have physical consequences. In an earlier sermon, dated 402-404, Augustine describes her motivation more fully when he adds her expectations to her belief, saying: "She touched [him] so that what she believed might happen; she did not touch [him] so that she might prove something she did not believe. [...] O touching! O believing! O demanding! (*Tetigit ut quod credidit consequeretur; non tetigit ut quod non crediderat probaretur. [...] O tangere! o credere! o exigere!*)."[49] This passage reveals another crucial difference with the Ostia experience. Augustine is now emphasizing that touching Christ can be

---

47   For a modern assessment of the dynamics of meditation, mental imaging and representation of the invisible through the visible see David Freedberg, *The Power of Images. Studies in the History and Theory of Response* (Chicago: University of Chicago Press, 1989), 161-91.

48   Powerfully shown by Conybeare, "Beyond," passim.

49   *Sermo* Mai XCV.6.6-7, 13 (*Misc. Agost.*, 1: 345).

done with the expectation of healing. The further addition of "demand-ing" is an even more marked difference: it points to a deliberate strategy, modelled upon Christ's words in the Gospel "Knock and it will be opened to you" (Mt 7:7, Lk 11:9). Is Augustine advising the "demanding" of a mir-acle here? As already indicated, in contrast to Ambrose's having initiated the western ecclesiastical propagation of martyrs' miracles in 386,[50] he for a long time thereafter continued to hold that no miracles were happen-ing, at least not at the African shrines of the martyrs. In the period before 424, accordingly, he points emphatically to the superiority of the interior miracle of the purification of the heart to merely physical cures.[51] Thus another sermon, dated to the year 408-409, says similarly that the woman "touched in faith, and the health which she had anticipated [indeed] fol-lowed. In short, [this was done] so that we might know what true touch-ing is (*Fide tetigit, et sanitas subsecuta est, quam praesumpsit. Denique ut nossemus quid sit vere tangere*)."[52] The real "touching," then, is now the spiritual one and its healing is spiritual purification.

In a later sermon, however, Augustine may be referring to the physical cures then taking place when he says that the woman was cured according to her faith: "Grace went out [from Christ], so that she might be healed. [...] We all touch [him], if we believe (*Gratia processit, ut illa sanaretur. [...] Tangamus omnes, si credamus*)."[53] What he is here holding out to everyone is the hope that a self-initiated imaginal communion–through what, for most people, is almost certainly a mental image–with the invisible interior pattern of Christ as the loving divine Healer can also precipitate a palpa-ble physical effect.[54] If the dating is correct this sermon would have been held in 428, well after miracles had begun to happen around Stephen's relic in Hippo. Even in his sermons about the martyr in this period, then, Augustine keeps emphasizing that it is Christ or God, and not as ordinary

---

50   As in his *Epistola* X.lxxvii.9 (CSEL 82.3, pp. 132, ll. 89-91).

51   As in *Sermo* 88.II.3 (PL 38, col. 540C). Ambrose describes inner healing from God when he says to widows: *tanget interiora tua dei manus [...] pulset dei dextera secreta cordis* (*De viduis* X.62 [PL 16, col. 266B]).

52   *Sermo* 243.II.2 (PL 38, col. 1144B). For the date: Kunzelmann, "Chronologie," 499, 514.

53   *Sermo* 245.III.3, IV.4 (PL 38, 1152D, 1153A,C). For the date: Kunzelmann, "Chro-nologie," 428, 514.

54   For an overview of the theme of *Christus medicus* in Augustine's writings, see Paul van Geest, "'Inveni medicus, qui in caelo habitat et in terris spargit medicamenta'. Augusti-nus van Hippo over ziekte en genezing [Augustine of Hippo on illness and healing]," *Leid-schrift. Historisch Tijdschrift* 17 (2002): 29-51. Ambrose too stressed this theme, as in *Exp. ev. sec. Luc.* VI.57.580 (CCSL 14, p. 194).

folk might assume the saint by himself, who does the actual healing.[55] As will now be seen, however, his actual description of these cures is more often than not surprisingly matter-of-fact.

III. Dum orans cum magno fletu cancellos teneo: accessing the divine through physical touch

Knowledge of the new miracles associated with the remains of the first martyr Stephen discovered in 415,[56] that in the years thereafter began to occur in all the Mediterranean countries, appears to have reached Augustine only in 424. In this year he visited his long-time friend bishop Evodius in the city of Uzalis, north of Carthage, in which Stephen's relic had arrived in 418 and from then on had been associated with many miracles.[57] Augustine appears to have been given a particle of it, or perhaps something that had been in contact with the relic, to take back with him to his own city, where it precipitated a tidal wave of miracles. These events forced him to reverse his long-time stance that no such events were happening in Africa into an insistence that these new ones should be actively made known to all by having them recorded in written statements or pamphlets to be read in church regularly.[58] In 426, citing them as evidence to support his discussion of the future resurrection in the last book of his *City of God*, Augustine adduced a number of short summaries of the almost seventy miracles that had been recorded in Hippo in the preceding two years as proofs that the martyrs had already risen, and thus that their faith was true: for their remains were seen to be conduits of effective divine grace.[59]

The first few miracles which Augustine lists, however, do not involve the martyrs. They happened during or after ecclesiastical ritual acts that involved the enactment of a power-laden symbolism combined with a specific kind of contact to achieve the presencing of the divine. Thus the sign of the Cross healed a cancer, the rite of baptism cured gout and paral-

---

55 As in *Sermo* 285.5 and 7 (PL 38, col. 1235D and 1297A).

56 See on this Meyers, *Miracles*, 11-25.

57 *De civitate dei* 22.8.36-65 and 22.8.353-54 in the edition of Bernardus Dombart and Alfonsus Kalb, CCSL 48 (Turnhout: Brepols, 1955), 824 (subsequent citations from this edition). Cf. Lancel, "Miracle," 70, citing in n. 56 Othmar Perler and S.L. Maier, *Les voyages de saint Augustin* (Paris: Études augustiniennes, 1969), 373-80, and 75. A full discussion of these miracles will appear in my *Poetics of Wonder*.

58 *Civ. dei* 22.8.345-53 (p. 824).

59 *Civ. dei* 22.8 (pp. 815-27).

ysis, and the celebration of the Eucharist expelled evil spirits. The holiness inherent in the ecclesiastical status appears to be transmitted into a material object when the tears of a priest praying for a woman fell into the oil with which she anointed herself–possibly following the ancient instructions for treating the sick in the letter of James 5:14-15–and effected her cure; another priest, however, cured someone by prayer at a distance. This connection or "touch" would have been spiritual. In almost all of these miracles, then, physical touch or proximity "triggers" the cure. Is the mere proximity of Stephen, through his relic, now transmitting a new grace into the community that spreads into the whole ecclesiastical sphere?

Indirect contact with Christ through earth brought from Jerusalem, however, effectively expelled and protected against evil spirits; Augustine himself accepted such material from a landowner and buried it in a special place, perhaps a chapel. Later a paralytic came to this now "holy place (*locu[s] sanctu[s]*),"[60] prayed and was cured. This shows that the power coming through a relic was experienced as radiating not only into the altars themselves but also into their surroundings. Similarly, at the memorial shrine (*memoria*) of the Milanese martyrs Gervasius and Protasius, a possessed young man, who had been laid there while unconscious, woke up when hymns were sung and began clutching the altar–presumably containing the relics–as though he could not let it go, while the evil spirit in him confessed all its crimes; when it finally departed, however, it left one eye dangling out. Trusting in the intercession of the saints, a relative bound it up, and after seven days it was found to be healed. The physical presence, then, of an object regarded as a conduit to holy power sparked a trust that healing would occur, and it did.

While one bishop "was cured immediately (*repente sanata est*)" of a fistula simply by carrying the, presumably encased, relics of Stephen,[61] other stories tell of cures effected by more extensively mediated contact. Thus touching the flowers carried by a bishop leading a procession of relics cured blind eyes: "she applied them to her eyes and at once began to see (*oculis admovit–protinus vidit*)."[62] And a Spanish priest at Calama was cured of a kidney stone when he had been carried to the shrine of Stephen there; praying and being in that place, near his relics, may have been enough. When he later died at home, however, his tunic was taken to the shrine, and after presumably having been laid on the altar containing the

---

60   *Civ. dei* 22.8.212 (p. 820).
61   *Civ. dei* 22.8.277 (p. 822).
62   *Civ. dei* 22.8.269 (p. 821).

relics, taken back and laid on him: he revived. Flowers that had been temporarily placed on the altar presumably containing Stephen's relics and then placed next to the sleeping head of a dying nobleman, who had up to then obstinately resisted conversion, suddenly changed his mind about this. Contact too is central when a small boy who had died after his head had been crushed by a wagon wheel, revived without apparent injury when his mother "placed [him] at the same shrine (*ad eandem memoriam posuit*)"[63]–again, presumably near or on the altar, for two other stories report this specifically as having been done with dead children who revived. There are two stories of women reviving from death through contact with one of their dresses that had been placed on the altar (containing the relics). And a tax-gatherer revived when he was anointed with "the martyr's oil (*oleum martyris*),"[64] almost certainly from a lamp on or near the altar. What we see in all these stories too is that the physical touching of a material object that is or has been in contact with the holy has been added to prayer as the way to connect with the divine healing power. The use of dresses and anointing may point to the whole body being involved in this mediated contact.

The only extant first-person testimony, or pamphlet, of a miraculous cure survived because it was read in church and commented upon in a sermon recorded by one of Augustine's always attending stenographers. In it the beneficiary Paul of Caesarea, who had been afflicted with a bodily tremor, says that after having prayed at Stephen's shrine every day for two weeks, on Easter day, while everyone stood around watching,

> when I was praying with profuse weeping and holding on to the railing [around the altar], I suddenly fell. Removed from my senses, I do not know where I was. After a little while I stood up again and did not find that tremor in my body.[65]

Augustine's own report of the event in his *City of God* notes that he lay "precisely as if asleep but not trembling as he used to do even in sleep (*dormienti simillimus iacuit, non tamen tremens, sicut etiam per somnum solebat*)."[66] Such a temporary collapse–in which the mind-body fundamentally rearranges and reorganizes its energies–has also been described

---

63 *Civ. dei* 22.8.314 (p. 823).
64 *Civ. dei* 22.8.333 (p. 823).
65 *Sermo* 322 (PL 38, 1414D): *[D]um orans cum magno fletu cancellos teneo, subito cecidi. Alienatus autem a sensu, ubi fuerim nescio. Post paululum assurrexi, et illum tremorem in corpore meo non inveni.*
66 *Civ. dei* 22.8.429-30 (p. 826).

as frequently occurring in the context of present-day faith healing as a "slaying in the Spirit" or "resting in the Spirit."[67]

Three days later, after Paul's pamphlet had been read to the community, and he and his sister Palladia–who was still suffering from the same kind of tremor–had withdrawn to the adjoining chapel for Stephen while Augustine commented upon the event, jubilant cries were suddenly heard from there. Everyone ran to them and saw that Palladia too had just been cured. According to what was told to Augustine, "as soon as she had touched the railing, she similarly collapsed as if falling asleep, [and then] arose healed (*mox ut cancellos adtigit, conlapsa similiter velut in somnum sana surrexit*)."[68] The phrase "as soon as she had touched" is crucial here. It looks as though the earlier miracle had established a pattern of expectation that, when similar circumstances occurred, precipitated its replication. For more clearly than in her brother's case, her touch is said to have induced a shock of power that released the body from the lock-grip of its involuntary trembling. The prehistory of these young people–their tremors, they said, had been brought on by their aggrieved mother's curse–makes it likely that their ailment had a psychological origin.[69]

The continuous groaning and weeping described as taking place during Paul's preceding prayer was then customary and understood as a ritualized entreaty and simultaneous purification from sin; it is likely to have preceded other cures too.[70] Like Augustine's own attention to breathing, it appears to have functioned as a sensory bridge to transformational spiritual experience. For its extremely strenuous, if ritualized, enactment of utter self-abasement is likely to have induced the intense emotion it makes visible and therefore also what in cultural anthropology is now called a trance or transgressive, "liminal" state. In traditional societies, this state is often brought about through exhausting or acutely painful rituals. They initiate a state of extreme emotional excitement that tends to shut off ordinary sensory perception or even consciousness altogether, and shatters fixed habits as well as debilitating emotional cramps; this releases up to

---

67   On the idea of "slaying in the Spirit": Morton T. Kelsey, *Discernment – A Study in Ecstasy and Evil* (New York: Paulist Press, 1978), 10-50; on "resting in the Spirit": Martien F.G. Parmentier, *Rusten in de Geest: God houdt ons de spiegel voor* [Resting in the Spirit. God holds up a mirror to us] (Hilversum: Stichting 'Vuur', 1992). Cf. William Sargant, *The Mind Possessed. A Physiology of Possession, Mysticism and Faith Healing* (Philadelphia: Lippincott, 1974), 4-5, 45.

68   *Civ. dei* 22.8.468-69 (p. 827).

69   Cf. Sargant, *Mind*, 40-41, on possession through guilt.

70   See P. Adnès, "Larmes," *Dictionnaire de Spiritualité* (Paris: G. Beauchesne, 1932-), 9: 287-303.

then constricted vital energies so that they can resume their function of building up and maintaining the body.[71] If, while praying, Paul and Palladia moreover had visualized a smiling saint Stephen–he is recorded as having been seen with "a smiling and serene face (*vultus [...] hilar[us] seren[us]*)" in a contemporary dream cure in Uzalis[72]–the affectively assimilated image of the healing energy made visible in this image would have activated the corresponding pattern in their bodies to effect the sudden cure.

"Moment of rupture and rapture"

To summarize and conclude: Augustine's description in the *Confessions* of the theophanic moment at Ostia appears to indicate that he then thought of what he supposed to be the "gap" between sensory and spiritual experience as capable of being leapt over only momentarily and by divine initiative. Rather than the conscious mental matching of images of sensory impressions with the innate exemplars of divine Truth which Augustine describes elsewhere as able to access it, the Ostia experience is described as an involuntary affective communion with a living, creating spiritual movement that must simply be awaited.

In his later sermons, however, Augustine makes the Gospel story of the woman with the issue of blood a model for a self-initiated imaginative experience of "touching," not the invisible divine Wisdom, but the visualizable person of the divine Christ. I have suggested that Augustine's implicit passing over here of what he had earlier experienced so painfully as the "gap" between sensory experience, as imaged in the mind, and the experience of numinous presence, must be ascribed to his now–implicitly–turning to another late antique presupposition. *It is that of the mutual attraction and natural merging of the similar: someone's affective surrender to* a true mental representation, then, would spontaneously merge his or her state of mind-heart with its corresponding invisible eternal ontological pattern. Although Augustine, as far as I know, did not formulate this explicitly, he shows the people in his miracle stories simply acting it out:

---

71 See on this, for instance, René Devisch, *Weaving the Threads of Life. The* Khita *Gyn-Eco-Logical Healing Cult Among the Yaka* (Chicago: University of Chicago Press, 1993), and Sargant, *Mind*, 44-57.

72 *Miracula sancti Stephani* 2.2.6 in *Les miracles de saint Étienne. Recherches sur le recueil pseudo-augustinien (BHL 7860-7861)*, Hagiologia 5, ed. Jean Meyers (Turnhout: Brepols, 2006), 322.

trusting in the loving, healing power of Christ to work through the palpable relics of his martyrs who, resembling him, were therefore thought to be spiritually connected to him.[73] Their trust is likely to have been mentally imaged in and as the healing Christ himself, or as his power channelled through a dead saint whose appearance too could be imagined. This leap from the sensory, through the mental image, to the numinous, and back again to the body, seems to qualify in its own way as–but, significantly, also to resolve the aporia in–what Burcht Pranger refers to as Augustine's notion in the *Confessions* of a spiritual "moment of rupture and rapture, the transformation of the visible into the invisible and *vice versa.*"[74] The connection, then, between the subject's affective assimilation to a mental image and the corresponding pattern in the interior reflection of the divine image would be an essential similarity that naturally causes them to coalesce. The miraculous cures would show how this coalescence could allow the divine pattern's latent healing power to extend itself into the whole mind-body, just as the woman's touch had done.

In case this model of healing seems far-fetched: ancient as well as present-day shamanic practice and modern clinical psychotherapy have convincingly shown that in our time too the affective assimilation to an image exhibiting a creative life-force–accomplished through the contemplation of a picture, or through enactive ritual or meditative visualization–can and does heal through stimulating what must be latent corresponding vitalizing energy patterns in the body.[75] That is not to say, however, that this image-logic alone explains how miracles happen. Especially in the cases of unconscious persons, but also in other cures, modern evidence shows that the existence can be surmised of as yet not scientifically registerable but demonstrably effective invisible energies, possibly stored in material objects and communicated through contact, but also channelled

---

73 This notion is central in a contemporary sermon about relics: Victricius Rotomagensis, *De laude sanctorum*, ed. Iacobus Mulders and Roland Demeulenaere, CCSL 64 (Turnhout: Brepols, 1985), 69-93.

74 Pranger, "Return," 62.

75 A very full and scientific report on this is that of Jeanne Achterberg, *Imagery in Healing. Shamanism and Modern Medicine* (Boston: Shambala, 1985). Results of bio-medical research on the neurological transmitters of image/emotion-messages are given in Candace B. Pert, *Molecules of Emotion. The Science Behind Mind-Body Medicine* (New York: Scribner, 1997).

through living persons.[76] Entering the quantum age, we are finding that our cognitive and affective capacities are less circumscribed and that the world perceived by the physical senses is less inert than we thought.[77]

---

76   On energies stored in material objects, see Lyall Watson, *The Nature of Things. The Secret Life of Inanimate Objects* (Rochester, VT: Destiny, 1990). There are many books on the subject of mind-body healing. I have found useful: Deepak Chopra [M.D.], *Quantum Healing. Exploring the Frontiers of Mind/Body Medicine* (New York: Bantam, 1989). Including historical miracles are: Morton T. Kelsey, *Psychology, Medicine and Christian Healing* (San Francisco: Harper and Row, 1988), and Maria Wittmer-Busch and Constanze Rendtel, *Miracula. Wunderheilungen im Mittelalter. Eine historisch-psychologische Annäherung* (Cologne: Böhlau, 2003). Specifically concerning healing through touch, in faith healing: Agnes Sanford, *The Healing Light* (New York: Ballantine Books, 1983), and as a clinical practice: Dolores Krieger, *The Therapeutic Touch. How to Use Your Hands to Help or Heal* (Englewood Cliffs: Prentice-Hall, 1979).

77   On different kinds of awareness, see, for instance, William James, *The Varieties of Religious Experience* (New York: Mentor, 1958); and Pim van Lommel [M.D.], *Eindeloos bewustzijn. Een wetenschappelijke visie op de bijna-dood ervaring* [Infinite consciousness. A scientific view of the near-death experience] (Kampen: Ten Have, 2007); on the scientific evidence of the transparency of the material world to patterns of a not directly knowable creative energy: David Bohm, *Wholeness and the Implicate Order* (London: Routledge, 1980).

THE FAME OF FAKE, DIONYSIUS THE AREOPAGITE: FABRICATION, FALSIFICATION AND THE 'CLOUD OF UNKNOWING'

BRAM KEMPERS

Introduction

Few texts enjoyed such a varied, volatile, contradictory and long afterlife as those that were ascribed to the enigmatic author, known as Dionysius the Areopagite. An enormous variety of meanings have been attached to a relatively small group of texts of limited length. In the later stages of their reception more and more focus has been given to the identity of the author. The in the end successful falsification of the author as the Athenian pupil of the apostle Paul became the primary focus of scholarly attention.

In this essay I will argue that the question about the author's identity is part of a more complicated *Rezeptionsgeschichte* during a very long period, which started in the early sixth century and lasts until the present day. The convincing conclusion that the texts cannot have been written by Paul's Greek companion somehow became a handicap in understanding the wider context of the huge attention that the texts happened to attract, not least because they suggested Dionysius the Areopagite to be their author. On the whole the vast secondary literature on Pseudo-Dionysius tends to emphasize the sudden and effective falsification of the purported author rather than acknowledging the complicated continuity in the reception as a crucial source of wisdom.

Step by step the Dionysian texts, originally written in Greek, acquired almost unprecedented authority in the Latin West. After the Bible itself, these texts were considered to be of prime importance since the twelfth century, even more so than either the Greek philosophers or the Church fathers.

The surprisingly positive reception of Dionysius in the fifteenth century hardly became an issue in the extensive secondary literature, which tends to focus far too much on the favourable reception of Valla's falsification. In fact, ever more meaning was attached to the Dionysian texts. They were marginalized only at a much later stage.

Precisely because Pseudo-Dionysius became a niche within specialized scholarly discourse, mainly within the modern disciplines of theology and to a lesser extent philosophy, it became increasingly difficult to establish his extensive cultural impact in the long run. Relying on modern editions and translations, using the secondary literature, and reading many primary texts again or for the first time with this theme in mind, I will try to reconsider Dionysius' role in our cultural history.

Invention and renovation of traditions from Greek into Latin

An intriguing group of Greek texts suddenly made its appearance in the early sixth century: four treatises and ten letters. The longest text bears the title *Divine Names*, a short one is called *Mystical Theology*. According to the titles the two other treatises deal with the *Celestial Hierarchy* and the *Ecclesiastical Hierarchy*. Ten letters are addressed to various persons, Titus and John the apostle and evangelist among them. Timothy is frequently mentioned in the texts. In some of the manuscripts Timothy appears as the addressee of the treatises. Few persons are mentioned by name in the texts: Jesus Christ and the apostles Paul, Peter, Jacob and Bartholomew. All these names suggest a specific context: the early Christian Church. According to the New Testament both Titus and Timothy received letters by Saint Paul; they participated in the early historiography of the church. The author mentions Paul himself as his main teacher, together with the enigmatic Hierotheus. In this way the author suggested that he knew the apostles personally and that he was directly inspired by them. This suggestion proved to be a successful literary strategy. In fact, it was a widespread literary strategy, well known from the Bible itself and many other texts circulating in Antiquity. A little earlier fourteen letters appeared, presented as a correspondence between Seneca and Saint Paul.

Immediately this group of four treatises and ten letters was ascribed to a single author: Dionysius the Areopagite. In Acts 17, describing Paul's discussion with the philosophers in Athens, his first convert there was referred to by the name of Dionysius, a member of the Council called the Areopagus. Only a few years after its first appearance, this alleged authorship was doubted at the synod of Constantinople in 533. It was claimed that the newly discovered texts could not belong to the era of Saint Paul and his first converts, thereby denying their ancient authority. An apostolic pedigree, implied by the names of Timothy and Dionysius the Areopagite, met with critique in the Byzantine context of the sixth century. In the Greek world the reception of the texts, ascribed to Dionysius the Areopagite, failed to become an absolute success story, yet Dionysius came to be described, depicted and revered as a saint and a bishop.

Within Latin literature the same group of texts received an even more favorable reaction than in the Greek era. Pope Gregory the Great mentioned Dionysius in his 34th *Homily*. In western Europe Dionysius Areopagita became a celebrity, especially since the ninth century when a manuscript with the Greek texts travelled from East to West. With the arrival in France in 827, three centuries after their first appearance in the Byzantine East, the same texts acquired different meanings, in another language and in a new context.

Without much discussion, his name as an author came to be attached to these texts, which were more and more presented as a Latin corpus with a single author, named Dionysius. The distance in time, space and language allowed for more virtual certainties, which enhanced the authority of the manuscript and the growing corpus of texts that surrounded the original texts. John Scottus Eriugena made an influential translation, revising the slightly earlier one by Hilduin, abbot of Saint Denis, who paved the way for the fame of Dionysius. His *Life* and *Passion* of Saint Dionysius became a canonical text. Both Hilduin and Scottus contributed to the emergence of an ever more independent Latin tradition, sustained by a sequence of revised translations, commentaries and references in other treatises. An expanding number of allusions to Dionysius the Areopagite circulated in widening circles, from Rome to Paris and beyond, reaching the British Isles as well. Changing the geographical setting meant transforming the content as it was understood in the new world. Readers assigned new meanings to the texts and gave the author another identity.

Several new elements were added to the author's persona. In France he was identified with the Parisian bishop of the same name: Saint Dionysius or Denis. Readers from the ninth century onwards, already familiar with Augustine, Jerome and Boethius, were especially receptive to the harmonious mixture of Christian and pagan elements. The mystical depth of Platonic ideas embedded in a Christian context added to the repute of the Dionysian *Corpus*. Authors welcomed such a visionary synthesis between the classical tradition, tracing its roots to Athens, and the New Testament, which they saw culminating in the tradition of the medieval West. The invented identification with the legendary bishop Denis and the interest in fusing pagan and Christian thought gave a new impetus to the reception of the Dionysian texts.

In Dionysian thought European readers recognized a solid understanding of the Greek philosophers within a Christian paradigm, at the same time using names, concepts and metaphors derived from the Old Testament. Knowledge of that newly assembled tradition was increasingly transmitted in Latin translations, not only of the Bible but also of Plato and his followers. As such the oeuvre of Dionysius proved to be more a product of the Latin West than a creation from the Greek Middle East, where his tradition had been originally invented. On the basis of a three-fold, in itself heterogeneous, invention of tradition–making the texts as if they had an apostolic origin, linking them to the name of Saint Paul's first Athenian disciple, and connecting them to an early French martyr-bishop–an impressive academic building was erected in the Latin West.

For an interesting mixture of reasons Dionysius acquired almost un-surpassed authority as an eloquent source of the earliest Christian philos-ophy, which was grounded in classical literature, the Old Testament and the New Testament. Dionysius, dying for his faith, seemed to be the pupil of Saint Paul himself, benefiting as well from Hierotheus, his alleged men-tor; he was a friend of the slightly younger Timothy to whom he dedicated the texts, at least according to the later manuscripts. In the texts Timothy, Titus, and the apostles John, Paul, Peter, Jacob and Bartholomew appear alongside the prophets Moses, David, Ezekiel, and Zechariah. Their focus is the teaching of Jesus to whom the author comes very close due to his implied personal link with the apostles, while its vocabulary resembles the Platonic tradition. In the Latin literature Dionysius was continuously re-invented and recreated after his initial appearance in the Greek context of the early sixth century.

Dionysius continued to attract attention from the leading scholars in western Europe, Hugh of Saint-Victor, Richard of Saint-Victor, Alan of Lille, Thomas Gallus, Bonaventure, and Albert the Great among them. His fame was so widely spread that Dante allowed him to appear twice in his *Paradise*, which further enhanced his renown. In his widely read *Golden Legend*, Jacopo de Voragine assigned Dionysius the Areopagite pride of place as his chief intellectual authority. Thomas Aquinas mentioned Di-onysius time and again, even more often than Aristotle, quoting him some seventeen hundred times. Within the limited number of libraries in the Latin West, each boasting only part of the Greek literary heritage, the Dionysian texts really meant a cornerstone to the intellectual elite. From the ninth century to the fifteenth few other authors were mentioned as frequently as Dionysius, and few other texts received as much commen-taries as his four treatises and ten letters. In the Latin tradition, Dionysius the Areopagite hardly had any rivals. In the canon, he directly followed authors like Paul himself and preceded both Plato and Aristotle and even

Augustine, Jerome, Ambrose and Gregory the Great, one of the first in the Latin tradition to mention Dionysius the Areopagite.

Due to dozens of leading poets, theologians, philosophers, and historians Dionysius' fame remained firmly established in the fourteenth century. A great diversity of authors, writing either in Latin or in one of the emerging vernacular languages, confirmed the authority of the Dionysian texts, which had made their first appearance around 520 in the Byzantine world. There, they continued to be read and commented upon, but within a cultural tradition, which in no way could rival the impressive series of renaissances and recreations in the Latin West. It was partly due to the scarcity of texts in Western Europe, in combination with the fortunate transmission of the Dionysian texts, that they could acquire such an exceptional authority.

Renaissances and re-inventions in print

In the secondary literature the fifteenth century is usually presented as a turning point, marking the scientific discovery of the false identity of Dionysius. For a number of reasons, this is highly misleading. Both the rise of the vernacular languages and the introduction of printing added to the repute of Dionysius' writing. He was not at all put aside and marginalized. In addition, the arrival of many more Greek texts from the East provided new means to interpret his texts and assign ever more meaning to them. Within the dominant intellectual traditions, Dionysius ruled as a unique source in the field of universal wisdom, to which the leading humanists from many nations added substantial new elements. Still another renaissance was to take place, ensuring his unique authority.

In the fifteenth century the Latin versions of the Dionysian texts continued to enjoy unsurpassed authority, confirmed by esteemed authors such as Ambrogio Traversari, Angelo Poliziano, Bessarion and Nicolaus Cusanus. They mentioned his name, commented upon his ideas, and occasionally discussed his identity as an author of the apostolic age. Some scholars expressed doubts about his personal link with Saint Paul, most notably Lorenzo Valla, but such philological concerns did not at all diminish the interest in Dionysius' texts.

Printed editions and revised commentaries added to their repute. In his *World Chronicle* of 1493, Hartmann Schedel reconfirmed Dionysius as a major historical figure. He mentioned him immediately after Timothy, bishop of Ephesus. In Athens they spoke of Jesus and his passion. Saint Paul baptised Dionysius, who became bishop of Athens. In France he died as a martyr and came to be revered and depicted as a saint. Schedel continued his story with Titus, the first bishop of Crete, and with the apostle and evangelist John. In this way the German scholar gave a new life to the earlier ideas that Dionysius belonged to the world of the New Testament and to the world of the early Church, from Greece to France.

In the late fifteenth century Marsilio Ficino retranslated the *Divine Names* and the *Mystical Theology*, providing extensive commentaries on them. Ficino's focus was an intellectual one rather than a historical interest like Schedel's. In Italy Ficino could use the impressive libraries of Florence and Rome, recently enriched by a flood of manuscripts, which Greek émigrés had brought with them flying from Constantinople and Athens. His contribution to the reception of Dionysius went further than the transformation from a manuscript tradition into a printed transmission in an increasing number of copies and re-editions. Ficino gave Dionysius a more explicit philosophical and theological content, elaborating upon his Platonic roots. In his *Christian Religion* Ficino explicitly praised Dionysius as the apotheosis of Plato's teaching and the foundation of Christian theology. Dionysius appears to be the crucial historical figure in Ficino's printed treatise on the *Christian Religion*, in which he discusses the gentile sibyls, the Hebrew prophets, the Platonists and the oldest pagan theologians such as Hermes Trismegistus and Zoroaster. As no one before him, Ficino went beyond Dionysius' texts, giving them a new intellectual context. He proceeded with his re-invention in extensive commentaries to the Dionysian texts retranslated by him, in his monumental *Platonic Theology*, and in his other publications, from those on Hermes Trismegistus to his letters.

Throughout his monumental oeuvre Ficino provided many new dimensions to Dionysius. This framework consisted of new translations and commentaries devoted to the Platonic oeuvre, only known to a very limited degree among earlier generations. In addition Ficino presented a number of other authors and texts, largely unknown to his predecessors. They knew some of their names but hardly any of their texts. Ficino's spiritual context for Dionysius consisted not only of a Platonic renaissance, extending well into the ideas of Ammonius, Porphyrius, Iamblichus and Proclus, but also of the spectacular introduction or re-introduction of legendary authors of the greatest antiquity, considered as old as Moses or even older. Ficino created a new framework for his hero, Dionysius, consisting of Hermes Trismegistus, Zoroaster, Orpheus, Pythagoras and the sibyls. He attached recently imported texts, rediscovered in the Byzantine world, to a new canon of ancient authors, purported to be as old as the oldest Hebrew prophets.

For Ficino the newly recreated tradition of these old sages, male and female, found its fulfilment in Dionysius the Areopagite, who became the corner stone of his paradigm, synthesizing Eastern wisdom, Hebrew religion, pagan learning, and western Christianity. In a monumental series of printed texts, Ficino went much further than Augustine, Jerome or Boethius had done in arguing for a harmony between Greek, Egyptian and Persian philosophies and Christianity with its roots in the Hebrew religion.

To Ficino and his Italian fellow scholars, the French connection of Dionysius lost its attraction. Schedel accepted the connection, introduced in the ninth century, with the French bishop, but the Italian humanists tended to reject this link. For them Dionysius became an apostolic humanist rather than a martyr bishop.

In his manuscripts and printed treatises Giovanni Pico della Mirandola, a dedicated reader of Ficino, confirmed Dionysius' crucial role in the context of the Hebrew prophets, Plato, Hermes, Zoroaster and the other *prisci theologi*, as he, Ficino and others often called them. Pico mentioned Dionysius frequently, presenting him as the pupil of both Saint Paul and Hierotheus, much as Ficino had done. Dionysius appears in all treatises published by Pico, who mentioned him by name, quoted from his work and referred to the Latin titles of his treatises. Pico mentioned Dionysius just slightly less than Moses, Plato and Aristotle, and as often as Paul, John and Augustine. Count Pico re-synthesised early Christian thought, Greek philosophy and the old theologies from Israel and Egypt to Persia and India. His approach was similar to that of Ficino, to whom he paid tribute. His vocabulary, literary style and rhetoric differed from Ficino's. Pico's highly original oeuvre showed the great vitality of the Dionysian ideas and their enormous intellectual attraction.

In the sixteenth century this paradigm, constructed by Ficino and Pico, enjoyed great authority, also due to printed editions of their collected works. Their ideas acquired the status of normal science, albeit not totally uncontested.

A slow revision and the emergence of new perspectives: from faith to science

Dionysius remained highly esteemed, but doubts were re-expressed about his identity. Falsifying texts and authors happened to be an equally complicated social process as their initial fabrication; for centuries critique and re-fabrication went hand in hand. In the Latin West, Lorenzo Valla, a generation older than Pico, was one of the first to seriously challenge

Dionysius' apostolic identity. Valla did so in his commentary on the New Testament, discussing Acts 17, and in an encomium of Aquinas. His critical glosses, presented at several occasions between 1442 and 1457, remained moderate in scope. Valla rejected the reading of Acts as if Luke implied that the members of the Areopagus were philosophers. On the contrary, Valla maintained, they possessed juridical authority. So, he claimed, Dionysius could not be a philosopher, and hence Saint Paul's first Athenian convert was not the author of the corpus of such high repute. In choosing this emphasis, Valla did not at all question the intellectual value of the treatises and letters.

Falsification turned out to be a slow process. Valla's critical remarks failed to attract much attention. They influenced only some of the leading scholars. Valla's argument against the authenticity of Dionysius as Saint Paul's pupil was far less polemical than his attack on the authenticity of the *Donation of Constantine* to Pope Sylvester. According to Valla this text could in no way belong to the era of Constantine, for several historical and philological reasons, which Valla presented so eloquently. But even this spectacular falsification attracted limited attention, until it gained relevance in the context of the German reformation during the sixteenth century.

Textual criticism, to which Valla added so much, was not an isolated scientific phenomenon; both the invention of new ideas and their reception proved to be highly politicised. Valla's critique on the Dionysian identity received some positive reactions from Erasmus' printed publication of Valla's handwritten material. Luther, Grocyn, Calvin, and others expressed doubts about the apostolic roots of Dionysius. Returning to Scripture itself they tended to ascribe less value to Dionysius than Ficino and Pico had done. Protestant scholars were less inclined to attach much meaning to Dionysius than Catholic authors. On the whole critical reading did not inspire an intellectual revolution; the technique of textual criticism as such became more and more the subject of critique within the higher echelons of the Roman Catholic Church. Within the reformation movements Valla's arguments against the authenticity of the *Donation of Constantine* really became an issue, as did some of Erasmus' glosses on Jerome's translation of the Bible.

However, the question whether or not Dionysius was the philosophically trained author of the corpus ascribed to him proved to be of limited relevance to most authors from the sixteenth to the nineteenth centuries. The religious and political relevance of the issue was too restricted to pave the way for a thorough revision of the Dionysian Corpus. Valla's sharp remarks and Erasmus' positive reception failed to produce a profound reconsideration of the construction that had been built up in the previous centuries. Prolific orators and authors such as Egidius of Viterbo, Raffaele Maffei, Domenico Jacobazzi and Tommaso Inghirami accepted the Ficino-Pico paradigm. In many short orations and some extensive treatises these leading scholars assigned great authority to Dionysius the Areopagite. They failed to follow the philological hermeneutics laid down by Valla and Erasmus. With striking continuity Dionysius was read, mentioned, translated, retranslated, edited, commented, quoted, analyzed, used, and praised.

For a very long time the 'cloud of unknowing', as it was called in a meteorological metaphor in the *Mystical Theology*, designated the corpus of which this treatise was a short but visionary part. Whoever its inventor, the concept of unknowing as a crucial part of human insight proved to be an important scholarly contribution, christianizing the Socratic doubt as it was codified by Plato. In the Dionysian texts, this insight was connected to the idea of negative theology: an interest in the limits of human knowledge as the basis of his Christian mysticism and the true understanding of the divine. For various philosophical and theological reasons many readers continued to value the Dionysian mode of thought, considering the question of his direct link with Saint Paul of limited relevance. They also appreciated his literary value; writing as a celebrity was considered more a sophisticated and accepted poetic device than a controversial act of historical forgery.

In 1895 the theologian Stiglmayr and the philologist and classicist Koch returned once again to the Dionysian Corpus. Meticulously comparing these texts with those of Proclus, they argued, independent of one another, that the Dionysian texts were derived from Proclus, and were therefore later than about 480, a hypothesis introduced by Engelhardt in 1820. This link explained the Platonic content, about which Pico and Ficino were so enthusiastic. Stiglmayr and Koch marked the decisive turning point in the reception of Dionysius. Valla, Erasmus and Luther were for a long time less influential than Ficino and Pico, but finally textual criticism triumphed over speculation and syncretism.

Ever since the late nineteenth century various authors have been proposed but no consensus was attained, save that the texts had been written in Syria around 500. Various names have been put forward, but none has been generally accepted. Hence the author's name was step by step transformed into Pseudo-Dionysius or Ps. Dionysius. Under those new names another new life was created for him, because scholarly interest in his oeuvre continued, focusing on its relevance for the history of ideas since the sixth century. Pico and Ficino happened to be the main victims in this context.

The reinterpretation of Dionysius followed the path of earlier falsifications. In the meantime the correspondence between Seneca and Saint Paul was considered to be a forgery. Many of Ficino's and Pico's heroes lost their purported pedigree. Step by step critique was launched and accepted on the ancestry of the texts circulating under the names of the sibyls, Hermes Trismegistus, Zoroaster, Orpheus and Pythagoras. This process of de-canonisation took four centuries, Dionysius being the last to acquire a new identity and diminishing meaning.

Conclusion

Taken together, these revisions from Hermes and the sibyls to Pythagoras and Dionysius contributed to the creation of a new myth: the scientific revolution starting with Valla and the spectacular triumph of humanist textual criticism as an early proof of Popper's principle of falsification and thus the root of a paradigmatic transformation from religion to science, leaving aside changing conventions of literary construction.

Indeed, the scholarly revolution increased our understanding of the fact that Dionysius the Areopagite was not the author of the four treatises and ten letters, which were ascribed to him from the early sixth century onwards. Yet the focus on this successful falsification has not been favourable to our understanding of the wider cultural context during the *longue durée*. Texts, for a long time considered to be of prime cultural importance, have been marginalized precisely because of this scientific specialisation. In this way Dionysius has become a niche only accessible to a small group of specialists. He shared this fate with many others who have been of prime importance in our cultural history. Their invented identities are still a crucial part of our cultural heritage.

For much more than a millennium, the sibyls, Hermes Trismegistus, Zoroaster, Orpheus and Dionysius the Areopagite, fabricated and refabricated as they were time and again, represented the shining stars of our knowledge. As such they were all depicted by Raphael in the *Stanza della Segnatura*, Dionysius with Hierotheus, Timothy and Titus to the right and the *Disputa* directly below Saint Paul in heaven.

Bibliographical note

For this article I could rely on the vast corpus of secondary literature on the subject. Aspects of the reception have been dealt with in encyclopaedic articles and in introductory chapters to editions and translations. For the first and third sections I used in particular: P. Rorem, *Pseudo-Dionysius. A Commentary on the Texts and an Introduction to their Influence* (Oxford: Oxford University Press, 1993); *Pseudo-Dionysius Areopagita. Über die himmlische Hierarchie, Über die kirchliche Hierarchie; Die Namen Gottes; Über die Mystische Theologie und Briefe*, introd. and trans. Adolf Martin Ritter, 3 vols., *Bibliothek der Griechischen Literatur*, 22, 26 and 40 (Stuttgart: Hiersemann, 1986, 1988 and 1994); T. Boiadjiev, G. Kapriev and A. Speer, *Die Dionysius-Rezeption im Mittelalter* (International conference, Sofia 1999) (Turnhout: Brepols, 2000); Ch. Schäfer, *The Philosophy of Dionysius the Areopagite. An Introduction to the Structure and the Content of the Treatise* On the Divine Names (Leiden: Brill, 2006); S. Klitenic Wear and J. Dillon, *Dionysius the Areopagite and the Neoplatonist Tradition. Despoiling the Hellenes* (Aldershot: Ashgate, 2007). For the material of the fifteenth and early sixteenth centuries, dealt with in the second section, I consulted the original manuscripts and editions. In *De Christiana Religione*, Marsilio Ficino introduces him on page 13 of the *Opera Omnia* (Basel: Froben, 1576), as "Dionysius Areopagita philosophorum Atheniensium praestantissimus," returning to him several times afterwards. In his *Argumentum* to the *De Mystica Theologia*, Ficino calls him on page 1013 "Dionysius Areopagita Platonicae disciplinae culmen, & Christianae Theologiae columen, quaerens divinum lumen." Both Ficino and Pico accept Hierotheus, whom Dionysius calls his mentor, as a historical figure and not as a literary invention; Dionysius mentions him by name five times, and as "our master" twenty-one times, being the author of *Elements of Theology* and *Hymns of Yearning*. Pico addressed Dionysius in: *De hominis dignitate, Heptaplus, De ente et uno*, and *Commento sopra una canzone De amore composta da Girolamo Benivieni*. See the edition and translation by Eugenio Garin (Florence: Vallecci, 1942). Research for this article followed my attempts to discover Dionysius, his heroes and his companions in Raphael's *Stanza della Segnatura*.

TWO FEMALE APOSTOLIC MYSTICS:
CATHERINE OF SIENA AND MADAME JEANNE GUYON

Bernard McGinn

"Greet Andronicus and Junia, my fellow countrymen and comrades in captivity, who are eminent among the apostles and were Christians before I was" (Rom. 16:7). Few of us have probably paused over this verse among the list of greetings Paul puts at the end of the Epistle to the Romans. Among those who obviously did was the scribe who substituted "Junias," a man's name, for the female "Junia."[1] How could a woman be an apostle, our shocked scribe probably asked? Of course, *apostolos*, literally "one who is sent," is used so variously in its eighty appearances in the New Testament that it is difficult to speak of a single biblical meaning for the word. In general, we can distinguish generic uses (anyone who is sent: e.g., 2 Cor. 8:23, Phil. 2:25, Heb. 3:1) from the semi-technical sense of a group of leaders vested with some authority in the community.[2] While the Synoptic Gospels, especially Luke (see, e.g., Lk. 6:13, 9:10, 17:5, 22:14), tend to use the term of the original twelve of Jesus's followers, John does not know this usage. We might think that Paul barged his way into the club in his claim, "I am the least of the apostles" (Rom. 15:9; see Rom. 1:1, 11:13; 1 Cor. 1:1, 9:1; 2 Cor. 1:1; Gal. 1:1; etc.), but he was willing to see others besides the twelve and himself as apostles, as his reference to the otherwise unknown Andronicus and Junia demonstrate. In Hebrews 3:1 Jesus himself is described as "the apostle and high priest of our confession."

As the early Christian church developed the notion of a line, or succession, of leaders, the successors of the apostles came to be restricted to the episcopal office, a long and complex development not discussed here,

---

1 'Junias' is found, for example, in the uncial manuscripts B2 (6th-7th cent.) and D2 (9th cent.). Almost all scholars today see Junia as a woman, probably the wife of Andronicus. See E.J. Epp, *Junia* (Minneapolis: Fortress, 2005); and R. Bauckham, *Gospel Women* (Grand Rapids, MI: Eerdmans, 2002).

2 For a summary of the New Testament usages and references to the large literature, see Jeannine K. Brown, "Apostle. I. New Testament," in *The Encyclopedia of the Bible and Its Reception* (Berlin/New York: Walter de Gruyter, 2009), 2: 471-76.

since it has often been written about.[3] What we should remember, though, is that the institutional and official sense of apostle never totally cancelled out the functional, more charismatic, sense of apostle as one called by Christ and sent out to spread the gospel, as we can see from the way in which certain missionaries came to be hailed as apostles, for example, Patrick the 'Apostle of the Irish,' Ansgar, the 'Apostle of the North,' and Cyril and Methodius, the 'Apostles of the Slavs.' This charismatic understanding of *apostolus* might be thought of as merely metaphorical, and it was certainly secondary to the status of the twelve and their successors, but it is interesting to note that even the theological understanding of apostle, as set forth, for example, by Thomas Aquinas, made room for the special charisms given to the original twelve, which might, by extension, be granted to others through grace. Thomas noted the infused knowledge and wisdom given the twelve apostles for their mission to convert the world. "The apostles," Thomas says, "had all the knowledge necessary to convert the world."[4] That means, he explains elsewhere, that "God gave the apostles knowledge of scripture and of all the languages men are able to acquire by study or custom, although not as perfectly."[5] Although Thomas does not explicitly discuss the issue, he gives no reason why those called to continue the work of conversion might not also be accorded special graces (*gratiae gratis datae*) to aid them in spreading the gospel.

Both the institutional sense of *apostolus* enshrined in the twelve and their episcopal successors (*viri apostolici*), as well as the charismatic sense of later apostles as missionaries endowed with special knowledge to preach and convert the world, were for the most part assigned to men, so we can see why the unknown scribe decided to change Junia to Junias. Given that the twelve and their missionary successors were men, how could a woman be an apostle? Only with great difficulty, one supposes! There was, however, a tradition of female apostles in the history of the church that has all-too-often been neglected. It is worth exploring one aspect of this story, concentrating on the lives, claims, and fates of two mystical female apostles: Catherine of Siena in fourteenth-century Italy and Jeanne Guyon in seventeenth-century France.

---

3 On apostolic succession in early Christianity, see especially Francis A. Sullivan, *From Apostles to Bishops. The Development of the Episcopacy in the Early Church* (New York: Paulist Press, 2001).

4 Thomas Aquinas, *Summa theologiae* (STh), IIaIIae, q. 176, a. 1, ad 1; cf. IaIIae, q. 106, a. 4, ad 2.

5 STh IaIIae, q. 51, a. 4c.

A significant aspect of the Christian story that made it possible for some women to claim, or have claimed for them, the status of *apostola* is the fact that there was one very well-known example in Christian origins of a female apostle, the *apostola apostolorum*, Mary Magdalene. 'Magdalene-mania' is not a new phenomenon in church history, but I will adhere to the historical record, so you need not fear a plunge into "Da Vinci Code" foolishness. Nor will I touch on the role of the Magdalene in Gnostic writings, because these documents were unknown to later tradition until their retrieval in modern scholarship. What is important for our purpose is the hagiographical picture of Mary Magdalene, one which built upon the texts relating to the Magdalene in the New Testament, but, as is usual with hagiography, filled in the gaps and extended and improved the story.[6]

Since at least the time of Gregory the Great at the end of the sixth century, the Western church conflated the Mary Magdalene who ministered to Christ, stood at the cross, sought him in the garden, and brought word of the empty tomb to the twelve (Lk. 8:1-2, Mt. 28:1-10, Jn. 20:11-18) with the sinful woman who anointed Christ's feet (Lk. 7:37) and the sister of Martha and Lazarus (Lk. 10). Gregory does not call Mary *apostola*, but the gist of his praise for her in the twenty-fifth and thirty-third of his *Gospel Homilies* comes down to very much the same thing. For Gregory, as for later tradition, Mary combined supreme ecstatic love for Jesus with a God-given mission to spread the good news. In other words, Mary Magdalene was a mystical apostle. From the ninth and tenth centuries on, a distinctive Western hagiography expanded on the Gospel accounts. According to this legend, Mary and her siblings Martha and Lazarus were set adrift in a rudderless boat by the Jewish authorities and miraculously wafted over the Mediterranean to the Riviera, where they disembarked and began the work of converting Southern France.[7] In the twelfth-century *Life of Saint Mary Magdalene and her Sister Saint Martha*, the Magdalene is portrayed as a great contemplative, who, nevertheless, feels compelled to give up the delights of inner communion with God to preach to the pagan Gauls. And

---

6   There is a large literature on the Magdalene. Foundational for the medieval understanding is Victor Saxer, *Le Culte de Marie Madeleine en Occident des origines à la fin du moyen âge* (Auxerre-Paris: Clavreuil, 1959). In English, see Susan Haskins, *Mary Magdalene. Myth and Metaphor* (New York: Harcourt and Brace, 1993); and Katherine Ludwig Jansen, *The Making of the Magdalen. Preaching and Devotion in the Later Middle Ages* (Princeton: Princeton University Press, 2000).

7   The earliest written testimony appears to be the *Vita apostolica Mariae Magdalenae*, probably of the tenth century, which can be found in Etienne-Michel Faillon, *Monuments inédits sur l'apostolat de S. Marie-Magdaleine en Provence*, 2 vols. (Paris: J.P. Migne, 1848), 2: 433-36.

what a preacher she was! The *Life* says, "It was fitting, then, that just as she had been chosen to be the apostle of Christ's resurrection and the prophet of his ascension, so she also became an evangelist for belief throughout the world."[8] Mary Magdalene was at least the equal of the twelve in this regard. In good early medieval fashion, of course, contemplation is always superior to action, so after years of preaching Mary gave up her active life for a thirty-year stint of solitude and contemplation in the desert, clothed only with the abundant hair that later artists delighted to portray as a titillating experiment in veiled unveiling.

This hagiographical picture helps us understand how the Magdalene became a model for women who sought to combine contemplative rapture and some kind of active teaching. In one sense, Mary Magdalene offered a more accessible model than the Virgin Mary, whose life was sinless and who lacked any public role. We can see this influence in the case of women both historical and fictional. The historical beguine, Marguerite Porete, burned as a heretic in Paris in 1310 for continuing to disseminate her mystical book, *The Mirror of Simple Souls*, took the Magdalene as a model for what she called the 'sad souls,' that is, those who are aware that there is a higher form of life, that of total annihilation in God, but who do not yet know how to attain it.[9] As long as Mary Magdalene sought Jesus out of her own will (*Mirror*, Chap. 93) and led an active life of asceticism and preaching (Chap. 124), she remained on the level of the sad souls. It was only during her final years in the desert, according to Marguerite, that she reached annihilation and became a 'simple soul' (Chap. 93). In one sense, Marguerite Porete undercuts the importance of the Magdalene's apostolic role, but the paradox is that she herself was condemned to death for following the Magdalene's model of combining contemplation and preaching.

Several decades after Marguerite Porete's execution Mary Magdalene was taken up again as a model, this time by a fictional mystical woman. The Middle High German treatise known as *Sister Katherine*, or sometimes *Meister Eckhart's Strassburg Daughter*, tells the story of an anonymous beguine and a learned friar through a series of dialogues. Initially,

---

8 The *Vita*, probably a Cistercian product, can be found among the works of Rabanus Maurus in PL 112: 1431-1508. I cite from the translation of David Mycoff, *The Life of Saint Mary Magdalene and of her Sister Saint Martha* (Kalamazoo: Cistercian Publications, 1989), 96.

9 The Middle French and Latin versions of the work (neither is the original text) have been edited by Romana Guarnieri and Paul Verdeyen, *Marguerite Porete. Le Mirouer des simples ames*, CCCM 69 (Turnhout: Brepols, 1986). There are several English versions; see especially Ellen Babinsky, *Marguerite Porete. The Mirror of Simple Souls* (New York: Paulist Press, 1993).

the beguine learns about the inner life from the friar's instruction, but she becomes dissatisfied with his advice and goes off into an internal exile to seek a more perfect way. When she returns, he hears her confession and recognizes that she now knows more than he does. After a three-day trance, or 'mystical death,' she attains a state of 'being established in God,' a union of action and contemplation in which she now gives the friar lessons on the spiritual life and the mysteries of contemplation. Her model for this is Mary Magdalene, whom she praises both for her active preaching and her contemplative wisdom. As she puts it:

> [The Magdalene] did everything the apostles did in a perfect life. She went into all the lands in which she could preach Christianity and reveal the truth. You must know that Mary Magdalene accomplished more in a shorter time than any of the apostles. Now I will explain to you why she went into the forest.... She went into the forest so that she would not have any comfort from creatures and that she would stay solely in the eternal good which is God.[10]

Here, too, the Magdalene's contemplation is given a higher status, but not to the detriment of her previous apostolic action. The author of *Sister Katherine*, whether a friar or a learned beguine or nun, had no qualms about portraying a woman as a superior teacher of contemplation and mystical truth.

Catherine of Siena (1347-1380), co-patron of Italy and since 1970 a 'Doctor of the Church,' was another woman who aspired to follow the model of Mary Magdalene and combine active preaching and contemplative rapture. Although Catherine's letters, her mystical treatise called the *Dialogue of Divine Providence*, and the popular *Large Life (Legenda major)* written by her confessor Raymond of Capua, portray her as devoted to many saints, there is no question that the Magdalene had a special role for the young Italian woman.[11] This was not just because of the status of the Magdalene in the general religious life of the late Middle Ages, but also due to the fact that the Dominican order, to which Catherine belonged as a *mantellata*, or 'veiled woman' under the protection of the friars, had

---

10 The *Sister Katherine* treatise was edited by Franz-Josef Schweitzer, *Der Freiheits-begriff der deutschen Mystik* (Frankfort: Peter Lang, 1981), 322-70. There is an English translation by Elvira Borgstädt, *The "Sister Catherine" Treatise*, in Bernard McGinn, ed., *Meister Eckhart. Teacher and Preacher* (New York: Paulist Press, 1981), 347-87. The quotation is at 380 (for other passages on the Magdalene, see 352, 371-75, and 380-81).

11 For the relation between Catherine and the Magdalene, as well as a sketch of her mystical apostolate, see Bernard McGinn, "Catherine of Siena: apostle of the Blood of Christ," *Theology Digest* 48 (2004): 329-42.

developed a particular devotion to the Magdalene since the late thirteenth century when the order supported the claim of Charles II of Sicily who discovered the 'true' relics of the saint at the church of St. Maximin at Aix-en-Provence and turned them over to the Dominicans for protection (thus rejecting the traditional claims of the Benedictines to be in possession of her relics at the basilica named after her at Vézelay in Burgundy).[12]

Catherine's claims to be an *apostola* go beyond both the hagiographical picture of Mary Magdalene, as well the apostolic aspects found in Marguerite Porete and the fictional beguine of *Sister Catherine*.[13] First of all, in Catherine the apostolic life is not inferior to the contemplative life, so that preaching needs to be abandoned at the end of life for contemplative solitude. Catherine reversed this paradigm in that the last decade of her life, especially the final five years, become a time of growing activity and wider public influence. Catherine, like a number of late medieval mystics, though in her own way, did not see apostolic action and deep contemplation as necessarily opposed or in tension; rather, she was convinced that with divine grace a person could become, as was later said of Ignatius of Loyola, 'active in contemplation' (*in contemplatione activus*). Second, Catherine claims to have been given her apostolic mission directly by God, as we will see below. Third, and perhaps most significant, is the fact that Catherine did indeed have a remarkable impact on both the Western Church and late medieval society. It was unprecedented that a woman of her class managed to attain the role she did. However we wish to evaluate her success or failure, Catherine's 'saintly politics,' as F. Thomas Luongo termed it,[14] was an integral part of her message about love of God and love of neighbor.

In his *Large Life* Raymond of Capua wrestled with Catherine's unusual form of sanctity, especially for a woman. On the whole, we must admire his success in confronting head on the issue of how to present a female saint who did not conform to the usual model of the secluded ecstatic. Raymond's solution for beginning the drive for Catherine's canonization was to structure the main narrative part of the *Life* into two books, the first of which was traditional in picturing Catherine as a visionary, miracle-working, private contemplative from her childhood down to about

---

12   See Neal Raymond Clemens, *The Cult of Saint Mary Magdalene in Provence in the Thirteenth and Fourteenth Centuries* (PhD diss., Columbia University, 1996).

13   For a good sketch of Catherine's self-identity as an apostle, see Karen Scott, "St. Catherine of Siena, 'Apostola,'" *Church History* 61 (1992): 34-46.

14   F. Thomas Luongo, *The Saintly Politics of Catherine of Siena* (Ithaca: Cornell University Press, 2006).

1370 when God called her out of seclusion to begin taking on a more active role, first among the Dominican 'veiled women.'[15] Raymond shaped his material in Book 1 to show that anything other women had claimed by way of mystical favors and graces was also true of Catherine. Even some of her special graces, such as her espousal with Christ described in Chapter 12 of Book 1, include a look forward to the apostolic part of her career. Raymond tells us, probably following Catherine herself, that she saw this grace as a sign that she was "to follow lines far different from those of other women.... She was to be sent out to live in the public eye, working for the honor of God and the salvation of soul."[16]

The major innovation in the *Long Life* comes in Book 2 where Raymond argues that it was at God's command that Catherine undertook her public apostolic career for the welfare of the church. Raymond sets this up in the first chapter of Book 2, where God tells her:

> Dearest daughter,...it is right for you to fulfill all justice, for my grace in you must now begin to bear fruit not only in yourself but in other souls as well. I have no intention whatever of parting you from myself, but rather of making sure to bind you to me all the closer, by the bond of your love for your neighbor.[17]

This message was to be central to all Catherine's teaching, both in her treatise the *Dialogue* and in the almost four hundred letters she sent to a host of correspondents from every level of society. God's reason for this unusual command was also emphasized by Raymond-the Pauline reversal theme of God choosing the weak things of the world to confound the strong (1 Cor. 1:27). Because human pride, especially that of the 'wise and learned,' had passed beyond all bounds, God says that just as he once did with the Jews and the Gentiles, "So I will do now, sending to them, to humble their pride, mere women-women who of themselves will be ignorant and frail, but whom I will fill with the power of God and the wisdom of God."[18] The result of this commission is that Catherine is now

---

15 Raymond, as is the custom with all hagiographers, tailored the facts to suit his non-historical genre. Thus, his account has Catherine entering the *mantellate* ca. 1362, whereas the actual date was probably ca. 1369.

16 Raymond of Capua's *Legenda major S. Catharinae* is found in AA.SS., Aprilis 3: 862-967. For an English version, see *Raymond of Capua. The Life of Catherine of Siena*, trans. Conleth Kearns (Washington, DC: Dominica Publications, 1980). This text is found at 1.12.116 (trans. Kearns, 108).

17 *Legenda major* 2.1.121 (trans. Kearns, 115-16).

18 *Legenda Major* 2.1.122 (trans. Kearns, 117). For other texts emphasizing Catherine's apostolic mission and her ability to combine action and contemplation, see, e.g., 2.2.125-30, 2.5.165, 2.6.178, and 2.6.216 (trans. Kearns, 120-25, 159, 173-74, and 205).

sent forth from her cell in her father's house, first to minister to her circle
of followers in Siena, and by 1375 to leave her native city and take to the
road spreading her message throughout Italy, to the pope at Avignon, and
to many of the rulers of Europe through her letters. Raymond says of this
apostolic period of her life: "From that time on, the Lord began to show
himself familiarly and openly to his spouse [i.e., Catherine], not only in
secret, as he had formerly done, but also while she was traveling or staying
in some place [abroad]."[19]

Raymond's artful construction of Catherine's mystical and apostolic
career is, if anything, heightened in her own writings. The long *Dialogue*
that she composed between 1377 and 1378, a series of conversations with
God, contains ample evidence for her conviction that God had given her
a special mission to work tirelessly for the correction of Christian life, the
reform of the church, the return of the papacy to Rome, and the mounting
of a new crusade.[20] Catherine's almost frenetic five years of writing, travelling, letter writing, advising, condemning, and cajolling testify to a life
lived in a tearing rush to fulfill what she saw to be God's will. Her sense
of apostolic mission is even more evident in her letters. Let us look at just
one, a letter so unusual in its claims that Raymond of Capua says nothing
about it in his *Life*, although it was written to him.

Catherine wrote at least sixteen letters to Raymond, more than to anyone else, and she revealed her inner life to him with great directness in
these communications. In a letter written to Raymond probably in early April of 1376, as she was getting ready to leave first for Florence and
then for Avignon to meet with Pope Gregory XI, Catherine told Raymond
about a vision she had received on April 1.[21] The letter describes a new
divine authorization for this stage in her career-an investiture with the
task of universal reform of the church and missionary outreach to both
believers and unbelievers. Catherine begins the letter with the wish that
Raymond and her other followers be nailed to the cross with Christ, "so

---

19   *Legenda Major* 2.6.177 (my trans.). Chapter 2.6 has an extended description of the
role of Mary Magdalene as a model for Catherine in paragraphs 183-86 (trans. Kearns, 177-
80).

20   For an edition, see Giuliana Cavallini, O.P., *S. Caterina da Siena. Il Dialogo* (Rome:
Edizioni Cateriniane, 1968). The best English translation is that of Suzanne Noffke, O.P.,
The Dialogue of Catherine of Siena (New York: Paulist Press, 1980).

21   This letter, T 219, can be found in *S. Caterina da Siena. Le Lettere*, ed. Umberto
Meattini (Milan: Edizioni Paoline, 1987), 1127-30. I cite the translation of Suzanne Noffke,
O.P., *The Letters of St. Catherine of Siena* (Binghamton: SUNY, 1988), 1: 206-09. For an
analysis, see Thomas McDermott, *Catherine of Siena. Spiritual Development in her Life and
Teaching* (New York: Paulist Press, 2008), 64-67.

engrafted that neither the devil nor anyone else can ever separate you." Echoing a constant theme of her teaching, she advises the recipients to continue throwing the wood of self-knowledge on the fire of charity and to bear with each other's shortcomings. Then she turns to her vision:

> On the night of April first God disclosed his secrets more than usual. He showed his marvels in such a way that my soul seemed to be outside my body and was so overwhelmed with joy that I can't really describe it in words. He told me and explained bit by bit the mystery of the persecution holy church is now enduring, and of the renewal and exaltation to come.

Christ tells her that just as he once drove the money-changers from the Temple (Mt. 21:13), so too he is now using a "whip of certain [unnamed] people" to purify the clergy from their "shameful disordered way of life." As Catherine's holy desire increases, the vision shifts to a universal dimension. She says:

> And I saw the people, Christians and unbelievers, entering the side of Christ crucified. In desire and impelled by love I walked through their midst and entered with them into Christ gentle Jesus. And with me were my father Saint Dominic, the beloved John, and all my children. Then he placed the cross on my shoulder and put the olive branch in my hand, as if he wanted me (and so he told me) to carry it to Christians and unbelievers alike. And he said to me: "Tell them, 'I am bringing you news of great joy'!" [cf. Lk. 2:10]

Catherine goes on to say that her soul "was immersed in the divine essence with those who taste God through union and the feeling of love," that is, the blessed in heaven. She is, therefore, claiming a direct, if temporary, vision of God. The letter closes with Catherine reiterating her commitment to her universal mission and summoning Raymond and his companions to "drown yourself in the blood of Christ crucified"-a central motif of her apostolic mysticism. By giving her both the cross of suffering (and crusade, let us remember), as well as the olive branch of peace, Christ is making Catherine almost a kind of co-redemptrix for both believers and unbelievers-something more than an *apostola*. Most puzzling of all, as mentioned above, is that Raymond does not refer to this vision in the *Life*. Although he describes a wide range of the special graces given to Catherine, and uses a variety of biblical texts and other arguments to build the case for her apostolic authority, perhaps this vision went further than he was prepared to go.

Catherine's sanctity and mystical message, including its apostolic claims, were controversial, though ultimately successful. Hers was scarcely a case of *santa subita*! Catherine's version of the Guelph politics of the papal party in Italy had many detractors in her own day; some of the claims

that Raymond made for her, such as that concerning her invisible stigmata, were attacked by the Franciscans until various popes stepped in and
approved them. It is interesting to note that the other major text pushing
for Catherine's canonization, the so-called *Little Supplement Book (Libellus de supplemento)* written by the Dominican Thomas of Siena between
1412 and 1418, deliberately tones down the apostolic aspects of Catherine's career to present a more traditional hagiographical picture concentrating on her mystical gifts. Raymond's *Long Life*, however, was popular,
being translated into a number of languages and widely read. Catherine
was eventually canonized by the Sienese pope Pius II in 1461, and, of
course, has remained a pillar of Catholic mystical teaching and theology
over the centuries. Quite a different fate awaited our second example of an
apostolic female mystic.

Jeanne Marie Bouvières de la Motte, to give her full name, was born
into an upper-class French family in 1648, married to a husband twenty
years older in 1664, and, after a difficult marriage, left the widow Madame
Guyon at his death in 1676. (She refused pressure from relatives at this
time to enter a convent and give her wealth to the church.) Her life was
to last until 1717 amidst a divergence of viewpoints that has not ended
to this day.[22] Ronald Knox, in his classic work of 1950, *Enthusiasm*, gave
a full, though largely negative, portrait of Guyon. He begins his account
of her character with the rhetorical question, "What was this woman
like, a woman who has been represented so variously, as saint, devil, or
lunatic?"[23] Saint and lunatic, perhaps (the combination is not unknown
in the history of Christianity), but few today would think that Guyon
consciously intended evil. What Guyon actually wanted to achieve was
an apostolic renewal of Christianity, though it was not, alas, one that had
much effect, given the fact that she and her close associate and disciple,
Archbishop François Fénelon (1651-1715), were both subject to ecclesiastical condemnation for mystical error. As the key figures in the French
chapter of the Quietist Controversy, Guyon and Fénelon have come down
in history as proponents of the error that perfected souls could surpass
ordinary hopes and fears for salvation and reach a state of quiet and total
surrender to God in which everything, even final salvation, is left up to

---

22 The best recent life of Guyon is Marie-Louise Gondal, *Madame Guyon (1648-1717).
Un nouveau visage* (Paris: Beauchesne, 1989). In English, see Marie-Florine Bruneau, *Wom-
en Mystics Confront the Modern World. Marie de l'Incarnation (1599-1672) and Madame
Guyon (1648-1717)* (Albany: State University of New York Press, 1998).

23 Ronald A. Knox, *Enthusiasm. A Chapter in the History of Religion with Special Reference to the XVII and XVIII Centuries* (Oxford: Oxford University Press, 1950), 322.

the divine will. We need not enter into the issue of whether they actually did hold this (though they did, at least in some way), or the extent to which some forms of such claims might still be said to be within the bounds of 'orthodoxy.' Rather, for our purposes we need to look at how Madame Guyon's teaching on the annihilation and pure love that lead the soul to giving up the will for salvation also, and perhaps paradoxically, has a distinctly apostolic dimension.

Since Madame Guyon is less well known than Catherine of Siena, a brief sketch of the development of her spiritual life is helpful for setting the stage for her notion of apostolicity. Much of what we know comes from her three-volume autobiography, the *Life* that she began writing in 1682, though the original manuscript and its additions were not published until 1720.[24] Guyon tells us that she experienced a conversion to the deeper life as early as 1667 and subsequently received a series of mystical graces (not unlike Catherine of Siena), including marriage to the baby Jesus on the Feast of Mary Magdalene, July 22, 1672. After undergoing a seven-year trial of inner suffering and aridity, she was delivered from this trial also on the Feast of Mary Magdalene in 1680. She was then ready to begin her public career. God's instrument for this new stage in her life was the Barnabite priest, François La Combe (1643-1715), who had become her confessor and soon also was her companion on the apostolic preaching tours she undertook in France and Switzerland between 1681 and 1687, as she sought to spread the message of her new mode of praying enshrined in the treatise *The Short and Very Easy Method of Prayer*, first published in 1685. In October 1687 she and Fr. La Combe were arrested on suspicion of heresy and immorality. She was imprisoned for half a year, but released through her political connections; he was to spend the rest of his life in jail. In the autumn of 1688 Guyon met Bishop Fénelon, the tutor of Louis XIV's grandson and one of the most important clerics of France. He became her friend and supporter as Guyon continued her apostolic work, supported by a circle of influential *dévots* who called themselves the 'Confraternity of Pure Love.'

Guyon's situation changed in 1693, when her supporters at court turned against her and attacks on her teaching, especially by Jacques Bénigne Bossuet, the influential bishop of Meaux, increased. Guyon then asked for a theological commission to clear her name and a group of bishops met at

---

24 The *Life* was first published by Guyon's Protestant disciple, Pierre Poiret, at Amsterdam in 1720 under the title *La vie de Madame J. M. B. de la Mothe Guion, écrit par elle-même*. There are many later reprints of Poiret's text. On the role of the text in the history of autobiography, see Bruneau, *Women Mystics Confront the Modern World*, chap. 8.

Issy between July and September of 1694 to examine her teaching. Eventually, in March 1695 thirty-four articles were issued by the commission, condemning Quietist views found in her writings by declaring the Catholic truth on each issue. Guyon submitted to the articles, as did Fénelon. Doubts soon arose, however, about the proper interpretation of the articles, as well as to whether Guyon, who continued her teaching, had really submitted, so she was imprisoned again in December of the same year. From 1697 through 1699 a lengthy barrage of claims, counter-claims, letters and pamphlets convulsed the religious scene in France, with Fénelon supporting Guyon, and Bossuet and his followers attacking her and him, while meanwhile working behind the scenes in Rome for a papal condemnation of their errors. (The French, with a penchant for understatement, speak of this as 'the Battle of the Olympians.') On March 12, 1699, Pope Innocent XII issued a relatively mild condemnation of twenty-three articles drawn from Fénelon's defense of Guyon. The Archbishop immediately submitted to the condemnation. Guyon herself gave in in 1703, to live out the rest of her days under what amounted to house arrest.

Madame Guyon's writings fill thirty-nine volumes. Her mystical itinerary is complex and controversial. Suffice it to say that at the core of her doctrine is an insistence on a love of God so pure that it can only find expression in the subject's total self-annihilation. In her *Life*, as well as in her major mystical treatises, such as *The Spiritual Torrents* (1682), *The Short and Very Easy Method* (1685), *The Commentary on the Song of Songs* (1687), and *The Justifications* (1694), she shows how the loving soul progresses from letting go of the perception of the self, through an annihilating of all personal sensation, through a time of inner and outer trials where she despairs of self, to finally arrive at the state of spiritual marriage conceived of as a melting into the ocean of divinity where all distinction is lost. Commenting on Song of Songs 6:4, she puts it this way:

> The distinction I now refer to is that between God and the soul. Here the soul cannot and ought not any longer make such a distinction; God is she and she is God, since by the consummation of the marriage she is absorbed into God and lost in him without power to distinguish or find herself again. The true consummation of the marriage causes an admixture of the soul with God so great and so intimate that she can distinguish and see herself no longer, and it is this fusion that divinizes, so to speak, the actions of a creature arrived at this lofty and sublime position.[25]

---

25 Using the adapted version of the translation of James W. Metcalf, as found in Bernard McGinn, *The Essential Writings of Christian Mysticism* (New York: Random House, 2006), 44. For the French text, *Madame Guyon. Les Torrents et Commentaire au Cantique des cantiques de Salomon 1683-1684*, ed. Claude Morali (Grenoble: Jerôme Millon, 1992), 276.

Like many mystics before her, Guyon qualifies such strong statements of a union of identity by stating in other places that this union does not involve a total loss of the soul's created essence. However we may judge the success of these qualifications, her inquisitors at Issy were more worried about the effect that a sense of total indistinction might have upon the practice of everyday religious life-could an annihilated person still be willing to follow the obligations of Christian faith designed to lead the soul to the reward of heavenly bliss? Their concern is evident from the fact that they asked Guyon to submit to the orthodoxy of several articles that insisted that one can never abandon hope for heaven. For example, Issy article five states, "Every Christian in every state, although not at every minute, is obliged to will, desire, and explicitly ask for his eternal salvation...,"; article nine is equally clear: "A Christian is not allowed to be indifferent with regard to his salvation, nor to the things related to it."[26]

It might be supposed that someone who stressed annihilation, total indifference, and supreme inner quietude would be content to retreat into an obscure corner and do anything to avoid public notice. The paradox of Quietism, however, especially as realized in Madame Guyon, was that the reverse side of annihilation was the acceptance of the divine gift which she referred to as 'the apostolic state.' In a number of texts Madame Guyon constructs a mystical itinerary of three stages of faith, beginning with the cognitive stage of the 'faith of light,' moving on to the affective 'faith of tasting,' and culminating in the 'pure or naked faith' in which the soul dies and is annihilated. Beyond all these, however, is the grace that Guyon calls the 'state of resurrection,' that is the 'apostolic state' in which God acts in and through the soul which remains totally at rest in itself-a form of what she called 'active passivity.'[27]

In her *Life*, as well as in her *Commentary on the Song of Songs*, Guyon claimed that through her marriage with Christ she had attained the status of an 'apostolic bride,' someone sent forth to spread the message of the true form of prayer to the world. The second part of the *Life* is filled with descriptions of her apostolic calling and actions, activities that she defended in her examination by Bossuet prior to the Issy meetings. In her own words:

---

26 "The Issy Articles," as translated in McGinn, *The Essential Writings*, 506.

27 For a detailed consideration of Guyon's views on the relation of activity and passivity, as well as the three forms of faith and 'resurrected life,' see Henri Bourgeois, "Passivité et activité dans le discours et l'expérience de madame Guyon," in *Madame Guyon* (Grenoble: Jerôme Millon, 1997), 235-67, who cites texts on Guyon's view of 'passivité active' on 254.

The Bishop of Meaux raised great objections to what I had to say in my *Life* regarding the apostolic state. What I meant to say is that persons (as, for instance, lay people and women), who by their state and conditions are not called upon to aid souls, ought not to intrude into it of themselves; but when God wished to make use of them by his authority, it was necessary that they should be put into the state of which I have written…. That this state is possible, we have only to open the histories of all times to show that God has made use of laity and women without learning to instruct, edify, conduct, and bring souls to a very high perfection.[28]

Guyon concludes her defense with the same Pauline verse that Raymond of Capua had used of Catherine of Siena, "He [God] has chosen weak things to confound the strong" (1 Cor. 1:27).[29]

The contrasting fates of Catherine of Siena and Madame Guyon provide food for thought as we consider the role of the apostolic charism at the beginning of the twenty-first century. I by no means want to claim that these two women advanced the same message or were of equivalent standing. I would note, however, that we read them through the filter of their reception, historically and ecclesiastically. There is much in the 'heretic' Madame Guyon that is strange, excessive, at times even bizarre. Catherine of Siena is a saint and a doctor of the Roman Catholic church, though anyone who takes a full look at her life and teaching will also find much that is excessive and troubling, such as her unrelenting support of the crusade and the refusal to eat that did much to hasten her demise at age thirty-three. Our task is not judgment, but reflection. Both these women-very much products of their time-felt called to an apostolic life that was, if not forbidden, at least problematic for women. Bossuet, for example, in his satiric attack on Guyon and Fénelon entitled the *Relation on Quietism* ridiculed his fellow bishop for finding excuses "for the enormous boasts of a woman who claimed to be a prophetess and apostle,… full of overflowing grace and endowed with such an eminent perfection that she could not tolerate the rest of mankind."[30]

We may think that we have gone beyond the prejudices of the past regarding the apostolic dimension of the lives of women. After all, women

---

28 Quoted from the English version of the *Life* entitled *Selections from The Autobiography of Madame Guyon*, ed. Warner A. Hutchinson, trans. Thomas Taylor Allen (New Canaan, CT: Keats, 1980), 348-49 (part III, chap. 14).

29 For more on Guyon's notion of the 'apostolic state' and how she defended it, see Gondal, *Madame Guyon*, 104-10; and Bruneau, *Women Mystics Confront the Modern World*, 163-64.

30 Bossuet, *La Relation sur le quiétisme*, in idem, *Oeuvres*, ed. Abbé Velat and Yvonne Champailler (Paris: Gallimard, 1970), 19: 1157, using the translation in Bruneau, *Women Mystics Confront the Modern World*, 187.

today are active in many official ways in Christianity all over the world. But have women *really* been allowed positions of effective apostolic leadership in the ways claimed by Catherine and Jeanne Guyon? You will note that this essay has hinged on a distinction between institutional apostolicity and charismatic apostolicity, so I make no claims or case about women's ordination, a common practice in many Protestant denominations, but still forbidden in the Catholicism of Catherine and Guyon, as well as in Orthodox Christianity. Abstracting from theological debates over female priests and bishops, it seems to me that Christianity in its various denominations has to strive to deal more directly and honestly with the issue of women taking on roles of charismatic apostolic leadership in the ways that Catherine achieved and Jeanne Guyon attempted. Too often today woman are welcomed into the infantry of a rapidly-depleting army whose generals are busy fighting the last war, oblivious of the challenges and opportunities of the present. I do not pretend to be a prophet, or even the 'son of a prophet,' as Amos said many centuries ago (Amos 7:14), but I am convinced that in these early years of Christianity's third millennium there is need more than ever for truly apostolic women whose insight and leadership can provide hope and direction in challenging and difficult times.

DE OBITU VALENTINIANI: ABELARD, BERNARD OF CLAIRVAUX, AND THE CANONIZATION OF AMBROSE OF MILAN ON BAPTISM BY DESIRE

Marcia L. Colish

The most recent Roman Catholic catechism treats baptism by desire as a standard and uncontroversial truth. While affirming that the church "does not know any means other than baptism that assures entry into eternal beatitude,"[1] it also states that baptism by desire conveys the fruits of ritual baptism: "For catechumens who die before their Baptism, their explicit desire to receive it together with repentance for their sins, and charity, assures them the salvation they were not able to receive through the sacrament."[2] Citing the decree *Lumen gentium* proclaimed 2 November 1964, this teaching, the catechism asserts, is one on which "the church has always held a firm conviction."[3] Such a retrojection of current theology into earlier church tradition, if not unique, is notable. For, historically, the defense of baptism by desire began only in the late fourth century, and had a checkered medieval career before reaching its present safe haven in the Catholic consensus. Baptism by desire first gained extended discussion and vigorous support in Ambrose of Milan's *De obitu Valentiniani* (hereafter *DoV*) of 392, a funeral oration on the western Roman emperor Valentinian II delivered in a decidedly unsettled political situation. Without citing Ambrose, Augustine gave this doctrine equivocal treatment. It then lay fallow until the turn of the twelfth century. When theologians revived it, they targeted Ambrose's text as its sturdiest support. While not first out of the gate, both Peter Abelard and Bernard of Clairvaux played a

---

1   *Catechism of the Catholic Church*, 2nd ed., ed. Peter Cardinal Gasparri (Rome: Libreria Editrice Vaticana, 1994), 6.1257 (p. 320).

2   Ibid. 6.1258-6.1260; quotation at 6.1260 (p. 321).

3   Ibid. 6.1281 (p. 325), citing *Lumen gentium*; cf. *Lumen gentium* 2.14-2.16 in *The Documents of Vatican II (1963-1965)*, ed. and trans. Joseph Gallagher (New York: Guild Press, 1966), 32-35. See, in particular, at 2.14 (p. 35): "Catechumens who, moved by the Holy Spirit, seek with explicit intention to be incorporated into the Church are by that very intention joined to her. With love and solicitude Mother Church already embraces them as her own." On this point see also the post-Vatican II Dutch catechism, in *A New Catechism: Catholic Faith for Adults*, trans. Kevin Smyth (New York: Seabury Press, 1965), 249.

key role in canonizing the *DoV*, setting the stage for its citation as an authority on this issue in the scholastic sequel.

As a valid substitute for the font, it was baptism by blood that drew earliest attention. The first to offer a theological rationale was Tertullian, who locates the equivalence of these alternative modes of baptism in the water and blood flowing from the side of the crucified Christ: "These two baptisms He sent forth from the wound in His pierced side, in order that those who believed in His blood might be washed with water, and those who had been washed with water might carry the stain of His blood."[4] Cyprian of Carthage agrees while negating the efficacy of both baptism and martyrdom for heterodox Christians. It is only catechumens of the true church, crushed before they can receive the rite, who "are not deprived of the pledge of baptism on the grounds that they are baptized with the glorious and highest baptism of blood."[5]

Heterodoxy remained a problem after the legitimization of Christianity and the influx of converts, many of whom delayed baptism and the intellectual and moral reforms it required. Fourth-century bishops stressed the need of catechumens to proceed to the font. Closest in time to Ambrose, Gregory Nazianzen makes this point in his Epiphany sermon in 381. He outlines five modes of baptism. First is the Israelites' baptism in the Red Sea, prefiguring the Christian rite. Next is the baptism of John the Baptist, involving repentance for sin but water alone. Third is the baptism of Christ, involving water and the Holy Spirit; Gregory does not specify when he thinks it was instituted. Fourth is the martyrs' baptism by blood. Fifth and last is what he calls the baptism of tears. Gregory does not mean

---

4 Tertullian, *De baptismo*, ed. J.G.P. Borleffs, CCSL 1 (Turnhout: Brepols, 1993), 16.1-2 (pp. 290-91): "Proinde nos facere aqua vocatos sanguine electos duos baptismos de vulnere percussi lateris emisit, quia in sanguinem eius crederent aqua lavarentur, qui aqua lavissent et sanguine opporterent;" Tertullian, *Concerning Baptism*, trans. Alexander Souter (London: SPCK, 1919), 66. Most useful on Tertullian's influence on this point in early and patristic theology is Franz Josef Dölger, "Tertullian über die Bluttaufe: Tertullian, *De baptismo* 16," *Antike und Christentum: Kultur- und religionsgeschichliche Studien*, 2nd ed. (Münster: Aschendorff, 1974), 2:117-41. See also Peter Cramer, *Baptism and Change in the Early Middle Ages, c. 200-c. 1150* (Cambridge: Cambridge University Press, 1993), 73-86; G. Barielle, "Baptême d'après les pères grecs et latins," *DthC* 2/1:208-11.

5 Cyprian, *Epistulae*, ed. G.F. Diercks, CCSL 3C (Turnhout: Brepols, 1996), 73.22.2 (pp. 556-57): "nec privari baptismi sacramento, utpote qui baptizentur gloriossisime et maximo sanguinis baptismo . . .;" Cyprian, *On the Church: Selected Letters*, trans. Allen Brent (Crestwood, NY: St. Vladimir's Seminary Press, 2006), 212. See most recently Attilio Carpin, *Battezati nell'unica vera chiesa? Cipriano di Cartagine e la controversia battesmale* (Bologna: Edizioni Studio Domenicano, 2007), 11-77, and for Cyprian's later influence, ibid., 78-251 with emphasis on episcopal vs. Roman jurisdiction.

by this formula that compunction and repentance can replace ritual baptism. What he wants to emphasize is that baptism is not a free pass, nor is post-baptismal sin either impossible or unforgivable. Rather, just as candidates for baptism must renounce sin, so sin, and repentance for it, are ongoing features of the Christian life, for which the church provides a remedy.[6]

Against this background, and his own stress on the importance on ritual baptism in his other works, we can appreciate Ambrose's argument in *DoV* as the innovation it is. Most of the literature on this text focuses on Ambrose's Latin style and his use of classical and biblical rhetoric[7] or

---

6 Gregory of Nazienzen, *Oratio*, ed. Claudio Moreschini, trans. Paul Gallay, Sources Chrétiennes 358 (Paris: Les Éditions du Cerf, 1991), 39.17-18 (pp. 186-93). This text was preserved faithfully in Latin translation by Rufinus of Aquileia, *Orationum Gregorii Nazianzeni novem interpretatio*, ed. Augustus Engelbrecht, CSEL 46 (Vienna: F. Tempsky, 1910), 129-31. For background on the polemics involved in Gregory's argument, see Claudio Moreschini, "Il battesimo come fondamento dell'istruzione del cristiano in Gregorio Nazianeno," in *Sacerdozio battismale e formazione teologica nella catechesi e nella testimonianza dei Padri*, ed. Sergio Felici (Rome: Libreria Ateneo Salesiano, 1992), 73-82; idem, *Introduzione a Gregorio Nazienzeno* (Brescia: Morcelliana, 2006), 51-52, 85, 88, 92, 100, 121; John A. McGuckin, *St. Gregory Nazianzus: An Intellectual Biography* (Crestwood, NY: St. Vladimir's Seminary Press, 2001), 337-48; Susanna Elm, "Inscriptions and Conversions: Gregory of Nazianzus on Baptism (*Or.* 38-40)," in *Conversion in Late Antiquity and the Early Middle Ages: Seeing and Believing*, ed. Kenneth Mills and Anthony Grafton (Rochester, NY: University of Rochester Press, 2003), 1-35; Brian E. Daley, *Gregory of Nazianzus* (London: Routledge, 2006), 127; Christopher A. Beeley, *Gregory of Nazianzus on the Trinity and Knowledge of God: In Your Light We See Light* (Oxford: Oxford University Press, 2008), 34-35, 43, 69, 71-72, 76-77, 102, 177. At 43, Beeley claims that Epiphany Sunday was the date on which Gregory baptized catechumens; but this was the normal date in the fourth century for enrolling those to be baptized the following Easter, on which see Victor Saxer, *Les rites de l'initiation chrétienne du IIe au VIe siècles: Esquisse historique et signification d'après leur principaux témoins* (Spoleto: Centro Italiano di Studi sull'Alto Medioevo, 1988), 242-54, 263-64, 294-95, 303-14, 323-26, 329-32, 341-48, 350-57, 372. On the general issue of patristic objections to the delay of baptism, see Éric Rebillard, "La figure du catéchumène et le problème du delai du baptême dans la pastorale d'Augustin," in *Augustin prédicateur (395-411)*, Actes du Colloque international de Chantilly, 5-7 septembre 1996, ed. Goulven Madec (Paris: Institut d'Études Augustiniennes, 1998), 285-92.

7 The fullest and most recent analysis is by Martin Biermann, *Die Leichreden des Ambrosius von Mailand: Rhetorik, Predigt, Politik*, Hermes Einzelschriften 70, ed. Jürgen Blänsdorf, Jochen Bleiken, and Wolfgang Kullmann (Stuttgart: Franz Steiner Verlag, 1995), 12, 21-24, 44-49, 51-57, 87-103, 121, 134-42, 151-78, 195. See also Franz Rozynski, *Die Leichtreden des hl. Ambrosius inbesondere auf ihr Verhältnis zu der antike Redekunst und den antiken Trostschriften untersucht* (Breslau: Buchdruckerei der Schlesischen Volkszeitung, 1910), 71-94; Yves-Marie Duval, "Formes profanes et formes biblique dans les oraisons funèbres de saint Ambroise," in *Christianisme et formes littéraires de l'antiquité tardive en Occident*, ed. Alan Cameron et al., Entretiens sur l'Antiquité classique 23 (Geneva: Fondation Hardt, 1977), 249, 254, 257, 258-74, 277, 286-93, 298-99.

on its political context.[8] This political context is indeed important. When Valentinian II succeeded his half-brother Gratian as western emperor he was a minor dominated by his mother Justina. Her hostility to Ambrose and her effort to undermine Nicene Christianity led to the famous basilica crisis of 386. In 388 Justina died and Theodosius I, emperor in the east, decided that his sons should succeed the present rulers, Arcadius in the east and Honorius in Italy. He assigned Gaul to Valentinian, but under the tutelage of his *magister militum* Arbogast. On 15 May 392, at the age of 21, having sought to assert his independence, Valentinian was found strangled. Was he a suicide? Was he assassinated by Arbogast, and, if so, at the behest of Theodosius or on his own initiative? This last possibility is suggested by the fact that on 22 August 392 Arbogast named Eugenius, his own candidate, as emperor in the west. Warfare with Theodosius ensued and Arbogast and Eugenius were both defeated and put to death.

The truth concerning Valentinian's death and the political fall-out of these events were up in the air when Ambrose presided over the young emperor's obsequies, his body having been returned to Milan for burial. That Ambrose was walking on eggs in his funeral oration is manifest in its rhetoric.[9] At various points he addresses God; the Milanese Christian community; Justa and Gratia, Valentinian's sisters, his surviving relatives and chief mourners there; Gratian; and Valentinian himself, as a saint in Heaven along with Gratian. The beatified Gratian also gets a speech, confirming Christ's assurance of that happy outcome. Throughout, Ambrose skirts the details of Valentinian's early anti-Nicene policy and the question

---

8   For political background on Valentinian II's reign, see Neil B. McLynn, *Ambrose of Milan: Church and Court in a Christian Capital* (Berkeley: University of California Press, 1994), 84-91, 98-102, 105, 154-55, 160-61, 165-66, 170-208, 218, 279, 296-97, 337-41. On the basilica crisis of 386, see Marcia L. Colish, "Why the Portiana? Reflections on the Milanese Basilica Crisis of 386," *Journal of Early Christian Studies* 10 (2002): 361-72, reprt. in eadem, *The Fathers and Beyond: Church Fathers between Ancient and Medieval Thought* (Aldershot: Ashgate, 2008), no. VIII. For the debates of patristic authors concerning the suicide/assassination issue (assassination being the more widespread view) and those of modern scholars, see Thomas A. Kelly, intro. to his ed. and trans. of Ambrose, *De consolatione Valentiniani*, Catholic University of America Patristic Studies 58 (Washington: Catholic University of America Press, 1940), 38-41.

9   Ambrose, *De obitu Valentinii*, ed. and trans. Gabriele Banterle in *Le orazioni funebri*, Sancti Ambrosii episcopi Mediolanensis opera 18 (Milan: Biblioteca Ambrosiana, 1985), 162-209. Good English translations include Ambrose, *Consolation on the Death of Valentinian*, trans. Roy J. Deferrari in *Funeral Orations by Saint Gregory Nazianzus and Saint Ambrose*, FC 22 (New York: Fathers of the Church, Inc., 1953); Ambrose of Milan, *Political Speeches and Letters*, trans. J.H.W.G. Liebeschuetz and Carole Hill, Translated Texts for Historians 43 (Liverpool: Liverpool University Press, 2005). I have consulted these works with profit but translations of this text and others in this essay are my own unless otherwise indicated.

of how he died. Accenting the virtues he imputes to him, Ambrose merely says that, seeing the error of his ways, the emperor corrected them. Once he was his own master, Ambrose asserts, Valentinian committed himself to orthodox Christianity, postponing his baptism only because of the conflicts among bishops in Gaul and because he wished to receive the rite at Ambrose's own hands: "He often intimated, when I was absent, that he wanted to be initiated into the sacred mysteries by me."[10] Far from being a non-believer receiving a posthumous, surrogate baptism,[11] Ambrose's Valentinian was a fully-instructed catechumen hastening to the font when he was cut down by his unexplained death.[12]

Thus, Valentinian's sisters should not worry about his lack of ritual baptism. For Gratian, Ambrose imparts, has assured Valentinian that Christ Himself granted him baptism by desire: "It was not just anyone," says Gratian, "but Christ, who illuminated you with spiritual grace. He has baptized you, since human rites were not present in your case."[13] Given Valentinian's upright faith and morals and his repeated requests and yearning for baptism, this validation by the Lord should allay all anxiety. So, to Justa and Gratia, Ambrose observes, "I hear your lament that he did not receive the rites of baptism.... But did he not have the grace he desired? Did he not have what he requested? And because he requested it, he received it."[14]

At the close of his oration, Ambrose wraps up his argument syllogistically, again addressing Valentinian's sisters: "But if you are troubled by the fact that the mysteries were not solemnly celebrated, not even the martyrs were crowned, if they were not catechumens. For they are not crowned if they are not initiated. But since the martyrs have, in fact, been washed by

---

10 Ambrose, *DoV* c. 6, 9-21, 25, 34-38, 41, 46, 54-57, 64-79b; the quotation is at c. 13 (p. 176): "Illa privata, quod saepe me adpellabat absentem et a me initiandum se sacris mysteriis praeferebat."

11 This is the opinion given by Jeffrey A. Trumbower, *Rescue for the Dead: The Posthumous Salvation of Non-Christians in Early Christianity* (New York: Oxford University Press, 2004), 4, 33-41, 104, 155. Cf. Marcia L. Colish, "The Virtuous Pagan: Dante and the Christian Tradition," *The Fathers and Beyond* (as in n. 8), no. XVII.

12 Ambrose, *DoV* c. 25-26.

13 Ibid. c. 75 (p. 204): "Hoc est: non quicumque te, sed Christus inluminavit gratia spiritali. Ille te baptizavit, quia humana tibi officia defuerunt."

14 Ibid. c. 51 (pp. 192-94): "Sed audio vos dolere, quod non acceperit sacramenta baptismatis. . . . Non habet ergo gratiam, quam desideravit, non habet, quam poposcit? Et quia poposcit, accepit." See also c. 30 (p. 180): "Sed ille non amisit gratiam, quam poposcit?"

their blood, so also his piety and desire have washed him."[15] Here, Ambrose presents the validity of baptism by desire as an irrefutable logical conclusion, and as fully efficacious as baptism by blood.

That this Ambrosian doctrine breaks fresh ground has received only scant scholarly attention.[16] Ambrose's editors note that, aside from one fourteenth-century codex containing this text, it was transmitted in manuscripts from the Carolingian period through the twelfth century;[17] yet scholars have not tracked its later fortunes. Despite its availability, there is no known reference to the *DoV* before ca. 1100. Until then, the main treatments of baptism by desire are by Augustine, and with far less clarity than Ambrose.

In his early *De diversis quaestionibus octoginta tribus*, reflecting no particular polemical agenda, Augustine foregrounds two biblical figures destined to loom large in this account, Cornelius [Acts 10:1-44] and the good thief on the cross [Luke 23:43]. Cornelius, he agrees, was granted faith by the Holy Spirit. And, as St. Peter ruled, he should have, and did, proceed to ritual baptism. As for the good thief, "baptism was granted to the believing thief, considered as having received it in his free mind since he could not receive it bodily on the cross."[18] But Augustine takes a different line in his anti-Donatist *De baptismo*, cited more frequently by later theologians. Agreeing with Cyprian that we should distinguish heterodox from orthodox baptism and martyrdom, he contrasts Cornelius more crisply with the good thief. The good thief, indeed, received baptism by desire; but we should not regard him as a martyr: "Again and again

---

15   Ibid. c. 53 (p. 194): "Aut si, quia sollemniter non sunt celebrata mysteria, hoc movet, ergo nec martyres, si catechumeni fuerint, coronatur; non enim coronatur, si non initiantur. Quodsi, suo abluuntur sanguine, et hunc sua pietas abluit et voluntas."

16   Noted by Banterle, intro. to his ed. and trans. of *DoV*, 15; Dorothea Sattler, "Begierdetaufe," in *Lexikon für Theologie und Kirche* (Freiburg: Herder, 1994), 2:143; Ernst Dassmann, *Ambrosius von Mailand: Leben und Werken* (Stuttgart: W. Kohlhammer, 2004), 178.

17   Banterle, intro. to his ed. and trans. of *DoV*, 22; most recently Michaela Zelzer, "Quelques remarques sur la tradition des oeuvres d'Ambroise et sur leurs titres originaux," in *Lire et éditer aujourd'hui Ambroise de Milan*, ed. Gérard Nauroy (Bern: Peter Lang, 2007), 21-35 at 25-26, 31; see also eadem, "Zur Überlieferung und Rezeption der Kaiserreden des Ambrosius im Mailänder Raum," in *"Chartae caritatis": Études de patristique et d'antiquité tardive en hommage à Yves-Marie Duval*, ed. Benoît Gain, Pierre Jay, and Gérard Nauroy (Paris: Institut d'Études Augustiniennes, 2004), 113-25. The manuscripts preserving this text are: S. Omer 72 (8th/9th c.), Paris BN lat. 1913 (9th c.), Paris BN lat. 1719 (11th c.), Durham Cath. Bib. B.II.6 (11th c.), Milan Bib. Ambrosiana 371 sup. (12th c.), Heiligenkreutz 254 (12th c.), and Paris BN lat. 1920 (14th c.).

18   Augustine, *De diversis quaestionibus octoginta tribus*, ed. Almut Mutzenbecher, CCSL 44A (Turnhout: Brepols, 1975), q. 62 (p. 133): "etiam baptismum credente latrone, et pro accepto habitum in animo libero quod in corpore crucifixo accipi non poterat."

I find on consideration that, in addition to martyrdom for the name of Christ, faith and conversion of heart can supply what is lacking if the rite of baptism cannot be celebrated for lack of time. That thief was crucified not for the name of Christ but for his crimes. He did not suffer because he believed, but believed while he was suffering. It is evident how powerful this is in the thief's case,... even without the visible sacrament, for baptism is accomplished invisibly when its administration is omitted by reason of necessity, not through contempt of religion."[19]

In his anti-Pelagian *De natura et origine animae* Augustine shifts his tactics yet again, since his opponents invoke the good thief in arguing that ritual baptism is unnecessary. For them, the thief believed before his crucifixion and was, simply, saved thereby. Alluding to Tertullian in his rebuttal, Augustine observes, "It is not beyond belief to say that the thief crucified next to the Lord then believed, and received a most holy baptism by the water flowing from His wounded side;" but, he adds, "none of us knows this for sure or can prove it."[20] As a sidebar, Augustine refers to Dinocrates, prayed out of Hell by his sister St. Perpetua. Her *vita* gives no evidence concerning his faith. But, could not Dinocrates, albeit a child, have already converted?[21] Not to mention Christ's own apostles. Scripture is silent on when they were baptized; but it would be shameful to think that this never occurred.[22]

Yet another argument surfaces in Augustine's commentary on Leviticus, sparked by the typology of the Red Sea event. In the Christian era, too, the Holy Spirit sanctifies invisibly as well as visibly. Maintaining as

---

19 Augustine, *De baptismo libri VII*, ed. M. Petchenig, CSEL 51 (Vienna: F. Tempsky, 1908), 4.22.29 (p. 257): "Quod etiam atque etiam considerans invenio non tantum passione pro nomine Christi id quod ex baptismo deerat posse supplere, sed etiam fidem conversionemque cordis, si forte ad celebrandum mysterium baptismi in angustiis temporum succurri non potuit neque enim latro ille pro nomine Christi crucifixus est, sed pro meritis facinorum suum, nec quia credidit passus est, sed dum patitur credidit, quantum itaque valeat etiam sine visibili baptismi sacramento . . . in illo latrone declaratum est, sed tunc impletur invisibiliter, cum ministerium baptismi non contemptus religionis, sed articulus necessitatis excludit."

20 Augustine, *De natura et origine animae*, ed. Carolus F. Urba and Josephus Zycha, CSEL 40 (Vienna: F. Tempsky, 1913), 1.9.11 (pp. 311-12): "non incredibliter dicitur latronem qui tunc credidit iuxta dominum crucifixum aqua illa, quae de vulnera lateris eius emicuit, tamquam sacratissimo baptismo fuisse perfusum; . . . quoniam nemo nostrum novit, nemo convicit."

21 Ibid. 1.10.12, 3.9.12. In the latter passage Augustine raises the (unprovable) possibility that the good thief might have been ritually baptized before his crucifixion.

22 Ibid. 3.9.12. For a rich discussion of the debate from the early church through the twelfth century on when the apostles were baptized, see Ernst Kantorowicz, "The Baptism of the Apostles," *Dumbarton Oaks Papers* 9/10 (1956): 203-51.

undeniable the good thief's invisible sanctification and subsequent bliss, Augustine now presents him as a unique case, not as a precedent for current practice. Indeed, times had already changed by Cornelius' day. For him, as for us, "visible sanctification is not judged superfluous even if invisible precedes it."[23] But, preaching on John 3:3-5, the conversation between Christ and Nicodemus, Augustine takes a harder line. This sermon was delivered on Palm Sunday, 30 March 413, as the catechumens in his congregation entered the final week of their pre-baptismal preparation. Augustine thus stresses the universal need for ritual baptism: "Now is the time to exhort you catechumens, who, even though you believe in Christ, are still encumbered by your sins. No one will reign with Christ unless they are forgiven him, and no one can be forgiven unless reborn of water and the Holy Spirit;" he adjures them, literally, to lay down their burden and to take the plunge.[24] Nicodemus, he continues the following day, is an exact parallel with these catechumens: a believer, but not yet cleansed in the font.[25] Here, Augustine's anti-Pelagian brief joins hands with the pastoral needs of his audience at this particular liturgical season.

When he updated his oeuvre in the *Retractationes*, the only works on this topic which Augustine reviewed were the *De diversis quaestionibus* and the *De baptismo*. On the good thief, he says, he has done further research, and has new thoughts about his pre-crucifixion state: "I do not know that this documentation can prove that the thief was not baptized."[26] Again, he observes, "it is uncertain whether he had been baptized or not."[27] For further discussion Augustine refers readers to his anti-Pelagian considerations of the thief. While now dismissing the thief as no longer a good model for current practice, even as Augustine sets aside his example he does not obviate the possibility that Christ accepted the thief's conversion on the cross as the equivalent of baptism.

---

23   Augustine, *Quaestiones Levitici* 3.84 in *Quaestiones in Heptateuchum libri VII*, ed. J. Fraipont, CCSL 33 (Turnhout: Brepols, 1958), 228: "nec superflua iudicata est visibilis sanctificatio, quam invisibilis iam praecesserat."

24   Augustine, *In Iohannis Evangelium tractatus libri* CXXIV, ed. D. Radbodus Willems, CCSL 36 (Turnhout: Brepols, 1954), 109: "Tempus est enim ut vos exhortemur, qui adhuc estis catechumeni, qui, sic creditistis in Christum, ut adhuc vestra peccata portetis; quia nisi cui dimissa fuerint, non regnabit cum Christo; dimitti non possunt nisi ei qui renatus fuit ex aqua et Spiritu Sancto."

25   Ibid. 11.3-6, 12.1-6.

26   Augustine, *Retractationes*, ed. Almut Mutzenbecher, CCSL 57 (Turnhout: Brepols, 1984), 1.26 (p. 83): "sed quibus documentis satis posit ostendi, quod non fuerit ille latro baptizatus, ignoro."

27   Ibid. 2.18 (p. 104): "quia utrum non fuerit baptizatus incertum est."

This ambiguous Augustinian legacy on baptism by desire, like Ambrose's forthright support of it in the *DoV*, was not put to use for over half a millennium. The first author to reopen the question of baptism by desire was Bonizo of Sutri, best known for his writings as a canonist and his travails in support of Matilda of Tuscany. Most of the sources on which Bonizo draws in his *Liber de vita christiana* of 1089/90 are earlier canonical texts. Addressing the problem of sacraments administered by heretics, schismatics, and excommunicates given a high profile by the investiture controversy, Bonizo adds his own theological and pastoral concerns.[28] He prefaces his remarks on baptism with Augustine's *De baptismo* statement that the good thief was no martyr. He died for his crimes, not for the name of Christ. "Nor did he suffer because he believed, but believed while he suffered."[29] Bonizo is certain that baptism was imputed to the thief. At he same time, he agrees with Augustine that Cornelius, who did not omit ritual baptism, is the relevant contemporary model.[30] Bonizo indicates that Gregory of Nazianzen on the baptism of tears has entered the Latin tradition, although without noting Gregory's concerns. He reads this notion as signifying God's acceptance of the repentance of Old and New Testament figures alike.[31] Given that Bonizo is laying down the canonical and liturgical norms for ritual baptism in this work, despite the authorities cited he concludes by dismissing baptism by desire as such: "We do not believe that a catechumen, however much he dies with good works, has eternal life, unless the sacrament [of baptism] is fulfilled in him by martyrdom."[32]

Shortly after Bonizo wrote, a new chapter was opened on the subject of baptism by desire by Anselm of Laon and his followers, although without yet giving Ambrose a hearing.[33] While they support the necessity of bap-

---

28 On the nature of this work, its place in Bonizo's career, and its sources, see Ludovico Gatto, *Bonizone di Sutri e il suo Libro ad Amicum: Ricerche sull'età gregoriana* (Pescara: Editrice Trimestre, 1968), 63-69; Bonizo of Sutri, *Liber de vita christiana*, 2nd ed., ed. Ernst Perels, Nachwort by Walter Berschin (Berlin: Weidemann, 1998), xvi-xxxiii, 405*.

29 Bonizo, *Liber*, praeambula 3 (pp. 2-3): "nec quia credidit passus est, set dum patitur credidit."

30 Ibid., 3-5.

31 Ibid. 1.3 (p. 15); for the whole passage, see ibid. 1.42 (pp. 17-31).

32 Ibid. 1.33 (pp. 28-29): "Catechumenum quamvis in bonis operibus defunctum vitam eternam non credimus, excepto dumtaxat, nisi martirii sacramentum in eo compleamur."

33 Earlier studies include Artur Michael Landgraf, "Das sacramentum in voto," *Dogmengeschichte der Frühscholastik*, 4 vols. in 8 (Regensburg: Friedrich Pustat, 1952-56), 3/1: 210-53 at 218-20; Ludwig Ott, *Untersuchungen zur theologischen Briefliteratur der Frühscholastik unter besonderer Berücksichtigung des Viktorinerkreises*, Beiträge zur Geschichte der Philosophie und Theologie des Mittelalters 34 (Münster: Aschendorff, 1937), 495-548; Marcia L. Colish, *Peter Lombard*, 2 vols. (Leiden: Brill, 1994), 2: 532-39.

tism, they also offer strategies for circumventing the anti-Pelagian Augustine which they bequeath to twelfth-century successors who do cite the *DoV*. One tactic, acknowledging Augustine's reconsideration of *De baptismo* in the *Retractationes*, is to affirm that he retained his earlier teaching even if he rejected the example of the good thief. Baptism by desire is thus efficacious and Augustine supports this position. A second gambit it to reinterpret both Augustine and the Acts of the Apostles in the light of a distinction which the Laon masters helped to make standard, between the *sacramentum*, the external rite, and the *res sacramenti*, its spiritual content and effects. While agreeing that infants require the *sacramentum*, adults, they observe, sometimes receive the *res sacramenti* without it.[34] The thinkers in this group do not speak with one voice on the good thief. Some regard him as saved and glorified but as a unique case, not pertinent to current practice.[35] Others think that the thief's beatitude is by no means unique. He possessed a full complement of the faith, hope, and charity needed by all who are glorified.[36] The Laon masters are quite willing to invert Augustine's argument concerning Cornelius. For them he is a classic illustration of the availability of the *res sacramenti* before, and apart from, the *sacramentum*: "Before Peter arrived, Cornelius had the *res sacramenti*. Peter added the *sacramentum*."[37] And, Cornelius is not a biblical one-off. Rather, he models those persons later granted baptism by desire: "For if, before they can be baptized, death prevents them, by reason of necessity and not out of any negligence on their part, good will alone suffices for

---

34 On infants: *Sententie divine pagine* in *Anselms von Laon systematische Sentenzen*, ed. Franz Bliemetzrieder, Beiträge zur Geschichte der Philosophie des Mittelalters 18/2-3 (Münster: Aschendorff, 1919), 42-43, 46; *Liber Pancrisis* no. 46; Sentences of the School of Anselm of Laon no. 366, 369; *Antequam quicquam fieret* no. 7, ed. Odon Lottin, *Psychologie et morale aux XIIe et XIIIe siècle*, 6 vols. (Gembloux/Louvain: J. Duculot/Abbaye de Mont César, 1948-60), 5: 42-43, 275, 337-38. On baptism by blood as the only alternative to the font, Sentences of the School of Laon no. 365 in Lottin, 5: 273-74; *Dubitatur a quibusdam* in *Das Schrifttum der Schule Anselms von Laon und Wilhelm von Champeaux in deutschen Bibliotheken*, ed. Heinrich Weisweiler, Beiträge zur Geschichte der Philosophie und Theologie des Mittelalters 33/1-2 (Münster: Aschendorff, 1936), 347.

35 Sentences of the School of Laon no. 367 in Lottin (as in n. 34), 5: 274.

36 *Deus hominem fecit perfectum* in Weisweiler (as in n. 34), 297, repeated verbatim in *Dubitatur a quibusdam*, ibid. 317: "Tribus de causis latro paradisum introivit: Fidem habuit, quando hominum secum morientem regnaturum credidit; spem, quando aditum celi ab eo petiit; caritatem, quando confratrem et conlatronem iniquitatis sue redarguit."

37 Sentences of the School of Laon no. 364 in Lottin (as in n. 34), 5: 273: "Cornelius antequam Petrus venisset, habuit rem sacramenti. Petrus addidit sacramentum." See also *Sententie Atrebatensis*; *Liber Pancrisis* no. 52 in ibid., 5: 49, 428.

their salvation and brings them into union with the church."[38] Whether citing Augustine positively or citing Augustine against Augustine, these masters open wide the door to the efficacy of sacramental grace for those prevented from receiving the rites by extenuating circumstances. And this position applies not only to baptism by desire but to sacraments in general. In a position that, reformulated by Peter Lombard, had a long career ahead of it, the author of the *Liber Pancrisis* asserts, "God, Who alone can do all things, and Who forgives the sins of whomever and however He wills, in no way has to remit them with the help of the sacraments."[39]

Those familiar with Peter Abelard will not be surprised to learn that he does not credit the Laon masters either for their willingness to criticize authorities with whom they disagree or for their tactics in subverting them. Yet, in the event, neither did Abelard receive the credit he deserves for supporting baptism by desire. Rather, he was cast by Bernard of Clairvaux as the villain of the piece, the chief opponent of that doctrine. Abelard and Bernard are equally central for yoking the *DoV* to this question, even if problematically in Abelard's case. How their basic agreement became, and was seen to be, a doctrinal stand-off is critical for the canonization of Ambrose's text as an authority on this subject, wherever later thinkers came down on it.

Abelard places the *DoV* front and center in both his *Sic et non* and *Theologia christiana*. In the earliest versions of the *Sic et non*, he treats only the doctrine of God, the Trinity, and Christology. He includes the sacraments only in versions produced between 1121 and 1126.[40] *Quaestio* 106 asks whether ritual baptism is always required for salvation. Oddly, given the wealth of patristic possibilities, on the negative side he lists one sole authority, Gennadius, who admits only the baptism by blood exception standard since Tertullian. On the positive side, Abelard presents two fig-

---

38 *Sententie Anselmi*, ed. Bliemetzrieder (as in n. 34), 84: "Sed tamen, antequam baptizari possint, si morte preventi fuerint, ita quod necessitas et nulla eorum negligentia impediveret, sola bona vountas eis sufficit ad salvationem, et hec eos in ecclesie unitatem facit." See also *Liber Pancrisis* no. 59, in Lottin (as in n. 34), 5: 54: "salvi sunt et bene possunt dici baptizati;" *Sententia divine pagine*, ed. Bliemetzrieder (as in n. 34), 46: "Si non contemptus religionis sed articulus excludit necessitas."

39 *Liber Pancrisis* no. 57, in Lottin (as in n. 34), 5: 53: "Deus qui omnia solus potest et qui, cui vult et quomodo vult, peccata dimittit, nullius indiguit ad illa remittenda auxilio sacramenti." Cf. Peter Lombard, *Sententiae in IV libris distinctae* 4.d.4.c.4.10, 3rd ed., ed. Ignatius C. Brady (Grottaferrata: Collegium S. Bonaventurae, 1971-81), 2: 258: ". . . Deus, qui suam potentiam sacramentis non alligavit."

40 Constant J. Mews, "On Dating the Works of Peter Abelard," *Archives d'histoire doctrinale et littéraire du moyen âge* 52 (1984): 73-134 at 121-23, 131; reprt. in idem, *Abelard and His Legacy* (Aldershot: Ashgate, 2001), no. VII.

ures who, he claims, demonstrate the posthumous salvation of pagans. In so doing, he reflects his departure from the sage rules for validating the accuracy and relevance of authorities which he outlines in the preface of the *Sic et non*.[41] One of these pagan examples is the infant Dinocrates. Ignoring Augustine's hypotheses concerning his pre-mortem state, and claiming no salient virtues for him, Abelard simply reports that Perpetua prayed Dinocrates out of Hell as related in her *vita*. His second example, on the other hand, is a genuine virtuous pagan, Trajan. There already existed several versions of the *vita* of Gregory the Great, deemed to have rescued Trajan from Hell. Abelard cites as his authority John the Deacon's *vita* of Gregory. However, the version of the Trajan legend which he presents is found neither in John the Deacon, nor anywhere else for that matter, prior to the *Sic et non* itself.[42] Abelard then moves to authorities who support baptism by desire in living adult Christian converts. After citing the general observation in I. Corinthians that the Holy Spirit bloweth where it listeth, he presents the two authorities who really count: Augustine's *De baptismo* as modified by the *Retractationes*, and then a lengthy verbatim quotation from chapters 51 and 52 of the *DoV* where Ambrose nails down his final argument.[43] If Abelard can be thought of as listing his positive authorities in ascending order of importance, then Ambrose's Valentinian is his weightiest support for baptism by desire.

Quite possibly Abelard wanted his pupils, as they worked their way through the *Sic et non*, to find persuasive the salvation of virtuous pagans and not just Ambrose's position on baptism by desire for adult Christian converts, since he reprises the theme of the virtuous pagan, as the context in which he defends baptism by desire, in other works. He presents Cornelius as a virtuous pagan, saved by faith prior to baptism, in *Scito te ipsum*.[44] In his commentary on Romans, he makes the more general point that those predestined to salvation will be saved, whether they can be baptized ritually or not.[45] But it is in his *Theologia christiana* that Abelard

---

41 Peter Abelard, *Sic et non*, ed. Blanche Boyer and Richard McKeon (Chicago: University of Chicago Press, 1976), q. 106 (pp. 341-50); for the preface, see ibid. (pp. 89-104); trans. in *Medieval Literary Theory and Criticism, c. 1100-c. 1375*, ed. A.J. Minnis and A.B. Scott with the assistance of David Wallace (Oxford: Clarendon Press, 1988), 87-100.

42 Abelard, *Sic et non* q. 106 (pp. 348-49). On these figures, see Colish, "The Virtuous Pagan" (as in n. 11), no. XVII, at 2 for Perpetua and Dinocrates; at 4-11, 20-22 for the Trajan legend and Abelard's treatment of it.

43 Abelard, *Sic et non* q. 106 (pp. 349-50).

44 Peter Abelard, *Scito te ipsum*, ed. R.M. Ilgner, CCCM 190 (Turnhout: Brepols, 2001), 42-43.

45 Peter Abelard, *Commentaria in Epistolam Pauli ad Romanos* 2, ed. Eligius M. Buytaert, CCCM 11 (Turnhout: Brepols, 1969), ch. 2 (p. 119).

shows his clearest reliance on Ambrose. In contrast with the *Sic et non*, he cites here only the authorities who buttress his desired solution, and streamlines his argument, limiting himself to two.[46] One is the garbled reference to the Gregory/Trajan story which he again attributes erroneously to John the Deacon.[47] The other is the *DoV*. Dismissing John 3:3-5 and the martyr exception as irrelevant without further ado, he offers the following assessment: "But evoking still greater admiration is what blessed Ambrose himself wrote to the emperor's sisters in the *Consolation on the Death of Valentinian*. There, the aforesaid saint indicated that everyone knew that he [Valentinian] had already been catechized by him, but not yet baptized. Before that act, on account of his life's good works, he was granted grace without baptism, and, after death, numbered among the elect.... Did he not receive what he requested?"[48] As with Ambrose, Abelard treats the rhetorical question as an affirmation. But he then dragoons this argument to the defense of one of his most controversial positions. True, both Trajan and Valentinian lived during the Christian era. But what should we think about the philosophers who lived before that age, but whose virtues were exemplary and whose writings forecast the gospel? Should they not also be included among the blessed, thanks to God's goodness and mercy?[49]

Prudently, Abelard's disciples did not go this last mile with him, although they supported his stress on intentionality over ritual.[50] The author of the *Ysagoge in theologiam* is the Abelardian who presents the crispest defense of baptism by desire, citing both the *DoV* and Augustine's unmodified *De baptismo* in his clinching argument. He considers the fate of just persons who possess faith and love but who cannot receive the rite

---

46 Peter Abelard, *Theologia christiana*, ed. Eligius M. Buytaert, CCCM 12 (Turnhout: Brepols, 1969), 2.112-115 (pp. 182-84).

47 Ibid. 2.112 (p. 182).

48 Ibid. 2.113-114 (pp. 182-84): "Sed fortasse illud maiori admiratione suscipitur quod *In consolationem super morte Valentinani* imperatoris ad sorores ipsius beatus scripserit Ambrosius. Ubi quidem praedictus sanctus omnino adstruere intelligitur eum a se iam catechizatum sed nondum baptizatum, ex ante actae vitae bonis operibus veniam impetrasse post mortem et sortem electorum sine baptismi gratia percepisse; . . . non habet quam poposcit?"

49 Ibid. 2.115 (p. 184).

50 [50] See in general, Richard E. Weingart, "Peter Abailard's Contribution to Medieval Sacramentology," *Recherches de théologie ancienne et médiévale* 34 (1967): 159-78 at 168-69, 177; idem, *The Logic of Divine Love: A Critical Analysis of the Soteriology of Peter Abailard* (Oxford: Clarendon Press, 1970), 186-92; Constant J. Mews, *Abelard and Heloise* (Oxford: Oxford University Press, 2005), 129-30, 190, 122; Mews extends this judgment to the *Sententie Hermannus*, which he reads, at 218ff., as a *reportatio* of Abelard's teaching, not as the work of a disciple.

by reason of necessity, and concludes, "With respect to these good people, who are prevented, both authority and reason can confirm that they proceed to eternal rest; ...faith without the sacrament must be valid."[51]

Given this evidence, it is paradoxical indeed that, starting with Hugh of St. Victor and Bernard of Clairvaux, twelfth-century supporters of baptism by desire posit what they take to be Abelard's position as the one demanding refutation.[52] A key text in promoting this outcome is Bernard's *Epistola 77*, dating to 1125 or 1126/28. He wrote in response to Hugh's request for clarification on a number of theological points, among them the necessity of ritual baptism. Recent scholars have made considerable headway in turning around the earlier judgment of Bernard as a conservative wet blanket in relation to nascent scholasticism, flagging various doctrinal questions to which he made a positive contribution.[53] But it is to Hugh Feiss and his followers that we owe an appreciation of Bernard's role in placing baptism by desire at the center of scholastic debates, in stigmatizing Abelard as that doctrine's most toxic opponent, and in rescuing

---

51   *Ysagoge in theologiam*, ed. Artur Michael Landgraf, *Écrits théologiques de l'école d'Abélard* (Louvain: Spicilegium Sacrum Lovaniense, 1934), ch. 2 (pp. 184-88); at p. 184: "alii iusti dum in articulo necessitatis fides cum dilectio prevenitur;" at pp. 188-89: "Nam de bonis, qui preveniuntur, et auctoritas vel ratio afferri potest, quia ad requiem transeunt; . . . fides sine sacramento debet valere."

52   David E. Luscombe, *The School of Peter Abelard: The Influence of Abelard's Thought in the Early Scholastic Period* (Cambridge: Cambridge University Press, 1970), 210, 225, 246.

53   Jean Châtillon, "L'Influence de S. Bernard sur la pensée scolastique au XIIe et au XIIIe siècle," in *Saint Bernard théologien*, Actes du Congrès de Dijon, 15-19 septembre 1953, Analecta Sacri Ordinis Cisterciensis 9 (Rome: Tipografia Pio X, 1953), 268-88; reprt. in idem, *D'Isidore de Séville à saint Thomas d'Aquin: Études d'histoire et de théologie* (London: Variorum Reprints, 1985), no. V, which notes Bernard's response to Hugh at 276-77, 279-80, 287 but without specifying its content; likewise Artur Michael Landgraf, "Der hl. Bernhard in seinem Verhältnis zur Theologie des 12. Jahrhundert," in *Bernhard von Clarivaux, Mönch und Mystiker*, ed. Joseph Lortz (Wiesbaden: Franz Steiner Verlag, 1955), 44-62 notes this correspondence at 45-46, 53 but without discussing its doctrinal content; that topic is not mentioned at all by John R. Sommerfeldt, "Bernard of Clairvaux and Scholasticism," *Papers of the Michigan Academy of Sciences, Arts, and Letters* 48 (1963): 265-77; William J. Courtenay, "Sacrament, Symbol, and Causality in Bernard of Clairvaux," in *Bernard of Clairvaux: Studies Presented to Jean Leclercq*, Cistercian Studies Series 23 (Kalamazoo: Cistercian Publications, 1973), 111-22; or Robert Baumkirschner, "Bernhard von Clairvaux als Kirchenlehrer in dogmengeschichtlicher Schau," *Cistercienser Chronik* 86, n.F. 145 (1979): 85-102. Most recently, Matthew A. Doyle, *Bernard of Clairvaux and the Schools* (Spoleto: Centro Italiano de Studi sull'Alto Medioevo, 2005) reprises earlier literature at 8-9 nn. 25-31; at 72-73 he simply notes Bernard's "dexterous use of the Fathers and the Bible" in this letter but does not discuss its teaching on baptism. Doyle's chief concern is Bernard's friendly relations with early scholastics, not doctrinal influences.

the *DoV* as its solid foundation, purged of the idiosyncratic opinions with which Abelard associates it.[54]

Hugh's letter to Bernard does not survive although Bernard reprises its content in his reply. Hugh adverts to an unnamed current thinker whose insistence on the unqualified necessity of ritual baptism he finds problematic. Nor does Bernard name this thinker, although he treats his identity and teaching as common knowledge. The consensus, then and now, is that he is Abelard, rather than some other contemporary proponent of Augustine's anti-Pelagian position.[55] Bernard launches his defense of baptism by desire not by analyzing and refuting the unnamed opponent's argument but simply by advancing the authorities who, he thinks, most strongly support his own case. They are also the ones Abelard and the author of the *Ysagoge in theologiam* cite, Augustine's *De baptismo* and the *DoV*. These, he says, are the foundation on which his conclusion rests. And, their teaching is identical: "Both give the same opinion, which we also affirm."[56] Taking a leaf from the book of the Laon masters, Bernard argues that Augustine's *Retractationes* do not nullify the force of his *De baptismo*. The good thief, he agrees, was not a martyr. But he did undergo conversion of heart on the cross. Thus, he received the invisible grace of baptism without the rite, not out of contempt for religion but because of imminent necessity and lack of time. Bernard dismisses out of hand Augustine's later efforts to problematize the good thief's status by positing that he could have been baptized before his crucifixion. This hypothesis he judges to be both unfounded and distasteful, a debater's trick that seeks to put Augustine's antagonists into the position of proving a negative. Bernard recognizes this move as a mere rhetorical ploy, as unavailing as it is transparent. Even more important, this shaky claim conflicts with Augustine's sounder

---

54 Hugh Feiss, "*Bernardus Scholasticus*: The Correspondence of Bernard of Clairvaux and Hugh of Saint Victor on Baptism," in *Bernardus Magister*, ed. John R. Sommerfeldt, Cistercian Studies Series 135 (Kalamazoo: Cistercian Publications, 1992), 349-78; P. Marek Chojnacki, *Il Battesimo e l'Eucharistia: Fonti rituali della vita cristiana secondo San Bernardo di Chiaravalle* (Rome: Pontificia Università Gregoriana, 2002), 80, 96-97, 216; Emero Stiegman, intro. to Bernard of Clairvaux, *On Baptism and the Office of Bishop*, trans. Paulina Matarasso, Cistercian Fathers Series 67 (Kalamazoo: Cistercian Publications, 2004), 85-147.

55 Stiegman, intro. to Bernard, *On Baptism* (as in n. 54), 90-92, 94-97, 109, 119-26, 145 gives full details on adherents of this consensus position.

56 Bernard of Clairvaux, *Epistola* 77.2.7 in *Opere di San Bernardo*, ed. Ferruccio Gastaldelli, trans. Ettore Paratore, 6 vols. (Milan: Scriptorum Claravallano, 1984-2000), 6/1: 352: "uterque idem profecto sensit, quod fatemur et nos." Text also in *Sancti Bernardi opera*, ed. Jean Leclercq et al., 8 vols. in 9 (Rome: Editiones Cistercienses, 1955-77), 7: 984-200.

and more basic teaching that some people receive grace and sanctification by invisible means.[57]

Bernard then turns to the quotation and discussion of the *DoV*. His first step in defense of Ambrose's position is to castigate the unnamed opponent as a misinformed and negligent scholar: "He certainly should read Ambrose's book *On the Death of Valentinian*, if he has not read it. If he has already read it, he should bring it to mind. If he recalls it, he should not dissimulate, but should focus without doubt on the fact that the saint granted salvation to a man who died unbaptized, by faith alone, confidently conceding to good will what was lacking to opportunity."[58] It is incredible, Bernard asserts, that this unnamed opponent should fail to take seriously "these two columns, I mean Augustine and Ambrose," on which correct doctrine rests, "with whom," he says, "I also believe that a man can be saved by faith alone, through his desire to receive the sacrament, in the event that it is forestalled by imminent death or any other insuperable force."[59] The good thief shows that faith sufficed in biblical history. Valentinian shows that faith suffices in the post-biblical age as well. Just as martyrdom can still replace ritual baptism in the here and now, so also baptism by desire continues to remain an efficacious option. Now, as always, God scrutinizes the convert's inner intention and continues to accept his faith and repentance without the shedding of blood or the pouring of water. Provided that such a person does not spurn the font if it is available to him, he assuredly gains salvation.[60]

Hugh of St. Victor takes Bernard's argument to heart and incorporates it into his *De sacramentis*, which in turn puts it into scholastic circulation in the twelfth century. Hugh adopts a more academic approach than Bernard, citing authorities who would exclude baptism by desire before wielding the weapons forged by Augustine's *De baptismo* and Ambrose's *DoV* to refute them.[61] He offers two modest departures from Bernard. In

---

57   Ibid. 6/1: 352-54.

58   Ibid. 6/1: 352: "Librum certe Ambrosius *De morte Valentini* legat, si non legit; recolat, si iam legit; non dissimulet, si re colit, et advertet sine dubio, sanctum homini non baptizato et morte fidenter de sola fide salutem praesumere, et tribuere indubitanter bonae voluntati quod defuit facultati."

59   Ibid. 6/1: 354: "Ab his ergo duabus columnis, Augustinum loquor et Ambrosium; . . . Cum his, . . . credens et ipse sola fide hominem posse salvari, cum desiderio percipiendi sacramentum, mors anticipans seu alia quaecumque vis invincibilis obviarverit."

60   Ibid. 6/1: 374-75.

61   Hugh of St. Victor, *De sacramentis Christianae fidei*, ed. Ranier Berndt, Corpus Victorinum 1 (Münster: Aschendorff, 2008), 2.6.7 (pp. 385-88). This edition supersedes that in PL 176.

Hugh's eyes, martyrdom, more glorious even than ritual baptism, may involve modes of death other than the shedding of blood, such as suffocation, strangling, or drowning.[62] This last point suggests Hugh's awareness that Valentinian met his death by strangulation, whether by his own hand or not. Also, having added this new wrinkle to the understanding of martyrdom, Hugh, agreeing with the Laon masters, states that baptism by desire occurs not by faith alone but on the merits of a fuller complement of theological virtues: "Thanks to true faith and true charity it [baptism by desire] can be gained by one to whom the visible sacrament of water is not available;" along with the authorities already cited, Hugh avers, "there are many others who could be adduced to support it."[63]

Scholastics after Hugh repeatedly cited Ambrose's *DoV* as a canonical authority side by side with Augustine's *De baptismo*, salvaged from his anti-Pelagian polemics, as debates on baptism continued in the twelfth century. Baptism by desire had its critics as well as its defenders among the early scholastics. Masters often drew on different arguments even when they supported the same conclusions.[64] The early scholastic strategy of invoking historical context and authorial intention in order to limit or annul the force or relevance of an authority with whom the master disagrees had its effects on the *DoV* as well. For instance, the anonymous author of the Porretan *Sententiae divinitatis*, writing in mid-century, argues that the validity of non-ritual baptism is limited to baptism by blood, and disallows baptism by desire except for those individuals personally assured of it by Christ before His death. He thus rules out baptism by desire entirely as a post-biblical option. His technique is to de-legitimize the *DoV* by observing that this work was not intended by Ambrose as a statement of positive doctrine, a text in which he aimed at laying down a universal rule. Rather, the *DoV* was an occasion piece, whose goal was simply to minister to the bereaved, in a genre, the funeral oration, in which one does not speak ill of the dead. Ambrose's words in the *DoV* were "words spoken in condolence, not as an assertion but as a consolation."[65]

---

62 Ibid., 387.

63 Ibid., 388: "Nisi forte dicere velis neminem fidem veram et caritatem veram habere posse qui visibile sacramentum aque non sit habiturus; . . . multa sunt alia que super hoc approbandum adduci potuissent."

64 On these debates, see Ott, *Untersuchungen*, 496-97, 499-526, 540; Landgraf, *Dogmengeschichte*, 3/1: 210-37 with discussion of thirteenth-century figures at 237-53; Colish, *Peter Lombard*, 2: 532-39.

65 Bernhard Geyer, ed., *Die Sententiae divinitatis: Ein Sentenzenbuch der gilbertischen Schule*, Beiträge zur Geschichte der Philosophie des Mittelalters 7/2-3 (Münster: Aschendorff, 1909), (pp. 115-16*): "Consolatoria verba sunt; non assertio sed consolatio."

Even more contextually sensitive, and illustrative of how this debate, and the *DoV*, impressed a more generally educated and less specialized twelfth-century audience, is Otto of Freising's *Two Cities*. Despite his pressing duties as a prelate, Otto remained informed on the theological issues that had excited attention since his student days in Paris. Written in 1143/47 and revised before 1157 with only minor changes, this updating of Augustine's *City of God* rehearses Roman history before addressing more recent events. Ancient Rome is of particular concern to its German imperial successors. Otto sets the entire story of Valentinian's death and of Ambrose's eulogy on him in the year 388.[66] Although he does not mention Valentinian's move to Gaul, Otto reports the disagreements of his sources on whether he was assassinated by Arbogast or took his own life. He then moves to Ambrose's funeral oration and is forthright in stating his own personal opinion of its teaching, in a passage that deserves quotation at some length:

> This is the Valentinian who, though he was made a catechumen by Ambrose, was prevented by a death of this sort from receiving the sacrament of baptism. The aforesaid bishop wrote a mournful letter with regard to this matter.... And therein we find written, by the same man: ... 'He has not lost the grace which he asked for.' With this utterance as authority certain theologians of our time reason, even after the express statement of the Gospel [John 3:3-5]... that one may be saved without the sacrament of baptism, whether by the pouring out of blood for a witness to Christ's passion, or, as it may be, by the Lord's declaration. They argue this because... they do not consider with proper care under what circumstances authors speak: what it is they say merely by way of opinion, what by way of assertion, what by way of consoling themselves in the extremity of their grief. But, although it is true that God's power is not restrained by ecclesiastical rules or by the sacraments, it will yet be necessary for me, who am bound by the Christian rule, to believe that no one can be saved except by such things. Wherefore, although it may be possible for God on His own express testimony... to save Jew or Gentile or unbaptized person without the pouring of water, yet it will be impossible for me to believe this. And so in such matters the divine power is limited, not for Him but for me.[67]

---

66   Otto of Freising, *The Two Cities: A Chronicle of Universal History to the Year 1148 AD*, ed. Austin P. Evans and Charles Knapp, trans. Charles Christopher Mierow, intro. by Karl F. Morrison (New York: Columbia University Press, 2002), 4.18 (pp. 298-99). Latin text: *Historia de duabus civitatibus*, ed. Adolfus Hofmeister, MGH, Scriptores rerum germanicorum in usum scolarum 45 (Hannover: Hahn, 1912), 205-6. Noted by Ott, *Untersuchungen*, 522-24.

67   Otto of Freising, *The Two Cities* 4.18 (trans. Mierow, pp. 298-99).

It must be said of both Otto of Freising and the author of the *Sententiae divinitatis* that they do a better job of applying Abelard's stated criteria for contextualizing authorities in their treatment of the *DoV* than does Abelard himself, although in aid of the opposite side of the question. In defending or opposing the doctrine of baptism by desire, it is clear that twelfth-century theologians-and their alumni in the secular clergy-have come to regard Ambrose's work as a canonical source for its support, whether or not they supplement the *DoV* with Augustine's *De baptismo* shorn of his anti-Pelagian polemics. How that debate continued to develop in medieval scholastic thought and how baptism by desire emerged the victor, to become the standard Catholic doctrine noted at the beginning of this paper, are subjects for other studies. What this investigation has shown is both the innovative character of Ambrose's teaching in the *DoV*, whatever its generic and situational qualifications, and the central contributions of Abelard, in fact and by negative imputation, and of Bernard of Clairvaux, in canonizing this text for their contemporaries and successors.

THE 'WHOLE ABELARD' AND THE AVAILABILITY OF LANGUAGE

BABETTE HELLEMANS

Function of music: personal integration.
Harder to listen to music than to write music
Pierre Boulez (letter to John Cage, 20-24 May 1949)

In 1121, the thinker Peter Abelard was condemned at the council of Soissons, having returned to Paris seven year earlier as a master of the school of Notre-Dame. In the French capital Abelard had lived a splendid career as a teacher in dialectics and he had experienced the famous but tragic love-affair with Heloise (ca. 1098-1164). The story is described by Abelard himself in the *Historia calamitatum*, the first part of a tripartite literary project–it occupies a prominent place in the canon of Western literature.[1] The *Historia* is supposed to represent a letter of consolation to a dear friend (*dilectissime frater in Christo*), a specific *topos* in the medieval epistolary genre. The expression 'history', or 'story', is provided at the very end of the text, when Abelard concludes:

> So, most beloved brother in Christ and, through divine conversation, closest companion, this is the story of my misfortunes which have afflicted me almost since I left my cradle; let the fact that I have written it with your affliction and the injury you have suffered in mind suffice to enable you [...]

---

1 The *Historia* is the first text of this literary project, followed by the exchange of letters between Abelard and Heloïse. The third part is constituted of the *Problemata Heloissae*, a monastic rule for women. The *Historia* narrates Abelard's life, from his childhood until approximately 1130-1132. The story has often been told, (re)written, published and translated entirely on the internet, and it is not the purpose of this article to describe the events in detail. For a historical account of the story, see Michael Clanchy, *Abelard. A Medieval Life* (Oxford: Blackwell Publishers, 1997). For the 'history of misfortunes' as being part of a larger project, possibly the design of a monastic rule for women, see the hypothesis of Peter von Moos, "Abaelard, Heloise und ihr Paraklet: ein Kloster nach Maß. Zugleich eine Streitschrift gegen die ewige Wiederkehr Hermeneutische Naivität," in G. Melville and M. Schürer, eds., *Das Eigene und das Ganze, Zum Individuellen im mittelalterlichen Religiosentum*, Vita regularis 16 (Münster: LIT Verlag, 2002), 563-620. For the problem of 'identity' and 'self-awareness' in the twelfth-century renaissance, see Peter Godman, *Paradoxes of Conscience in the High Middle Ages. Abelard, Heloise, and the Archpoet* (Cambridge: Cambridge University Press, 2009).

to think of your trouble as little or nothing in comparison with mine, and to bear it with more patience when you can see it in perspective. Take comfort from what the Lord told his followers about the followers of the devil: "As they persecuted me they will persecute you. If the world hates you, it hated me first, as you know well. If you belonged to the world, the world would love its own.[2]

Consolation was indeed desired, since at Soissons Abelard's opponents were numerous, and a condition of his absolution was that he had to burn his *Theologia "summi boni"*, probably written in the year before this event, and now lost. The *Historia* (§83) provides us some information about the conflict and the trial, during which Abelard was accused of heresy. In sum, the argument had to do with the way in which Abelard exposed a new method ("theology-to-be") in this book, arguing dogmatic positions concerning the ontology of the Trinity by drawing his arguments from a logical set of instruments borrowed from the *artes liberales*. These arguments, roughly speaking, concerned the various notions of 'sameness' and 'difference' that Abelard introduced in order to explain the relationship between the three divine persons.[3] The difference was first described by Abelard as a distinction in definition, a position he refined in his later work (*Theologia Christiana*), stressing that difference was to be understood as 'difference in property.' The notion of sameness was to be understood in essence (*essentia*), meaning in the context of Abelard's learned culture a concrete, particular thing. So when he says that *A* and *B* are essentially the same, he means that *A* and *B* are the same *thing*.[4]

---

2 Translations are generally my own, although I have consulted the translation in the Penguin Classics series by Betty Radice, revised by Michael Clanchy; see *The Letters of Abelard and Heloise* (Harmondsworth: Penguin Books, 2003). For the quotation see Pierre Abélard, *Historia Calamitatum*, ed. Jean Monfrin (Paris: Vrin, 1979), ll. 1560-72 (pp. 107-08): "Hec, dilectissime frater in Christo et ex divina conversatione familiarissime comes, de calamitatum mearum hystoria, in quibus quasi a cunabulis iugiter laboro, tue me desolationi atque iniurie illate scripsisse sufficiat: ut, [...] oppressionem tuam in comparatione mearum aut nullam aut modicam esse iudices, et tanto eam patientius feras quanto minorem consideras; illud semper in consolationem assumens, quod membris suis de mebris diaboli Dominus predixit: 'Si me persecuti sunt, et vos persequentur. Si mundus vos odit, scitote quoniam me priorem vobis odio habuit. Si de mundo fuissetis, mundus quod suum erat diligeret.'"

3 On the words "sameness and difference," cf. esp. book 2 of *Theologia "summi boni"* and the paragraph dealing with "the ways in which we say 'sameness.'" See Abelard, *Theologia "summi boni"* (=the Theology that begins with the words 'The Highest Good'), in *Petri Abaelardi Opera Theologica*, vol. 3, ed. C.S.F. Buytaert and C.J. Mews, Corpus Christianorum, continuatio mediaevalis 13 (Turnhout: Brepols, 1987), 309-549. I used the very accessible French translation of Jean Jolivet, in *Abélard. Du bien suprême* (Paris: Vrin, 1978).

4 Jean Jolivet, *Arts du langage et théologie chez Abélard*, 3rd ed. (Paris: Vrin, 2000), 293ff.

After his condemnation, Abelard was held under house arrest at St Médard in Soissons. From there he went to the distinguished monastery of St Denis where he–'pertinently'–questioned the authenticity of their patron saint. He incurred the wrath of abbot Suger of St Denis and had to leave again, this time to Provins. Here he stayed a while under the protection of Thibaud de Champagne. About a year later, in 1122, he was able to establish a hermitage near Nogent-sur-Seine, at first dedicated to the Trinity as a whole (sic!), but which he renamed before long in a sphere of new-found placidity after God's particular manifestation as a 'consoler': the Paraclete. The historian and biographer of Abelard, Michael Clanchy, has put it this way: "He [Abelard] explains that it was an after-thought, intended as a thank-offering for the consolation he had received there. (This in itself suggests that Abelard had found life in his hermitage very satisfying.) As he makes no mention of the Paraclete's role as 'consoler' in *Theologia Christiana*, he may not have taken an interest in this idea until 1123 or later."[5] The change of names is discussed at length in the *Historia*. In addition, Abelard continuously claims to be simply 'rational' and he takes the ignorance of others as an inevitable part of what I would like to call his 'epistemological project.'[6] Historians of intellectual history hold the view that Abelard, although he never obtained the status of authority in the medieval sense of *auctoritas*, nevertheless marks the beginning of an era in the history of logic and language philosophy. What stands out in this context is his distinctive and challenging method of enquiry.[7] In essence, this method consists of questioning procedures concerning knowledge in which the probing itself is the nucleus of philosophizing. In other words, Abelard's writing technique is fundamentally shaped by his way of questioning (*inquirere*), both originating in and struggling against the culture in which he was born. This type of *quaestio* is not driven by ignorance, nor is it meant to bring about a better understanding of reality. Instead, its rhetoric is directed towards a sheer theoretical illumination of a problem stated for its own sake.

In what follows I want to point out the 'philosophical' implications that a distinctively Abelardian 'questioning' of the status of language and its provision might involve. This singular type of inquiry in order to under

---

5 Clanchy, *Abelard*, 243. The change of names is described in detail by Abelard in the *Historia calamitatum*.

6 The exploration of this 'singular epistemological project' represents the nucleus of my forthcoming book, bearing the preliminary title *Varieties of the Self. The Notion of Intention in the Work of Peter Abelard*.

7 The *Stanford Dictionary of Philosophy*, available on-line, provides an up-to-date overview of Abelard's impact on scholastic thought.

stand the human condition is what I mean by Abelard's 'epistemological project.' My hopes are modest, since the topic is extremely complex. So when I speak of 'Abelard', the topic is selected with the intent of demonstrating his skeptical method of understanding language within a specific historical context.[8] Such an investigation cannot be based upon some consenting or dissenting reference to Abelard in some of his works, or on the status of his work as it was shaped by the nature of his 'profession' (master, logician, philosopher, theologian, lover and so forth). Thus, to get a grip on Abelard's epistemological project, I will refrain, as far as possible, from applying external categories to his work. Instead, the hermeneutical problem which underlies the (in)accessibility of 'Abelard', in his works as well as in the factual information concerning his historical *persona*, is my approach of understanding his epistemological project. My position is based on three different perspectives which I will try to explain briefly, following a sliding scale. (1) First, I wish to make it clear that I comply with a temporal, that is, historiographical distance, acknowledging the fact of not being able to know 'Abelard.' I therefore do not intend to prove progression or recession in the history of philosophy by selecting some of Abelard's key-thoughts. No attempt will be made to prove anticipation (or rediscovery) of any other patterns of thought. (2) In line with this first argument the next perspective concerns the (in)-accessibility of Abelard's language. Within the realm of a medieval institutional background, dominated by the seven liberal arts (the *artes liberales*), language is examined and performed in distinctive ways. When trying to understand Abelard's language, I am confronted with the problem of translating (in the medieval sense of *translatio*, that is, to transfer) the twelfth-century context to our modern context, 'post-everything' so to speak, dealing with symbols, semantic fields, deconstruction, conceptual *mythèmes*, etc.[9] A turn to ordinary language within our everyday usage would hardly be satisfying, for the theories at issue are quite different in both periods, because they function within completely different versions of academic scholarship. In the days of Abelard, the study of language was governed by rules and divided into disciplines we do not

---

8 I use the term 'skeptic' and 'skepticism' with the *caveat* that we do not mean quite the same thing when we speak of skepticism as conceived by a thinker conditioned by a Christian *Weltanschauung* as when we speak of skepticism as a philosophical enterprise. In the case of Abelard, his skeptical method of questioning can be illustrated by his famous aphorism in the prologue of *Sic et Non*: "By doubting we come to examine, and by examining we reach the truth."

9 Cf. the attempt to compare Abelard with Frege: Klaus Jacobi, "Abelard and Frege: the Semantics of Words and Propositions," in *Atti del Convegno Internazionale di Storia della Logica*, San Gimignano, 4-8 dicembre 1982 (Bologna: CLUEB, 1983), 81-96.

have today. This has, naturally, repercussions on the (im)possibility of getting a firmer grip on the matter. (3) The third perspective of understanding my object of study, following from the first two criteria, requires a delicate touch. Manifesting itself as almost invisible, there is the unavailability of language as such since the past is transformed, repudiated, and there is the fact that one's own practice and ambition can be identified only against the continuous experience of the past. This puts quite a heavy burden on the critical attitude that a scholar working with sources coming 'from beyond' wishes to take. One has no choice here but to simulate our own humble presence in the company of someone actually living (since reception is very much circumscribed by a 'living scholarship' itself) for some nine hundred years.[10]

What can one say about a specific kind of philosophy in that case? It is for example a reality that an isolated analytical article on a very specific topic is the common form of academic expression in the humanities as much as it is a fact that textbooks on intellectual history are clustered *a posteriori* around themes. Often, the argument is to cater to cultural and intellectual expectations, transmitting knowledge without taking into account that a specific need for knowledge is developing in time as well. In that sense philosophies of the past are used as an accomplished set of names and ideas selected by criteria of usefulness in contributing to the present or in setting the terms in which present knowledge and intellect has acquired its meaning and standards. The inaccessibility of language in this sense also concerns the question of the 'anthropology' of language, that is, the human nature of language, as being insufficient to articulate metaphysics. In the historical context of Abelard, this inability to articulate God is neither skepticism nor a matter of negative theology. It is philosophical, I think, in the sense that it has to do with the intelligibility of the *condition humaine*. Consequently, some of the arguments of scholarship levelled against

---

10 By way of example I would like to refer to Claude Lévi-Strauss. Because of his longevity he was a rare example of living history, and I was moved by one of his last interviews with *Le Monde* in 1999. One has to take into account that his brightness did not fade until the end – a condition to be able to formulate with such strength and lucidity. Celebrating his ninetieth birthday he described his own life and memory as a 'broken hologram' (*hologramme brisée*) in which reminiscences of the past (his own, that is) stay intact but can no longer function in the actual circumstances, while at the same time, he is the only person alive to be able to see the whole. In addition, he pointed out that one cannot imagine beforehand what it is to reach extreme old age – an experience which he described as one of the most fascinating adventures of his life, even though a solitary one. Our problem with Abelard is quite the same, since he *is* alive as long as we take him as our discussion partner. But we can only see him (and his work) as a broken hologram. I will come back to Lévi-Strauss at the end of this paper.

an integral interpretation of Abelard (which I consider to be essentially hermeneutic) are on the whole irrelevant to their main concerns. I would speculate that Abelard articulates a language project for human consolation that honours the complexity of the individual human condition in which the soul is neither damned nor saved, while promising a transformation that preserves the affective dimensions of these conditions. In this line of argument, I also think that a chronological study of Abelard's epistemological project is no longer relevant. This essay therefore takes the following shape: the next two sections will discuss the two underlying layers of skepticism with regard to 'knowing the whole Abelard' (the surface level being the self-evident historiographical distance). First, coming back to the second type of 'perspective' (2) I will discuss the problem of disciplines and philosophy governed by the 'rules' of the *artes liberales*. By way of a case study, I will try to bring up some alternative interpretations of Abelard's ideas on the notion of intention. In order to do justice to the third level of understanding (3), I will conclude with the most delicate part of this paper, dealing with rules and the availability of language, by introducing some criteria for further examination, illuminated by the problem of structures and Stanley Cavell's interpretation of Wittgenstein's view of language, as well as Claude Lévi-Strauss' understanding of difference and sameness, which may help us to grasp aspects of Abelard's typical 'articulation' and style of arguing.

Decisions about Form, Style and Rules

What I find most noteworthy about modern, historical accounts of the events of Abelard's life as described in the *Historia* is not the great admiration in which Abelardian rationalism is held or the pretentiousness of a kind of criticism by which his oeuvre is divided into disciplines, but the pervasive absence of any concern that some remark or thought of Abelard may not be wholly obvious in its meaning and implications.[11] This

---

11 One of the exceptions is the work of Peter van Moos; see esp. *Mittelalterforschung und Ideologiekritik, Der Gelehrtestreit um Heloise*, Kritische Information 15 (Munich: Fink, 1974) and "Le silence d'Héloïse et les idéologies modernes," in *Pierre Abélard-Pierre le Vénérable*, colloque de Cluny, juillet 1972, colloques internationales du CNRS 546 (Paris: CNRS, 1975), 425-468, revised in *Entre histoire et littérature. Communication et culture au Moyen Âge* (Florence: Edizioni del Galluzzo, 2005), 3-43. I also find the work of Klaus Jacobi extremely refined and to the point in this regard. See for instance: "Peter Abelard's investigation into the meaning and functions of the speech sign 'est,'" in Simon Knuuttila, ed., *The Logic of Being: Historical Studies* (Reidel: Dordrecht, 1986), 145-180.

absence of concern is all the more striking considering the fact that the work of Abelard is almost without exception divided into two categories: the brainy scholar (logic, philosophy, theology) and the smooth-operating poet-lover (Heloise, letter-exchange, hymns, *Historia*). At the beginning of this essay I mentioned the multiple difficulties one faces in approaching the philosophical 'Abelard.' Let us by way of exercise have a look at the best treatment there is of these issues, presented by John Marenbon's analytical study *The Philosophy of Peter Abelard*. This book provides us with an analysis of Abelard's 'philosophical' work (that is, the writings on logic and ethics, the theological texts). In addition, the study aims to combine the accepted categories of Abelardian scholarship by interpreting the love-story with Heloise as part of what Marenbon calls the 'theological project.' When I read on the opening page discussing the 'philosophical' section of the book: "Abelard was a logician, a theologian and a moral thinker: how far, outside the area of ethics, was he also a philosopher?" (p. 99), and then in the opening line of the next part dealing with his 'theology': "The system which Abelard elaborated as the second phase of his work was (in a broad sense) a theological one: an explanation of Christian doctrine" (p. 213), I was impressed, although critically so.[12] Those would be large attributions and categories to introduce and sustain for any difficult thinker of the period we subsequently call 'the twelfth-century Renaissance.' In the case of Abelard this claim of knowing his 'identities' without worrying about the fact that the meaning of what he says might not always be obvious is, so to speak, 'trebled up'. First, there are elements in the representation of his 'epistemological project' that are inconsistent with the rationalistic approach originally outlined in his language philosophy and according to 'scholarly rules' (the approach which made him legendary in the first place). Second, one is faced with obvious surface difficulties concerning authorship and historical and literary content, such as the epistemological problem of *auto*-biography or the sincerity and truthfulness of the fragmented literary project undertaken with Heloise. This issue of 'the self' as a concept referring to 'interiority' is especially complicated to categorize within the tight context of the *artes liberales*, as, for instance, Peter von Moos has pointed out time and again. Finally, one is met by a new theological concept of 'difficulty'

---

12 John Marenbon, *The Philosophy of Peter Abelard* (Cambridge: Cambridge University Press, 1997).

itself: the difficulty of 'theologizing' language.[13] My hope for a refined synthesis of these different claims concerning the 'personae' of Abelard, provided by Marenbon in a recently published survey, faded away as I found
the most famous ideas of this composite figure, such as his theory of mo-
dality and potencies, the problem of universals and the *dictum* as well as
his highly obscure theory on intention as a moral act, enumerated in a
linear way, described as though a linear account of this kind really *was* a
satisfactory explanation of his 'identities.'[14] I became increasingly worried
that such a refined synthesis, that is, a free eclecticism of method as an
intellectual commitment to a wider traditional problem of human culture,
might not be guaranteed when I read Marenbon's concluding remark:

> Is it worthwhile for other individual scholars to contribute to the path fol-
> lowed by Clanchy and Mews and try to present to their readers the whole
> Abelard? Many Abelardians, especially those with logical interest, may feel
> that it is more important to pursue "the whole Abelard" in a different sense.
> There are still hundreds of pages of dense argument in the logical com-
> mentaries and the *Dialectica* (and to some extent in the theological works
> too) which have never been properly analyzed or seen in relation to other,
> similar discussions of the time. Abelard cannot be said to be known as a
> whole as long as these large areas of his writing, though published, remain
> uncharted by intelligent and informed commentary (and by translations?).
> There is value, I would suggest, in trying to reclaim the whole Abelard in
> both these different senses. Detailed analysis of individual texts will cer-
> tainly further sharpen awareness of Abelard's range and power as a thinker,
> though perhaps also show his closeness to other thinkers of the time and

---

13   The book of Jean Jolivet, *Arts du language et théologie*, which I already quoted
above, shows very convincingly the complexity of the 'theological genre.' I find it bewilder-
ing that the most 'theological' section of the *Cambridge Companion to Abelard* (on the Trinity) only refers marginally to this important work and its effort to stress the complication of
'theologizing' language. See Jeffrey Brower, "Trinity," in *The Cambridge Companion to Abelard* (Cambridge: Cambridge University Press, 2004), 223-257. This book is generally based
upon Anglo-Saxon analytic scholarship and largely ignores continental erudition. Some
important works for the progress of Abelardian scholarship, such as the CNRS volume on
the conference held in 1972 on Peter Abelard and Peter the Venerable, is not mentioned
at all. The important and sensitive work of De Gandillac and Von Moos, just to name two
examples, appears only in a few isolated footnotes. The work of Clanchy, by the way, also
deserves more attention than this companion suggests. I will repeatedly come back to the
scholarly problem of claims and the lack of interest in historical approaches. See *Pierre Abélard, Pierre le Vénérable. Les courants philosophiques, littéraires et artistiques en occident au
milieu du XIIe siècle*, conférence Abbaye de Cluny, 2 au 9 juillet 1972 (Paris: CNRS, 1975).
On the role of Scripture and its relation to the self, see Willemien Otten, "In Conscience's
Court: Abelard's Ethics as a Science of the Self," in István Bejczy and Richard Newhauser,
eds., *Virtue and Ethics in the Twelfth Century* (Leiden: Brill, 2004), 53-73.

14   John Marenbon, "The Rediscovery of Peter Abelard's Philosophy," *Journal of the
History of Philosophy* 44 (2006): 331-351.

even his dependence on them. Studies which succeed in connecting the detail of Abelard's logic and theology with the unusually full (though un-straightforward) accounts we have of his life and feeling should, for their part, help to make his world of thought more vivid to us and overcome some of its strangeness. The rediscovery of Abelard, though well under way, is still far from complete.[15]

This plea may be justified in itself since one can simply embrace or reject the status quo of academic disciplinary research. Yet the question whether Abelard is whole or scattered as an explanation of his 'identities' is not primarily my concern. As far as conventions are concerned, where Marenbon, in my view, misses the point is in applying a one-dimensional interpretation of rules dictated by a discipline-based philosophical approach. In my view, the comparison of language with disciplines turns on their both 'observing rules.' Abelard does this his own way: he brings into play rules not as contexts in which it is clear what the observation contributes to, but contexts in which observation can be investigated. Like any concept of rules, its correctness would have no function unless these concepts already had a meaning. I think that for Abelard, a rule (within the realm of the *artes liberales*, or precisely *out of the realm*) is as much a training in language as it represents a joust, that is, the playing of a game, which includes 'playing with loaded dice.' This invites us to explore the problem of *mores* or standards and rules a bit further, and ask ourselves how confusion occurs when prescriptive utterances are only considered as typical instances of normative utterances. Of course we can point to rules and norms, but we must realise that most of the time this is only *approximately* pointing to rules and norms. We have a certain picture of a concept, in the academic world very often claimed absolute and complete. And some concepts as they function within rules cannot be paraphrased without pulling loose the aesthetic or blowing up the rules themselves. Furthermore, from a moral point of view, the foundation of a norm is not telling us how the action is done, i.e., how it relates to the description of what it *is* to act morally. It is telling how we ought to perform an action.[16]

Within this context, one has to recognize as a basic principle that Abelard's exposé is permeated with Christian reverberations, while our academic habits of speech are supposed to be *secular*–suggesting 'impartial-

---

15 Ibid., 351.
16 The issue of rules and 'language games' is reminiscent of Wittgenstein's language philosophy. My introduction on this matter serves as a prelude to the last section of this essay on Stanley Cavell's interpretation of Wittgenstein.

ity'–supported strenuously by footnotes and resting firmly on a tradition
of interpretation. Interestingly enough, Abelard somehow serves as a straw
man within this contorted posture of 'believers' versus 'non-believers'–
whether in God or in the Enlightenment. But this is actually not the point
I want to stress here (although it indeed has a huge impact on Abelardian
scholarship and it is fundamental to the way I try to find ways to unravel
the complex issue of rules in the reception of Abelard's oeuvre). Abelard's
historical inheritance and the way it handles 'rules' is the aspect I want to
emphasize now: if a normative utterance is one used to create or institute
rules, then what are we to make of the whimsical and not fully straight-
forward situation of early twelfth-century scholarship? In this period of
Abelard's life, the practice of norms and rules arising from different shapes
of life was put under pressure. New monastic rules were developed or reformed, such as the Cistercian order, while the monastic monopoly on erudition and knowledge was challenged. Within the twelfth-century context,
the notions of game and rule are not at all to be understood neutrally. The
mocking connotation of the learned monk as God's 'juggler' (*ioculator*), for
instance, refers specifically in the case of Bernard to his clerical profession,
as he operated between the 'tightened up' and the 'free floating,' controlling
the rules of monasticism as well as rhetoric.[17] While the supremacy of a
'universal' monastic education was waning, the professional institutionali-
zation of the urban intellectual was not yet fully in place.

As for Abelard, his intellectual profile as a dialectician was shaped by
his teachers, Roscelin of Compiègne and William of Champeaux. The
study of logic (the *ars dialectica*, one of the triplet composing the *trivium*,
the 'language section' within the seven liberal arts) was influenced by a
confined corpus of texts which, despite its narrowness, was used as a basis for further reasoning.[18] In matters of dialectics, Abelard relied on the

---

17 This is especially the case for Bernard. However, the possibility that Abelard played
with the monastic jargon should not, I think, be excluded. His adopted name (referring to
abaier, to yawn, meaning 'loud-mouthed') is already ironic in itself. For the notion of juggler see Dom Jean Leclercq, "Le thème de la jonglerie dans les relations entre saint Bernard,
Abélard et Pierre le Vénérable," in *Pierre Abélard, Pierre le Vénérable*, 671-688. The discussion after this paper led to the problem of irony and the name Abelard ascribed himself; see
p. 686. For the notion of playfulness in Abelard and Bernard, see M.B. Pranger, "Elective
Affinities," in Stephen Gersch and Bert Roest, eds., *Medieval and Renaissance Humanism.
Rhetoric, Representation and Reform*, (Leiden: Brill, 2003), 55-72, and of course, Pranger,
Bernard of Clairvaux and the Shape of Monastic Thought. Broken Dreams. (Leiden: Brill,
1994).

18 This fixed *capita selecta* consisted of Aristotle's *Categories* and *On Interpretation*,
Porphyry's *Isagoge* (the introduction) and Boethius' *On Division*, together with some of his
textbooks.

work of his predecessors and for this reason he dealt with much the same issues as many other grammarians and dialecticians at the time. They all based their work on the fixed corpus of texts in the *artes*-education system. We know little about his following except that his teaching was principally intended for clerics and that there was no strict control over its contents.[19] Furthermore, Abelard stands at the outset of the scholastic development in logic, and he therefore does not find a finished terminology at his disposal for his philosophical investigations. This rather ambivalent state of affairs has far-reaching consequences for his designation as a 'theologian,' a profession which, regardless of the type of church, is heavily indebted to the scholastic method of questioning, a technique which obviously did not exist in his time.[20] His language does not have the crystalline clear conciseness of the later scholastic thinkers.

One could even say that Abelard tediously spins around the same casuistic position, that is, that words can never be a 'thing' (*res*) since they are in each case definite and singular. Not only within the argumentation itself, but also in his centrifugal style there is no process of *Verdinglichung* in Abelard's thought.[21] The agility of Abelard's articulation is noticeable again in the way he tries to elaborate a distinction between cognition (*significatio intellectus*) and ontology (*significatio rei*). Thus Abelard writes in his *Commentary on Aristotle's "Peri ermeneias"*: "when the mind attends to some characteristic of a thing, inasmuch as it is a thing or it exists or it is called substance or a body or white or Socrates, this is then called understanding (*intellectus*)."[22] Reducing the performance of giving meaning through language to its tiniest parts, he focuses on the smallest units of speech, considering cognition as a primary

---

19 Cf. D.E. Luscombe, *The School of Peter Abelard. The Influence of Abelard's Thought in the Early Scholastic Period*, Cambridge Studies in Medieval Life and Thought (Cambridge: Cambridge University Press, 2008), and Jacques Verger, "De l'école d'Abélard aux premières universités," in Jean Jolivet and Henri Habrias, eds., *Pierre Abélard. Colloque international de Nantes* (Rennes: CNRS, 2003), 17-28.

20 See for the development of theology as a scientific discipline within the context of early scholasticism: Willemien Otten, *From Paradise to Paradigm. A Study of Twelfth-Century Humanism* (Leiden: Brill, 2004).

21 For the intrinsic logical discussion, see L.M. De Rijk, *Pierre Abelard (1079-1142). Scherpzinnigheid als hartstocht* (Amsterdam-Oxford-New York: KNAW, 1981), 19. The issue of centrifugal style is my addition.

22 *Glossae super Peri hermeneias* [*Super Peri herm.*], in *Peter Abaelards Philosophische Schriften*, vol. 1.3: *Die Logica 'Ingredientibus': Die Glossen zu Peri hermeneias* [in Greek characters], ed. Bernard Geyer, Beiträge zur Geschichte der Philosophie des Mittelalters 21.3 (Münster: Aschendorf, 1927), p. 317, ll. 12-13. Further references will also be to this edition.

function while assigning to ontology a subordinate function.[23] When Abelard makes his distinction between the two types of signification, he seeks to create priorities, taking the intelligible as his starting point. The importance of this priority occurs not only in scholarly language but also in ordinary language. For there is something outside the mind for which these strings of words stand, so Abelard concludes, a notion that is to some (however limited) extent comparable to our notion of a 'semantic context.'[24] While further elaborating on the distinction between cognition and ontology, Abelard turns his thoughts towards a question which occupied grammarians and logicians in general, that is, how and why speech opens up reality. He introduces the notion of "complex concept" (*intellectus compositus*), enquiring whether the composition of words just created actually means something, or nothing. I think that, keeping his centrifugal language style in mind, it is important to emphasis that Abelard is essentially *not* interested in descriptive linguistics. The relation between speech and reality is entirely vertical. In other words, the question for Abelard is *not* a horizontal and descriptive one of the kind 'on which distinguishable ways speech or language opens up reality.' Instead, the usage of a vertical 'pictogram' also has an impact on his other obsessions, such as his dealing with copula and the way they function as a logic hinge within the phrase composed–exerting pressure on the ontological status of the subject and direct object. The apagogical nature of Abelard's thinking (i.e. proving indirectly by showing that the antithesis would be absurd) is therefore essential, since he *needs* his specific language style as a form with which to express himself inversely, proportional to the true and false procedures he so thoroughly examines. Hence his important conclusion is that pure knowledge (cognition) is not available to humankind.[25] To us, there is a certain awkwardness in his language style and the apagogical, enveloping, movement of thought which I believe to be essential for the understanding of his thinking. This style has nothing to do with an education curriculum though: there is no set of characteristics available which everything we call 'disciplines' shares.

---

23 As explained in detail in Jacobi, *Abelard and Frege*, 85-86.

24 For the so-called 'contextual approach' of Abelard, see Klaus Jacobi, *Sprachtheorie in Spätantike und Mittelalter*, ed. Sten Ebbesen (Tübingen: Gunter Narr Verlag, 1995), 79.

25 De Rijk, *Scherpzinnigheid als hartstocht*, 26.

Intermezzo: Shooting without the Intention to Kill

For all that, we are still occupied with our fundamental enquiry into the degrees of accessibility concerning Abelard's language and thought. Let us have a look at another example in which Abelard's language may not be wholly obvious in its meaning and implications. Probably the most well-known 'cognition-experience' regards his rather obscure ethics of the so-called *intentio*, also called 'the consent to sin,' treated in a later work called *Scito teipsum*–a title which refers to the Socratic *know thyself*. In essence, Abelard attributes sin, when identified, to the consent to sin rather than to the act, thus holding a theory that actions are indifferent.[26] He declares that,

> God considers only the mind in rewarding good or evil, not the result of deeds, and [...] he judges the mind itself in the purpose of its intention (*ipsum animum in proposito suae intentionis*). Deeds [...] are equally common to the damned and to the elect [and] are in themselves indifferent. They are not to be called good or bad, except according to the intention of the doer (*pro intentione agentis*), that is to say, not because it is good or bad to be done for them to be done, but because they are well or badly done, that is, done with the intention whereby they are done properly, or not.[27]

This example demonstrates how lively things are in Abelard's moral playground, with assessments and evaluations passing and retorting in different directions. This is indeed quite a shaky matter to work with from a methodological point of view. It becomes even more intriguing for our question concerning the accessibility of Abelard's language, especially if we consider that he stressed the importance of the 'transgressing conscience' (*scienter transgrediendo*), which is *qualitate qua* not to be pin-

---

26 The most detailed account of Abelard's theory is to be found in Robert Blomme, *La doctrine du péché dans les écoles théologiques de la première moitié du XIIᵉ siècle* (Louvain: Publications Universitaires de Louvain, 1958); cf. esp. the sections on 'le consentement' and 'l'intention' at 118-164.

27 *Ethica seu Scito teipsum*, 44 (my translation): "Solum quippe animum in remuneratione boni uel mali, non effecta operum, Deus adtendit, ne quid de culpa uel de bona uoluntate nostra proueniat pensat, sed ipsum animum in proposito suae intentionis, non in effectu exterioris operis, diiudicat. Opera quippe que [...] eque reprobis ut electis communia sunt, omnia in se indifferentia sunt nec nisi pro intentione agentis bona uel mala dicenda sunt, non uidelicet quia bonum uel malum sit ea fieri, sed quia bene uel male fiunt, hoc est, ea intentione qua conuenit fieri, aut minime." I used here the edition (and I refer to the page) of D.E. Luscombe, *Peter Abelard's Ethics* (Oxford: Oxford University Press, 1979), in addition to the more accessible translation of Paul Vincent Spade in Peter Abelard, *Ethical Writings. His Ethics or "Know Thyself" and His Dialogue Between a Philosopher, a Jew and a Christian* (Indianapolis and Cambridge: Hackett Publishing Company, 1995).

pointed by human cognition.[28] All this, it goes without saying, is complex and demands further clarification. Let us return to Marenbon's study on Abelard's philosophy and examine how he describes the morality of intention. For the sake of practicality I select here Marenbon's explanation of the so-called *root of intention*, which is the one most easy to 'identify' within Abelard's continuously turning argumentation:

> Although [...] Abelard holds that actions in themselves are indifferent, [...] he does not strip actions of ethical value, but he insists that it is a derivative value. Actions are rightly described as good or bad, but only by virtue of the intentions from which they spring. But intentions, although they belong to the life of the mind, are sinful only in relation to a definitely intended (although perhaps prevented) action. This view is, therefore, in one way the direct opposite of that which underlies the stages theory. Instead of holding that intentions and acts should each be evaluated, Abelard believes that acts cannot be judged except through the intentions which inform them and that intentions cannot be judged except in relation to the acts which result from them, or would have resulted had they not been thwarted. [...] Unlike many of his contemporaries, Abelard held that neither disposition to act sinfully, nor any physical or mental process or attitude other than the final mental act of choosing to perform the sinful act, were blameworthy.[29]

So far so good. But what purpose is served by this description of *intentio* as a means of understanding Abelard as a 'philosopher'? What does this passage of Marenbon's discussion reveal about the meaning of acts within the rationalistic approach originally outlined in Abelard's language philosophy? And what, according to Marenbon, would Abelard mean to say when he is not "stripping actions of ethical value" but insists that it is a "derivative value"–is Abelard's language *really* not stripped off? What does the "unlike many of his contemporaries" look like? What kind of proof is provided to us? I think it is worth trying to understand what we are to make of the fact that Abelard constantly compares moments of speech, thought and acts with *cognitive* moves in the mind, not to speak of the problem of a composed understanding. The last two sections of *Scito teipsum* entitled 'how many ways is something called a "sin"?' and 'is every sin forbidden?' illustrate the way in which Abelard's language style coincides with morality. Beginning, of course, with the intelligibility of sin (exploring the whole range: sacrifice *for* sin, deeds *of* sin, consent *to* sin etc.), showing all kinds of arguments from authoritative texts (Athanasius, the Bible) and the apagogical technique of the absurd by including

---

28 Abelard comments here in *Scito teipsum* on the passage of the slave receiving slaps from his master in Luke 12:47, and on Romans; cf. Blomme, *La doctrine du péché*, 154.
29 Marenbon, *Philosophy of Peter Abelard*, 256.

the extreme in his argumentation (i.e. the persecution and crucifixion of Christ), Abelard states:

> [F]or instance, if someone perhaps slays with an arrow a person he doesn't see in the forest, while meaning to shoot wild beasts or birds. While we nevertheless say he "sins" out of ignorance (*per ignorantiam*) just as sometimes we confess to "sinning" not only in consent but also in thought, speech and action, in this context we aren't using the word properly for a fault, but are taking it broadly for what is not fit for us to do, whether it is done out of error, out of negligence or in any other inappropriate way. Therefore this is what sinning out of ignorance is: not to have any fault in it, but *doing* what isn't appropriate for us. Sinning in thought (that is, in will) is willing what isn't appropriate for us. Sinning in speech or in action is speaking or doing what we ought not, even if this happens out of ignorance, against our will. Thus those who persecuted Christ or his followers, and believed they *should* be persecuted, we say sinned through action (*per operationem peccasse*). Nevertheless, they would have sinned more seriously through fault if they had spared them contrary to conscience (*si contra conscientiam eis parcerent*).[30]

Shooting without intention to kill. Saying things without knowing. Doing things without understanding what you cause. Sinning without thinking, thinking without sinning. What could there be, finally, to be concerned about? Is intellect a *conditio sine qua non* of the consciousness that one has sinned? Although Abelard introduces sin as a kind of oxymoron, stressing the problem of doing things we should not do, he does not say how utterances and acts *ought* to be performed. The problem for Abelard is, I believe, not sin as objectified and absolute. On the contrary. He is conscious of the anthropological nature of language–a kind of 'must we be a sign of what we do?'; I shall come back to this in the next section. He thus amplifies the problem of sin, spinning out the consequences of understanding sin, an intellectual operation of a kind which would imply that we act

---

30 *Scito teipsum*, 66 (trans. Paul Vincent Spade, 28; as in n. 27): "[...] ueluti siquis forte hominem, quem non uidet in silua sagitta interficiat dum feris uel auibus sagittandis intendit. Quem tamen dum peccare per ignorantiam dicimus, sicut nos quandoque fatemur non solum in consensu uerum etiam in cogitatione, locutione, operatione peccare, hoc loco non proprie pro culpa ponimus, sed large accipimus pro eo scilicet quod nos facere minime conuenit, siue id per errorem siue per negligentiam uel quocumque modo inconuenienti fiat. Tale est ergo per ignorantiam peccare, non culpam in hoc habere, sed quod nobis non conuenit facere, uel peccare in cogitatione, hoc est, uoluntate, quod nos uelle minime conuenit, uel in locutione aut in operatione loqui nos uel agere quod non oportet, etsi per ignorantiam nobis inuitis illud eueniat. Sic et illos qui persequebantur Christum uel suos quos persequendos credebant per operationem peccasse dicimus, qui tamen grauius per culpam peccassent si contra conscientiam eis parcerent."

against God's will, meaning against ourselves, which would imply a reduc
tion of the human creature. Self-consciousness (*scito teipsum!*) includes
many kinds of sins, just as judgment is to be located in two different
meanings: in each self and in heaven. Adding moral, that is, prescriptive
components, to Abelard's concept of *intentio* would suggest that a debate
would be necessary on either whether human beings ought to behave
as creatures we conceive of as human (which is, as we just saw, not possible for Abelard), or whether the earthly world could be different from
what it actually is (which is, as we already briefly observed, impossible for
Abelard as well since 'skepticism' about the world is not an option when
Creation is involved). Since Abelard's investigations of knowledge of the
self and of things depends on his methodical language style as an intrinsic
part of his epistemological project, apagogical and centrifugal without articulating the core-substance, it is worth noting that, although Marenbon
undertakes a discussion of Abelard's 'identities' (fortunately, to his credit,
he is not mixing this up with 'inner experiences' which is the worst case
of romanticising Abelard and a real trouble in scholarship), he withholds
any opinion about the role of knowledge of the self in those 'identities.'
When concluding the chapter dealing with contempt, law and conscience,
Marenbon does suggest that Abelard considered words to have a meaning
as though Abelard supposed the users of language, that is, men including
himself, to be knocked out of the playground:

> [The theory of sin and ignorance] is a sophisticated theory. Its greatest
> weakness has already been suggested–the unsuitability of the traditional
> idea of venial sin for the very different use Abelard makes of it, and the
> vagueness with which [A performs *s* voluntarily but without thinking about
> it, and he habitually know[s] that L forbids *s* ('venial sin'–Interpretation ['sin
> of ignorance']: reduced blame], especially, is developed. By so firmly identi-
> fying sin with a mental act in which we choose to go against what we believe
> divine law commands us to do or not do and to scorn God, Abelard makes it
> impossible for himself to give any satisfactory place in his account to actions
> which we do not think about but for which it is reasonable to think we are
> fully responsible.[31]

Marenbon does suggest that Abelard "makes it impossible for himself" as
though Abelard meant to provide a rule to solve the problem, in order to
"give any satisfactory place in his account to actions." I believe what Abelard says, is that what is experiential in the use of a word cannot (logically)

---

31 Marenbon, *Philosophy of Peter Abelard*, 281.

be an element, not one identifiable reappearance whose presence insures the signification of a word, or whose absence deprives it of a meaning (cf. the absence of *Verdinglichung* in Abelard's thought).[32] With these blurred outlines of Abelard's "intention" to investigate the rules of language, we can prudently say that his very "wholeness" (to come back to Marenbon's idea of future scholarship on Abelard) allows him to formulate a source of a 'deformed' conception of language, a deformation that is 'backed' by theorizing (whether philosophical, semantical, logical or rhetorical).

Unlike his contemporaries but not univocally so, Abelard does not consider a verb of existence (*esse*) to have a semantic ambiguity: *to be* semantically embraces all meanings or, to put it more accurately, it has one single meaning which is "something from among the multitude of things which exists"–i.e., substance, quality and quantity.[33] Regardless of the philosophical intricacies of this view, this 'awareness' of language shows how inessential the request for rules is as an explanation of language.[34] As such, language has no essence. Or put the other way round, as Abelard is reasoning apagogically again in his *Super "peri ermeneias"*: "every concept, whether simple or complex, through which we heed how the thing behaves, is valid (*sanus*)".[35] For instance, the word 'man' produces a valid concept as long as (at least) a man exists. Chimera, on the other hand, is an example of a word of which the concept does not signify any existing thing–so if there were no thing such as man, the concept of 'man' too would be empty.[36] In the same text Abelard makes a distinction between the form of an expression (a string of words, *oratio*) and its content, that

---

32 Within the limits of this paper, it goes too far to examine more thoroughly the notion of the not-spoken or not-meaning in Abelard, which is a crucial element in his logic. This will be a subject for further investigation.

33 *Super Peri herm.*, p. 347, ll. 23-26; see also p. 346, ll. 25-28. Discussion on the topic in Jacobi, "Abelard's Investigations into the Meaning and Functions of the Speech Sign 'est,'" in Simon Knuuttila, ed., *The Logic of Being: Historical Studies* (Dordrecht: Reidel, 1986), 145-180, esp. 151-152 for the present context; and L.M. De Rijk, "Die Wirkung der neuplatonischen Semantik auf das mittelalterliche Denken über das Sein," in *Sprache und Erkenntnis im Mittelalter*, Miscellanea Mediaevalia 13.1 (Berlin and New York: De Gruyter, 1981), 19-35.

34 Abelard demonstrates this through the care with which he explains the function and status of non-denotive words (words that have a meaning but do not refer to anything which exists); see Jacobi, "Abelard's Investigations."

35 *Super Peri herm.*, p. 326, ll. 30-31: "Sanus autem est omnis intellectus tam simplex quam compositus, per quem attendimus, ut res se habet." See Jacobi, "Abelard's Investigations," 160.

36 *Super Peri herm.*, p. 326, ll. 33-34: "...ut 'homo' quamdiu homo subsistit, sanum intellectum generat." See Jacobi, "Abelard's Investigations," 160.

is, its understanding (*intellectus*).[37] Over and over, Abelard insists on the fact that words can never capture a thing in its complexity, but that they always reveal some aspects of the whole, the particularity of the signified thing.[38] The semantic distinction between the signification of things and signification of understandings (*significatio rerum/intellectum*) is connected to Abelard's statement, which is not at all self-evident, that only the signification of understandings is relevant. Signification of things, instead, can be neglected or is at best of secondary interest.[39] What Abelard says about decisions, acts, properties and so forth is difficult enough, as we saw, but not sufficiently so to cause one to hesitate before saying that Marenbon has not tried to understand what Abelard has most painstakingly wished to say about language (and meaning and understanding). That is to say that theological and philosophical language *does* depend upon a structure and concepts of rules (whether in the practice of the *artes liberales* or in the soul) and yet that the presence of such a structure in no way impairs its functioning in the human condition. In other words, Marenbon's claim to examine the identities of Abelard is not the same as trying to understand his characteristics in thought, his texts, his language. For Marenbon's decision, as of many others here, seems to imply that correctness is only determined in a *constructed* language. Then what are we to make of the fact that Abelard constantly compares moments of (articulated) thought or speech with moves in the intellect (that is, the complete or incomplete perception of it)? The complexity of constructing language itself and the understanding of its meaning is his thread of Ariadne.[40]

---

37   See the lucid and helpful article of Klaus Jacobi, Christian Strub and Peter King, "From *intellectus verus/falsus* to the *dictum propositionis*: The Semantics of Peter Abelard and His Circle," *Vivarium* 34 (1996): 15-40. See also H.A.G. Braakhuis and C.H. Kneepkens, eds., *Aristotle's Peri hermeneias in the Latin Middle Ages. Essays on the Commentary Tradition*, Series Supplementa Artistarium 10 (Turnhout: Brepols, 2003).

38   Jean Jolivet pointed out that the dialectical reasoning of Abelard (rooted in an Augustinian Manichaeism) is his ever-present underlying principle, referring to Porphyry, in *Pierre Abélard. Arts et théologie*, 86. I will come back to this.

39   *Super Peri herm*, p. 308, ll.19-22. The selection of texts and the edition is from the article of Jacobi, Strub and King, "From *intellectus verus/falsus* to the *dictum propositionis*, 16-17. This team of scholars has recently re-edited a new and complete version (including both the Milan and Berlin mss.) of the text in the *Corpus christianorum* series.

40   It is the main topic of the *Tractatus de Intellectibus*. See, for instance, the commentary of Patrick Morin in Abélard, *Des Intellections*, ed. and trans. Patrick Morin (Paris: Vrin, 1994), 126: "Le contenu du *Tractatus* [et les] divisions principales soulignent l'unité de l'opuscule, et les grand thèmes en font ressortir des points saillants. La préoccupation, qui obsédait Abélard, de démontrer les relations continues qui existent entre la pensée et le langage, a été, on l'espère, mise en évidence."

I conclude this intermezzo. Where I take issue with an interpretation suggesting that Abelard the logician thinks according to certain rules, is not that it takes too literally what Abelard says of semantics or about himself being 'rational.' An obsession with thinking according to rules (whether according to the *ars dialectica* or *retorica*) is just not what Abelard reveals when dealing with 'his education system,' be it as a teacher or as a student. Although he elaborates his thoughts within the codes laid down for him by his education, he does not reveal an active awareness of their being restrictive or that his argumentation *must* be applied in such and such a way. Taking that stance would imply that there would be an alternative to something strictly technical. But the technical side of rules is not a problem for him as they are for us, with their "awkwardness." Abelard's excellent mastery of the *artes*, contrariwise, enables him to go beyond the technical matter and to think more freely. While his *topos* of being misunderstood sounds problematic, one should wonder as well if it might not be entirely rhetorical. I have the impression that drawing an analogy between moral conduct and 'language rules' such as is the case within the *trivium* is sometimes felt as misleadingly simple–or even inconsequential–because there are no rules in moral conduct corresponding to the technical rules of oratory or grammar, or even more challenging to suggest, the observance of a monastic rule. But this is actually not the point of analogy. The actions, intentions and speech have to be done correctly, which is not the same as suggesting that every movement, desire or utterance *is* correct. In other words, promising or integrity is not just a matter of following rules; this is also why the problem of interiority and the self in the twelfth century is extremely complex. One of Marenbon's claims seems to be shared by many others who are in awe of Abelard's 'rationalism': that we have access to the knowledge of Abelard, and that there is no obscurity in his meaning. This claim often snaps at the hint of a 'historical (re-) construction'–deconstruction would be a sacrilege!–the 'path' Mews and Clanchy would have chosen, because of fear that it denies philosophical, that is, 'sound', reasoning. I agree about the risk of interpreting Abelard within the standards of Romanticism of which the solemn act of bringing Abelard and Heloise together at Père Lachaise is the most embarrassing example. As regards content, I also agree that reticence is required concerning Abelard's playfulness as if the Rubik's cube of his language style would be applicable unilaterally to his moral philosophy (with the conditional addition that this philosophy itself is not prescriptive per se, as I described above). But what is problematic in such discussions is not the word 'historic', 'construction' and again, 'wholeness', it is rather the

unexamined use of them, a use in which the concept of discipline and decision is disengaged from its (grammatical) connections with the concepts
of mutuality (e.g. Heloise), acknowledgment (e.g. *Historia*), consolation
(e.g. the Paraclete). Moreover, I believe that part of the claim-problem is
due to differences in academic tradition. For instance, the Anglo-Saxon
analytical tradition has never fully digested the 'Hegelian' (self-)awareness
of history as a form of human knowledge. In that respect it is worthwhile
trying to elucidate the relation of Abelard's *procedure of intention*–which
is usually entered as summary of ethical 'truth and/or false' procedures–to
the idea that grammar tells us what kind of object intention is.[41] In other words, we learn and we apply words in certain contexts. We are aware
that erudition is extremely difficult to grasp in the twelfth-century context
of autodidacts engaged on hairsplitting subtleties, for what would be the
meaning of 'auto-' in this context anyway? And, we are presuming to be
able to project such container-concepts to other contexts of rules (which
one to choose: philosophy or theology or logic or institutions, such as the
artes or a monastic rule?). Nothing guarantees that this projection will
take place in *particular* (grasping the universals, the notion of *intentio*, the
rule of observance) just as nothing guarantees that we will make the same
projections "to help to make his world of thought more vivid to us and
overcome some of its strangeness," giving back the last word to Marenbon.

Stanley Cavell, Claude Lévi-Strauss and the Claim of Knowledge

By way of conclusion–*da capo al fine*–, I should perhaps add a few words
about the way in which in my view context, construction and framework
should be developed in order to get a better understanding of the Abe-
lard-corpus. In language philosophy it is *communis opinio* that you cannot separate the meaning of a word from the entire context. This impossibility of separation concerns not only the actual linguistic condition of
words, but also the meaning of feelings, beliefs and hopes of the speaker,
as well as of the listener, including the social, historical and ideological
contexts. If we had to go on about 'context' as such, including the prob-

---

41 The 'reassessment' of Jean Porter seeks to overcome only partly the problem of
moral intention by introducing the notion of 'interiority.' Porter stresses the necessity of a
connection between philosophical criteria and (Christian) ethics in the thought of Abelard
by focusing on the notion of 'consent,' which is for Abelard consent to an act; see "Responsibility, Passion and Sin. A Reassessment of Abelard's Ethics," *Journal of Religious Ethics* 28
(2000): 367-393.

lem of 'projection' we discussed above, the discussion would get bogged down. While on the other hand, the contrary result–a radical isolation between the meaning of a word and the context–creates a feeling of 'something strange' (it represents perhaps even the origin of the absurd) and the awareness of a meaningless meaning might lead to an academic disorientation or empirical confusion. Taken in a more lyrical sense, to do justice to the motto of this article, the absolute isolation in modern music–such as in Boulez's or in Cage's–, of an utterance or a sound from its context, for instance by a dissonance or muteness which is disconnected from its context (a song, a composition), kindling a feeling of strangeness, is here applied on purpose to express a feeling of alienation. Hence, it is worth examining the exact status of the type of alienation described by Marenbon. For it is my conviction that the radical experiment in the language style of Abelard, his tireless effort to circumvent concepts about language, the problem of articulation (act-speech), and meaning (understanding) creates our modern feeling of 'something strange' about his notion of intention: the hunter in the forest, killing without knowing, is at some moment connected with the persecution of Christ. The official rhetoric might be rational, but the common use of words reveals something different in our consciousness. In other words, what does an average twelfth-century Christian think when he hears that Christ was persecuted and died to save sinners? Abelard does not say anything about what the hunter *saw* when he shot; he just states that he *was not able to see* and why it was a transgression, or at least, as he explains, partly transgressive. As I understand Abelard in this example, there is an open-ended structure of the past and the future surrounding a concept (or action). Marenbon seems to feel that it is only an underlying structure or rules of a grammatical and logic framework of language which can give force to our interpretation of Abelard's 'normativity.' Our intermezzo demonstrated how there are several ways to be skeptical about the 'possibility of knowing Abelard' and how these are bound by epistemological confusion (i.e., the odd feeling). Marenbon, by eliciting criteria revealing the sophisticated grammatical structure of understanding 'the whole Abelard,' does not reveal the separate order controlling the claim of agreement between different disciplines in the understanding of 'Abelard.'

Let us observe this claim of objectified knowledge ('X') in more detail. In response to epistemological confusion ('to overcome the strangeness of X') we may produce for ourselves an open-ended articulation of our criteria informed by the epistemological disorientation (the difficulties concerning the 'wholeness of X'), reflecting on our criteria. This is what academic discipline and academic language represents. But the problem of skepticism the academic faces is not that it is impossible for him to have reasons to claim knowledge of X, examining carefully the texts written by X. The question is rather that *whatever* reasons he may have (or that we, colleagues, imagine him to have), he will be remarking on his particular epistemic condition, and on how or why he happens to be *in a particular condition to know*. The *real* problem is, however, that the academic wants his considerations on 'X' to be wholly applicable, to reveal the nature of his human epistemic position as such. In other words, the problem of skepticism met with by the academic is not that context (his 'lyrics') which militates against him. It is his own project that prohibits him from accepting what he means by the various perfectly intelligible claims that he makes–so that he is unavoidably driven into unintelligible speech the moment he says anything in particular.

Some brief reference to the modern language philosopher Stanley Cavell as well as to the 'father of ethnology' Claude Lévi-Strauss will prove to be useful in elaborating the problem of intelligibility and alienation. While I am more familiar with Lévi-Strauss than with Cavell, both helped me immensely to 'learn to listen' to strangeness and otherness, to understand modernist mechanics of academic discipline as well as the importance of artistic engagement in the study of humanities if one is to understand the *rapport* of this study with (my) reality (as a scholar). I start with Cavell. Heavily influenced by Austin and Wittgenstein, he tries to find ways to solve the problem of Wittgenstein's 'language games' in which there are two ideas of language games regarding its rules within the framework of language. Roughly, the first is like the 'language games of physical objects, colours, sensations, beliefs', a specific discourse supporting the idea of language as a frame of rules. The second language game is about judgement and truth-falsehood procedures (cf. also Abelard's *intellectus verus/falsus*), and does not support such a framework.[42] In our examination of Marenbon's 'language game', the first idea is clearly present: there is a framework of rules applied to the understanding of Abelard's philosophy, determining the latter's 'language game' within and *outside* the liberal arts. The second idea, the 'not speaking' or, in the example of Abelard's description of intention, the 'not seeing' does not have any importance in Marenbon's analysis. Cavell's approach seeks to understand the use of language which allows

---

42   Cf. for instance §228 in Ludwig Wittgenstein, *Philosophical Investigations*, trans. G.E.M. Anscombe (Oxford: Blackwell, 1958), 180, 224-226; and the discussion of it in Steven G. Affeldt, "The Ground of Mutuality: Criteria, Judgment, and Intelligibility in Stephen Mulhall and Stanley Cavell," *European Journal of Philosophy* 6 (1998): 1-31.

us to describe the possibilities of our philosophical grief (alienation) and epistemological disorientation. Subsequently, he introduces possibilities to overcome a dissatisfaction with our language as a framework of rules. He asserts a certain modernist ambition, stating that there is a constant need to define philosophy against its past accomplishments in order to preserve those very accomplishments.[43] This is also why the process of writing itself and 'modes of writing' are essentially part of his project. My reading of Cavell is that he reveals the constant tension between the 'object' (piece of art, text) and the context in which a 'commitment to the object' (writing, reading, sculpting) occurs. Take this aphorism: "The context in which I make a martini with vodka is no less complex than the context in which I make a statement with 'voluntary.'"[44] Here, Stanley Cavell puts his finger on the weakest theoretical spot of language. Again, without pretending to be 'familiar with Cavell' and to be able to give a full account of his philosophy, I think the foregoing aphorism indicates the need for room for the not-quite-knowing. This is not motivated by skepticism as such (cf. his essay *Coriolanus and the Interpretation of Politics*–i.e. sheer skepticism as a form of narcissism) but it is a necessity for academic speech, especially for the commitment to the meaning of humanities in our culture.[45] Few people use the full range of perception which language provides, just as they do not use that full range with regard to the rest of cultural heritage.

One of the major concerns of this essay is the need for skepticism as far as the facts of (auto-)biography and the claim of 'wholeness of identities' are concerned. I briefly want to pinpoint this problem in the case of the historical Cavell. Here as well, the claim of completeness as if knowledge were possible from only one angle (which would make the shape of "wholeness" very flat and anti-monumental) would, I think, be missing the point of Cavell's efforts completely. In that respect, Michael Gorra, in his essay on intellectual autobiographies, misses the point too. He states that Cavell's autobiographical exercises in his *A Pitch of Philosophy*, are "marked by a degree of self-referentiality unusual even for him [...] and they [the exercises] assume so thoroughly a grounding in Cavell's own

---

43   For a clear essay on Cavell's philosophy as possibly being part of the academic canon (*quod non*), see Timothy Gould, "Present Tense: Working with Cavell," *The Journal of Aesthetics and Art Criticism* 65 (2007): 229-233.

44   Stanley Cavell, *Must We Mean What We Say? A Book of Essays* (1969; Cambridge: Cambridge University Press, 2000), 17.

45   For his understanding of skepticism, see Stanley Cavell, *Disowning Knowledge in Seven Plays of Shakespeare* (Cambridge: Cambridge University Press, 2003), 143-144.

earlier work as to be impenetrable to those who don't know that work well, and superfluous for those who do."[46] Whereas he is perhaps right that a well-prepared reader is able to discern the different philosophical layers of the text, this disappointment suggests that Gorra does not take into account the language style of Cavell as an essential part of his philosophy. What if someone who does not know his language philosophy were to miss the point entirely? Which point exactly does this person miss? Is this person not able to understand the historical Cavell (who learned to play piano from his mother, who changed his Jewish name into 'Stanley Cavell')? Or is he neglecting to understand Cavell's philosophy? I think that this autobiography is not be read as an account of his life or his philosophy, but as an exercise in his commitment to philosophy, that is to maintain the difficulty of self-knowledge and the complexity of learning the world and language together. What I want to stress (again) is that it is not always obvious what the activity of "my-finding-out-what-I-mean-by-a-word would be. But there obviously is finding-out-what-a-word-means."[47] With this in mind, I suggest reading a bit more Cavell:

> If you feel that finding out what something is must entail investigation of the world rather than of language, perhaps you are imagining a situation like finding out what somebody's name and address are, or what the contents of a will or a bottle are, or whether frogs eat butterflies. But now imagine that you are in your armchair reading a book of reminiscences and come across the work "umiak". You reach for your dictionary and look it up. Now what did you do? Find out what "umiak" means, or find out what "umiak" is? But how could we have discovered something about the world by hunting in the dictionary? If this seems surprising, perhaps it is because we learn language and the world *together*, that they become elaborated and distorted together, and in the same places. [...] When we turned to the dictionary for "umiak" we already knew everything about the word, as it were, but its combination: we knew what a noun is and how to name an object and how to look up a word and what boats are and what an Eskimo is. We were all prepared for that umiak. What seemed like finding the world in a dictionary was really a case of bringing the world to a dictionary.[48]

So what purpose is served by this Cavellian *finale*, as far as an understanding of Abelard's thought is concerned? I would contend that it is significant in Cavell's philosophy in general that he tries to 'de-claim' the obvious,

---

46   Michael Gorra, "The Autobiographical Turn. Reading the New Academic Autobiography," *Transition* 68 (1995): 146.
47   Cavell, *Must We Mean What We Say?*, 39.
48   Cavell, *Must We Mean What We Say?*, 19-20.

that is, to undermine the claim of knowing knowledge by emphasising the need for skepticism and limitation (the condition of thinking about context and meaning in the first place) and ultimately, the importance of the acknowledgement of such a limitation.[49] De-claiming the obvious is one of the most difficult things to realize. But so is 'acknowledging.' In his impressive discussion of Wittgenstein's language philosophy (dealing especially with the *Investigations*), Cavell incessantly stresses the importance (that is, Wittgenstein's) of a shared knowledge through a shared language game, depending on criteria. Perhaps one of the most difficult criteria is 'emotion,' both difficult in the sense of sharing language and in the case of Abelard's anthropological status of language, which seems to be caught in a 'historical' cage of rules, in the sense of distance and formality. It is by finding out new criteria, in response to the crisis of alienation, set by the multiple and subtle distortions of emotion and expression, that either the confusion in the face of some epistemological phenomenon (availability of Abelard's language) or the disorientation (wholeness) can be overcome and we begin to recover ourselves by recounting the forms that our speech can take. I think, in that regard, that it is beneficial to understand that language is learned together with the world.

I come to my final point and to Claude Lévi-Strauss. The selected example of Cavell illustrates how language, semiotics and lending meaning to the world (as it is, as it has been in the past or on another continent) is as much an ethnological problem as a philosophical one. It also illustrates why Lévi-Strauss in essence never renounced his philosophical mind (as if that would be a hanging-matter for him) or why Abelard never renounced his 'whatever-kind-of-mind' (idem). There is something intriguing going on in these three very different examples–Abelard, Cavell and Lévi-Strauss–, concerning the way they are thinking about language, meaning and structures (or rules). In 1984, Lévi-Strauss was interviewed by Bernard Pivot for the thirtieth anniversary of his *Tristes tropiques* on the popular French television literary program on literature, *Apostrophes*. The famous first phrase of this major piece of art sets up, like the sound of the kettledrum, the indefinite character of this report of a journey to Brazil, in which it is impossible to pinpoint where a contemplative literature starts and where an academic observation of the ethnologist takes over:

---

49   His fundamental work is Stanley Cavell, *Claim of Reason: Wittgenstein, Skepticism, Morality and Tragedy* (Oxford: Oxford University Press, 1979).

I hate travelling and explorers. Yet here I am proposing to tell you the story
of my expedition. But how long it has taken me to make up my mind to do
so?[50]

Pivot starts his interview by bringing to mind how the jury of the prestigious literature prize Prix Goncourt at the time was puzzled by the ambiguous character of the report, in which the problem of genre remained
unresolved. Ultimately, the prize was not awarded to Lévi-Strauss. The
incorporation of his oeuvre in the prestigious *Pléiade* series in 2008 (including even the author's 'ethnological' works) proves, however, that judgments and criteria change. In the same interview Lévi-Strauss is asked
about his own explanation of 'structuralism.' He instantly replies with
the typical French rhetoric of being 'highly surprised' about all the fuss
on this topic, that structuralism is as old as the world and that he almost
does not dare to pronounce himself about the subject anymore. He pur-
sues his argument in an interesting direction, artistically kindred to the
one we just saw with Cavell, that structuralism is 'just' a method of skeptical empiricism conducted in order to examine man with a little more
rigor, since the object of study is complicated to such an extent that it is
impossible to describe it in a totally satisfactory way. Lévi-Strauss gives
the example of Marcel Proust describing the face of the duchess of Guer-
mantes. After many pages of reading Proust, the reader still is not able to
see the face empirically, only imaginatively. The painter Albrecht Dürer,
continues Lévi-Strauss, already understood that the exact description of
one face compared to another face would create a simple *rule of transformation*, in which the passage of description 'face *A*' to 'face *B*' would
create a *deformation in meaning*, which in itself would be fairly easy to
realize and to grasp. But, Lévi-Strauss warns, such a rule of transformation as providing new dimensions in meaning is not the same thing
as the procedure of describing objects in the most detailed way possible: "one single life would not be enough to describe one hour of existence within a society of fifty people/une vie ne serait pas suffisante
pour décrire une heure de la vie d'une société de cinquante personnes"
(my own transcription). It is telling that Lévi-Strauss felt himself misunderstood in the way in which *he* intended to employ structures to
understand societies, similar to his missing out on the Prix Goncourt
(he never concealed his artistic ambitions, desiring to be most of all a
composer or, second best, a conductor). What comes to the fore is that

---

50 Claude Lévi-Strauss, *Tristes tropiques*, trans. John Weightman and Doreen Weightman (New York: Penguin, 1992), 1.

freedom of expression seemed most important to him as it functions within the double mechanism of 'language games,' rather than, say, a formalistic 'structuralism.' As such, 'structuralism,' describing objects, colours, masks or infanticide was never meant to become merely a 'grammar system.' Is not the first line of *Tristes tropiques* somehow reminiscent of the exclamation of Abelard at the beginning of his *Historia Calamitatum*, which is itself close to the last passage of this letter, the quote I started this essay with? In the first lines, Abelard writes:

> Often example is better than words for stirring or soothing human feelings; and so I propose to follow up the words of consolation I gave you in person with the trials of my own misfortunes, hoping to give you comfort in my absence. In comparison with mine you will see that your own are nothing, or only slight, and will find them easier to bear.[51]

Acknowledging a second dimension of 'language games' introduces a new kind of intelligibility concerning the grammar of concepts, as they function within a specific frame of reference. The difference between our understanding of reality and the reality of Abelard is that our structure of relations amongst concepts is not understood to be given *a priori*. As we saw before, skepticism as such is not an option when creation is involved. For Abelard, within his 'Platonic' worldview, the grammar of a concept is always existing in knowledge prior to and apart from judgments employing concepts. The structure of relations is given beforehand, in the sense that it is established by specific paradigmatic uses of concepts, thus determining the meaning of words governed by a pre-intelligence. Cavell reminds us–in his reading of Wittgenstein–that a framework is not a structure on which agreement is based, but it is the performance of *saying* which does the trick, just as Lévi-Strauss stresses the process of *deformation* between 'face A' and 'face B,' which gives meaning. In all cases, agreement in language is the pivot point, not in opinions, but in forms of life. When there are specific contexts, say, the academic or the mathematical or the logical, there might be something like a framework, making it possible to check whether a rule has been obeyed or not. These frames allow us to count, measure or find the grammatical function of a word. There are specific contexts which make it possible to make further agreements, taking the framework of language as a foundation and not as its final stage, restoring

---

51 *Historia Calamitatum*, ed. Monfrin, ll. 1-7 (p. 63, as in n. 2): "Sepe humanos affectus aut provocant aut mittigant amplius exempla quam verba. Unde post nonnullam sermonis ad presentem habiti consolationem, de ipsis calamitatum mearum experimentis consolatoriam ad absentem scribere decrevi, ut in comparatione mearum tuas aut nullas aut modicas temptationes recognoscas et tolerabilius feras."

one's voice through listening and writing, thus developing new judgments about the world and about our knowledge of the past: *harder to listen to music than to write music.*

TEMPUS LONGUM ... LOCUS ASPER ... :
CHIAROSCURO IN HUGH OF SAINT-VICTOR

Ineke van 't Spijker

In his magnum opus, *De sacramentis Christianae fidei*, Hugh of Saint-Victor discusses the question whether love of God can be lost. Countering those who hold the position that, once someone has it, this person cannot lose *caritas*, Hugh points to the changeability of our earthly, temporal state: "We are in time, where all things unravel in uncertainty, and you make for me eternity out of time?" *Nos in tempore sumus ubi incerta volvuntur omnia, et tu mihi de tempore aeternitatem facis?*[1] 'Making eternity out of time' was exactly what was supposed to be the purpose of the life to which religious communities such as Saint-Victor were dedicated, eminently in their liturgy, but also in their thought, through works such as those of Anselm of Canterbury. The exact character of this dedication in various authors is explored in much of Burcht Pranger's work.

Although they were canons, not monks, the community of Saint-Victor was characterized by an effort to combine the learning for which they became famous with a monastic way of life. What then are we to make of Hugh's objections against 'making eternity out of time'? Of course, Hugh's exclamation is part of an argument here. Yet, in its dramatic tone it is also indicative of a concern with temporality which underlies Hugh's work. Hugh wants to keep time and eternity separated. Time cannot be eternal, as Hugh argues in his *In Ecclesiasten Homiliae*, against those who posit an 'eternal return.'[2] Confusing the creator and creation is to be avoided: *ut... nec deum concludat tempore, nec creaturam tendat eternitate.*[3] Earlier

---

1   I would like to thank Cédric Giraud for reading this article and offering some helpful suggestions. Throughout this essay, I will quote the edition of *De sacramentis Christianae fidei* in Patrologia Latina [PL] 176 (Paris: Migne, 1844-55) and will give the location in the new edition of Rainer Berndt, *Hugonis de Sancto Victore De sacramentis Christianae fidei*, Corpus Victorinum, Textus historici 1 (Münster: Aschendorff, 2008). For this quote, see *De sacramentis* 2.13.11 (PL 176:541A; ed. Berndt, p. 500, ll. 3-4).

2   *In Ecclesiasten Homiliae* 2 (PL 175:144D).

3   *De sacramentis* 1.10.5 (PL 176:334C; ed. Berndt, p. 231, l. 19).

in *De sacramentis* Hugh deals with the difficult issues surrounding God's eternal will, where man distinguishes between God's goodness and will, his wisdom and his power and their role in the creation of the temporal world: whereas in man there is a temporal sequence, in God goodness, wisdom, power as well as disposition and operation are one. As confusion threatens, Hugh, in his effort to find an answer, exclaims: "But what do we do? Shall we dare to introduce time into eternity?"[4]

Again, this is part of an argument, which probably would be shared by the more philosophically inclined Anselm as well as by the monk *par excellence*, Bernard of Clairvaux. Yet it also fits in Hugh's very history-suffused concerns. For him, there is no *punctum*, in which time contracts, as there was in the work of Augustine or Anselm, nor a *figura* equally reflecting "eternity's hold over time," as in Bernard's work. And if Augustine's work shows a lack of plot, the work of Hugh, the *alter Augustinus*, is full of it.[5] I do not wish to construe too strong a contrast between Hugh and Augustine, who of course had a well-developed historical consciousness as well as a strong sense of eternity's grip on history. However, Hugh's concept of history is characterized more by *chiaroscuro* than by the lightning flash of eternity.

This does not mean that Hugh does not search for concentration, away from distractions and for the recuperation of a lost unity, as becomes clear, for example in the introduction to his treatise on the Ark. Hugh eloquently evokes a scene of his students asking for the reasons for a very

---

4   *De sacramentis* 1.2.10 (PL 176:210CD; ed. Berndt, p. 65, ll. 18-25): "Et videtur quasi quaedam esse distinctio et successio temporalis; et demonstrat se considerationi prima bonitas, quia per eam voluit Deus, deinde sapientia, quia per eam disposuit, novissime potestas quia per eam fecit; quoniam ordo videtur esse, et fuisse voluntas prima, et post eam dispositio, et novissime operatio subsecuta ... Et occurrit magna ratio, quia semper in hominibus precedit voluntas consilium, et consilium opus subsequitur. Sed quid facimus? Nunquid audebimus inducere tempora in aeternitatem?"

5   On Bernard's *figura* see M.B. Pranger, *Bernard of Clairvaux and the Shape of Monastic Thought: Broken Dreams* (Leiden: Brill, 1994). On Anselm's Meditations see M.B. Pranger, *The Artificiality of Christianity. Essays on the Poetics of Monasticism* (Stanford: Stanford University Press, 2003), 107-150; for "eternity's hold over time" ibid., 100. On Augustine's 'plotlessness' see M.B. Pranger, "Time and Narrative in Augustine's *Confessions*," *Journal of Religion* 81 (2001): 377-393. For Hugh as *secundus Augustinus, alter Augustinus* see PL 175:166D, 168A. See also Dominique Poirel, "'Alter Augustinus – der zweite Augustinus'. Hugo von Sankt-Viktor und die Väter der Kirche," in Joannes Arnold, Rainer Berndt, Ralf M.W. Stammberger, Christine Feld, eds., *Väter der Kirche. Ekklesiales Denken von den Anfängen bis in die Neuzeit*. Festgabe für Hermann Josef Sieben SJ zum 70. Geburtstag (Paderborn: Schoeningh, 2004), 643-668 (esp. at 664, n. 66).

Augustinian sounding unrest of the human heart.[6] In the Prologue to *De sacramentis* Hugh states the purpose of this work, which he wants to offer as a brief summary, "that the mind may have something definite to which it may fix and conform its attention (*intentio*), lest it be carried away by various volumes of writings and a diversity of readings without order or direction."[7]

However, *De sacramentis* is not so much a 'brief summary' as a 'rhapsody' of treatises, discussions and extracts.[8] Its organising principle is indeed historical, and it reflects in its very structure its author's appreciation of and attitudes to man's temporal condition. In his *Homilies on Ecclesiastes* Hugh articulates this, commenting on and echoing Ecclesiastes' verses *Omnia tempus habent* (Eccl. 3:1-8): "Nothing is to be rejected in its own time, and nothing not to be chosen in its own time, but the mind should be so prepared for the use of time that it yet does not change with time's changeability."[9] The right 'use of time' is at the heart of Hugh's work, and the changeability that comes with it is less solidly rejected than this quote predictably suggests, loosening 'eternity's hold' over time, over man in time. It is this historical perspective that distinguishes Hugh's work, which in this way exemplifies a tendency in the twelfth century (although

---

6 *De archa Noe*, ed. Patrice Sicard, Corpus Christianorum Continuatio Medievalis [CCCM] 176 (Turnhout: Brepols, 2001), 1.1 (p. 3, ll. 1-5): "Cum sederem aliquando in conuentu fratrum et, illis interrogantibus meque respondente, multa in medium prolata fuissent, ad hoc tandem deducta sunt uerba, ut de humani potissimum cordis instabilitate et inquietudine ammirari omnes simul et suspirare inciperemus."

7 *De sacramentis*, Prologus (PL 176:183-184; ed. Berndt, p. 31, ll. 1-8): "Hanc enim quasi brevem quamdam summam omnium in unam seriem compegi, ut animus aliquid certum haberet, cui intentionem affigere et conformare valeret, ne per varia Scripturarum volumina et lectionum divortia sine ordine et directione raperetur."

8 Dominique Poirel, "*Symbolice et anagogice*: l'école de Saint-Victor et la naissance du style gothique," in Poirel, ed., *L'abbé Suger, le manifeste gothique de Saint-Denis et la pensée victorine*, Actes du Colloque organisé à la Fondation Singer-Polignac (Paris) le mardi 21 novembre 2000, Rencontres Médiévales Européennes 1 (Turnhout, 2001), 141-170, at 151. See also H. Weisweiler, "Die Arbeitsmethode Hugos von St.Viktor. Ein Beitrag zum Entstehen seines Hauptwerkes De Sacramentis," *Scholastik* 19-24 (1944-1949): 59-87 and 232-267.

9 *In Ecclesiasten* 13 (PL 175:206CD): "Nihil ergo suo tempore abjiciendum, et nihil non suo tempore eligendum, sed sic animus ad usum temporis praeparetur ut tamen ad mutabilitatem temporis non mutetur."

not in Anselm or Bernard): a growing historical conscience.[10] This, in a way, enables man to play his part in time, and in this sense perhaps contributes to a certain subjectivity.[11]

The sacraments at the centre of *De sacramentis* are part of the underlying and ongoing drama of the Word, who came into the world to fight with the devil.[12] In two Books, Hugh discusses what he calls the *opera conditionis* and the *opera restaurationis*, creation and redemption, to help man on his way to achieve, by interpreting Scripture, "virtue and knowledge." After the Fall man's life, between the beginning and the end of the world, is the time in which reparation will happen; this world is the place; the sacraments are the remedy. The time is long, the place is difficult, but the remedy is adequate.[13]

Sometimes seen as a first summa, or at least a proto-summa of theology, *De sacramentis* is very different from the much more systematic treatment of theological issues in the work of Peter the Lombard and his followers. It seems unfinished: the last parts of the second Book, dealing with 'last things,' are mostly quotations from Augustine and Gregory the Great. The parts that make up *De sacramentis* vary in length and style. Apart from the last books just mentioned, parts of Book Two also lean

---

10 Among the many studies discussing this aspect of Hugh's work see especially M.-D. Chenu, "Conscience de l'histoire et théologie," in *La théologie au douzième siècle* (Paris: Vrin, 1957), 62-89; trans. as "Theology and the New Awareness of History," in Chenu, *Nature, Man and Society in the Twelfth Century. Essays on New Theological Perspectives in the Latin West,* ed. and trans. by Jerome Taylor and Lester K. Little, Medieval Academy Reprints for Teaching (Toronto: University of Toronto Press, 1997), 162-201; Joachim Ehlers, *Hugo von St. Viktor. Studien zum Geschichtsdenken und zur Geschichtsschreibung des 12. Jahrhunderts* (Wiesbaden: Steiner, 1973); Grover A. Zinn, "*Historia fundamentum est*: the role of history in the contemplative life according to Hugh of St. Victor," in George H. Shriver, ed., *Contemporary reflections on the medieval Christian tradition. Essays in honor of Ray C. Petry* (Durham, NC: Duke University Press, 1974), 135-158; Charlotte Gross, "Twelfth-Century Concepts of Time: Three Reinterpretations of Augustine's Doctrine of Creation *Simul*," *Journal of the History of Philosophy* 23 (1985): 325-338.

11 On the connection between subjectivity and historical consciousness see Marcel Gauchet, *La condition historique* (Paris: Stock, 2003). Although Gauchet posits subjectivity in a narrow sense as a distinct phenomenon of modernity, his broad overview of Western developments perhaps allows for a certain extrapolation as implied in my evaluation of Hugh.

12 *De sacramentis* Prologus (PL 176:183B; ed. Berndt, p. 32, ll. 2-3).

13 *De sacramentis* 1.8.1 (PL 176:305D-306C; ed. Berndt, p. 194, ll. 12-16): "Tria ergo hic in reparatione hominis primo loco consideranda occurrunt: tempus, locus, remedium. Tempus est praesens vita ab initio mundi usque ad finem saeculi. Locus est mundus iste. Remedium in tribus constat: in fide, in sacramentis, in operibus bonis. Tempus longum, ne imparatus praeoccupetur. Locus asper, ut praevaricator castigetur. Remedium efficax, ut infirmus sanetur."

heavily on other sources. Part Two, on the Church, and Part Three, on the orders in the Church, consist mainly of quotations from Ivo of Chartres and other authorities. In many other parts, however, Hugh discusses matters that were on the agenda of contemporary debates in a very lively manner. He offers a rationale for the diversity in his treatment in the Prologue to Book Two.

> As not everyone has received the same grace of understanding, Scripture itself contains that with which it nourishes the faith of the simple, which joined with deeper things, constitutes one rule of truth. Thus in the treatment of Scripture the same form of saying should not be maintained throughout, as the deeper sacraments of faith are to be treated reverently with a more elevated discourse, worthy of holy things; the lesser instruments of the divine sacraments to be explained in accordance with the capacity of the more simple people in a humbler kind of speech ...[14]

The diversity of discourse in *De sacramentis* consists not so much in different levels of difficulty, as in differences between various parts. In some, Hugh gives a clear exposition of some issue–indicating where caution is called for in matters that may not be easily accessible to human understanding;[15] in others, he engages his readers in his endeavour to understand, or invites them to reconsider their own arguments, as in both discussions mentioned above. It is throughout both these parts that his "musical" style can be observed, a style which sets his work apart from more scholastic summas, and which has been masterfully analysed by Baron.[16]

Apart from this style, there is also a distinct tone to his work, often connected to an imaginary dialogue, which lends a sense of drama to the discussions, as in the question of *caritas* and its loss, with which we began. Another example can be found when Hugh turns to define the sacraments, in Part Nine of Book One. Hugh methodically presents his own famous definition (... *sacramentum est corporale, vel materiale elementum, foris sensibiliter propositum ex similitudine repraesentans et ex institutione*

---

14 *De sacramentis* (PL 176:363-354; ed. Berndt, p. 271, ll. 1-8).

15 E.g. on the question whether Christ at the Last Supper gave his mortal or immortal body, *De sacramentis* 2.8.3 (PL 176:462D; ed. Berndt, p. 401, ll. 4-5): "Ego in ejusmodi (sicut et in aliis professus sum) divina secreta magis veneranda quam discutienda censeo."

16 Roger Baron, "Le style de Hugues de Saint-Victor," in *Études sur Hugues de Saint-Victor* (Paris: Desclée de Brouwer, 1963), 91-132, at 106: "Le style musical cependant n'est qu'un accompagnement de la pensée. Il peut surgir au cours d'un développement, ou même le commencer ou le conclure; mais il ne l'arrête pas ..."

significans, et ex sanctificatione continens aliquam invisibilem et spiritu-alem gratiam), explaining the three reasons for their institution (*humili-atio, eruditio,* and *exercitatio*).[17] He then goes on to address an imaginary reader, who supposedly could suggest that someone who is not able to receive a sacrament could not be saved. Hugh points to the difference be-tween on the one hand God's power to save without the sacraments and, on the other hand, man's need to obediently honour them:

> What do you think then, you, whoever honours God's sacraments, when you think you honour God's sacraments, and dishonour God? You judge the necessity of the sacraments while abrogating the sacraments' author his power, and denying piety? You tell me that he who does not have God's sac-raments cannot be saved; I tell you that whoever has the power (*virtus*) of the sacraments cannot perish ... But you say, how are we to understand what is written: unless someone is born again from water and the Holy Spirit he cannot enter the kingdom of God (John 3, 5)? And I ask you, how do you imagine that we should understand what is written: he who believes in me shall not see death in eternity (John 11, 25)?[18]

The dramatic quality resulting from such dialogue distinguishes his work from the summa-literature after him, and also from the contem-porary sentence-collections, or the work of his contemporary Abelard. Yet his work is also different in tone from an author such as Anselm of Canterbury, or Bernard of Clairvaux, although both these writers could be equally dramatic, as Pranger has often shown in his work. It is its his-torical perspective, already mentioned, which distinguishes Hugh's work from these authors. Moreover, despite his strong sense of the underlying unity as the goal–the point of *reditus* of the human quest–, Hugh often praises the manifold beauty and plurality of creation, a plurality which is realised through time: "Physical nature, whose beauty is realised accord-ing to diverse species and forms, is embellished by its very changeability with more and more grace, when through the intervals of time and altera-tion of things passing by in time and succeeding in time it receives what it cannot receive simultaneously ..."[19]A historical dimension is not only the

---

17 Hugh's definition is in *De sacramentis* 1.9.2 (PL 176:317D-318B; ed. Berndt, p. 209, l. 22 – p. 210, l. 2); for the sacraments' institution see *De sacramentis* 1.9.3 (PL 176:319A-322A; ed. Berndt, pp. 211-214). See on Hugh's definition of sacraments and its context Irène Rosier-Catach, *La parole efficace. Signe, rituel, sacré* (Paris: Seuil, 2004).

18 *De sacramentis* 1.9.5 (PL 176:324C-325A; ed. Berndt, p. 218, ll. 8-23).

19 *In Ecclesiasten* 1 (PL 175:119b). See on Hugh's theological aesthetics Lenka Karfíko-va, *"De esse ad pulchrum esse". Schönheit in der Theologie Hugos von St. Viktor*, Bibliotheca Victorina 8 (Turnhout: Brepols, 1998).

underlying structure in *De sacramentis*, it also comes to the fore in Hugh's well-known interest in the historical sense as the necessary foundation for any further interpretation of the Bible. And it suffuses some of his more meditational works. The last two books of *De vanitate mundi* consist of an overview of salvation history up to the Church Fathers.[20] *De archa Noe*, meant to investigate the causes of the unrest of the human heart and offer a remedy for it, does not end so much with a unifying climax, but with the suggestion to "enter the works of restoration as it were as an ark," proposing biblical history as the content for the thought with which to build one's inner man, and praising this inner ark for the variety of its delights.[21]

Thus, allied with this life's 'time and place' are variation and multiplicity. They not only distract the mind away from its original focus; much more they are also the product of divine dispensation, transparent, for those with the right view, to the invisible reality behind. Yet, at the same time, the variety of the sacraments (reflecting the variety that Hugh observed in Scripture) for all their symbolical meaning function also as a varied 'exercise' in which silence and singing, singing and reading, alternate. They are thus part of a positive *mutabilitas* that is opposed to man's inevitable changeability.[22]

This positive value of variety runs through much of Hugh's work, causing a tension of course with the negative distractions it also provides. This tension contributes to and aggravates man's fragility due to his fall. At a more basic level, there is a hint of fragility even before the Fall, when Hugh imagines that someone could ask why God made man in the first place, as he did not need any help from his creation, nor was there anyone else for whom he could have made anything: man seems to be made as

---

20 *De vanitate mundi* 3-4. In anticipation of a new edition by Cédric Giraud I refer to PL 176:723C-739B. I thank Cédric Giraud for enabling me to see his thesis, "Le *De vanitate mundi* d'Hugues de Saint-Victor († 1141). Édition critique et commentaire," (PhD diss., École nationale des chartes, Paris, 2002); résumé in *Positions des thèses de l'École nationale des chartes* (Paris: École nationale des chartes, 2002), 63-71.

21 *De archa Noe* 4.8 (CCCM 176, p. 110, ll. 158-159; as in n. 6): "... et nunc in opera restaurationis quasi in archam ingredimur." See also 4.9 (p. 115, ll. 132-133): "Hec archa similis est apothece omnium deliciarum uarietate referte." See on the connection between history and contemplation, Zinn, "*Historia fundamentum est*" (as in n. 10).

22 *De sacramentis* 1.9.3 (PL 176:321A; ed. Berndt, p. 213, ll. 16-19: "Quia ergo vita hominis hic sine mutabilitate esse non potest, contra illam (quae defectum generat) mutabilitatem alia ei mutabilitas quae profectum parit opponitur; ut, quia stare non potest ut semper idem sit, moveatur et promoveatur semper ut melior sit."

it were for nothing.[23] The ensuing discussion of God's will and his wish to have rational nature participate in his goodness does not cancel this fragility. Existence, from this perspective, is fully gratuitous.[24] Moreover, it is impermanent, things disappearing from our presence before they disappear even from our memory.[25] Hugh's Platonic background feeds into this ephemeral character of the world, for example when he sees existing things as only imitating real beings: they only seem to touch reality, that they are not totally nothing, having their being by participation.[26]

However, this fragility is not just part of an ongoing medieval *contemptus mundi*.[27] Rather than that, it is implied by Hugh's sense of history. It is this same sense of fragility and changeability that underlies Hugh's view of the possibilities (including impossibility) of 'enduring love'. And it is equally the obverse side of something more positive, man's potential development.

Let us return to Hugh's possibly sarcastic rhetorical question quoted in the beginning of this article: "... and you want to make for me eternity out of time?" This was a provisional conclusion within a complicated discussion–in which perhaps Hugh does not demonstrate a very charitable approach to his opponents, suggesting that they do not have this *caritas* in the first place. Neither do Hugh's counter arguments meet plausible standards of logical consistency, for example when he states that, if a good per-

---

23 *De sacramentis* 1.2.1 (PL 176:206C; ed. Berndt, p. 60, ll. 16-19): "Sed dicet aliquis: Quare deus creaturam fecit si juvari ipse non potuit per creaturam? qui alteri fecit quod sibi non fecit quando alter nemo erat nisi ipse qui fecit. Quasi enim pro nihilo factum esse videtur et causam non habuisse, ut fieret quod ita factum est; ut inde nec juvaretur qui fecit quia perfectus non eguit ..."

24 A similar hint of gratuity can be found in Hugh's *De arrha anime*, in *L'Oeuvre de Hugues de Saint-Victor I. De institutione novitiorum. De virtute orandi. De laude caritatis. De arrha animae*, ed. H.B. Feiss and P. Sicard, trans. D. Poirel, H. Rochais and P. Sicard (Turnhout: Brepols, 1997), 226-300, at 252: "Primum cogita, anima mea, quod aliquando non fueris et, ut esse inciperes, hoc eius dono acceperis. Donum ergo eius erat ut fieres ...gratis accepisti ab eo ut fieres."

25 See also *In Ecclesiasten* 2 (PL 175:147D-148A): "Et tamen fluunt omnia, nec permanet quidquam sub sole ... Nam prius a praesentia nostra subtrahuntur, ut non subsistant per speciem; deinde etiam a memoria oblivione delentur, ut nec subsistant saltem per recordationem." See also PL 175:149AB: "In vera igitur consideratione hoc solum quasi non esse vidit, quod solum esse videtur. Quia dum simul et esse incipit ex eo quod nondum est, et esse desinet (*sic*) in id quod jam non est; pene nihil est quod est."

26 *In Ecclesiasten* 13 (PL 175:208AB).

27 See for a nuanced view of this *contemptus mundi* H.R.Schlette, *Die Nichtigkeit der Welt. Der philosophische Horizont des Hugos von St. Viktor* (München: Kösel-Verlag, 1961). See also Giraud, "Le *De vanitate mundi* d'Hugues de Saint-Victor," 278: *De vanitate* is an exercise in meditation, based on *admiratio*, rather than on *contemptus mundi*. This applies to Hugh's work in general.

son, that is one who has *caritas*, cannot lose what he has, a bad person cannot acquire it: *Si ergo bonus qui habet non potest amittere nec malus qui non habet potest acquirere*. Even if one would accept the identification between having love and being good, and its opposite, it does not follow, from the fact that someone who has something cannot lose it, that someone else who does not have that same thing cannot acquire it.[28]

What is at stake here and elsewhere for Hugh, however, is a wide-ranging pastoral concern. If the opponent were right, there would be no reason for caution, or for hope: *Quod si verum esse constiterit nec stanti timendum est nec sperandum jacenti.*[29] As to the question why some people, who, according to Hugh, had real charity but lost it, have not been given the necessary perseverance, Hugh (following Augustine) puts his hands up–he does not know.[30] As he had said before, "Here, as long as life is lived in changeability, a bad person can be good and a good person can be bad."[31] Hugh emphasizes that what we are dealing with here is not an issue of feigned love–the lost rightness, *justitia*, as he, quoting Augustine, now

---

28 *De sacramentis* 2.13.11 (PL 176:540A-541A; ed. Berndt, p. 499, l. 3- p. 500, l. 4): "Dicunt quod charitas semel habita, deinceps nunquam amplius amittatur. Ego igitur illos interrogo si ipsi charitatem nunquam perdiderunt, et utinam idcirco charitatem non perdidissent quia habitam retinuissent. Sed vereor quod ideo potius non perdiderunt quia nunquam habuerunt. Si autem nunquam habuerunt neque gustaverunt, quomodo asserere presumunt quod nesciunt? Si autem charitatem aliquando habuerunt, habent adhuc ipsam charitatem quam habuerunt, quia secundum sententiam ipsorum semel habitam amittere non potuerunt. Si autem habent charitatem, ambulant secundum charitatem et non operantur iniquitatem (Psalm 118, 3). Si autem operantur iniquitatem non habent charitatem. Si enim Deum non diligit qui mundum diligit, et ea quae in mundo sunt, quomodo non multo magis non Deum diligit qui iniquitatem diligit? *Qui diligit iniquitatem, odit animam suam* (Psalm 10, 6). Qui animam suam odit seipsum non diligit, vel si diligit, male diligit, quia secundum solam carnem diligit. Qui autem non diligit seipsum, non diligit proximum sicut seipsum. *Qui autem non diligit proximum quem videt, quomodo potest diligere Deum quem non videt* (1 John 4:20)? Isti ergo qui aliquando operantur iniquitatem dicant quomodo habeant charitatem ... Dicunt quod qui semel charitatem habet, deinceps illam amittere non potest, hoc est dicere, qui bonus est, malus esse non potest. Quare ergo similiter non dicemus quia qui malus est bonus esse non potest, si dicimus quod qui modo bonus est, malus esse non potest? Qui enim charitatem habet bonus est, et qui charitatem non habet bonus non est. Si ergo bonus qui habet non potest amittere, neque malus qui non habet potest acquirere; quod si verum esse constiterit nec stanti timendum est nec sperandum jacenti. Nos in tempore sumus ubi incerta volvuntur omnia, et tu mihi de tempore aeternitatem facis?"

29 *De sacramentis* 2.13.11 (PL 176:541A; ed. Berndt, p. 500, ll. 2-3).

30 *De sacramentis* 2.13.12 (PL 176:550A; ed. Berndt, p. 510, ll. 13-15): "Hic si a me quaeratur cur eis Deus perseverantiam non dederit ... me ignorare respondeo." Quoted from Augustine, *De correptione et gratia* 8.17 (PL 44:925-926).

31 *De sacramentis* 2.13.11 (PL 176:541B; ed. Berndt, p.500, ll. 16-17): "Hic autem quandiu mutabiliter vivitur, et bonus malus, et malus bonus esse potest."

calls it, was real enough–, but of lack of perseverance.[32] It is not for nothing that in the next part Hugh discusses confession and penance. (If this is
not quite to say *Così fan tutte*, Hugh would probably applaud Tito's Clem-
enza: *Il vero pentimento, di cui tu sei capace, val più d'una verace costante
fedeltà*, "the true repentance of which you are capable, is worth more than
a true and constant loyalty," surely more so than a precocious certainty
which is the implication of his opponent's position, more like Fiordiligi's
Como scoglio or even her later *Per pietà*.)

Instead of seeking the philosophical precision which Abelard and others–not necessarily less interested in the pastoral consequences of their
positions–would apply to such questions, Hugh resorts to a rhetoric of
highly dramatic dialogue, here and elsewhere.

In the issues surrounding God's will in Book One, Hugh had equally
addressed philosophically and theologically urgent questions, namely
whether God could have made a better world. This issue was discussed
by Abelard and answered in the negative.[33] Hugh denies any limitations
on God's will, dismissing those who think otherwise: "Let them go away
now, and take pride in their own understanding, those who think that
they can take apart the divine works with reason and constrain his power
within their limit."[34] With these words he enters upon a philosophical digression but he changes the stakes of the debate and introduces his interest in historical development: "And he who has made things, can make
them better, not in correcting what has been made badly, but by promoting what has been made well into something better; not that he [God],
as to himself, would make a better job of doing things, but that what he
has made, through his very doing, and with him persevering in the same,
becomes better."[35] A sense of development, of plot, is inherent in Hugh's

---

32 *De sacramentis* 2.13.12 (PL 176:550B; ed. Berndt, p. 510, ll. 21-22): "Non quia justitiam simulaverunt, sed quia in ea non permanserunt." The same in Augustine, *De correptione et gratia* 9.20 (PL 44:928).

33 On this debate see Marcia Colish, *Peter Lombard*, vol. 1 of 2 (Leiden: Brill, 1994),
290-302.

34 *De sacramentis* 1.2.22 (PL 176:214B; ed. Berndt, p. 70, ll. 12-13): "Eant ergo nunc et
de suo sensu glorientur qui opera divina ratione se putant discutere, et ejus potentiam sub
mensura coarctare."

35 *De sacramentis* 1.2.22 (PL 176:216B; ed. Berndt, p. 72, ll. 20-22): "Et ipse quod fecit
melius facere potest; non tamen corrigens male factum, sed bene factum promovens in
melius; non ut ipse quantum ad se melius faciat, sed ut quod fecit ipso identidem operante
et in eodem perseverante melius fiat."

views, from the beginning of creation, where *esse* precedes, or was meant to precede, *pulchrum esse*.[36]

Man was supposed to develop in Paradise, even before any Fall. And, as if there never was a before or after, the matter of Scripture, to which *De sacramentis* offers 'a basis for interpretation,' is the *opus restaurationis*, that is "the incarnation of the Word with all its sacraments, either those that came before from the beginning of the world, or those that follow until the end of the world."[37] Historical development is almost projected backwards. Before giving his famous definition of the sacraments in the beginning of Part Nine of Book One, Hugh explains the time of the institution of the sacraments. Indeed, the sacraments of Christian faith, with faith and good works constituting the remedy for human guilt, were instituted once man had fallen into this world's exile, but even then one sacrament, that of marriage, had already been given before, as a symbol of the union between God and the soul; its *officium*, the physical union between man and woman, a symbol of the unity between Christ and the Church.[38]

It is through this telescoping of a pre-lapsarian but temporal perspective into 'this our time' that an overarching unity of perspective remains, more than through time being shot through with eternity's moments. This does not mean that the visible world is not also appreciated in its symbolical value as "opening a space for the reminiscence of the divine," as it was for Augustine.[39] Yet, Hugh's world is not exhausted by its symbolical character, leaving him perhaps with a sense of exile which is the more melancholic as his world is more separate from the homeland it symbolizes.

Hugh's historical perspective, his view of the beauty of the multiple, but also his sense of fragility are all intertwined in *De sacramentis*, and are, I would suggest, related to his predilection for a dramatic style. Part of man's fragility is his incapacity to understand and talk properly about God.[40] Hugh is aware of the problem of theological language, but does not

---

36 *De sacramentis* 1.1.3 (PL 176:189AB; ed. Berndt, p. 38, ll. 12-16).

37 *De sacramentis* Prologus (PL 176:183B; ed. Berndt, p. 32, ll. 2-3).

38 *De sacramentis* 1.8.13 (PL 176:314CD; ed. Berndt, p. 205, ll. 17-26).

39 Guy-H. Allard, "Arts libéraux et langage chez Saint Augustin," in *Arts libéraux et philosophie au Moyen Âge*. Actes du quatrième congrès international de philosophie médiévale (Montréal / Paris: Vrin, 1969), 481-492, at 485.

40 Hugh presents his epistemology in his theory of the 'three eyes' in the context of his treatise on faith. See, for example, *De sacramentis* 1.10.2 (PL 176:329C-330A; ed. Berndt, p. 225): after the Fall, the eye of contemplation was lost, the eye of reason became blurred, and only the bodily eye remained functional.

treat this problem in a systematic way.[41] Instead of struggling with seman
tic precision, he poses rhetorical questions. Sometimes these questions reveal what Hugh presents as the absurdity of a position, and although he is
usually seen as a peacefully calm and balanced author, he is sometimes as
acerbic as a Bernard of Clairvaux, as we saw already in some of the examples quoted above.[42]

Even when he is not pouring scorn on some opponents his discussion
often has a dramatic tone, brought about by the dialogue with an imagined reader. This can be much like the traditional pedagogical dialogue,
just as in his *De arrha animae*, or *De vanitate mundi*, or in questions-
and-answers as we saw in the discussion of God's power to save man even
without his sacraments. In his discussion of the names of the Trinity, the
use of which caused Abelard such problems, Hugh explains their application–this time without a side-swipe at Abelard–while signalling the problem, that our words for the divine are taken from man: *quoniam ab hominibus sumpta sunt vocabula*.[43] As he remarks when trying to explain the
union of God and man in Christ, man labours, as he can hardly understand anything except what he can say and according to what he can say.[44]

As in the discussion about the possibility of losing *caritas*, the stakes
are equally high in the First Part of Book Two, on the Incarnation, where
the questions raised are related to man's salvation through Christ's death.
Thus, for example, there is the question regarding Christ's 'merit'. Some
say that Christ could not have come to the glory of immortality unless he
had first earned it by suffering death. Hugh counters that God as man was
indeed mortal, but by his will, not by necessity. If he had only achieved
immortality by dying necessarily, he would have died for himself. Hugh

---

41 See Giraud, "Le *De vanitate mundi* d'Hugues de Saint-Victor," who offers a fine investigation of Hugh's language, which goes beyond a stylistic analysis, as it connects this
language to Hugh's pedagogy of salvation. Giraud, ibid., 289, points to Hugh's "play with the
expressive possibilities of language at the same time as his subtle suggestion of its limits."

42 Cf. also Hugh's opposition to those who say that true love of God does not wish
for any reward. *De sacramentis* 2.13.8 (PL 176:534 BC; ed. Berndt, p. 492, l.15-19): "Audite
homines sapientes. Diligimus, inquiunt, ipsum, sed non quaerimus ipsum. Hoc est dicere
diligimus ipsum, sed non curamus de ipso. Ego homo sic diligi nollem a vobis. Si me sic di-
ligeres ut de me non curaretis ego de vestra dilectione non curarem. Vos videritis si dignum
est ut Deo offeratis quod homo digne respueret."

43 *De sacramentis* 1.3.26 (PL 176:228A; ed. Berndt, p. 88, l. 7), reading *omnibus* instead of *hominibus*. See on the debate about the trinitarian appropriations Dominique Poirel, *Livre de la nature et débat trinitaire au XIIe siècle. Le De tribus diebus de Hugues de
Saint-Victor*, Bibliotheca Victorina 14 (Turnhout: Brepols, 2002).

44 *De sacramentis* 2.1.11 (PL 176:405C; ed. Berndt, p. 324, ll. 1-2): "Magna involutio
dicendi est circa haec; et laborat homo in suo, qui pene nihil intelligere novit, nisi hoc et
secundum hoc quod dicere novit."

introduces Christ as one of the speakers, in a tone of familiarity not unknown in Bernard of Clairvaux:

> Yet, what does he say? I, he says, am going to be sacrificed for you. Pay atten-
> tion to this: I am going to be sacrificed for you. Why does Christ not say: I
> am going to be sacrificed for you and for myself? If he has only died for us,
> where is, what you say, that he has died for himself? Thus, listen. Christ says
> that he has died for us, and if we say that he has died for himself, we deny
> the benefit because we do not wish to give thanks. If he has died for himself,
> what do we owe him? Let him give thanks to himself. *Ipse sibi congratuletur.*
> For himself he sustained and for himself he received ... [45]

Nor did Christ suffer for us *and* for himself, as the opponents say, trying, in vain, to save their position: "While they fear to fall, they hurl down
headlong."[46]

Hugh's concern in *De sacramentis* is with the remedy of the sacraments
playing out in time and place. Time has its own irrevocability, of course–
what has happened cannot be undone.[47] Yet–and this is perhaps again an
implication of Hugh's plot–only up to a certain point. Hugh's argument
here, in the context of a discussion of the possibility of renewed penitence,
is partly a discussion of Jerome's famous *dictum* that God, although he
can do anything, cannot make a virgin out of a woman who has lost her
virginity.[48] Hugh is cautious in evaluating Jerome's words, as he is bound
by respect for the Church father, but does not want to diminish God's
power. Unlike Augustine's "It is one thing to rise rapidly, another thing
not to fall,"[49] Hugh emphasizes that falling is inevitable (and Augustine
would agree), and more than that: many have fallen, but have risen better
than before, having learned from their experience. If Hugh, for the sake of

---

45 *De sacramentis* 2.1.6 (PL 176:384CD; ed. Berndt, p. 299, ll. 5-10): "Quid autem dicit? "Vado, inquit, immolari pro vobis." Hic intendite: "Vado, inquit, immolari pro vobis."
Quare non dicit Christus vado immolari pro vobis et pro me? Si enim pro nobis tantum
mortuus est, ubi est quod dicitis mortuum pro se? [Berndt: quare non dicis et pro te? Si pro
nobis mortuus es ubi est pro te?] Audite ergo: Christus dicit quod pro nobis mortuus est; et
nos si dicimus quod pro semetipso mortuus est, beneficium negamus, quia gratias referre
nolumus. Si pro se mortuus est, quid ei debemus? Ipse igitur sibi congratuletur. Pro se sustinuit, sibi recepit."
46 *De sacramentis* 2.1.6 (PL 176:385A; ed. Berndt, p. 299, l. 24).
47 *De sacramentis* 2.14. 4 (PL 176:558B; ed. Berndt, p. 522, l. 8-9): "Quod idcirco fieri
non potest, quia sicut tempora transacta amplius non redeunt, ita quae semel perpetrata
fuerint, amplius non facta esse non possunt."
48 See Jerome, *Epistula*, ed. Isidorus Hilberg, Corpus Scriptorum Ecclesiasticorum
Latinorum [CSEL] 54 (Vienna: Verlag der Österreichischen Akademie der Wissenschaften,
1996), 22.5 (p. 150).
49 Augustine, *Confessiones* 10.35.57. Pranger discusses the passage in his "Time and
Narrative" (see n. 5).

completeness, has to acknowledge that although it is great to rise, it is better never to have fallen, this can be seen as an interpretation which "does
not close the door to penitents, while yet demonstrating the danger of
falling." As he had explained much earlier, if "the first good was to stand
in the highest place, the second is to ascend to higher things."[50]

Although "anything appearing in time has been disposed before time
in eternity,"[51] what resonates in Hugh is not 'eternity's hold over time,'
but man turning temporal things to 'good use.' Hugh never loses sight of
the enduring good that lies behind it–nor of the ultimate and inscrutable
divine judgment which is behind some people's lack of perseverance in
caritas. Life's consolations often do not outweigh the trouble in seeking
them.[52] Yet, whatever Hugh's appreciation of the *vanitas mundi*, he envis-
ages man in his temporal predicament, in a *tempus longum* and a *locus
asper*–as a subject preparing himself for the 'use of time.' It is this resulting subjectivation, to use this word in a slightly anachronistic sense–man,
that is, confronting his predicament–,which has as its reverse side Hugh's
melancholy awareness of man's fragility and his precarious position–as it
resonates especially in Hugh's *Homilies on Ecclesiastes*:

> All things are good in their own time for him who uses them well, and yet
> all that is subject to mutability, although it may provide some consolation in
> man's misery, cannot confer any easiness. Nothing in its own time is to be
> rejected, and nothing to be chosen in what is not its own time, but the mind
> should be prepared for the use of time in such a way that in the end it is not
> changed at the mutability of time.[53]

In this time, and this place, such immutability is illusory. "It does not per-
tain to this life's rightness ... that he who is good never falls, but that when
he falls, he rises again."[54] Plot implies the possibility of falling–and rising

---

50 *De sacramentis* 1.9.3 (PL 176:321A; ed. Berndt, p. 213, ll.19-20): "Primum enim bonum erat in summo stare. Secundum bonum est ad superiora ascendere."

51 *De sacramentis* 1.2.8 (PL 176:210A; ed. Berndt, p. 65, ll. 2-3): "Quidquid enim in
tempore apparuit ante tempora in aeternite dispositum fuit."

52 *In Ecclesiasten* 1 (PL 175:124D): "Vidit quanta affectione ac miseria quotidie sine
cessatione vita humana atteritur, etiam in iis quae pro sui consolatione operatur, et que-
madmodum semper fere plus detrimenti patitur in quaerendo remedio, quam recipiat con-
solationis in percipiendo fomento."

53 *In Ecclesiasten* 13 (PL 175:206): "Omnia enim suo tempore bene utenti bona sunt, et
tamen universa quae mutabilitati subjacent, licet in miseria qualemcunque consolationem
praebeant, facilitatem tamen conferre non possunt. Nihil ergo suo tempore abjiciendum, et
nihil non suo tempore eligendum, sed sic animus ad usum temporis praeparetur ut tamen
ad mutabilitatem temporis non mutetur."

54 *De sacramentis* 1.10.6 (PL 176:335C; ed. Berndt, p. 232, l. 26- p. 233, l. 2): "Neque
enim ad justitiam hujus vitae pertinet ... ut qui bonus est nunquam cadat; sed, cum ce-
ciderit ut resurgat ..."

again. If it also implies that *caritas* can be ultimately lost, that does not mean that it was not real. Perhaps it is embracing history's *chiaroscuro* that enables Hugh to accept such aporia.

OBEDIENCE SIMPLE AND TRUE:
ANSELM OF CANTERBURY ON
HOW TO DEFEAT THE DEVIL

Arjo Vanderjagt

Succinctly, Giles Gasper has remarked that "[i]ntegrated and consistent thought are hallmarks of Anselm's working habits."[1] This consistency in grammar, logic, and also rhetoric is evident to every reader of his writings such as the *Tres tractatus*, the *Cur deus homo* or the *Monologion*, and perhaps in particular of his *Proslogion*. It is this methodological, systematic rigor that makes Anselm's thought the object of more than only historical interests. His is a very special exercise in systematics, and contemporary philosophers intent on logic and language still debate not only the stringent logical and grammatical analysis of his various arguments for God's existence but also the general deontology of this late-eleventh and early-twelfth century monastic writer.[2] In systematic theology, too, Anselm's doctrine of the atonement of Christ and his salvific teleology continue today as points of departure for lively discussions. In different fashion, however, from modern philosophers, who tend to respect if not admire the consistency of his arguments, whether or not they agree with him, contemporary theologians often regard his method and the substance of his ideas as inhumanly logical, as legalistic and mechanical, and especially as "realist," a term, of course, of opprobrium to modern constructivist ap-

---

1 Giles E.M. Gasper, *Anselm of Canterbury and his Theological Inheritance* (Aldershot: Ashgate, 2004), 198.

2 See, for example, Desmond P. Henry, *The Logic of Saint Anselm* (Oxford: Oxford University Press, 1967) and his *Medieval Logic and Metaphysics. A Modern Introduction* (London: Hutchinson, 1972); Alvin Plantinga, *God, Freedom and Evil* (Grand Rapids: Eerdmans, 1977); Hubertus G. Hubbeling, *Principles of the Philosophy of Religion* (Assen: Van Gorcum, 1987); see also Brian Davies and Brian Leftow, eds., *The Cambridge Companion to Anselm*, (Cambridge: Cambridge University Press, 2004).

proaches.[3] Whatever these different modern valuations of his intellectual procedure, Anselm's precision and the inexorability of his argumentation would seem to leave no room for a serious consideration of the less than logical uncertainties and vicissitudes of the practicalities of day-to-day life, in his case of the fears and doubts of his monastic brothers and sisters and his own, as well.[4] Indeed, Anselm's theory–even, logic–of knowledge has been described in terms of an ethical imperative which leads to the ultimate goal of the Christian life: "Anselm never loses sight of the fact that the pursuit of understanding constitutes an act of obedience, since the Christian is commanded to know the basis of his faith (I Peter 3:15). And obedience in itself fosters the experience of joy by being a necessary condition for its presence."[5]

Friends obey each other spontaneously, as I learned well many years ago in my very first meeting with the honoree of this festschrift. It is thus fitting to here examine one of Burcht Pranger's intellectual heroes on this point. I will first examine Anselm's insistence on the *spontaneity* of true obedience and secondly his idea of obedience as the best defense against the onslaughts of the devil. Most discussions of Anselm's thought are based upon his treatises, but the present article especially in its second section will give an important place to the letters.[6] It seems to me that through their dialectic between the writer and his reader, and thus their personal style, but also by their broader meaning because Anselm intended them as well for dissemination to a wide audience, the letters are an

---

3 Eastern Orthodox theology has generally seen Anselm's doctrine of the atonement as legalistic. Modern Christian theologians often agree; an important example is Gustaf Aulén's originally Swedish, *Christus Victor. An Historical Study of the Three Main Types of the Idea of the Atonement* (1930; New York: Macmillan, 1975), which is particularly influential because the English translation was introduced by Jaroslav Pelikan. Recently, Anthony W. Bartlett, *Cross Purposes. The Violent Grammar of Christian Atonement* (Harrisburg: Trinity Press International, 2001), has presented the "appearance of seamless and irresistible logic" of the *Cur deus homo* "as displaying some of the most destructive tensions" in the tradition of the atonement (introduction and 76-89).

4 Cf. my "The Devil and Virtue. Anselm of Canterbury's universal order," in István P. Bejczy and Richard Newhauser, eds., *Virtue and Ethics in the Twelfth Century*, (Leiden: Brill Academic Publishers, 2005), 33-51.

5 Jasper Hopkins, *A Companion to the Study of St. Anselm* (Minneapolis: University of Minnesota Press, 1972), 40.

6 The critical edition of Anselm's letters is in *S. Anselmi Cantuariensis Archiepiscopi Opera Omnia*, ed. Franciscus S. Schmitt, vols. 3-5 of 6 (Edinburgh: Nelson, 1946-1961). For an English version: *The Letters of Saint Anselm of Canterbury*, trans. Walter Fröhlich, 3 vols. (Kalamazoo: Cistercian Publications, 1990-1994). An invaluable study of the letters is Sally Vaughn, *St Anselm and the Handmaidens of God. A Study of Anselm's Correspondence with Women* (Turnhout: Brepols, 2002). Unless otherwise noted, references to Anselm's works in the following are the standard ones of the *Opera Omnia* cited above.

excellent source for his ethical thought and moral practice.[7] Moreover, the discursive style of treatises, especially evident in the method of dialogue much favored by Anselm, demands a far more formal and logically necessary intellectual argumentation than the strongly personal and exhortative form of his pedagogical letters, which cut more nearly to the quick, and to the personal moral fiber both of his readers and of himself.

Is there in the emphasis which scholars have generally placed on Anselm's treatises what Stuart Hampshire in another context has called "a snobbery of abstract thought at the expense of perception of the contingent, of the concrete, of the particular, of the historical accident, of the objects of the presumed lower reaches of the mind"?[8] And even, are Anselm himself and his thought victims of this tension in later historiography, philosophy and theology? This contribution as such already affirms the earlier question, but with regard to the latter it will demonstrate that far from falling into a snobbery of intellectualism, Anselm's construct and injunction of obedience, strict as it is, yet allows his correspondents sufficient room for their personal needs, moral decisions and more generally for their freedom of choice without diminishing its logical or, to be sure, its cosmological rigor.

The spontaneity of true obedience

Things in the infralapsarian world are not as they ought to be, and this is most clear for Anselm when he analyses the concept of "obedience." Richard Southern has pointed out that for him obedience is "the fundamental rule of the universe," but Anselm himself is rather more subtle.[9] This ruling obedience is not at all associated with force or even violence in the sense that reasoning creatures are pressed by some external, metaphysical power to be obedient to it. They are, in fact, members of the ordered reality created by a personal God even if the devil ultimately does not want to accept his particular place in that hierarchy of created beings. For Anselm, obedience rather is an act of internal freedom that totally acknowledges

---

7 In his intellectual biography of Anselm, Richard W. Southern, *Saint Anselm. A Portrait in a Landscape* (Cambridge: Cambridge University Press, 1990), makes extensive use of the letters. The present article takes a similar approach, although I believe the letters are more systematically coherent than Southern does; cf. my "The Devil and Virtue" (as in n. 4).

8 Stuart Hampshire, *Morality and Conflict* (Oxford: Blackwell, 1983), 152-153.

9 Southern, *Saint Anselm*, 218 (as in n. 7); Southern writes extensively about Anselm and obedience, mainly from a biographical stance: see chapter 11 (pp. 254-276).

with praise and love the well-structured cosmological plan of the Creator and the assigned positions in it reserved for rational beings, whether angels or humankind. "Original obedience"–if a pun might be allowed– is simple and true, and it stands in opposition to the multiplicity caused by the Fall, by the original sin.[10] In Anselm's terminology this simplicity and truth are literally such because freedom of choice–choosing freely to be obedient–allows for only one choice, namely a choice for the good. Freedom in Anselm's definition does not mean to have the option of choosing between good and evil.

Free will as an option of willing either for good or for evil is for Anselm not a real choice at all. Such a "free" will might well under certain circumstances lead to evil, and once mired there it would be impossible to escape its sinking sands. In *Cur deus homo* Anselm puts it this way: "For simple and true obedience occurs when rational nature freely (*sponte*) and without necessity keeps the will which it has received from God."[11] "Rational nature" here takes the angels and humankind together as freely thinking and willing creatures. "True obedience," in the first instance supralapsarian obedience, that is, and the obedience restored to man through Christ, then, are unrestrained, spontaneous–that is: originating in an ordered fashion from within the rational being who chooses to be obedient. Alexander the Monk reports Anselm to have said that he who does not obey from the heart (*ex corde*) and through love (*ex amore*) but only on account of outside pressure does not have the gift of obedience.[12] Obedience is especially a graceful, natural–in Anselmian terminology, God-given to and received by rational beings–activity of thanksgiving to the Creator which fully acknowledges the original *and* also the once again repaired beauty of the universe.[13] This is *not* mere, coerced submission to the order of creation and recreation on the pain of eternal death. Far more than this,

---

10　For the concept of "multiplicity" in connection with sin and the fall of rational creatures, see my "The Devil and Virtue" (as in n. 4).

11　Cu 1.10 (p. 65): "Nam tunc est simplex et vera oboedientia, cum rationalis natura non necessitate, sed sponte servat voluntatem a deo acceptam." The English translation is from *Anselm of Canterbury*, vol. 3, trans. Jasper Hopkins and Herbert Richardson (Toronto: Mellen Press, 1976), 65, which is closer to the Latin (and more elegant) than Richard Regan's (see n. 15, below).

12　Alexander the Monk, *Liber ex dictis Beati Anselmi*, ed. Richard W. Southern and Franciscus S. Schmitt, *Memorials of St. Anselm* (Oxford: Oxford University Press, 1969), 105-195, esp. 161.

13　Cf. my "*Propter utilitatem et rationis pulchritudinem amabilis*. The aesthetics of Anselm's *Cur deus homo*," in Paul Gilbert, H. Kohlenberger and E. Salman, eds., '*Cur deus homo*'. *Atti del Cognresso Anselmiano Internazionale. Roma, 21-23 maggio 1998* (Rome: Pontificio Ateneo S. Anselmo, 1999), 717-730.

it is a joyful acclamation of God's order of being, and the reward of this is in that joy itself.

Anselm wants nothing to do with coerced obedience. The spontaneity that he ascribes to willing or choosing is not an unordered one; it is the result of a rational creature's internal deliberation that derives from the ordered love of God's creation which lies at the very heart of the beauty of the cosmos.[14] For Anselm the paragon of spontaneous, non-coerced obedience is that of Christ. Although Christ in his penultimate prayer in Gethsemane prayed to the Father "Not according to my will, but yours" (Matt. 26, 39), he underwent death voluntarily, and was not forced into it by anything other than by his own love. In his vivid discussion with Boso, his interlocutor, in *Cur deus homo* I, 8, Anselm states categorically that "the Father did not coerce (*invitum coegit*) Christ to face death against his will, or give permission for him to be killed, but Christ himself of his own volition (*sponte*) underwent death in order to save mankind."[15] Boso will have nothing of this and calls up a host of texts (Phil. 2,8; Heb. 5,8; Rom. 8,31; John 6,38; 14,3 and 18,11; Matt. 26,39 and 26,42) to counter Anselm's point. A little shrilly like a student, he concludes that it is overtly clear (*plus*) that "Christ endured death under the compulsion of obedience, rather than through the intention of his own free will."[16] Not one to be caught out by logical analysis and linguistic distinctions, Anselm at the beginning of chapter 9 immediately reiterates that Christ died voluntarily, and he proceeds here and in the next chapter to carefully parse the texts which Boso has adduced to bolster his idea in order to prove the student wrong. He does this against the backdrop of what he had earlier written about the logical and grammatical use of the notions of truth, rectitude, and willing or choosing in the *Three Treatises* (*De veritate, De libertate arbitrii, De casu diaboli*).

Anselm then concludes his argument in this chapter on a synthetic level, discussing with the help of his typical use of the negation what we mean when we say that someone wishes for something: "For we often say that someone wishes something because there is something else that

---

14 Cf. my *"Propter utilitatem"* (as in n. 13).

15 Cu 1.8-9 (esp. pp. 60-64), for the Biblical texts Boso and Anselm debate; the quotation is on p. 60. The translation is by Richard Regan in Anselm of Canterbury, *The Major Works*, ed. Brian Davis and Gillian R. Evans (Oxford: Oxford University Press, 1998), 275ff.. The Latin reads: "Non enim eum invitum ad mortem ille coegit aut occidi permisit, sed idem ipse sponte sua mortem sustinuit, ut homines salvaret."

16 Cu 1.8 (p. 61): "In his omnibus plus videtur Christus oboedientia cogente quam spontanea voluntate disponente mortem sustinuisse."

he does not wish for, the reasoning being that if he did not wish for this second thing, his first alleged wish would not be fulfilled."[17] In his way of approaching philosophical and theological problems from an analysis of ordinary language, he gives as an example what we say about someone who finds himself in a draughty room lit by a candle: "He wants the lamp to go out," when properly speaking he does not want to close the window through which the draught is coming which is putting out the candle. Applied to the problem of the voluntary obedience of Christ, Anselm reiterates a point made earlier in *Cur deus homo*. The Father did not will to save the world by any other means than by the death of the Son in the sense that he did not want to see the world saved by any other means than that a man should perform a deed of such magnitude. But this still left for the Son a *spontaneous* obedience: "Since no one else could perform the deed, this consideration was as weighty, from the point of view of the Son, in his desire for the salvation of mankind, *as if (quantum)* the Father were instructing him to die." But Christ *could* have not obeyed; it was only his love for the Father and at the same time for humankind that allowed him freely to will this obedience. Thus we might say inexactly that God wanted to save the world by the death of his Son, but precisely speaking that would be wrong. Precisely speaking, God does not want the world not to be saved, but it is the Son, not the Father, who positively offers himself up to do so out of the innate spontaneity of his love which is proper to him. This we *call* the Son's obedience.

In *De libertate arbitrii* Anselm had already put down his ideas on what it is in principle for rational beings–humans and angels, including the angel who was still to fall, and even God–to choose. Free choice or willing freely and spontaneously has two elements: it is always for the good and it always functions beyond the reach of external compunction or force. At the beginning of the dialogue, the Teacher states unequivocally: "I don't think freedom of choice is the power to sin and not to sin. After all, if this were its definition, then neither God nor the angels in their present state,

---

17 Anselm's use of the negative to drive home philosophical points and to analyse ordinary language is treated masterfully by Desmod P. Henry, *The Logic of St Anselm* (Oxford: Clarendon Press, 1967), 207-219. See also Marinus B. Pranger, *Consequente Theologie. Een Studie over het Denken van Anselmus van Canterbury* (Assen: Van Gorcum, 1975). My own translations into Dutch of the Three Treatises emphasize the importance of this procedure for understanding Anselm on truth and the will (successively Kampen: Kok Agora, 1990; Kampen: Kok Agora, 1997; Kampen: Klement, 2002).

who cannot sin, would have free choice–which it is impious to say."[18] We must, says Anselm, if we are to make sense, use philosophical terms un-equivocally. Thus to will obedience to God is–by the definition which ap-plies to God as well–to will it freely and spontaneously, something that is a given to rational beings inasmuch as they are creatures and exist. Anselm goes very far in emphasizing the power and extent of the willing of ration-al beings both before and after the Fall. At the close of De casu diaboli in chapter 28, he argues that even the devil's power to will what he ought not to will was always good with respect to its essence, which it received from God. The devil only fell when he did not use that power to will correctly. For Anselm, willing correctly or with rectitude is willing itself. When, in other words, that angel did not will, he fell into the nothingness of evil.[19] He fell because he did not spontaneously–out of his own essence–act in an obedient way. Properly (proprie) speaking, Anselm would say that the devil did not will evil but rather that he did not choose for the good, and thus he fell.[20] Over and against the devil's not willing stands Christ's spon-taneous willing–with respect not to his Godhead but to his position as a rational human but sinless creature–to obedience, although he could have not willed. In the last case, however, he would not have been love, and as such he would not have been Christ.

Anselm argues for all of this with an inexorable logic and analysis of language. He is utterly clear that even not willing the good for an instance immediately led to the fall into evil of the erstwhile good angel. This evil is so terrifying to both the Teacher and the Student of De casu diaboli that they almost fall from their roles as intelligent, faithful enquirers into the problems of truth and evil, showing a rare bit of existential angst. They shudder with dread at the mere mention of this evil. At the beginning of winding up their discussion in Chapter 26 both use the Latin word "horreo," to tremble with fear, and only in the analysis do they employ the

---

18   L 1 (p. 207). The translation is by Thomas Williams, Anselm. Three Philosophical Dialogues (Indianapolis: Hackett, 2002), 32. Anselm argues in chapter 25 of De casu diaboli that after the fall of the devil, the good angels can no longer fall.

19   On the "nothingness of evil" in Anselm see Christian Schäfer, Unde Malum. Die Frage nach dem Woher des Bösen bei Plotin, Augustinus und Dionysius (Würzburg: Königs-hausen & Neumann, 2002), esp. 478-481.

20   For Anselm's use of the term 'proprie,' see Eileen Serene, "Anselm's modal concep-tions," in Simo Knuuttila, ed., Reforging the Great Chain of Being, (Dordrecht: Reidel, 1980), 117-162, and Desmond P. Henry, "St Anselm and the linguistic disciplines," Anselm Studies 2 (1988): 319-332; brief but extremely helpful comments in Ferdinand E. Cranz, "Augustine and Anselm of Canterbury," in Cranz, Reorientations of Western Thought from Antiquity to the Renaissance, ed. Nancy Struever (Aldershot: Ashgate Variorum, 2006), section IV, 78-83.

more neutral term "timeo," to fear. Even here the last term is colored by the former one.[21] This is the kind of utter fear with which we are familiar from the early medieval monastic experience such as that of Otloh of St. Emmeram (c.1010-c.1070), who writes extensively about the mental and even extreme physical anguish caused him by the devil in the course of his "real" conversion.[22]

True obedience is particularly, of course, the attribute and attitude of Christ who chooses to become a sacrifice out of pure love for the Father and for the rational beings–humankind–who have fallen from grace through the machination of the devil and themselves. At the same time, true obedience is so exacting that it is not only, strictly speaking, the not willing of the good or willing more than it is allotted by God that leads to the fall into the nothingness of evil. Even willing the good *at the wrong time*, that is to say willing it at the time which is not yet God's time, leads to damnation. In the middle of chapter 4 of *De casu diaboli*, the Student has just affirmed that the fallen angel ought to have willed what he received from God and that of course he did not sin by willing that. The Teacher replies, "Then he willed something that he did not have and that he ought not to have willed at that time (*tunc*), just as Eve willed to be 'like the gods' before (*priusquam*) God willed that."[23] We might paraphrase Anselm's idea of the fall of the angel by saying that he sought the goal of existence *too* much rather than too little, so much so that he jumped the gun, so to speak. He willed before he was allowed to will what was good. A good, contemporary example can illustrate this up to a point. Jon Drummond, the 100-metre sprint athlete, during the Ninth World Championships in Athletics (2003), wanted so much to get to his goal that he could not abide the order of things, made a false start just before the pistol fired, and disqualified himself. Summing up the Teacher says, "the devil spontaneously stopped willing what he ought and justly lost what he had, since he spontaneously and unjustly willed what he didn't have and what he ought not to have willed."[24] It must be pointed out, then, that it is not only the single-mindedness toward the good and the putting aside of "un-

---

21　Ca 26 (p. 274).

22　Cf. my "The Devil and Virtue," 37-39 (as in n. 4); for Otloh's description of his experience: Otloh of Sankt Emmeram, *Liber de temptatione cuisdam monachi*, ed. and trans. Sabine Gäbe (Bern: Lang, 1992); for further analysis: Ineke van't Spijker, "Saints and Despair: Twelfth-Century Hagiography as 'Intimate Biography'," in Anneke B. Mulder-Bakker, ed., *The Invention of Saintliness* (London: Routledge, 2002), 185-202.

23　Ca 4 (p. 241; trans. Williams, 63, as in n. 18).

24　Ca 4 (p. 242; trans. Williams, 64, as in n. 18).

orderedness," which inform the ethical, virtuous rational being, but also a reckoning with the ordered flight of time's arrow. Thus, Anselm's ethical order would seem to be unrelenting in the working as such of willing and choosing for the good, and it is also relentless in the historical timing of that will and choice. Who can possibly live this out in practice, even if it is in the relative protection of the monastic life of the eleventh century?

Obedience as defense against the devil

In his *Morality and Conflict*, Stuart Hampshire takes to task most of the history of ethical thought because according to him it ignores the individual moral conflicts of people and demands that they accede to a "timeless," general categorical imperative. He writes:

> Whether it is Aristotelian, Kantian, Humean, or utilitarian, moral philosophy can do harm when it implies that there ought to be, and that there can be, fundamental agreement on, or even a convergence in, moral ideals–the harm is that the reality of conflict, both within individuals and within societies, is disguised by the myth of humanity as a consistent moral unit across time and space. There is a false blandness in the myth, an aversion from reality. We know that we in fact have essential divisions within us as persons and that we experience moral conflicts arising from them. A person hesitates between two contrasting ways of life, and sets of virtues, and he has to make a very definite, and even final, determination between them. This determination is a negation, and normally the agent will feel that the choice has killed, or repressed, some part of him.[25]

Indeed, at first sight Anselm, too, would seem to fall among those whom Hampshire castigates. Closer examination, though, shows that Anselm's ideas must be clearly delineated from the kind of 'intellectualist' ethics of the 'western,' 'Greek' tradition which is fundamental to the systems Hampshire criticizes. Anselm–and I am sure, too, many others medieval and Christian thinkers–distinguish themselves clearly from this mainstream intellectualist movement (which the history of western philosophy has accentuated since its invention in the late eighteenth century, an era of unmitigated rationalism). Anselm not at all believes that rational beings must be seen as consistent moral units down through history. It is precisely the *lack* of such a moral consistency that caused the devil to not will what he ought to have willed. Moreover, after the fall of the devil, hu-

---

25 Hampshire, *Morality and Conflict*, 155 (as in n. 8).

mans have constantly to make final determinations between choosing for the good and, properly speaking according to Anselm, not choosing at all, which in ordinary locution we call choosing for evil. For Anselm there is no single choice or even inborn inclination once and for all for an ineffable Good. Christians and in particular the monastics entrusted to his care must constantly and unfailingly choose for the good which is clear from the injunctions of God through Scripture in the middle of a multitude of very real temptations and uncertainties. It is evident from his letters that he has an excellent insight into the divisions and hesitations which prey on his correspondents, and also often into their misgivings about having chosen to "negate" their earlier, non-monastic lives.

Out of many, here is an example from a letter Anselm wrote to the novice Ralph at Le Bec while he was himself traveling on Le Bec's business in England:

> For I know the malicious jealousy of the devil who is grinding his teeth, wasting away with envy at the thought that you are escaping from his hands, nay rather from his jaws. So I am certain he will attempt to deceive you in countless ways, by showing you either the hardship of the service of God which you have chosen or the delights of serving himself through love of the world which you have relinquished. Therefore, ...by God's grace I hope I can guard you against all his sly tricks–which abound in fallacies and folly...[26]

Other letters, too, further attest to his understanding of the hesitations and often grievous worries which plague his fellow monks. Thus from Lyon he writes a letter partly on politics but also as a counselor of souls to Farman, Ordwy and Benjamin, monks of Christ Church, Canterbury.[27] Benjamin has terribly alleged to Anselm the loss of his soul because he is unable to speak to him, being so far away. Anselm tells him that this complaint has placed both his own soul and Anselm's in grave danger, because his request is impossible to grant. He continues sternly but understands exactly what is needed:

> For it is not rational to follow wherever the impulse of our soul drives us without discrimination, even if with a good intention. I cannot perceive that your soul is in danger of perdition just because you are not able to speak to me... Therefore I beseech and advise you, dearest son, to bear what God's providence has in store for your soul without offence, and according to how you see him dispose of us and what belongs to us strive, as one who is reasonable and who has trust in God, to save yourself.

---

26 E 99 (1079/1080) (ed. Schmitt, 3: 230; trans. Fröhlich, 1: 248, as in n. 6).

27 E 355 (1104/1105) (ed. Schmitt, 4: 296; trans. Fröhlich, 3: 93-94, as in n. 6), from which the following quotation is taken.

Yet, for Anselm it is neither rationality nor logic which determines ethics and the moral life; neither is it–paradoxically in the light of the central place of it in the history of philosophy–knowledge which ultimately shows the way to Truth. In a letter to Walter, a monk of St. Wandrille near Fontenelle, he gently teases him about his questions which *rational knowledge* might answer, and he then continues, slightly jesting:

> I pray you, therefore, lest by despising my foolishness you refuse to have regard for our charity. Charity should be loved more than knowledge. *For knowledge puffs up but charity edifies* (1 Cor. 8:1). Moreover, since all useful knowledge depends on charity–on it indeed *depend all the law and the prophets* (Matt. 22:40)–and since where *two or three are gathered together in the name* of Truth, it says that it is *in the midst of them* (Matt. 18:20), I trust in the promise of Truth, that, if we come together in its name with the affection of *charity*, the knowledge of the Truth be with us.[28]

Georgi Kapriev has dialectically remarked that this insight of Anselm's does not mean that knowledge is of no importance, but that knowledge-of-the-real-kind follows chastity, the charity of God's commandments and humility: "Dementsprechend legt er in den Grund der Gotteserkenntnis nicht die Ausbildung des Intellekts, d.h. seine dialektische oder hermeneutische Schulung, sondern die Reinigung des Herzens durch den Glauben, die Erleuchtung der Augens duch das Einhalten der Gebote Gottes und der demütigen Gehorsam (*humilis oboedientia*), da die erreichte Selbstverringerung zur Weisheit führt. Damit schreitet man zum Geist. Auf diese Weise ist der Gehorsam auch eine Erhebung zur Befriedigung des Intellekts,... "[29]

In another letter, this time to the monks of the monastery of Saint Werburgh at Chester, Anselm again emphasizes the very importance of this obedience:

> Obedience could have kept man in paradise from where he was expelled through disobedience, and nobody will reach the heavenly kingdom except through obedience. Consider that if man was thrown out into the extreme misery we suffer in this world for one single act of disobedience, how much we ought to abhor it and strive for the good of obedience. Therefore show your abbot obedience in all things, not merely in deeds but also in intention, and maintain peace and unity among yourselves through mutual love. You

---

28 E 85 (1077/1078) (ed. Schmitt, 3: 210; trans. Fröhlich, 1: 221, as in n. 6).

29 Georgi Kapriev, *...ipsa vita et veritas. Der 'ontologischee Gottesbeweis' und die Ideenwelt Anselms von Canterbury* (Leiden: Brill, 1998), 291.

will be able to foster and maintain this love if each one strives *not to bend the other to his will, but to bend himself to the will of the other.*[30]

In slightly different words, paraphrasing much of Anselm's thought on true obedience and obedience, we might say that now that the simple and true obedience of Paradise has been lost, the *strict* obedience of monks and nuns to their abbots and spiritual directors, points the way back to Paradise, that is, to the heavenly kingdom, and that once we realize this we may "practice" this obedience in the charity that we duly bear towards our brothers and sisters, to each in their own various ways. This is the practical ethic of the monastery, which as a *hortus conclusus* both etiologically remakes lost Eden and teleologically foreshadows that heavenly garden where the child plays freely with the serpent.

It is clear that Anselm does not take obedience seriously only in his theoretical works. It is of great concern to him also in daily practice. The monastic profession of obedience to the Rule and to one's superiors once one had entered into the monastery was not in the least to be trifled with by anyone, least of all by himself. His own biography demonstrates how carefully and circumspectly Anselm treated his personal vows of obedience and mutual charity both to his fellow monks and to his superiors when he was called upon to leave Le Bec for the primacy at Canterbury of the Church of England.[31] It was only after much tearful soul-searching and an extended and sometimes dramatic dialogue with his brother monks that he gave heed to that vocation and they, on their part, allowed him to loosen his ties of obedient charity to them.

The monastery, they were sure, attempts to safeguard its denizens against the violent attacks of the devil in society outside its walls. The vows of chastity, poverty, *stabilitas loci* and obedience served to demarcate the space in which monks might be safe, but this does not mean that they did not have to work at perseverance in their godly profession. It is especially the obedience to their superior and ultimately to the abbot–the "stand-in" for God himself–in the monastic, temporal safe haven which Anselm emphasises time and again in his letters. This obedience is an important shield of the monastic against evil both without and in particular from within. Thus, for example, Anselm writes to Eulalia, abbess of Shaftesbury, and her nuns that true obedience (*vera oboedientia*) occurs when the will

---

30   E 231 (1102) (ed. Schmitt, 4: 137; trans. Fröhlich, 2: 202, as in n. 6); and see similar remarks in C 3.1.9-14.

31   Southern, *Saint Anselm*, esp. 264-274 (as in n. 7).

of the subordinate obeys the will of the superior in such a way that "wherever the subordinate may be, she wishes what she knows the superior wishes, as long as it is not against the will of God."[32] In fact, their monastic community is to be a temple of God. This is demonstrated by their living in a holy manner, and "you live in a holy manner if you diligently keep your rule and your intention"–in other words, if you are obedient to your profession. Tellingly, Anselm exhorts the nuns to "dread regress with all your heart," and here he again uses the word "horreo," which he has much earlier associated with the chilling shudder Teacher and Student feel when they are confronted even with the mere term "evil." They are to strive to keep their works and hearts always as if they are in God's sight. By using the word "to strive," Anselm signals that keeping the good–keeping truth and rectitude, as he puts it in De veritate–takes conscious effort. After the fall, obedience has become exceedingly difficult and this is why the protection of the monastery and its strict rules is essential to the ultimate well-being of the monastics. As everyone in the eleventh century knew, the devil can be defeated by leading a virtuous life and the best place to do this is in the monastic environment.[33]

If for anyone in the Middle Ages, Hampshire's contention holds for Anselm and his coreligionists: "My claim is that morality has its sources in conflict, in the divided soul and between contrary claims, and that there is no rational path that leads from these conflicts to harmony and to an assured solution, and to the normal and natural conclusion."[34] By "rational" Hampshire is referring to abstract thought which loses sight of particular, contingent experience. Anselm is highly aware and extremely sensitive to the dialectic between the cosmological order of creation and the duty of created, rational beings to hold fast to their positions in it by spontaneously choosing for what they ought, the good which God affords them. Morality for him is indeed born out of conflict, namely that between choosing or not choosing what ought to be chosen; yet morality is not in that conflict itself–which appears to be Hamphsire's position–but it lies in the ultimate choice for God's will, which is Truth and Rectitude.

For Anselm there is no such thing as an absolute demand of a mechanical, rationalist obedience, say in the sense of Spinoza or Kant. More than a few times he gives advice on the 'elasticity'–one might say–of the rule of obedience. A telling example is in a letter of 1100-1109 to Odo, a monk

---

32   E 403 (1106) (ed. Schmitt, 4: 347; trans. Fröhlich, 3: 167, as in n. 6).
33   Cf. my "The Devil and Virtue" (as in n. 4).
34   Hampshire, *Morality and Conflict*, 152 (as in n. 8).

and cellarer, who is old and feels his obedience is lagging, and is literally terrified about that.[35] Anselm tells him soothingly:

> Do not fear that because of the weakness of your body you will not be able to work and care for the things which have to be done in that obedience as effectively as you once could in good health and youth. God does not demand from you more than you can do. *Do not let any adversities, from wherever they may come, with which the enemy of your soul wants to vex and tire you, disturb you so that you give up before the end and lose the reward of perseverance.*

In fact, here as elsewhere, Anselm is saying that the devil may even use the injunction of absolute obedience as a way to tire out and vex the true believer. Similarly he writes to the religious sisters Seit, Edit, Thydit, Lwerun, Dirgit and Godit, their abbot Robert and chaplain William that they need not be overly worried if their emotions are unbecoming: "Do not fear that such emotions or thoughts will be imputed to you as sins as long as your intention does not associate itself with them on any account."[36] At the same time he admits that it is very difficult to "quench" such thoughts once we have admitted them to our mind, and he beseeches his readers "with my whole heart to persevere in this holy and pious intention." Nonetheless, it is clear from these examples that Anselm has a sharp eye for the evil desires that plague those leading the religious life. These desires are multiple and they vary with the individuals who are their victims. In many of his letters, he tries to give his correspondents individual counsel and aid so that they are able to withstand these false desires and to not consent to them. Thereby they can learn more and more to aim their spontaneous intention towards the single good of willing what and as they ought.

Obedience in this infralapsarian world can never attain to true heavenly obedience. In the end, only the perseverance given at Creation to the freedom of choice which is inalienable from rational, human beings–given, that is, with their being truly rational and directed to rectitude–must be revivified by God through the trust the believer puts in him. An analogy may be drawn from the process which Anselm describes in his argument for the existence of God in the *Proslogion*. After his performative

---

35 E 436 (1100-1109) (ed. Schmitt, 4: 384-385; trans. Fröhlich, 3: 217-18, as in n. 6).

36 E 414 (1106-1109) (ed. Schmitt, 4: 359-362; trans. Fröhlich, 3: 184-87, as in n. 6). Simo Knuuttila, *Emotions in Ancient and Medieval Philosophy* (Oxford: Oxford University Press, 2006), 222, has pointed out that "paraphrasing Augustine, Anselm of Canterbury stated that sin does not consist in having desires but in consenting to them."

demonstration of God's existence, he at once doubts it, and he cries out to God to help him. It is then God himself who demonstrates his own existence.[37] Thus, too, true obedience in this fallen world needs the help of God if it is to attain its goal of beatitude and aesthetic union. It is in this obedient tension between the limits of our own obedience and that which God requires of us that the devil is defeated.[38] It is in the spontaneous choosing for what one ought to will within this moral conflict that a virtuous life can be led, which leads everyone but which, too, takes account of one's *own capacity.*

---

37 See my "The performative heart of St Anselm's *Proslogion*," in D. Luscombe and G.R. Evans, eds., *Anselm: Aosta, Bec and Canterbury* (Sheffield: Sheffield University Press 1996), 229-237.

38 Cf. my "The Devil and Virtue" (as in n. 4).

THE MONASTIC CHALLENGE: REMARKS

HELMUT KOHLENBERGER

"I called my son out of Egypt," runs Hosea 11:1, and the son is Israel. Egypt is the land from which Israel is called. Mary and Joseph's flight with Jesus to Egypt and then their return from Egypt are an echo of this calling. When Freud put forward his thesis that the "man Moses" brought the Jews into being out of Egypt, the sovereignty of spirit, the call into the Word of God was asserted once more against the claim of origins, but now in the form of a question. This sovereignty as a questioning of the traditional bond is seen rightly as a provocation, which establishes a new kind of bond.[1] The connection with the God of Abraham, Isaac and Jacob, and so with the sacrifice of Abraham and with "Joseph and his brothers," transformed fatherhood into the calling of a single one; it raised fatherhood up over genealogy. Israel must pass through Egypt and the desert. With his world-historical spectacles on, Jacob Burckhardt saw in monasticism the late child of the spirit of ancient Egypt. (Monasticism, after all, lives by spiritual paternity.) Culturally, Burckhardt tells us, the monks had their own version of colonisation when they spread to Europe, which was quite distinct from the early Christian missions in the communities across the Mediterranean from Paul through to Augustine. Within Augustine's calling, as we read it in the *Confessions*, there are the twin strands of St. Anthony's *Life*–the way of the hermit–and the command to take up and read.

The monastic life was radical. It ran against the grain of the ancient world; against Alexandria, whose marshes proved too much for Origen. There was an antiquarianism in the older civilisations which stifled word and life out of anything that looked forward. Defying the pallid city, drained of life, the natural procession of generations fashioned a life for

---

1 Cf. Jan Assmann, *Die Mosaische Unterscheidung* (Munich: Hanser, 2003). In the Mosaic distinction the telling apart of justice and injustice is brought directly into relation with God. This process establishes a tissue of links among the sacred texts relating to the law. The same discernment appears, trenchant as ever, in the New Testament, for example in the sayings about the fire cast down on the earth (Lk 12:49) and the sword (Mt 10:34).

itself around a contradiction: the contradiction by the word of the flesh, which was thus withdrawn from corruption and temptation. Word was to become flesh in the *ruminatio* of Holy Writ. Separating himself from the old ties, from their dispersal and half-truths, the solitary set out on a constant battle with himself.[2] And so the solitary became above all the disciple of a teacher. The way from world's ruin led to a new life, a second life, a Utopia. It led to the refuge in the desert, the occupying of an uninhabited landscape. The simple conditions required to live gained a hitherto unknown intensity. Under the sovereignty of the Word, the flesh became the object of vigilance and discipline. Fasting, wakes, manual labour.[3] A life-long sacrifice begins. By going to the very edge of his physical existence, the solitary goes beyond himself. Some defining frankness or simplicity in Anthony, it was said, meant you could identify him straightaway in the middle of a crowd.[4] Or to put it another way: we are told the monks were like angels; and later on it became a point of discussion whether men took the places, one for one, left vacant by the fallen angels in heaven.

The monk lives at the rim of the civilised world. His marginal existence was not likely to become a way of life for all. It is hardly surprising that the church of the bishops had its misgivings, and only with time became accustomed to these steadfastly independent monastic colonies. Against the monks' world-denying ordinance, meanwhile, the memory of the always-present reality of everyman continued to assert itself, not least in the remembrance of the dead. The dead found a place among the living.

Cassian was no doubt the greatest of those who translated the Egyptian desert tradition for the western church.[5] His first concern was for the discernment of spirits and for a frankly technical apprenticeship in the ascetic life, in which the Word of God became a kind of second nature. His writings and *Conferences* say nothing of material organisation, only of a strenuous inner listening and speaking. Through listening and speaking the monk is to come to an equilibrium, and on this state of things the happy few would found their life. Later, this apparently Utopian project would be given organisational structure. The *Rule of Benedict*

---

2 The command to "make yourselves separate bodies" (Neh 8:15) is quoted by Peter Brown, *The Body and Society. Sexual Renunciation in Early Christianity* (New York: Columbia University Press, repr. 2008), 241, as a motto of the ascetic movement.

3 Ibid., 237: "In the desert tradition, the body was allowed to become the discreet mentor of the proud soul."

4 Ibid., 226.

5 For what follows, see Conrad Leyser, *Authority and Asceticism from Augustine to Gregory the Great* (Oxford: Clarendon Press, 2000).

brings together the art of self-discipline in speaking and living with the
need to answer to the various wills of the monastery, all pressing to be
heard. With this the question of authority arises. The *Rule* stresses both
the subjection of everyone to the abbot and of the abbot to the *Rule*, to the
Rule as master; and it requires the basic duty of obedience of each member of the community to all the others. The monastery is not an attempt
to make a paradise on earth, and for this reason authority is a precarious
thing. Only with Gregory the Great, the monk on the throne of Peter, did
the monastic become the grounds of a spiritual teaching reaching beyond
the monks to the world, and this with an eschatological and missionary
earnest, despite another old and formative tradition in the western church
which made it open not only to the spiritual elites, but from the time of
the fall of Rome, to everyman. The monasteries became transitional to the
new age. With their sustained repetition of the Psalms, they recalled the
passing over of Israel. They recalled the heavenly Jerusalem. The aloofness
of the monastery from its surroundings could not survive the later build-
up of regional lordships. It is in this phase that the work of Anselm of
Canterbury was accomplished; and Anselm's pattern of thought, erected
on the matrix of the monastic life, has exemplary status. The principle of
libertas (cf. *libertas ecclesiae*) was one he made his own, above all in his
activity as archbishop. In the shadow of the Norman conquerors' abbey
at Canterbury, a world of kings and bishops took shape. In the enthusiasm of its incipient rationalism, this world reached into every aspect of
life, including that of the cloister. The tracing of borders by the Word, in
which the monk finds his calling, runs right through Anselm's thinking.
The monk is now one who both walks across and guards the borders.

Anselm forsook the house of his father, and later, in his prayers, he addressed St. Paul as father and mother in the life of faith.[6] It is faith that
drives him. Already in the *Monologion*, the inner disquiet that characterises his prayers pushes the old Augustinian question about God and the
soul, the question of the *imago dei*, to the edge of thought's possibility,
seizing it in the Word of creation from nothing, in other words in the episode in which the emptying out of meaning reveals all there is to be utterly dependent, and so to appear under a new light. The disquiet gives rise
to the phrase: *quomodo illa similitudo quae in acie mentis rem ipsam cogi-
tantis exprimitur.*[7] This word has the effect of framing the thought of non-

---

6   See Oratio 10, in Anselm, *Sancti Anselmi Opera omnia*, 6 vols., ed. Franciscus Sale-
sius Schmitt (Seckau-Rome-Edinburgh: Thomas Nelson and Sons, 1938-1961), 3: 39-41.
7   Anselm, *Monologion* 10, in *Sancti Anselmi Opera omnia*, 1: 25 (ll. 20-21).

being, takes the Word of God as the grounds of distinction of all that is and is not. This Word cannot be grasped as itself, it must be accepted. Yet it gives shape to the wandering back and forth of thought. In the *Proslogion*, Anselm condensed the power of distinction into the *id quo maius cogitari nequit*. And this *id quo maius...* is an insight into the borderland where thought is at home, whence it comes "somewhat to understand" (*aliquatenus intelligere*).[8] At the same time, it holds in check, with a formal method, the risk that self-doubt might decline into an endless eddying. It is a method which forces Gaunilo (who responds to Anselm's argument) to his confession: that he does not know whether he can think his own not-being, as long as he knows with the greatest certainty that he is.[9] Even this certainty does not exist if one follows Anselm's next argument in the dialogue with his disciple, which is itself an example of the monk as teacher in the sense given by the *Rule*. Gaunilo's doubt, in strictest logical sequence, is thrown back onto the human condition and thus onto the limits of formal method: "What do you have which you have not received?" It was a commonplace of monastic thought to convey the make-up of creation and of its freedom through the example of the angel, and to see this make-up in its *perseverantia*, in its "holding to the truth." Self-will (*propria voluntas*) in this scheme of things, is a fall into non-being, and in speech this corresponds to the blind automatism of merely formal reductionism.[10] In the closed system of evil, the gesture of a freedom which is given is left to the province of the imaginary. In the activity of freedom, there is no such thing as mechanical predictability. (In this light, it is no doubt odd to speak of men replacing fallen angels, one for one.)

The angels' fall and the need to re-establish *rectitudo*, right-ordering, between God and man, lie behind the experience of evil in the world. In the soul, these conditions give speech. This forms the background to the teacher's rationalising task. He does not shy away from the last questions which, in prayer and meditation, have the form of speech. His method is one of monastic *discretio*, and this in turn is a form of life. It is called a

---

8   Anselm, *Proslogion* 1, in *Sancti Anselmi Opera omnia*, 1: 100 (l. 17); and see *Proslogion* 14, in ibid., 1: 111 (ll. 20-21).

9   Anselm, *Pro insipiente* 7, in *Sancti Anselmi Opera omnia*, 1: 129 (ll. 14-15).

10   See M.B. Pranger, *The Artificiality of Christianity: Essays on the Poetics of Monasticism* (Stanford: Stanford University Press, 2003), 108ff. Burcht Pranger's readings of Anselm, in the second part of the book, have the effect of liberating the text from the often narrow philosophical approaches to Anselm's thought.

militia.[11] In Anselm's mind this military life had nothing to do with the crusade which was going on around him. He handles the link with the earthly Jerusalem with elegant economy in his letter to the King of Jerusalem, warning against the seductions of flight into the imaginary and setting against this the monastic turn towards a heavenly Jerusalem. But he is careful to avoid the other obvious mistake, of supposing the monastery might be made an earthly paradise.[12] The *militia* to which the monk belongs keeps alive, for teacher and disciple alike, a spiritual fatherhood which becomes a teaching office; and it provides with a family all those who have left behind their own. Anselm went so far–anticipating a later age–as to compare the monk with a coin.[13] Yet he was himself unable to live out fully the life of a monk by his duties as archbishop, painfully construed by him as a further demand on his obedience.[14] A little later, Bernard of Clairvaux sounds the last chord of monastic *militia*, and by now an ambiguity has crept into its usage, a metaphorical sweep which tends to reify the heavenly Jerusalem.

In Anselm and Bernard we can see the two great figures at the twilight of the monastic age, with its constant leaning to the limits of human existence. After it came the decay of medieval Christianity into the rationalism of, for example, the Nominalist elite of the universities; into the mystical movements and the mathematics-based arts and sciences, none of which the Conciliar Movement was able to prevent. In the cognitive domain Descartes supposed he had found in Anselm's argument, once removed from its monastic context, the very grounds of thought, and so began one of the chief strands in modern philosophy.[15] Monasticism out-of-context

---

11   See Anselm's simile of monk as soldier (*miles*) in *Memorials of Saint Anselm*, ed. R.W Southern and F.S. Schmitt, Auctores Britannici Medii Aevi 1 (Oxford: Oxford University Press, 1969), 97-102.

12   Anselm's letter to King Baldwin, epistle 324, in *Sancti Anselmi Opera omnia*, 5: 255; and see the advice given by Anselm to Bishop Osmund of Salisbury concerning monks making the journey to Jerusalem (ep. 324, 85-6).

13   See *Memorials of Saint Anselm*, 76: *Tria cuique bono insunt denario, quae cuique bono monacho inesse debent. Denarius quippe bonus puro ex aere, recto pondere, monetaque legitima debet constare. Si enim ex his unum defuerit, venalis esse non poterit* ....

14   On this, R.W.Southern, *Saint Anselm. A Portrait in a Landscape* (Cambridge: Cambridge University Press, 1990), 186-94; and Eadmer, *Vita Anselmi*, ed. R.W. Southern (Edinburgh: T. Nelson, 1962), 21ff, on Anselm's obedience to Archbishop Maurilius of Rouen.

15   Karl Jaspers observed this with especial clarity in *Aus dem Ursprung denkende Metaphysiker* (München: Piper, 1957), 116 ff., esp. 132-136. Jaspers argues that Kant is opposing Anselm's argument which he did not know in its original form, while the structure of his thinking is comparable to Anselm's. Cf. Jaspers, *Anselm and Nicholas of Cusa*, vol. 2 of *The Great Philosophers*, ed. Hannah Arendt (New York: Harcourt Brace Jovanovich, 1974).

still operates as a social device in a setting where the repudiation of the traditional family is the norm. In circumstances where social bonds are weakened, it leads–this device–to a more or less latent totalitarian social structure, whose only (vain) hope of legitimacy is in rationalisation. The legitimacy is self-referential, can as a result never gain general assent, and so becomes the cause of permanent revolution. Perhaps the hooded figures who stalk the *banlieues*, and who are spoken of in the same breath as the 'coming insurrection,' are a replay (with all the artificiality the word suggests) of the monastic past. The monastic was no game; its command still has its sting.[16] "The desert grows/Woe to him who bears deserts within."[17]

---

16 See Elias Canetti, *Masse und Macht* (Frankfurt a.M.: Fischer Verlag, 30th ed., 2006), 357ff.

17 Friedrich Nietzsche, "Die Wüste wächst: weh Dem, der Wüsten birgt!" in *Werke*, ed. Karl Schlechta (München: C. Hanser, 6th ed., 1969), 2:540.

INDEX OF PERSONAL NAMES

Brill's Studies in
Intellectual History

Series Editor: A.J. Vanderjagt

142. Davenport, A.A. *Descartes's Theory of Action*. 2006. ISBN 978 90 04 15205 2
143. Mazzocco, A. *Interpretations of Renaissance Humanism*. 2006. ISBN 978 90 04 15244 1
144. Verbaal, W., Y. Maes & J. Papy (eds.). *Latinitas Perennis*. Volume I: The Continuity of Latin Literature. 2007. ISBN 978 90 04 15327 1
145. Boulton, D'Arcy J.D. & J.R. Veenstra (eds.). *The Ideology of Burgundy*. The Promotion of National Consciousness, 1364-1565. 2006. ISBN 978 90 04 15359 2
146. Ruler, H. van, A. Uhlmann & M. Wilson (eds.). *Arnold Geulincx* Ethics. With Samuel Beckett's Notes. Translated by M. Wilson. 2006. ISBN 978 90 04 15467 4 (Published as Vol. 1 in the subseries *Brill's Texts and Sources in Intellectual History*)
147. Radding, C.M. & A. Ciaralli (eds.). *The* Corpus Iuris Civilis *in the Middle Ages*. Manuscripts and Transmission from the Sixth Century to the Juristic Revival. 2007. ISBN 978 90 04 15499 5
148. Birkedal Bruun, M. *Parables: Bernard of Clairvaux's Mapping of Spiritual Topography*. 2007. ISBN 978 90 04 15503 9
149. Lehner, U. *Kants Vorsehungskonzept auf dem Hintergrund der deutschen Schulphilosophie und -theologie*. 2007. ISBN 978 90 04 15607 4
150. Warnar, G. *Ruusbroec*. Literature and Mysticism in the Fourteenth Century. Translated by D. Webb. 2007. ISBN 978 90 04 15869 6
151. Treschow, M., W. Otten & W. Hannam (eds.). *Divine Creation in Ancient, Medieval, and Early Modern Thought*. Essays Presented to the Rev'd Dr Robert D. Crouse. 2007. ISBN 978 90 04 15619 7
152. Juste, D. *Les* Alchandreana *primitifs*. Étude sur les plus anciens traités astrologiques latins d'origine arabe (Xe siècle). 2007. ISBN 978 90 04 15827 6 (Published as Vol. 2 in the subseries *Brill's Texts and Sources in Intellectual History*)
153. Chardonnens, L.S. *Anglo-Saxon Prognostics, 900-1100*. Study and Texts. 2007. ISBN 978 90 04 15829 0 (Published as Vol. 3 in the subseries *Brill's Texts and Sources in Intellectual History*)
154. Melve, L. *Inventing the Public Sphere*. The Public Debate during the Investiture Contest (c. 1030–1122). 2007. ISBN 978 90 04 15884 9
155. Velema, W.R.E. *Republicans*. Essays on Eighteenth-Century Dutch Political Thought. 2007. ISBN 978 90 04 16191 7
156. Boone, R.A. *War, Domination, and the* Monarchy of France, *Claude de Seyssel and the Language of Politics in the Renaissance*. 2007. ISBN 978 90 04 16214 3
157. Smith, P.J. *Dispositio*: Problematic Ordering in French Renaissance Literature. 2007. ISBN 978 90 04 16305 8
158 . Heddle, D.C. *John Stewart of Baldynneis' Roland Furious, A Scots Poem in its European Context*. 2007. ISBN 978 90 04 16318 8 (Published as Vol. 4 in the subseries *Brill's Texts and Sources in Intellectual History*)
159. Schuchard, M. (ed.). *Bernhard Varenius (1622-1650)*. 2007. ISBN 978 90 04 16363 8
160. Bejczy, I.P. (ed.). *Virtue Ethics in the Middle Ages*, Commentaries on Aristotle's *Nicomachean Ethics*, 1200-1500. 2008. ISBN 978 90 04 16316 4
161. Stern-Gillet, S. & K. Corrigan (eds.). *Reading Ancient Texts. Volume I: Presocratics and Plato*. Essays in Honour of Denis O'Brien. 2007. ISBN 978 90 04 16509 0
162. Stern-Gillet, S. & K. Corrigan (eds.). *Reading Ancient Texts. Volume II: Aristotle and Neoplatonism*. Essays in Honour of Denis O'Brien. 2007. ISBN 978 90 04 16512 0
164. Stefaniak, R.'*Mysterium Magnum*'. Michelangelo's Tondo Doni. 2008. ISBN 978 90 04 16544 1 (Published as Vol. 1 in the subseries *Brill's Studies on Art, Art History, and Intellectual History*)

165. Catana, L. *The Historiographical Concept 'System of Philosophy'*. Its Origin, Nature, Influence and Legitimacy. 2008. ISBN 978 90 04 16648 6

166. Goodare, J. & A.A. MacDonald (eds.). *Sixteenth-Century Scotland*. Essays in Honour of Michael Lynch. 2008. ISBN 978 90 04 16825 1

167. Van Bunge, W. & H. Bots (eds.). *Pierre Bayle (1647-1706), le philosophe de Rotterdam: Philosophy, Religion and Reception*. Selected Papers of the Tercentenary Conferenceheld at Rotterdam, 7-8 December 2006. 2008. ISBN 978 90 04 16536 6

168. Dixhoorn, A. van & S. Speakman Sutch. *The Reach of the Republic of Letters*. Literaryand Learned Societies in Late Medieval and Early Modern Europe (2 Vols.). 2008. ISBN 978 90 04 16955 5

169. Cohen, S. *Animals as Disguised Symbols in Renaissance Art*. 2008. ISBN 978 90 04 17101 5 (Published as Vol. 2 in the subseries *Brill's Studies on Art, Art History, and Intellectual History*)

170. Lennon, T.M. *The Plain Truth*. Descartes, Huet, and Skepticism. 2008. ISBN 978 90 04 17115 2

171. Lehner, U.L. (ed.). Beda Mayr, *Vertheidigung der katholischen Religion*. Sammt einem Anhange von der Möglichkeit einer Vereinigung zwischen unserer, und der evangelisch-lutherischen Kirche (1789). 2009. ISBN 978 90 04 17318 7 (Published as Vol. 5 in the subseries Brill s Texts and Sources in Intellectual History)

172. Rothkamm, J. *Institutio Oratoria*. Bacon, Descartes, Hobbes, Spinoza. 2009. ISBN 978 90 04 17328 6

173. Richardson, C.M. *Reclaiming Rome*. Cardinals in the Fifteenth Century. 2009. ISBN 978 90 04 17183 1

174. Dyson, R.W. (ed.). *James of Viterbo*: De regimine Christiano. A Critical Edition and Translation. 2009. ISBN 978 90 04 17597 6 (Published as Vol. 6 in the subseries *Brill's Texts and Sources in Intellectual History*)

175. Lærke, M. (ed.). *The Use of Censorship in the Enlightenment*. 2009. ISBN 978 90 04 17558 7

176. Vall, R. van de & R. Zwijnenberg (eds.). *The Body Within*. Art, Medicine and Visualization. 2009. ISBN 978 90 04 17621 8 (Published as Vol. 3 in the subseries *Brill's Studies on Art, Art History, and Intellectual History*)

177. Sauter, M.J. *Visions of the Enlightenment*. The Edict on Religion of 1788 and the Politics of the Public Sphere in Eighteenth-Century Prussia. 2009. ISBN 978 90 04 17651 5

178. Verbaal, W., Y. Maes & J. Papy (eds.). *Latinitas Perennis*. Volume II: Appropriation by Latin Literature. 2009. ISBN 978 90 04 17683 6

179. Miert, D.K.W. van. *Humanism in an Age of Science*. The Amsterdam Athenaeum in the Golden Age, 1632-1704. 2009. ISBN 978 90 04 17685 0

181. Maia Neto, J.R., J.C. Laursen & G. Paganini (eds.). *Skepticism in the Modern Age*. Building on the Work of Richard Popkin. 2009. ISBN 978 90 04 17784 0

182. Cruz, L. & W. Frijhoff (eds.). *Myth in History, History in Myth*. 2009. ISBN 978 90 04 17834 2

183. Ben-Tov, A. *Lutheran Humanists and Greek Antiquity*. Melanchthonian Scholarship Between Universal History and Pedagogy. 2009. ISBN 978 90 04 17965 3

184. Talbot, A. *"The Great Ocean of Knowledge"*. The Influence of Travel Literature on the Work of John Locke. 2010. ISBN 978 90 04 18115 1

185. Almási, G. *The Uses of Humanism*. Johannes Sambucus (1531-1584), Andreas Dudith (1533-1589), and the Republic of Letters in East Central Europe. 2009. ISBN 978 90 04 18185 4

186. Von Stuckrad, K. *Locations of Knowledge in Medieval and Early Modern Europe*. Esoteric Discourse and Western Identities. 2010. ISBN 978 90 04 18422 0

187. Baumgold, D. *Contract Theory in Historical Context*. Essays on Grotius, Hobbes, and Locke. 2010. ISBN 978 90 04 18425 1

188. Otten, W., A. Vanderjagt & H. de Vries (eds.). *How the West Was Won*. Essays on Literary Imagination, the Canon and the Christian Middle Ages. 2010. ISBN 978 90 04 18496 1